LESSONS AND LEGACIES VI

LESSONS AND LEGACIES VI

New Currents in Holocaust Research

Edited and with an introduction
by Jeffry M. Diefendorf

NORTHWESTERN UNIVERSITY PRESS   EVANSTON, ILLINOIS

Northwestern University Press
Evanston, Illinois 60208-4170

Copyright © 2004 by Northwestern University Press. Published 2004. All rights reserved.

Printed in the United States of America

10 9 8 7 6 5 4 3 2 1

ISBN 0-8101-1999-4 (cloth)
ISBN 0-8101-2001-1 (paper)

Library of Congress Cataloging-in-Publication data are available from the Library of Congress.

The paper used in this publication meets the minimum requirements of the
American National Standard for Information Sciences—Permanence of Paper for
Printed Library Materials, ANSI Z39.48-1992.

DEDICATED TO HENRY S. BIENEN, PRESIDENT,
NORTHWESTERN UNIVERSITY

In gratitude to Henry S. Bienen for his recognition that the Holocaust should serve as a lesson to humanity rather than a forgotten piece of history and for his unstinted support of Holocaust study at Northwestern University.

Contents

Theodore Zev Weiss

Foreword

This is the sixth volume of scholarly papers published as an out-growth of the Lessons and Legacies Conferences that the Holocaust Educational Foundation sponsors in partnership with major centers of higher learning. As with Lessons and Legacies Conferences I and II, Northwestern University was our partner in the sixth Lessons and Legacies Conference. We are very pleased to acknowledge the help of Northwestern's academic officers, in particular President Henry Bienen and Dean Donald Jacobs of the Kellogg Business School. The chair of Lessons and Legacies VI was Professor Peter Hayes of Northwestern University. His hard work and dedication made the conference a great success. Volumes from the five past conferences have all been published by Northwestern University Press.

The success of the Lessons and Legacies Conference is only one area in which the work of the Holocaust Educational Foundation has made gratifying strides in recent years. The number of colleges and universities teaching courses on the Holocaust with the foundation's help has grown from twenty to more than four hundred. Moreover, the foundation has established the biannual summer seminar trip to Holocaust sites in Central and Eastern Europe, enabling, to date, some one hundred scholars who teach courses on the Holocaust to acquaint themselves on an immediate basis with the "topography of terror" of the Nazi regime. Finally, the annual Summer Institute on the Holocaust and Jewish Civilization, held at Northwestern University and established years ago by the foundation, educates current and future college and university professors about the history of the Holocaust and the faith and culture of the Jewish people, whom Nazism targeted for extinction. All of these efforts have brought us into ever more fulfilling contact with a growing "family" of decent and dedicated academicians who share our conviction that learning remains the best antidote to humanity's more inhumane impulses.

This year we have started a new program that awards fellowships to graduate students who wish to pursue a doctorate in Holocaust studies. This important step ensures the Holocaust will be taught to future generations.

I want to take this opportunity to express my deep gratitude to the board members who have contributed so generously to the foundation's work and have made all this possible.

My personal thanks to the scholars who participated in and contributed so greatly to the success of the Lessons and Legacies Conferences.

Finally, as always, my strongest sense of gratitude is to my wife, Alice, and my children, Deborah and Gabi, and Danny and Jodi, who have encouraged the work of the foundation at every juncture and replenished my energies at every step.

Acknowledgments

When I entered Stanford as an undergraduate, I had no knowledge or awareness of the Holocaust. My mother's family was Jewish, my father's evangelical Christian. The compromise was to raise me with no religion whatsoever, and neither parent displayed much interest in recent history. To fulfill my college language requirement, I took German, and in my sophomore year I went to Germany, a way to fulfill other requirements and experience Europe. I found my maternal grandmother's distress that I was going to Germany rather odd. Equally odd to me was the fact that the student scheduled to be my roommate in Germany dropped out at the last moment. He was Jewish and had deep anxiety about the trip. It was a sign of my ignorance and naïveté that I had no understanding of what Germany meant to Jews living safely and happily in America.

The nine months spent in Germany were exciting, and puzzling. Classes on modern German history and a visit to Dachau raised the specter of the horrors perpetrated by Nazism, but this was offset by friendships formed with Germans. By the time I entered graduate school, trying to understand German history and the Germans became the focus of my study and, eventually, my profession. Convinced that not everything prior to 1933 led to Nazism and that not everything since 1945 resulted from Nazism, I resisted making the Third Reich the centerpiece of German history. I also resisted making the Holocaust a primary subject in my teaching.

That I now teach a course on the Holocaust, have raised money for an endowment for Holocaust education at the University of New Hampshire, and was asked to edit this current volume is a demonstration of the remarkable work of Zev Weiss. A dozen years ago, quite out of the blue, Theodore Zev Weiss called me, introduced himself as the spokesman of the Holocaust Education Foundation, and asked if there was anything he could do to help me make the Holocaust a part of my teaching. He then offered to subsidize my attendance at a conference on the Holocaust to take place near Chicago. Not being a Holocaust scholar, I went to learn, not to present anything of my own. Learn I did, at this and several subsequent conferences and at the first summer institute on Judaism and the Holocaust held at Northwestern University. In the process I got to know many of the leading Holocaust scholars, among them Peter Hayes and Christopher Browning, historians and the principle academic advisors to Zev Weiss and the Holocaust Education Foundation. Hence I want to express my gratitude to Zev, Peter, and Chris and to the Holocaust Education Foundation for stimulating my efforts to study and teach about the Holocaust. I also want to acknowledge the extraordinary efforts of those who have presented their work at the Lessons and Legacies conferences. These conferences have become a premier venue for the presentation of current Holocaust research and the exchange of ideas about how best to teach about the Holocaust. Finally, I would like to thank Jill Silos, for her help in preparing the manuscript for publication, and the Endowed Fund for Holocaust Education at the University of New Hampshire, for its support for my efforts.

This book is dedicated to my maternal grandparents, Ben and Rose Rosenfield Mindlin, and to their ancestors and descendants on both sides of the Atlantic.

Jeffry M. Diefendorf

Introduction

Like the five earlier books in this series, this volume is a record, at least in part, of a Lessons and Legacies Conference on the Holocaust, in this case the meeting held at Northwestern University in November 2000. The sheer size of these conferences, and the range and quality of the papers presented at them, have made the Lessons and Legacies conferences among the most important meetings anywhere of Holocaust scholars and educators. This book represents but a selection of the more than fifty presentations at this conference. The selections have been clustered around significant themes. Without having to read the entire volume, established scholars, graduate students, and students can follow current historiographical debates or gain exposure to current directions of research by both leading scholars and new scholars just starting to make a mark in the field.

As those who labor in this field know, recent years have seen an avalanche of scholarly publications on the Holocaust, and controversies about the Holocaust swirl in the media, evidence that popular interest is equally high. At the 2002 meeting of the German Studies Association, over thirty papers dealt with the Holocaust, about the same number that dealt with Nazism, and this is indicative of the degree to which Hitler's war against Europe's Jews is now seen as one of the central features not just of the Third Reich but also of World War II. While important new research is in fact appearing in many countries, the extent to which the Holocaust has commanded the attention of both scholars and the public in the United States has itself become a subject of scholarly controversy, as epitomized by Peter Novick's *The Holocaust in American Life,* which raises the issue of the supposed instrumentalization of the Holocaust for selfish or sectarian ends.

The sources of the intense contemporary interest in the Holocaust are many. Court cases involving perpetrators (or alleged perpetrators) such as Maurice Papon are still in the news, even though the individuals involved are now very elderly. The scholarly and legal communities, large corporations, governments, and international agencies and commissions have energetically addressed one unresolved legacy of the Holocaust—the unexceeded theft of material assets and uncompensated labor. Here the issue of historical truth about those who gained from the Holocaust has been joined with efforts to restore "lost" property to rightful owners or their descendants, compensate at least some who had worked as slave or "forced" laborers, and find the owners of "dormant" bank accounts or "unclaimed" insurance policies. Such tales cannot fail to make headlines. Nor can stories that purport to reveal actions by the Nazis' victims, or by the Allied soldiers who defeated the Third Reich, that embody what some would see as equivalent evils. Thus the *Boston Globe,* in a series on "The Secret History of World War II," ran a front page story on July 2, 2001, on what was claimed to be the summary executions by shooting of already-surrendered Nazi soldiers and camp guards by the American soldiers who liberated Dachau. Jan T. Gross's work on the tragedy in the Polish village of Jedwabne, where Poles, not Germans, apparently killed large numbers of their Jewish neighbors in July 1941, has sparked an intense discussion involving both scholars and the public in Poland and within the Polish community abroad.

The intersection of the pursuits of the scholarly community and the interests of the broader public can be seen in several other instances that have also generated widespread publicity. One was certainly the libel trial in which the British writer David Irving sued the American historian Deborah Lipstadt and her publisher for having described him as a Holocaust denier. To his consternation, the British court became a forum for demonstrating the difference between good and fraudulent history; Irving lost his suit, and the media interpreted the verdict as a repudiation of Holocaust denial. (The historian Richard Evans, a key witness against Irving, has written of his experience of the trial in his book *Lying about History: History, Holocaust, and the David Irving Trial,* and in May 2003, U.S. public television aired *Holocaust on Trial,* an hour-long program on the trial that combined documentary and docudrama.) Surely the biggest spotlight has been trained on the work of Daniel Goldhagen, whose *Hitler's Willing Executioners* attributed the Holocaust to a deeply rooted, centuries-old "eliminationist anti-Semitism" that constituted an integral part of German national character. Though attacked by nearly all historians, Goldhagen's sensational, simplistic explanation generated enormous press coverage and huge sales, forced scholars to reexamine German anti-Semitism, and guaranteed his place as a foil to appear in footnotes for years to come. The decision of the Catholic Church to move forward on the beatification of Pope Pius XII shone another spotlight on the role of the Pope and the Church in the Holocaust both outside and inside Italy. Having an acute sense of the market, Goldhagen has now inserted himself into this debate with a new book, *A Moral Reckoning,* which roundly condemns Catholics (and other Christians) as the fundamental source of anti-Semitism.

Still another reason for the continued interest in the Holocaust has been the appearance of new sources. In an effort to record the testimonies of remaining survivors, major archives of oral accounts have been constructed, including that sponsored by film producer Steven Spielberg. These accounts are not just of camp survivors but also of Jewish refugees intent on enlarging the story to include their fates. A vital role has been played by the growth of the United States Holocaust Memorial Museum, not just in its function as exhibitor but also as an archival depository of records from all over Europe and as a sponsor of research and publication. Its efforts have been furthered by the declassification of enormous numbers of records in American (and British) archives, permitting new perspectives on both events in Europe and Allied knowledge of those events. The collapse of the former Soviet Union has brought the discovery of archival sources previously unaccessible or thought lost throughout Eastern Europe, and the vastly greater academic freedom throughout Eastern Europe, Russia, and the Soviet successor states has stimulated new scholarly study of the Holocaust in Western and Eastern Europe, Israel, and the United States.

In spite of the great advances in scholarly knowledge about the Holocaust, and in spite of the constant presence of the Holocaust in the news, education about the Holocaust still has a long way to go. I recently taught a course that dealt with the Holocaust to a group of twenty freshman and sophomore honors students. Though all knew a little, none knew very much about the subject. Judging from this small group, I suspect it probably would not be unusual for a college freshman to think that most of the Jews who perished were Germans, that nearly all Holocaust victims were gassed in the concentration camps, and that all of the perpetrators were black-shirted Nazis. Furthermore, of this group of students, only two regularly followed the daily news and hence noticed Holocaust-related stories, such as the release of Maurice Papon in France. Few students perceive that the crimes of the Third Reich have been invoked as a justification for the International War Crimes Tribunal at The Hague as well as for the assertion by the administration of American president George W. Bush that the United States now has a right and obligation to engage in unilateral, preemptive action against states that might perpetrate equivalent crimes. Students are surprised to see that the specter of British and French appeasement in the 1930s, used in the 1960s as rhetoric to defend the war in Vietnam, has found new life in the aftermath of the terrorist attack on the World Trade Center on September 11, 2002.

Moreover, many people both inside and outside academic life see the Holocaust as something that concerns primarily Jews, and they are mystified and sometimes affronted by the numbers of visitors to the United States Holocaust Memorial Museum. They fail to see that the Holocaust is not simply a Jewish issue or an issue for Germans and Jews. In one way or another, it involved nearly all of the nations and ethnic and religious groups that participated in World War II. But its significance goes beyond that. One can, I think, argue that the main thrust of Western civilization since the middle of the eighteenth century has been the pursuit of values articulated by the Enlightenment and assumed to be of universal importance: social and economic progress, the ascendance of reason and rationality in domestic political affairs and international relations, the spread of democracy, the growth of a civic culture taking place in the public sphere, the rise of science, and so forth. If this is true, then the Holocaust was surely the most fundamental challenge to this prolonged project of the Enlightenment. It was a challenge to Western civilization that originated at the heart of that civilization. For that reason, the ongoing scholarly efforts to understand the many dimensions of those horrible events deserve our close attention.

As noted, this book is divided into several sections, beginning with three papers that examine certain Nazi policies in new ways. Paul B. Jaskot explores the close relationship between cultural policy as embodied in the program of monumental state and party architecture, the economic policies of the SS in managing the concentration camp system, and the Nazi policy of genocide through labor. The SS sought to profit from the building program by utilizing forced labor in stone quarries and brick factories. The location and management of camps like Sachsenhausen, Buchenwald, Mauthausen, and Flossenbürg were initially tied to Göring's Four Year Plan, but the SS then linked the productive capacities of these camps to the architectural projects of Albert Speer, who contracted with the SS for a supply of building materials. In April 1938 the SS created the German Earth and Stone Works as a quasi-private company to handle these lucrative contracts, and Jaskot shows that the production of stone and brick for Speer continued throughout the war in spite of a ban on construction not related to war necessities. And since the SS could obtain an apparently unlimited supply of forced labor, the oppression and murder of parts of the concentration camp labor force, even when this reduced its efficiency, did not matter. For the SS, profiting from the monumental building projects and murdering the workers under its control went hand in hand.

Sybille Steinbacher looks at the most infamous concentration camp, Auschwitz, not as a site of mass exploitation of labor and mass murder but in its relationship to life just outside the camp. She notes that while the town had been Polish prior to the war, that part of Silesia was quickly annexed to the Reich. It was not, as is commonly stated, in the "East"; instead it was a part of the expanded Germany, and Himmler initially planned to relocate the native population of Poles and Jews and replace them with Germans from South Tirol. Even as German administrators and businessmen moved in, Jews were collected there from other parts of the Kattowitz government district. The concentration camp, three kilometers from the town, was built by Jewish laborers in spring 1940 to house Polish political prisoners. A year later the IG Farben plant brought further Germanization of the town and the expulsion of its Jews to other assembly points or to ghettos. By 1943 the town was twice its prewar size, but the Jews, the largest part of the prewar population, were gone. There were 7,000 Reich Germans living and working in Auschwitz, with plans on the drawing board for some 70,000 to 80,000 Germans to inhabit a comfortable new city. By January 1945, there were 4,481 SS personnel working in the concentration camp, and many of these were accompanied by their families. In other words, the town of Auschwitz and the concentration camp complex were parts of the German acquisition of new living space, the vast program of population resettlement, *and* the evolving campaign to exterminate the Jews.

The recent controversies about Pope Pius XII and anti-Semitism in the Catholic Church have brought renewed attention to the fate of Italy's Jews. Richard Breitman, who has been closely involved in the declassification of formerly secret documents held in American archives, focuses on the role of Herbert Kappler, an intelligence officer in the German embassy in Rome who reported to the Reich Security Main Office. Recently declassified radio intercepts show that Kappler was a central figure; it was to Kappler that Himmler gave the order to round up and deport Rome's Jews in September 1943. Kappler was exonerated in 1948 by an Italian court, which accepted his claim that he opposed Himmler's orders. Breitman argues that the chronology and substance of the decoded intercepts make Kappler's claim dubious. If Kappler hesitated in carrying out Himmler's orders, it was because he felt he lacked sufficient resources to do the job thoroughly, not because of some principled objection. Kappler realized that Italian public opinion was turning against the Germans to such an extent that a complete roundup of Rome's Jews was not possible. In contrast to the situation in northern Europe, conditions in Italy meant that Himmler's policies could not be implemented.

The second section of the book offers new perspectives on both resistance to the persecution of Jews and efforts to rescue Jews. Yehuda Bauer asks whether the accounts of resistance in places like Warsaw, Lodz, and Vilna hold true for the majority of places where Jews lived or were forced into ghettos, and whether the experience of Jews in fact differed from or paralleled that of other victim groups. He looks, in particular, for what he calls nonarmed *amidah,* or "standing up against" the Nazis, and he argues that scholars must resist easy generalizations, because the experiences in different places under different circumstances varied so widely. Thus in Brest-Litovsk, where a thriving, diverse Jewish community was destroyed by the Soviets in September 1939, well before the Germans arrived in 1941, there was almost no *amidah* to speak of. In the small *shtetl* town of Kurzeniec, a town also first occupied by the Soviets, there was both armed and unarmed *amidah,* which derived from a combination of the existence of a tight Jewish community, help from local non-Jews, and a preexisting left-wing Zionist youth movement. For his third example, Bauer chooses the Ukrainian town of Kosow Huculski, where the Jews faced first the Soviets, then Hungarians who arrived as part of Operation Barbarossa, and then the Germans in September 1941. Here the hostility of the Ukrainians made *amidah* almost impossible. These different stories of resistance make it clear that much more research is needed on the actual experience of Eastern European Jewry between the beginning of the war in 1939 and the virtual liquidation of the Jews by the war's end.

If help from non-Jews was crucial in encouraging resistance, it was even more important in rescue efforts, but Jonathan Goldstein shows that not enough is yet known about the motives of those who did help rescue Jews. In his essay, Goldstein examines the activities of Jan Zwartendijk, a Dutch businessman in Lithuania who issued 2,345 so-called "Curaçao visas" to allow Jews to make a safe transit to the Dutch West Indies. Zwartendijk's efforts thus were the first step and were followed by the issuing of Japanese transit visas by Consul Sugihara Chiune and then Soviet transit visas approved by Molotov's deputy Vladimir Dekanozov, perhaps with Stalin's approval. It may be the case that Sugihara acted as part of intelligence-gathering activities and that the Russians had various nonhumanitarian motives, but Goldstein argues that Zwartendijk was motivated by a straightforward humanitarian sensitivity. In other words, the willingness to act to try to rescue Jews, like resistance, defies simple generalization.

Similarly, one key to the rescue of some 425 to 450 Jewish adolescents from Holland (the subject of Yehudi Lindeman's essay) was the aid given by non-Jews. A central figure here was Joop Westerweel, the principal of a Montessori school in Rotterdam. A socialist and anarchist, Westerweel may have been motivated by the school's progressive, anti-authoritarian orientation. He was one of several non-Jews who helped this group of children, which included German and Austrian emigrants who had been preparing to go to Palestine when the war began. The adult Jews in charge of the children had to organize their escape from the Westerbork internment camp, move them from the Low Countries across France into Spain, and then on to Palestine. They needed false documents, money, hiding places, food, guides, and escorts, much of which was provided by non-Jews, including members of the French resistance. Moreover, the children needed common sense, resolve, and solidarity, which Lindeman argues was derived from their involvement in the preinvasion enthusiasm and planning for emigration. It also helped that the Jews who had fled from Germany were better informed about German intentions and atrocities than were Dutch Jews.

Resistance and rescue is also the subject of Lenore Weitzman's study of the women who bravely served as couriers while Eastern European Jews were confined in ghettos. These women—and girls—carried documents, news, money, and weapons. They helped establish and maintain contacts between the Jews isolated in the ghettos and Jews still outside, and they obtained information about German plans and actions, all of which helped active resistance and furthered rescue efforts. Knowing that they faced torture and death, they lived in terror of what would happen if caught while engaging in illegal travel and exposed as both Jews and couriers. Weitzman is interested in exploring what helped these women succeed as couriers and also what motivated them to risk their lives in this way. She identifies a number of factors. The couriers had to be able to speak Polish without accent, not "look Jewish," and have sufficient acting ability to get out of tight spots. Jewish girls were more likely than boys to have attended Polish schools, where they not only mastered Polish but picked up Polish slang and mannerisms that helped them pass as Polish. As young women, they could project innocence or sexuality. It was normal for women to shop and move around. Finally, Weitzman argues, the motivation and commitment of couriers came from their involvement in prewar Zionism and political organizations.

The next three parts of this book deal with scholars and the Holocaust. Patricia von Papen-Bodek examines the Nazi Institute for the Study of the Jewish Question, which was founded under the umbrella of Alfred Rosenberg's Foreign Office. Led initially by Wilhelm Grau, this institute confiscated the municipal Judaica collection of Frankfurt am Main and then added material taken from private and public libraries and holdings in Germany, France, and other conquered areas, building up a library of some 350,000 volumes. The institute put out a pseudo-scholarly journal and other publications that helped the Foreign Office and other agencies in their anti-Jewish activities. For example, the institute sought to clarify whether Sephardic or Iranian Jews in France were racially Jews or gentiles practicing Judaism as a religion. Thus, through this institute and institutes like it that were subsequently established in Poland, Paris, and Budapest,

Nazi scholars could further their careers by utilizing their skills to promote the active persecution of Europe's Jews.

Konrad Jarausch examines another group of scholars who collaborated with Nazism, namely historians like Theodor Schieder, Werner Conze, and Karl-Dietrich Erdmann. In the 1930s and 1940s these men engaged in research on culture and ethnicity on and beyond Germany's prewar borders. Though it is unclear exactly how much of a contribution this research made, certainly their findings provided a potentially legitimate scholarly underpinning for the vast demographic relocation policies that the Nazis sought to impose. The careers of these scholars have, as Jarausch discusses, become the subject of controversy. First, Schieder, Conze, and Erdmann all became prominent after 1945; indeed, all became presidents of the German Historical Association. Second, their students—particularly those who formed the left-liberal Bielefeld school of social historians—failed to confront their intellectual "fathers" for their Nazi-era labors, thereby leading a new generation of German historians to attack the previous cohorts for having maintained a silence about the true past of the historical guild. Without denying any of these charges, Jarausch notes that Schieder, Conze, Erdmann, and their students in the end contributed a vital critical perspective that helped undercut radical nationalism in Germany and strengthened the democracy of the Federal Republic.

Using history and historians as tools both to elucidate the true nature of Nazism and to buttress democratic institutions in the new Germany is also the subject of Devin Pendas's paper on the Frankfurt Auschwitz trial. When attempting bringing to justice twenty-two defendants for their crimes at Auschwitz, the prosecutors utilized five historians to provide expert testimony "to counter historical distortions" about the Nazi era. Hans Buchheim, Martin Broszat, Helmut Krausnich, Hans-Adolf Jacobson, and Jürgen Kuczynski (the latter from the German Democratic Republic) offered a general background on Nazism and anti-Semitism and detailed information about specific policies and actions, such as the Commissar Order at the beginning of the onslaught against the Soviet Union. Here the prosecutors and historians sought to turn historical scholarship into legally proven knowledge; historical scholarship was intended to bolster the moral and pedagogical impact of the trials before the German public, not just to convict the defendants. In focusing on the SS and the concentration camp system, and in portraying the latter as an SS anti-state serving Hitler outside the realm of normal law, politics, and even German history, the historians presented an early version of what has come to be known as the "intentionalist" interpretation of the Holocaust, whereby Nazi criminality is derived directly from Hitler and his minions. Historical scholarship thus provided "a structural anatomy of the institutional context of the individual guilt of the trial's defendants."

From the uses and misuses of scholarship, the book turns in the fourth section to consideration of current historiography. The first two papers in this section examine the contribution of Christopher Browning, perhaps the best known among American Holocaust scholars. (A chapter of what became his book *Ordinary Men* appeared in the first Lessons and Legacies volume.) As Dan Michman notes, most of Browning's work other than his study of the actions by the Order Police units concentrated on the decision-making process that produced the Final Solution. He argues that Browning has staked out a position between the "intentionalists," who focused on Hitler, Nazi ideology and anti-Semitism; and totalitarian organizations, and "functionalists," who saw the murder of the Jews as something growing incrementally and being partly initiated from the bottom up, something made possible by the chaos of the Nazi regime. Browning, Michman contends, leans more toward the functionalists, but he also believes that Hitler did indeed make the key decisions to move ahead toward mass murder. These decisions were not made when Hitler formed the Party, when he came to power, or even when he launched the war on Poland, but rather in July and then early autumn of 1941. Hitler made these decisions while influenced by a sense of euphoria derived from actual and anticipated victories in the war with the Soviet Union; the "euphoria of victory" provided the context in which the decisions were made. According to Michman, Browning thereby blends intentionalism as the "essence" and functionalism as the "climate" for choosing mass extermination to solve the "Jewish question," with the special mood swings of Hitler and his entourage serving to hold it all together.

In his brief and pithy essay, Gerhard Weinberg praises Browning not for specific interpretations but rather for his insistence on careful scholarship using new materials in new ways. Whether it is in his analysis of decision making in the Foreign Office, in the treatment of the Order Police, in the "differentiated analysis of ghettos," or in the experience of those held in labor camps, Browning has stimulated new scholarship and provided a solid basis for rejecting what Weinberg sees as the "nonsense" offered by Arno Mayer and Daniel Goldhagen. Weinberg would place greater emphasis than Browning on the broader nature of the war, which from the beginning, Weinberg thinks, included the destruction of Europe's Jews, but he values Browning's close attention to exact chronology and empirical evidence.

Dariusz Stola offers a survey of current Holocaust research in Poland. Polish Jews were the largest group of Holocaust victims, much of the killing took place there, and many of the witnesses were Poles. Moreover, the Holocaust took place within the context of complex Polish-Jewish relations long tinged with anti-Semitism. Stola begins by tracing scholarship in communist Poland, which was sometimes anti-Zionist and anti-Semitic, but he notes that the real breakthrough came during the sixteen months of Solidarity in 1980–81, which called for a search for truth and new discussions between Polish and Jewish historians. After 1989 there has been a virtual flood of interest in Jewish culture and history, including the Holocaust, and Polish scholars have become aware of scholarship from abroad. Key debates have focused on the role of Poles as perpetrators, on comparisons between the martyrdom of Poles and that of Jews, and also on the absence of Jews in postwar Polish culture. Polish scholars have been busy publishing primary documents, testimonies, and interviews from both Jewish and Polish sources, and they have prepared detailed studies of such subjects as the Polish police, provincial Jewish communities, and cases of Poles themselves murdering Jews. Stola notes that it is not surprising that such sensitive and controversial topics have been accompanied by regrettable instances of Holocaust denial.

The essays by Christian Gerlach and Susannah Heschel go beyond examining current scholarship to raise new questions to be addressed and to confront interpretations now enjoying some currency. In his essay, Gerlach insists that German historians rework the ways in which they contextualize the Holocaust. He begins with the story of Quartermaster General Eduard Wagner to demonstrate the problematic nature of any oversimplified approach. Wagner was both a leading perpetrator of the Holocaust, playing a central role in demographic and food policies in Eastern Europe that entailed genocide, and a resister, participating in the failed coup attempt of July 20, 1944. In this single person, then, one finds a complex mixture of motives and actions, where military service, bureaucratic rationality, the extermination of Jews, other genocidal policies, and patriotism come together in strange ways. Gerlach then surveys new studies that include regional analyses of the German occupation of Europe, work on political centralization and decentralization, and fresh work on perpetrators, but his main interest is in the attempt to situate both decision making and implementation of policy within the broader political, demographic, and economic policies of the occupation. At the same time, he pleads for more scholarship on such policies and actions as the mass starvation of Soviet POWs, something that he contends, could usefully be compared with the euthanasia campaign and the Holocaust.

Susannah Heschel's contribution suggests that historians need to rethink the use of concepts of gender and femininity when analyzing the behavior of female perpetrators. She notes that while women were influential at lower levels in the Nazi hierarchy and thus did not make broader policy decisions, women did serve as camp guards, and other women lived at the camps as spouses of male camp personnel. At Auschwitz, for example, there were 200 women guards, compared to the 7,000 male camp personnel, but elsewhere the percentage of women among camp personnel reached 20 percent. Furthermore, some 240,000 women married SS men, 500,000 worked for the army, and 6 to 9 million belonged to Nazi organizations. Herschel argues that not enough has been done by historians to account for acts of cruelty by women, and little is known about the private lives of women guards outside the camps. Did they also retreat to some sort of domestic sanctuary after a day's work? At the few postwar trials, "testimony was presented and evaluated in gendered and sexualized mythological language," but this testimony may not in fact really explain the behavior of women perpetrators. Heschel challenges feminist theory to confront the issue of women committing violence against other women. In committing atrocities, were women participating in male gender roles, challenging them, or redefining female gender roles within Nazism?

The first four sections of this book deal with policies and actions that transpired during the period of the Third Reich or with various dimensions of the evolving scholarship on the Holocaust. The fifth section of the book examines ways in which the aftermath of the Holocaust played out in postwar legal systems. The first two papers, that by Hilary Earl on the Einsatzgruppen trial and that by Rebecca Wittmann on the Auschwitz Trial, both illuminate how the German criminal justice system, while pursuing the admirable goal of bringing Nazi perpetrators to justice, also served to distort Holocaust history.

In the Einsatzgruppen Trial of 1947, evidence was presented about the supposed existence and timing of an order from Hitler to kill Soviet Jews. Otto Ohlendorf testified that such a *Führerbefehl* was issued in the summer of 1941, but other evidence suggested he lied. Nevertheless, he was believed for several reasons. The legal system favored credible oral testimony, and Ohlendorf's willingness to talk gave him credibility. Both the defense and the prosecution, each for different reasons, focused on this Hitler order, which may not have existed. The prosecution assumed that there was early, planned, top-level decision making, and hence it found its position corroborated by Ohlendorf. In the course of his interviews in jail, Ohlendorf elaborated and refined his story about superior orders. The defense, on the other hand, sought to use the existence of superior orders, along with the claim that executions were justified to defend Germany against Soviet attack, to get the defendants acquitted. This did not work. The issue before the court was whether the defendants had committed crimes, and the court had from the start declared the defense's arguments inadmissable. That Hitler had ordered the killings, however, became a historical "fact" given a measure of legal sanction, and this in turn became a part of the later intentionalist-functionalist debate. As Earl observes, this trial shows that obtaining convictions of criminals in a court of law and obtaining historically accurate information are "frequently incompatible."

In the 1963–65 Auschwitz Trial in Frankfurt, as Wittmann shows, the prosecutors used prewar precedents and Nazi standards of illegality to convict defendants of torturing and killing camp inmates. The 1871 penal code, which remained on the books after 1945, required that prosecutors prove inner motivation, individual initiative, and knowledge of illegality to convict someone for murder. To make this case, the prosecutors turned to evidence gathered by the Nazis themselves. The SS in fact had written rules controlling punishments, including torture, which were supposed to make the actions of camp authorities less arbitrary. In 1943 the SS had authorized an investigation headed by Judge Konrad Morgen into corruption at Auschwitz, but Morgen focused only on acts that he considered illegal because they violated SS rules and were not derived from orders from Hitler or Himmler. The evidence collected in the investigation thus could be used by prosecutors in the 1960s to show that individual guards exceeded the kinds of behavior "legally" mandated by the Nazi regime, thereby proving motivation, initiative, and awareness of criminality. That the court in the 1960s used Nazi standards and evidence to show that the defendants had disobeyed *Nazi* orders and thus to convict them for individual criminal acts may have provided some measure of justice, but it made it all the more difficult to find a legal basis for judging those who created the camp system and used it for genocide on a large scale. The implication was that the makers of SS policy and the creators of the camp system had acted legally.

The Nazi war on the Jews was not only a program of mass murder; it was also a program of mass theft and exploitation. Survivors of the Holocaust, their descendants, and postwar organizations representing the victims have rightly sought compensation for lost property and livelihoods and, in cases where victims had worked as slave labor, some measure of restitution of lost wages. They have also, when possible, sought the return of looted assets. These are matters that have occupied both the courts and politicians for decades, and the remaining three papers in this section throw light on this subject.

As Constantin Goschler notes in his essay on German compensation to Jewish victims, the issue of compensation was very complicated after the war. The claims of Holocaust victims competed with those of German refugees, veterans, and those whose property had been damaged in the war. The German government was concerned that compensation claims might burden the future in the way that reparations had burdened the Weimar Republic. The victorious Allies had their own competing ideas about reparations, but the Americans particularly pressured the Germans to face the need to compensate Jewish victims. The Germans focused first on the restitution of "identifiable" Jewish property expropriated by the Nazi state directly, not property alienated through sale, even if forced. Even so, who would be compensated if the original owners and their heirs had disappeared? Successor organizations? In Europe only, or organizations based in the United States or Israel? How might the government deal with the opposition to restitution from non-Jewish "last owners" who claimed to have obtained property in good faith? What should be done about looted property whose original owners could not be identified?

As Goschler shows, the most easily resolved claims for restitution of "identifiable" property were settled in the 1950s. Moreover, in September 1952 the Federal Republic and Israel agreed on a compensation payment to Israel of DM 3.45 billion, 65 percent to be paid in goods and oil. In 1965 a "final" West German compensation law was passed, under which perhaps DM 80 billion have been paid to date to Jewish victims. Even this program proved not to be final after all. The East Germans had put compensation for communist victims ahead of compensation for Jews, and unlike West Germany, required that those receiving payments be resident in the German Democratic Republic (GDR). After unification of the two German states, new payments were needed for victims in the former GDR, and the whole issue of restitution of lost property had to be reopened. With the end of the Cold War, the enlarged Federal Republic and German corporations in the 1990s also have reached agreements with its now non-communist neighbors regarding some measure of compensation for non-Germans—Jews and non-Jews—who had been forced laborers.

The willingness of Germans to reconsider and expand compensation and restitution programs since 1990 has been motivated not solely by moral reasons. Jonathan Steinberg discusses the path taken by the largest German bank, the Deutsche Bank, in joining the compensation program. In the mid-1990s there was a flurry of research into the wartime activities of the Swiss, who purchased gold from the Third Reich, and various German corporations. In part this was due to the availability of new archival sources found in the former GDR and in other formerly communist states from Poland to Russia; in part it was because newly liberalized governments were prepared to examine the question of culpability for the Holocaust; and in part it was because a large number of elderly victims in Eastern Europe were now legally able to make restitution claims. Equally important, however, was the fact that German firms wishing to participate in the globalized economy had to do business in the United States, and this opened them up to class-action civil lawsuits in American courts. Firms like the Deutsche Bank decided to commission independent historians to examine their wartime activities, promising scholars like Steinberg full access to records and an unrestricted right to publish their findings. In fact the Deutsche Bank did serve as an agent to transfer gold from the Reichsbank to Switzerland, and at least 16 percent of the gold could be shown to be from concentration camp victims. Most of the rest had been looted from banks in occupied countries. On the other hand, this business activity, while profitable, was only a "tiny part of the bank's activities." Still, by owning up to their wartime activities and joining the compensation program, even though embarrassing and costly, the Deutsche Bank and other German firms cleared the way for future business activities on the world stage.

Further details to this story are added by Helen Junz in her essay on the globalization of the restitution and compensation issue. She notes that while the United States had taken the lead between 1943 and 1947 on establishing restitution laws to be applied in former Axis countries, it had not shown similar initiative in pursuing the restitution of property that had landed in its own, Allied, or neutral hands. The Federal Republic of Germany had, indeed, paid massive sums, 96 percent of which was compensation for damaged health and lost pensions and wages, but only 4 percent for the loss of property. The gigantic 1995 class-action suit filed in a New York court by the American lawyer Edward Fagin for $18 billion, spurred on by outspoken personalities such as Edgar Bronfman Sr., of the World Jewish Congress, and Senator Alfonse D'Amato, led to the creation of the so-called Independent Committee of Eminent Persons, chaired by banker Paul Volker, to investigate the charges that Jewish assets were still hidden in Switzerland. This, in turn, led to establishment of investigative committees in twenty-five nations, plus the corporate histories mentioned by Steinberg. In other words, legal and moral pressure joined forces with economic and political interests to force governments and corporations to try to resolve remaining restitution and compensation issues even as the survivor generation was rapidly disappearing. Junz makes one last important point. It would be wrong to consider restitution as a manifestation of greed by survivors or their heirs. Real individuals had lost real assets, and restitution should be understood as a part of the restoration of the individuality of those victims.

In the final section of the book, five scholars look at complicated and problematic attempts to come to grips with the Holocaust after 1945. Ian Buruma begins with a twelve-year-old child's brief, eyewitness account of the Holocaust in Poland. It is terse and relentlessly bleak, describing hunger and death. Buruma then contrasts this statement with the sentimental, ahistorical morality tales of childish innocence to be found in fiction, film, some memoirs, and even the uses of Anne Frank's diary. The Dutch, Buruma argues, have made Anne Frank into their Joan of Arc, representing the heroic victim of Nazism, even though she was German and her family was betrayed by a Dutch person. The popular film *Life is Beautiful,* by Roberto Benigni, presents the Holocaust as a fable, a comedy wherein an innocent Jewish son is saved by his buffoon-like father. Steven Spielberg's *Schindler's List* is a sentimental story of redemption. This childlike use of an innocent perspective is problematic, even an exercise in bad faith, because it represents a "refusal to look truth in the face," avoiding not just real horror but also "ducking responsibility" for what happened.

In his essay, Jeffrey Herf raises questions about Peter Novick's assessment of the place of the Holocaust in American culture. Herf reject's Novick's claim that Holocaust memory in America is simply either an effort to define identity in terms of victimization or a rather cynical instrumentalization of the Holocaust by neoconservatives on behalf of an embattled Israel in the mid-1960s. Instead Herf points to other forces that stimulated both popular and intellectual interest in the Holocaust. These include connections with the civil rights and antiwar protests of the 1960s and the advancement of both survivors and their children to positions in academia and the media. Such individuals now had the possibility to make the Holocaust a central theme. Indeed, Herf argues that work on the Holocaust was more closely tied to traditional liberalism than to either the political left or right. The 1960s saw an increase in liberalism and a decrease in anti-Semitism appear alongside the growing self-confidence and prosperity of the survivor generation, which believed that its story needed to be told for its own sake and not to help Israel or to buttress the American Jewish community. In other words, while Novick's work has served to encourage reflection on the explosive growth of Holocaust study in the United States, Herf's arguments suggest that more needs to be done to place this phenomenon within the context of Jewish and American intellectual and political history.

Pieter Lagrou surveys the relationship between national history and national responsibility in France and the Low Countries. Approximately 200,000 West European Jews were deported and killed—half from the Netherlands, 75,000 from France, and 25,000 from Belgium—and collaboration with the German occupiers made this possible. The Netherlands' Jews had been socially segregated by confession, and their social isolation made persecution easier but also made it easier for the Dutch to obscure what had happened. Postwar Dutch memory focused on images of occupation, sacrifice, and resistance shared by all citizens, overlooking the fact that 55 percent of all war-related deaths were part of the Holocaust. Jews received no special recognition or compensation, and of the Netherlands' 40,000 surviving Jews, one-fifth emigrated to Israel or the United States, leaving behind a small Jewish community. Not until the 1970s did the Netherlands begin to face up to Dutch complicity in genocide. In postwar France, unlike in the Netherlands, there was no monopoly on wartime memory. With France's polity fragmented right after the war, and with a strong Communist Party, many organizations representing POWs, the resistance, and the persecuted sought recognition and made claims for restitution. And in contrast to the case of the Netherlands, where the Jewish community declined further after the war, a high demographic growth rate among France's Jews was augmented by considerable immigration of Jews from North Africa. Jewry in France, then, was not invisible, and its claims to special recognition were initially recognized after the war, even if the French had difficulty coming to grips with their own collaboration with the Nazis. However, when de Gaulle reemerged as France's leader in 1958, the resistance and national unity became the dominant modes of understanding the war years, and special claims by Jews for recognition and compensation were forced into the shadows. Finally, Lagrou argues that Jewish claims in Belgium were obscured by fundamental political cleavages. Belgium was divided, on the one hand, between secular/democratic/antifascist forces and royalist/Catholic/traditionalist forces, and between pro-French and pro-Flemish factions on the other. In this context, while in the early postwar years Jewish victims were given special status in claiming reparations benefits, increasingly anti-Fascism became a stronger basis for making claims on Belgian memory of the experience of German occupation, and for seeking reparations, than did Jewishness. The distinctive wartime experience of Belgian Jews and non-Belgian Jews trapped in that country became "assimilated" into the experience of the nation, much as was the case in France under de Gaulle.

In her discussion of the response to Cardinal Aloisius Muench's essay *One World in Charity,* Suzanne Brown-Fleming shows how the views of an American Catholic prelate were used by German Catholics to relativize the Holocaust and thereby diminish a sense of German responsibility for what had happened. Muench, the bishop of Fargo, N.D., was appointed Pius XII's personal diplomat in Germany from 1946 to 1959, making him the most powerful American Catholic in Germany and a central figure in creating a myth of Catholic innocence. Drafted by Muench as a pastoral letter for Lent in December 1945, *One World* blamed Nazi crimes on a small number of Germans and then went on to compare the Allied occupation of Germany with Hitler's policies. In the same breath it condemned the concentration camps, the bombing of Hiroshima and Nagasaki, the bombing of German cities by the Allies, and the ethnic cleansing of Germans in Eastern Europe at the end of the war. There was no special mention of Jews, but instead Muench called for charity and forgiveness toward Germans and urged the Allies to avoid replicating their crimes. By early 1947 a truncated version of *One World* was circulating in Germany to great acclaim by German Catholics. Its spread, Brown-Fleming argues, was a grass-roots phenomenon, and it was especially popular among the so-called Reich Germans expelled from the East. The reason for the essay's popularity was obvious: composed by an American, not a German, it was a repudiation of any idea of collective guilt. The circulation of *One World* among German Catholics made it easier for them to avoid facing up to the fact that the Holocaust had been perpetrated not just by a small number of fanatical unreligious Nazis but by large numbers of Germans of all kinds, including practicing Catholics.

The final essay in this volume is by James E. Young and tells the story both of the debate over the design of a Holocaust memorial on a five-acre site near Berlin's Brandenburg Gate and of his own role in that debate. Over 500 entries were submitted in the 1994 design competition. The choice made the following year to construct a monumental, tilted gravestone met quick criticism and was abandoned. Starting in 1997 a series of public colloquia was held, and Young participated as an expert on memorial iconography. Eventually he was invited to join the "Findungskommission," a five-member body to reconsider the designs and find a solution, even though he was the only non-German, a Jew, and not an architect or designer himself. In the process by which the commission selected the design by Peter Eisenman and Richard Serra, Young moved from being a skeptical critic to an "arbiter, critic, and advocate," using his knowledge of Holocaust memorials elsewhere and his unique perspective to suggest modifications. The memorial is currently under construction, and only time will tell how well it reaches its multiple goals of memorializing the victims, educating visitors, and helping Germans come to grips with their history.

Young's essay is a fitting conclusion to this book. As suggested at the beginning of this introduction, the Holocaust is not a subject that disappears into history books. Nearly sixty years have passed since the fall of the Third Reich, but the events of that period have continued resonance in the present. The calling of Holocaust scholars is to understand the past, but everyone engaged in Holocaust scholarship is sensitive to the role that the history of the Holocaust still plays. James E. Young's part in helping shape the monumental Holocaust memorial in central Berlin can serve as a model for the constructive engagement of scholars with the public.

LESSONS AND LEGACIES VI

I. RETHINKING NAZI POLICIES

Paul B. Jaskot

Concentration Camps and Cultural Policy: Rethinking the Development of the Camp System, 1936–41

IT HAS LONG BEEN RECOGNIZED THAT ONE OF THE DEFINING CHARAC-
teristics of the National Socialist regime was its ability to infiltrate,
mobilize, and radicalize every major aspect of German public life.
Scholars have often used this point to indicate the complexity of the
development of policies leading to the destruction of the European
Jews. Moving beyond the debates concerning policymaking that
searched for the specific orders directly related to the murder of the
Jewish populations, scholarly trends have more recently been interested in exploring the ways seemingly non-Jewish policies, institutions, and administrations led to a cumulative enactment of state-
sponsored violence that paved the way and enabled the ultimate
violent policies of the genocide.[1] Looking at complex causal factors
and institutional opportunities created outside the specific focus on
anti-Semitic policy has not meant, however, that we need to ignore
the importance of individual agency, nor has it meant that we must
see the Holocaust as structurally preordained. Rather, it has meant
analyzing the ways in which actors had choices within given institutional and structural limits, and that they then made decisions which
in turn created new political, economic, and social conditions that
allowed for other choices and an expansion beyond previous limitations. This dynamic historical process allowed for the intersection of
specific anti-Semitic interests with the general promotion of developments in other spheres of the Nazi state. The SS, as one of the primary institutions with foremost responsibility for the implementation of the genocide, was just as subject to this dynamic as were other
administrative powers. The ways in which cultural policy influenced

the setting of priorities within the SS is a crucial example of how a more complex understanding of the National Socialist past helps us to clarify the complicated road that led to Auschwitz.

In the past ten years, we have seen scholars extend their analyses to include an understanding of how National Socialist policies were used to influence and manipulate culture.[2] As the public role of culture has been more and more under scrutiny, it has become evident that here, too, the interests of key Nazi leaders and specific aspects of the dominant political ideology became inextricably linked to everything from advertisements in the daily newspaper to the elite culture displayed at the "Great German Art Shows." This process by which National Socialist policies and politicians influenced public culture was not a linear development but rather, as with much in the Nazi regime, was sporadic and often inconsistent. Not surprisingly, the contradictions as well as the points of consensus that marked the internal development of the Party and state had their complementary expression in the development of public culture. Hence, public culture was yet another sphere that could be taken advantage of at particular moments and by specific individuals to push their own intrapolitical influence as well as to promote the radicalization of state-sanctioned policies such as anti-Semitism. While culture was never the determining realm of political power and ideology, it was nevertheless a high-profile area of work that could effectively be the means by which seemingly noncultural political, economic, and social policies could be extended and enacted.

Such a dynamic becomes clear if we look at what Hitler considered to be his most important public cultural policy—monumental state and Party architecture—in relation to the Nazi state's most devastating policing weapon: the SS-controlled concentration camp system. Across historical and art historical scholarship, Hitler's involvement with architectural projects has been well researched. The extent of his plans was massive, not only for the redesign of the so-called Hitler cities of Linz, Hamburg, Munich, Berlin, and the Party Rally Grounds at Nuremberg, but also for thirty-five other sites that, by 1941, had been added to the official registry of German cities to be redesigned.[3] Albert Speer controlled the two major projects of the Berlin redesign and the Nuremberg rally grounds, and the majority of the monumental buildings here and elsewhere favored Speer's and Hitler's preferred aesthetic of stripped-down neoclassicism with large-scale masonry construction.

Many scholars have noted that it is exactly here, in the masonry-building economy, that SS interests intersected with state cultural policy. But the precise connection between the two has nevertheless remained underresearched, especially as it concerns the initial decision of SS administrators to reorient the concentration camp forced labor in the late thirties. Most scholars have relied on the early and important work of Enno Georg, who analyzed the SS forced-labor industries through a summation of documents available through the Nuremberg Tribunals. More recent close studies of particular camps, such as Hermann Kaienburg's work on Neuengamme, have also depended on Georg's research when dealing with the prewar phase of forced-labor policy.[4] Yet because the SS never efficiently mobilized its forced labor for the building industry, the importance of public cultural policy is generally dismissed as a side issue to the history of the brutally effective policing practices established in the camps leading into the war.

But the distinction between productive forced labor and oppression is not quite as clean, particularly in the war years, as scholars have more recently recognized (including, most notably, Michael Allen in his study of the administrative organization of SS engineers and bureaucrats within the Wirtschaftsverwaltungshauptamt [WVHA]).[5] It is neither easy to argue that forced labor in the camps was simply a means to annihilate unwanted ideological and political enemies (Jewish and non-Jewish), nor possible to argue that the SS mobilized its control over forced labor at the expense of policies and practices of oppression.[6] But in spite of this reconsideration, little attention has been given to a new assessment of the initial stages of the systematic use of forced labor in the late thirties. Clearly, in these years, the *efficient* mobilization of forced labor was never achieved due to the cruelty of the treatment of prisoners at the camp sites themselves. Nevertheless, the lack of efficient treatment did not mean that inmates were not compelled to be *productive.* Hence, the period of concentration camp development beginning with the reorganization of the camps in 1936 needs to be looked at anew.

Issues of efficiency, productivity, and oppressive policy not only are crucial to the present study but also have broad resonance with other areas of Holocaust research, particularly those devoted to labor policies in occupied Eastern Europe.[7] However, in the prewar labor camps studied here, the vast majority of prisoners were non-Jewish

inmates defined by other political or ideologically generated categories (communists, socialists, labor leaders, Jehovah's Witnesses,
gay men, etc.). For example, in the largest quarry concentration camp
at Mauthausen (founded in 1938), the first Jewish inmate to be recorded in SS records was sent to the camp because he was a gay man
from Vienna. He died in the camp from unknown causes in March
1940.[8] Yet the point here would be that the kinds of decisions implemented in the forced-labor camps in the late thirties allowed for and
influenced the timing and enactment of practices of oppression directed at a specifically Jewish population later in the war. In this sense,
the conjunction of cultural policies and brutal policing measures indicated one way that SS administrators could extend their power over
individuals by institutionalizing a strong connection between economic practices and ideological policies of oppression. Later policies
of labor and oppression could take advantage of this institutionalized
structure, even while they dramatically adapted it to more brutal
goals. Understanding the role of productivity within this matrix of
contradictory and inconsistently applied economic practices gives us
insight into the radicalization of the SS that prepared the way for a
further extension of its power over the Jewish populations of Europe
during the war. Issues of productivity and cultural policy form a crucial component that makes our analysis of how state leaders were able
to incarcerate, punish, and kill more complex, and hence, more historically comprehensible.

Productivity was a planned result of oppression, not simply a by-
product of the conditions implemented by SS camp personnel. In the
late thirties and the early war years, the productive goals of SS administrators and the success or failure of productivity at camp sites
themselves depended most clearly on the major public peacetime initiative of the Nazi state, its monumental architecture. Taking the
goals of the SS administration seriously means looking beyond the
propagandistic and ideological function of culture and reconsidering
its political-economic effects. It is here that the development of the
policing function of forced-labor concentration camps intersects most
clearly with the public architectural goals of the state.

Soon after Himmler was appointed to head the German police in
June 1936, two major state-driven initiatives began to dominate the
industrial and cultural management of public policy: (1) rearma-

ment, with its demands on the German economy, especially after the introduction of the Four Year Plan; and (2) the prioritization of architectural policy and its focus on specific key sites, above all the Party Rally Grounds at Nuremberg and Hitler's developing ideas around the rebuilding of Berlin. The short-term militarist goal of rearmament paralleled the long-term peacetime goal of monumental state architecture, and each held a strong interest for Hitler. Further, each goal provided a focus for competition or coordination of a variety of policies initiated by individual state and Party institutions, policies that included the development of anti-Semitic measures as well as the continued oppression of designated ideological or political enemies of the Party.[9]

The potential to take advantage of broad state policy allowed for the radicalization of key institutions that sought to increase their control over German life or extend their popularity (and hence, power) with Hitler. The SS was one such institution and, in a crucial decision, Himmler directed the reorganization of the camp system in the late thirties precisely toward one of the key, publicly stated goals of Hitler: the redesign of German cities. After 1936, the extension of the camps and choice of sites indicate that Himmler's goal was not simply to set up an effective penal system but to establish the long-term viability of the camps as political and economic tools of the SS. For example, Sachsenhausen and Buchenwald were chosen for their proximity not only to population centers (Prussia, Saxony/Thuringia), but also to clay deposits suitable for brick making.[10] In the initial stages, these economic plans remained vague in terms of how they were to be implemented; nevertheless, the interest in the economic use of forced labor for the building economy influenced this extension of the concentration camp system.

By 1937, the political authority won by the SS enabled the pursuit of other interests that would contribute to the consolidation of the concentration camps as integral institutions in the German state. Himmler, through his head administrator Oswald Pohl, began to place increasing emphasis on securing the permanence of the camps by adapting them to a comprehensive economic program. It was already clear to Himmler that larger camps would be needed in times of war, but a growing emphasis on economic enterprises would give the SS a reason to expand the camps in peacetime as well. Though the intent to exploit penal labor was part of the organization of the camps from the very beginning, it was only in 1937–38 that the SS addressed the economic potential of forced labor as a key means of guaranteeing its role in a peacetime Germany. After regulations concerning who could be taken into custody were broadened, the SS could and did actively target prisoners who met its economic needs.[11] Prepared as they were to select prisoners based on political, ideological, *and* economic criteria, the SS could attempt to maximize its economic potential. This policy was also clearly in line with the need to extend the productivity of all labor as defined by the state's economic goals and those of Göring's Four Year Plan.[12]

Extending the function of the camps to include grander schemes of developing an economic empire occurred first with the brickworks established at Buchenwald and Sachsenhausen in 1938. It was in this period, a time when severe labor and material shortages were common in the building industry and other segments of the German economy, that the SS began seriously to orient forced-labor operations to the building materials market. At first, SS brickworks were linked only to the necessities of the Four Year Plan.[13] Yet by the time construction began on the brickworks in 1938, the SS had turned to the more exclusive and increasingly powerful patronage of Speer by linking the new forced-labor quarries and some of the brickworks to Speer's needs as head of the Inspector General of Building for the Reich Capital Berlin (Generalbauinspektor für die Reichshauptstadt Berlin [GBI]).

The decision to focus the majority of forced-labor operations on the production of large-scale brickworks and stone quarries came at the initial meeting of Speer, Himmler, and Hitler, which occurred after Buchenwald opened in July 1937 but before Pohl's trip to Flossenbürg and Mauthausen in March 1938.[14] With the support of Speer and Hitler, the use of the prisoners to make bricks and to quarry stone became institutionalized in the founding of the German Earth and Stone Works (Deutsche Erd- und Steinwerke [DEST]) on April 29, 1938. The business was officially registered on June 10, 1938 under the management of SS-Obersturmbannführer Arthur Ahrens (who in September 1938 appointed Walter Salpeter as deputy manager). On paper, the business always had a double organization. DEST personnel administered the concern as a private enterprise but, as SS members, they were also politically responsible to the SS-Verwaltungsamt under Pohl. At this stage, however, Pohl played little more than an oversight role of the firm.[15]

Such a company was of dubious legality as it involved a Party institution getting involved with the private economy, a point that had been ignored with the small-scale SS operations prior to 1937–38 but now became of crucial importance to Nazi Party Treasurer Francis Xaver Schwarz as the SS expanded into the national building materials markets. The German state had such a restriction on economic activity because, obviously, a political institution was perceived as having an unfair advantage and, hence, must be banned from investing in the private market. While the line between a state or party organization and ownership of a private concern had always been fuzzy even before the Nazi era, specific challenges were made concerning the legal status of DEST that forced the SS to respond. SS administrators avoided the legal critique by claiming the loophole that their concerns were not like private businesses engaged in maximization of profit but rather served the dual political goals of punishing or "reforming" inmates through labor as well as providing needed materials for the monumental building projects prioritized by Hitler. Specifically, Speer's plans for Berlin were cited continuously by the SS in its reports and contracts as a justification for the unlawful entry of a Party institution into private business.[16]

In its first year, DEST struggled with Ahrens and his unprofessional staff, which bungled operations, particularly in the brickworks at Sachsenhausen.[17] Furthermore, DEST lacked significant funding for development in the concentration camps. Yet, this situation changed when DEST received a major contract from the GBI on July 1, 1938. This was to be the first of many contracts, large and small, that the SS made and attempted to make with the GBI, establishing a predominantly architectural orientation to DEST's economic concerns.[18]

The GBI was the first and largest single patron of DEST during its entire history as a provider of building materials. Beginning with base payments in 1938 for preapproved brick orders and additional payments through 1941 totaling over RM 9 million, no other customer was so crucial to DEST's success. Though credit funds were received from other sources, including the Reichsbank, the GBI retained its role as the predominant architectural client through its payments to the SS.[19] Financing the enterprises at the camps rested largely on the advantage taken by the SS of the GBI's need for an ever larger share of the building materials market in Germany—that is to say, on the advantage the SS took of public cultural policy initiatives.

Bank credits and advances from the GBI allowed the SS to build and develop its ventures from 1938 to the beginning of the war in September 1939. Construction had begun on the brickworks at Sachsenhausen and Buchenwald by the summer of 1938 and the initial quarries at Flossenbürg and Mauthausen were either leased or acquired by this time. The 1938 annual report showed a loss, but in 1939 the operating budget jumped and a small profit of RM 135,850 was achieved. These initially optimistic figures were compromised by the mistakes made at Sachsenhausen, but nevertheless reflect the growth of the concerns. Payments were also received in these years for relatively small orders from (among others) the Reichsautobahn and the "Buildings at Adolf Hitler Platz" Association in Weimar. Both of these orders were for stone, as the brickworks were not yet operational, and indicate the relative success of the granite works in this period (profit of over RM 390,000) in relation to the brickworks (loss of more than RM 390,000).[20] Thus, by the time the war began, four of the six concentration camps were producing or being readied to produce building materials, some of which were already making their way to the monumental building projects of the Party and state. The SS attempt to obtain a major share of the building materials industry in Germany was well underway before September 1939 due to consistent financial backing and the increased authority to arrest extended categories of people. With Speer's GBI and the centralized organization of the seemingly unlimited forced labor, these concentration camps were filled and the inmates put to work.

The outbreak of war in September 1939 did little to dampen the development of DEST and the pursuit by the SS of a share in the German building economy. Not only did the SS expect the war to end quickly, but it had been exempted from turning over its economic operations to armaments industries. Hence, DEST extended its operations, acquired new quarry sites and brick-making facilities, and directed its production to specific monumental projects. Punishing prisoners through the development of the forced-labor camps continued at a rapid pace.

Whereas the brickworks provided the impetus for the SS's entrance into the building materials industry, the stone quarries were more specifically aligned with particular building projects, especially in the early war years when peacetime projects continued only at the privileged sites of Berlin, Linz, Hamburg, Munich, and the Party

Rally Grounds. In fact, while the brickworks were important for DEST, the hard labor of stone quarrying and the relative success in productivity rates meant that the quarry camps were the sites at which cultural policy and punitive practices were most directly integrated. In addition to Mauthausen and Flossenbürg, Natzweiler and Gross-Rosen were also set up around quarry systems in 1940. A quarry at Marburg was acquired by DEST in 1942, though it employed only civilians. DEST, under the guidance of Speer's administration, also established a stone-processing center (Oranienburg II) in 1941 near Sachsenhausen. Oranienburg II used prisoners to cut stone in preparation for the monumental building projects in Berlin. The SS created similar stonemason programs for inmates at Flossenbürg, Gross-Rosen, and Natzweiler, and by the end of 1942 it controlled more stonemasons through forced labor than the entire mason-labor population of prewar Germany.[21] Himmler and Pohl's decision to erect a system of quarries connected to concentration camp labor was quite practical in relation to the overwhelming importance of stone to the monumental buildings in National Socialist Germany. It also corresponded to the general conditions of the early-war building economy in which Hitler continued to privilege his high-profile peacetime public projects.

It goes without saying that, not surprisingly, DEST administrators located the new quarries on high-quality granite deposits based on Hitler and Speer's aesthetic demands. The SS specifically targeted the monumental representational building sites, acquiring contracts for (among others) Speer's German Stadium in Nuremberg and Wilhelm Kreis's Soldiers' Hall in Berlin. The focus of quarrying efforts on Hitler and Speer's major projects also provided a reason for justifying further developmental funds for DEST. From 1938 to 1943, the total turnover of the granite works was at least double that of the brick producers.[22]

But this history of organization and production goals raises the question of how productive the very inefficient exploitation of forced labor actually was. As Michael Allen has pointed out, SS middle managers might have had grand schemes, but they were often ignored at the camp site by the commandants and SS personnel, who were not going to stop abusing and killing the prisoners simply to serve some bureaucratic economic agenda.[23] To take one example of the granite quarry at Flossenbürg, production goals were never efficiently carried out and did not achieve Himmler's dreams of a total capacity for the camps of 100,000 cubic meters (cbm) of granite per year. Nevertheless, in the process of oppressing the inmates, certain production objectives were, after all, achieved. For example, because of the punitive function of the camps, Flossenbürg had little problem in maintaining adequate numbers of prisoners and, while Speer via Hitler could still make architectural policy a priority, in procuring necessary stone contracts. Having set a goal of 2,200 forced laborers for Flossenbürg, by the end of 1942 DEST was using almost 2,000 men, 1,108 of whom were apprentices being trained to cut stone. Wanting to increase production to 5,000 cbm in 1941 and again in 1942, however, they succeeded only in approximately sustaining the 1940 rate of production (2,848 cbm). Yet the DEST work at Flossenbürg continued to receive credit and, above all, to obtain regular orders for the Soldiers' Hall until Quarry II closed in the fall of 1943. The DEST quarry manager, Heinz Schwarz, had predicted that 10 percent of Flossenbürg's production would eventually be dominated by the high-profile commission of Kreis's Soldiers' Hall, a monumental memorial structure planned for Speer's North-South Axis in Berlin. But by the end of the war, at least 16 percent of all granite quarried at the camp can be accounted for based on Soldiers' Hall contracts.[24] Hence, from 1939 to 1943, DEST administrators at Flossenbürg were partially successful in increasing productivity to match the public peacetime goals of Hitler's Germany.

As an important economic sector of prewar and wartime Germany, the building economy itself was integrated into the developing political economy of the state. But as long as this political economy could be adapted and expanded to include the variable needs of monumental state architectural projects, the development of DEST around high-quality granite concerns and brickworks could continue. Further, these concerns could be extended during the war due to the increased control of new numbers of forced laborers sent to the concentration camps as a result of military operations. Only in 1942–43 did DEST administrators reluctantly give up this politically determined advantage of controlling the largest labor force of any building materials concern in the German economy.

The results of this institutional development would prove crucial for the day-to-day life of the prisoners in the key forced-labor camps geared to the production of building materials for DEST. At Mauthausen, as productivity at the granite quarry expanded into the early war years, so, too, did the death rate. Not only were more prisoners being brought to Mauthausen by the thousands (including hundreds of Jews from occupied Western Europe) but, because of the ideologically driven optimism and extension of power over human life, these prisoners were being killed or worked to death faster and faster. In relation to forced-labor practices, Mauthausen had its highest death rate per capita precisely in these years of German victories. At this point in the war, the SS had no need to worry about the capacity of an individual worker, as the individual worker seemed replaceable.[25] A focus on productivity became the way in which DEST administrators could concentrate on economic operations while avoiding the obvious contradiction between an interest in efficiency and destroying one's own labor force. Such a lesson had brutal results for the approximately 30,000 people who were killed at the camp between 1938 and the full transition to armaments work in 1943; it would also establish a pattern of concentration camp practices that could be repeated and adapted to the larger death and labor centers established in the east for the exploitation and destruction of the Jews.

My argument here is based on the historical premise that National Socialist policies of oppression were formulated and achieved through a step-by-step process in which ever more radical alternatives to what Henry Friedlander has identified as a "politics of exclusion" could be achieved.[26] Within this process of radicalization, individuals and institutions could position themselves, taking advantage of particular openings within developing state policy or pushing forward specific ideological goals not yet made official at the state level. Radicalization thus allowed for a great deal of flexibility on the part of SS administrators. It also allowed for the targeting of public architectural policy at the moment in which Himmler and Pohl were reorganizing and extending the economic function of the camp system. Certainly, if they had not chosen the building economy, some other large-scale government initiative would have been targeted by SS leaders, much as the armaments trade was incorporated into forced-labor operations later in the war. But, in the formation of DEST in 1938, the SS (not surprisingly) chose the most high-profile peacetime interest of Hitler, a move that seemed anything but a gamble. That the results of such a reorientation of forced labor were variable is an understatement.

But, that the results did include an increasing level of productivity *and* an intensification of oppression—granite is, after all, a very labor-intensive and difficult stone to quarry and cut—is a factor that explains the continued pursuit of the building economy by the SS well into the early years of World War II.

From this conjunction of culture and oppression, the SS expanded its influence with Hitler as well as socialized its camp personnel into the deadly practices of forced labor. Such factors cannot be overlooked in terms of the later development of the death camps during the war. They indicate the willingness of SS personnel to maneuver in any attempt to gain a political advantage over key policies and spheres of influence. Sometimes they were effective at this, sometimes not. But the cumulative violence of the camps as they grew from centers of incarceration and random punishment to centralized institutions of forced labor to the grotesque facilities of mass murder was a dynamic enabled by the ability of the SS to prove itself as, literally, a productive contributor to the state as well as to make use of developing political economic conditions. The implementation of ideological goals that encompassed the creation of monumental architecture is inextricable from the economic decisions and punitive practices that influenced forced-labor operations. Understanding this dynamic is key to our analysis of how the Holocaust was ultimately possible.

DEST took advantage of political and economic developments to expand its economic enterprises through the oppression of a seemingly unlimited labor force. Production for the building industry and for monumental building projects in particular was inseparable from and achievable only through the physical oppression of the inmates. DEST administrators emphasized production totals over any concern for maximization of labor potential while taking advantage of the promotion of architectural policy by Speer and Hitler during the war. The intersection of SS economic interests with Nazi architectural policy gave the initial impetus to the reorganization of the concentration camp system after 1936 and facilitated the punishment of prisoners through the production of building materials for the public peacetime monuments of Hitler's Germany. By 1941, such economic goals were expanded into the exploitation of vast populations of European Jews and others. At this point, however, economic interests were already giving way to the brutal practices of oppression that resulted in the genocide. These practices of oppression expanded out of such possibilities as those created by the conjunction of cultural policy and the development of the concentration camp system into the early war years.

NOTES

My thanks to Peter Hayes and Robert Gellately for their invitation to participate in the Lessons and Legacies conference as well as for their critical comments on my presentation. I am grateful as well to the trenchant editorial advice of Jeffry Diefendorf.

1. A model study of this phenomenon is Henry Friedlander, *The Origins of Nazi Genocide: From Euthanasia to the Final Solution* (Chapel Hill: University of North Carolina Press, 1995). For an argument concerning how cultural policy contributed to cumulative violence, see O. K. Werckmeister, "Hitler the Artist," *Critical Inquiry* 23 (winter 1997): 270–97.

2. For notable examples, see Jonathan Petropoulos, *The Faustian Bargain: The Art World in Nazi Germany* (New York: Oxford University Press, 2000); Pamela Potter, *Most German of the Arts: Musicology and Society from the Weimar Republic to the End of Hitler's Reich* (New Haven, Conn.: Yale University Press, 1998); Peter Reichl, *Der schöne Schein des Dritten Reiches: Faszination und Gewalt des Faschismus* (Munich: Carl Hanser Verlag, 1991); Alan Steinweis, *Art, Ideology, and Economics in Nazi Germany: The Reich Chambers of Music, Theater, and the Visual Arts* (Chapel Hill: University of North Carolina Press, 1993).

3. See the useful summary of Hitler's interest in architecture and the extension of redesign policies in Klaus Backes, *Hitler und die bildenden Künste* (Cologne: DuMont, 1988), 117–81. The scholarship on architecture during the National Socialist era and its effects on postwar German developments is extensive and encompasses both art historical as well as historical studies. For useful examples of particular debates, the reader is directed to Jeffry M. Diefendorf, *In the Wake of War: The Reconstruction of German Cities after World War II* (Oxford: Oxford University Press, 1993); Werner Durth, *Deutsche Architekten: Biographische Verflechtungen 1900–1970* (Braunschweig: Friedr. Vieweg und Sohn, 1987); Debórah Dwork and Robert Jan van Pelt, *Auschwitz: 1270 to the Present* (New York: Norton, 1996); Paul B. Jaskot, *The Architecture of Oppression: The SS, Forced Labor and the Nazi Monumental Building Economy* (London: Routledge, 2000); Gavriel Rosenfeld, *Munich and Memory: Architecture, Monuments, and the Legacy of the Third Reich* (Los Angeles: University of California Press, 2000); and Alex Scobie, *Hitler's State Architecture: The Impact of Classical*

Antiquity (University Park: Pennsylvania State University Press, 1990). The standard overview of architecture during this period remains Barbara Miller Lane, *Architecture and Politics in Germany, 1918–1945* (Cambridge: Harvard University Press, 1968).

4. Even the very careful work by Ulrich Herbert generally schematizes the prewar history and refers the reader to Georg, focusing instead on the brutal conjunction of forced labor with the wartime economy and armaments build up. So, as Herbert stated in a 1993 article on labor policy: "Even in 1938, when the S.S. began to organize camp inmates to work in stone quarries, brickyards and repair workshops run by the S.S. itself, the non-economic character of this labour was largely maintained." Ulrich Herbert, "Labour and Extermination: Economic Interest and the Primacy of *Weltanschauung* in National Socialism," *Past & Present*, no. 138 (February 1993): 154. Herbert cites Georg as his evidence here (Enno Georg, *Die wirtschaftlichen Unternehmungen der SS* [Stuttgart: Deutsche Verlags-Anstalt, 1963]). See also Hermann Kaienburg, *"Vernichtung durch Arbeit": Der Fall Neuengamme* (Bonn: Verlag J. H. W. Dietz Nachf., 1990).

5. Michael Thad Allen, *The Business of Genocide: The SS, Slave Labor, and the Concentration Camps* (Chapel Hill: University of North Carolina Press, 2002). I am, as always, grateful to the many conversations that Allen and I have had on this topic over our years of working on the SS.

6. For a study of this dynamic, see Michael Allen, "The Banality of Evil Reconsidered: SS Mid-Level Managers of Extermination through Work," *Central European History* 30, no. 2 (1998): 253–94.

7. For a specific analysis of labor policy and the genocide, see Götz Aly and Susanne Heim, "The Economics of the Final Solution: A Case Study from the General Government," *Simon Wiesenthal Center Annual* 5 (1988): 3–48. See also the essays in Dieter Stiefel, ed., *Die politische Ökonomie des Holocaust: Zur wirtschaftlichen Logik von Verfolgung und "Wiedergutmachung"* (Munich: R. Oldenbourg Verlag, 2001).

8. An excellent overview of Mauthausen's development and its camp population can be found in G. Rabitsch, "Das KL Mauthausen," *Studien zur Geschichte der Konzentrationslager* (Stuttgart: Deutsche Verlags-Anstalt, 1989), 50–92.

9. See the discussion of the economy during this period in R. J. Overy, *The Nazi Economic Recovery 1932–1938,* rev. ed. (Cambridge: Cambridge University Press, 1996), 52–65. For architecture during these years, see Paul B. Jaskot, "Anti-Semitic Policy in Albert Speer's Plans for the Rebuilding of Berlin," *Art Bulletin* 77, no. 4, (1996): 622–32.

10. In the case of Buchenwald, for example, the location near Weimar was suggested by the Thuringian Geological Provincial Examination office (Thüringische Geologische Landesuntersuchung) because of the avail-

ability of clay deposits. *Konzentrationslager Buchenwald* (Buchenwald: Nationale Mahn- und Gedenkstätte Buchenwald, 1990), 14–16; Johannes Tuchel, *Konzentrationslager: Organisationsgeschichte und Funktion der "Inspektion der Konzentrationslager" 1934–1938* (Boppard am Rhein: Harald Boldt Verlag, 1991), 2, 6–8. See also Karin Orth, *Das System der nationalsozialistischen Konzentrationslager: Eine politische Organisationsgeschichte* (Hamburg: Hamburger Edition, 1999). Orth, however, spends little time on the prewar years of the concentration camp system. Tuchel's remains the strongest analysis of this period.

11. Martin Broszat, "Konzentrationslager 1933–1945," in *Anatomie des SS-Staates*, vol. 2 (Munich: Deutscher Taschenbuch Verlag, 1967), 68–76. The opening of Buchenwald, for example, was aided by a direct order in June 1938 from Reinhard Heydrich, chief of the SS-Reich Security Main Office (Reichssicherheitshauptamt [RSHA]), to the effect that every local police district arrest at least 200 male so-called asocials who also were considered ready and able to work. Broszat discusses several orders Himmler used to fill Buchenwald at this time. For information on these SS administrators and others as well as their development of individual and collective interests, see the biographical studies in Ronald Smelser and Enrico Syring, eds., *Die SS: Elite unter dem Totenkopf* (Paderborn: Ferdinand Schöningh, 2000).

12. For an overview of the early development of forced labor, see Klaus Drobisch, "Hinter der Torinschrift 'Arbeit macht frei,'" in *Konzentrationslager und deutsche Wirtschaft 1939–1945*, ed. Hermann Kaienburg (Opladen: Leske & Budrich, 1996), 17–27.

13. For example, Hellmuth Gommlich (Minister of the Interior in Thuringia) wrote in a letter dated April 24, 1937: "The camp inmates should be occupied, within the framework of the Four Year Plan, with the production of bricks." Cited in *Konzentrationslager Buchenwald*, 16.

14. For Pohl's statements supporting this dating, see BA (Bundesarchiv), NS1/547, 4. As Kaienburg points out, it is unclear who initially suggested the use of prisoners for the production of building materials. Speer named Himmler as initiator (Albert Speer, *Inside the Third Reich* [New York: Macmillan, 1970], 144) while DEST administrator Hans Mummenthey named Speer in the Nuremberg Tribunals (*Trials of War Criminals before the Nuernberg Military Tribunals*, "The Pohl Case," vol. 5 [Washington, D.C.: USGPO, 1950], 567). The SS referred to Hitler's orders in its correspondence. Cf. Kaienburg, *"Vernichtung durch Arbeit,"* 74 n. 19.

15. For a complete analysis of DEST and the building economy, see Jaskot, *Architecture of Oppression*. Administratively, DEST was organized at first under Pohl's SS-Verwaltungsamt. However, with the rapid expansion of the economic enterprises, this office quickly developed into the SS-

Central Administration and Economic Office (Hauptamt Verwaltung und Wirtschaft [SS-HAVW]), established April 20, 1939, on the organizational model of Heydrich's RSHA. The HAVW had three divisions corresponding to Pohl's areas of authority: legal, economic, and a department for the inspection of all SS administrations and concerns. The economic division oversaw the bureaus that managed the SS-controlled businesses. In terms of the general administrative and managerial development of the SS, Allen is the best source. See Allen, *Business of Genocide*. For an additional analysis of the SS administration, see Jan Erik Schulte, *Zwangsarbeit und Vernichtung: Das Wirtschaftsimperium der SS* (Paderborn: Ferdinand Schöningh, 2001).

16. See, for example, the memorandum to Schwarz from Pohl, in BA, NS1/547, 4–6. Note that profit appears never to have been either an officially proclaimed or an actual motivation in SS policy, as Michael Allen makes clear. See also the discussion of the legality and formation of the early business operations of the SS in Allen, *Business of Genocide*, 57–96.

17. Allen, *Business of Genocide*, 78–92.

18. See the renegotiated contract in BA, NS 3/36, 199–203. For a brief summary of the early failure of the brickworks at Sachsenhausen, see BA, NS3/719, 3–10.

19. See the list of GBI payments for 1938, 1940, and 1941, respectively, in BA, R2/4499, R43II/1183, R120/729. For an overview of DEST's credit situation (August 22, 1939), see BA, NS3/1532, 1–11.

20. For budget statements and payments, see BA, NS3/1345, 8–9; NS3/32, 1–25; NS3/1009, 4–6.

21. Summary of DEST quarries, in BA, NS3/32, 13–24. See also the analysis of SS stonemason operations in Jaskot, *Architecture of Oppression*, 71–9.

22. Georg, *Die wirtschaftlichen Unternehmungen*, 56. Georg cites the statements made at the Nuremberg Tribunal by Schwarz and Mummenthey concerning Speer's involvement in choosing the location for Natzweiler and Gross-Rosen based on the type of stone. This is supported, particularly in reference to Natzweiler, through the documentation on the Nuremberg Party Rally Grounds (see Jaskot, *Architecture of Oppression*, 47–79). For production statistics from 1939 to 1940, see BA, NS3/1009, 321–2.

23. See in particular Allen's discussion of the "primacy of policing" in regulating the camp environment in Allen, "The Banality of Evil Reconsidered," 260–8.

24. Jaskot, *Architecture of Oppression*, 108–13.

25. Ibid., 43–6.

26. Friedlander, *Origins of Nazi Genocide*.

Sybille Steinbacher

The Relationship of the Auschwitz Camp to the Outside Environment, Economy, and Society

WHILE IN THE 1950S THE NAME "AUSCHWITZ" WAS ALREADY HEARD often in both West Germany and the German Democratic Republic (GDR), for both countries it simply served as a cipher. In the GDR, it was basically shorthand for the criminal consequences of the capitalist system: a system that took on monstrous reality in the IG Farben factory in Auschwitz-Monowitz. In West Germany, at least by the start of the Auschwitz Trial in Frankfurt (1963–65), it had become a symbol and synonym for the mass crimes of the Nazi state.[1] In both the media and scholarly discussions, "Auschwitz" presently serves as a metaphor of the Nazi regime's atrocities: a putatively concrete stand-in for what is also termed "the inconceivable," "the unsayable," "nameless crimes against humanity" committed "in the name of Germany."

It is striking that document-based, empirical historical research on the major locus of Nazi mass murder is hardly manifest: aside from memoirs and literary renderings by former inmates, we in fact find the catchword "Auschwitz" mainly appearing in relation to moral-ethical reflections and cultural criticism. At the same time, we find a migration of discourse on Auschwitz within the academy from departments of history to sociology and pedagogy, and, outside the academy, its frequent presence within political journalism. In general, the Auschwitz discussion thus runs a risk of becoming a simple vehicle for expressing moral disturbance. Put more pointedly, over the past few decades, there has been more reasoning about, than research on, Auschwitz. To a great extent, the organization and realization for the mass murder committed there, as well as both the political and societal responsibility for it, have remained obscure.

West German historiography first focused on the exterminatory process in the report prepared at Munich's Institut für Zeitgeschichte by the Frankfurt public prosecutor's office, under the direction of Fritz Bauer, in the framework of the Frankfurt Auschwitz Trial. The genesis and structure of the crime were here explored on an analytic level only to be reached again two decades later.[2] In any event, in the 1980s the scholarly debate became swallowed up in the controversy between "intentionalists" and "structuralists" over Hitler's role in developing the "Final Solution to the Jewish Question." And while the historiographically fruitless Historikerstreit was concerned with classifying and explaining the Nazi mass murder, as well as with the question of its singularity ("Auschwitz" being its metaphor), reconstructing the event's empirical details was certainly not at its center.[3] The misleading impression thus emerged that the facts were sufficiently well known.

The opening of the Eastern European archives in the course of the last decade has, however, marked a change in this situation. A variety of new historical insights now promises to emerge against a backdrop of altered accents and perspectives, itself the result of detailed research on an empirical, documentary basis.

Such an expanded research horizon, making space for both a political and social-historical perspective, is apparent in the four-volume series whose title in translation would be something like "The History of Auschwitz: Accounts and Sources."[4] This project was initiated by Professor Norbert Frei of the Ruhr University in Bochum. Its goal is to consider the mass murder in the Auschwitz concentration camp and death camp in two contexts: on the one hand, in developments in the war; on the other, in Nazi policies regarding the economy, the society, and the domination of conquered Poland. The volumes are not meant to replace a specialized and comprehensive study of the camp's history, in its multilayered, complicated reality.

The classical themes of concentration camp research (i.e., the living conditions, forced work, resistance, and extermination)[5] do not stand at the center of these volumes. Rather, the main focus is on three problems: the ideological and practical linkage between "Germanization" policies and mass murder; the entanglement of the private German economy in the crime; and—not least of all—the behavior of the German civilian population in face of the terror and mass murder taking place within the camps. The history of the town of Auschwitz under the German occupation and the direct coexistence of town and camp is the theme of my own study, forming the project's second volume. In line with what I have suggested, I am not concerned there with "Auschwitz" the metaphor, but with—for the first time in an extended manner—the concrete historical-political space in which the mass murder and other crimes took place.[6] My study's purpose is to consider the conceptual and temporal unity of "Germanization" *(Eindeutschung)* and genocide: this against the backdrop of interwoven German policy strands—*Lebensraum,* conquest, extermination.

Scrutiny of the town and the ever-expanding camp complex makes it clear how centrally important Auschwitz, in fact, was in that policy framework: both of the chief ideological concepts of the Nazi state (the "Final Solution to the Jewish Question" and "conquest of *Lebensraum* in the East,") were here simultaneously set into action in the most narrow of spaces.

The close look at town and camp is meant to increase the depth of focus. As much as the kind and extent of linkage to such environs would differ from one camp to the next, it is clear that in general, ties would form between a camp's SS personnel and the outside inhabitants and officials—ties that would condense successively and have many expressions. In the case of Auschwitz, exploring the social setting of the locus of terror reveals how blurred the border was between normality and crime. It becomes clear that here as elsewhere, the camp was no impenetrable "closed-off cosmos."[7] Rather, the intensive administrative, infrastructural, economic, and social contacts with the immediate environs were necessary for the camp's existence.[8]

In the conquered East, the moment of distancing and aggressivity vis-à-vis everything foreign played a far more significant role than in the old German Reich as a pillar of *Volksgemeinschaft* ideology. Thus the concentration camp and its terror apparatus here served the purpose not only of eliminating political "enemies of the state," but also, and especially, of assuring "the new ethnic order," hence the creation of the "racially" homogenous *Volksgemeinschaft.*[9] In this regard, Auschwitz was the guarantee of a folkish future in the conquered *Lebensraum,* and the crimes being committed in the camp were bracketed out of the perceptive field of both the functionaries and the civilians who settled there. To the contrary: the ideological task of racial restructuring and purification legitimized all rigorism.

THE ROAD TO THE GERMAN REICH

Auschwitz was among the places in Poland that the Luftwaffe attacked in the first days of the war. The Germans were concerned with the strategically important train station, as well as with the barracks for the sixth battalion of the Polish cavalry; under pressure from the attack, the battalion withdrew sixty kilometers east to Krakow. After a number of civilians were killed in a hail of bombs, many of the town's residents also fled.

In September 1939, Auschwitz had roughly 14,000 residents. Something more than half were Jews; the rest (around 6,000) were Catholics. The town had had a mainly Jewish population since the end of the nineteenth century. The Jews spoke proudly of "Oświęcimer Jerusalem." In the days following the war's beginning, Jews, above all, left the town in droves. Meanwhile, the Wehrmacht had started moving toward Auschwitz; behind it was the Einsatz squad "for special usage" (Einsatzgruppe z.b.V.) that Himmler had hastily put together in order to suppress the Polish defenders in the Upper Silesian industrial zone. The Germans took the town on September 4, overcoming an intensive Polish defense effort.

Only a week later, the marketplace of the Polish- and Yiddish-speaking town had been renamed "Adolf-Hitler-Platz," and the Polish place-name "Oświęcim" (derived from *święty,* or "saint") was itself quickly changed to "Auschwitz." The town had last possessed that German name at the end of the previous century—it still belonged then to the Austro-Hungarian empire. The Germans saw to it that streets, bridges, and squares quickly had German names.

But it was still not clear to which political-geographic area Auschwitz was to be assigned: to the eastern part of Silesia—so-called eastern Upper Silesia—meant to be speedily "Germanized" and annexed to the German Reich; to the "Reichsgau Beskidenland" that was still under discussion then; or to the legally undefined General Government. A decision in favor of the first option was reached only with the October 1939 fixing of the German Reich's new borders by the commission on borders of the Reich Interior Ministry.

In dividing conquered Poland in two, Hitler's intention was not so much a final confirmation, already, of German claims in the East, but rather, set the stage as quickly as possible for two processes: first, a Germanization of the regions of western Poland, which, along with eastern Upper Silesia, included Danzig–western Prussia, the Wartheland (Warthegau), and eastern Prussia; and second, an economic exploitation of the General Government.

Intent on establishing a new territorial and economic order, the border commission mapped out the German Reich according to military and economic criteria as well as those related to transportation. The Reich was allotted 90,000 square kilometers of territory that, to a large extent, had been strictly Polish; 80 percent of Polish industry was located here, as were approximately 10 million inhabitants. This meant that far more territory than had been claimed by Germany since the First World War now belonged to the German Reich.

Auschwitz was directly affected by the annexation of western Poland. The town was now part of the Reich—it was located in the Bielitz Landkreis, in the newly formed governmental district of Kattowitz, province of Silesia. It cannot be stressed enough that Auschwitz was not located in a nebulous "East": something anchored in German postwar consciousness and still frequently suggested. Along with the Chelmno death camp in the Wartheland, the Auschwitz of the Final Solution was established on what was then German soil.

THE "NEW ETHNIC ORDER"

At the time of Auschwitz's annexation into the German Reich, practically no one living there aside from a few ethnic Germans could pass as German according to Nazi racial criteria. This fact illuminates the dimensions of the task facing the German conquerors in Auschwitz regarding what was termed "population policy." Historically sharpened through references to the medieval eastward settlement-movement, the programmatically violent "Germanization policy" became the occupiers' ideological program everywhere in annexed western Poland. In the framework of Nazism's "new European order," "Germanization" signified a "regrouping of peoples" that lacked all scruples: a radical denationalization and ruthless supplanting of the native population. The territories of western Poland were meant to be restructured as quickly as possible into a "purified," ethnically homogenized, and—tied to initial measures taken in the direction of the new social-economic order—economically efficient terrain. This planning called not only for the settlement of "racially valuable Germans," but also for the establishment of a German administration. The central goal was to drive all the Jews and most of the Poles out of western Polish territory, and to "bring in" Germans and persons of German origin under strict segregation from the remaining Poles.

In October 1939, Hitler granted Himmler, in his new capacity as Reichskommissar für die Festigung deutschen Volkstums (Reich Commissioner for the Consolidation of German Nationhood), far-reaching additional powers to set in motion the settlement of persons of German origin in the western Polish territories and removal of the "racially inferior" native population. In Himmler's first resettlement plans, Auschwitz was to become the political, economic, and cultural center for Germans from the South Tirol. The precondition for this was a "removal" of Jews and Poles from the town—something supported zealously by Vienna's Southeast German Research Society (Südostdeutsche Forschungsgemeinschaft). The society's area planners, architects, historians, and anthropologists were responsible for the socio-geographical and cultural research accompanying the Nazi resettlement policies.

However, the plans for Auschwitz were not ripe for implementation: after the victory over France, Himmler favored Burgundy as the new settlement zone for the southern Tiroleans; later, there was talk of lower Styria and even the Crimea. Eventually, a realization set in that the Germanization of the Auschwitz region was not as problem-free as originally anticipated. The entire eastern part of the Kattowitz governmental district, named the "eastern strip," was proving to be very difficult because of its almost entirely Polish and Jewish population. The settlement strategists in the civil administration and the SS were quick to agree that the region was unsuitable as an "inception" point for racial Germans. Separated from the governmental district's western area by the so-called police border—a guarded wall—the eastern strip had legally second-rank status. The terrain was thus at least provisionally exempted from Germanization. This was of some importance for Auschwitz's residents, since the town's location in the eastern strip meant them being free, for the time, from deportation.

For this reason, the Jewish population of Auschwitz did not diminish but rather increased with the start of the Nazi resettlement program: the town now became a collection-point for those Jews deported to the eastern strip from the western parts of the Kattowitz governmental district, which had been designated for accelerated Germanization. Having no choice but to shelter and care for these people,

the town's Jewish council of elders soon found itself facing utterly insoluble problems. In the spring of 1940, the city of Auschwitz contained one of the largest Jewish communities in the eastern strip. Jews
lived narrowly herded together in the alleys of the old town, isolated
from the other residents and strictly controlled by German guards.

Gradually settling in Auschwitz, the Germans included administrative officials, businessmen, and custodians of previously Jewish
and Polish firms. The move to the annexed eastern regions opened
many possibilities of social advancement to these people. Anarchic
circumstances prevailed in occupied Poland in the phase between the
termination of military administration in the fall of 1939 and the
consolidation of civil administration in the spring of 1940. Legal insecurity spread quickly in the confusion of authority at work between
countless departments and offices of state and party. Other than in
the old Reich, political and personal corruption was here in the conquered east the rule for Germans in this "plunder period" of the occupation. The euphoria of war, assurance of victory, and pioneering
mood together found their expression in an absence of moral inhibi-
tions. Not restrained by standard norms and not subject to effective
controlling forces, in Auschwitz the functionaries also freely exercised
their caprice—an approach understood as a self-evident right. This
"master race" behavior, informed by ideology and personal greed,
propelled the corruption forward, rendering it an endemic, structural
problem for the German occupation.

THE CONCENTRATION CAMP AND ITS EFFECTS

In the spring of 1940, the first concentration camp within Poland's
prewar borders was erected, a little less than three kilometers from
Auschwitz's old town. The site was a former barracks area, used in
World War I to shelter Polish seasonal workers. The choice of site was
connected to a general search initiated by Himmler: areas in the
Reich's border regions that were suitable for concentration camps
needed to be located, for the sake of interning political opponents
and bolstering German power.[10]

Auschwitz was chosen only after repeated inspections—the barracks were decayed and the general area lay in a flood zone. But in
the view of the competent SS experts, the advantages outweighed
the drawbacks, since the former camp for seasonal workers was in-

frastructurally developed and easily closed off.[11] At the beginning, Auschwitz was simply one of many similar Nazi camps. The only unusual thing about it was its calculated capacity of up to 10,000 prisoners, the occupiers counting on many political prisoners in conquered Poland. In the initial phase, most prisoners were not Jews but members of Poland's intelligentsia and other groups seen as part of the Polish national resistance.

The first persons who had to endure labor on the camp's construction were 300 Jewish men recruited by the SS with the forced assistance of the elders' council.[12] The Jews remained in the dark concerning the purpose of the construction, and they were strictly isolated from the arriving prisoners. The roughly 1,200 unemployed and impoverished Polish refugees living in the barracks next to the camp site were also directly affected by the construction: camp Kommandant Rudolf Höss was troubled by the "asocial elements" and wished the barracks area to be incorporated into the camp's terrain; he thus demanded the Poles' immediate evacuation. However, these individuals forestalled the planned "cleansing action," leaving the site quietly in night and fog, and taking the barracks' usable parts with them. Some time after, the SS confiscated apartment buildings of Polish families in the vicinity of the camp, and the residents were deported. More than a hundred buildings were also dynamited in order to create a "free-fire field" in the case of attempted escapes.

The companies profiting from the construction of the Auschwitz camp were exclusively German, with Höss relying on firms in the Silesian old Reich for suitable personnel and material. In June 1940 he enlisted the first firm: the well-construction specialists Wodak, from Beuthen. Soon after, he enlisted the above- and below-ground construction firm Kluge, from Gleiwitz. By the summer of 1944, more than 500 larger and smaller firms from the entire Reich had helped build and maintain the camp through various kinds of construction, installation, and supply. As has recently become well publicized, the Deutsche Bank had a substantial role in financing the Auschwitz extermination facilities: the bank furnished credit to ten construction firms doing work there for both the Waffen-SS and IG Farben. Since some of the amounts involved were so high they required approval from the bank's Berlin directors—it is to be assumed that its chief managers at least suspected what the money was for.[13]

THE SS SETTLEMENT

In the summer of 1940, Auschwitz became a seat for troops from the SS—the start of a macabre idyll. The men were first housed in a former barracks block outside the protective-custody camp, as well as in the Gymnasium by the Kasernenblock, on the Sola bridge. Additional houses, sometimes even whole streets, were gradually confiscated for the SS. In the end, the so-called SS settlement was extended into a distinct part of the town. In August 1944, 3,342 SS personnel were serving in the camp; a highpoint of 4,481 would be reached for a two-week period in January 1945. At the war's end, a total of around 7,000 SS members had served in Auschwitz, including around 200 female SS supervisors.[14]

In the initial period, wives and dependents of SS members were not allowed in the camp. But soon the policy changed to one of encouraging brides and wives to follow their husbands to Auschwitz, accompanied by children, in order to make a normal family life possible. As various internal directives and reports from the camp commanders to the guard units make clear, the camp administration approved countless residency applications.[15] Living in the SS settlement had many pleasant aspects. For instance, SS garrison doctors would see to the needs of SS families and were thus referred to as "family doctors," their consultations as "family office hours." It was by no means unusual for children in an SS family to run outside the area demarcated by the great chain of guardposts while playing; in this context, the directives refer indignantly to children marching alongside the inmate columns during the daily entry and exit of the work detachments. The commander's office warns of mortal danger to the children in the case of escape attempts, on account of the "use of firearms by the accompanying guards that is necessary here." And alarm comes through in the reference to the "moral deficits" ensuing from "contact of the children with the prisoners"—and the parental irresponsibility thus involved in such contacts.[16]

At the peak of the mass-murder process, the number of SS family members rose strikingly. Moves into the camp increased to the point that the commander's office was forced to refuse any additional living-space to SS families.[17] In June 1944, the commander had to strictly instruct the camp guards that "entry to the camp-zone by strangers is not allowed"[18]—at this time, hundreds of thousands of Hungarian Jews were being gassed to death there.

"BULWARK OF *DEUTSCHTUM*"

It was shown that on account of its "racial" structure and location in the legally inferior eastern strip, the town of Auschwitz initially played only a marginal role vis-à-vis Nazi policies of Germanization. But in the spring of 1941, this situation changed in a basic way, due to the construction of the IG Farben factory, one of the largest, most expensive, and most ambitious investment projects undertaken by the German Reich in World War II. With breathtaking speed, a policy of industry-led urban planning emerged that rendered Auschwitz a "model of Eastern settlement"[19] or, put otherwise, an exemplar of the Germanization of conquered *Lebensraum.*

IG Farben was the most important private German company and had one of the largest chemical plants in Europe. Construction of the Auschwitz factory not only marked fulfillment of an urgent goal of the Nazi German government's economic policy; at the same time, it marked fulfillment of an equally urgent goal of population policy: erection of a "bulwark of *Deutschtum*" on the eastern edge of the German Reich.

The firm's policy-leitmotif was a profitable linkage of race-ideological dogma and economic interest. IG Farben was the first private enterprise in the Reich to construct a concentration camp—that of Monowitz. The firm entered without any qualms into intimate complicity with the SS. Beyond this, in the service of Germanization, the firm initiated the violent racial restructuring of the town's population, its Jewish residents being deported as a direct consequence of the factory's construction. On April 7, 1941, notables from politics and industry celebrated the founding of the new plant with a ceremony in Kattowitz. At the same time, the Jews of Auschwitz were forcibly expelled from their town, its more than 700-year-old Jewish tradition coming to an abrupt end. They were transported to the assembly areas and eventual ghettos of Sosnowitz and Bendzin (Bendsburg), from where most later returned—to the death camp at the gates of their own town. The Polish residents remained in Auschwitz in order to serve as a work force constructing of the IG Farben plant.

According to the plans (which would not be realized), as soon as they had served their purpose, they were also to disappear.

Entire villages were emptied in spring 1941, after Himmler ordered erection of a mammoth agricultural estate—the so-called *Interessengebiet*—in the immediate vicinity of the Auschwitz camp. In fall 1941, a camp complex was built on the site of the former village of Birkenau, which had been inhabited by around 3,800 Jews and Poles.[20] This new complex was far larger than the original camp. First planned as a camp for Soviet war-prisoners—the construction order was issued on September 26, 1941—Birkenau almost certainly had already become the locus for the mass murder of European Jewry in the early summer of 1942.

Simultaneous with this, as part of the "civilizational development" of the town of Auschwitz, chief architect Hans Stosberg, specially called in for the purpose, was working there on gigantic construction plans for the future German residents: broad residential streets, magnificent party buildings, a "residential city" for the "following" of IG Farben; and also stadiums, swimming pools, and parks. Entire neighborhoods of the town were conceived anew, with room for 70,000 to 80,000 German residents being on the drawing board.

Even if Stosberg's larger design was hardly realized, it is the case that Auschwitz became the new center of life for several thousand "Reich Germans." It is striking that the settlers arrived in the town at around the same time that the camp's extermination process reached a first apogee in 1943. Most of the arrivals were staff members of IG Farben from cities in which the concern had branches. Later, settlers would come from all over the Reich, for—like all of Silesia—the region around Auschwitz had gained in attraction by still being spared from bombing.

In 1943, the roughly 28,000 residents of the town of Auschwitz represented twice as high a population as in 1939. Jews, to be sure, no longer lived in the former "Oświęcimer Jerusalem." In their place, around 7,000 "Reich Germans" were spreading themselves out. We do not, in fact, know very much about them. For example, it is unclear whether—and, if so, in what way—IG Farben forced their resettlement. Still, it is evident that the "Reich Germans" enjoyed extensive tax advantages in the annexed eastern regions— and also that the individuals moving there included many young people apparently meant to complete some of their training in the new plant.

As we know from many historical sources, much partial information concerning the camp, as well as rumors, hunches, and suspicions, circulated among Auschwitz's German population. In addition, there was a dull feeling that the frequent sweetish stink of burnt flesh, too penetrating not to be noticed, had an evil source. Until the startup of the new, large crematoria in the spring of 1943, the persons murdered with poison gas in Birkenau were burnt in the open air. But whoever wanted to could find simple explanations: those, for instance, who reasoned that "self-evidently" there was a higher mortality rate in the camp and that the corpses had to be cremated. Such self-comfort made possible an overcoming of cognitive dissonance; and certainly latent angst contributed to inquiries' being omitted. Indifference was frequent; the degree of approval is unclear. Protest was in any case not loud; rather, what is significant is the lack of action.

The main attention of the German residents was reserved for furthering professional and private existence. The camp entered the picture only when, for instance, the SS issued an invitation for a "community meal followed by a big bright afternoon" on the SS grounds, for the so-called Wehrmacht Day at the end of March 1943. The continuation of normal, relaxed life in the town is also apparent in the noisy celebrations that took place in the marketplace's main inn, the Ratshof, on New Year's Eve 1943–44. The establishment was managed by a man from Wuppertal, who proudly reported to a friend in the old Reich that the admission tickets were as eagerly desired "as the press ball in Berlin."

When it comes to awareness of the crime of mass murder, we certainly need to ask how detailed the knowledge could be, as well as whether any possibilities for regulating conflict were in fact available. What is certain is that some groups of people in Auschwitz had very precise knowledge of what was transpiring: employees of the Reichsbahn, for example, who regularly accompanied the arriving death-trains from the train station to Birkenau. And the gassing of prisoners who were no longer "capable of work" was an open secret to the managers of IG Farben in particular, who denied all guilt at Nuremberg for the murder of 25,000 slave laborers.[21]

CONCLUSION

In its relation to general Holocaust research, two aspects of this evaluation of the Auschwitz camp's concrete historical-political space—Auschwitz was not situated in the "distant East" but belonged to the German Reich—and the camp's social ambiance are particularly salient.

First, the planning for a new social and economic order had an important function in the legitimation of the mass murder of the Jews. Serving the Germanization process, the "scientifically" supported plans for social transformation of towns and cities offered a (pseudo-)objective justification of proceeding against the Jews in a radical manner. However, the plans for modernization and reconstruction were not the cause of the mass murder. Rather, they were the situative expression and practical, murderous application of a deeply internalized race-ideological conviction. In the name of so-called modernization, functionaries down to the level of town mayors demanded the "disappearance" of the Jews. Far-reaching impulses for the murder policy's realization emerged precisely from low- and middle-ranking administrative offices.

Second, since the murder of "racially inferior" people was the key to the Germans' long-term future in the East, and since the German claim to domination justified the crime ideologically, neither the daily lives of the German residents in the town of Auschwitz nor their sense of right and morals were affected by the horrific crime. To the contrary: the extermination received moral legitimation as ensuring the existence of the "Aryan race," and was defined as necessary against the backdrop of a biological-genetic order of values.

Against the backdrop of the "racial purification" of the conquered East, the Auschwitz concentration camp and death camp was nothing less than a complimentary supplement to the exemplary settlement town. The proximity of town and camp shows one thing very clearly: mass murder and German reconstruction did not stand in opposition. Rather, policies of Germanization and extermination formed a conceptual, spatial, and temporal unity. The camp itself was not secret, even if some activities were supposed to be and even if residents did not know everything. Resettlement and urban and economic development went side by side with depopulation, forced labor, and genocide. The killing of "racially unworthy" individuals furthered the emergence of a "racially pure folk-community." In essence, the "German reconstruction" in the East was entirely inconceivable without the simultaneous program of extermination.

NOTES

1. Cf. Norbert Frei, "Auschwitz und Holocaust: Begriff und Historiographie," in *Holocaust: Die Grenzen des Verstehens. Eine Debatte über die Besetzung der Geschichte*, ed. Hanno Loewy (Reinbek, 1992), 101–9, here p. 101. For an up-to-date review of the research, see Waclaw Dlugoborski and Franciszek Piper, eds., *Auschwitz 1940–1945: Studien zur Geschichte des Konzentrations und Vernichtungslagers Auschwitz*, vol. 1, *Aufbau und Struktur des Lagers* (Oświęcimer, 1999), 25–40.

2. Cf. Hans Buchheim, Martin Broszat, Hans-Adolf Jacobsen, and Helmut Krausnick, *Anatomie des SS-Staates* (Freiburg, 1965; Munich, 1994).

3. *"Historikerstreit": Die Dokumentation der Kontroverse um die Einzigartigkeit der nationalsozialistischen Judenvernichtung* (Munich, 1988).

4. Cf. Norbert Frei, Thomas Grotum, Jan Parcer, Sybille Steinbacher, and Bernd C. Wagner, eds., *Standort und Kommandanturbefehle des Konzentrationslagers Auschwitz 1940–1945* (Munich, 2000); Sybille Steinbacher, *"Musterstadt" Auschwitz: Germanisierungspolitik und Judenmord in Ostoberschlesien* (Munich, 2000); Bernd C. Wagner, *IG Auschwitz: Zwangsarbeit und Vernichtung von Häftlingen des Lagers Monowitz, 1941–1945* (Munich, 2000); Norbert Frei, Sybille Steinbacher, and Bernd C. Wagner, eds., *Ausbeutung, Vernichtung, Öffentlichkeit: Neue Studien zur nationalsozialistischen Lagerpolitik* (Munich, 2000).

5. Dlugoborski and Piper, *Auschwitz 1940–1945*, vol. 1, *Aufbau und Struktur des Lagers;* vol. 2, *Die Häftlinge: Existenzbedingungen, Arbeit und Tod;* vol. 3, *Vernichtung;* vol. 4, *Widerstand;* vol. 5, *Epilog* (Oswiecim, 1999; original Polish publication: Oswiecim, 1995).

6. Although it is thematically related, the study by Debórah Dwork and Robert-Jan van Pelt of Auschwitz's urban history is in many respects insufficient. Its strength lies in the discussion of the architectural history of the Birkenau camp and the connected question of the start of the mass murder. But the study's weaknesses are more prominent, since the conceptual and temporal parallelism between "Germanization" and genocide are not considered. The authors draw a direct line between the medieval settler-movement and Nazi policies of extermination; the mass murder is thus teleologically interpreted as a culmination of the German "drive toward the

East." Cf. Debórah Dwork and Robert-Jan van Pelt, *Auschwitz: 1270 to the Present* (New York, 1996).

7. This contra Wolfgang Sofsky, *Die Ordnung des Terrors: Das Konzentrationslager* (Frankfurt am Main, 1993), 24.

8. The relation between concentration camp and environs in the conquered eastern territories has not been previously investigated; there has been some work on the social framework of some camp sites in the old Reich (the German Reich in its 1937 borders). Cf. Sybille Steinbacher, *Dachau—die Stadt und das Konzentrationslager in der NS-Zeit: Die Untersuchung einer Nachbarschaft* (Frankfurt am Main, 1994; 1993); Jens Schley, *Nachbar Buchenwald: Die Stadt Weimar und ihr Konzentrationslager 1937–1945* (Cologne, 1999); Gordon J. Horwitz, *In the Shadow of Death: Living outside the Gates of Mauthausen* (New York, 1990); Isabell Sprenger, *Groß-Rosen: Ein Konzentrationslager in Schlesien* (Cologne, 1996), 153ff. See also *Dachauer Hefte* 12 (1996), focusing on the theme of "Lebenswelt und Umfeld," and *Dachauer Hefte* 17 (2001), focusing on "Öffentlichkeit und KZ: Was wußte die Bevölkerung?"

9. On the Volksgemeinschaft as an identifying factor, cf. Detlev Peukert, *Volksgenossen und Gemeinschaftsfremde: Anpassung, Ausmerze und Aufbegehren unter dem Nationalsozialismus* (Cologne, 1982), 233ff.

10. The notion that Silesian prison conditions led to the construction of Auschwitz is incorrect. The lack of room in the prisons played no role in Himmler's reflections. The first author to suggest this was Alfred Konieczny, "Bemerkungen über die Anfänge des KL Auschwitz," *Hefte von Auschwitz* (1970) H. 12, 4–44. The notion was then assimilated into subsequent research without scrutiny, most recently by Franciszek Piper, "Die Entstehungsgeschichte des KL Auschwitz," in Dlugoborski and Piper, *Auschwitz 1940–1945,* vol. 1, 43–71, here pp. 59ff.

11. Cf. Karin Orth, *Das System der nationalsozialistischen Konzentrationslager: Eine politische Organisationsgeschichte* (Hamburg, 1999), 76ff.

12. We are mistakenly informed in many studies that the mayor of Auschwitz placed the Jews "at disposal," most recently in Irena Strzelecka and Piotr Setkiewicz, "Bau, Ausbau und Entwicklung des KL Auschwitz und seiner Nebenlager," in Dlugoborski and Piper, *Auschwitz 1940–1945,* vol. 1, 73–99, here p. 73. The error's source is a misunderstanding of the term "community" *(Gemeinde),* the word by which the Jewish witnesses who were relied upon for information about the forced recruitments designated the *Jewish* community, not the larger political community. The reason for Polish workers' not being enlisted for the camp's construction is unknown.

13. Detailed information concerning the role of the Deutsche Bank in the financing of the Auschwitz camp can be expected from the historical commission now researching the bank's history during the "Third Reich."

Cf. Michael Hepp, "Deutsche Bank, Dresdner Bank—Erlöse aus Raub, Enteignung und Zwangsarbeit 1933–1945," in *Zeitschrift für Sozialgeschichte des 20. und 21. Jahrhunderts* 15, no. 1 (2000): 64–116, here p. 95f.

14. Cf. Aleksander Lasik's sociological-demographic analysis "Die SS-Besatzung des KL Auschwitz," in Dlugoborski and Piper, *Auschwitz 1940–1945,* vol. 1, 321–84.

15. For this and the following, cf. Frei et al., *Standort- und Kommandanturbefehle.*

16. Ibid., Kommandanturbefehl 8/43, 20.4.1943; Standortbefehl 25/43, 1[2].7.1943.

17. Cf. ibid., Standortbefehl 22/44, 18.8.1944.

18. Cf. ibid., Standortbefehl 17/44, 9.6.1944.

19. *Muster der Ostsiedlung*—this was the literal term used in the founding meeting of the *Interessengemeinschaft* Auschwitz, which took place in Kattowitz on April 7, 1941. Nürnbg. Dok. NI-11117, 1–12, here p. 9, printed in *Nürnberg Military Tribunal (Trials of War Criminals),* vol. 8, 383–8, here p. 386.

20. Cf. Strzelecka and Setkiewicz, "Bau, Ausbau und Entwicklung," 73–99, here pp. 84ff.

21. Cf. Bernd C. Wagner, "Gerüchte, Wissen, Verdrängung: Die IG Auschwitz und das Vernichtungslager Birkenau," in Frei, Steinbacher, and Wagner, *Ausbeutung,* 231–48.

Richard Breitman

The Nazis and the Jews of Italy: New Sources on the Responsibility for the Holocaust in Italy

ON JULY 23, 1943, IN RESPONSE TO RUMORS ABOUT A PLOT TO OVER-throw Mussolini's government, Herbert Kappler set up a short-wave radio in his office in Rome and established contact with his superiors in Berlin.[1] Technically a police attaché within the German embassy in Rome, the thirty-six-year-old Kappler was placed with German diplomats as a cover. In actuality, he performed functions in Rome for the Gestapo and Security Service (Sicherheitsdienst [SD]) Foreign Intelligence: he reported not to the German Foreign Office, but to officials of Departments IV and VI of the Reich Security Main Office (Reichssicherheitshauptamt [RSHA]).

Kappler's radio connection came just in time. Two days later a palace coup in Italy did unseat Mussolini and install Marshal Pietro Badoglio in office. Anxious authorities in Germany wanted immediate information about the Italian political and military situation, and Kappler used his radio to describe the maneuvers of the Badoglio government, the Italian military, and the Vatican, as well as to report on the status of trusted fascist officials. After Italy secretly negotiated an armistice with the Allies and the British and Americans landed troops in southern Italy, Germany responded by rushing large numbers of troops and some policemen into Italy and taking control of the capital. Italy was no longer a German ally, but an occupied country—and a battleground.

Finding himself at the focal point of attention in Europe, Kappler relied heavily on radio communication: it gave him independence from Italian (and local German) officials and a means to reach Ernst Kaltenbrunner, chief of the RSHA, and even Heinrich Himmler. Although some mail went by courier and some phone calls may have been made, from early September until late October 1943 Keppler and various RSHA and SS authorities in Germany exchanged radio messages each day. These messages provide a running log of SS and police reactions to, and activity during, the Italian crisis, and they include small but revealing bits of information about the first stage of the Holocaust in Italy.

The radio messages between Kappler and authorities in Germany have hardly been used as a historical source, for a very obvious reason. Most of the file copies did not survive on either end, or they have not yet surfaced. But many of the messages were plucked out of the air at the time. As F. H. Hinsley and his team of historians indicated in the 1980s,[2] British intelligence intercepted these transmissions and quickly deciphered them. Translations were distributed within days, and among the recipients were some American intelligence officials. With the emergence of the translated messages in releases at the Public Record Office in Kew, London, and the National Archives in College Park, Maryland, during 2000,[3] it is now possible to exploit more fully what British and American intelligence learned at the time.

This article draws primarily upon these decodes of SD messages and certain other recently declassified documents, and secondarily upon some primary sources available earlier, in order to complement and verify recent accounts of the beginnings of the Holocaust in Italy. These primary sources help to clarify the timing of certain Nazi decisions and the authority behind them. They also give a better picture of the attitudes and actions of some of the key perpetrators than is available in even the most detailed monographs.

In some established accounts the Final Solution came to Rome on September 12, 1943, when Heinrich Himmler's office called Kappler and ordered him to round up and deport the Jews of Rome. Kappler had misgivings about carrying this action out under the eyes of Pope Pius XII and an unsupportive Italian population, and stalled as a result. Another, more detailed order came from Himmler on September 24.[4] At Kappler's trial in 1948, an Italian military tribunal agreed with Kappler's claim that he had opposed Himmler's plan.[5]

Although they are not complete or conclusive, the newly available primary sources do not support this received version, particularly the chronology. (Himmler's telephone log of September 12 also has nothing about a phone call to Kappler.)[6] The decodes of SD messages (hereafter called SD decodes) indicate that during the days before September 12 Himmler was obsessed with the rescue of Mussolini from Italian captivity. Infuriated by a refusal from General Karl Student, commander of a parachute battalion, to divide his troops and try to free Mussolini from captivity, Himmler ordered Kappler and other local authorities to override Student and carry out the rescue of Mussolini with the use of all available SS and police forces; all other activities should be deferred.[7] (Otto Skorzeny led the team of commandos that freed Mussolini on September 12.) These sources suggest that orders for deportations of Jews from Rome came later than September 12. With Rome not under full German control then, any deportation order was implausible anyway.

The first traces of the Final Solution in Italy appearing in the SD decodes came on September 18 with the arrival of Karl Wolff, formerly Himmler's chief of staff and now Highest SS and Police Leader for Italy, in Rome.[8] Wolff immediately ordered the transfer to Rome of 100 policemen from a police battalion in northern Italy, giving Kappler the nucleus of a force of his own.[9] It would be important during the next month, since Kappler recognized that he could not depend upon the Italian police to cooperate in deporting Jews. In fact, the general unreliability of Italian police in Rome forced Kappler to take some Roman police officials into custody.[10]

By September 24 Kappler was familiar with Himmler's goal of deporting Italian Jews. On that day Kappler warned Berlin that Spanish diplomats were about to leave Rome on a special train, and that the Vatican had sold Spanish, Argentinian, Portuguese, and Mexican visas to Jews trying to escape Rome on this train.[11] Whether the Vatican had actually done what Kappler reported is doubtful; in any case, there is no independent evidence to confirm the sale of visas to Jews. But Kappler's warning that some Jews were escaping, and his promise to find out who the purchasers of visas were, cast doubt on his postwar testimony of resisting Himmler's order.

It is possible that Kappler had earlier received Himmler's order to arrest and liquidate the Jews of Rome by a message that the British failed to intercept or decode, but it is more likely that any such order came via courier. (In fact, one likely bearer of such a message was Karl Wolff himself.) On September 25 the RSHA circulated a list of Jews of different nationalities who could now be deported—Italian Jews were first on the list.[12] By this time, Nazi policy was set.

On September 26 Kappler met with two leading Italian Jews—

Dante Almansi, president of the Union of Italian Israelite communities, and Ugo Foa, president of the Jewish community of Rome—to demand fifty kilograms of gold from the Jewish community of Rome within forty-eight hours. Otherwise 200 Jews would be deported to Germany. Following Kappler's postwar testimony, both historian Meir Michaelis and Richard Lamb, author of a study of the war in Italy 1943–45, suggested that Kappler turned to extortion as an alternative to deportation—he hoped to show his superiors how profitable it would be to exploit Rome's Jews.[13] Historian Susan Zuccotti summarized Kappler's explanation, but expressed great skepticism about it. (She most recently dismissed it entirely.)[14] The decodes do not conclusively establish Kappler's motivation, but they do show that Kappler was concerned about a rise in anti-German sentiments among the Italian population: his measures against the Jews of Rome were adding to the problem.[15] Nonetheless, he collected the gold and, as the decodes reveal, shipped it off to Kaltenbrunner's office on October 7.[16]

In an October 6 radio message decoded by the British,[17] Kappler alerted Wolff, who had returned to Germany, that SS Hauptsturmführer Theodor Dannecker had arrived in Italy with orders to seize all Jews quickly and ship them off to Germany. In the rest of the message, the interception or decoding was partly garbled, Kappler warned that German officials in Rome were going to Field Marshal Kesselring to suggest that Jews could be better used as laborers in Italy.[18]

In postwar testimony Kappler claimed that Dannecker arrived with authorization signed by Heinrich Müller to deport the Jews and to draw on all available police: it was a sign that Kappler's foot-dragging had failed.[19]

In actuality, Dannecker's arrival in Rome in early October seems to mark the point when resistance either began or intensified. German Foreign Office records indicate that the main lobbyist against deportation was the German consul in Rome, Eitel Friedrich Möllhausen, who was the senior embassy diplomat in the absence of Ambassador Rahn. Möllhausen contacted Ribbentrop on October 6 to try to cancel deportation: according to a document later smuggled into Switzerland by an anti-Nazi official in the German Foreign Office, Möllhausen also addressed his same message to Hitler.[20] The text suggested that General Stahel, the German commandant of Rome, was opposed to deportation; it was ambiguous about Kappler's view. Möllhausen's cable specified that he was about to go to Kesselring: he had not already done so. (Historian Michaelis expressed bewilderment in a footnote; he thought Möllhausen had acted ten days earlier.[21] But the newly available sources do not support that version — or Kappler's postwar spin.)

While awaiting resolution from above, Kappler passed along to Berlin another report that a businessman named Morini from Alessandria was traveling around Italy helping to smuggle Jews into Switzerland. (Nothing else is known about this Morini. It is possible that this report was a garbled version of the activities of Settimo Sorani, an official of the Jewish assistance organization Delasem. Sorani sometimes used cover names.)[22] Kappler sent this report to help his superiors shut this activity down. This message again suggests that if Kappler were opposed to deporting the Jews of Rome, it was only because he had concern about whether he could pull it off without full support of German authorities in Italy and in the face of Italian public opposition.

On the evening of October 7, Karl Wolff met with Hitler in the Führer's headquarters.[23] Whatever his own views, Wolff knew Hitler well enough not to recommend lesser punishment for Italian Jews. On October 11 Kaltenbrunner sent Kappler a very firm order that undoubtedly reflected both Hitler's and Himmler's heart-felt views:

> It is precisely the immediate and thorough eradication of the Jews in Italy which is the special interest of the present internal political situation and the general security in Italy. To postpone the expulsion of the Jews until the Carabinieri and the Italian army officers have been removed can no more be considered than the idea mentioned of calling up the Jews in Italy for what would probably be very improductive [*sic*] labour under responsible direction by Italian authorities. The longer the delay, the more the Jews[,] who are doubtless reckoning on evacuation measures[,] have an opportunity by moving to the houses of pro-Jewish Italians of disappearing completely. [Garbled word — Einsatzkommando?] Italy (has been) instructed in executing the RFSS orders to proceed with the evacuation of the Jews without further delay.[24]

This message survives only because of British interception: we have no other evidence of Kaltenbrunner's intervention. Kappler could now have no doubts that he was expected to fulfill this order regardless of its difficulties or repercussions. The next day Kaltenbrunner added a sweetener with his message that Kappler had been awarded not only the Kriegsverdienstkreuz, first class, but also the Iron Cross, second class.[25]

According to Robert Katz and more recently Michael Phayer, German Embassy personnel also contacted the German ambassador to the Vatican, Baron von Weizsäcker, who notified the Vatican of the impending action against the Jews of Rome.[26] Although a number of monasteries and convents opened their gates to Jews seeking to go underground, there is no clear evidence that the Vatican issued a warning or ordered Vatican institutions to offer sanctuary. There was no surge of Jewish applicants for sanctuary before October 16.[27]

Would anyone else warn the Jews of Rome? Almansi and Foa, the two Jewish leaders, did not do so—they hoped for the best from Kappler—but they got only misleading information from him. British intelligence was not in the practice of talking publicly about what it gleaned from German radio messages. The anti-Nazi German diplomat Albrecht von Kessel later claimed to have issued warnings to some of Rome's Jews that they would be exterminated, but his words met only disbelief.[28]

Kappler's preparations for the action of October 16 in Rome do not appear in the decodes of messages to Berlin. But once 365 police and SS managed to round up 1,259 Jewish men, women, and children and imprison them within a military school near the Vatican, Kappler quickly sent off a radio report that evening. His tone was slightly defensive—he had planned as well as possible, all available German police were used, the Italian police were unreliable, and it had not been possible to cordon off whole blocks in an open city to prevent Jews from escaping. Above all, the Italian public had resisted passively, and there were some instances of active opposition.[29] The results, he seemed to be implying, were as good as possible under difficult circumstances. Whether his superiors would rejoice in the seizure or bemoan the number of those not apprehended (more than 6,700), he did not know. (This report, largely but not entirely intercepted and decoded by the British, also went north by courier, and a copy survived in Himmler's files.[30] We are thus in a position to compare the full German original with the British translation.)

Kappler's men screened the Jewish prisoners, releasing those non-Jews arrested by mistake, Jews in mixed marriages, and some other special cases, such as Jews from countries where Germany had not yet started deportations. The Vatican secretariat of state sought to win the release of converts to Catholicism defined as Jews under racial laws, but without success.[31] On October 18 the remainder left Rome on a train numbered X70469. Wilhelm Harster, commander of the Security Police and SD for Italy, requested Kappler to radio Vienna and Prague (as well as Berlin) to arrange relief of the police escort when the train arrived there. Harster's radio message specified the transport's ultimate destination: Auschwitz—British intelligence read that quite clearly.[32] Dannecker also used Kappler's radio to report to his office (and thus to Eichmann) the departure of 1,007 Jews accompanied by a detachment of guards under SS-Oberscharführer Arndze, who had two copies of a list of the passengers.[33] Upon their arrival at Auschwitz, all but 196 Jews on the transport were immediately gassed, and only 15 of the 196 were to survive the war.[34]

On October 21 Dannecker's men headed off to Florence under the temporary command of SS-Untersturmführer Eisenkolb, Dannecker himself being ill.[35] They all had done what they could in Rome under the circumstances. But Kappler was not finished explaining his problems in Rome. In response to a message that some of his earlier transmissions had been garbled, on October 27 Kappler retransmitted an earlier assessment: for a long time, the Vatican had been assisting Jews to escape, and the population of Rome was turning increasingly anti-German—fearing that seizures of Italian laborers might follow the roundup of Jews. Kappler urged better German propaganda and more use of pro-German Italians to sway Italian public opinion.[36]

Kappler's assessments were a combination of his own perceptions and his own excuses for a job very partially accomplished. The action of October 16 captured about 15 percent of the total Jewish population in the city. The Final Solution in Italy took a toll of about 6,800 Jews—about 20 percent of the total, but more than what Nazi officials might have seized in the face of open defiance and publicity from the Vatican. Still, it is worth noting that Kappler would hardly have agreed with one recent author that Pius XII was "Hitler's Pope."[37] As far as Kappler was concerned, the Vatican represented a hostile influence on the Jewish question. That was undoubtedly what his superiors felt, too. It could hardly hurt to tell them what they already believed.

Kappler might have taken comfort in his superiors' appreciation of his situation if he had been able to listen in on an October 16 conversation between Heinrich Müller, head of the Gestapo, and a Foreign Office bureaucrat named Eberhard von Thadden. Their topic of discussion was implementation of the Jewish question in newly occupied territories. Von Thadden pointed to the escape of most Danish Jews in early October: To avoid repetition of failure, future actions against Jews should be carried out with sufficient planning and forces, so that serious political complications could be minimized. Conceding that the RSHA had learned something from events in Copenhagen, Müller responded that for the duration of the war it would not be possible to raise forces sufficient to carry out actions in one blow *(schlagartig)*. The only recourse was to do as well as possible with the forces that were available. Reflecting the view of the Foreign Office, von Thadden specifically argued that the influence of the Catholic Church in Italy made it important to strike rapidly there. But Müller stuck to his same approach: the purge of Jews would have to begin behind the line of battle (in the south) and spread to the north. There were not enough forces to do it any other way. Nonetheless, von Thadden noted that Müller apparently was concerned about the planned seizure of 8,000 Jews in Rome—an action that was in progress as they spoke. Müller referred to it as a *Führerbefehl*.[38] Kaltenbrunner had instructed Kappler harshly on October 11 because this order came from the highest possible authority.

Could the Allies have used information obtained from the SD decodes to help save some Italian Jews? This question is linked to a broader debate about what can or cannot be done with intelligence during a war. Every use of intelligence carries risks to intelligence gathering, but there were ways of using information publicly without revealing specific sources. Of course, few people in the fall of 1943 had access to information classified as "Most Secret."

There is no current information to suggest that Franklin Roosevelt received information about Nazi intentions in Italy in time to influence the outcome of events in Rome on October 16. The president did receive a translation of Möllhausen's appeal to Ribbentrop and Hitler, but only by way of a copy smuggled to Allen Dulles in Switzerland some two months after the event and then sent on to Washington.[39]

Winston Churchill had a better chance of gaining access to timely information about the Holocaust in Italy, but nothing in the intelligence files of the prime minister's office indicates that he learned of the plan for a Final Solution in Italy.[40] But two days after the SD message of October 6 from Kappler to Wolff announcing Dannecker's arrival in Rome and clearly revealing Dannecker's mission in Italy, Winston Churchill happened to discuss with his war cabinet the idea of issuing another public statement denouncing Nazi atrocities. Perhaps if the Allies publicly committed themselves to punishing those who carried out atrocities, massacres, or killings, it would deter future crimes. Foreign Minister Anthony Eden dissented from Churchill's proposal, arguing: "I am most anxious not to get into the position of breathing fire and slaughter against War Criminals and promising condign punishment, and a year or two hence having to find pretexts for doing nothing."[41] Churchill ultimately got his way on the principle, but the Moscow Declaration of November 1, 1943 (emanating from the Moscow Conference attended by the British and Soviet foreign ministers and the secretary of state), made no mention of killings of Jews and offered no warning to those still in danger of being deported.[42]

What ultimately happened to the perpetrators of the Final Solution in Italy? RSHA chief Ernst Kaltenbrunner was included among the major war criminals tried by the International Military Tribunal at Nuremberg. The prosecutors did not know, one assumes, about his order of October 11, 1943, or they would have used it as evidence against him. Nonetheless, there was enough other evidence to secure a conviction and a death sentence.

The fate of Theodor Dannecker, head of the deportation experts in Italy, remained obscure for some time after the war. (Even in 1985, Raul Hilberg was willing to claim only that Dannecker was believed to have died in American hands.)[43] Dannecker went into hiding to help organize Nazi resistance to an Allied occupation of Germany. Before doing so, he instructed his wife to poison their two children. One of the children died; the other was rescued by outside intervention. Dannecker led a small band of Nazis in the Black Forest and then migrated to Bad Toelz. Benefiting from a tip, American forces captured him, jailed him, and interrogated him. Dannecker conceded having played a role in deportations of Jews from several countries, and he admitted to being in Italy from September 1943 until February 1944. Given time to write his life history the next day, he hanged himself in his cell in December 1945. He did not get to the point of writing about his Italian activities.[44]

Herbert Kappler was captured by British forces and interrogated at some length in June 1945 about his recruitment of intelligence operatives, his treatment of political prisoners, and his plans for resistance to the Allied occupation of Italy. The Combined Staff Detailed Interrogation Center's summary of June 8, 1945, does not indicate that his interrogators asked questions about Nazi Jewish policy or that Kappler volunteered any information. Was this lack of attention to Kappler's role in the Holocaust the result of lack of interest, or of unfamiliarity with the most relevant intelligence records? Without further information, it is impossible to judge. The interrogator assessed Kappler as an intelligent, ruthless man, with the mentality and mannerisms of the "cold, correct Prussian militarist," who was prepared to justify his actions in Rome, partly at the expense of his superiors Karl Wolff and Wilhelm Harster. (It is not clear from files currently available whether he did so.) The interrogator, who thought Kappler's testimony reliable, indicated that Kappler might be wanted as a war criminal.[45]

Kappler was turned over to Italian authorities and tried in 1948 by an Italian military tribunal. Published accounts indicate that the court found insufficient evidence to convict Kappler for his role in deporting Jews from Rome—though he was given extra time for extorting gold from Rome's Jewish community. Kappler was convicted, however, for directing an execution of 320 prisoners in the Ardeatine Caves on March 24, 1944, as a reprisal against acts of sabotage by Italian partisans. Some of those to be executed were selected because they were Jews. Kappler had claimed that Harster had ordered him to include Jews among the victims, but Wolff placed blame for this decision on Kappler himself.[46] Kappler remained for many years in an Italian prison, but escaped in 1977 and made his way to West Germany, which refused to extradite him. He died not long afterward.

Kappler was not the only one responsible for reprisals in Italy. According to Kappler, Karl Wolff arrived in Rome on the evening of March 24, 1944, and complained that the execution of 320 people was not nearly enough: he wanted to blow up a section of the city dominated by communists. Wolff's account, given in London in November 1946, had been quite different. When he arrived, the executions had already been carried out on the basis of an order directly from the Führer to the Fourteenth Army. Kappler had taken the initiative to reach the specified number of executions by including some Jews. But Kappler was suffering so much from the psychological burden of carrying out the shootings that Wolff did not give him any trouble.[47] American intelligence officials had independent evidence implicating Wolff in other German reprisals in Italy,[48] but it was never used in proceedings against Wolff. Wolff had the distinct advantage of having helped to arrange an early surrender of German forces in northern Italy with Allen Dulles, head of the Office of Strategic Services in Switzerland. Although Dulles had made no promise of immunity to Wolff, he had been impressed with the man and spoke up for him afterward. Wolff nonetheless had a number of postwar difficulties. In a climate where world public opinion was shocked by photos of corpses and survivors from concentration and extermination camps, there was no way for Himmler's former chief of staff—one of the highest ranking SS officers to survive—to escape imprisonment. Wolff was moved from one internment camp to another and regularly interrogated. He was almost named as one of the major defendants at the International Military Tribunal at Nuremberg, but was passed over.[49]

In early 1946 Wolff was diagnosed as paranoid and was confined in a mental institution: he thought he was pursued by Jewish demons. After considerable American hesitation about prosecuting him because of his participation in Operation Sunrise, the British proposed to try him together with Field Marshal Kesselring. But they changed their plans and instead held a little-publicized trial in Hamburg in 1949, in which Wolff's partners in Operation Sunrise wrote affidavits or testified on his behalf. He was convicted, but on appeal his sentence was reduced to the time he had already served in internment. It was the equivalent of an acquittal. After the Eichmann trial, however, West German prosecutors turned up evidence that Wolff had helped to speed deportations of Jews to Treblinka. In 1962 he was convicted and sentenced to fifteen years, of which he served ten.[50]

Wilhelm Harster, commander of the Security Police and SD in Italy, was captured and interrogated immediately after the war. There is no reference in the interrogation summary to the Nazi actions against Italian Jews—Harster apparently did not have to answer questions about directing transports of Jews to Auschwitz.[51] But Harster had earlier served as commander of the Security Police in the Netherlands; he was turned over to the Dutch, who tried him for his crimes there. Harster was convicted and given a twelve-year sentence, of which he served six. Afterward he became a civil servant in Bavaria.[52]

For numerous prominent Nazi officials, the availability of top-quality intelligence regarding their crimes in Italy played no part in their treatment or their fate after the war. They benefitted to some degree from the fact that information available to Allied intelligence analysts in 1943 was not available for postwar prosecutions. It is, however, available in part for us to use today in trying to describe and to understand the Holocaust in Italy. The SD decodes and other recently declassified documents used for this paper do not revolutionize our understanding of the Holocaust in Italy. The main reason is that Kappler's report of October 16 survived in paper form; evidence from the decodes fills in the picture around it. If decodes of later messages turn up, and if they contain details of how police in other cities prepared for and carried out deportations, that would be striking new information, but there is little prospect of such sources appearing. At present, the new sources allow us to see a significant difference of opinion between the RSHA and SS authorities in Italy, on one side, and some German diplomats, on the other. They help us to discount self-serving and self-exculpating postwar testimony. In combination with other sources, they permit us to connect Karl Wolff and especially Ernst Kaltenbrunner to the Holocaust in Italy much more directly than has been done before. And they reinforce our understanding of the hierarchy involved in the Final Solution: in cases of difficulty, authorization came from the very top.

One important facet of the new information is that it shows how Italian public opinion—or Kappler's perception of it—affected very directly how much he tried to do. Relatively late in the war, when German forces were stretched thin, Nazi officials really needed outside help or at least a neutral environment. The climate in Italy was not favorable for an efficient Final Solution. With regard to Herbert Kappler, there is little reason to dissent from the assessment made by British and American intelligence analysts during the war: Kappler was a powerful figure in Italy, but he was always pessimistic.[53]

NOTES

A longer version of this article appeared in *Holocaust and Genocide Studies* 16, no. 3 (2002): 4002–14.

1. Kappler's radio transmitter was later moved into the German embassy after he was no longer forced to operate under cover. British intelli-

gence report entitled "German Policy towards Italy," undated, but apparently late Oct. 1943, copy in U.S. National Archives (NA), Record Group (RG) 226, Entry 210, Box 80, Folder 891. The first decode in the surviving American file is from 3 Aug. 1943, but the original British collection was considerably larger, as British analyses indicate. The American collection is in RG 226, Entry 122, Box 1.

2. F. H. Hinsley, E. E. Thomas, C. F. G. Ransom, and R. C. Knight, *British Intelligence in the Second World War: Its Influence on Strategy and Operations,* vol. 3, pt. 1 (New York: Cambridge University Press, 1984), 487.

3. For the American copies, NA RG 226, E 122, Box 1.

4. Meir Michaelis, *Mussolini and the Jews: German-Italian Relations and the Jewish Question in Italy 1922–1945* (Oxford: Clarendon, 1978), 352; Susan Zuccotti, *The Italians and the Holocaust: Persecution, Rescue, Survival* (New York: Basic Books, 1987), 109.

5. Michaelis, *Mussolini,* 353 n. 3. Zuccotti, *The Italians,* 300 n. 27.

6. Copy in NA RG 242, Microfilm T-84, R 25.

7. Schellenberg to Rome, 8 Sept. 1943, decode no. 5498; Hoettl to Rome, 10 Sept. 1943, decode no. 5696; Kappler to Berlin, 12 Sept. 1943, decode no. 5763; Schellenberg to Rome, 12 Sept. 1943, decode no. 5797. NA RG 226, E 112, Box 1.

8. Wolff (Rome) to Himmler, 18 Sept. 1943, decode no. 6253.

9. Wolff also used Waffen-SS units to reorganize the fascist militia. Wolff to Mussolini, 18 Sept. 1943, decode 6260; Kappler to Harster via Berlin, 18 Sept. 1943, decode 6261.

10. The Italian police chief of Rome, his deputy, and some other police officials were arrested, as were some Italian military officers in the city. Rome to Berlin, 23 Sept. 1943, decode no. 6671.

11. Kappler to Berlin, 24 Sept. 1943, decode no. 6728.

12. Raul Hilberg, *The Destruction of the European Jews,* vol. 2 (New York: Holmes and Meier, 1985), 669. If Kappler had not received word about the Final Solution in Italy earlier, this RSHA circular directed German officials in Italy to start at once with Italian Jews.

13. Michaelis, *Mussolini,* 354–5. Richard Lamb, *War in Italy 1943–1945: A Brutal Story* (New York: DeCapo, 1993), 40.

14. Zuccotti, *The Italians,* 111. Zuccotti's most recent work, *Under His Very Windows: The Vatican and the Holocaust in Italy* (New Haven: Yale University Press, 2000), 53ff., is unqualified: Kappler received orders on September 25 and engaged in a policy of deception with the Jewish representatives.

15. Kappler to Berlin, 29 Sept. 1943, decode no. 6921.

16. Kappler to Berlin, 5 Oct. 1943, decode no. 7185; Kappler to Berlin, 7 Oct. 1943, decode no. 7256.

17. The message was decoded the next day. This decode (cited below in n. 18), in combination with the decode of October 20 (cited below in n. 29), made it plain that the purpose of shipping Jews to Auschwitz was to eliminate them. This conclusion is at variance with the general interpretation in Martin Gilbert, *Auschwitz and the Allies* (1981; reprint, New York: Henry Holt, 1990).

18. Kappler to Wolff, 6 Oct. 1943, decode no. 7244.

19. Michaelis, *Mussolini*, 362.

20. Hilberg, *The Destruction*, vol. 2, 671–2; Michaelis, *Mussolini*, 363; Bern (Dulles) to OSS, 30 Dec. 1943, and Bern (Dulles) to Director OSS, 30 Dec. 1943, NA RG 226, E 210, Box 463, Folder 2. The OSS documents were declassified in 2000.

21. Michaelis, *Mussolini*, 363 n. 1. Zuccotti's chronology, *Under His Very Windows*, 156–7, is more elaborate: Möllhausen tried shortly after September 25 to prevent deportations, then sent telegrams to the Foreign Ministry on October 6–7, receiving word that he was not to get involved. Finally, he tried to work through Baron von Weizsäcker, German ambassador to the Vatican, who notified the Vatican about the impending deportations.

22. Kappler to Berlin, 10 Oct. 1943, decode no. 7412. On Sorani and Delasem, see Zuccotti, *Under His Very Windows*, 176, 181–6.

23. Hitler's appointments in NA RG 242, Microfilm T-84, R 387.

24. Kaltenbrunner to Kappler, 11 Oct. 1943, decode no. 7458.

25. Kaltenbrunner to Kappler, 12 Oct. 1943, decode no. 7512.

26. Robert Katz, *Death in Rome* (Cambridge: Harvard University Press, 1967), 25. Michael Phayer, *The Catholic Church and the Holocaust, 1930–1965,* (Bloomington: Indiana University Press, 2000) 98.

27. Zuccotti, *Under His Very Windows*, 175–201. Michaelis, *Mussolini*, 364–5. Following Italian scholar Michael Tagliacozzo, Michaelis states that 477 Jews were sheltered within the Vatican and another 4,238 within monasteries and convents. Although questioning statistics compiled by Catholic authorities indicating somewhat larger numbers of Jewish refugees given sanctuary, Zuccotti's main emphasis is to demonstrate that the demand for sanctuary increased dramatically after the roundup of October 16 and that Catholic institutions inside and outside Vatican territory acted independently and often spontaneously. There was no carefully coordinated Vatican policy issued from the top.

28. Phayer, *The Catholic Church*, 99. I have found no contemporary evidence to confirm von Kessel's claim.

29. Rome to Berlin, 16 Oct. 1943, decode no. 7668.

30. A copy of Kappler's radio message was given to Wolff, and it ended up in Himmler's files. Copy in NA RG 242, T-175, R 53/frames 2567133–4.

31. Zuccotti, *Under His Very Windows*, 155.

32. Harster to Berlin, via Rome, 20 Oct. 1943, decode no. 7732.

33. Dannecker to RSHA IV B 4, 21 Oct. 1943, decode no. 7754.

34. Zuccotti, *The Italians,* 123–5.

35. Kappler to Harster, via Berlin, 23 Oct. 1943, decode no. 7834.

36. Rome to Berlin, 26 Oct. 1943, decode no. 7927.

37. John Cornwell, *Hitler's Pope: The Secret History of Pius XII* (New York: Penguin, 2000).

38. Summary of the meeting in Foreign Office records, copy in NA RG 242, microfilm T-120, R 2720/E 420790–3.

39. See the OSS documents cited in n. 20 above. All the reports from Fritz Kolbe, code-named Wood, were judged to be so important that they were distributed to the president.

40. Information courtesy of Stephen Tyas, who searched the intelligence files of the prime minister's office available at the Public Record Office. In daily digests of information from intercepts, Churchill did receive some items about the SD in Italy later in October.

41. Gilbert, *Auschwitz and the Allies,* 158–9.

42. Richard Breitman, *Official Secrets: What the Nazis Planned, What the British and Americans Knew* (New York: Hill and Wang, 1998), 215.

43. Hilberg, *The Destruction,* vol. 3, 1093.

44. Army Investigative Repository Records (IRR) file on Theodor Dannecker, NA RG 319, XE 009228.

45. CSDIC Interrogation of Herbert Kappler, 8 June 1945, copy in NA RG 226, E 194, Box 63, Folder 280.

46. Zuccotti, *The Italians,* 300 n. 27; Hilberg, *The Destruction,* vol. 3, 1098; CSDIC Interrogation of Kappler, 8 June 1945, NA RG 226, E 194, Box 63, Folder 280; voluntary statement by Karl Wolff, 2 Dec. 1946 (London), copy in NA RG 332, Entry ETO-MIS-Y, Box 127, Folder 4.

47. See Wolff interrogation in "Germans in Italy" file.

48. Wolff to Oberbefehlshaber Suedwest, 29 Dec. 1944, NA RG 226, E 92, Box 619, Folder 2.

49. Bradley F. Smith and Elena Agarossi, *Operation Sunrise: The Secret Surrender* (New York: Basic Books, 1979), 189.

50. Smith and Agarossi, *Operation Sunrise,* 189–91.

51. CSDIC Interrogation of Wilhelm Harster, 20 May 1945, NA RG 226, E 194, Box 63, Folder 6.

52. Hilberg, *The Destruction,* vol. 3, 1096.

53. OSS report entitled "German Policy towards Italy" (n.d., late 1943), NA RG 226, E 210, Box 80, Folder 891; British report entitled "The Sicherheitsdienst—Recent Development," 9 Oct. 1943, copy in NA RG 226, E 108B, Box 286. Both reports draw heavily from the SD decodes.

II. R·E·S·I·S·T·A·N·C·E AND R·E·S·C·U·E

Yehuda Bauer

The Problem of Non-Armed Jewish Reactions
to Nazi Rule in Eastern Europe

THERE IS A GENERAL HISTORIOGRAPHIC TRADITION, TO WHICH I MY-
self have also contributed, that deals with Jewish reactions to German
policies in Eastern Europe in World War II in terms that sometimes
seem to approach hagiography.[1] Not that the facts on which this is
based are inaccurate; these traditions certainly have a very solid foundation in the source materials that we all use. We know a great deal
about the Warsaw ghetto, and that includes the work of over a thousand house committees, many of whom did a tremendous amount of
self-sacrificing welfare work; we know about the underground educational efforts in the so-called *complets*—small groups of children
who were taught by people whose reward often was a piece of bread;
we know of the high school organized by the Dror Zionist youth
movement, which prepared ghetto youngsters for the *abitur,* the Polish state exams at the conclusion of high school studies, with the help
of some of the best experts in Poland who were Jews. We know about
many *minyanim,* groups of religious Jews that maintained their traditions of prayer in closed rooms and attics. We know about the soup
kitchens organized not only by the Judenrat but also by a coalition of
underground political parties headed by the historian Emmanuel
Ringelblum, known as *Zetos,* and of course about the underground
archive of Oneg Shabbat that the group around Ringelblum organized, and two-thirds of which ultimately came down to us. This,
and much more, about Warsaw ghetto alone. We know about con-
certs and theater plays in Vilna, about strikes and other manifestations of workers' demands in Lodz and Czestochowa. And these are
just a few of very many such demonstrations of the Jewish will to survive as civilized human beings. But our descriptions have not really

been followed up by analysis, and, furthermore, opposite pictures have not been properly considered.

My topic is not the usual topic of Holocaust research. Most follow the usual themes of the history of the perpetration of the genocide, on the one hand, and on the other, the aftereffects of the Holocaust in public consciousness and in literature, film, art, and other such themes, which in themselves of course are very important. The problem, as I see it, is that all this is lopsided. The victims are described, to be sure, with great empathy; their armed rebellions are celebrated; there is increased understanding of their dilemmas; the Judenräte are no longer devil figures or traitors—but we face two lacunae, and one overarching problem of analysis. The two lacunae are these: (1) that we have not tried to see whether the picture we have of Warsaw, Lodz, Vilna, Kovno, and a few other places of this kind holds true for the majority of the ghettos or places of concentration of East European Jews, who were the vast majority of the Holocaust's victims; and (2) that we have made no serious attempts to compare the reaction of these Jews with the reactions of other groups in situations that may not have been exactly parallel to that of the Jews, but that sometimes came pretty close to it—Gypsies, Poles, and some others during the Nazi era, as well as Armenians, Khmer, Ibo, Tutsi, American Indians, and others. The overarching problem is that the history of the perpetrators captures the imagination; evil is fascinating; suffering is something one shies away from, if one can, except for the purely emotional and, very often, outright shmaltzy elements. Collective weeping and the attached catharsis are wonderful, and in the United States, for instance, many Jews do their Holocaust bit twice a year: on Kristallnacht memorial night, and on Holocaust Memorial Day. That is when one can have one's catharsis, and swear to that rather inane slogan "never again," and that leaves 363 days where one is left at peace. Lots of repeated quotations and lots of burnt-out cliches float around, and I am reminded of the Polish proverb that says that a quote is an interval between two thoughts. Now, it is undoubtedly absolutely essential to find out as much as we can about the murderers and the societies they came from, and about the problem of evil in general. But if we do not balance it by examining that which *all of us* may become in certain situations—namely, the victims—and their reactions, and the whys and the wherefores of such reactions, we simply do not deal with this or any other genocide, but only with some aspects of it. Don't we all know that there will always be more victims than perpetrators, and that therefore the study of the victims, both before they became victims and afterward, is crucial for our understanding of ourselves? What I am trying to do here is to make a very, very small contribution to such a redressing of the balance. In other words, this is my modest contribution to the perpetuation of the Holocaust industry, that lopsided invention of Jewish intellectuals at their worst.[2]

In both North America and Israel the problem is aggravated by the fact that in neither country is there a minimal critical mass of researchers who can read the necessary languages and are interested in the subject of East European Jewry during the Holocaust. Find me ten young scholars, on either side of the water, who can read Yiddish, Polish, Hebrew, and German, at least, if not also Russian and French, and who want to research the Holocaust where most of it actually happened, and I will be both surprised, and happier than I now am.

In order to examine Jewish reactions to the Holocaust in Eastern Europe, let me use the Hebrew term *amidah,* which in this context means, roughly, "standing up against"—there is no accurate English translation, and the Hebrew term fits the situation exactly: to stand up against real or merely perceived German policies. Jews in Eastern Europe are said to have employed, generally speaking, two strategies— namely, unarmed and armed resistance. A definition of all these terms must be attempted. By "Eastern Europe" I mean the Polish-Soviet area, the Baltic countries, Romania, Hungary, Slovakia, and Subcarpathian Russia. "Armed resistance" should, properly speaking, include anything from the collection of arms and the group organization for using them, to local rebellions and partisan warfare. The difficulty lies with a definition of non-armed *amidah.* A new book of mine that has appeared in the meantime goes into greater detail,[3] but here I would repeat a version of a definition that I have offered in the past: *amidah* is any action that ran counter to real or perceived German policies. This sounds easier than it is, so here are a few examples: education, insofar as it was forbidden (e.g., in Warsaw, until September 1941); organized food smuggling; maintenance of religious life when it was forbidden; maintenance of social welfare to help the poorest; organization of medical help; cultural life in its various forms; underground political activity; protection of the weaker parts of the community; and similar activities. It is relatively easier to deal with group phenomena of this kind than with individual actions. Thus, when parents protected their children, this could be counted as *amidah,* though others will argue that it is nothing more than the natural, instinctive reaction of parents to a situation threatening their children.

What are our sources? German sources are of very limited use, as the Nazis were not interested in these activities, except for the smuggling of food, and possibly medical activities. In postwar interrogations in Germany, the obvious emphasis was on testimonies that would clarify the murderers' culpability. Internal Jewish issues were of no interest.

We do have a huge number of personal testimonies, taken at various times during the past fifty-five years or so, but some people tell us that personal testimonies are useless. My contention is that, if crosschecked and found to converge, they are at least as reliable as contemporary German documents that were often created to mislead.

As I said, the question I like to pose is whether the behavior we characterize as *amidah* is typical for all or most of the East European Jewish communities. The answer to this obviously has to rely on detailed research on as large a number of such communities as possible. The current situation is that we do not have a critical mass of such research. In my seminar at Hebrew University, my students and I have examined a number of such places, especially in what used to be eastern Poland and is now western Belarus and western Ukraine. We examined, superficially, larger communities such as Brest-Litovsk, Baranowicze, Przemysl, and Tarnow, and small *shtetlach* such as Kosow Huculski, Rokitna, Hrubieszow, and Kurzeniec. These smaller places are probably unknown to most of you, but they were the typical small *shtetlach* of the former Pale of Settlement. In a very real sense, what I am saying here is in the character of a research report, because I hope to continue to work on a very detailed examination of some of these communities.

Let me pick three contrasting examples from among them. The first is Brest-Litovsk, or Brisk de-Litte in Yiddish, a large community of perhaps close to 30,000 in 1939, 17,000 of whom were in the local ghetto in 1942. Brest was an ancient Jewish community, dating from the fourteenth century at the latest. From it came such contemporary luminaries as the Soloveichik family of American orthodox rabbis, Menachem Begin and Ariel Sharon, and Yakov Chazan, a leader of the leftist Mapam in Israel. It had the full complement of

Jewish interwar organizations—ultraorthodox synagogues, Bundists, Zionists of all hues and shades, communists; Polish, Yiddish, and Hebrew educational institutions; a Free Loan Bank subsidized by the Joint Distribution Committee (JDC), and more. All this collapsed like a house of cards upon the occupation by the Soviets on September 22, 1939.

Young Jews enthusiastically welcomed the new regime, which opened for them the gates of education, whereas many of the former leaders were arrested and exiled, and all the Hebrew institutions closed without any opposition and changed, in part, into Yiddish schools promoting the cult of Stalin. There were some fairly elementary underground organizations throughout the region, but none in Brest. Soviet Jewish security agents penetrated groups and even families. Refugees streamed in from German-occupied Poland, and many of these were deported to the gulags before Operation Barbarossa. There certainly was no *amidah* under the Soviets, and the ease with which all this happened is quite amazing. The beginnings of an analysis of this were attempted by Ben-Cion Pinchuk and Dov Levin in Israel,[4] but I have found no satisfactory explanation for this phenomenon, which was repeated, more or less, in all the places east of the Curzon line that I know of.

When the Germans occupied Brest on the first day of their invasion of the Soviet Union, they found a basically disorganized Jewish population with no communal structure. The Judenrat they nominated in August was headed by a former merchant, Hersh Rosenberg. There was a former minor functionary of the community, and some intellectuals, including a couple of doctors. I do not have to detail the disasters that now began, because that is something that was repeated all over Eastern Europe. But in Brest, immediately upon its occupation, members of Einsatzgruppe C murdered a large number—perhaps a few hundred—of male Jewish intellectuals, and Police Battallion 307 then murdered close to 5,000 male Jews, probably on July 3, 1941. That of course means that there were few young males left after that, and that no armed underground should have existed. The ghetto was finally closed on December 15, 1941. Rations were 150 grams per day of very poor bread, and later 100 grams per day. Forced labor took place at the railroad station, in some stores for captured Soviet arms, at the former Jewish (now German military) hospital, and outside town in certain outlying villages. No pay was given, and little food, much of which was smuggled into the ghetto—which was, as you can imagine, starving in the most horrible way. There was no education, and social welfare was limited to the Judenrat's soup kitchens; one soup kitchen was organized by the orthodox, and one very old rabbi who managed to organize prayers in 1942 for Jewish holidays, for a small number of the devout. There was a rudimentary health clinic, and the doctors tried to help as best they could. In the testimonies I have found, they and the Judenrat get very high marks for self-sacrifice and willingness to help. The German boss of the ghetto, Polizeistandortführer and Major of the Police Friedrich Wilhelm Rohde, was, by all accounts, a corrupt and sadistic individual. A so-called contribution of RM 2 million was exacted; anything of value was confiscated; and then uncounted so-called presents were given, including a birthday cake with a diamond ring, and quite possibly the sexual services of four Jewish girls who were viewed by the survivors as real heroines. Contrary to logic, there were two resistance groups. One probably never got beyond the talking stage, and was composed of former members of the Hebrew Tarbut school. The other, much larger, reputedly some eighty people strong, was led by Soviet-Jewish communists who had not managed to get away in time (though the only name we know, one Arie Sheinman, might well have been a Zionist, judging by his name). They acquired arms and were in contact with the Polish, and perhaps also the Soviet, underground in the city. Attempts to get groups of young people into the forests failed; they were murdered by bandits posing as partisans. When the liquidation of the ghetto occurred, on October 15, 1942, the underground was surprised and rendered ineffective, probably by a traitor who brought the Germans to the arms cache. A few people managed to join the partisans, and a few others were saved by friendly non-Jews; the total number of survivors cannot be higher than twenty-five. I have identified twenty-one.[5] The rest were murdered, either in the ghetto itself by Rohde and his local garrison or, most of them, at a place on the railway line between Brest and Baranowicze called Bronnaya Gora. We don't know who did the actual murdering there, except that the Security Police (Sicherheitspolizei [SIPO]) and Security Service (Sicherheitsdienst [SD]) from the area were—of course—involved.

One can say that of the actions characteristic of *amidah*, education and cultural activities were absent; religious activity was on a very small scale; social welfare was limited to the Judenrat's soup kitchens, with food smuggling done on an individual basis; political underground activity was absent; and only armed resistance was planned, and failed.

My second example comes from the small *shtetl* of Kurzeniec, a short distance from Vilejka, which lies east of Vilna and is now in Belarus. There were some 2,500 Jews there in 1939, and they constituted about 60 percent of the total population. Their ancestors had been living there from the eighteenth century at least, and they really consisted of a small number of clans, so that the same family names repeat themselves constantly. They had a community like those everywhere else, and the usual array of welfare organizations, Zionist youth movements (mainly the Marxist-Zionist Hashomer Hatzair), and a well-attended synagogue. However, the religious element was definitely on the decline, as the young generation espoused secular causes, very largely left-wing ones.[6]

When the Soviets came, the same collapse of institutions can be observed as in Brest, but here several youngsters, members of Hashomer Hatzair, established an underground group complete with a flag and secret meetings. A central figure from the movement's leadership, Yosef Kaplan, later the central figure in the Warsaw Jewish Fighting Organization—before Anielewicz—visited Kurzeniec and met with the group, thus assuring them of some kind of backing in the leadership. Other youths, however, went to study at Soviet institutions of learning, and accepted the Soviet regime, while their much more conservative parents were increasingly unhappy. A refugee from Austria, by the name of Schatz, made his appearance in the *shtetl*. The head teacher of the Polish school, Matoros,[7] continued to teach and established close relationships with his Jewish students.

The Germans came on June 28, 1941, and the usual persecutions started. Matoros was nominated burgomaster, much to the dislike of the majority Belorussians in the town and the surrounding villages. In neighboring Vilejka the murders started early, and soon the Germans discovered that they needed labor. Jews from Kurzeniec were marched to Vilejka and put to work there. In Kurzeniec, a small Judenrat was set up, with Schatz as the head, probably because of his fluency in German. In the town market square, a transit camp was established for Soviet POWs on the way to more permanent stalags. Torn and desperately hungry and thirsty, they were the object of help extended by both Jews and non-Jews. The Jews were forced to bring food from German stores, and water, to the POWs. Some POWs were helped to escape. One of the Hashomer Hatzair members[8] gave civilian clothes to a Soviet captain, included him as a member of the Jewish crew of workers there, and smuggled him out of the camp. His name was Pyotr Michailovich Danilotchkin, and he was a teacher from Rostov on the Don, not a party member. He assumed the *nom de guerre* of Volodia, and immediately began organizing a Soviet underground. He was helped by villagers from the small village of Volovchizna, and he encouraged the underground group in Kurzeniec to organize as well. The Kurzeniec youths expanded their membership and obtained, bought, and stole some weapons—a few guns and ammunition, and some handguns. One of the mothers of one of the members was particularly helpful in this. On instructions from Volodia, they stole printing type from Vilejka and printed a series of propaganda leaflets attacking the Germans. German murderers— and I have not yet found out their identities—supervised the killing of smaller groups of Jews by Belorussian police during 1941 and in early 1942, including the much-beloved rabbi, Moshe Aharon Feldman, but left the majority alive, obviously because they needed their labor. This in spite of the demands of Belorussian collaborators, especially of course the local police, to kill as many Jews as possible. However, in and near the town there were also quite a number of peasants who were willing to help. As long as Matoros was the mayor—he was killed in the summer of 1942, clearly because he had organized Polish resistance—Jews could expect some help. The town seems to have been a German supply base, and Matoros employed some of the underground members in the food stores. They used this to build up a supply of food in the forests, again on Volodia's instructions. In December 1941, Volodia organized a mass meeting of his group in Vilejka, on a Sunday, under the noses of the Germans. The cover was a Sunday feast. He even produced a Soviet parachutist who said some unkind words about the Jews; Volodia immediately corrected him, and applauded the work of the Kurzeniec youngsters.

There was no educational activity in the town. Welfare was based on mutual support, in a small town where everybody was connected to everybody. Religious life was very limited, and ceased, more or less, when the rabbi was murdered. However, there are testimonies telling us of increased individual observance and ardent belief among the older generations. Schatz is viewed as a victim by the survivors, though members of the underground also accuse him of trying to prevent their activities. However, he knew about the conspiracy, and did not betray them, and later on even tried to organize a breakout. In the spring of 1942, a group of some dozens of youngsters joined Volodia in the forests. They participated in the burning of German objects, and the killing of Germans and their collaborators. A central figure among the partisans was a Jewish girl, Bertha Dimanshtein, from a tiny village near Kurzeniec. However, in the summer they were attacked by a large German force—again, I do not yet know their corporate identity—and had to disperse. The Jewish youths returned to Kurzeniec.

The underground was, by that time, known by many and suspected by the rest. Jews tried to get arms, and organized escape possibilities. As elsewhere, underground hiding places were prepared. Nevertheless, the mass slaughter on September 9, 1942, caught them by surprise. It was executed largely by the Belorussian police, under the eyes of what the survivors identified as "the Gestapo." Whoever was caught was brought to the market square and marched from there to be shot outside the town, or they were burnt alive in the square. Because of prior preparation, many tried to flee, and a total of about 300 persons managed to escape, while others who tried were shot.

Life in the *puszcza,* the East European primeval forest, was anything but easy, and depended on protection by the partisans, among whom Volodia now served as a commissar, and the goodwill of the peasants in the area. When winter came, conditions became impossible, and an attempt was made to move all the Jews to a partisan-controlled area near Polotzk in the east. Some managed to get there, and many joined the partisans; some had to retrace their steps, and tried to survive in the Kurzeniec forest area. About 120 survived.

My third example is Kosow Huculski in the Carpathian foothills, now in the western Ukraine. This had been the area where the founder of Chassidism, Yisrael Baal Shem Tov, or the Besht, wandered before he started spreading his message; and the Huculs, a people who live in the area and speak a language between Polish and Ukrainian, were still telling tales about him in the twentieth century. Kosow had about 2,500 Jews, and about 1,500 non-Jews, Ukrainians, and Poles—the latter mainly government officials. The town was quite prosperous, boasted a carpet industry, and became a tourist center for wealthy Polish families; however, there were also some very poor Jews there.

The Soviets, when they came, prefered to deal with the Ukrainian majority in the area rather than the Jews. Factories and businesses were confiscated, and some Jews were sent to Siberia. Communal life was destroyed in a fashion parallel to that which we find in other places in the region. Then the Hungarians came, in the framework of Barbarossa, and occupied Kosow for about two months. When some 16,000 Jews from the territories occupied by Hungary between 1938 and 1940 were murdered at Kamenetz Podolsk, a few hundred kilometers east of Kosow, 2,000 others fled. About 150 of them arrived at Kosow, where they were maintained by the local community, now organized by a committee. The committee became a Judenrat when the Germans occupied the place in early September, 1941. As in Kurzeniec, the main problem was the attitude of the surrounding population; but the Ukrainian attitude was much worse than that of the Belorussians. A major problem was the Austrian wife of the Ukrainian police chief, nominated by the Germans. As elsewhere, the Judenrat, headed by a former factory owner, Chaim Steiner, and his deputy, Yehoshua Gertner, also a former business owner, supplied forced labor to the Germans, and had to pay large sums of money and all the valuables of the Jews to Germans and Ukrainians. As in Kurzeniec, there was never a ghetto in Kosow. Jews had to move into a certain section of the town, which basically consisted of one very long street. There is evidence of some effort to supply extra rations to children, aided by what had been the JDC center at Cracow and was now known as the Jüdische Unterstützungsstelle (JUS). There is no evidence of any educational effort, though, and religious life mirrored what I described for Kurzeniec. There was a problem of refugees, as the Germans crammed 1,500 Jews from outlying villages into the Jewish section, so the total number of Jews was about 4,000. The Judenrat seems to have dealt with this in a manner that the survivors remember with satisfaction.

As we know from the excellent work of our German colleagues, Dieter Pohl, Thomas Sandkühler, and Christian Gerlach,[9] murder of Jews in the area was a local initiative blessed by the center in Lvov and in Berlin, and the major event was the mass murder of Stanislawow Jews in October. Parallel with that, and at the demand of the local Ukrainian authorities, the Germans came in mid-October and murdered over 2,000 Jews, or one-half of the Jewish population of Kosow—men, women, and children, including some Judenrat members. There was therefore no place for any illusions on the part of the Jewish remnant. The hostility of the Ukrainians prevented not only any underground armed activities, but also any possibility for most people to hide with non-Jewish neighbors. However, as in practically all these places, some non-Jews—including a new mayor of the town, an engineer by the name of Lopatin—were willing to hide Jews.

In April 1942, on the eve of Passover, the Judenrat met to arrange for some semblance of keeping the holiday, when a phone call—peculiarly enough, the Nazis never cut phone lines, anywhere in the East—came from a Polish official friendly to the Jews, who was working for the Labor Office (the *Arbeitsamt*) at the other end of the long village street. The guests, he said, had arrived: SS men in tarpaulin-covered lorries. Clearly, the end of Kosow had come. Steiner told the Judenrat members to go and alert the Jewish population so they could try to hide or escape, if they could. He called for volunteers to stay with him in the building, to hold up the Germans for maybe another short while—apparently he thought they would need maps, and orientation about the buildings harboring Jews. Three men stayed with him; then one of them fainted, and Steiner told him to go home, because he would be of no use when the Germans came. Three Judenrat members stayed to face the Germans.[10]

This story about the Judenrat in Kosow is mentioned by the survivors sort of *en passant*. I think it is an example of non-armed resistance that is of no less import than any rebellion could have been.

One may ask, of course, what happened next. The answer is: the Germans never came. It was a false alarm, and that is basically why we know about it. Jewish Kosow was murdered in September 1942, and there is one testimony—actually, a book in German by a survivor by the name of Ignatz Lipinsky, who accuses the Judenrat of knowing about that *aktzia* and not warning the Jews in time. I am not sure regarding this accusation, although it is repeated by one other witness, a close relative of Lipinsky. Even if true, the accusation does not necessarily contradict the Judenrat's behavior in April 1942. The problem with Kosow is the narrow documentary basis: I have uncovered, so far, about twenty testimonies altogether. However, the detailed testimonies of some of the survivors may compensate for that. They were deposited within about ten years of the events themselves.

Some members of the Judenrat managed to get away or to hide and escape over the nearby frontier, to either Hungary or Romania.

Steiner was apparently caught by Hungarian guards and handed over to the Germans. But Gertner managed to reach to Bucharest, and on October 21, 1942, he wrote the first authentic report on the destruction of a Jewish community that we possess. The report, written in Yiddish, reached Jerusalem in November, just as the information about what we call the Holocaust reached Palestine through the sixtynine European Jews exchanged for Germans living in Palestine. Gertner's testimony was published in a news sheet of the Jewish Agency because the British censors in Palestine did not permit such reports to be published in the newspapers because in their eyes it might have caused panic. In any case, the testimony was overshadowed by the information then being received, from the exchangees and from London—news that formed the background to the Allied declaration of December 17, 1942, recognizing the fact of the destruction of European Jewry.

What are we to make of all this? The Judenrat in Brest received high marks for its steadfastness and honesty. The one in Kosow is described as either traitorous or heroic—and both these judgments may be accurate. Schatz in Kurzeniec is not criticized sharply; sometimes, quite the contrary. *Amidah* was marginal (practically nonexistent in Brest and Kosow) in the fields of education, welfare, and underground activity. In Kosow, for instance, there is no evidence of any revival of youth-movement activity after the Germans occupied the place. In Brest it probably did not exist either. Smuggling of food was done on an individual basis in Brest, and was not an issue in Kurzeniec and Kosow, where food was scarce, but there are no reports of actual hunger. All this is of course quite different from what we know about the large ghettos, or at least most of them. But when I say "large ghettos," I am not being accurate, because Brest with 17,000 ghettoized Jews was about the same as Vilno with its 20,000, and Kovno with a roughly similar number of Jews. Yet there was very little *amidah* in Brest. The fact that the Soviets had destroyed Jewish communal life is no answer, because the same happened in Kovno, Vilno, and Shiauliai (or Shavli, in Yiddish), the third-largest ghetto in Lithuania. There was terrible starvation in Brest, but there was starvation in Lodz and Warsaw as well. In Brest, the traumatic murder of most of the young males right at the beginning of the German occupation may be a good part of the explanation, and despite what I just said about Lodz and Warsaw, horrible starvation is another.

In Kurzeniec we are dealing with a tightly knit community of poor people whose families provided the base for resistance activities. One might almost be tempted to say that non-armed *amidah* was not necessary there. In Kosow, nestling in the foothills of the Carpathian mountains, resistance was probably possible, but it did not happen. Why? I simply have no answer so far.

Finally, armed resistance: there was the prepared uprising in Brest, contrary to all expectations one has in such conditions, spurred not by a Zionist underground, but apparently largely by Jewish communists. There were about eighty members, according to the evidence we have. The tragedy of a prepared uprising that did not take place — either because there were Judenrat members who tried to sabotage it (which was not the case in Brest), or because of excellent work by the Gestapo intelligence who recruited Jewish agents, promising them life in return for treason — happened in quite a number of places, for instance in Baranowicze. There is a wide spectrum there, between Kosow on the one end of it, and Kurzeniec, where there was real and significant armed resistance by Jews who fled to the partisans, on the other. What was crucial in the smaller places was the presence of at least some minimal support by the local non-Jews. This was more forthcoming in the forested areas of Belarus, where Jews had lived for centuries in close proximity to their non-Jewish neighbors, than in the overwhelmingly hostile Ukrainian plains. There was no armed resistance in Kosow, though, despite the closeness to the Carpathian mountains and forests.

The case of Kurzeniec is an extreme one, and we see there a combination of crucially important local help and a preexisting, underground Zionist youth movement of a marked left-wing nature. Had there been no Volodia, the picture might have been quite different, and of course Volodia was a Russian from the eastern Ukraine, and an intellectual to boot. Like many, but not all, of his Jewish partisans, he accepted Soviet society, though like them he was not a party member. The Zionist core group started out with both sympathy for, and opposition to, the Soviet regime. Some of them were even flown to the Russian interior by the Soviets, in 1943 and 1944, trained there, and returned to their partisan units. After the war, most Kurzeniec survivors immigrated to Palestine, but then so did most of the survivors from Brest and Kosow, though some came to the United States as well. The survival ratio varies widely: about 25 people, or 0.15 percent, for Brest; about 120, or 5 percent, for Kurzeniec; and about 20, or 0.5 percent, for Kosow.

This is, as I said initially, a first research report. But one thing is crystal clear: Jewish reactions to Nazi conquest in Eastern Europe differed very widely, and it is impossible to reach glib generalizations the way we have done so far. One Brest survivor told me: When you are hungry, you don't think of anything else but food; when you are hungry, you don't play Beethoven, even if you have a violin and know how to play. There was little of what we usually see as *amidah* in Brest. And yet, the three men of Kosow provide a shining example of *amidah* at its best. And the partisans from Kurzeniec translated Hersh Glick's famous partisan song into reality— *mir sennen do,* we are here.

NOTES

1. Alfred Katz, *Poland's Ghettos* (New York, 1970); Reuben Ainsztein, *Jewish Resistance in Nazi-Occupied Europe* (London, 1974); and Yehuda Bauer, *Jewish Reactions to the Holocaust* (Tel Aviv, 1989) are some examples.

2. Norman Finkelstein, *The Holocaust Industry* (London, 2000).

3. Yehuda Bauer, *Rethinking the Holocaust* (New Haven, Conn., 2001).

4. Ibid., 149–63.

5. I myself published a figure of nineteen survivors who returned to Brest immediately after the war (Bauer, *Rethinking,* 158), but there were a few survivors who did not return to Brest at all.

6. Shalom Cholavsky, *Meri Velochama Partizanit* (Resistance and Partisan Struggle) (Jerusalem, 2001), 128–37; idem, "Machteret uPartizanim Migetto Kurnietz" (Underground and Partisans from the Kurnietz [Kurzeniec] Ghetto), in *Yalkut Moreshet,* no. 59 (1995): 63–74; Christian Gerlach, *Kalkulierte Morde* (Hamburg, 1999), 541, 545–6, and elsewhere, on the Wilejka region.

7. I have not been able to find out the first names of Schatz, Matoros, or Lopatin (see below).

8. Nachum Alperowicz.

9. Dieter Pohl, *Nationalsozialistische Judenverfolgung in Ostgalizien 1941–1944* (Munich, 1996); Thomas Sandkühler, *Die "Endlösung in Galizien" und die Rettungsinitiative von Berthold Beitz, 1941–1944* (Bonn, 1996); Gerlach, *Kalkulierte Morde.*

10. G. Kessel and L. Olicki, eds., *Sefer Kosow* ([Memorial] Book of Kosow) (Tel Aviv, 1964); Jehoschua Gertner and Danek Gertner, *Der Untergang von Kosow und Zabie* (Vienna, 1998); Ignatz Lipinsky, *Zwischen Tod und Leben* (Frankfurt am Main, 1981).

Jonathan Goldstein

_____

Motivation in Holocaust Rescue: The Case of Jan Zwartendijk in Lithuania, 1940

_____

IN THEIR SEMINAL WORK ON THE 1938–40 FLIGHT OF APPROXIMATELY 20,000 German, Austrian, and Czech Jews to Shanghai, mainly via Italian and French seaports, Hebrew University historians Avraham Altman and Irene Eber discuss both individual motivation and the political, diplomatic, and economic context that enabled that exodus to take place. They also describe factors that inhibited escape of an even larger number of Jews from the same areas.[1] This chapter applies similar considerations about individual action and inaction and political, diplomatic, and economic setting to the exodus of approximately 2,200 Jews from Poland and Lithuania overland via the Soviet Union and thence by sea to Japan. About 1,100 of this group then proceeded to Shanghai. This escape route was not examined by Altman and Eber.

This chapter considers the role Jews played in the creation of the Soviet Union–Japan–Shanghai escape route. It also probes the motivation of Jan Zwartendijk (1896–1976), a Dutch gentile businessman who risked the lives of himself, his wife, and their three young children in order to help thousands of Jews to flee. A final concern is the motives of the governments involved: the Dutch government-in-exile, Japan, and perhaps most interestingly, the Soviet Union, which absorbed unoccupied Lithuania in the summer of 1940 and from whose territory the Jews were technically escaping.

WHAT MOTIVATED THE JEWS TO FLEE?

In March 1939, Germany occupied the Klaipeda (Memel) region of independent Lithuania. By late 1939, under the terms of the Hitler-

Stalin pact of August 23, Germany completed its occupation of western Poland and paused there, turning its attention temporarily westward. Also in late 1939, the Soviet Union occupied eastern Poland.[2] A series of draconian laws and murderous events had begun in Poland as early as September 3, two days after the German invasion. According to historian Martin Gilbert, "as the German forces advanced, and within hours of their occupation of a town or village, Jews were singled out for abuse and massacre by special SS operational groups."[3] On September 8, Hans Frank, the chief civilian administrator attached to the German army command, ordered all Jewish enterprises, including shops, workshops, cafes, and restaurants, to bear mandatory and distinct markings.[4] On October 9, Hitler appointed Heinrich Himmler as Reich Commissar for the Strengthening of German Folkdom (RKFDV). This decree made Himmler, in historian Lucy Dawidowicz's words,

> the *de facto* master and chthonian monarch of occupied Poland. All non-Germans were to be expelled from those areas of Poland that would be integrated into Germany proper. The Jews were to be concentrated in a few large centers and then segregated from the non-Jewish population as a first step in a long-range plan that would end in their annihilation.[5]

By the end of 1939, the first Jewish ghetto was established in Piotrkow in the General Government region of Nazi-occupied Poland.[6] By January 1940, M. W. Beckelman, the Vilna- (Vilnius- or Wilno-) based representative of the American Jewish Joint Distribution Committee (JDC), reported back to his home office that, in German-occupied Poland and German-occupied Lithuania, murder, brutal forced labor, expulsions, and ghettoization of Jews were commonplace. He observed that

> the killing of hundreds monthly continue[s] unabated. Forceful expulsions during the arctic spells of December and January of children, aged, and ill from Jewish institutions requisitioned by German authorities have resulted in additional hundreds of deaths. The general intent seems to be to expel all Jews from those provinces which have been officially annexed to the Reich and to make life for them in the so called Gouvernement [General Government of German-occupied but unannexed Poland—ed.] so unbearable that they will leave it by flight, suicide or death.[7]

Beckelman's observations have been corroborated by eyewitnesses Mary Berg and Chaim A. Kaplan and by historians Yisrael Gutman, Shmuel Krakowski, Leni Yahil, Gilbert, and Dawidowicz.[8]

Many thousands of Jews who were subjected to this brutality were determined to flee to any safe haven. Many who already held end visas or certificates to enter Palestine and who had sufficient funds or could get subsidies from relatives or from the JDC took the opportunity to emigrate.[9] Still other Jews fled German-occupied Poland for Soviet-occupied Poland, where they quickly discovered, in Beckelman's words, that "some Jewish groups—Bund members, Zionists, Rabbis, [and] yeshivah students—face specific persecution as political undesireables."[10] Polish Zionist leader and later Israeli Minister of Religious Affairs Zorach Warhaftig quoted the adage coined by Jewish inhabitants of Soviet-occupied eastern Poland, that "though rescued from the death penalty, we have been sentenced to life imprisonment."[11] Beckelman's and Warhaftig's observations about Jewish suffering under the Soviets have been corroborated by historians Ben Cion Pinchuk and Masha Greenbaum.[12]

Therefore, by early 1940, as a result of both Nazi and Soviet oppression, many thousands of Polish and Lithuanian Jews had fled into unoccupied Lithuania from Memel, from the regions of Poland that had formally been annexed into the Third Reich, and from the German-controlled but unannexed General Government region of Poland. Some even had fled from as far away as Koenigsberg, in East Prussia. The refugees concentrated in or near Vilna, which had been incorporated into independent Lithuania on October 10, 1939. Beckelman reported that of the 9,824 Jewish refugees registered with his committee as of January 31, 1940, "3153 came from territory now occupied by the Russians [and] 6671 from German-occupied Poland."[13]

On June 15, 1940, the Soviet Union annexed all of unoccupied Lithuania. Jews who had fled to unoccupied Lithuania precisely to escape Nazi and/or Soviet cruelty felt especially vulnerable during the annexation process. Those who had fled Soviet rule once now found themselves under Soviet rule a second time. By July virtually all the foreign embassies and consulates in the now ex-Lithuanian capital of Kovno were closing, and therewith the refugees' last probable hope of getting documents to settle abroad. At this point Zwartendijk took on a role that quickly evolved into the unpredictable business of rescuing Jews.

Since May 1939 Zwartendijk had been representing Philips, the Dutch electronics manufacturer, in Lithuania.[14] In May 1940, when the Germans overran the Netherlands, a Dutch government-in-exile was established in London. L. P. J. de Decker, based in Riga, Latvia, represented this government in all of the Baltic states. Ambassador de Decker, suspecting the Dutch consul in Kovno (a Lithuanian citizen but ethnic German named Dr. Tillmanns) of pro-Nazi sympathies, dismissed him and, in June 1940, only days before the Soviets occupied Lithuania, asked Zwartendijk to take over as consul in Kovno. In spite of the fact that Zwartendijk had no diplomatic experience, he accepted this assignment, expecting only such minor chores as occasionally extending some Dutch resident's passport.[15]

Zwartendijk's work quickly evolved into the rescue of Jews. In July 1940 Pessla Lewin, a former Dutch citizen who was then a Polish-Jewish refugee living in Lithuania with her husband Isaac and son Nathan, wrote to de Decker, who was still the Dutch ambassador, requesting immigration authorization for the Dutch West Indies. She learned that no immigration visas were required for that area, but she would need a landing permit from the local governor. Such permits were rarely issued. Nevertheless the ambassador tried to help by inscribing in her Polish passport a French-language statement that "for the admission of aliens to Surinam, Curaçao, and other Dutch possessions in the Americas, an entry visa is not required."

This stipulation, dated July 11, 1940, came to be known among the refugees as a "Curaçao visa." It gave the impression of being as good as a visa since it omitted the key phrase that a landing permit was required. On July 22 Isaac Lewin approached Zwartendijk in Kovno. Lewin writes in his 1994 memoir that Zwartendijk, after seeing what Ambassador de Decker had done, "copied [the "Curaçao visa"] into my Lithuanian safe-conduct pass."[16] This "visa" also covered the Lewins' three-year-old son, Nathan. Armed with this documentation, Pessla and Isaac Lewin, plus her mother and brother, who were still Dutch citizens, went to the Japanese consulate in Kovno, where they were issued seven- to fifteen-day transit visas to travel through Japan en route to Curaçao. They also went to the Soviet authorities, where they were issued permission to travel by train across the Soviet Union to Vladivostok, where they would leave the country for Japan.

The Japanese consul, far better known in the twentieth and

twenty-first centuries than Zwartendijk, was Sugihara Chiune (1900–86), who later changed his name to Sugihara Senpo. He has been featured in the movies *Escape to the Rising Sun, Sugihara: Conspiracy of Silence,* and *Visas That Saved Lives;* in the play *Virtue: Senpo Sugihara;* and in a published imaginary dialogue with Boston University Judaic Studies Professor Hillel Levine.[17] Nevertheless, apart from a relatively small number of genuine destination visas for entry into the United States, Palestine, Canada, and elsewhere, it was the 2,345 fictitious "Curaçao visas" that would be issued by Zwartendijk that enabled Sugihara to issue correspondingly large numbers of Japanese transit visas. Zwartendijk's action also would enable the Soviet authorities to issue correspondingly large numbers of their necessary travel permits.

How did the Lewins' single-family trip turn into a mass exodus of beleaguered Jews? Unaware of the Lewins' experience, Nathan Gutwirth, a legitimate Dutch citizen who was then a student at the Yeshiva of Telz (Telsiai), Lithuania, asked Zwartendijk if several of his fellow students, non-Dutch citizens, could accompany him to Curaçao. Zwartendijk said he was willing to provide Gutwirth's several friends with the same helpful notation he had given the Lewin family. According to Gutwirth, this help to his friends had de Decker's concurrence. Gutwirth then told Zorach Warhaftig what had been accomplished. When Warhaftig inquired of Zwartendijk, he let it be known that he was willing to give a Curaçao visa to anyone who asked. There is no evidence whether Zwartendijk sought or received authorization to issue Curaçao visas *en masse.*

Word of this possible escape mechanism spread quickly through the religious Zionist community in Lithuania and eventually to the broader Jewish refugee communities in Kovno and Vilna. It did not reach some of the more isolated Lithuanian Jewish communities.[18] Within hours, dozens of petitioners lined up at Zwartendijk's Kovno office. Zwartendijk issued 2,345 visas between July 24 and August 3, when the Soviets commandeered his office, obligating him and his family to return to the Netherlands in September.

Ultimately, not a single Jew to whom Zwartendijk issued a phony visa showed up in Curaçao. Armed with these notations, which could masquerade as the equivalent of end visas, about half of the roughly 2,200 refugees who reached Japan succeeded in moving on to the United States, Palestine, Canada, and other final destinations. It is unclear precisely how many of the 2,345 visas issued by Zwartendijk were actually used, and how many people actually travelled on each visa. Infants, for example, could travel on a parent's visa, as happened with the Levin family. What is clear is that after December 7, 1941, due to wartime conditions, very few of the refugees already in Japan were able to exit Japanese-held territory. The Japanese government interned approximately 1,000 of these stranded individuals in Japanese-occupied Shanghai for the duration of the war, including 250 faculty and students from the Yeshiva of Mir, Poland. That academy, through its own efforts and a sequence of events beyond its own control, is the only Eastern European Jewish institute of higher learning whose members escaped the Holocaust virtually intact.[19]

Dutch Governor Kasteel, in 1942 of Curaçao and Surinam, much later became ambassador to the state of Israel when Warhaftig was minister of religious affairs. Warhaftig records the following interview with Kasteel:

> After describing to him the type of visas we had received in 1940 for Curaçao, I asked him how he would have reacted had a ship actually arrived in Curaçao with hundreds of Jewish refugees aboard holding such "visas." Would he have accorded them asylum? "Nothing of the sort," he answered promptly. He would have forced the ship back into mid-ocean as had the American and Cuban authorities in the case of the *St. Louis*.[20]

On June 22, 1941, less than a year after the Kovno exodus, the Nazis overran Lithuania as part of their overall attack on the Soviet Union. The remaining Jews of Lithuania were almost entirely annihilated. Zwartendijk's action thus saved approximately 2,200 Jews from almost certain destruction.

It is clear that the Lewins, Gutwirths, Warhaftigs, and many others with direct knowledge of life under the Nazis and/or Soviets were determined to leave no stone unturned in their efforts to locate avenues of escape. For many of the Jews who ultimately fled across Siberia in 1940 or 1941, that trip would be their second, and in some cases, third, desperate exodus within a period of twelve to twenty-four months. But how to explain the behavior of other Jews who did not make vigorous efforts to leave? Were those individuals firmly rooted by a feeling of home and security that they did not wish to jeopardize? Did they underestimate the diabolical, ultimately genocidal, nature of European anti-Semitism in spite of impassioned warnings from Vladimir (Zev) Jabotinsky and other Zionist leaders that Europe was not safe for a Jew? With respect to Zwartendijk's specific exit scheme, were some terrified by the idea of having to cross Siberia to get to Japan? Were some convinced they would end up as slave laborers in Siberia? Were some simply unaware that an avenue of escape was available? Mrs. Betty Goodfriend lived in the *shtetl* of Velki (Vilkija), approximately thirty kilometers from Kovno, during the Zwartendijk episode. In a 1999 interview she reminded me that "we never heard of Sugihara. We never heard of Zwartendijk."[21]

Quite remarkably, in the remaining war years Zwartendijk and his family escaped repercussions from the Kovno incident. As already noted, the family returned to the Nazi-occupied Netherlands in September 1940. Once the Germans had decided upon their "Final Solution to the Jewish Question" in January 1942, German High Commissioner Artur von Seyss-Inquart (1892–1946) set about the systematic extermination of the Dutch Jews. The Gestapo might well have come across a file mentioning Zwartendijk's name as the signer of 2,345 sham declarations that had in 1940 enabled many Polish and Lithuanian Jews to flee. Zwartendijk would then have been in deep trouble. In fact, in 1941 or 1942 Zwartendijk was interrogated by the Gestapo about an unrelated matter. He was released, to his great relief. As his elder son Jan recalls and records the incident:

> Two Gestapo officers came to see him at home. He feared the worst—that they had found out about the Kaunas affair. But it turned out that the Germans had killed an old friend of his from Prague "trying to escape" in Romania ["'auf der Flucht erschossen'"— a common German euphemism for tortured to death during interrogation]. This man had Zwartendijk's name and address in his pocket. There was no connection with Kaunas and there were no further consequences of this visit. It was nerve-wracking because drawing attention for any reason meant scrutiny of Gestapo files. Miraculously, his Kaunas activities must have escaped their intelligence. But Zwartendijk did not feel safe until the Allied liberators arrived in southern Holland in September 1944.[22]

In summation, Zwartendijk accepted what he thought would be a routine, quasi-diplomatic assignment. Very shortly thereafter he became involved in the rescue of Jews, endangering himself, his wife, and their three small children. The text beneath which he put his signature 2,345 times was a deliberately deceptive declaration. The nature of the inscription plus the number of times he issued it on his own volition could certainly qualify as an abuse of his consular authority. At the time he signed the "visas" no one knew how the ever-unpredictable Soviets would react, not to mention the Nazis once he returned to the Netherlands. Germany did not recognize the Dutch government-in-exile, and the Soviet Union and the Netherlands had no diplomatic relations; so Zwartendijk could not hope for diplomatic protection. As it turned out, against expectations at the time and for reasons that remain unclear, the Germans never caught onto his scheme and the Soviets decided to permit Jewish refugees to leave Lithuania. The "visas," valid or invalid, turned out not to constitute an irritation for the Soviets. But that was not foreseeable and it was always dangerous to stick one's neck out in the Soviet Union.

WHAT MOTIVATED ZWARTENDIJK?

What motivated a Dutch businessman with a wife and three young children to almost instinctively partake in a dangerous scheme to rescue Jews when his own country was already overrun by the Nazis? Although Philips Company president Dr. Frederik Philips took the initiative in sheltering some 500 Jewish employees from the Nazis and ultimately went into hiding himself, neither Dr. Philips nor his company were even aware until 1997 of Zwartendijk's activities to rescue Jews.[23] Because Zwartendijk had to destroy all his consular files before leaving Kovno, there are few documents that can cast light on the key question of his motivation. One clue emerges in a July 5, 1940, letter from Zwartendijk in Kovno to Philips headquarters in Eindhoven in the Nazi-occupied Netherlands. Zwartendijk writes obliquely of trying to help folk who were "*in de puree*," colloquial Dutch for "in hot water" or literally "in the soup." Even this reference, however, casts little light on the motivation behind Zwartendijk's altruism.[24]

One possible motivation would be religious faith. Carl Lutz, the Swiss consul in Budapest from 1942 until the end of the war, protected Jews through legal and illegal channels. According to his step-daughter, "he was a committed Christian and felt that he had been sent to Budapest for a purpose."[25] The Calvinist citizens of Le Chambon sur Lignon, almost in the shadow of Vichy, the capital of unoccupied but pro-Nazi France, sheltered many thousands of Jews throughout the war due to a deeply held Calvinist faith and historical acquaintance with religious intolerance.[26] Was Zwartendijk also motivated by a religious belief system? According to his oldest son, Jan, who witnessed the events in Kovno, that was not the case. That son wrote in 1998:

> My father was not religious in the sense of participating in religious activities or going to church. His parents had been strong Protestants, inclined toward the socially-liberal side. He himself never felt comfortable with organized religion and never went to church. I think he could be described as a "humanist seeker" in his beliefs. I believe that what guided him in Kaunas was a set of strong personal convictions about what for him was right and what wasn't. He always stuck to his own code without hesitation or compromise, even if that occasionally got him into trouble. But he did not have the slightest inclination to lecture anybody about his values, nor even to discuss them. He just did what he felt he ought to do, period. No discussion or commentary called for, before or after.[27]

Zwartendijk's younger son Robert, although only an infant during the Kovno episode, has corroborated his brother's version of events. Robert stated categorically that Jan Sr. "did what he felt he had to do as a human being, nothing more and nothing less."[28] Perhaps the most telling evidence of Zwartendijk's selflessness is that between 1945 and his death on September 17, 1976, he never spoke about or made any attempt to publicize or glorify his role. Nor did he know how many people he aided had actually made it out of Lithuania. Indeed, he did not know that anyone at all had made it out until 1963, when he learned that there were survivors living in the Los Angeles area. Conversely, most of those whom he rescued did not know his name and referred to him as "Mr. Philips Radio" or "The Angel of Curaçao." Some thought "Philips Radio" was his actual name. In March 1976, through the efforts of Shanghai survivor Ernest G. Heppner and others, Zwartendijk was finally located.[29] Pinhas Hirschprung, Av Beth Din (Chief Judge) of the Montreal Rabbinical Court, wrote Zwartendijk in June 1976 that "not only have you saved us, but you literally saved the generations coming from us."[30] Several months before Zwartendijk's death he was notified by historian David Kranzler about the magnitude of his rescue mission.[31] Survivor

Samuel Orlansky, of Bene Berak, Israel, wrote Jan Zwartendyk Jr. in 1996: "Our first aider and supporter was your late father. . . . What a great feeling it must be if one is privileged to save the life of even one person. And what great merit more was it to save a whole community from the clutches of death."[32]

Finally, in October 1997, through the efforts of Kranzler, Heppner, Israeli diplomat Moshe Yegar, this author, and others, Jan Sr. was recognized as "Righteous among the Nations" by Yad Vashem, the state of Israel's official Holocaust Martyrs' and Heroes' Remembrance Authority. Dr. Mordecai Paldiel, the head of the Department of the Righteous and arguably the individual with the most intimate knowledge of the motivation of some 18,000 other righteous gentiles, has drawn the following conclusion about motivation in the majority of cases he has examined. It would also seem to apply to Zwartendijk:

> The exceptional response of the rescuers to the plight of the Jews is predicated upon the presence of a deeper and more primal disposition, perhaps rooted in our genes, which causes some of us to respond instinctively and instantaneously when confronted with a situation that is so upsetting to our senses as to constitute a traumatic experience. This is especially the case when the potential rescuer is witness to a situation in which the principle of the right to life is called into question, as it was for Jews on the European continent during the Nazi reign of terror.[33]

WHAT MOTIVATED THE DUTCH, JAPANESE, AND SOVIET GOVERNMENTS?

With respect to the motivations of governments, the Dutch government-in-exile had been in existence only a matter of weeks when its ambassador to the Baltic States asked Zwartendijk to take the place of the suspected pro-Nazi Dutch consul in Kovno—clearly a conscious, anti-fascist choice. The ambassador also, without asking or informing his government, acquiesced in the issuance of phony visas for the Lewin family and for Gutwirth's friends. In addition to Zwartendijk's voluminous visa-writing, Dutch diplomats in Stockholm (A. M. de Jong) and Kobe (N. A. G. de Voogt) later on issued identical Curaçao visas to Jewish refugees. The issuance of such "visas" was a heroic and commendable act but in all cases the individual decision of the diplomat himself. There was no governmental policy to issue phony documents to Jewish refugees. Indeed, the Dutch government did not know about the Kovno rescue scheme until about 1963, when they first heard about it and asked Zwartendijk for an explanation. He privately provided the information that was requested without seeking any broader publicity or recognition.

What motivated Sugihara? Unlike Zwartendijk, he was a professionally trained diplomat and intelligence officer. His granting of transit visas to Jews should be seen in that context, as has been suggested in several articles by Boris Bresler, archivist of the Tel Aviv–based Association of Former Jewish Residents of China (Igud Yotzei Sin).[34] In an unpublished memoir, Sugihara explained that he was assigned to open a new Japanese consulate in Kovno in 1939 because "General Oshima [Lieutentant General Hiroshi Oshima, the Japanese ambassador in Berlin—ed.] wanted to know whether the German army would really attack the Soviet Union." The Japanese General Staff wanted to withdraw its army from the Soviet-Manchurian border and move it to the South Pacific. Therefore, in Sugihara's words, his primary task in Kovno was to establish the foreseeable date of a German attack on Russia. He wrote:

> It was obvious why the Staff had insisted that the Foreign Office open a consulate in Kaunas. As a consul in Kaunas, where there was no Japanese colony, I understood that my main task was to inform the General Staff and the Foreign Ministry about the concentration of German troops near the border.[35]

Upon his arrival in Kovno, Sugihara set about establishing an intelligence-gathering network to ascertain regional troop movements. His activities received a major boost in the autumn of 1939 when agents from the Polish underground and the London-based Polish government-in-exile, along with many other Poles, crossed into unoccupied Lithuania when Poland was overrun. Large numbers of Polish troops were interned by the Lithuanian government in camps in Kolotowo, Birsztany, and Polaga. Sugihara helped get some key Polish officers and operatives out of internment and indeed out of Lithuania and into third countries, in several cases issuing them Japanese identity documents and loaning them his official vehicle. One of Sugihara's closest informants was Polish Lieutenant Leszek Daszkiewicz, whose memoir reveals the close connection between Sugihara's intelligence operations and his rescue of Polish Jews. Daszkiewicz wrote:

> Apart from supplying the Japanese consul with information from the territory of the U.S.S.R., I was to receive a reply from him as to the decision concerning the issue of Japanese transit visas to enable Polish refugees to travel via Russia and Japan to America or to one of the islands off the South American coast. . . . There had been a positive reply from the Japanese government and he was only awaiting instructions from the Foreign Ministry [concerning refugees who had final destination visas—ed.]. . . . The honorary consul of that state in Kaunas agreed to issue residence permits [inaccurate; he issued only Curaçao visas—ed.] against payment, even though he knew that none of the refugees would go there [he did not know that—ed.]. Once in Japan, with the help of the still-operating Polish Embassy there, they would go elsewhere.
>
> When the time came and the Japanese Consulate started issuing visas, it was the Jews who came in great numbers, while there were very few [ethnic—ed.] Poles. Only a dozen or so applied and I arranged for them to be treated as priority in all matters. . . . Sugihara told me that it was quite difficult for him to write the customary formula in Japanese in all passports and that caused delays. I suggested making a rubber stamp. He agreed and gave me a master copy. I then gave this to [Polish Army intelligence officer] Captain Jakubianiec who ordered a stamp to be made from it. However, we had two copies made and one sent to Vilnius where Japanese transit visas were issued later following the departure of the consul from Kaunas, but backdated.[36]

Polish documents make clear, then, that apart from any humanitarian motives, Sugihara's involvement with Polish Jewish refugees was part of a coordinated operation to get Jewish and non-Jewish Poles out of Lithuania. It was a by-product of his intelligence-gathering operations with the Polish government-in-exile. That cooperative effort was endorsed by the Japanese Foreign Office and military. After the Soviets closed Sugihara's consulate in Kovno, he went on to equally sensitive postings in Berlin and Koenigsberg and then went on to become Japanese consul general in Prague, an even more prestigious posting than the job he'd held in Kovno.[37] The motivation for Sugihara's activities was fundamentally different from that of Zwartendijk, who was not a salaried or professional diplomat and who was certainly not acting in conjunction with an intelligence-gathering operation.

The Soviet Union's motives in the Kovno rescue are far more complex. Here we are no longer dealing with an individual's choice or even the collective choice of a family or a small community. Instead, we are dealing with the machinations of what was at that time one of the world's two largest totalitarian states. Who permitted approximately 2,200 Polish and Lithuanian Jews to travel thousands of miles across Siberia in order to leave the "paradise" of the Soviet Union? These highly unusual activities almost certainly could not have been authorized by local party functionaries in Kovno or even by Pozdniakov, the Russian representative in Kovno, whose task was to implement the incorporation of Lithuania into the Soviet Union.[38] Who were the higher authorities, and why might they have gone along with the scheme?

According to former USSR United Nations Ambassador Victor Israelyan, who is also a historian of the Soviet Union in the World War II period, one individual, Vladimir Dekanozov, would have been responsible in 1940 for approving exit visas for Polish and Lithuanian Jews and allowing them to travel across the Soviet Union to Vladivostok. Dekanozov was Lavrenti Beria's man when both were still in Soviet Georgia in the mid-1930s. When both were called to Moscow, Dekanozov became Foreign Minister Vyacheslav Molotov's long-time deputy (1939 to November 1940, and 1941–48) with a short stint as the Soviet Union's ambassador to Germany (November 1940–41). In 1938 Beria became head of the NKVD (the Soviet secret police, later named the KGB). Dekanozov became Beria's deputy in March 1953. Both were executed in December 1953.

The broader context in which Dekanozov had to decide about the visas was the August 1939 Hitler-Stalin nonaggression agreement, which Victor Israelyan calls "the pact between two scorpions in a bottle."[39] That treaty stipulated that the Baltic republics were to be within the sphere of influence of the Soviet Union and not that they were to be annexed by the Soviet Union. Nevertheless, the Soviet Union annexed the Baltic republics in 1940 while Hitler was preoccupied overrunning France and the Low Countries on his way to invading Britain.[40] Stalin thought he could get away without a German reaction, and he did. Still, Stalin did not want to push his luck. According to Victor Israelyan, it would have been inconceivable for Dekanozov to allow 2,200 Polish and Lithuanian Jews to escape across Siberia without Molotov's approval, and Molotov would not have approved it without Stalin's approval.[41]

The question then becomes: why would Stalin have approved this? Humanitarian sentiments can be ruled out. What was the deal? With whom? One possible Soviet motive was that permitting the rescue mission was a convenient way of eliminating the burden of several thousand desperate and impoverished Jews in freshly annexed Lithuania. Warhaftig wrote that "the local government was interested in ridding itself of the refugee burden with maximum speed and was prepared to assist us, mainly in issuing passports and travel documents."[42] A second possible motive was that the escape scheme provided a good opportunity to induce some of the more desperate refugees, through intimidation or blackmail, to spy for the Soviets in the United States, Canada, Palestine, Japan, Shanghai, or elsewhere. (No one realistically expected the refugees to wind up in Curaçao.) Warhaftig writes that some of the applicants for Soviet transit and exit permits

> were called in for screening by an official of the NKVD. Two of the students from the Grodno yeshivah informed me [about] their screening. The NKVD suggested [to one of the students] that he might act as their agent, whatever his destination. The issue of an exit permit was made dependent on his acceptance of the offer, but he claimed to have declined.[43]

Yet another possible Soviet motive was that this was an easy way to raise more than half a million dollars for Intourist, the Soviet state travel agency. Each refugee was charged between 170 and 240 U.S. dollars. The money was collected and the tickets bought with the assistance of American Jewish relatives, the JDC, and the Vaad ha-Hatzala, an Orthodox Jewish relief and rescue organization based in New York City.[44] Perhaps all three factors played a part.

According to Israelyan, there are probably no Soviet Foreign Office officials left alive who were involved in the authorization. Dekanozov's name was purged from all official Soviet histories and published Foreign Office documents. He "never existed." Only surviving KGB agents or recently opened KGB or Foreign Office files could tell us more.[45] While such research is beyond the scope of this chapter, answers to these questions could clarify one episode in Chinese, Dutch, Japanese, Jewish, Lithuanian, Polish, and Russian history and contribute to an understanding of motivation in one of the most intense periods of personal and political crisis in the twentieth century.

NOTES

West Georgia's Learning Resources Committee provided funds, and Dean of Arts and Sciences Richard G. Miller provided released time, which enabled the author to complete the basic research for this study at the Oxford (U.K.) Centre for Hebrew and Jewish Studies, of which Peter Oppenheimer is president and David Patterson is president emeritus. The author also greatly appreciates the research assistance of Jeffry M. Diefendorf of the University of New Hampshire; Ambassador (Emeritus) Victor Israelyan of State College, Pennsylvania; Marvin Tokayer of Great Neck, New York; and Jan Zwartendyk of Tucson, Arizona. (Zwartendijk's eldest son Jan has altered the spelling of his last name to Zwartendyk.)

1. Avraham Altman and Irene Eber, "Flight to Shanghai, 1938–1940: The Larger Setting," *Yad Vashem Studies* (Jerusalem) 28 (2000): 51–86.

2. A. J. P. Taylor, *The Origins of the Second World War* (New York: Atheneum, 1983), 208ff.

3. Martin Gilbert, *The Holocaust* (New York: Holt, 1987), 15.

4. Yisrael Gutman and Shmuel Krakowski, *Unequal Victims: Poles and Jews During World War Two* (New York: Holocaust Library, 1986), 30–1.

5. Lucy Dawidowicz, *The War against the Jews 1933–1945* (New York: Bantam, 1986), 112–4.

6. Gutman and Krakowski, *Unequal,* 31.

7. "Mr. Beckelman," "The Refugee Problem in Lithuania." February 1940, sixteen-page typescript in American Jewish Joint Distribution Committee (JDC) Archives, New York City, file number JDC: 1937–1950.730, p. 2.

8. For additional descriptions of the persecution of Jews in the General Government region of Poland as well as in areas formally annexed into Germany proper, see Mary Berg, *Warsaw Ghetto* (New York: L. B. Fischer, 1945), 12–37; Chaim A. Kaplan, *Scroll of Agony* (Bloomington: Indiana University Press, 1999), 12–236; Leni Yahil, *The Holocaust: The Fate of European Jewry, 1932–1945* (New York: Oxford University Press, 1990), 128ff.; Gilbert, *Holocaust,* 84–98; Gutman and Krakowski, *Unequal,* 29ff.; and Dawidowicz, *War,* 112ff.

9. David Kranzler, *Japanese, Nazis & Jews: The Jewish Refugee Community of Shanghai, 1938–1945* (Hoboken, N.J.: Ktav, 1988), 310; Efraim Zuroff, *The Response of Orthodox Jewry in the United States to the Holocaust* (New York: Yeshiva University Press, 2000), 81–2.

10. "Beckelman," "Refugee," 2.

11. Zorach Warhaftig, *Refugee and Survivor: Rescue Efforts during the Holocaust* (Jerusalem: Yad Vashem, 1988), 118.

12. Ben Cion Pinchuk, *Shtetl Jews under Soviet Rule* (Oxford, U.K.: Basil Blackwell, 1991); Masha Greenbaum, *The Jews of Lithuania* (Jerusalem: Gefen, 1995), 288–301.

13. "Beckelman," "Refugee," 2.

14. Documents about Philips' presence in Lithuania in 1939 have been preserved in Lithuania's Central State Archives in Vilnius. These are mainly Finance Ministry records bearing original tax stamps plus photos of Zwartendijk and his wife. I am grateful to Archives Director Riorardas Cipas and Deputy Director Grazine Sluckaite for making these papers available to me during my June 1998 research trip. The Kaunas Regional Archives, Juozas Rimkus, director, contains some Finance Ministry and other commercial documents from 1940–41 and telephone books from the years 1939 to 1940. For additional background on Orthodox Jewish organizations and their contacts with Zwartendijk see Zuroff, *Response, passim.*

15. There are two retrospective letters from Zwartendijk himself confirming the basic facts of his appointment and activities in Kovno. Letters: Jan Zwartendijk, Rotterdam, to Benjamin Gray, Los Angeles, August 21, 1963, and to H. Shapiro, Baltimore, January 22, 1967, both courtesy of Jan Zwartendyk.

16. Isaac Lewin, *Remembering Days of Old: Historical Essays* (New York: Research Institute of Religious Jewry, 1994), 171–6; Nathan Lewin, "Memories of My Father," *Washington Jewish Week,* September 7, 1995, p. 53. Most residents of the Soviet Union needed official permission to travel across their own country (e.g., from Kovno or Vilna to Vladivostok). They had to have an additional permit to leave their country, a document known correctly or incorrectly as an "exit visa." They also needed an entry visa issued by a foreign power to gain admittance to that country. And, in the case of refugees traveling across Japan to Shanghai or elsewhere, a Japanese transit visa was necessary. Warhaftig devotes several chapters to the intricacies of procuring each of these documents.

17. Sugihara told Warhaftig in 1969 that he had been aware of the fictitious nature of the Curaçao visas. But, as long as his action was not in any way illegal, he was prepared to aid the refugees. Warhaftig, *Refugee,* 110 and *passim.* Other accounts about Sugihara include Hillel Levine, *In Search of Sugihara* (New York: Free Press, 1996); Christopher Lehmann-Haupt, "Tackling a Mysterious Mass Rescuer," *New York Times,* December 23, 1996, p. C16; Ernest G. Heppner, "Sine Qua Non," *Hadassah Magazine,* November 1997, p. 41; and Mel Gussow, "Sugihara's List: A Play about 6,000 Saved Jews," *New York Times,* January 21, 1998, p. B3. A widely published but unsourced account about Sugihara appears in Marvin Tokayer and Mary Swartz, *The Fugu Plan: The Untold Story of the Japanese and the Jews during World War II* (New York: Paddington Press, 1979; reprint, New

York: Weatherhill, 1996), also published under the title *Desperate Voyagers* (New York: Dell, 1980) and translated into Chinese by Gong Fangzhen, Zhang Letian, and Lu Haisheng as *Hetun yu jihua: Dierci shijie dazhan qijian Ribenren yu Youtairen de mimi jiaowang shi* (Shanghai: Shanghai sanlian shudian, 1992).

18. Letters: Jan Zwartendijk, Rotterdam, to Gray, Los Angeles, August 21, 1963; to Shapiro, Baltimore, January 22, 1967; Nathan Gutwirth, Antwerp, to Mordecai Paldiel, Jerusalem, May 28, 1996; to Jan Zwartendyk, State College, Pa., July 16, 1996, all courtesy of Jan Zwartendyk. Kranzler, *Japanese,* 311–2; Zuroff, *Response,* 80–7. As noted later in this chapter, Mrs. Betty Goodfriend was living with her family in a *shtetl* some thirty kilometers from Kovno.

19. Until 1941, when the Japanese occupiers shut the gates of Shanghai (having earlier kept them open), Shanghai was the only place on earth just prior to the Holocaust where a foreigner could legally walk ashore without any documentation whatsoever. The absence of passport controls in Shanghai has often mistakenly been described as the "nonrequirement of visas." The absence of controls was due to the absence of authority in Shanghai of both the Chongqing-based Chinese nationalist government of Chiang Kai-shek and the Nanjing-based Japanese puppet government of Wang Jingwei. On how intricacies of governance and nongovernance in Shanghai created a haven for Jews, see Ernest G. Heppner, *Shanghai Refuge: A Memoir of the World War II Jewish Ghetto* (Lincoln: University of Nebraska Press, 1993), 40 and *passim,* translated into German by Roberto de Hollanda as *Fluchtort Shanghai: Erinnerungen 1938–1948* (Bonn: Weidle Verlag, 1998); Altman and Eber, "Flight," 51–86.

20. Warhaftig, *Refugee,* 104–5. Despite Warhaftig's record of his meeting with Kasteel, there is at least one recorded instance of Jewish refugees' being admitted to Curaçao and not being turned back to sea. After the German invasion of the Netherlands in May 1940, several Jews with Austrian and German passports were interned on the Dutch West Indian island of Bonaire. In late 1941 a League of Nations refugee official in London prevailed upon the Dutch government-in-exile in London to cable the governor of Curaçao to admit to Curaçao an additional eighty-two Jewish refugees aboard the Spanish ship *Cabo de Hornos,* and the refugees were admitted. The *Cabo de Hornos* incident was a twentieth-century replay of the arrival of the first Jewish refugees in New Amsterdam in 1654. On that occasion, twenty-three Jewish refugees from Brazil were, on orders from Amsterdam, admitted to New Amsterdam over the protestations of Dutch Governor Peter Stuyvesant. Beckelman, then stationed in Asuncion, Paraguay, to JDC, New York, December 13 and 23, 1941, JDC Archives; "High Seas," *Time Magazine,* December 1, 1941, p. 30; Pamela Rotner Sakamoto, "The Policy

of the Japanese Ministry of Foreign Affairs toward Jewish Refugees" (doctoral diss., Fletcher School of Law and Diplomacy, Tufts University, 1996), 297–300; Walter Laqueur, *Generation Exodus* (Hanover, N.H.: Brandeis University Press, 2001), 219; David de Sola Pool and Tamar de Sola Pool, *An Old Faith in a New World* (New York: Columbia University Press, 1955), 4–31; Arthur Herzberg, *The Jews in America* (New York: Simon and Shuster, 1989), 19–26.

21. Betty Goodfriend, interview with author, Atlanta, Ga., October 1999. On Jewish fears of deportation to Siberia, see Menachem Begin, *White Nights* (New York: Harper and Row, 1977), *passim.*

22. Jan Zwartendyk, "Jan Zwartendijk: His Activities as Dutch Consul in Lithuania, 1940" (Ms., October 1, 1996), 7; courtesy of Jan Zwartendyk.

23. Even though the Holocaust rescue activities of Zwartendijk and Dr. Philips were unrelated, on November 4, 1997, the Israeli charitable organization Boys Town Jerusalem sponsored a dinner in Amsterdam to jointly honor both. At this event, Zwartendijk's children received his posthumous "Righteous among the Nations" medal from Yad Vashem. The same honor had been bestowed on Dr. Philips earlier that year. Letter: Mordecai Paldiel, Jerusalem, to Jan Zwartendyk, State College, Pa., October 7, 1997, copy to author.

24. Letter: J. Zwartendijk, Kaunas, to Philips head office, Eindhoven, the Netherlands, July 5, 1940, courtesy Jan Zwartendyk.

25. Ruth Rothenberg, "Belated Honor for Swiss Diplomat Who Saved Jews," *Jewish Chronicle* (London), April 7, 2000, p. 19.

26. See interviews with wartime survivors of Le Chambon in Pierre Sauvage's documentary film *Weapons of the Spirit,* produced by Friends of Le Chambon. For general background, see Gilbert, *Holocaust,* 403–4 and Yahil, *Holocaust,* 589–90.

27. E-mail: Jan Zwartendijk, Tucson, Arizona, to the author, December 29, 1998, courtesy Jan Zwartendyk.

28. Robert Zwartendijk, quoted in "The Man Who Saved Judaism," *Jerusalem Post International Edition No. 1860* (June 29, 1996), 1.

29. E-mail: Jan Zwartendyk to author, September 23, 2001. On the efforts of Heppner, Kranzler, and others, see letters from J. Zwartendyk and Ernest G. Heppner in *The Jewish Post and Opinion,* April 30, 1976, p. 2; Ed Stattman, "Japanese Granted Dutch Denied Laurels for Saving Jews," *Jewish Post and Opinion,* June 21, 1995, NAT 4; Ed Stattman, "Dutchman to be Honored for 1940 Rescues," *Jewish Post and Opinion,* May 8, 1996, NAT 2; Steve Lipman, "The Decent Thing," *Jewish Week* (New York), May 10, 1996, p. 1; Letter: Paldiel to Jan Zwartendyk, October 7, 1997; and Phyllis Braun, "Yad Vashem Gives Righteous Gentile His Due," *Arizona Jewish Post* (Tucson), May 1, 1998, pp. 1, 8.

30. Letter: Pinhas Hirschprung, Montreal, to Jan Zwartendyk, State College, Pa., June 12, 1976, in Boys Town Jerusalem testimonial volume dedicated to Jan Zwartendijk, New York City, September 9, 1996, n.p.

31. E-mail: Jan Zwartendyk to author, September 23, 2001.

32. Letter: Samuel Orlansky, Bene Berak, Israel, to Jan Zwartendyk, May 19, 1996, in Boys Town volume, n.p.

33. Mordecai Paldiel, "The Face of the Other: Reflections on the Motivations of Gentile Rescuers of Jews," in *Remembering for the Future: The Holocaust in an Age of Genocide,* vol. 2, ed. John K. Roth and Elisabeth Maxwell (Basingstoke, U.K.: Palgrave, 2001), 334.

34. Boris Bresler, "Sugihara Story: Facts, Mystery, Myth," *Bulletin of the Igud Yotzei Sin* (Tel Aviv) no. 350 (June–July 1997): 12–14, no. 351 (September–October 1997): 8–11; reprinted in *Points East* (Menlo Park, Calif.) 13, no. 2 (July 1998): 1, 6–10.

35. Sugihara Chiune, "Report on the Activity in Kovno and on Cooperation with the Polish Forces" (unpublished report, in Russian), 1–2, cited in Ewa Palasz-Rutkowska and Andrzej T. Romer, "Polish-Japanese Cooperation during World War II," *Japan Forum* (London) 7, no. 2 (Autumn 1995): 287–8.

36. Sugihara, "Report," 5, in Palasz-Rutkowska, "Polish," 289; Leszek Daszkiewicz, *Placowka wywiadowcza "G" Sprawodania i dokumenty* (Polish: Intelligence Agency "G." Reports and Documents), unpublished, England, 1948, in Palasz-Rutkowska, "Polish," 292–93.

37. Sugihara Yukiko, *Rokusennin-inochi-no biza* (Life Visas for 6,000 People) (Tokyo: Asahi-sonorama, 1990), 73, in Palasz-Rutkowska, "Polish," 293–4.

38. Warhaftig met with Pozdniakov on at least one occasion. Zuroff, *Response,* 85.

39. Victor Israelyan was, as of 1996, a Fulbright Scholar at Pennsylvania State University. Jan Zwartendyk, notes on a conversation with Victor Israelyan, June 4, 1996, courtesy of Jan Zwartendyk.

40. Gerhard L. Weinberg, *A World at Arms* (Cambridge: Cambridge University Press, 1999), 100–7.

41. Zwartendyk, notes on Israelyan, June 4, 1996.

42. Warhaftig, *Refugee,* 92.

43. Ibid., 104–5.

44. Kranzler, *Japanese,* 312, 338.

45. Zwartendyk, notes on Israelyan, June 4, 1996.

Yehudi Lindeman

Against All Odds: Successes and Failures of the Dutch Palestine Pioneers

AS EARLY AS 1961, THE DUTCH HISTORIAN JACOB (JACQUES) PRESSER DEfended the notion that, contrary to popular belief, Jewish men and women in the Netherlands played significant roles in every phase of resistance against the occupying Germans.[1] Those resistance activities consisted of armed acts of sabotage; raids aimed at freeing imprisoned comrades; creating forgeries of German and Dutch seals, stamps, identification papers, and so on; and the publication and distribution of underground pamphlets and newspapers. They also included the physically and emotionally demanding enterprise of rescuing, hiding, and looking after Jewish adults and children marked for deportation. In a limited number of cases, these rescue attempts were rooted in two-sided coordination between Jews and non-Jews.

One instance of such cooperation was the removal of between 700 and 1,000 Jewish children (mostly babies and toddlers) from the Amsterdam "crèche" (day-care center), an extended rescue effort that covered a period of eight months. The crèche housed children whose parents had been arrested and were about to be deported. The adults were penned up across the street in the Hollandse Schouwburg (Holland Theater), used by the Germans as a temporary prison for arrested Jews on their way to camp Westerbork. It was a complex and delicate rescue operation involving Jewish day-care workers, Jewish Council personnel, non-Jewish members of three fledgling resistance groups, students at the Protestant teacher-training college next door to the crèche, and even one SS man, Alfons Zündler. After being smuggled out one or two at a time, each child had to be taken to a hiding address. For the intervention to be successful, the child's name had to be removed from the theater's registration list, a dangerous task that required cool-headed precision, timing, and luck. In sum, the entire process demanded close coordination of the various illegal activities and a sophisticated pattern of Jewish–non-Jewish trust and cooperation.[2]

Yet little credit has been given to date to the historically unique situation of Dutch Jews and non-Jews working side by side in the underground. Right from the end of World War II the assumption took hold that the Dutch Jews, as targets and victims of Nazi aggression, had been absent from, or at best underrepresented in, the areas of armed and non-armed resistance. Yehuda Bauer's verdict that "Jews in the Dutch resistance were few" reflects the generally held position.[3] Whatever its relation to objective fact or documentation, it is an impression that lingers and has assumed the status of a myth. Like other myths regarding ethnic or national minorities, this one, too, should be reexamined. Thus it is a pity that Amsterdam's most famous resistance monument, Mari Andriessen's impressive statue of the city's longshoreman, opposite the venerable Portuguese synagogue, does not reflect the sort of two-sided cooperation of which I am speaking. On the contrary, it is clearly, and is clearly intended to be, a tribute to the city's resolute shipyard workers and the many others who proclaimed a strike on behalf of their Jewish brothers on February 25, 1941.

That tribute is, of course, entirely deserved. The statue's posture, expressing outrage and determination, embodies an act of defiance against any further German attempts to attack and arrest the Jewish part of the population. But in that case, it should probably be recalled that the "February strike" was prompted by the violent German raid on the Jewish quarter of February 22 and 23—and also that this German assault was itself a reaction against the actions of the *knokploegen,* mostly Jewish neighborhood gangs or action groups composed of young street toughs who physically opposed the gangs of pro-Nazi hoodlums or organized Dutch Nazi youth bent on harassing Jewish merchants and individuals.[4] In its portrayal of a brave working-class hero, Andriessen's moving statue in fact perpetuates, however unintentionally, the postwar myth of robust non-Jews supporting their defenseless Jewish fellow-citizens in one-sided solidarity. It supports a narrative that my observations on Jewish/non-Jewish underground cooperation intend to remedy somewhat.

My subject is the rescue, "against all odds," of between 425 and 450 Jewish youngsters in Holland, the so-called Palestine Pioneers, through the coordinated efforts of Jews and non-Jews. "Against all odds" was the self-conscious motto the youngsters had chosen, and refers to the obstacles they needed to overcome to avoid deportation and reach freedom. These Zionist youngsters were members of the Dutch *Chalutz* or *Hechalutz* (pioneer) movement who were headed for life on a kibbutz in Eretz Yisrael until the war interfered in their plans. Though they spoke Dutch, most were born in Germany or Austria and had come to Holland as immigrants or refugees. By working on the land, either the community's or that of farmers in the region, and living in a community home, they were actively preparing themselves for a collective agricultural future life in Palestine. Except for their leaders, they were still in their teens at the moment when the Germans began deporting Jews to Auschwitz, in the summer of 1942. The well-documented but little-known resistance initiative of their group is probably the only clear instance of active underground activity to which the label of centralized Jewish resistance can be fairly applied.

By choosing to rally behind the motto "against all odds" (my free translation of the Hebrew *af al pi chen*), the pioneers expressed their firm intention to achieve their goal, which for all of them, as dedicated Zionists, was *aliyah* (i.e., immigration to Palestine), even if it involved great risks and meant that uncertain numbers of them would die on the way. In the end, of those who opted for hiding, many would survive the war in various hideouts in Holland. Their estimated number is 240. At least eighty of the pioneers would be discovered at their hiding addresses, or otherwise betrayed or captured. Over 100 pioneers, after crossing national borders twice, would be aided in finding hiding places in France or would, after crossing the Pyrenees, find safety in neutral Spain. Most of those who managed to reach Spain—about seventy—would sail for Palestine by boarding two different ships in the course of 1944, a triumph over odds by all definitions, given the European state of affairs.[5] This article focuses on the pressures and dilemmas of the Jewish organizers and their non-Jewish partners of two groups, the youth *aliyah* center in Loosdrecht and the Beth Hechalutz (Pioneers' House) in Amsterdam. I will focus on the dilemmas they faced, the factors that made them opt for escape and/or resistance, and the solutions they found to each obstacle on their way.

These obstacles were many and of all sorts. We begin with the Loosdrecht group, which was the first to choose hiding and resistance in July and August 1942: their youth *aliyah* center had to be evacuated, and hiding places found for each of the fifty young men and women. This also involved finding considerable sums of money. Next, there was the need to keep the liaison between the youngster in hiding, his or her hosts, and the organizers of the resistance. Besides the need for money and ration cards, one of the organizers' constant preoccupations was to provide new hiding places whenever the need arose. One special obstacle was to orchestrate the organized escape of *chaverim* from camp Westerbork, to which I will come back later. Crossing the border into Belgium and France presented formidable new challenges, one of which was the need to possess legitimate (i.e., forged) identity and border-crossing papers. As a result, some of the *chaverim* (comrades) became masters at counterfeiting documents. Crossing the Pyrenees into Spain presented a physical and logistics challenge of even larger proportions, not to mention the need to find the colossal amounts of money to pay for guides and supplies. Finally, and most important of all, was the pioneers' dependence on networking with other resistance groups. For their stay in France and for crossings into Spain, the pioneers required the help of organizations that were familiar with the local conditions and terrain. Here they were fortunate to find ways to mutually trade favors and support. Indeed, very little would have been achieved without the consistent help and mutual support of pioneers and French underground networks (Jewish and non-Jewish) working together. The most notable support came from the French underground Armée Juive. Even after successfully making the often grueling crossings into Spain, there were obstacles that kept the pioneers from reaching Palestine.[6] Eventually those too would be overcome, so that about seventy *chaverim* were able to reach Haifa, on two ships sailing from Spain—the *Niassa* and the *Guinée*—in early and late 1944, respectively.

To overcome some of these obstacles, such as the immediate need for a hiding place, required speed, initiative, and an ability to improvise. Forging papers or planning escapes from camp Westerbork required ingenuity, patience, and meticulous preparation. One ingredient that was often but not always forthcoming was luck. The single most essential ingredient was to establish careful and secure networks.

Though nearly all of the pioneers' principal leaders would eventually be captured, by that time proven routes and connections had usually been established. Even after an unexpected interruption, gaps in routes or contacts would be reestablished, and the work resumed by others. Thus, as a result of the the untimely capture and death in January 1943 of Joachim ("Schuschu") Simon of the Loosdrecht and Amsterdam group, important contacts with French resistance workers were terminated. Yet within a few months, Kurt Hanneman, Norbert Klein, and Kurt Reilinger were able to continue the work, using some of the contacts pioneered by Schuschu. Again, after the capture and execution of Joop Westerweel a year later, others carried on in his footsteps. In each instance, and in spite of the setbacks, the network was able to recuperate itself. Hence it can be stated that networking with non-Jewish bystanders was the key element in all of the pioneers' operations, just as finding reliable contacts in the Netherlands and abroad was their greatest challenge. This is in keeping with recent findings.[7]

The manuscript that contains the record of the pioneers' collective story includes many personal testimonies, on which I draw freely.[8] Those personal witness accounts are invaluable for two distinct reasons. They evoke the time, place, and personal feelings and motivations of the young men and women trying to escape the German dragnet, thus giving the story of their planned escape a personal element and bringing it to life. Equally important, the personal accounts present precise and chronological records of how problems were dealt with and resolved. In other words, by depicting the chain of events, they indicate in detail how each new step toward freedom led to new possibilities, or dangers, inviting new solutions. Those personal documents also reveal the pioneers' realistic assessment of the precise obstacles that lay between them and personal and collective freedom. They show the extent to which most of the pioneers, despite their young age, were guided by common sense rather than romantic expectations or adventurism. One sure cause of this was their firm sense of solidarity and belonging.

This bonding experience had been further strengthened over the years as they prepared themselves for a collective farmer's existence in Eretz Yisrael. It is no surprise, therefore, to learn that of those who were captured, no one ever betrayed a comrade. To cite just one example, by using precise timing and taking calculated risks, Jewish and non-Jewish pioneers from outside and inside camp Westerbork worked together to liberate small groups of fellow pioneers from the camp without being discovered. The testimonies of both Jewish and non-Jewish members draw a clear picture of how this was done. On a deportation night, it was possible to hide a few of those scheduled to go to Poland. Since their names were at that point deleted from all the lists, their escape would remain unnoticed. Thus the Jewish Lore Durlacher and non-Jewish Frans Gerritsen, among others, worked just outside camp Westerbork in close coordination with *chaverim* inside the camp to get people out. They then supplied them with bicycles and with train tickets and other documents and accompanied them to a nearby railway station. The key person in those escapes was Kurt Walter, who was in charge of a small industrial rail transport. As machinist of a small locomotive, he was able to hide two people at a time. And since he worked both inside and outside the camp, he was able to smuggle the pioneers across the boundary line when he left the camp.[9]

Solidarity, trust, and precise coordination were important factors in all documented rescue efforts. The pioneers soon learned that only by sticking together and placing their trust exclusively with those within the Jewish–non-Jewish network could they maximize successes and minimize betrayal. Both the Jews and non-Jews participating in the work sooner or later had to go "underwater" (*onderduiken*—i.e., being "immersed," Dutch for going into hiding). By operating in hiding and with false identity papers, and by staying clear of the Dutch civilian authorities and the Jewish establishment, they minimized their chances of being arrested and deported. In all of their underground activities, Jews and non-Jews worked together closely and in solidarity so that it is probably appropriate to say that the two (or, as we shall see, three) networks worked together as one.[10]

This account is incomplete without a glance at the prevailing situation in occupied Holland during the war, and during the period following liberation. As I mentioned before, the extent of Jews and non-Jews in Holland working side by side in resistance activities had been underestimated in the period after the war, and their stories suppressed. The same may well be true for other occupied countries too, though the history, profile, and size of Dutch Jewry differed significantly from that of neighboring countries. A soft but tenacious postwar anti-Semitism most likely accounted for the widely held resentment against those Jews who would return from the camps or from hiding.[11] That plus the need to explore and record versions of Dutch collective experience during the war (from which the Jews were by definition virtually excluded) were certainly factors contributing to the suppression of the share of Jewish underground activities. In case after documented case, the Jews were only grudgingly received back into the towns and places from which they had been deported or gone into hiding. By minimizing the extent of Jewish anti-Nazi resistance, especially within the context of a wider Dutch resistance network, the Dutch may have been compensating, both collectively and personally, for the rather lackluster treatment of their Jewish fellow-citizens during the war, and the failure of Dutch society to protect them during the months and years of their greatest need. In no other West European country was the persecution of the Jews so well organized on every societal level, and the fatality rate so high. An estimated 75 percent of the prewar Jewish population perished during the war. The high number of deported Jews has been the issue dominating Dutch historiography of World War II.[12]

In partial defense of the Dutch civilian population at the time, it may be pointed out that due to the monarch's, and subsequently the government's, hasty departure in May 1940, the entire country came under direct German civilian administration. Their flight and the ensuing German intervention had serious social consequences for the country's more than 140,000 Jews, and it constitutes a series of events still an issue prompting fierce debates on the part of Dutch historians and political scientists. Partly as a result of the successful German subversion of the civil service, and of the Nazi regime's ferocious suppression of any form of resistance, Holland had a high degree of collaboration. This was true especially at the highest levels of the Dutch *ambtenarij* (civil service). Basically it kept, through a trickle-down effect, all rank-and-file civil servants from resisting German orders. A slightly more generous interpretation would have it that any meaningful resistance was limited to the lowest ranks of the bureaucracy. Either way, it had the effect of turning the entire Dutch civil service, from local and government employees to transport personnel and police, municipal and nationwide, into pliant and effective tools of the German civil administration, which helped create a deceptive and lethal web for the increasingly isolated Jewish part of the population that only few individuals and very few groups were willing or able to escape.[13]

Another possible factor limiting the perceived Jewish contributions to the resistance may be that the names of Jewish persons are not always obviously and recognizably Jewish. It is also important to realize that, for ideological and safety reasons, many of these Jewish men and women would not necessarily have wanted to be known as Jewish rather than Dutch resisters. Also, a good deal of what is known is dependent on oral documentation that until recently appeared suspect to many historians. Lately there have been some efforts to reopen the debate about the Jewish share of the resistance.[14] My focus on the Palestine Pioneers is also intended as a contribution to this dialogue. Meanwhile, to the extent that these matters can be quantified, the available record indicates that, quantitatively speaking, the Dutch Jews, relative to their numbers, supplied more resistance workers than the non-Jewish population as a whole. Or as J. Presser put it in 1965, "There can be no doubt that resistance by Jews was proportionately greater than that of other Dutchmen."[15]

In July of 1942, the leaders of the Youth Aliyah House in Loosdrecht, home to about forty-eight (some say fifty) youngsters between the age of fifteen and seventeen, were faced with a serious dilemma: Should the young people be advised to obediently go to camp Westerbork, and from there to Poland, once their call-up notices arrived, or should an attempt be made to hide them? It was the group leaders' dilemma to formulate an answer, as did their colleagues at pioneer youth centers in other parts of the country. It was indeed the dilemma facing the vast majority of the Jews of Holland.[16] To better understand their fears and hesitations, I will draw on some of the leaders' personal testimonies that mirror both their despair and their determination to arrive at a solution. In the spring of 1942, the isolated and stigmatized Jews of Holland were like sitting ducks. In the words of one of the Loosdrecht leaders, things were now at a point where "the preparations for the 'final solution of the Jewish problem' having been completed, the stage was set for the actual destruction of the Dutch Jews."[17]

As the young leadership pondered the question of what to do, several memories weighed on their minds. One was the sudden deportation of over sixty agricultural trainees from the pioneers' work farm at Wieringen to Mauthausen, in June 1941, through German duplicity. None of them had survived. Another was the frightening experience of their colleague and friend Joachim "Schuschu" Simon, who had been an inmate of a German concentration camp as recently as 1938. Another memory was the 1941 meeting, at the youth *aliyah* home, with Mr. Edelstein, a community leader from Prague. (He later became a prominent leader at Theresienstadt.) His words and bearing made a deep impression on the leaders who attended, judging from the fact that three of them mention it in their testimony. In the incongruously rural setting of Loosdrecht, Mr. Edelstein had expressed his complete pessimism about the fate and the survival chances of the Jews of Europe.[18]

These were some of the considerations on the minds of the Loosdrecht youth leaders in June and early July 1942. During those days and weeks the existence of the Dutch Jews hung in the balance. In June, the Jewish Council, during a joint meeting with the German authorities, was put on notice that the entire Dutch Jewish population would soon be deported to the east, and that people should prepare themselves for imminent departure. Then, still unexpectedly, the first deportation notices arrived on July 5. A total of 4,000 people, at this point mostly German Jews, were scheduled for deportation to Westerbork, and then to Poland. Next came the random and violent *razzias* (raids) and mass arrests of July 14 and 15, 1942. Simultaneous with the *razzias* came the departure, in the early morning of July 15, of the first transport to Poland. The Loosdrecht boys and girls would surely be next in line to be deported. Nearly all of them were German or Austrian by birth and had come to Holland as refugees. The problem was what to do about it.

There was a consensus in favor of escaping arrest through hiding, but none of the pioneers had non-Jewish community contacts that would lead to shelter for so large a number of young people. Then Miriam Waterman, a young Jewish woman who lived nearby, introduced them to some of her non-Jewish friends who appeared willing to hide individual Jews. It came as a revelation, says Menachem Pinkhof, one of the leaders. Suddenly, and at the moment of their greatest need, there was the "fantastic idea of starting a hiding action on a large scale." Soon various potential hiding places were found through the persistence and hard work of Miriam Waterman and her sister Elli, and of Bouke Koning and Jan Smit, who were non-Jews.[19]

Although Miriam had joined the Zionist organization in 1938, she came from an assimilated Jewish background, and many of her friends and acquaintances were non-Jews. She had taught for two and a half years at the progressive "Werkplaats" school under its director,

Kees Boeke. At the Kees Boeke school she met Bouke Koning, a gardener and landscaper, and Jan Smit, an art teacher. There she also learned about the problems facing the European Jews, through her meetings with pupils who were German-Jewish refugees. After being forced to leave the Werkplaats in late 1940 (when all Jewish teachers were fired), Miriam started a small Jewish school in Loosdrecht, near the pioneers' home. After meeting some of the leaders, she responded to their urgent requests by successfully asking for help from her non-Jewish friends. But it was not enough: many more addresses were needed and time was pressing. The turning point came in early August, when she arranged a meeting between Menachem and Joachim (Schuschu) of the pioneers, and Joop Westerweel, principal of a Montessori school in Rotterdam and a former head teacher at the Kees Boeke school. Once he was informed of what was needed, Joop immediately activated his wide circle of friends and took over the task of organizing and finding addresses for all the remaining pioneer youngsters. That August connection between the leadership of the Loosdrecht house and Joop Westerweel effectively signals the start of the resistance activities of the Palestine Pioneers and what would later be known as the Westerweel group.

Joop's first action was to provide addresses for those youngsters still without a place to hide. Next, one of their main concerns was to raise money and obtain false papers. It was agreed that the pioneers would have to raise the money and find ration cards to support those in hiding. A constant flow of money would also be needed to support the children in hiding with food and clothes, and to pay for those traveling by bus and train to visit children and locate new hiding places for those youngsters who were hidden only provisionally and were forced to move on. By selling the entire Loosdrecht food supply on the black market, they raised 7,000 guilders, a significant amount of money and enough to keep the work going for the next two months. Nobody dared to look any further ahead than that.[20]

Meanwhile the pioneers and their friends remained on high alert, for it was uncertain when the deportation orders would come. They were lucky enough to have a reliable ally within the ranks of the Jewish establishment. Erika Blueth was secretary of the Youth Aliyah Department and sat on several committees of the Jewish Council. In that capacity she had access to confidential information, including the sending of deportation notices. She was reliable and never spoke to anybody about the planned escape, knowing full well the extent to which the Jewish leaders were opposed to any such initiative on the part of individuals, let alone groups. Erika Blueth also promised to let Loosdrecht know, through a telephone message in code, when the pioneers' evacuation to Westerbork was scheduled to take place.

The expected phone call came on a Thursday in mid-August 1942, indicating that the youth house would be forcibly vacated on the following Monday. That same day, the leaders convened a meeting at which they revealed the new plans to the startled young people. Until then, the youngsters had believed that they would go to Poland as a group, and continue their pioneer work in a work camp there. Many thought that by working hard and sticking together as a group, they would prevail, *af al pi chen*, whatever the conditions might be. This kind of thinking was not rare. Many people thought that even in Poland young and healthy Jews with the right work ethic would survive. One month earlier, the Zionist socialist leader Sam de Wolff had addressed some of those about to be deported, at the Amsterdam Hechalutz House. He told them to have courage, for "whatever the fate of the individual, socialism will conquer, and Eretz Yisrael will be built."[21] For reasons of safety, and to ensure secrecy, the leaders had told none of the children about the change of plans.

It had been a spring and summer of rapid changes for the Loosdrecht youth *aliyah* pioneers. One of the leaders remembers a late May meeting to honor the festival of Shavu'ot, celebrated by the pioneers in Zionist fashion as Bikkurim, the harvest festival of bringing in the first fruits or crops. There had been much singing, and some of the sixteen- and seventeen-year-old girls had performed dances. It was a touching ceremony, and all the *chaverim* had been full of good cheer. Now they were sad and confused, as they were told that they were about to leave the youth *aliyah* house. It seemed especially painful to them that in going under, or "underwater" *(onderduiken)*, they would have to stay in one location for a long time, maybe for years, without any chance of meeting other group members or of having any contact with the outside world. That meant no letters could be written, either. Everything had to remain secret. That way, even in the eventuality of an arrest, they would be able to claim ignorance. One rightly wonders what went on in the young people's minds. We know from the record that there was an emotional discussion, at the end of which Schuschu spoke about his terrible experiences in the

Buchenwald concentration camp. He then asked the young people who would prefer to stay behind, rather than go into hiding. Nobody volunteered to stay. That same Thursday evening, the first number of children was taken to nearby hiding addresses, on the backs of bicycles. By Sunday, all forty-eight, forty-nine, or fifty children had been moved to their hiding places, and all books, furniture, and personal possessions had been given away. Even so, the leadership realized that this was only the beginning.[22]

Many people lent a helping hand during those first few weeks. Some of the leaders assumed the task of visiting the youngsters in their new places, and brought them clothes and books and other items for their personal needs, as well as money and ration cards for their keep. Forged identification cards were prepared for those who sometimes moved outside, or who needed to be moved from one address to another. Local clerks in different towns were found who were willing to take personal risks by illegally registering youngsters under assumed names in their new municipalities.[23] Soon the Amsterdam pioneers asked the leaders of the Loosdrecht group to assist them in finding hiding addresses for those *chaverim* who had received deportation notices. Addresses for them were quickly found as well, in spite of Joop's protests that this was more than the network could handle. Eventually Joop agreed, and so the resistance group expanded to include a third group. The leaders of the Amsterdam Hechalutz were Kurt Hanneman, Norbert Klein, and Gideon Drach. Later, after those three had been arrested (Norbert was rescued, but was gravely wounded), the leaders who continued the rescue work were Kurt Reilinger, Ernst Hirsch, and Betty Brits, among others. They were all from the Amsterdam Chalutz Center and played major roles, alongside Joop Westerweel, Bouke Koning, and other non-Jewish activists, in moving the operational center to France. After Joop's arrest in March 1944, the rescuers converged on Toulouse, the center of the French Zionist resistance, and the place from which cross-border exits to Spain were organized.

Meanwhile, Erika Blueth, through her various connections, was able to obtain more money for the pioneers and much-needed travel permits for some of their members. Nevertheless there was a perception that soon grew into a conviction that hiding inside the Netherlands was only a partial solution. There were several reasons for this. One was the temporary nature of many of the hiding addresses. Provisionary stays meant frequent changes involving dangerous travel missions for those on their way to a new place, and added to the already heavy burden on the leadership. Another reason was the high incidence of betrayals by informers or ordinary bystanders. Add to this the high vigilance of the local civilian authorities, and the efficient dragnet with its frequent raids on the part of the German and Dutch police, and one cannot avoid the conclusion that it was a dangerous thing to be hidden in Holland. Yet the alternatives were equally as dangerous or more so. In all the pioneers' discussions, over the autumn of 1942, the only serious alternatives were border crossings into either neutral Switzerland or Vichy France.[24] This resulted in the pioneers' first organized transborder rescue operation abroad, which was a complete failure.

Nobody knows what went wrong with the carefully planned convoy of the ten or thirteen *chaverim* who aimed to cross into Switzerland. It had been a complex journey to organize, and involved several untested and therefore potentially unreliable outsiders and a great deal of money. Though the circumstances remained unclear, it is likely that one of the organizers betrayed the group to the Germans. It was a hard lesson, to lose so many people, but the fiasco strengthened the leaders in their resolve to control every part of the journey inside and outside the country. From now on, *af al pi chen* would mean relying on one's own wits. This had two consequences. It forced the pioneers (i.e., the Loosdrecht, Amsterdam, and Westerweel groups) to run a fully independent rescue network, and to scout for completely secure contacts abroad. Operating their own route or routes through Belgium into France, and eventually across the Pyrenees into Spain, would be a challenge, but also the only way to minimize betrayals.[25] With this in mind, and with the backing of the leaders, Schuschu Simon set out in the autumn of 1942 to make the route a reality, to find secure hiding places in France, and to search for reliable French networks to assist future crossings into Spain.

Schuschu's search mission constituted the effective break with the past that the pioneers had looked for, but had been unable to achieve. It meant that there would be an alternative to hiding in Holland, but it also meant much more than that. In spite of the relative safety that hiding in Vichy France would provide for the *chaverim,* this was not seen as a goal in itself. The goal was getting to Spain, and arrival in Eretz Yisrael. This in turn would place new obstacles in their way, including the need to get support from the local Spanish, American, and Palestinian authorities. But first there was the need for reliable contacts with French underground networks, prior to attempting to traverse the formidable physical and security obstacle presented by the mighty Pyrenees. Second, these projects would be in need of being supported by lots of money and counterfeit documents. While key members of the pioneer network focused on creating forged papers and documents, Joop and Schuschu, over the autumn of 1942, mastered the art of moving in and out of Belgium and France. With the help of other pioneers, they successfully accompanied many children and adults across to Belgium and France. Upon arrival, they were given money, contacts, and places to stay, but had to give up their papers. Those would be used, in turn, by *chaverim* of the next transport. To cross, the groups also received help from local underground smugglers.

In January 1943, Schuschu and Joop prepared the first border crossing into neutral Spain, with a small group of pioneers. At that point, Schuschu had already succeeded in making contacts with the French Jewish underground, especially the Zionist youth movement *(Mouvement de la jeunesse sioniste).* Useful as these contacts were, they were considered a necessity for crossing into Spain. But later in January 1943, Schuschu was arrested at the Dutch-Belgian border. He took his own life while in a Dutch prison, rather than risk betraying his friends under German torture. It was left to Joop to lead the group to southern France and, with the services of a Maquis guide, help them reach Spain in February 1943. The missions to France of pioneer youngsters and adults would continue regularly so that by the summer of 1943 increasing numbers had found shelter in Paris, or further south in Vichy France. While this was a successful achievement and owed everything to the work of Joop Westerweel, Betty Brits, Ernst Hirsch, and others, Schuschu's valuable contacts with the French underground were lost. It would take another four months before new contacts were made, this time between Kurt Reilinger and others, with the Armée Juive (AJ), the underground "Jewish Army." And it would take another four to six months before further crossings of by now larger groups into Spain would be attempted.[26]

The headquarters of the AJ were in Toulouse, which was also the place from which most of the crossings into Spain took place. The greatest obstacles were now the need for money and valid travel documents. The Maquis guides, who were needed to traverse the mountains, were very expensive. While some of the necessary money was obtained from the Jewish National Fund and through various French underground organizations, the bulk came from the U.S. Joint Distribution Committee (JDC.) Without the generous financial assistance from the JDC, the very expensive crossings into Spain could not have been realized. As for the travel documents, that was yet another story.

The original idea had most likely been Schuschu's, but it was Kurt Reilinger's genius to put into practice a bold scheme ensuring the Dutch *chaverim* of free passage through a fair part of occupied Europe, while at the same time endearing them to their comrades in the French Jewish underground. The pioneers had been increasingly successful at creating counterfeit documents and had several masters of forgery in their ranks. Two of them were the non-Jewish Frans Gerritsen, a talented designer who had worked in advertising; and the Jewish Karli Oroslan, from the Amsterdam *Chalutz* group, who expertly copied and altered documents, stamps, and signatures from a variety of German offices and organizations. Karli Oroslan often worked at night, using the offices and office equipment of the Amsterdam Jewish Council, to which he had a key.

From the spring of 1943 till the end of the war, the Dutch pioneers used documents showing that they worked for the German Wehrmacht, and belonged to the labor battalions of the Organisation Todt. It was a brilliant device, because that way they were able to pass for regular Dutch laborers, thousands of whom worked throughout Belgium, Germany, and France. Their task in France was to build fortifications for the Wehrmacht. As a result, pioneers could travel in groups, and identify themselves without fear. They were even able to stay in specially designated hotels or hostels, and eat in the restaurants and cafeterias open only to those employed by the Wehrmacht. Even apart from the security it provided, it also saved them large amounts of money. In an ironic twist, it also supplied a number of *chaverim* with paid employment—for instance in Lyon, where some worked in an office, and in Bordeaux, where a number of them worked in the Wehrmacht kitchen. Also, by sharing these documents with AJ members, they offered something in return for the money and services provided them, namely a safe alibi and a protective shield for members of the AJ.[27]

With the help of members of the French Zionist underground and, among others, Joop Westerweel, Kurt Reilinger, Ernst Hirsch, Betty Brits, and Lore Siesskind of the pioneers, about seventy youngsters and young adults illegally crossed into Spain between February 1943 and July 1944. While in France, they had found temporary work, or were active in the Maquis. Their intended goal was not only to reach safety in Spain, but also to join their comrades in Eretz Yisrael. Many of the adults also intended to join the fight against the Nazis, under British command. Of all the pioneer youngsters, youth leaders, and young adults who reached Spain, sixty-one set sail in 1944 on board two ships, the *Niassa* and the *Guinée*. They arrived in Haifa in February and November 1944, respectively. If one puts the number of children who went into hiding from the Loosdrecht house at forty-eight, one must conclude that 70 percent of them survived. Eleven of them were smuggled into Spain and reached Palestine before the end of the war. Of the thirty-seven youngsters in hiding, fourteen were deported and killed. Nearly all of the other twenty-four left for Palestine after the end of World War II, along with those of their pioneer leaders who had survived.[28]

Looking back, there were at least three factors that pushed the Loosdrecht leadership to opt for hiding the children, with all the risks that that would entail. The first factor was the traumatic experiences of those group leaders whose German background and personal knowledge of persecution inside the Third Reich had prepared them for the full measure of German anti-Semitism and anti-Jewish violence. Such experiences were unique to the recent German and Austrian refugees, and unavailable to most Dutch Jews, who had been living a comparatively sheltered existence. In this context, Schuschu Simon's stay in a German concentration camp may have been crucial for the future of the children. Having been imprisoned in Buchenwald, he had no illusions about the German plans for solving the "Jewish problem," and was squarely in favor of hiding the boys and girls. Moreover, Schuschu, who divided his time between Loosdrecht and Amsterdam (where he helped run the pioneers' *Chalutz* house), had close personal ties with some of the young German and Austrian refugees who lived there. This may have further reinforced his view that the children had to be hidden.[29]

The second factor in favor of hiding had to do with the newly available non-Jewish network of rescuers led by Joop Westerweel, his wife, Wil (herself at this point pregnant with their fourth child), Bouke Koning, Jan Smit, and a small circle of their trusted associates and friends, which also included Jaap Lambeck and Giel Salomé. Several recent historians emphasize the importance of such a network of rescuers as a condition for Jewish survival.[30] The third factor concerns the nonconformist and nonestablishment orientation of both the Loosdrecht and Amsterdam pioneer groups, and their weak links with the rest of the Dutch Jewish community. Most of them were new to Holland, but even the young Dutchmen among them had effectively severed their traditional ties with the Dutch Jewry, whether comfortably middle class, religious, Zionist, social democrat, or revolutionary socialist.

By contrast, the native Dutch committee members of the "establishment" wing of the pioneer movement were set against all forms of hiding. They cited several motives. It would be too dangerous for the children, for oneself, and for the rescuers. One source speaks of the Jewish Council's fear of German punitive measures.[31] It might endanger the future acquisition of "exemptions" and other privileges that could be obtained only through smooth cooperation with the Jewish Council. The entire future of the JCB (the Jewish Training Center for Crafts and Trades) might be put at risk, and with it the ability of that center to provide exemptions and privileges. Ru Cohen director of the JCB, brother of Jewish Council president David Cohen, and the éminence grise of the Dutch pioneer movement, was especially and adamantly opposed to any group hiding. He was left in the dark about the Loosdrecht plan but strongly and successfully opposed hiding the forty youngsters under his care at the youth *aliyah* house in Elden, in the east of the country. With the exception of four youngsters who privately arranged hiding addresses, all were deported to Westerbork. Even Sam de Wolff, the dean of socialist Zionism in Holland, was strongly opposed to hiding.[32]

And what about the more than 120 pioneer children and young adults in camp Westerbork? They were in danger of being deported to Poland at any given time. Most of them left Holland on one transport that left on September 14, 1943, of which we have extensive reports. How did they feel about their situation, and why did they not try to escape? They must have been aware of the successful rescue efforts by the Amsterdam *chalutzim* who, together with their non-

Jewish colleagues, smuggled about twenty *chaverim* out of Wester-bork during 1943. They seem to have accepted the position of the official pioneer leadership in the camp. They remained firmly set against any participation in the escapes. It is unclear whether this stemmed from their distaste for anything illegal, or their hopes for getting last-minute exemptions or delays through the official German channels. In the end, the Dutch-born leaders' position may have been just a matter of temperament. Successfully hoodwinking the German authorities was not something that came easy to them. They also put their hopes in obtaining Palestine certificates for some of the pioneer children, and with some reason. Even so, the pioneer leaders in West-erbork were powerless to prevent the deportation to Poland of nearly all of the *chaverim* in the camp. As already mentioned, many went into the unknown with the transport of September 14, 1943.[33]

The Loosdrecht pioneers and their Amsterdam colleagues at the Pioneer House were far removed from the fear of giving offense and the search for accommodation that marked the positions of practically all those with ties to the Dutch Jewish establishment. Never having had such communal ties to begin with, their principal community connection was with their own youth *aliyah* house, the Amsterdam Chalutz house, and their fellow pioneers. Also, in contrast to most other Dutch Jews, they were primarily less concerned with saving their own lives, and more with group solidarity, countering injustice, and resistance. With *af al pi chen* as their motto, all they needed was a network that was willing and able to match their intentions and as-pirations. This they found in the young teachers associated with the Kees Boeke school. In Miriam Waterman's words, their plan to rescue the entire youth group became a reality when the pioneers' "will to re-sist" joined forces with the "will to resist" of Joop and his associates.[34]

One may ask what motivated Joop Westerweel's decision to join forces with the pioneers, in mid-August 1942. Since August 1941, he was principal of the Rotterdam Montessori school, and his family re-sponsibilities included looking after three children and his pregnant wife. How did that leave him with the time and energy to rescue forty-eight children, and look after all their future needs? And why did he put his career, family, and life at risk for the sake of saving Jew-ish children? The key to an answer may lie in Joop's earlier experi-ences at the Kees Boeke school in Bilthoven. The school's teaching methods were modern and progressive. The teachers were called by

their first names, and students had to be self-motivated and were expected to spend much of their time in extracurricular activities. They
also learned how to use their hands, hence the name of the school, De
Werkplaats (The Workshop). Most of all, the school's entire pedagogical philosophy was anti-authoritarian. Joop had been a teacher
there from 1930 until 1940, and had been active in teaching and
counseling the children in a special class for German Jewish refugees
established in 1939. That is the way in which he had gotten to know
those young refugees, with their fears and special needs. The motivation to resist the German occupation and oppression may well derive
from the school's principles promoting freedom and self-development.
The atmosphere at the school was humanitarian, anti-fascist, and pacifist. Joop espoused all those principles and was also a socialist and
somewhat of an anarchist. Thus he refused to pay taxes to the Dutch
government, arguing that much of the money would be used to make
war, which he opposed. In an earlier stage of his life he had been a
conscientious objector. When the government made it mandatory to
have a personal identity card, Joop refused his on the grounds that it
was an intrusion on his personal freedom. Later he accepted one, but
only to give it away to a Jewish person. In keeping with the school's
radical educational principles, Joop's chief reason for actively opposing National Socialism may well have been its suppression of personal
freedom. Though he could not guess what it would lead to, it is probably fair to say that Joop's encounter with the pioneers provided the
opportunity he had been looking for to translate his feelings of passive resistance into action.[35]

CONCLUSION

For the past ten or twelve years, the single issue dominating Dutch
historiography of World War II has been the very high numbers of
Jews killed during the war in comparison to the numbers in other
West European countries. Exploring the reasons is beyond the scope
of this article, but two reasons frequently cited are the speed of the
Germans in persecuting the Jews combined with the Dutch state's inability to protect them, and the isolated Dutch Jews' inability to find
non-Jewish social networks to save them. What the Jews needed and
lacked the most were reliable hiding addresses, and the necessary transportation to get them there. Recent historical research has empha-

sized this point. Speaking plainly, the links in the chain connecting the Jews in need of hiding places with one of the fledgling resistance groups were too weak. And "without a social network containing non-Jewish Dutchmen, their chances for hiding, and thus surviving the occupation, were very poor."[36] No formulation better captures the plight of the Loosdrecht children who were saved by non-Jewish families willing to hide them in their homes, and the swift and coordinated rescue efforts of all those involved. However, the key element that saved them was their timely connection to the network of non-Jews around Joop Westerweel.

Yet as I have tried to show, each solution also led to new obstacles and challenges. The need to locate additional hiding addresses for those Amsterdam pioneers facing immediate deportation was a burden on the fledgling rescue network, but it added important new personnel to the total operating force. Initially, the hiding of the children was a goal in itself, but it led to the realization that hiding and servicing more and more children and young adults was beyond the group's ability. This prompted the decision to expand the rescue effort and move it across national boundaries, which in turn increased the need for counterfeit travel documents and foreign identity papers. This search for and production of sophisticated illegal and forged documents allowed pioneers to safely hide and work in France alongside other foreigners legally employed by the German Wehrmacht.

A few words need to be added about the way the three groups worked together. The pioneers' successes, limited as they were, were made possible by the intelligent and fearless ways in which three distinct groups operated together. One thing the groups had in common was a distrust of the Dutch and Jewish authorities, all of whose dealings with the Germans were based on compliance and accommodation.[37] For different reasons, they shared an antiestablishment position and were unaffected by the traditional awe of authority shared by most other Dutch and Jewish citizens. Given the selfless way in which the members of the three groups worked together, and the solidarity and trust that marked each new rescue initiative, it seems appropriate to speak in the future of one collective group. Hence I propose using one name for the Jewish and non-Jewish resistance and rescue groups that originated in July 1942 around Schuschu Simon and Joop Westerweel: the Palestine Pioneers.

Finally, what about the children? What were their hopes and expectations? How many were saved, and how many killed? How do we imagine them during their last months and weeks in camp Westerbork? If we look at the numbers, all of the Loosdrecht children were successfully hidden, but fourteen of those perished after being betrayed or otherwise discovered. Of 821 pioneers of different ages in Holland, 452 (or 56 percent) were killed.[38] Of those saved, most survived in hiding while a minority returned after surviving one or more of the camps. There are well-documented reports about those who ended up in camp Westerbork. We also have photographs of them working on a farm near the camp, or folk-dancing in a tight circle, arms wrapped around each other, inside the camp. Other photographs taken in Westerbork show them lighting the candles of the festival of Chanukah, or celebrating the harvest festival of Shavu'ot. We know from their testimonies that for these young, secular pioneers with their agricultural orientation, the late May or early June festival of the "first fruit of your work, of what you sow in the field" (Exodus 23:16) held special significance.

Staying together as a group of close friends, the pioneers were considered a remarkable presence in the camp. The pioneers were respected because of their hard work, group solidarity, and generally upbeat attitude. Yet the circle that united them was not able to protect them as their time in the camp drew to a close. After a year in Westerbork, much of their earlier optimism had faded, and they despaired at ever reaching Eretz Yisrael.[39] The fact that others would survive "against all odds" must have been a comfort to them. Yet I fail to see how much it helped them as the train carrying them crossed the border into Germany and beyond. In the spring of 1942, the Loosdrecht children had been together to celebrate Bikkurim ("First Fruit"), as they called the Shavu'ot festival. The atmosphere had been idyllic, and the weather lovely. They ate outside, and the young women performed a dance evoking the gathering of the first fruit. At night there had been games, dances, singing, and much laughter.[40] It would be their last joint gathering, and their last festival celebrated in freedom. Sixty years later, I think of my young brothers and sisters, cut off before their prime, and remember all those who perished. May the memory of them be a blessing to us all.

—Shavu'ot, 1942–2002

NOTES

1. See Jacob Presser, "Het verzet van joden in Nederland 1940–1945," in *Schrijfsels en schrifturen* (Amsterdam: Moussault, 1961), *passim*. See also J. Presser, *The Destruction of the Dutch Jews* (New York: Dutton, 1969), 279–83. In Presser's own words, from the English translation (which is an abbreviated version of the two-volume Dutch edition): "there was no branch of the Dutch resistance in which Jewish men and women were not active" (283).

2. See Debórah Dwork, *Children with a Star* (New Haven: Yale University Press, 1991), 49–51; and Bob Moore, *Victims and Survivors: The Nazi Persecution of the Jews, 1940–1945* (London: Arnold, 1997), 173–4.

3. Yehuda Bauer, *A History of the Holocaust* (New York: Franklin Watts, 1982), 277.

4. For a detailed description of the events leading up to the February strike, see Moore, *Victims and Survivors,* 71–2.

5. See Presser, *Destruction of the Dutch Jews,* 282–3; Moore, *Victims and Survivors,* 168, 296; and B. A. Sijes, "Several Observations Concerning the Position of the Jews in Occupied Holland during World War II," in *Rescue Attempts during the Holocaust,* ed. Israel Gutman. (Jerusalem: Yad Vashem, 1976), 551–2.

6. See Haim Avni, "The Zionist Underground in Holland and France and the Escape to Spain," in *Rescue Attempts during the Holocaust,* 555–90.

7. See Henk Flap and Marnix Croes, eds., *Wat toeval leek te zijn maar niet was: De organisatie van de jodenvervolging in Nederland* (That which appeared to be but was not an accident: The organization of the persecution of the Dutch Jews) (Amsterdam: Het Spinhuis, 2001), 12.

8. The typed Netherlands Institute for War Documentation (NIOD) document "Palestina-Pioniers," map (file) II (1969), contains a large number of personal accounts. It is cited henceforth as "Palestine Pioneers." The sources of much of the document are the German *Vom Ringen des holländischen Hechalutz* (n.p., 1954), and the Hebrew *Hamachteret hachalutzit beholland hakevushah* (Tel Aviv: Kibbutz Hameuchad Publishing House, 1969).

9. See "Palestine Pioneers," file II (NIOD), pp. 155, 242.

10. Cf. Sijes, "Several Observations," 552.

11. For a recent summary, see Bob Moore, "Postwar Antisemitism," chap. 11 of *Victims and Survivors,* 249–52. A reliable Dutch source is D. Hondius, *Terugkeer: Antisemitisme in Nederland rond de bevrijding* (The Hague: SDU, 1990). Some of the stories by Gerhard Durlacher provide good case studies on the degree of hostility accorded many Dutch Jewish survivors upon their return. See Gerhard L. Durlacher, "Liberations," in

Stripes in the Sky: A Wartime Memoir (London: Serpent's Tail, 1991), 71–
101, translated from the Dutch, and his story "After 1945," in *Quarantaine:
Verhalen* (Amsterdam: Meulenhoff, 1993), 73–110, which is available only
in Dutch. See also Yehudi Lindeman, "Abandonment, Adjustment and
Memory: Reflections on J. Presser, Elie Cohen and Gerhard Durlacher," in
*Reflections on the Holocaust: "Festschrift" for Raul Hilberg on His Seventy-
Fifth Birthday,* ed. Wolfgang Mieder and David Scrase (Burlington: Center
for Holocaust Studies, University of Vermont, 2001), 96–7.

12. See Flap and Croes, *Wat toeval leek te zijn maar niet was,* vii, 1.

13. See Flap and Croes, *Wat toeval leek te zijn maar niet was,* 7, 183
n. 3. See also P. Romijn, "De oorlog (1940–1945)," chap. 8 of *De geschiedenis van de joden in Nederland,* ed. J. C. H. Blom et al. (Amsterdam: Balans,
1995), 345–7; and Moore, *Victims and Survivors,* 1–14.

14. See, for instance, B. Braber, *Zelfs als wij zullen verliezen: Joden in
verzet en illegaliteit 1940–1945* (Amsterdam: Balans, 1990). Cf. Moore,
Victims and Survivors, 11, 168–9.

15. Presser, *Destruction of the Dutch Jews,* 279.

16. Sources for what follows are Avni, "The Zionist Underground,"
See also Igal Benjamin, *Faithful to Their Destiny and to Themselves: The
Zionist Pioneers' Underground in the Netherlands in War and Holocaust* (Beth
Lochamei Haghetaot, 1998), a Hebrew work with a brief summary in En-
glish, based on the author's doctoral dissertation for Bar-Ilan University.
The best source is the already-mentioned "Palestine Pioneers" in the library
of NIOD, the Netherlands Institute for War Documentation.

17. Account of Menachem Pinkhof, "Palestine Pioneers," file II
(NIOD), chap. 3, p. 59.

18. Ibid., chap. 3, pp. 59, 63, 67.

19. Ibid., pp. 60–1, 63–4.

20. Ibid., p. 61.

21. See the testimony of Lore Siessdkind-Zimmels in Ibid., p. 77.

22. See Ibid., pp. 64–8.

23. Ibid., p. 64.

24. See "Palestine Pioneers," pp. 65, 74, 79; and Avni, "The Zionist
Underground," 558.

25. See "Palestine Pioneers," p. 74; and Avni, "The Zionist Underground," 558.

26. See "Palestine Pioneers," chap. 8, pp. 7–9; and Avni, "The Zionist
Underground," 561–2.

27. See "Palestine Pioneers," chap. 8, pp. 7–8.

28. See J. Presser, *Ondergang; de vervolging en verdelging van het Ned-
erlandse Jodendom, 1940–1945,* vol. 2 (The Hague: Martinus Nijhoff,
1965); Avni, "The Zionist Underground," 584–5.

29. "Palestine Pioneers," p. 66.

30. P. Romijn, "De oorlog (1940–1945)," chap. 8 of *De geschiedenis van de joden in Nederland,* 337; Flap and Croes, *Wat toeval leek te zijn maar niet was,* 12.

31. Romijn, "De oorlog (1940–1945)," 337.

32. "Palestine Pioneers," pp. 67–8. For Sam de Wolff, see p. 77.

33. See Ibid., pp. 239, 242.

34. See Ibid., p. 64.

35. See Ibid., chap. 3, p. 63, and chap. 4, pp. 140 and 155–6. See also Presser, *Destruction of the Dutch Jews,* 282–3.

36. See Flap and Croes, *Wat toeval leek te zijn maar niet was,* 5, 12; see also 168, 175.

37. See Moore, *Victims and Survivors,* 201; and Romijn, "De oorlog (1940–1945)," 346.

38. See Presser, *Ondergang,* 15–6. Though these figures date from 1965, they have not been challenged.

39. "Palestine Pioneers," p. 239.

40. Ibid., pp. 68–9.

Lenore J. Weitzman

Women of Courage: The *Kashariyot* (Couriers) in the Jewish Resistance During the Holocaust

THE *KASHARIYOT* WERE YOUNG WOMEN WHO TRAVELLED ILLEGALLY ON missions for the Jewish resistance in Nazi-occupied eastern Europe during the Holocaust. Using false papers to conceal their Jewish identities, they smuggled underground newspapers, forged identity cards, secret documents, money, food, medical supplies, guns, ammunition—and other Jews—in and out of the ghettos of Poland, Lithuania, and parts of Russia. They were called *kashariyot* because they provided the isolated ghettoized Jews with a *kesher,* a connection to the outside world: they became the "voice radio" for news and information, the human contact for supplies and resources, and the personal inspiration for hope and resilience.

Diaries and chronicles of the ghetto period describe the *kashariyot* as courageous heroines and proudly recount their death-defying exploits. In fact, it is impossible to begin a chapter on the *kashariyot* without quoting from the well-known tribute to their heroism written by Emmanuel Ringelblum, the distinguished historian who organized the Warsaw ghetto's underground archive:

> These heroic girls, Chaika and Frumka, are a theme that calls for the pen of a great writer. Boldly they travel back and forth through the cities and towns of Poland. They carry "Aryan" papers identifying them as Poles or Ukrainians. . . .
>
> They are in mortal danger every day. . . . Without a murmur, without a moment of hesitation, they accept and carry out the most dangerous missions. Is someone needed to travel to Vilna, Bialystok, Lvov, or Radom . . . to smuggle in contraband such as illegal publications, goods, money? The girls volunteer as though it

were the most natural thing in the world. Are there comrades who have to be rescued from Vilna, Lublin, or some other city? They undertake the mission.

Nothing stands in their way. Nothing deters them. . . . How many times have they looked death in the eyes? How many times have they been arrested and searched? . . . [T]hese girls are indefatigable.[1]

Ringelblum went on to predict that "The story of the Jewish woman will be a glorious page in the history of Jewry during the present war. And the Chaikas and Frumkas will be the leading figures in this story."[2]

However, the "glorious page" of the *kashariyot* has not been written. Instead of being recognized, as Ringelblum predicted, as "leading figures," they have typically been ignored. While the amazing feats of individual couriers are applauded, the *kashariyot,* as a group, have received relatively little attention and have rarely been the subject of academic research.[3]

My aim is to undertake a comprehensive study of the *kashariyot*—who they were, what they did, and the role they played in the Jewish resistance. This chapter is the first report from that larger project and is limited to their activities during the ghetto period. It draws primarily on my own in-depth interviews with former *kashariyot;* testimonies from the archives of Yad Vashem and the United States Holocaust Memorial Museum; materials from the archives of the Zionist youth groups; Yizkor Books from the towns and cities where they lived; letters they wrote (during the Holocaust) to friends and relatives abroad; and published memoirs.

This chapter begins by locating the *kashariyot* demographically: the first section describes their social characteristics and the patterns of their recruitment. The second section examines the nature of their work and how it changed over time. The last section analyzes their contribution to the Jewish resistance during the Holocaust.

The Hebrew words *kashariyot* (plural) and *kasharit* (singular) and the English words "couriers" and "courier" are used interchangeably in this chapter, even though the English translation fails to capture the heroic connotation of the Hebrew words.

WHY WERE *KASHARIYOT* NECESSARY?
AN OVERVIEW OF THEIR ROLE

Before I proceed with this analysis, it may be helpful to explain why
the *kashariyot* were necessary—and important—in the ghetto period.
The Jewish resistance needed *Kashariyot* to circumvent the forced-
isolation of Jews in ghettos. The German policy of ghettoization was
designed to segregate and isolate Jews in self-contained communities:
they forced the Jews into ghettos, erected walls and gates to cut them
off from the outside world, instituted the death penalty for Jews who
escaped, and *cut off communication between Jews in different ghettos.*
Because the Nazis wanted to wall the Jews off from any information
or contacts that might help them survive, the Jews in Poland were segregated not only from Poles, they were also cut off from other Jews.

The first task of the *kashariyot* was to break through those walls by
gathering and sharing information. They were sent out to establish
contacts with Jews in ghettos throughout the vast territory that was
formerly Poland, and to gather information and intelligence about
Nazi activities. Mordechi Tennenbaum, the leader of the Jewish resistance in the Bialystok ghetto, captures the massive scope of their
missions in his portrait of the Dror courier Tema Schneiderman:

> Over 20 times she crossed borders that separated different parts of
> Poland. . . . Tema visited every ghetto, knew Jewish life and troubles
> in every town and city.
>   She was a living treasure of information. . . . She brought mes-
> sages from the movement to every area. . . . Even Poles and Ger-
> mans could not reach every part of Poland as she did. And when
> she came, there was such joy.[4]

In the early months after the German invasion of Poland, before restrictions were imposed on travel for Jews, the young men and women
who first set out on these reconnaissance missions were the leaders of
pre-war Jewish organizations who were hoping to re-organize their
local groups and to reestablish a national communication network to
link their members in cities and towns throughout Poland.

But once the ghettos were formed and Jewish travel was forbidden, it became much more dangerous for the male leaders to travel,
and the couriers became predominantly female. Although the regulations were instituted in different spheres of German administration

at different times, once the Germans instituted the death penalty for any Jew who was found outside the ghetto, the *kashariyot* had to smuggle themselves out of the ghettos and travel illegally. Because they had to use false identity cards and forged travel permits, they had to bluff their way through multiple inspections and police patrols. They were always at risk of being unmasked and were always under the threat of death. It was a job that required great courage, quick wits, and nerves of steel.

In light of these risks and dangers, it is not surprising that the *kashariyot* were often welcomed as heroes by the local members of their organization. They were quickly surrounded and bombarded with questions. The local members were buoyed by their success in evading the Nazis, eager to hear about their families and friends in other ghettos, and excited to receive the underground newsletters and precious contraband the couriers had smuggled into the ghetto. The *kashariyot* also conducted educational seminars to encourage the local members, and to afford them a temporary escape from the stress of daily life in the ghetto. Equally important was the psychological impact of the *kashariyot* as symbols of Jewish resilience, as "beams of light." These were the words that Rushka Korczak used to describe the emotional response of her besieged colleagues in the Vilna underground when Tosia Altman, one of the most famous *kasharit*/leaders, arrived from Warsaw in December 1941:

> Tosia came.
> It was like a blessing of freedom.
> Just the information that she came.
> It spread among the people.
> That we have Tosia visiting us from Warsaw.
> As if there was no ghetto.
> As if there were no Germans.
> As if there was no death around.
> As if we were not in this terrible war.
> A beam of love.
> A beam of light.[5]

The second, and the most critical, mission of the *kashariyot*, built on the skills and contacts they acquired in these early missions. But it required them to shift gears and to deliver a very different type of message—and a terrifying warning. When the leaders of the Jewish underground learned about the mass shootings of Jews (in places like the forest of Ponary near Vilna), they slowly began to understand the comprehensive nature of the Nazis' plans. They realized they had to find a way to get this news to Jews in other ghettos, and to warn them of the real danger they were facing. Relaying that news, and sounding that warning, became the all-important mission of the *kashariyot*.

It was hard for the *kashariyot,* who had always encouraged others to believe in life and hope, to find themselves travelling on the same dangerous routes to speed the news of impending death. It was a hard message to convey, and a hard message to hear. How could anyone believe that families who boarded trucks to be "resettled" were instead taken to killing sites where they were shot and buried in mass graves? The Nazis went to great lengths—using both secrecy and deception—to prevent the Jews from finding out about the mass killings, because they were keenly aware of just how dangerous this information would be. The Germans knew that if the Jews in each ghetto believed they were being resettled, they would be caught unaware and would not mount any resistance. But if the couriers got there first, and if the Jews knew the trains were headed for killing sites, they would be less likely to report for deportation, and more likely to resist.

Although that reasoning may sound straightforward, one of the major challenges the couriers faced was that of convincing other Jews to believe that the Nazis were really planning to *kill them.* It was only when (and if) the *kashariyot* could convince them to accept the grim news that they themselves were really targeted for murder, that the *kashariyot* would be able to also convince them to try to resist—by trying to hide, or to escape, or to join together to fight the Nazis.

The third mission of the *kashariyot* focused directly on mounting that resistance. Because the *kashariyot* had the expertise and contacts for working outside the ghetto, they became responsible for a range of dangerous missions that could be carried out only on the "Aryan" side. At the top of this list was the all-important assignment of acquiring guns, explosives, and ammunition for the ghetto revolts—and for smuggling them into the ghettos. They were also involved in gathering intelligence, negotiating with the Polish underground, and smuggling money, supplies, ammunition, and other resources to those who were organizing resistance in other ghettos, factories, and camps.

At the same time, the *kashariyot* were given a fourth mission—to save Jewish lives. In the final months of the ghettos, efforts to save as many Jews as possible became an all-consuming passion. As seasoned operatives on the Aryan side, the *kashariyot* were the obvious choice for organizing this massive undertaking. They helped children and adults escape from the ghetto, located rooms for them to stay on the Aryan side, equipped them with new identity cards, and supplied them (and those who were hiding and helping them) with financial support.

The *kashariyot* also provided support for leaders of the Jewish underground who were working on the Aryan side by securing "safe" houses, rooms, and apartments for their work; shielding them from scrutiny; helping them plan their missions outside the ghetto; preparing false papers and certificates of employment to facilitate their mobility; relaying their messages, money, and supplies; and by becoming their personal escorts and local guides on the Aryan side.

After the ghettos were liquidated, the *kashariyot* who survived continued their resistance activities by working with the partisans and engaging in ever-more daring missions to save and support Jews still in hiding, imprisoned in forced labor camps, or living in the forests. But that chapter of their lives is beyond the scope of this chapter.

WHO WERE THEY? HASIA'S STORY

The young women who became couriers shared a set of social characteristics and prewar experiences that are illustrated by the example of Hasia Bornstein.[6] Hasia was born in 1921 in Grodno, a city near Bialystok, which was part of Poland between the First and the Second World Wars. Half of Grodno's 60,000 inhabitants were Jewish, and the community supported a wide variety of Jewish cultural events and institutions, including many synagogues, a Jewish hospital, bank, and orphanage, and several Jewish schools.[7]

Hasia's parents were observant Jews who spoke only Yiddish at home. Their lives revolved around the Jewish holidays and the weekly Sabbath. The highlight of their week was Friday night, when the family would gather for a special Shabbat meal with joyous singing. They lived in a large house with a garden of flowers and fruit trees on the outskirts of the city. Her father owned a small factory for making sodas and they were comfortably middle-class. But his business suffered in the depression of 1928–29. As a result, they could not afford the tuition to send Hasia to the Jewish school (where classes were taught in Hebrew). Instead she went to a public school, where Polish was the language of instruction. This simple fluke—going to a Polish school and being forced to speak colloquial Polish—provided Hasia with essential skills and contacts for her wartime missions on the Aryan side. Ironically, her family's economic situation improved in time for her younger sisters to enroll in the Jewish school. As Hasia recalls: "While they learned Polish that was grammatically correct, they still had a Jewish accent. I was the only lucky one (who spoke like the Poles), but, at the time, I thought I was unlucky because I so wanted to go the (Jewish) Tarbut school."[8]

The Zionist movement was very active in Grodno, and, like most teenagers, Hasia joined a Zionist youth group, Ha-Shomer Ha-tsa'ir (i.e., the Young Guard), along with her younger sister. Their after-school meetings became the center of their lives: they learned about Palestine and Jewish history, sang Hebrew songs, and socialized.

When the Nazis marched into Grodno on June 22, 1941, Hasia had just finished a sewing course sponsored by the Jewish Organization for Rehabilitation and Training (ORT). Five months later, when the Grodno Jews were forced into ghettos—and had to leave behind anything they could not carry—Hasia carried her sewing machine and a few clothes. It proved to be a wise choice. Hasia was soon conscripted for forced-labor in a German brick factory where she worked with non-Jewish Poles. She sewed for them at night in exchange for bread and cabbage, which she could smuggle into the ghetto for her family. Since only the workers were fed during the day, her family was always hungry and would not have survived without Hasia's sewing. In the ghetto, Hasia continued her active involvement in her Zionist youth group. When the Nazis closed the schools, they established an illegal school for children because "we wanted to help the children learn and to keep them busy and hopeful."

Their goal, in this first period, was to help Jews live through the occupation. Educational activities gave them a purpose, dignity, and hope. It encouraged them to invest in the future, so that they would not give up in despair.

But this strategy was called into question when *kashariyot* from the Zionist youth groups came to Grodno (in early 1942) and held secret meetings with the local members of their youth group. The couriers told them about the terrifying killings of the Jews of Vilna. As Hasia recalls:

They told us there were eyewitnesses who saw it. They took the
Jews out of the Vilna ghetto in trucks and brought them to a
nearby forest, at Ponary. There they were forced to dig their own
graves, big graves for hundreds and hundreds and hundreds of
people. And then they shot them. . . . It was a highly secret operation and no one knew what awaited them when they left the
ghetto. Families who were eating breakfast together in the morning were lying in mass graves by night.

It is not surprising that the story of Ponary had a profound impact on Hasia. It also marked the turning point for the Jewish underground. If the *kashariyot* were correct, and if the Nazis were really
planning to murder all the Jews, there was no point in helping people
cope with the hardships of the ghetto, because no matter what they
did, no one would survive in the ghetto. If all Jews had already been
sentenced to death, then the only activity that was important was to
warn them—and to try to thwart the Nazis' plans. As Hasia explained: "We decided to stop our educational work and start to prepare ourselves for fighting. To fight against the Germans. Not to go
like sheep . . . but to resist. We started to organize our movement in
a different way."

But everything happened too fast. Before they could organize
there was an *Aktion* (an organized and often brutal roundup of Jews
for deportation) and the Jewish underground realized that they did
not have enough time to get weapons to put up a fight. They therefore decided to move their members to the Bialystok ghetto, which
seemed much more secure. Bialystok was a major textile center and
most of its 50,000 Jews worked in factories, producing uniforms and
shoes and other supplies for the Wehrmacht, the German army.

One of the most prized possessions of the Grodno underground
was their "laboratory" for manufacturing false documents. The lab
consisted of special cards, papers, and inks for fabricating identity
cards, and official-looking stamps to authenticate them. The identity
cards they produced were more valuable than gold: they were "tickets
to life."

Hasia was given the job of transporting the laboratory to Bialystok. It was her first assignment as a courier. She had to smuggle the
materials out of the Grodno ghetto, keep them hidden through the
frequent inspections on route, and then smuggle them into the ghetto
in Bialystok. The assignment terrified her. It was not the danger

alone, it was having to leave all her friends and her family in the ghetto. It meant she was leaving her whole world. But she was committed to the movement, and it was an order. Hasia's reaction was common: Most of the couriers were upset when they were "chosen" for work on the Aryan side. As Vanda Ruttenberg explained:

> I was so unhappy. It sounds weird but here [in the ghetto], I was among friends, and whatever would happen to us together. To be together always has a special meaning. To be in the movement gives you strength, it gives you importance, and it takes care of you. . . . and they were sending me out into a hostile street. . . . The only thing they gave me was an address, and that was it. . . . They made me a farewell party and we all cried. We didn't know if we would ever meet again.[9]

On January 16, 1943, a blistering cold winter morning, Hasia waited at the ghetto gate at 5:00 A.M. It was her twenty-first birthday. The underground had arranged for her to join a group of Jews being taken for forced labor in a German factory. Because she was supposed to be a day worker, she could not carry a suitcase. So she hid the laboratory materials—the stamps, cards, and inks—at the bottom of her handbag, covered by her underwear and pajamas.

Aside from her courage, Hasia had very little preparation for this dangerous mission. The underground supplied her with a map of Bialystok—she had been there only once before—and with false papers that identified her as Halina Stasiuk, a Polish Catholic. But despite her lack of training, Hasia had three personal characteristics that made her an ideal courier: she did not "look Jewish"; she spoke Polish without an accent; and she had an attractive self-confident personality that included a talent for talking herself out of difficult situations. In addition, she was "blessed with lots of good luck."

Since this was Hasia's first mission as a courier, another young woman, Zila, was sent to accompany her. Zila was also a novice, but the underground assumed the two of them would be less suspicious than a young girl traveling alone. They stood in the middle of the group of workers, shivering from the icy wind that blew right through their cloth coats. Then the guards counted them and waived them through. No inspection, no questions. They could not believe their luck. As the group marched through the city, Hasia and Zila let themselves fall to the rear. When the group turned the corner of a narrow street the two women quickly ducked into a doorway. Hasia held her breath waiting for the shouts and guns. But the marching continued. They made it. They had escaped.

When they reached the train station the flush of their initial success quickly disappeared: no one knew when the train to Bialystok was due and they were forced to wait—exposed to the eyes of all the other passengers waiting at the station. These were the most terrifying hours for Hasia. If anyone recognized her, she "was finished." That was how her brother was killed: he was on a mission on the Aryan side when a Polish boy recognized him and pointed him out to two German policemen. The police seized him and dragged him back to the ghetto to shoot him. They did it intentionally, in broad daylight, where everyone could see what was happening, as a lesson to demonstrate the fate of Jews who try to escape to the Aryan side.

In fact, Hasia faced an even greater risk than her brother because she was well-known in Grodno. She not only attended the regular Polish schools, she had worked in the public library during school vacations. Because she was naturally gregarious and helpful, her library job brought her in contact with many Poles who knew who she was.

Hasia and Zila waited for the train for almost twelve hours. They were nervous, cold, and hungry. Finally it arrived, close to dusk, packed with women peasants carrying big bags of produce which they were smuggling into the city, hoping to make a handsome profit on the black market. But the Germans knew about the smuggling route and were waiting to catch them in Bialystok. Unaware of the trap that lay ahead, Hasia and Zila were worried about the 9:00 P.M. curfew. The train was due to arrive at 8:15 P.M.: the last thing they needed was to be caught on the streets violating the curfew.

When the train pulled into Bialystok, the platform was swarming with German police. Hasia, who was carrying the precious bag, found herself pushed into a group of women ordered to line up for an inspection. Each woman had to empty the contents of her bag on the table. After a year in the ghetto, Hasia was amazed to see so much food. It was only then that she realized that the police were searching for smugglers and confiscating their food. But still, they would force her to empty her bag and they would discover the cards and seals for making false documents. How could she get out of there? There was no break in the ring of Germans surrounding them. "This is it," Hasia thought. "They will probably shoot me on the spot."

The line moved forward slowly as the peasant women put up a good fight, screaming and yelling and insisting that they be allowed to keep some butter and eggs and potatoes. Hasia was stopped next to one of the guards and she could feel his eyes on her. So she started talking to him:

> Listen, I have to go very far to get to my aunt's place and tomorrow I have to take her to a doctor. I don't know what you want from me. You can look at my bag: I just have clothes to stay with my aunt. Look, I have only pajamas. And the curfew is just about to start and I will not be able to make it. I don't have anything to sell. I'm not a speculator.

The guard did not blink: he did not look at Hasia and he did not look at her bag. Five minutes later she tried again: this time she took the pajamas and underwear out of her bag to waive in front of him. Again, she told him about her sick aunt. Again, no reaction. By now Zila had disappeared. It was too dangerous for her to hang around. The line kept moving. Hasia was close to the table. It was her last chance. This time she tried pleading in a sweet, soft voice—not like the tough peasant women shouting at the police at the table. "Please, let me go. . . . You can see I have only pajamas. . . . I have to get to my aunt's house before the curfew." "All right," he said, "you can go!"

She stood there for a moment in disbelief, as if she were frozen. Then she ran off to catch up with Zila, who was standing alone on a small bridge and crying. She was was certain that Hasia had been shot. By then it was almost 9 o clock, the beginning of the curfew. The streets were deserted, except for the police. "We were afraid. . . . We were two young girls and every German, every SS man on the street, would start up with us."

Hasia quickly devised a plan. She saw a small house that had a warm look. They would knock on the door and ask for help—not as Jews, that would have been suicide—but as two young Polish girls trying to get away from the Germans. Most Poles would sympathize with the story of a late train and Germans hassling them. They would ask if they could sleep on the kitchen floor. Their luck held out: the young couple believed them (because "we were so young and looked so innocent"). Finally, fifteen hours after they left the ghetto, they were safe in Bialystok, lying on blankets near a warm kitchen stove.

The next day, they smuggled the precious laboratory into the ghetto (by joining a group of returning workers.)

THE MAKING OF A *KASHARIT*: SOCIAL
AND PHYSICAL CHARACTERISTICS

Most couriers shared five basic characteristics with Hasia. The first was their physical appearance—they did not look distinctively Jewish. They often had blond hair and blue eyes and could blend into the Polish population. For example, Chaika Grossman described Hasia "as a typical *shikse,* tall, blond, with light blue eyes."[10]

However, blending in to the local population and "looking Polish" involved much more than one's physical appearance. One had to look natural in the non-Jewish world. Like Hasia, many of the couriers had attended non-Jewish public schools (or had similar experiences) where they became familiar with Polish dress, style, manners, and demeanor. In contrast, because most Jews in Poland grew up in Jewish communities and lived in a Jewish mileu, they often "looked different" with distinctive clothing, shoes, hair styles, manners, and modes of behavior. While people like Hasia could look and feel comfortable in both worlds, according to Nechama Tec, most Polish Jews "felt like strangers in the world of the other."[11]

The second characteristic of the couriers was their fluency in the Polish language. Like Hasia, most of the couriers learned colloquial Polish in a non-Jewish public school. In contrast, most Jews in Poland grew up speaking Yiddish at home and in their everyday lives. In fact, in the 1931 Polish Census, 79 percent of the Jews in Poland listed Yiddish—not Polish—as their mother tongue.[12] While many Jews used Polish, they typically spoke it with an accent or with a "Jewish" inflection that immediately identified them as Jews. (Hasia's sisters were typical: the Polish they learned in the Jewish school was grammatically correct but they still had a Jewish accent.)

Because the way one spoke Polish revealed one's education and social-class background—very much like the way one's English did in Great Britain—Polish that was too "perfect" or too "intellectual" could also be a handicap for a courier. Vanda Ruttenberg; a courier in Crakow, made a conscious effort to "tone down" her speech because she worried about sounding "too well educated." As she said, "my

Polish was better than just good and that was a big fault because I
lived with simple people who spoke slang."[13] One's Polish not only
affected the impression one made on others, it also affected one's self-
confidence. That is why the ideal courier was someone who had
grown up speaking colloquial Polish and did not have to worry about
how she formed each sentence. Still, not every courier spoke flawless
Polish. For example, Bella Hazan was educated in Hebrew-speaking
schools and she knew her Polish was not impeccable. But, with her
picture-perfect Aryan looks, she was confident that she could "get by
on my face."[14]

The third characteristic of the couriers was their age: most of them
were in their late teens and early twenties.[15] In this respect their demographic profile was similar to that of the young men in the Jewish
resistance. As young people they were, collectively, more likely to be
strong, energetic, and idealistic. They were also single and therefore
less likely to be held back by responsibility for children or a spouse.

The fourth characteristic of the couriers was their gender: most of
them were female. Although there were a few male couriers, it is clear
that the underground leadership believed that young women made the
best couriers.[16] Their implicit rationale, although rarely articulated,
includes all of the factors noted in the discussion that follows.[17]

The first advantage of being a young woman who was trying to
pass in Nazi-occupied Poland was that one could *not* be unequivocally
identified as Jewish. Jewish men, in contrast, were physically marked
by their circumcision and they could be easily identified as Jews if
they were caught. As Antek Zuckerman wrote: "I had to keep from
being caught at any price, since all they had to do was pull down my
pants to prove I was a Jew . . . [and] I was sentenced to death."[18] Since
Polish and German males were not circumcised, Jewish men were, to
quote Helen Feigon, "physically handicapped from the start."[19]

A second advantage that women enjoyed was the result of their
traditional female socialization, which trained them to be sensitive to
the feelings of others, worried about their reactions, attuned to their
nonverbal cues, and responsive to their needs and wishes. Girls were
also more likely to be socialized to adapt and fit in, and all of these
skills were critical in passing.

In Poland many Jewish girls also had the advantage of greater exposure to the non-Jewish world. Although Hasia thought it was just
an economic "fluke" that led her to a Polish school, Jewish girls were,

in general, more likely to attend Polish public schools than their brothers. That was because a Jewish education was considered more important for males, and boys were often sent to special Jewish schools, the cheder and the yeshivah, while their sisters were sent to the "inferior" Polish schools.[20] These Polish schools, as noted above, not only equipped Jewish girls with colloquial Polish; they also helped them absorb Polish "mannerisms," how they did things, and the way they talked.[21] In addition, the Jewish girls were exposed to Polish customs, holidays, and religious rituals. For example, Vitka Kovner learned the Catholic prayers by heart because they were said out loud in school every morning. (As she said, she did not have to "learn them," she "lived with them.")[22] Finally, the Polish schools provided Jewish girls with networks of non-Jews—and sometimes with real friends—who might be helpful later on.

A fourth advantage is evident in Hasia's story: it is the natural appeal of a young woman in distress. Hasia ascribed her success with both the policeman and the young couple to the fact that "we were so young and looked so innocent." Other couriers talked about simply smiling and asking for a favor. For example, when Bronka Klibanski, the Dror courier, needed a ticket to board the train, she approached "a German officer and asked him very nicely if he could buy me a ticket. And he said, yes, why not."[23] Bronka describes herself as very polite. What she does not mention is that she was (and is) beautiful, with strawberry blond hair, a twinkle in her sparkling blue eyes, and a warm smile. It is not at all surprising that others—both men and women—responded to her smile and wanted to help her.

Because it is obvious that part of the appeal of some of these young women was their sexual attractiveness, it is important to note that most couriers consciously avoided using sexual enticement as part of their *modus operandi*. As Adina Szwajger explained, it was "just too dangerous." She was acutely aware of the potential hazards of arousing too much male interest, and that was the last thing she wanted.[24]

But each of the couriers had an appealing manner for evoking help. People responded to Hasia, as we have already seen, because she looked so innocent. Lisa Chapnik, a Jewish courier from a communist youth group, had large blue eyes and "little girl looks" that aroused women's maternal instincts. Bronka, as we have seen, had a more well-bred, ladylike style, inspiring men to be chivalrous and gentlemanly. Bella Hazan, the Dror courier with long blond braids, looked

like every German's ideal daughter. The Gestapo officers at the headquarters where she worked responded instinctively: they trusted her.

A final advantage of being a young woman was that one was given
more freedom and leeway in public spaces. It was considered normal
for women to be out shopping and walking in the streets during the
day, while men who were not working were viewed with suspicion. For
example, Itka Szwajger, the Bund courier who hid Jews on the Aryan
side of Warsaw, would set out to investigate potential apartments
with her partner Marysia, walking arm in arm, "smiling and chatting
like two young girls—just like all the other girls who filled the streets
of Warsaw."[25] But two young men on the street in the middle of the
day might be stopped by German patrols searching for members of
the Polish resistance. Since the police usually assumed that resistance
activists were male, men were subjected to more scrutiny and to more
frequent inspections. A Jewish male courier who was passing as a Pole
would face the same challenges. Since all couriers traveled with false
documents, these routine checks meant that male couriers had more
opportunities to be caught. In addition, young men were more likely
to be arbitrarily picked up for forced labor. All of this added up to a
more benign working environment for women couriers.

In light of the advantages of being a young woman, and the dis-
advantages of being a young man, it is not surprising that most of the
couriers were young women. There were, however, a few male couriers, and they shared the other physical and social characteristics noted
above: they too had an Aryan appearance, spoke fluent Polish, and
were youthful members of the Jewish resistance. For example, Kazik
(Simcha Rotem) described himself as a typical, Aryan-looking Warsaw kid with the Polish dialect of the city streets.[26]

The fifth and final characteristic of the couriers is critical for understanding why and how they were recruited to become *kashariyot*.
All of them had been active in Jewish organizations before the war,
and most were already recognized as leaders within their peer group.
It was natural to ask someone who was already involved in, identified
with, and considered a leader within the organization, to represent
the organization by becoming a *kasharit*. That is why the *kashariyot*
were usually identified by the group they represented, for example, as
a "Bund courier" or a "courier for Dror." And that is also how they
identified themselves: they were the voice of their movement, and they

were linked to their fellow members by history, ideology, friendship, and trust.[27]

It is difficult to convey the intensity and passion with which many young people identified themselves as a member of a particular organization or movement. The movement was the center of their lives: its ideology defined their goals; its activities filled their days; its leaders were their role models; and its members were their closest friends. The movement inspired ardent devotion, and most members were willing to undertake any mission on its behalf. As the war progressed, and as many young people lost their families, the movement often became even more important.

Each of the prewar organization that became involved in resistance recruited *kashariyot* from the ranks of their own leadership. In addition to the Zionist youth groups (such as Akiba, Dror, and Ha-Shomer Ha-tsa'ir), there were the youth groups linked to major political parties like the Bund (the Jewish-Socialist workers party), and the Communist party. While this chapter is devoted to the Jewish couriers, it is important to note that there were also non-Jewish couriers (such as Irena Adamowicz) who worked with the Jewish resistance. They were recruited from parallel Polish groups, such as the Polish scouts and the Communist party youth groups.

WHAT DID THEY DO? THE FOUR MISSIONS

As noted above, the tasks of the *kashariyot* changed as the Jewish underground responded to shifts in Nazi policy. At first, when they believed they could live through the Nazi occupation, they were involved in contacting and organizing their members and sustaining lives in the ghetto. Second, spurred by the news of the mass murders, they shifted gears and set out on missions to sound the alarm, warn others, and urge resistance. In the third phase they spearheaded resistance activities outside the ghetto, securing arms and ammunition, safe houses, and potential allies on the Aryan side. In the fourth and final phase, the *kashariyot* were consumed with rescue and saving lives: they helped people escape from the ghetto and sustained them with false papers, places to stay, visits, and money.

It is important to note however, that this sequence of activities did not begin at the same time, or proceed at the same pace, in all of

the territories that had been Poland before 1939, because the establishment, duration, and structure of the ghettos varied across and
within different zones of German administration.

First: Making Contact and Helping Others Survive

When the prewar political and Zionist groups reconstituted themselves in the ghettos, they believed they would survive the German
occupation. Their goal was to help others live, and to help them survive with dignity. Many of their activities were forbidden, and they
were part of a conscious effort to defy the Germans and affirm their
own values. For example, Bronka Klibanski explained that Dror established illegal schools precisely because they were forbidden:

> When the Germans forbid the Jewish children to study, our first
> reaction . . . was that *if the Germans forbid it, then we have to do
> it* [emphasis added]. . . . It was not important what subject. . . .
> What was important was not to lose our human dignity . . . be-
> cause we understood that the Germans were always trying to de-
> grade us.[28]

Since the primary goal of this period was to sustain Jewish life,
several groups sent couriers to the Aryan side of their own cities and
towns to find food and other supplies to smuggle into the ghetto—
in what Rich Cohen refers to as "waging a white resistance to keep the
ghetto Jews clothed, fed and alive."[29]

Other couriers were sent out to establish contact with Jews in
other communities, as noted above. Typically these first missions
aimed at finding the members of their own movement in other ghettos (whom they often knew from conferences, summer camps, agricultural training courses, etc.) and sharing news and information
with them. Those who were not yet confined in ghettos might also be
able to help with food and other resources.

At the same time, many of the young women who later became
couriers began smuggling food into the ghetto in a "private white
war" to keep their families alive, as Hasia did. Because the Nazis intentionally limited the supply of food in the ghettos, Jews who did
not have extra resources and who did not work (and who therefore
did not receive some soup or bread during the day) were being slowly
starved to death.

Like Hasia, Bronka Klibanski, the Dror courier, also began smuggling during this period. She would sneak out of the ghetto with clothes and other items to trade for food. For Bronka, it became a sport: she enjoyed discovering new ways to get in and out of the ghetto, and she made a point of "not following German orders."[30]

In retrospect, it is clear that this first period was a critical training period for the *kashariyot.* They acquired knowledge, skills, experience, and contacts. They studied the routines of the guards at the ghetto gates, and learned when and how they could get through; they honed their techniques for hiding and smuggling illegal goods; and they established useful contacts on the Aryan side. Equally important, they gained both confidence and experience in outwitting the Nazis.

Second: Carrying the Warning—and Urging Resistance

Once the Jewish underground accepted the news of the mass murders as German policy, it became clear that all their efforts to sustain life in the ghetto were pointless: the schools, the seminars, and even the smuggling of food were futile if they were all to be killed.

But what could they do? How could they stop the all-powerful German army? It seemed impossible. However, when they thought about their options they realized that even if they could not stop the Germans, they could organize some forms of resistance that would impede their plans and make their "work" more difficult. For example, they could sabotage and disrupt the orderly method in which the Germans planned to liquidate the ghetto.

They could also decide to fight the Germans. Even though they would be killed in the fighting, they would die with honor. In his famous speech calling for armed resistance in Vilna (on December 31, 1941) Abba Kovner declared: "Let us not go like sheep to the slaughter. . . . It is better to die as free men fighting. . . . Let us defend ourselves to the very last breath."[31] Kovner was the first underground leader to hear and believe an eyewitness who escaped the mass killings in Ponary and the first to understand what her story meant.[32] It was Kovner who dispatched the first couriers to Grodno, Bialystok, and Warsaw, to read the text of his speech as the inspiration for their call for resistance. (That is why one hears Kovner's dictum "let us not go like sheep to the slaughter" in so many testimonies.)

As fighters they could also take revenge by killing some of the

Germans before they themselves were killed. A final option for resistance was to thwart the Nazis' goals by rescuing and saving some Jews.
Although they knew they could not save everyone, each Jew who was
saved was a triumph. Rescue was a clear and concrete way of defying
the Nazis and sabotaging their plans.[33]

But no form of resistance was likely if the Jews were not fore-
warned and were not prepared. Thus *the most urgent priority* of the
Jewish underground was to send out *kashariyot* to warn and mobilize
Jews all over Poland. This became the most important mission of the
kashariyot: they were dispatched to carry the news from ghetto to
ghetto. Their first challenge was to survive the hazards of illegal travel
and reach the other ghettos. Their second challenge was to persuade
everyone to heed their warnings.

In order to travel outside the ghetto the couriers had to use false
documents that identified them as Poles, and to withstand the scrutiny
of both Polish and German policemen who were constantly patrolling
the trains and checking documents. Because the major Jewish ghettos
of Warsaw, Vilna, and Bialystok were in three separate zones of German administration, the *kashariyot* also needed special police passes
to cross those borders.[34] They therefore had to use two or more forged
documents and had to undergo a meticulous inspection at the borders. It was, to understate the case, extremely hazardous. The reports
of those who managed to get through leave one in awe of their quick
wits, resourcefulness, and amazing luck.

But many more did not make it.[35] The dual burden of having several sets of forged documents, and having to submit them for rigorous
scrutiny at multiple border controls, meant that they faced impossible odds. (See, for example, the story of two of the most successful
kashariyot, Bela Hazan and Lonka Kozibrodska, who were caught at
the Malkinia junction and sent to Auschwitz.[36])

As noted above, getting through to report the news of the mass
murders was only the first half of the challenge that the *kashariyot*
faced. They also had to convince the Jewish leadership that the Nazis
were really planning to murder all Jews, and that they themselves
were in imminent danger. It is important to underscore how difficult
that was. As Bronka Klibanski explained, the older leaders simply
could "not believe such a policy could exist . . . because it was so inhuman. . . . After all, the Germans were a civilized society and what
civilized society, even in wartime, would kill an entire people?"[37]

Bela Hazan, the Dror courier who was sent from Vilna to Grodno, provides a telling example of the difficulty she had in getting the members of the Judenrat to accept her message. She was so upset by her frustrating meeting with the Grodno Judenrat that she began to cry. As she reported: "I could see that they did not believe my story. . . . I saw their dismissive gestures, and I could tell that they were rejecting what I described. . . . [After the meeting] I stood in the corridor and broke out in tears."[38]

In addition, in each ghetto the leaders had specific reasons for explaining why what happened in Vilna, if it did really happen, could not happen in their ghetto. It could not happen in Warsaw, for example, because Warsaw was the capital of Poland, and one could not kill half a million Jews in the center of the capital.

These were the reactions that Chaika Grossman encountered on her first mission to Warsaw in January 1942.[39] Chaika, a national leader of Ha-Shomer Ha-tsa'ir, was sent to Warsaw as the official representative of the newly formed Vilna FPO, the United Fighting Organization of Vilna. Hers was a high-level mission to tell the Warsaw Jewish leadership about the mass murders in Vilna,[40] and to convince them to organize armed resistance.

The national leaders of most of the major Jewish organizations in Poland were in Warsaw—and in the ghetto—and they all came to the meeting with Chaika. Sitting around the table were representatives of the whole spectrum of political views. Chaika talked about the killings in Vilna, the importance of seeing this as a general Nazi policy, and the need to establish a Jewish "armed defense." But the Warsaw leaders were certain that Warsaw was different. As the Bund representative told her: "It would not happen in Warsaw. . . . Warsaw is a big metropolis in the middle of Europe. The world would be shocked and protest. Warsaw was not like Vilna. . . : the Germans won't want to anger the Western world because of the Jews."[41]

Similarly, in Bialystok, the head of the Judenrat, Ephraim Barash, assured Chaika that the Germans "would not dare" do what they did in Vilna, because the factories in the Bialystok ghetto produced essential materials for the German army.[42] Barash insisted that the Germans would never cut off their own supply lines! "They need us." Thus the biggest challenge the couriers faced was breaking through these paralyzing illusions.[43] They were, after all, women, and young women at that, and neither status was accorded great deference at the time. In addition, it was difficult for anyone to believe that they were slated for death, and the Nazis were masters of false assurances and skillful deception.

In fact, what is surprising, when one considers all the obstacles they faced, is how successful the couriers ultimately were and how much anti-German resistance they ultimately inspired. Even those who were initially greeted with skepticism planted seeds that grew into major uprisings. For example, as noted above, when Chaika Grossman first met with the Jewish leaders in Warsaw in January 1942, they were not ready to organize because they did not believe that they would be affected. But, by the fall of 1942, after the "great *Aktions*" in Warsaw, most of them accepted the agenda she had proposed.

The *kashariyot* had a much more direct and immediate impact on the young men and women who became the leaders of the ghetto uprisings. As noted above, the arrival of a courier was always an exciting "event" for the local members of her movement.[44] As word of her appearance spread, members rushed over to welcome her, and to hear the latest news. The *kashariyot* were already becoming legendary figures in their movements, and the stories of their courage and death-defying exploits accorded them a special status.[45]

For example, when Chaika arrived in Warsaw, she met Mordechai Anielewicz who took her to the "kibbutz," the "headquarters" of Ha-Shomer Ha-tsa'ir in the ghetto, and the place where many members lived collectively. After the excitement and joy of greeting her close friends—who were the national leaders of Ha-Shomer Ha-tsa'ir[46]— the others "all hurried in . . . they all wanted to receive me."[47] Their meeting lasted into the night: Someone found food, Tosya added some wood to the iron stove, and no one left to go home.

When Chaika talked about the murders in Vilna and the need to prepare for armed resistance she "did not have to convince them" because they, like Chaika, were the national leadership and "they understood" everything. However, at that time, they (and the national leaders of Dror, Yitzhak Zuckerman and Zivia Lubetkin, their partners in organizing armed resistance in Warsaw) were still thinking about "when and how." They were also unsure of how to unify groups that had been political opponents.[48] The days of Chaika's visit were nonstop discussions of like-minded leaders engaged in strategic and tactical planning.[49] One year later, in January 1943, the plans were worked out, and Anielewicz and Zuckerman were commanding the first uprising in the Warsaw ghetto.

A second aim of Chaika's mission in 1942 was to get the money Abba Kovner needed to buy guns for the Vilna uprising. Her Warsaw comrades helped her with contacts and strategy and she returned to Vilna with the money from the Joint Distribution Committee [JDC]. It was considered a great feat.

Chaika's meeting with the members of her Zionist youth group in Bialystok was similar. She described it as "exhilarating. . . . one of our most profound experiences."[50] When she read Abba Kovner's famous speech they were ready to act. While it would take some time before the Bialystok resistance was organized and unified, a core group of young people was already on board.

Although we noted the typical contrast between the responses of the ghetto "establishment" on the one hand, and the members of the zionist youth groups, on the other, to the message of the *kashariyot,* there was at least one ghetto establishment that stands out as different, and one courier who had an immediate impact on that ghetto's leadership. The ghetto was Kovno, and the courier was Irena Adamowicz.[51] Irena was a non-Jewish member of the Polish Scouts who had worked with the Jewish Scouts before the war. During the war she was active in the Polish resistance and used her position to help her Jewish friends. She also became one of the most important couriers for the Jewish resistance. According to Arad, she was the courier sent to tell the Jews of Kovno about the mass murders and to urge them to prepare for armed resistance. When she transmitted Abba Kovner's message, they immediately understood the urgency of her warning. They quickly shifted the focus of their activities away from culture and education, and began to formulate plans for resistance.[52]

Third: Mounting the Resistance

The third sphere of courier activities, which overlapped chronologically with the second, focused on mounting that resistance. Because the *kashariyot* had developed the expertise and contacts for working outside the ghetto, they became responsible for a wide range of difficult and dangerous tasks that had to be undertaken on the Aryan side. At the top of this list was the all-important job of acquiring guns, explosives, and ammunition for the ghetto revolts, and smuggling them into the ghetto. The couriers also provided critical guidance, escorts, false documents and safe houses for resistance workers on the Aryan side, and they smuggled money, supplies and ammunition to groups of Jews planning resistance in factories, prisons, camps, and distant ghettos.

Getting Weapons

Finding weapons was, for many couriers, their most difficult, most frustrating—and most important—assignment. As Vladka Meed, a Bund courier in Warsaw, wrote:

> [T]he main objective of our mission on the Aryan side—the goal for which we endured constant danger, hid like frightened animals, assumed false identities, moved from dwelling to dwelling to escape detection as Jews—was to obtain arms for the resistance in the ghetto.[53]

In retrospect, it is difficult to believe that the Jewish resistance had no weapons when they decided to fight the Germans. Yet this was true in each of the major ghettos. In Bialystok, for example, it had only one rifle by the summer of 1942: the rifle had to be carried to each unit of would-be fighters—always at great risk in the ghetto—so that each group could be trained with a real rifle.[54] In Vilna the fighters shared a single snub-nosed revolver for their training, "which was passed hand to hand like an icon."[55] In Cracow, they did not have a single gun.[56]

Nothing was as frustrating to the leaders of the resistance as their inability to get the arms they needed to fight the Germans. The lack of weapons was (in the judgment of both the participants at that time and later historians) their single biggest obstacle. In Warsaw, the leaders of the newly formed ZOB, the Jewish Fighting Organization, assumed they would get arms and military support from the Polish underground. Antek Zuckerman, the ZOB commander, requested help from three groups: the AK (Armia Krajowa), the major underground army in Poland; the Polish government-in-exile in London; and the Armia Ludowa (AL), the Polish-communist resistance. The responses, or, to be more accurate, the negative responses he received from the first two groups were insulting and infuriating. Despite his increasingly desperate appeals, the Poles, after long delays, turned him down with lame excuses (such as not believing that Jews would really fight).[57]

Although a thorough discussion of the attitude and actions of the

Polish resistance is clearly beyond the scope of this chapter, it is useful to note that both Zuckerman (the commander who negotiated with the Poles) and Israel Gutman (the eminent historian) believe that the AK command never really supported the Jewish uprising and had their own reasons for not wanting it to succeed.[58] Zuckerman writes about their misleading promises, deceptions, and ultimate betrayal of the Jewish uprising with great bitterness.[59]

The only branch of the Polish resistance exempted from this bitter assessment was the Polish-communist AL, which was genuinely supportive of the Jewish cause. But it did not have the resources, manpower, or weapons to really help. It gave the ZOB "the addresses and contacts with arms dealers" who, for high prices, sold the ZOB grenades and a few guns, "which were only good enough for show."[60] Then, in a devastating series of events, the ZOB's agent for these purchases, Aryeh Wilner (Jurek), was betrayed and caught by the Gestapo, and the supply lines were cut off.[61]

While the ZOB was negotiating with the national leaders of the AK and the AL, other Jewish organizations were seeking guns through their own networks. For example, the Jewish Bund maintained strong ties to Polish-socialist colleagues who promised to find guns for it. However, as the Bund courier Vladka Meed reported, they just kept making promises and urging the Bund to be patient.[62] In the end, in spite of the Bund's willingness to pay generously for the weapons, their Polish colleagues never came through.

It was in this bleak environment that the *kashariyot* were sent out to find weapons—on their own. Time was running out and the resistance desperately needed guns and ammunition. This was the ultimate challenge for the *kashariyot*. It was the point at which their expertise and Aryan contacts were most needed. Vladka Meed, the Bund courier, tells of the thrill of getting her first gun, which she arranged to buy from her landlord's nephew.[63] But because it was so precious, she was afraid to risk smuggling it into the Warsaw ghetto by herself. There were three sets of guards at the gates (German, Polish, and Jewish) and she might be searched. Instead Vladka chose to disguise her gun as an ordinary parcel and to use an "established" smuggling route, a hole in the ghetto wall.

Bronka Klibanski's "parcels" were considerably larger: she filled her suitcase with weapons she had bought from the peasants in the countryside near Bialystok.[64] They believed she was a member of the Polish resistance and went out of their way to help her. It was Mordechai Tennenbaum's idea, born in desperation, after months of trying to get arms from the AK. At first Mordechai, the leader of the Bialystok resistance, had assumed that the AK in Bialystok would be willing to provide weapons for the Jewish fighters. But when all his pleas were ignored, he too realized that the Jews were on their own.

So he devised an ingenious solution: if no one wanted to help the Jews, he would send Poles—or at least couriers who could pose as Poles—to solicit help for the Polish underground. It was rumored that there were peasants who had acquired weapons from the retreating Russians, and had managed to hide them before the German invasion. Mordechai needed someone who could appeal to the peasants, someone who would arouse their sympathy, someone who would gain their trust. That someone was Bronka Klibanski. Bronka always managed to win over people who were happy to help such a fine young lady.

Her next hurdle was getting her precious cargo back to Bialystok. As we know from Hasia's experience, many women were trying to smuggle farm products into Bialystok, and the Germans were on the lookout for them. Although Bronka had worked out a routine that usually avoided their searches, one day, with her suitcase loaded with a machine gun, she saw a tall German policeman as she approached the station. Her first instinct was to turn around. But Bronka realized he had seen her, so she had to proceed.

The German had a dog, a big dog, but Bronka knew she could not hesitate. So she approached him with a smile and asked if he knew when the train would arrive:

> He looked at my valise, and then at me, and he asked me what I had inside? So I told him, I have lard and eggs and butter. All these things were illegal—it was not permitted to bring them to the city. It was smuggling.
>
> And I asked him with a nice smile if he wants me to open it? And he said, no, no, no, thank you very much, because there was no need to open it, because I told him I had all of these things that I was not permitted to have. . . . So if I told him the truth, there was no need to open. It was finished.
>
> He told me to go with him to the station. We waited for the train together. I didn't know if I was under arrest or not.
>
> When the train arrived, he took me to the conductor of the train, and he asked him to give me a good place to sit where no one

would bother me. And he told the conductor not to let anyone look at my valise, that nobody should bother me. And so I got back safely to Bialystok with the arms.[65]

An amazing story. But equally amazing was the fact that Bronka's luck endured for all her future missions.

Itka Szwajger, a young doctor who was a courier for the Bund, was also extraordinarily lucky. One day she was carrying ammunition in her bag when she was stopped by an ordinary police patrol in Warsaw. The officer ordered her to open her bag. She smiled and opened the bag widely to show him the potatoes that were on top. When he saw the potatoes he waived her on.[66]

Because the AK and the AL (the two armies of the Polish resistance) were not homogeneous, the local units in some cities, such as Vilna and Cracow, were willing to help their Jewish comrades. In Cracow, for example, the Akiba group asked their colleagues in the communist AL to help them get weapons. The Crakow AL located a cache of weapons for them to "pick up" in Warsaw.

Hela Schupper was the Akiba courier selected for this all-important mission of buying and smuggling the guns.[67] Knowing she would have to spend twenty hours on trains, she prepared her appearance with great care. She dyed her hair to be really blond; borrowed an outfit that looked very Polish, very stylish, and very mature, from the mother of a non-Jewish friend; and splurged on a fashionable and elegant handbag. All together, it gave her the air of a carefree, chic, cultured lady off to an afternoon of theater. When she received the weapons, she carefully taped the five pistols to her body, under her clothing, to preserve her carefree appearance. She placed the explosives and bullets in her fashionable bag, covered by clothing. Although her stomach was tied in knots, her performance was a success and she returned to Crakow on the train without ever being searched.[68] Hela was a heroine. As Gusta Davidson wrote: "No one had ever been greeted with the outpouring of affection that was showered on Hela. . . . It is impossible to describe the ecstasy inspired by those weapons. . . . No one had really believed weapons would ever be found. . . . [I]t was truly a miracle . . . the start of a new era. . . ."[69] The hero's welcome that Hela received is echoed in other testimonies. For example, the ZOB commander Antek Zuckerman said he would never forget the celebration and drinks in honor of

Frumka Plotnitzka when she smuggled the ZOB's first weapons into the Warsaw ghetto.[70] Frumka had also escaped detection quite miraculously. She was carrying the weapons in a basket of potatoes when she was stopped by a German policeman. He put his hand in the basket, groped around, but, somehow, he did not find anything.[71]

Hasia Bornstein, the courier we followed from Grodno to Bialystok at the beginning of this chapter, was also welcomed as a savior when she later delivered a machine gun and 600 bullets to the partisans in the forest near Bialystok.[72] There was such excitement and rejoicing that they would not let her leave to return to the city. Although the partisans had "nothing," they somehow managed to find "gifts"—a small comb, a pretty ring—in an emotional outpouring of affection and gratitude.[73]

These couriers were, of course, the lucky ones. The Jewish resistance lost many other couriers who were caught buying and smuggling arms. Two of the most successful couriers, Bela Hazan and Lonka Kozibrodska, were caught because Lonka was smuggling guns. Although everyone assumed that Bela and Lonka could talk their way out of any difficulty, when the police suspected Lonka's ghetto-made papers, they searched her and found four pistols. They immediately "knew" she was a member of the Polish resistance. When they caught Bela as well, they tortured them to make them disclose the source of their weapons. Neither Bela nor Lonka broke. They were both able to maintain their Aryan cover, and neither one was unmasked as a Jew (despite the fact that both were carrying Hebrew materials when they were caught.) Their performances saved Bela's life because they were sent to Auschwitz as Poles, while they would have been shot if they were known to be Jews. Lonka, however, died in Auschwitz.[74]

Fourth: Saving Lives: Rescue as Resistance

The fourth mission of the *kashariyot* was to save Jewish lives. Once the ghetto were under seige, that could only be accomplished by finding places for Jews to live outside the ghetto, on the Aryan side. As those with the most practical knowledge and experience of the Aryan side, the *kashariyot* were the obvious choice for organizing and carrying out this massive undertaking. In the final months of the ghettos, efforts to save as many Jews as possible became an all-consuming passion. The *kashariyot* helped children and adults escape from the ghetto, located rooms for them to stay on the Aryan side, prepared their new identity cards and residential identification, and supplied them (and those who were hiding and helping them) with financial support.

In addition to saving and hiding "ordinary people," the *kashariyot* were also responsible for guiding and protecting the leaders and members of the Jewish resistance who were working on the Aryan side. The *kashariyot* located "safe" houses, rooms, and apartments for their work, and acted as the official tenant and front person in those settings. The couriers also provided resistance members with false papers and certificates of employment and helped them plan and carry out their missions outside of the ghetto. Finally, the *kashariyot* served as their emissaries, relayed messages to and from them, and often accompanied them on missions as their personal escorts on the Aryan side.

Because it was hazardous for male leaders of the Jewish resistance to be on the streets and to travel on the Aryan side, they were typically accompanied by a courier who acted as their "personal liaison" and escort. For example, Antek Zuckerman was always accompanied by a *kasharit,* like Lonka or Chavka, when he was outside the ghetto. The courier not only furnished him with a cloak of respectability (because a couple always looked more innocent than a single male); she often spoke better Polish and was equipped with local knowledge and experience.[75]

While some *kashariyot* worked as personal liaisons for male leaders, and others spent most of their time on the roads in long distance missions, in the final days of the ghettos, most of the *kashariyot* were involved in rescuing children and adults from the ghetto and making arrangements for them on the Aryan side. The couriers were responsible for finding safe accommodations, providing false documents, and for managing their care. For most couriers, these rescue activities consumed more time, energy, and psychological stress than anything else.

Each of these tasks—finding accommodations, getting false papers, and overseeing their care—was enormously time consuming, complicated, and risky. In addition, the arrangements were always falling apart and had to be redone: a neighbor would became suspicious, or a landlord would become nervous, or someone would be discovered by a blackmailer. The psychic stress was relentless. Adina (Itka) Szwajger, a Warsaw doctor who became a courier for the Bund, described her feelings on a typical day: from the moment she hid the forged ID cards in her handbag or tucked them into her clothes, she could feel the shivers of fear and anxiety spread throughout her body. "It was a cold feeling . . . an awareness that from that moment on every accidental search in the street might be the end."[76]

The couriers in Warsaw also had to cope with a particularly obnoxious and dangerous group of Poles, "the *schmalzowniks*"—the extortionists and blackmailers who were "in the business" of shaking down Jews on the Aryan side and who were, in Ringelblum's words, "the endless nightmare of Jews on the Aryan side in Warsaw."[77] They were in it for the money, and Jews on the Aryan side were easy prey. The *schmalzowniks* positioned themselves outside the ghetto walls and around the train stations to accost escaping Jews. Once they identified a Jew, they demanded a ransom for not turning him or her in to the Gestapo. The terrified Jew usually paid. But if one did not pay, or did not pay enough, or if the extortionist just felt like it, he would take the Jew to the Gestapo and collect the fee they offered for every Jew who was delivered. The blackmailers terrorized Jews on the Aryan side.

For the couriers responsible for hiding Jews on the Aryan side of Warsaw, a blackmailer's visit to one of their charges was "the ultimate disaster." Itka Szwajger never understood how they managed to find the addresses of people who were completely hidden.[78] But once the blackmailers visited a flat, they would return again and again, until the helpless victims had given them everything they had. As soon as an apartment was "burned" by being visited by a blackmailer, the courier had to move immediately to find a new hiding place for the unfortunate victim.

It would be reasonable to assume that since the couriers were not likely to be identified as Jews, they themselves would therefore *not* be targeted by extortionists. However, the couriers' work required them to be seen in places (such as leaving the ghetto) that made them suspect. Chaika Grossman, for example, was accosted by an extortionist who saw her leave the Warsaw ghetto.[79] He approached her politely at first, because he was probably not sure if she was Jewish since non-Jews also went into the ghetto for business. She ignored him, but he followed her. When she went into a courtyard, he waited until she came out. Chaika was sweating: she was carrying important documents and a substantial amount of money to buy guns for the Vilna resistance. The money was hidden, but she had pictures of the camps, which Dr. Ringelblum had put in her pockets. She berated herself for taking such risks. Maybe she should pay the extortionist off? No, the money belonged to the Jewish resistance, which it desperately needed to buy arms. She was furious at the very idea that he might get a zloty of their money. So she turned on him:

> "Why are you creeping behind me like a smelly dog?"
> "You are Jewish." His voice was threatening.
> Again she yelled at him and cursed him as a stinking dog.
> "Oh, how nervous we are." He was taunting her.

The man was about to summon a nearby Polish policeman when Chaika saw a German soldier. She knew she had a better chance with the German: she could speak to him in German. Most Poles were afraid of Germans. She announced she was going straight to the SS officer. The Pole hesitated. It was over. The Pole walked away.

Vladka Meed, the Bund courier in Warsaw, was also in the wrong place at the wrong time when three men saw her leaving a factory that employed Jewish workers from the ghetto. She also used intimidation. She refused to pay the enormous ransom they demanded and threatened to go to the police to make them pay for harassing her.[80]

Although this chapter is limited to the ghetto period, it is important to note that the couriers' activities intensified in the final days of the ghettos, during the final *Aktions,* rebellions, and liquidations. At the very last minute the couriers were propelled into a new whirlwind of activity: they were given the daunting task of finding hiding places and documents to save the fighters who could escape.

These rescue efforts were, in fact, an afterthought for those who were planning to fight in the ghetto. Because most of the fighters assumed that they themselves would be killed, they did not think about what would happen after the revolts. Their aim, from the beginning, was to control how they were going to die. And they assumed they would die fighting the Nazis. It was not until the end of the uprising, after they had achieved their goal of letting the world know that Jews had fought, that the fighters confronted the horrible choice that lay ahead: either they could either kill themselves to avoid capture, or they could surrender and be taken to the freight trains. It was only then that they allowed themselves to reconsider the possibility of escape. In short, it was only when the fighters realized that some of them would survive that they thought about getting help on the Aryan side.

The only thing that prevented these rescue activities from being totally ad hoc was the unexpected withdrawal of German troops from the ghetto (in both Warsaw and Bialystok) when the Jews began fighting. The hiatus between the first armed resistance and the final liquidation gave the resistance groups in these two cities more time to prepare to save some fighters. After the ghettos were liquidated the *kashariyot* who survived continued their resistance activities, focusing primarily on rescue and partisan operations. For example, Hasia's group of five couriers who survived in the Bialystok area[81] initiated and orchestrated the rescue of Jews from other ghettos, labor camps, and prisons. They also engaged in a wide range of partisan activities. As we follow their activities through the war we see them grow from young girls being "sent" on missions, into seasoned experts who are operating independently and orchestrating resistance activities in Bialystok in the final stages of the war. They were all honored as "national heroines" of the Soviet Union after the liberation.

EVALUATING THE IMPORTANCE OF THE *KASHARIYOT*

How important were the *kashariyot* in the larger context of Jewish resistance during the Holocaust?

If we examine the judgments of their contemporaries, such as the leaders of the Jewish resistance who were in the best position to judge their role, we find that they consistently placed the *kashariyot* in the indispensable core of the resistance. For example, the Dror leader Zivia Lubetkin, who was in the central command of the Warsaw ghetto uprising, devoted a chapter in her book to the women *kashariyot* and concluded that "one can not possibly describe this work of organizing the Jewish resistance, or the uprising itself, without mentioning the role of these valiant women."[82] Similarly, the written accounts of the activities of individual couriers are a mixture of glowing praise and reverence that approaches awe. Consider, for example, the description of Lonka Kozibrodska written by Yitzhak Zuckerman, a commander of the Jewish fighting organization in the Warsaw ghetto:

> Blue eyes, straight nose, blond hair with long braids arranged like a halo on her head. . . .[83]
>
>   She was sent to the places of greatest danger, places where no paths had been cleared and death was lurking on every road. She would go. Brave, and certain of her strength . . .[84]

Many *kashariyot* took upon themselves dangerous missions in those days, but she (Lonka) turned her work into an art . . . like a virtuoso who produces . . . magic.[85]

. . . . with talent . . . intelligence, wisdom, and charm.[86]

This mixture of reporting, praise and awe is also evident in the writings of Mordechai Tannenbaum, the commander of the Jewish uprising in the Bialystok ghetto. Although Tannenbaum was killed in the ghetto revolt in August 1943, less than a month before the uprising, he wrote a letter to his sister in Israel praising the fearless courier Tema Schneiderman:

> Wherever there was an *Aktion,* she had to be there at once. Whenever someone was caught in the camps—they had to be rescued! At the station, when a railway carriage is being suspiciously prepared, it was necessary to find out why, and where it was headed and to warn others to be careful. A fire in a village—money was needed there. Seek out partisans in the forest. Buy arms. Everything. . . .
>
> She was familiar with every ghetto in Poland, walls and barbed wire, every Judenrat. She was the real center of . . . all the Zionist and public federations. . . .[87]

The reverence reflected in these statements was not limited to mere words. The couriers were treated with great respect and deference at the time. For example, at the historic meeting when the representatives of all the movements in Vilna came together to establish the united Jewish resistance on December 31, 1941, Abba Kovner delivered his famous speech calling for armed resistance ("Let us not go like sheep to the slaughter. . . .") It is significant that Kovner first read his speech in Yiddish, and then turned to Tosia Altman, one of the most famous *kashariyot* leaders of Ha-Shomer Ha-Tsa'ir who had just arrived in Vilna on a mission from Warsaw, and Tosia delivered the same powerful speech in Hebrew.[88] The symbolic recognition and status accorded to Tosia reflected not only her own stature as a leader and a spokesperson from Warsaw, but also the heroic stature of the *kashariyot* as those who would carry the call for resistance.

As we noted above, the couriers were already legendary figures in the Jewish underground, where stories of their exploits and triumphs were a sorely needed source of solace and pride. Although they were, at first, known to members of their own movements, news of their miraculous feats spread to the wider circle of those who were involved in the resistance.

Emmanuel Ringelblum's remarks, cited at the beginning of this chapter, reflect this awareness of the heroic stature of the *kashariyot*. Ringelblum was a keen observer of both people and events in the ghetto, and his entry revealed his knowledge of the couriers' accomplishments (they carry out "the most dangerous missions," "smuggle contraband," and "rescue comrades"). It also attested to Ringleblum's unrestrained admiration for their bravery and courage (they are "heroic," "bold," and "indefatigable . . . nothing deters them").[89] Finally, his concluding evaluation accorded them a central role in history (a "glorious page in the history of Jewry during the present war. And the Chaikas and Frumkas will be the leading figures in this story."[90])

We must then ask why the *kashariyot*, who were clearly regarded as central and important participants in the Jewish resistance by their contemporaries, have rarely been accorded that status in subsequent historical accounts. Why would they be considered heroic at the time, but be neglected for the following sixty years?

It would appear that historians have adopted a much more restrictive definition of the key actors in the resistance and have, on the whole, focused only on those who engaged in direct combat with the Germans and died "with honor." Although some *kashariyot*—like Frumka Plotnitska who led the ghetto fighters in the Bendzin ghetto—did die fighting, most of the *kashariyot* who were still alive when the uprising began were immediately "ordered" to leave the ghetto (or to remain outside the ghetto) because their critical skills were needed on the Aryan side.

It may, nevertheless, be useful to examine this implicit standard. Is it appropriate to restrict the definition of a fighter (and a hero) to those who engaged in armed combat and died with honor? Did all of those honored as heroes meet this standard? In fact, the standard itself is seriously flawed, and, in addition, it has been applied inconsistently.

First, it is obvious that we often honor those who did not die. Some of those who fought in the ghetto revolts survived, but they are still recognized as "fighters" and considered "heroes" of the uprising. What then defines a fighter? Is it one who has taken the risk of being killed? If so, then the *kashariyot* should be considered fighters because they certainly shared that risk. Or is the definition of a fighter based on the number of days, or hours or minutes that one is "engaged" in life-threatening situations? If the amount of time one is at risk is critical, then, once again, there can be no doubt that the *kashariyot* were fighters, because they were in life-threatening situations for much longer periods of time than those who fought in the ghetto revolts.

For example, if we compare the amount of time the *kashariyot* spent at risk with the amount of time of the ghetto fighters were at risk, we see that the *kashariyot* were exposed to danger and death for much longer periods of time. In Warsaw the ghetto fighters were at risk, using the most liberal definitions of the time involved, for, at most, five months (January to May 1943). In Bialystok, they were at risk for, at most, 3 weeks (in August 1943.) In contrast, most of the couriers faced the risk of death for years.

Perhaps the implicit standard for being recognized as a fighter/ hero is not actually the risk of "death" or the amount of time at risk, but rather whether or not one has actually given one's life for the cause. But here too, it is clear that most of the couriers were also killed in the line of duty. For example, among the twenty-three women who started out as couriers in Hasia's group in Bialystok, only five survived.

Of course, one must recognize that this type of reasoned analysis may nevertheless be at odds with the popular judgment that accords more honor to those who had guns, even if they never fired them. But was holding and/or firing a weapon during an uprising more important than finding weapons or smuggling them into the ghetto? The "fighters" would not have had weapons to hold without the *kashariyot*. All armies recognize undercover agents who are lost on reconnaissance missions as fighters who lost their lives in battle. Similarly, the bomber-pilot who is shot down on his/her first bombing mission is still a bomber-pilot even if he/she never has a chance to fire: we would not doubt that he/she was a full-fledged fighter. It therefore seems reasonable to extend the term "fighter" to the women couriers who assumed similar roles, for they too bore the risk of death and many of them were also killed in the line of duty.

In summary, both this short analysis and the longer description of the activities of the couriers in this chapter point to the conclusion that the couriers were both essential and central to the Jewish resistance—whether one defines that resistance as a resistance of informing, persuading, and organizing others to resist, evade or thwart the

Nazis—or whether one defines that resistance as the armed struggle against the Germans. Even if they had done nothing else, their efforts to spread the news of the mass murders, and their effectiveness in mobilizing others, placed them at the very heart of the Jewish resistance. Without the voices and persuasion of the *kashariyot,* there would have been much less resistance. More ghettos would have remained isolated and ignorant of the Nazi plans; more Jews would have believed German assurances that the transports were for resettlement, and fewer would have resisted deportation. Whatever form of resistance the Jews in various ghettos eventually adopted—whether it was hiding in bunkers, or trying to rescue and save Jews on the Aryan side, or escaping from the ghetto to join the partisans, or organizing to fight the Germans in the ghetto—it is likely that not as much of it would have occurred if they had not been told about the Final Solution.

Even if one limits the definition of resistance to armed struggle, this chapter has shown that the couriers were as essential as those who fired the guns and threw the Molotov cocktails. In terms of the three measures considered above—the exposure to risk and death, the amount of time at risk of death (such as the amount of time they spent securing and transporting guns and ammunition for the uprising), and the loss of life in the line of duty—the *kashariyot* were more than equal to other participants in the ghetto resistance. It is, in fact, difficult to imagine a Jewish resistance during the Holocaust without them. It is therefore appropriate to correct the historical record to include what Dr. Ringelblum referred to as the *kashariyot's* "glorious page" in the history of the Jewish resistance during the Holocaust.[91]

NOTES

1. Emmanuel Ringelblum's entry of May 19, 1942 in *Notes from the Warsaw Ghetto: The Journal of Emmanuel Ringelblum,* ed. and trans. by Jacob Sloan (New York: Schocken Books, 1974) 273–4. (The entry is not dated in the English edition but is placed between the entries for May 12 and May 22, 1942. It is dated May 19, 1942 in the Hebrew edition, *Yoman U-reshimot Mi-tekufat Ha-Milhamah: Geto Varshah, September 1939–December 1942* [Diary and Notes from the Period of the War: Warsaw Ghetto, September 1939–December 1942] (Jerusalem: Yad Vashem, 1992–93), 365.

2. Ibid.

3. The major exceptions are Naomi Shimshi's comprehensive masters

thesis, "Ma'arkhot Ha-kesher Va-anshe Ha-kesher Bi-tenu'ot Ha-no'ar Ha-halutsiyot be-Polin Ha-kevushah" [The Communication Networks and the Couriers of the Pioneering Youth Movements in Occupied Poland] University of Haifa, Faculty of Humanities, November 1990; and Sara Bender's paper "Covert Activities of Young Jewish Women in Poland in the Underground Movement in World War II" presented at the Conference on Women in the Holocaust, Hebrew University, Jerusalem, June 1995.

To date, the only non-autobiographical book on an individual is Zivah Shalev's *Tosyah: Tosyah Altman, Meha-hanhagah Ha-rashit Shel Ha-Shomer Ha-Tsa'ir Le-mifkedet Ha-Irgun Ha-Yehudi Ha-Iohem* [Tosyah: Tosyah Altman, From the Leadership of Ha-Shomer Ha-Tsa'ir to the High Command of the Jewish Fighting Organization] (Tel Aviv: Moreshet, 1992).

4. Mordecai Tennenbaum *Dapim Min Ha-delekah: Pirke Yoman, Mikhtavim, U-reshimot* [Pages From the Fire: Chapters of a Diary, Letters, and Notes] (Tel-Aviv: Ha-Kibutz Ha-Me'uhad, 1947), 83.

5. Rushka (Reizl) Korczak, *Lehavot Ba-efer* [Flames in The Ashes] (Tel Aviv: Moreshet, 1965 edition), 31. [transl. by Michlean Amir, April 2003.]

6. The following pages are paraphrased from my interview with Hasia Bornstein-Bielicka, June 14, 1994, in Kibbutz Lahavot Ha-Bashan, Israel. I am indebted to Professor Anita Weiner for accompanying me and for helping both Hasia and me to find the appropriate words. See also Hasia's new book: Bornstein-Bielicka, *Ah-chat Me-matim* [One of the Few] (Tel Aviv: Moreshet, 2003).

7. Shalom Cholawski "Grodno" in *The Encyclopedia of the Holocaust,* ed. Israel Gutman (New York: Macmillian, 1990), 619. See also Tikva Fatal-Knaani *Zo Lo Otah Grodnoh: Kehilat Grodnoh U-Sevivatah Ba Milhamah Uva Sho'ah, 1939–1943* [Grodno is Not The Same: The Jewish Community of Grodno and its Vicinity During the Second World War and the Holocaust, 1939–1943] (Jerusalem: Yad Vashem, 2001).

8. This and all the direct quotes that follow are from my interview with Hasia Bornstein-Bielicka, June 14, 1994.

9. Personal interview with Vanda Ruttenberg, June 23, 1994, Tel Aviv.

10. Chaika Grossman, *The Underground Army: Fighters of the Bialystok Ghetto* (New York: Holocaust Library, 1987), 179.

11. Nechama Tec, *When Light Pierced the Darkness* (New York: Oxford University Press, 1986), 36.

12. Celia Heller, *On the Edge of Destruction: Polish Jews between the Two World Wars* (Detroit: Wayne State University Press, 1977), 68.

13. Vanda Ruttenberg interview, June 23, 1994, Tel Aviv.

14. Personal interviews with Bela (Ya'ari) Hazan, June 20, 1994, Tel Aviv; October 20, 2003, Jerusalem; and December 19, 2003, Jerusalem.

15. Their ages ranged from eighteen to twenty-five. In my current

sample, which is not final, the oldest courier was Frumka Plotnitzka, who was twenty-five in 1939.

16. Yitzhak Zuckerman, the commander of the ZOB (the Jewish Fighting Organization) in the Warsaw ghetto, flatly states, "I didn't think we should use men as couriers. It was always more convenient to use women." *A Surplus of Memory: Chronicle of the Warsaw Ghetto Uprising* (Berkeley: University of California Press, 1993), 485.

17. I discuss these factors more fully in Lenore J. Weitzman "Living on the Aryan Side in Poland: Gender, Passing and the Nature of Resistance" in *Women in the Holocaust,* eds. Dalia Ofer and Lenore J. Weitzman, New Haven, Conn: Yale University Press, 1988), 187–222.

18. Zuckerman *Chronicle,* 485.

19. Comments at the "Symposium on the Ghettos," U.S. Holocaust Memorial Museum, November 1, 2001, Washington, D.C.

20. The Jewish community's concern about the non-Jewish education their daughters were receiving led to the establishment of "Beys Ya'akov Schools" for girls. Personal conversations with Gershon Bacon and Paula Hyman about sex differences in secular education in Poland, September 1997.

21. Personal interview with Hela Rufheisen-Schupper, June 18, 1994, in Mosav Bustan Ha-Galil, Israel.

22. Personal interview with Vitka Kovner, October 19 and 20, 1997, in Washington, D.C.

23. Personal interviews with Bronka Klibanski, June 12, 1993, and June 21, 1994, Jerusalem.

24. Adina Blady-Szwajger, *I Remember Nothing More: The Warsaw Jewish Hospital and the Jewish Resistance* (New York: Touchstone, 1990).

25. Ibid., 83.

26. Personal interview with Simcha Rotem, June 6, 1994, Jerusalem.

27. Later on, when these groups joined forces, many couriers worked for the unified resistance organization, such as the ZOB in Warsaw.

28. Bronka Klibanski interviews, 1993 and 1994.

29. Rich Cohen, *The Avengers* (New York: Alfred Knopf, 2000), 34.

30. Bronka Klibanski interviews, 1993 and 1994.

31. Because the original manifesto was written in Yiddish and Hebrew, the words I have used in English may not be identical to those in other sources. See, for example, Yitzhak Arad, *Ghetto in Flames: the Struggle and Destruction of the Jews of Vilna in the Holocaust* (New York: Holocaust Library, 1982), 231–2 and accompanying citations.

32. This dramatic story is told in Cohen, *The Avengers,* 43–45.

33. The other option, not mentioned here, was to leave the ghettos and sabotage the Germans on the Aryan side, and/or to join the partisans.

At this time, however, it was considered most important to make a stand "as Jews" and that meant fighting from the ghetto. See, for example, Zuckerman, *Chronicle,* 232–243.

34. Arad, *Ghetto in Flames,* 221.

35. Their ghetto-manufactured travel permits could not withstand the scrutiny of serious inspectors. The Malkinia junction, which one could not avoid if one was travelling from Warsaw to Bialystok, Grodno, or Vilna, was particularly hazardous, and several couriers were caught there. Arad, *Ghetto in Flames,* 244–5. They were all taken to the Pawiak prison in Warsaw and executed. Of those captured at Malkinia, only Bela Hazan and Lonka Kozibrodska, who were not identified as Jews, were spared from execution. After they were tortured, they were sent from the Pawiak prison to Auschwitz (as Poles.) See text accompanying note 74 below.

36. See text accompanying note 74 below.

37. Bronka Klibanski interview, June 12, 1993.

38. Bela Hazan interviews, 1994, Tel Aviv and 2003, Jerusalem. These events are also confirmed by Yitzhak Arad, *Ghetto in Flames,* 224, and Tikva Fatel, *Zo Lo Otah Grodnoh,* 231. Arad reports that Bela Hazan was sent to Grodno to meet with Brawer, chair of the Grodno Judenrat, and she brought authoritative information on the massacres in Vilna and Ponary to show him.

39. Grossman, *Underground Army,* 68–84; Arad, *Ghetto in Flames,* 241–3.

40. Although Shomer member Edek Boraks had reached Warsaw with news of the killings in Ponary a few weeks earlier (in December 1941), Chaika Grossman was the first official emissary of the united FPO in Vilna. Grossman, *Underground Army,* 68–84; Arad, *Ghetto in Flames,* 241–3.

41. Grossman, *Underground Army,* 78.

42. Ibid., p. 64.

43. The phrase comes from Bronka Klibanski "In the Ghetto and in the Resistance: A Personal Narrative" in *Women in the Holocaust,* eds. Ofer and Weitzman, 179.

44. Personal interview with Naomi Shimshi (author of unpublished masters thesis cited in n.3 above), July 1994, Kibbutz Yagur, Israel.

45. Ibid.

46. In addition to Mordechai, Chaika mentions "Aryeh Wilner, Tosya [Altman], Shmuel [Breslau], and Edek [Boraks] who Abba told me to bring back to Vilna." She also met with Zivia Lubetkin of Dror and notes that Dror and Ha-Shomer were united (and alone) in understanding the need for armed resistance. Grossman, *Underground Army,* 74–9.

47. Grossman, *The Underground Army,* 74.

48. Ibid., 75.

49. Ibid., 74–76, quote on p. 76.

50. Ibid., 59–60.

51. Arad, *Ghetto in Flames,* pp. 245–46.

52. Ibid., 245–46.

53. Vladka Meed, *On Both Sides of the Wall,* English ed. (New York: Holocaust Library, 1993), 94.

54. Grossman, *Underground Army,* 96.

55. Cohen, *The Avengers,* 59.

56. Gusta Davidson Draenger, *Justyna's Narrative,* trans. by Roslyn Hirsch and David H. Hirsch (Amherst, Mass: University of Massachusetts Press, 1996), 70–71 (originally published in Polish in 1946).

57. Zuckerman, *Chronicle,* 219. This was in September 1942, four months before the Jews first attacked the Germans in January 1943.

58. If the uprising was successful and spread (beyond the ghetto), it would bring strong German military retaliation and could decimate the AK before they were ready to fight the Germans. Zuckerman, *Chronicle,* 374, and Yisrael Gutman, *The Jews of Warsaw 1939–1943: Ghetto, Underground, and Revolt* (Bloomington, Indiana: Indiana University Press, 1989).

59. Zuckerman, *Chronicle,* 201. The situation improved slightly (and briefly) after the first Warsaw ghetto uprising, in January 1943, when the AK gave the ZOB forty-nine revolvers, fifty hand grenades, and some explosives. But they stalled on further aid. By April 1943, the time of the final uprising, they had a new set of excuses. Zuckerman, *Chronicle,* 360.

60. Zuckerman, *Chronicle,* 201. Later, in April 1943, the AL offered them all of the twenty-eight rifles in their armory. In addition, in May, the AL promised help in getting the last fighters out of the ghetto. But it was too little, and too late, and led to the tragic ambush of a group of fighters who had escaped through the sewers.

61. Wilner was captured in March 1943.

62. Meed, *On Both Sides of the Wall,* 94.

63. Ibid., Meed, 96–99.

64. Paraphrased from Bronka Klibanski interviews 1993 and 1994.

65. Bronka Klibanski interview, June, 1993.

66. Szwajger, *I Remember Nothing More,* 82.

67. Paraphrased from Hela Schupper interview, June 18, 1994.

68. Chavka Folman-Raban also used a "social class" cover to smuggle false documents: "I was always dressed in nice clothing and looked middle class. When they heard me speak even the other passengers in the car would say you don't have to inspect this woman." Personal interview, July 9, 1993, Kibbutz Lochame Ha Ghetto-ot, Israel.

69. Draenger, *Justyna's Narrative,* 70–71.

70. Zuckerman, *Chronicle,* 201.

71. Ibid., 201.

72. Personal interview with Hasia Bornstein-Bielicka, June 14, 1994, Kibbutz Lahavat Ha Bashan, Israel. This event is also discussed in Grossman, *Underground Army,* p. 364.

73. Their gifts were for the six Jewish couriers working with the partisans (see n. 81 below). The partisans knew all of them were involved in this mission. (Hasia interview, 1994, and Grossman, *Underground Army,* 364.)

74. Bela Yari Hazan interview, June 20, 1994.

75. For example, the Dror courier Chavka Folman-Raban explains that when Antek Zuckerman decided to go to Cracow (from Warsaw), she went with him because "I knew the route because I had been to Cracow many times to get false documents. . . . and his Polish was not as good, even though his looks were very good." Chavka Folman-Raban interview, July 1993.

76. Szwajger, *I Remember,* 81.

77. Emmanuel Ringelblum, *Polish Jewish Relations During the Second World War* (New York: Howard Fertig, 1976 and Jerusalem: Yad Vashem, 1974), 125.

78. Szwajger, *I Remember,* 161.

79. This event is paraphrased from Grossman, *Underground Army,* 115–16.

80. Meed, *On Both Sides of the Wall,* 91–2.

81. They were Hasia Bornstein (then Hasia Belicka), Chaika Grossman, and Rivka Madajska from Shomer Ha Tza'ir; Bronka Klibanski (then Bronka Winicka) from Dror; Lisa Chapnik and Anya Rod from the communists. (Rivka was shot, but the other five survived.) Later Maryla Rozycka "joined" the group, but was based with the partisans, and worked with them to smuggle guns, food, medicine, and information to the partisans in the forests. Personal interviews with Lisa Chapnick, June 1994, Tel Aviv, October 19, 2003, Beer Sheva, and December 18, 2003 Jerusalem; personal interviews with Anya Rud, October 19, 2003, Beer Sheva, and December 18, 2003 Jerusalem; Hasia Bornstein interview, 1994; Bronka Klibanski interviews, 1993, 1994 and December 19, 2003, Jerusalem.

82. Zivia Lubetkin, *In the Days of Destruction and Revolt* (Tel Aviv: Beit Lo-cha-meh Ha-Ghetaot/Ghetto Fighters House, 1981), 75.

83. Yitzhak Zuckerman *Ba Ghetto Uva-Mered* [In the Ghetto and in the Uprising] (Tel Aviv: Kibbutz Lo-cha-meh Ha-Ghetaot, Israel, 1985), 69, trans. by Michlean Amir, March 2003.

84. Ibid., 68.

85. Ibid.

86. Ibid.

87. Mordecai Tennenbaum, *Daphim Min Ha-deleyka,* cited in n.4

above. This passage is from a letter to his sister in Israel, written from the Bialystok ghetto at the end of July 1943. The letter begins on p. 138, this passage begins on page 141.

88. Shalev, *Tosyah Altman, Meha-hanhagah Ha-rashit,* 127 and notes 28 and 29. Korczak, *Lehavot Ba-efer,* 53–6.

89. Ringelblum, *Notes from the Warsaw Ghetto,* entry of May 19, 1942, 273–74, from the 1974 Sloan translation.

90. Ibid.

91. Ibid.

III. G·E·R·M·A·N S·C·H·O·L·A·R·S A·N·D T·H·E H·O·L·O·C·A·U·S·T

Patricia von Papen-Bodek

Anti-Jewish Research of the Institut zur Erforschung der Judenfrage in Frankfurt am Main between 1939 and 1945

UNDER THE THIRD REICH, A NEW EXTRA-UNIVERSITY DISCIPLINE emerged: *Judenforschung,* or research on Jews and Jerusalem. In its wake, anti-Jewish research institutions mushroomed throughout the Reich, providing the regime with quasi-scholarly legitimization. If not directly employed by the Ministries of Propaganda or the Interior, or by the Foreign Office, the Reichsstelle für Sippenforschung, or the Reichssicherheitshauptamt (RSHA), their personnel closely collaborated with these state agencies. During the war, anti-Jewish institutions were also set up in France, Italy, and Hungary with German "support" as well. These institutes built on existing local anti-Semitic networks.

In this essay I will examine the work of one of these German institutes, Alfred Rosenberg's so-called Außenstelle der Hohen Schule der NSDAP, or Institut zur Erforschung der Judenfrage. Until its inauguration in Frankfurt in March 1941, the Berlin Reichsinstitut für Geschichte des Neuen Deutschland, with its branch the Forschungsabteilung Judenfrage in Munich, claimed to be the center for anti-Jewish historical research in Germany. However, The Institute for the Study of the Jewish Question in Berlin (after 1939, Antisemitische Aktion), affiliated with the Ministry of Propaganda, preceded the latter.[1] In April 1939, a number of state churches founded the Institute for the Study of Jewish Influence on German Church Life in Eisenach.[2] Figure 1 at the end of this chapter provides an overview.

Since we still lack a monograph on the Außenstelle, I will summarize the existing data, hitherto scattered in several studies by Reinhard Bollmus,[3] Max Weinreich,[4] and Helmut Heiber,[5] or, more recently, in works by Willem de Vries,[6] Maria Kühn-Ludewig,[7] Dieter Schiefelbein,[8] Anja Heuss,[9] and Gabriele Steinmacher,[10] as well as in my own.[11]

In January 1939, the city of Frankfurt combined its municipal Judaica collection into a library institute and lent it to the Party for scholarly purposes.[12] Thus the collection remained the city's property and its custodian was simultaneously a municipal employee as well as a staff member of the Party. On February 10, 1939, Martin Bormann, chief of staff for Hitler's deputy Hess, agreed to the library's merger with Rosenberg's office. Because of an impending lawsuit against his former employer Reichsinstitut's president Walter Frank, however, Wilhelm Grau could be employed only temporarily by the city. Both Dieter Schiefelbein and I[13] have shown the rivalries that existed between Frank and Grau over the leadership in anti-Jewish studies. As of December 1941, the Außenstelle incorporated private libraries from the confiscated apartments of deported Frankfurt Jews. On March 21, 1942, the Finance Ministry of the Reich decreed that confiscated Jewish libraries all over the Reich were to be sent to Frankfurt. Up until April 1943, the Außenstelle thus integrated 100,000 volumes into its holdings.[14] With Alfred Rosenberg's nomination as Minister for the Occupied Territories in the East in July 1941, in addition to his position as the representative for the Party's entire ideological training and education, and with the expansion of the war, the Außenstelle's library grew even more, due to the ever-increasing looting of Judaica. While the city paid for the library's organization, the Party financed its research until 1942, when it took over all salaries.[15]

After Grau's lawsuit against Frank was settled (January 1940), Rosenberg was able to nominate him as director of the Außenstelle. Thus Grau served as director of the Frankfurt Judaica library as well as of the Außenstelle until October 1942. Prior to his Frankfurt engagement, he had set up the Forschungsabteilung Judenfrage in 1936 and directed it until April 1938. Grau had already listed Frankfurt's holdings of 1936 for the Reichsinstitut, which wanted to incorporate them into its Forschungsabteilung. Mayor Krebs, however, wished to preserve the treasure for his city. A contemporary American observer thus called Grau the "spiritus rector" of the Nazification of Jewish history.[16] Incidentally, Grau's death in October 2000 passed by entirely unnoticed by the German—even the local—press.

Between mid-July and the beginning of October 1940, Grau led the Paris unit of the Einsatzstab Rosenberg,[17] which seized Judaica for the Frankfurt library. The Einsatzstab Rosenberg, founded in July 1940 after the campaign in the West, was assigned to seize archives and libraries of ideological adversaries and to transfer them to Germany for research purposes. After September 30, 1942, the Einsatzstab functioned officially as *Wehrmachtsgefolge*.[18] It was Grau who suggested, from the outset, that the Einsatzstab should also seize the private libraries of immigrants in Paris.[19] Dieter Schiefelbein has shown Grau's contribution to the Außenstelle's establishment. However, Mayor Friedrich Krebs[20] was also actively involved in that he advised Grau, whom he visited in Paris, to extend his search for Judaica to Bordeaux as well[21] and suggested that Rosenberg should seize Norwegian libraries and archives just as he had done in France, the Netherlands, and Belgium. He also started negotiating with the Gestapo for Polish Judaica.

INAUGURATION

Between March 26 and March 28, 1941, the Außenstelle was inaugurated in Frankfurt's city hall[22] in the presence of two members of the Reichsinstitut's expert committee, Professor Hans Günther and Eugen Fischer.[23] After the Foreign Office's explicit invitation, representatives of Germany, Hungary, Romania, Bulgaria, Denmark, Belgium, Holland, and Norway talked about anti-Jewish measures in their respective countries.[24] The Party covered their expenses via the Foreign Office. Hitler himself reviewed with Rosenberg what could be publicly proclaimed. The press covered the event extensively.

Grau's opening speech was a plea for a Jew-free Europe.[25] The topics of the work sessions included "Jewish Emancipation in Southeast Europe and Its End" (Klaus Schickert),[26] "The Jewish Question in the Near East" (Dr. Giselher Wirsing),[27] "Population-Policy and Economic Problems of a European Total Solution of the Jewish Question" (Peter-Heinz Seraphim),[28] and "Racial Political Preconditions of a Solution to the Jewish Question" (Walter Gross's topic as head of the Party's Racial Political Office).[29] Rosenberg's final address on "The Jewish Question as a World Problem," which also asked for a Jew-free Europe, was broadcast from Berlin as well as the radio stations at Frankfurt, Cologne, Vienna, Königsberg, and Weichsel[30] because of the coup d' état in Yugoslavia.[31] The *Rheinischen Blätter* summarized the Institute's goals as laying the scholarly foundations for preventive measures of a future return of Jewry. Frankfurt now claimed to possess the largest library on Jewry worldwide (350,000 volumes).[32]

PUBLICATIONS

In conjunction with Peter Heinz Seraphim, Grau edited the institute's journal, *Weltkampf: Die Judenfrage in Geschichte und Gegenwart,* which served as a platform for anti-Semites all over Europe. In 1941, 6,000 copies of the first issue appeared in Germany, where most subscribers were primary-school teachers. One thousand copies were also published in Romanian, since it included the address by the Romanian participant, Dr. Cuza. Issue 2 of 1942, which dealt with the Jewish Question in France as seen by French authors, appeared also in a 2,000-copy French edition. Both issues were well received in French and Romanian circles.[33]

Grau included bibliographical information on anti-Semitica in *Weltkampf,* which he had started in 1935–36 in the *Historische Zeitschrift,*[34] as well as a calendar of events regarding the Jewish Question worldwide. Just as all other journals of anti-Jewish institutes, the *Weltkampf* followed the political agenda: after the German invasion of the Soviet Union, it featured the "Tsarist Anti-Jewish Legislation and Its Effect on the Jewish Problem in East and Central Europe," Pohl's "Yiddish Literature in the Soviet Union," and Seraphim's report on the opening of the Institut für deutsche Ostarbeit, Cracow.[35] Members of the Außenstelle also published in the German-speaking European daily press.[36] While Johannes Pohl, for example, reviewed Latvian Yiddish journals on the front page of *Deutsche Zeitung im Ostland* in December 1942 in order to conclude that Bolshevism and the Jews had to be defeated, Otto Paul denounced Jews as warmongers in the *Deutsche Zeitung in den Niederlanden* in June 1943.

In 1941, the Außenstelle published a brochure entitled *Schrifttum zur Judenfrage* in collaboration with the Party's Amt Schrifttumspflege in its series for ideological instruction. The brochure praised Grau for pioneering work in this new field.[37] In 1937, he had provided a textbook entitled *Die Judenfrage in der deutschen Geschichte,* which—updated in 1942—accused the Jews of having launched the war, which would end only once the Jewish Question had been resolved. In 1943, he republished three essays in *Die Erforschung der Judenfrage: Aufgabe und Organisation*[38] and had his Frankfurt opening speech reprinted.[39]

STAFF

Grau's staff included Dr. Otto Paul,[40] who headed the institute's reading room between April 1942 and October 1943,[41] and Dr. Kuno Schmidt, who was in charge of the Judaica collection.[42] After January 1942, the historian Friedrich Cornelius[43] organized the institute's journals as well as its subject catalogue. In accordance with Grau's plan, he differentiated between non-Judaica and Judaica with such subdivisions as Talmud, ritual murder, and so on. Dr. Fritz Zschaeck, a Frankfurt *Sippenforscher* (genealogist),[44] built up the photo archive.[45] Grau systematically installed a press archive: eighty journals were read on a daily basis, forty-one of which were foreign.[46] In the *Zentralblatt für Bibliothekswesen*,[47] he admitted that his library lacked anti-Semitica (which the Forschungsabteilung in Munich was renowned for), and that the organization of Hebraica had been postponed in favor of work with Talmudic sources.

The Prussian State Librarian Johannes Pohl (1904–60) was hired for the acquisition of books and replaced by Dr. Erhard Selbmann after[48] having joined the Sonderkommando Rosenberg (as Haupteinsatzführer) in June 1940. In March 1941, he was appointed head of the Hebraica collection and charged with the edition of a Talmud lexicon.[49] Pohl, like Grau, represented the quintessential anti-Jewish expert, whose career thrived only during the Hitler regime: after contributions to the Propaganda Ministry's *Mitteilungen zur Judenfrage* and the *Nationalsozialistische Monatshefte*,[50] Pohl also produced more "scholarly" pieces for the *Zentralblatt für Bibliothekswesen*.[51] In March 1939, he had offered his expertise to Nazi lawyer Grimm for the impending Grynszpan trial.[52] After Reichsinstituts-member Kittel[53] had torn apart his draft for a *Habilitation in Talmudistik*, his chances for an academic career seemed to be over (March 1940). Instead of the Talmud lexicon,[54] Pohl's *Talmud-Geist* appeared in 1941,[55] its Lithuanian and Latvian translations and *Die Religion des Talmud* in 1942.[56] The first edition of *Talmud-Geist* sold 20,000 copies, and a slightly shortened version was distributed in 1944, again in 20,000 copies. His hopes for Serbian and Hungarian editions, however, never materialized.[57] Pohl wrote on Jews in his *Einsatzorte* in the Ukraine, Lithuania, and Greece, for the *Weltkampf,* and in 1942, on Lithuanian and Greek Jewish topics[58] in *Die Judenfrage,* the Propaganda Ministry's journal. In 1942, the ministry's Antisemitische Aktion commissioned him to work on a project on "The Jewish State as well as Plans to resettle the Jews."[59] In November 1943, he moved to another of Rosenberg's offices (under the jurisdiction of his office Überstaatliche Mächte), the Welt-Dienst: Internationale Korrespondenz zur Aufklärung über die Judenfrage (Bad Schwalbach), which had surpassed the Außenstelle's reach of foreign collaborators at this point.

AGENDA

After the annexation of the Sudetenland, Rosenberg requested that the Reich Commissioner for the Sudeten area, Konrad Henlein, confiscate all Jewish literature.[60] In May 1941, Grau suggested to Rosenberg that the Einsatzstab's activities ought to be extended to Spain, Italy, Romania, Hungary, and Slovakia.[61] Grau, his successor, Schickert, and Pohl supervised the Einsatzstab's lootings of Jewish libraries. Frits Hoogewoud has chronicled the Einsatzstab's theft of libraries in the Netherlands, going into great depth in the case of Amsterdam.[62] Pohl, Schmidt, Selbmann, and Ms. Hohlfeld participated in the plunder of Athens, Salonica,[63] and many Greek villages. Pohl transferred Greek Judaica, Yivo's holdings from Vilna,[64] and the Judaica collection of Lenin's library in Minsk[65] to Frankfurt. In Volo, he seized Rabbi Moshe Pessah's library.[66] By contrast, the institute's request to have the Lublin Yeshiva Library transferred to Frankfurt was turned down by the district governor.[67] Stanislao Pugliese's account describes the Einsatzstab's confiscations in Rome in October 1943.[68]

HISTORY OF JEWISH GHETTOS IN EUROPE

In early 1941, after the erection of Polish ghettos,[69] the Außenstelle addressed several municipal administrations for their ghetto maps. At the end of February 1942, it appealed to the Gebietskommissariate in "Reichskommissariat Ostland" to forward all plans of old and newly erected ghettos, since it elaborated a *Comprehensive History of Jewish Ghettos throughout Europe.*[70] So far, we know of only one response from Lithuania,[71] but the sole surviving spiritual leader of Salonican Jewry also reports on the Einsatzstab's inquiry into the place of the ghetto.[72]

COLLABORATION WITH THE FOREIGN OFFICE

Anti-Jewish experts, however, became even more directly involved in anti-Jewish persecution, since they stood in close contact with the Foreign Office and other anti-Jewish research institutions: the Foreign Office's Judenreferent Franz Rademacher sent them secret reports of German consulates, such as that of the German delegation to Copenhagen of January 7, 1942, on the Danish discussion of Jewry's influence in Denmark[73] as well as the report of September 21, 1940,[74] of the German delegation in Athens on the distribution of Jews in Greece, which he forwarded to the Reichsinstitut's genealogist, Euler. He also continuously informed them on anti-Jewish legislation worldwide.[75]

In return, the institute received expertise about Jewish descent. Let us consider, for instance, the case of the request of the German embassy in Paris of January 1942, regarding how Sephardic Jews in occupied France should be treated. The Association Culturelle Sépharadite de Paris had requested the exemption of all Sephardim residing in the occupied zone from anti-Jewish measures, since racially they were not considered Jews.[76] Since the German occupier of Salonica, it argued, treated Sephardic Israelites as Aryans of Mosaic faith, the Germans in France would certainly do likewise.[77] Subsequently, the delegate to the Parisian embassy from mid-June 1940 until the end of November 1943, Rudolf Schleier (who subsequently headed the so-called Infostelle XIV or Antijüdische Auslandsorganisation), had inquired at the Foreign Office on how to further proceed.[78] By mid-February 1942 Rademacher replied that special treatment of the Sephardim was out of the question. That Salonican Jews were treated differently seemed incredible; the German representative in Athens had been ordered to end "special treatment," if it was in fact in place. While the Reichsinstitut's genealogist, Euler, referred to a memorandum entitled "On the Question of Racial Categorization and History of the Sephardim" that his colleague Clemens Hoberg had elaborated for the Military Commander in France,[79] Grau felt that special treatment was "neither racially justified nor historically legitimized and especially not politically permissable."[80] On February 26, 1942, the Foreign Office forwarded to Euler and Grau the report of the German consulate in Salonica,[81] which argued that Jews in occupied France should not be treated differently from Jews abroad.[82]

In October 1942 the Foreign Office inquired about Iranian Jews in occupied France with Euler and Grau, at the Office of Racial Policy.[83] The Ministry of the Interior had asked the Foreign Office to examine a statement of the former Iranian consulate in Paris according to which Iranians of Mosaic faith were not Jews, but gentiles of Iranian descent. The ministry also wanted to have the descent of the Mosaic Georgians and Afghans examined.[84] On October 23, 1942, Euler sent two expert opinions to the Foreign Office.[85] The first, on the Persians and Afghans of Mosaic faith, assumed a much higher number of Persian Jews and stated that their racial and sociopolitical development clearly set them apart from world Jewry. The second essay, on Caucasian and Georgian members of Mosaic faith, suggested again that the number of Jews concerned was higher[86] and that the Nazi authorities should treat them *differently* from other Jews.

Otto Paul could but report that the Einsatzstab was currently examining Karaites[87] and confirmed that he had received statements by Euler, the head of the Security Police and the SD. On November 6, 1942, the Foreign Office forwarded Euler's statements to the Racial Political Office, to the delegate of the Party's organization abroad, and to Germany's ambassador to the Soviet Union.

Gerhard Kittel confirmed Euler's figures and suggested that anthropological examinations be made of the Parisian Iranians of Mosaic faith. In contrast to Iranian Jews, special treatment of Caucasian Jews was justified.[88] However, although Euler and Kittel pleaded for special treatment of the Caucasian Jews in contrast to the Office of Racial Policy, on June 2, 1943, the Foreign Office noted internally that, on the basis of expert reports, the questionable Jews had been included in the general measures.[89]

The Foreign Office sent Euler's memorandum "On the Genealogical Categorization of the So-called Portuguese Jews in the Netherlands" of January 1943,[90] on the occasion of a Dutch petition directly to its offices in The Hague and Brussels, to the Außenstelle and the Propaganda Ministry's Anti-Semitische Aktion.

EUROPEAN COLLABORATION OF ANTI-JEWISH INSTITUTES

By January 1942, anti-Jewish institutes had been founded in Ancona and Paris, which, like the Fascist Party's Racial Office under Dr. Giovanni Preziosi, the Belgian Lamprichts Movement, the Racial Office of the Dutch Ministry of Propaganda, and the Danish Anti-Jewish League, were in contact with the Außenstelle. The Italian Ministry for Popular Culture wanted to imitate its statutes. Initially used to promote racial consciousness, the Italian centers soon turned into organs for locating Jews.[91] In 1942, Romanians as well as Croats wanted to send fellows to Frankfurt.[92] In April 1943, the Palestinian *Großmufti* of Jerusalem visited the Institute.[93]

As of April 1940 the Außenstelle collaborated with the Institut für deutsche Ostarbeit, Cracow, which had been established by General Governor Hans Frank. In the autumn, its Referat Judenforschung was founded.[94] The Referat Judenforschung, under Dr. Sommerfeldt, limited its work to the Polish territory for which it intended to compile a bibliography on the Jewish Question as part of a more comprehensive bibliography on the question of Eastern Jewry. A project on the Jewish Question in Galicia, set up as a history of permanent struggle between German *Bürger* and Eastern Jews, was also planned. Further projects included a study of the Jewish Question in the Polish state and, copying the Frankfurt model, a collection of sources concerning anti-Jewish movements in Poland. The institute's first session coincided with the Außenstelle's inauguration (March 27–29, 1941); its director, Dr. Wilhelm Coblitz, as well as Heinz Seraphim belonged to the latter's corresponding members next to Friedrich Kienzl, the head of Tobis Filmkunst dramaturgy in Berlin, as well as the Tübingen historian Josef Vogt.[95] Seraphim spoke at Frankfurt's as well as at Cracow's inaugurations and published in their respective journals.[96]

Although the Parisian Institut d'Etudes des Questions Juives had a French secretary general, Paul Sézille, it was the brainchild of and thus supervised by SS-Hauptsturmführer Theodor Dannecker (1913–45), the head of the Judenreferat des Reichssicherheitshauptamtes in Paris, and was financed by the German embassy.[97] Dannecker considered himself to be an Außendienststelle of the European Judenkommissar Heydrich,[98] and as such was attached to the embassy as

Judenberater. Thus anti-Jewish propaganda was placed under a French umbrella. The retired aviation officer of colonial troops, Sézille, was one of the closest collaborators of Louis Darquier de Pellepoix, founder of the Rassemblement Anti-Juif de France in 1936 and Xavier Vallat's successor as Commissaire Général aux Questions Juives in 1942. As Secretary General, Sézille was thus connected to the embassy, the Propagandastaffel, and the Gestapo. He reported to Dannecker on a regular basis. It is possible that Sézille even aspired to replace the Commissioner General for Jewish Affairs,[99] Vallat. Originally Dannecker would have liked to install his institute in an Office Général Juif, but when the Commissariat was founded on March 29, 1941, it abstained from propaganda. On the part of the embassy, Legationssekretär Buscher, counsellor Schwendemann, and, as of October, Dr. Peter Klassen[100] of its information service, were charged with supervising the institute's activities.[101]

The institute's constitutive session took place in February 1941 in Dannecker's presence. Closely observing the regime's anti-Jewish politics, the institute wanted to bring it in line with the German model. At its inauguration on May 11, 1941, in a former building of the Jewish art dealer Rosenberg at 21, rue de la Boétie (which Dannecker had seized for the institute), the Security Service kept conspiciously absent in order not to reveal its role to the public. In addition to French and German members, the institute included Persian members as well.[102]

Dannecker suggested conversion of the institute into a branch of the Außenstelle, mainly in order to exclude the Propagandastaffel (subordinated to the Military Commander in France) from its activities. That the institute considered the Außenstelle its headquarters (*"Mutterhaus"*) is also confirmed by Dannecker's report of February 1942: "The offices concerned within the RSHA have agreed that the Institute is aided by the Frankfurt Institute (Reichsleiter Rosenberg) which is run by the Party. Since December 1941 a representative from Frankfurt is in Paris. He is equipped with a written order by Reichsleiter Rosenberg."[103] The institute's association with Frankfurt and the simultaneous elimination of the Propagandastaffel indicate a radicalization process.

From September 1941 to mid-January 1942, it organized the exhibition *Le Juif et la France* in the Palais Berlitz near the place de l'Opéra with documents about "The Eternal Jew,"[104] which had been shown previously in Munich, Berlin, and Rome.[105] It is noteworthy that *Weltkampf* author Schwartz reported that, although the public (roughly 600,000 visitors)[106] allegedly cut across all classes, French functionaries abstained from the exhibit. He noted further that the Minister of Culture had refused to recommend it to French schools[107] and that Parisian theaters did not put French anti-Semitic plays, which had been so popular at the turn of the century, on their agendas.[108] Not only did Schwartz describe the institute as a French project,[109] thereby purposefully camouflaging its real origin, he also falsely doubled the number of visitors of the exhibition in order to pretend that it enjoyed enormous popularity. In reality it was not a success.[110]

The institute's journal *La Question Juive en France et dans le monde* had originated from the collaboration of the German embassy (Dr. Peter Klassen) with the Einsatzstab.[111] Rosenberg had charged *Weltkampf* author Schwarz with launching and supervising *La Question Juive*,[112] which Schwarz modeled after the *Weltkampf*. The actual collaboration, however, was limited to three editions of *La Question Juive* between April and September 1942, with three articles by Gerhard Lehmann (1900–87) that were translated from German. In 1942, the journal was distributed in 5,000 copies, 2,000 of which went to personalities of public life. The rest were sold.

In addition, the institute recruited a task force that actively supported Aryanization measures. Next to its propaganda campaign, its *direct* involvement in the persecution of Jews needs to be emphasized. On July 1, 1941, Dannecker and Sézille formed a *section spéciale des recherches,* which consisted of two commissars and several inspectors whose task it was to verify the flood of denunciations before alarming either the French police or the Gestapo. These inspectors sometimes delivered their victims straight to their deaths. Consider, for example, the case of one of these men, Henri Lagarde, who had a M. Zilbermann arrested. Zilbermann was subsequently deported to Auschwitz, where he died.[113]

The closing of the institute in the summer of 1942 coincided with the beginning of the deportations. In May 1942, Vallat was replaced by Darquier de Pellepoix;[114] in August, Dannecker was replaced by Heinz Röthke. The institute was transformed, as Dannecker had planned from the very beginning,[115] into an entirely French tool. The successor institute, l'Institut d'Etude des Questions

Juives et Ethno-Raciales, was established by the propaganda services of the Commissariat. Louis Prax, its propaganda director between December 1942 and the summer of 1943, had been introduced there by Dr. Klassen. Thus it is safe to say that Prax acted as the embassy's agent. The new institute's director was Vallat's ethnoracial expert of 1941,[116] Dr. George Montandon, translator of Otmar von Verschuer's *Handbuch zur Rassenhygiene*. Montandon was feared for his *examens ethnoracials*, on which his clients' fate depended.[117] The institute was inaugurated in spring 1943.[118] It continued to publish *La Question Juive* and took on some of Sézille's staff.

Since the Commissariat aimed at legitimizing its persecutory politics by promoting "scholarly" anti-Semitism, Darquier de Pellepoix founded a chair for the history of Judaism at the Sorbonne in November 1942, to which Henri Labroue (1880–1964) was appointed.[119] Again, due to the embassy's support, Labroue had founded the Bordeaux Institute for the Study of the Jewish Question in 1941,[120] before teaching courses on anti-Jewish measures in France in past centuries as well as international studies on the Jewish Question. In an interview with the *Pariser Zeitung* in December 1942, Labroue stated his desire to become personally acquainted with the Frankfurt Institute.[121] In 1944, he travelled to Eppenheim/Taunus, Frankfurt, and Berlin for a series of conferences.[122] However, perhaps also as a result of the failure of his courses, Labroue was also a prolific journalist[123] who operated in a European context, launching his campaign not only in France but in the Netherlands and Hungary as well.[124]

While Sézille's research section denounced Jews to the police, Montandon's *examens* threatened or saved his clients' lives. Thus, both not only legitimized persecutory policies ideologically but participated in them personally. Both profited from the occupation in that they were able to pursue their very own agendas.

In July 1942, the Außenstelle established a branch in Litzmannstadt (Lódz) under the Breslau theologian Adolf Wendel,[125] who had been chosen for this task by Seraphim. The Party confirmed three employees to conduct racial as well as genetic research in the ghetto.[126] Wendel's and Grau's dismissals on October 28, 1942, appear to be interrelated. While Grau's fall was a result of his Catholic past, disclosed by Walter Frank, Rosenberg discovered that Wendel had belonged to the Verein zur Abwehr des Antisemitismus until December 1932 and therefore closed the branch altogether! As of January 1943, 3,000 volumes had been transferred to Frankfurt.[127]

On October 28, 1943, Rosenberg appointed Klaus Schickert interim director of the Außenstelle, an indication of the reinforced anti-Jewish campaign by the state.[128] The second, enlarged edition of Schickert's *Die Judenfrage in Ungarn: Jüdische Assimilation und antisemitische Bewegung im 19. und 20. Jahrhundert* (first published in 1937 by the Institut zum Studium der Judenfrage),[129] appeared in 1943.[130] That it did *not* constitute mere historical reading is shown by the fact that the German delegation in Bratislava/Pressburg requested it as "foundational work" (*Arbeitsgrundlage*),[131] and that Schickert thanked the Antisemitische Aktion for its support in his introduction.[132] On Easter 1944, the *Donauzeitung* (Belgrade) welcomed the second edition as a piece of support for the newly established anti-Jewish Hungarian Institute. After deportations from the Carpathians and Transylvania began, Schickert's publisher informed him of an augmented paper contingent of 15,000 copies for a third edition. The Ministry of Propaganda wanted him to write a second book to take into account the "purification of Hungary" then underway.[133]

Schickert collaborated with Zoltán Bosnyák, who, since 1942, had led the then privately funded Hungarian Institute for Research into the Jewish Question in Budapest.[134] He mentioned it in his essay, "Hungary's Jewish Question as an Economic and Spiritual Problem," in the May/June 1943 issue of *Volk im Osten* dedicated entirely to the Jewish question and edited by the Romanian Deutsche Volksgruppe. Next to essays from Peter Heinz Seraphim,[135] Otto Paul, Alexandru Cuza, and others, Schickert emphasized that Jewish private property had been left untouched so far by any legislation and argued that the elimination of all Jewish components from historical narratives had to precede the racial solution to the Jewish question.[136]

In November 1943, Bosnyák presented his institute in Wilhelm Ziegler's *Europäischer Wissenschaftsdienst*.[137] The translation of works by Bosnyák and by Kolosváry-Borcsa, the editor of the journal *Függetlenség*, and the president of the Hungarian Press-Chamber,[138] was among the works in progress that Schickert listed in February 1944. This translation was supposed to appear under the title *Zwei madjarische Autoren zur Judenfrage* in 5,000 copies.[139] In his report on the Außenstelle's activities of March 1944, Schickert argued "that anti-Jewish foreign states felt supported in their beliefs when they saw how much we participate in their efforts."[140] On July 2, 1944, Pohl argued in Kolosváry's journal[141] that, according to the Talmud, gentiles deserved death mercilessly and that there was a clear connection between the Talmud and the terror bombings. It is likely that he gave this interview at a meeting of the *Welt-Dienst* with Hungarian anti-Semites at Eppenheim/Taunus on June 23, 1944.[142]

After the German occupation of Hungary in March 1944, two members of the Hungarian Institute in Budapest, László Endre and Vitéz Kolosváry-Borcsa, were appointed undersecretaries of state in charge of Jewish affairs at the Hungarian Ministry of the Interior. Institute director Bosnyák, whose office was part of the Department for Jewish Affairs at the Ministry of the Interior, assisted in the planning and implementation of the subsequent anti-Jewish decrees.[143] The institute, closely connected with the Außenstelle, was used by the RSHA and the Foreign Office to expedite their *Judenaktion.* The new Reich Plenipotentiary Dr. Edmund Veesenmayer appointed Judenreferent of Amt VII of the RSHA, SS-Hauptsturmführer Dr. Heinz Ballensiefen, as his propaganda expert for Jewish matters. Like Schickert, he, too, was a member of the Antijüdischer Aktionsausschuß of the Foreign Office. Prior to entering the RSHA, Ballensiefen had worked for Ziegler's Institut zur Erforschung der Judenfrage. In mid-May 1944 the Hungarian Institute was transformed into a public institution. Ballensiefen supervised Bosnyák's institutional journal *Harc* (Combat).[144] *Harc* was a weekly of eight pages and appeared in 50,000 copies (its first edition even in 80,000 copies). By June 1944, 180,000 copies were distributed. The Information Division of the Foreign Office furnished material but also requested that Consul Dr. Grell, Judenreferent at the embassy, send the half-monthly *Mitteilungen* for the missions to the editors.[145] While the institute as well as its organ were financed by the SD, it looked as if its expenses were covered by individual and institutional contributions as well as by sales from publications.[146]

Schickert intended to invite foreign anti-Semitic lecturers to Frankfurt University to publish hand- and sourcebooks on the Jewish Question, especially on the history of European anti-Judaism. This *History of Anti-Judaism from Emancipation to National Socialism* was conceived as a collection of essays; a third of the appointed authors were foreign. Dr. Fritz Zschaeck, for example, compiled a bibliography of Wilhelm Marr's works.[147] A new edition of the *Handbuch zur Judenfrage* was supervised by library assistant Herwig Hnizdo, who had assumed the pen name of Hartner.[148] A *Lexikon der Juden in der Musik*,[149] compiled as a reference book at the request of the NSDAP-Reichsleitung, was published as volume 2 of the series *Veröffentlichungen des Institutes der NSDAP zur Erforschung der Judenfrage*.[150] It was supposed to be a guide to music instructors, journalists, and theatre directors, as well as cultural policymakers.[151] While the first edition of 1940—supported by the Reichsstelle für Sippenforschung—listed German and Eastern European Jews, the three consecutive editions, which were updated with the help of informers from Germany and abroad (the *Lexikon* appealed to its readers to denounce Jewish musicians who had escaped registration to the Dienststelle,[152] increasingly included Jews of the occupied territories[153] in order to indicate to the Wehrmacht or other NS agencies where Jewish musicians resided or where they had emigrated.[154] Schickert himself contributed Hungarian Jewish names.[155] His report of March 8, 1944, foresaw the publication of Elisabeth Frenzel's *Lexikon der Juden auf dem Theater*.[156]

Schickert supported the Gauleiter's efforts to establish a chair of anti-Jewish studies at Frankfurt University.[157] Between November 1943 and February 1944 he lectured in Stettin's Kulturamt, in Hesse-Nassau's Rassenpolitisches Amt, in front of Hesse-Nassau's Hitler Youth, in Darmstadt, in Worms, and at Tübingen University. He prepared his visits to Southeast Europe with a special *Weltkampf* article dedicated to "The Exploration of the Jewish Question in Southeastern Europe,"[158] in which he emphasized the necessity of collaboration and argued that the state ought to secure sources that still belonged to Jews or Jewish communities. Between March 15 and April 30, 1944, he scheduled a trip through Slovakia, Hungary, Romania, Bulgaria, Greece, Serbia, and Croatia in order to meet with the delegations' *Sachbearbeiter* and the Deutschen Wissenschaftlichen Institute to discuss future collaboration that he hoped to win through the publication of a special *Weltkampf* issue on Southeastern Europe. For this issue, which was supposed to appear in local languages,[159] Schickert hoped to secure local contributors. For Hungary he recommended the historian Elemar Malyusz, and for Romania, Georg Bratianu (who

planned a contribution on minority rights at the Versailles conferences, 1919) as well as the former foreign minister Michael Manoilescu.
In Bulgaria Schickert collaborated with Professor Lubomir Wladikin
of Sofia University. He believed that Bulgaria would furnish rich
materials for a monograph on Sephardic Jewry. In Serbia, Schickert
made contact with Professor Schmaus of the Deutsches Wissen-
schaftliches Institut.

THE ANTI-JEWISH CONFERENCE IN CRACOW

At the request of the Foreign Office, Schickert joined the Antijüdischer Aktionsausschuß in mid-February 1944. In his report, he testified that the foreign political activity of the Außenstelle was identical
with the official foreign policy: "The personal union is an advantage
for the latter because this field is professionally dealt with, and for the
institute because its possibilities are improved."[160] Schickert edited a
Yearbook of Jewish World Politics for the Foreign Office, which was to
appear without mention of any editors and to prove the existence of
a Jewish world policy and its responsibility for the war. This *Yearbook*
appears to have been part of the preparations for the supposedly historical congress on "Jewry in World Politics in Our Age," which
Rosenberg planned to hold in Cracow with Hitler's approval and in
collaboration with the RSHA, the Foreign and Propaganda Ministries, and the General Governor. That it was to function as an anti-
Jewish campaign was to be kept highly secret.[161]

PRELIMINARY CONCLUSIONS

1. We have seen the relatively small, yet tight network of anti-Jewish
experts and their interinstitutional exchange. *Judenforschung* clearly
provided a niche for frustrated and unaccomplished opportunistic
academics.

2. If we compare the actual availability of catalogued books of
both libraries, Forschungsabteilung and Außenstelle, the latter does
not come off as splendidly as its public self-promotion would have it.
Despite its immense lootings,[162] the Außenstelle's library carried only
roughly a quarter more catalogued titles than its rival—and its staff
appears to have grown *less* qualified as the war continued. The hold-

ings of their biggest rival, the RSHA, remain to be explored.[163] For the time being, the online bookseller Werner Schroeder has begun to reconstruct the Judaica holdings of the RSHA Library.[164] According to Dov Schidorsky's estimation, the Judaica Department's stock comprised between 200,000 and 300,000 volumes,[165] which is, of course, roughly only half of the Außenstelle's 550,000 items. A comparison, however, between the Außenstelle's and the RSHA's research output will be possible only after we have thoroughly analyzed to what extent and in which way these holdings were used by the respective institutions.

3. Members of the Außenstelle resuscitated the ritual-murder legend to revive anti-Judaism; they crafted pieces of expertise to legitimize the state's anti-Jewish persecution; and they actively confiscated Jewish property. Yet, they also tried to strengthen the party's ideological cohesion by producing handbooks mainly for internal purposes.[166] The goal of their massive press campaign was to forge a German *völkisch* consciousness.

4. Schickert and Pohl as well as Ballensiefen (RSHA) had, prior to their engagement with the Außenstelle, published for the Propaganda Ministry's Institut zum Studium der Judenfrage. Pohl continued to publish in its organ *Die Judenfrage* even as an employee of the Außenstelle. Schickert, too, was approached by the Ministry of Propaganda to update his *Judenfrage in Ungarn,* and it was in Ziegler's *Europäischem Wissenschaftsdienst* that Bosnyák presented his Hungarian Institute. This clearly shows that the Propaganda Ministry won over Rosenberg's authors.

5. The Außenstelle clandestinely helped to install anti-Jewish institutions and set up journals dedicated solely to the "Jewish Question." It thereby instigated and propelled complicity in its crimes. That the Hungarian *Harc* was financed by the SD[167] suggests that the RSHA had taken over the Außenstelle's lead in anti-Jewish "research" at the end of the war.[168]

6. There can be no doubt that the Außenstelle could not have had such an impact had it not been supported in its crimes by many regional anti-Semitic networks. Further research on these local networks is necessary in order to determine whether the history of the Außenstelle can also be written from another perspective—namely, from the angle of these diverse entities throughout Europe.

FIGURE 1: ANTI-JEWISH RESEARCH INSTITUTES IN EUROPE, 1935–1945

City	Name of Institute	Year	Sponsor	Director
GERMAN REICH				
Berlin	Institut zum Studium der Judenfrage, since 1939 Antisemitische Aktion	1935	Ministry of Propaganda	Wilhelm Ziegler
Berlin	Reichsinstitut für Geschichte des neuen Deutschland	1935	Ministry of Education	Walter Frank (–1941)
München	Forschungsabteilung Judenfrage (Branch of RGND)	1936	Ministry of Education	Wilhelm Grau (–1938), Karl R. Ganzer
Eisenach	Institut zur Erforschung und Beseitigung des jüdischen Einflusses auf das deutsche kirchliche Leben	1939	Evangelische Landeskirchen	Walter Grundmann
Nürnberg	Antijüdische Liga		Der Stürmer	Paul Wurm
Bad Schwalbach	Welt-Dienst. Internationales Institut zur Aufklärung über die Judenfrage	1939	Alfred Rosenberg, NSDAP	August Schirmer
Frankfurt	Außenstelle der Hohen Schule der NSDAP or Institut zur Erforschung der Judenfrage	1939	Alfred Rosenberg, NSDAP	Wilhelm Grau (–1942), Klaus Schickert (1943–1945)
GAU WARTHELAND				
Łódz (GG)	Branch of the Außenstelle	1942	Alfred Rosenberg	Adolf Wendel

GENERAL GOVERNMENT

Krakau (GG)	Institut für deutsche Ostarbeit—Judenreferat	1940	General Governor Hans Frank	Dr. Josef Sommerfeldt

ITALY

Ancona	Institute for the Study of the Jewish Question	1941	Fascist Party's Racial Office	Guido Podaliri, Dr. Giovanni Preziosi
Milano, Florence		1942	Ministry of Popular Culture	Alfredo Acito, Ugo Puccioni
Triest	Fascist Centro per lo Studio Problema Ebraico Centro Triestino per la Difesa della Razza	1942	Racial Office of the Ministry of Education	Ettore Martinoli
Bologna	Institute for the Study of Jewish Question	1943	Dr. Giovanni Preziosi	Dr. Mario Tirollo

FRANCE

Paris	Institut d'Etudes des Questions Juives (until 1943)	1941	RSHA, German Embassy	Paul Sézille
	Institut d'Etudes des Questions Juiveset Ethno-Raciales	1943		George Montandon
Bordeaux	Institute for the Study of the Jewish Question	1941		Henri Labroue

HUNGARY

Budapest	Hungarian Institute for Research into the Jewish Question	1944	RSHA, Heinz Ballensiefen	Zoltán Bosnyák

NOTES

1. By December 1939, the institute renamed itself Antisemitische Aktion, and, by February 1942, Anti-Jüdische Aktion. Its organ, *Die Judenfrage,* ceased publication in 1943.

2. Compare Susannah Heschel, "Theologen für Hitler: Walter Grundmann und das Institut zur Erforschung und Beseitigung des jüdischen Einflusses auf das deutsche kirchliche Leben," in *Christlicher Antijudaismus und Antisemitismus,* ed. Leonore Siegele-Wenschkewitz (Frankfurt am Main: Haag und Herchen, 1994), 125–70.

3. Reinhard Bollmus, "Zum Projekt einer nationalsozialistischen Alternativuniversität: Alfred Rosenberg's 'Hohe Schule,'" in *Erziehung und Schulung im Dritten Reich,* Bd. 2, ed. Manfred Heinemann (Stuttgart: Klett-Cotta, 1980), 125–52.

4. Max Weinreich, *Hitler's Professors: The Part of Scholarship in Germany's Crimes against the Jewish People* (New York: Yivo, 1946).

5. Helmut Heiber, *Walter Frank und sein Reichsinstitut für Geschichte des Neuen Deutschlands,* Bd. 13, *Quellen und Darstellungen zur Zeitgeschichte* (Stuttgart: DVA, 1966).

6. Willem de Vries, *Sonderstab Musik: Music Confiscations by the Einsatzstab Reichsleiter Rosenberg under the Nazi Occupation of Western Europe* (Amsterdam: Amsterdam University Press, 1997).

7. Maria Kühn-Ludewig, *Johannes Pohl (1904–1960) Judaist und Bibliothekar im Dienste Rosenbergs: Eine biographische Dokumentation* (Hannover: Laurentius, 2000).

8. Dieter Schiefelbein, "Das 'Institut zur Erforschung der Judenfrage Frankfurt am Main.'" Vorgeschichte und Gründung 1935–1939. Materialien Nr. 9 der Arbeitsstelle zur Vorbereitung des Frankfurter Lern- und Dokumentationszentrums des Holocaust, Fritz Bauer Institut in Gründung hrsg. In Zusammenarbeit mit dem Institut für Stadtgeschichte (Frankfurt am Main, 1994); and idem, "Das 'Institut zur Erforschung der Judenfrage Frankfurt am Main': Antisemitismus als Karrieresprungbrett im NS Staat," in *"Beseitigung des jüdischen Einflusses . . ." Antisemitische Forschung, Eliten und Karrieren im Nationalsozialismus, Jahrbuch 1998/1999 zur Geschichte und Wirkung des Holocaust,* ed. Fritz Bauer Institut (Frankfurt: Campus Verlag, 1999), 43–71.

9. Anja Heuss, *Kunst- und Kulturgutraub: Eine vergleichende Studie zur Besatzungspolitik der Nationalsozialisten in Frankreich und der Sowjetunion* (Heidelberg: C. Winter, 2000).

10. See Gabriele Steinmacher, "Jüdische Bibliotheken unter dem Nationalsozialismus: Bücherdiebstahl während des Zweiten Weltkrieges," in

Myosotis: Zeitschrift für Buchwesen 1 (1998): 3–12. Steinmacher, unfortunately, hardly indicates her sources.

11. Patricia von Papen-Bodek, "'Scholarly' Antisemitism During the Third Reich: The Reichsinstitut's Research on the 'Jewish Question,' 1935–1945" (doctoral diss., Columbia University, 1999); idem, "Schützenhelfe nationalsozialistischer Judenpolitik: Die 'Judenforschung' des 'Reichsinstituts für Geschichte des neuen Deutschland' 1935–1945," in *"Beseitigung des jüdischen Einflusses . . ." Antisemitische Forschung, Eliten und Karrieren im Nationalsozialismus: Jahrbuch 1998/1999 zur Geschichte und Wirkung des Holocaust,* ed. Fritz Bauer Institut (Frankfurt: Campus Verlag, 1999), 17–42; idem, "Vom engagierten Katholiken zum Rassenantisemiten: Die Karriere des Historikers der 'Judenfrage' Wilhelm Grau 1935–1945," in *Theologische Wissenschaft im 'Dritten Reich': Ein ökumenisches Projekt,* hrsg. von Georg Denzler and Leonore Siegele-Wenschkewitz (Frankfurt: Haag und Herchen, 2000), 68–113.

12. See Schiefelbein, "Antisemitismus als Karrieresprungbrett," 48, as well as Johanna Binder, "Stadtbibliothek 1939–1950," in *Bibliotheca Publica Francofurtensis: Textband 500 Jahre Stadt und Universitätsbibliothek Frankfurt am Main,* ed. Klaus Dieter Lehmann (Frankfurt am Main: Stadt und Universitätsbibliothek, 1984), 219–26. See also Ernst Loewy, "Die Judaica-Sammlung der Frankfurter Stadt- und Universitätsbibliothek," in *Bulletin des Leo Baeck Instituts* 8 (1965): 55–64.

13. See von Papen-Bodek, "The Radicalization of Anti-Jewish Historiography in the Work of Wilhelm Grau," in "'Scholarly' Anti-Semitism," 186–240, especially 210ff.; and idem, "Vom engagierten Katholiken zum Rassenantisemiten," 68–113.

14. See Anja Heuss, "Kulturgutraub im Nationalsozialismus," in *Newsletter* (Fritz Bauer Institut), Nr. 20 (Spring 2001): 42.

15. Aktenvermerk Wilhelm Grau vom 22. Dezember 1959 in IfZ Munich, 3857/67 Bestand ZS 1873, p. 18.

16. See Bernhard Weinryb, "Nazification of Jewish Learning," in *Jewish Review* 3, no. 1 (April 1945): 38.

17. On the Einsatzstab Rosenberg, see Joshua Starr, "Jewish Cultural Property under Nazi Control," in *Jewish Social Studies,* Nr. 12 (1950): 27–48; Donald E. Collins and Herbert P. Rothfeder, "The Einsatzstab Reichsleiter Rosenberg and the Looting of Jewish and Masonic Libraries during World War II," *Journal of Library History* 18 (winter 1983): 21–36; Yitzhak Arad, "Alfred Rosenberg and the 'Final Solution' in the Occupied Soviet Territories," *Yad Vashem Studies* 13 (1979): 263–86; Frits J. Hoogewoud, "The Nazi Looting of Books and Its American 'Antithesis': Selected Pictures from the Offenbach Archival Depot's Photographic History and Its Supplement,"

Studia Rosenthalia 261 (1992): 158–92; Peter M. Manasse, *Verschleppte Archive und Bibliotheken: Die Tätigkeiten des Einsatzstabes Rosenberg während des Zweiten Weltkrieges* (St. Ingbert: Röhrig Universitätsverlag, 1997); and Antje Rapmund, "Die deutsche Bibliothekspolitik in der Tschechoslowakei und in Polen während des Zweiten Weltkrieges" (doctoral diss., Berlin, 1993).

18. See Hoogewoud, "The Nazi Looting," 161.

19. See BA Berlin, NS 8/259, p. 17. On the plunderings of 38,000 Parisian private Jewish homes during the war and the redistribution of their belongings, see the account on the camp Tolbiac-Austerlitz under the Einsatzstab's command: Von Alexander Smoltczyk and Maurice Weiss, "Die Türme des Schweigens: Wo heute Frankreichs Nationalbibliothek steht, wurden einst die Bücher deportierter Juden gesammelt," in *Zeitmagazin,* Nr. 5 (January 24, 1997): 10–17, here especially 13–14.

20. For initiatives from below more generally, see Wolf Gruner, "Die nationalsozialistische Judenverfolgung und die Kommunen: Zur wechselseitigen Dynamisierung von zentraler und lokaler Politik 1933–1941," *VfZ* 48 (2000): 75–126; idem, "Die Grundstücke der 'Reichsfeinde:' Ein Überblick zur 'Arisierung' von Immobilien durch Städte und Gemeinden 1938–1945," in *Jahrbuch zur Geschichte und Wirkung des Holocaust,* ed. Irmtrud Wojak and Peter Hayes (Frankfurt am Main, 2000) 125–56.

21. See Monica Kingreen, "Raubzüge einer Stadtverwaltung: Frankfurt am Main und die Aneignung 'jüdischen Besitzes,'" in *Bürokratien: Initiativen und Effizienz,* ed. Wolf Gruner, vol. 17 in *Beiträge zur Geschichte des Nationalsozialismus* (Berlin: Assoziation A, 2001), 17–50, here 32.

22. See von Papen-Bodek, "'Scholarly' Anti-Semitism," 242; "Der Auftrag von Frankfurt," *Völkischer Beobachter (VB),* Berliner Ausgabe, March 25, 1941, front page; "Von der Eröffnung des Instituts zur Erforschung der Judenfrage," *VB,* No. 85, March 26, 1941, p. 2; "Institut zur Erforschung der Judenfrage," *Frankfurter Volksblatt,* No. 84, March 26, 1941, p. 5; "Nationalsozialismus und Wissenschaft," *DAZ,* Abendausgabe, March 26, 1941, p. 194; "Die Wissenschaft von Juden," *Deutsche Zeitung in den Niederlanden* Jg. 1, No. 292, March 26, 1941, front page; "Alfred Rosenberg sprach in Frankfurt am Main," *VB,* München, March 27, 1941; "Die Judenfrage im Spiegel der Wissenschaft," *Frankfurter Volksblatt,* March 28, 1941; "Eine geistige Kraftzentrale gegen das Judentum: Aufbau und Arbeitsziele des neuen Frankfurter Instituts," *FZ,* March 28, 1941; "Europäische Lösung der Judenfrage: Beginn der wissenschaftlichen Arbeitstagung in Frankfurt," *VB,* Berlin, March 28, 1941; "Mussert von Rosenberg empfangen," *Deutsche Zeitung in den Niederlanden* Jg. 1, No. 294, March 28, 1941, front page; "Europäische Lösung der Judenfrage," *VB,* Berlin, March 28, 1941; "Die Frankfurter Arbeitstagung," *Westfälische Landeszeitung,* No. 75, March 29, 1941; "Die Juden-Diktatur in Europa endgültig zerschlagen,"

Frankfurter Volksblatt, No. 87, March 29, 1941, p. 3; "Die Judenfrage als Weltproblem: Alfred Rosenberg auf der Schlußkundgebung des Frankfurter Kongresses," *Deutsche Zeitung in den Niederlanden* Jg. 1 Nr. 295, March 29, 1941, p. 2; Fritz Zschaeck, "Bericht über die Eröffnung und Arbeitstagung des Instituts zur Erforschung der Judenfrage vom 26.–28. März 1941," *Weltkampf,* no. 1/2, 106–12; "Die europäische Front gegen Juda: Abschluss der ersten Arbeitstagung des Instituts zur Erforschung der Judenfrage," *Westdeutscher Beobachter,* Abendausgabe, March 29, 1941; "Reichsleiter Alfred Rosenberg eröffnet als erste Außenstelle der Hohen Schule in Frankfurt am Main das Institut zur Erforschung der Judenfrage," *Welt-Dienst,* No. 8, April 15, 1941; Gottfried Schweitzer, "Die Hohe Schule zur Judenforschung in Frankfurt am Main," *Die Westmark: Monatsschrift für deutsche Kultur* 8 (May 1941): 553–4.

23. See "Die Erforschung der Judenfrage: Feierliche Eröffnung des neuen Instituts in Frankfurt," *FZ,* No. 158/159, March 27, 1941, front page and p. 2.

24. See "Die politische Entwicklung der Judenfrage in Europa," *Weltkampf,* Heft 1/2, April-September, 1941.

25. See Wilhelm Grau, "Geschichtliche Lösungsversuche der Judenfrage," *Weltkampf,* München, No. 1/2, April-September, 1941, 7–16.

26. Martin Broszat contextualized Schickert's lecture. See "Das Dritte Reich und die rumänische Judenpolitik," *Gutachten des Instituts für Zeitgeschichte* (Munich: Selbstverlag des Instituts für Zeitgeschichte, 1958), 134.

27. Between 1954 and 1970, Dr. Giselher Wirsing (1907–75) was editor in chief of the weekly *Christ und Welt.*

28. See Alan Steinweis, "The Appropriation and Exploitation of Jewish Social Science by Nazi Scholars: The Case of Peter Heinz Seraphim" (Paper given at the 1998 Oxford Conference on "Jews and the Social and Biological Sciences"). Seraphim suggested emigration as the best solution for both the European peoples and the Jews. See also his *Das Judentum im osteuropäischen Raum,* hrsg. unter Mitwirkung des Instituts für osteuropäische Wirtschaft an der Universität Königsberg (Essen: Essener Verlagsanstalt, 1938).

29. "Wege zur Lösung der Judenfrage: Vorträge auf der Arbeitstagung des neuen Frankfurter Instituts," *FZ,* No. 162/163, March 29, 1941, p. 2. See also Fritz Zschaeck, "Bericht über die Eröffnung und Arbeitstagung des Instituts zur Erforschung der Judenfrage in Frankfurt am Main," *Weltkampf,* no. 1/2, 1941, 106–12.

30. See "Von der Eröffnung des Instituts zur Erforschung der Judenfrage," *VB,* Nr. 85, March 26, 1941, p. 2.

31. See "Die Judenfrage als Weltproblem: Eine Rundfunkansprache von Reichsleiter Rosenberg," *FZ,* March 30. Also see B. A. Koblenz, NS 8/63, as well as copy from Klaus Schickert to Legationsrat von Thadden on

December 30, 1943, in NA Washington, 4651, and Hauptstellenleiter Scheidt/Organizational Office of the High School to the Culture Department of the Foreign Office, Berlin on July 4, 1941.

32. Karlheinz Rüdiger, "Das Institut zur Erforschung der Judenfrage," *Rheinische Blätter: Deutsche kulturpolitische Zeitschrift im Westen* 18, No. 5 (May 1941): 193–96.

33. See *Weltkampf,* Heft 2 (April-June 1942), which featured Georges Montandon, Jean Héritier, Gueydan de Roussel, Jean Drault, and Elisabeth de Gramont.

34. Volkmar Eichstädt had carried them on between 1937 and 1941, since Grau had lost this competence as a consequence of his dispute with Frank in the summer of 1938. Rosenberg called upon Karl Alexander von Müller, editor of the *Historische Zeitschrift,* to give the section on the history of the Jewish Question back to Grau, since the anti-Jewish research officially belonged to Rosenberg's domain. See Abschrift Dr. W. Koeppen an Pg. Müller am 6. Juni 1941, in BA Koblenz, R001/000006, Blatt 284.

35. *Weltkampf,* Heft 1 (October-December 1941). See also Pohl's "Die jiddisch-kommunistische Presse in Sowjetrussland während des Bürgerkrieges 1918–1921," *Weltkampf,* Heft 1 (January-March 1942): 55–6.

36. See Johannes Pohl, "Oifgerichtes jiddisches folk," *Deutsche Zeitung im Ostland,* Riga, December 14, 1942, front page and p. 2; idem, *Juden in der Sowjetunion zu Beginn der Herrschaft Stalins: Statistische Angaben aus jiddisch-sowjetischen Quellen* (Tilsit: Holzner Verlag, 1942); Otto Paul, "Der Anspruch des Judentums kulturschöpferische Leistungen vollbracht zu haben," *Volk im Osten,* Hermannstadt, May-June 1943; idem, "Jeder Krieg war ihnen Geschäft: Das Weltjudentum als Schürer und Nutznießer. Ein Beispiel aus den Niederlanden," *Deutsche Zeitung in den Niederlanden,* Amsterdam, June 25, 1943, p. 3; Klaus Schickert, "Ungarn's Judenfrage als wirtschaftliches und geistiges Problem," *Volk im Osten,* Hermannstadt, May-June 1943, 41–52.

37. *Schrifttum zur Judenfrage: Eine Auswahl,* Heft 4 der *Schriftenreihe zur weltanschaulichen Schulungsarbeit,* hrsg. vom Amt Schrifttumspflege der NSDAP unter Mitwirkung des Institutes zur Erforschung der Judenfrage in Frankfurt am Main, bearbeitet von Joachim Menzel (Munich: Zentralverlag der NSDAP, 1941).

38. *Die Erforschung der Judenfrage: Aufgabe und Organisation,* Kleine Weltkampfbücherei, Nr. 3 (Munich: Hoheneichen-Verlag, 1943).

39. *Die geschichtlichen Lösungsversuche der Judenfrage,* Kleine Weltkampfbücherei, No. 4 (Munich: Hoheneichen-Verlag, 1943). See also L. F. Gengler, "Kleine Weltkampfbücherei," *Die Judenfrage,* December 15, 1943, 387–8.

40. Expert on German literature and Iranian philology, employed since November 1, 1940.

41. For the institute's public presentation, see "Zum ersten Mal in der Geschichte: Judenforschung ohne Juden," *Illustrierter Beobachter,* München, April 30, 1942.

42. See Rachel Heuberger, *Bibliothek des Judentums: Die Hebraica und Judaica-Sammlung der Stadt und Universitätsbibliothek Frankfurt am Main— Entstehung, Geschichte und heutige Aufgaben* (Frankfurt: Vittorio Klostermann, 1996), 85–118, here especially p. 104.

43. See Kühn-Ludewig, *Johannes Pohl,* 142. I am especially grateful to Mr. Efroyim Grossberger, independent researcher on the Committee for the Search of the Góra Kalwaria Library, who shared with me some precious insights and sources on the Frankfurt staff. As of 1958, Friedrich Cornelius taught Ancient History at Munich University. See Jakob Seibert, *100 Jahre Alte Geschichte an der Ludwig-Maximilians-Universität München (1901– 2001)* (Berlin: Duncker and Humblot, 2002), 27–8, where Cornelius's prior activities at the Frankfurt Institute are not mentioned. According to Evelyn Adunka, a Frankfurt bookdealer Breiting, who had helped to supervise the Frankfurt holdings, opened an *Antiquariat* in Frankfurt after the war. See Evelyn Adunka, *Der Raub der Bücher: Über Verschwinden und Vernichten von Bibliotheken in der NS-Zeit und ihre Restitution nach 1945* (Vienna: Czernin Verlag, 2002), 180.

44. Zschaeck and his wife belonged to Frankfurt's staff until December 1944. See Adunka, *Der Raub Bücher,* 147.

45. See Wilhelm Grau, "Der Aufbau der Bibliothek zur Erforschung der Judenfrage in Frankfurt am Main," *Zentralblatt für Bibliothekswesen* 59 (1942): 489–94, here p. 492.

46. See Jahresbericht vom 10. Januar 1942 in CDJC Paris, XLIII–293, and "Der Aufbau der Bibliothek zur Erforschung der Judenfrage in Frankfurt am Main," *Zentralblatt für Bibliothekswesen* 59 no. 11–12 (November-December 1942): 489–94.

47. See "Der Aufbau," 489.

48. See Grau's organizational plan of April 1942 in BA Koblenz, NS 15/339.

49. See Rosenberg an Hess am 3. Mai 1940 betr. Forschungsaufgaben der Hohen Schule in CDJC, Paris CXLIII–366.

50. "Der Talmud," *Nationalsozialistische Monatshefte,* Heft 8, March 1939.

51. Grau knew of Pohl; most probably he had even reviewed Pohl's proposal, which the latter had sent to the Friedrich Wilhelms University in March 1937, asking for a research project. Pohl wanted to elaborate sys-

tematically the centrality of "Jewish-communist ideas" to the Bolshevik rulers on the cultural level. Although the Reichsinstitut as well as the university had turned down Pohl's proposal, he had been invited to introduce himself to Grau. See Kühn-Ludewig, *Johannes Pohl,* 48.

52. Herschel Grynszpan had assassinated Legationssekretär Ernst vom Rath of the Parisian German embassy in retaliation for the expulsion of Polish Jews. See Friedrich Kaul, *Der Fall des Herschel Grynszpan* (Berlin: Akademie-Verlag, 1965), 79. Ironically, Walter Frank would have used Pohl as an expert in his trial against Grau to demonstrate the latter's alleged Jesuit morale because of Pohl's article on Talmud and Jesuit morale in *Der Stürmer.* See Dr. P., "Talmud und Jesuitenmoral: Auffallende Ähnlichkeit zwischen der jüdischen und der jesuitischen Sittenlehre," *Der Stürmer* January, 1939. No. 2.

53. See Kühn-Ludewig, *Johannes Pohl,* 110.

54. See Grau an Bäumler am 7. November 1940 in CDJC, Paris CXLIII–307, and Grau an Rosenberg am 16. November 1940 in BA Koblenz, NS 8/264.

55. *Talmud-Geist* (Berlin: Nordland, 1941).

56. See Kühn-Ludewig, *Johannes Pohl,* 168–69.

57. See ibid., 169, 235.

58. See "Judenprivilegien in Litauen," *Die Judenfrage* 6, Nr. 15, August 1, 1942, 166–70; and "Saloniki: Die ehemalige griechische Regierung in ihren Freundschaftsbeteuerungen gegenüber den Juden," *Die Judenfrage* 6, No. 16–17, September 1, 1942, 177f.

59. Compare Kühn-Ludewig, *Johannes Pohl,* 198. Two of his *Weltkampf* essays seem to have been by-products of this project. See "Umbruch und Aufbruch," *Weltkampf* 1/2 January-August, 1943, 50; and "Der Judenstaat 'Ararat' des Mordechay Immanuel Noah," *Weltkampf* Heft 4, October-December, 1942, 285–7.

60. Henlein charged Dr. Suchy with this task. See Philip Friedman, "The Fate of the Jewish Book during The Nazi Era," in *Jewish Book Annual,* vol. 15. New York: 1957–1958, 3–13, here p. 7.

61. Ibid., p. 10.

62. See Hoogewoud, "The Nazi Looting," 161, 163–4.

63. See Von Bibliothekar Johann Pohl, "Die Zahl der Juden in Griechenland," *Weltkampf,* Heft 3, July-September 1942, 221f. See Yitzhak Kerem, "The Confiscation of Jewish Books in Salonika in the Holocaust," *The Holocaust and the Book: Destruction and Preservation,* ed. Jonathan Rose (Amherst: University of Massachusetts Press, 2001), 59–65, here especially pp. 60–2; and Josef Nehama, "Les Bibliothèques Juives de Salonique Détruites par les Nazis," in *In Memoriam: Hommage aux Victimes Juives des*

Nazis en Grèce, vol. 1, publié sous la direction de Michael Molho (Salonique: Imp. N. Nicolaides, 1948), 127–32.

64. See Dr. Koeppen am 3. Juni 1943 Stichwortprotokoll des Termins von Pg. Hagemeyer . . . beim Reichsleiter am 10. Mai 1943 in BA Koblenz, NS 8/131. The selection process ended in July 1943 with the liquidation of the Vilna ghetto. See Dov Schidorsky, "Das Schicksal jüdischer Bibliotheken im Dritten Reich," in *Bibliotheken während des Nationalsozialismus,* vol. 2, ed. Peter Vodosek and Manfred Komorowski (Wiesbaden: Otto Harrassowitz: 1992), 203–6.

65. It contained 21,086 volumes.

66. See Philip Friedman, "Fate of the Jewish Book," 8.

67. Compare Rapmund, Die deutsche Bibliothekspolitik, 199.

68. See Stanislao Pugliese, "Bloodless Torture: The Books of the Roman Ghetto under the Nazi Occupation," in Rose, *The Holocaust and the Book,* 47–58.

69. Lódz sealed its ghetto in April 1940, Warsaw in November 1940.

70. See von Papen-Bodek, "'Scholarly' Anti-Semitism," 246.

71. Kühn-Ludewig, *Johannes Pohl,* 175.

72. See Michael Molho, ed., *Israelitische Gemeinde Thessalonikis: In Memoriam,* trans. Peter Katzung (Essen: typescript, 1981).

73. See CDJC, Paris CDXLIV–37.

74. See NA Washington, 4668.

75. See ibid., 4661.

76. See Dt. Botschaft Paris an Auswärtiges Amt am 23. Januar 1942 betr. Behandlung der Sefarden in NA Washington, 4661.

77. See Association Culturelle Sépharadite de Paris am 13. Januar 1942 in PA-AA Bonn, 5625.

78. Schleier am 23. Januar 1942 an Auswärtiges Amt in PA-AA Bonn, 5625.

79. Compare Heiber, *Walter Frank,* 1166, as well as Euler an Rademacher am 14. Februar 1942 in PA-AA Bonn, 5625.

80. Grau an Auswärtiges Amt am 7. Februar 1942 betr. Behandlung der Sefarden in NA Washington, T120 4661.

81. See Deutsche Gesandtschaft an Auswärtiges Amt am 26. Februar 1942 in NA Washington, 4661, as well as Abschrift Schönberg/Deutsches Konsulat am 20. Februar 1942 in NA Washington, 4661.

82. See PA-AA Bonn, 5625.

83. Rademacher to Groß, Grau, Euler, and Reiffer am 15. Oktober 1942 in NA Washington, 4668.

84. See von Papen-Bodek, "'Scholarly' Anti-Semitism," 165.

85. Euler an Legationsrat Rademacher am 23. Oktober 1942 mit zwei

gutachterlichen Äußerungen zur Abstammung der persischen und afghanischen Angehörigen des mosaischen Bekenntnisses und zur Abstammung der kaukasischen und georgischen Angehörigen des mosaischen Bekenntnisses in NA Washington, 4668.

86. "The anthropological findings actually show all types of the Near Eastern/Semitic racial mixture, yet of a male-permeated, in no way specifically Jewish character. . . . However, the Slavic racial elements which otherwise characterize the eastern Jewish type are missing in this racial mixture." See ibid. On the fate of the Judeo-Tats see Rudolf Loewenthal, "The Judeo-Tats in the Caucasus," *Historia Judaica* 14 (April 1952): 61–82, here especially p. 79; and Hans von Herwarth, *Zwischen Hitler und Stalin: Erlebte Zeitgeschichte 1931 bis 1945* (Frankfurt: Propyläen, 1982), 271.

87. A Jewish sect with followers in Lithuania, whom the Einsatzstab encountered in Vilna.

88. See Prof. Kittel am 16. Februar 1943 über die persischen, afghanischen und kaukasischen Juden in NA Washington, 4668. and Groß an Auswärtiges Amt am 24. Mai 1943 betr. Gutachten von Prof. Kittel in Wien über die persischen, afghanischen und kaukasischen Juden in ibid.

89. See especially von Thadden zu Inland IIA 4328 am 2. Juni 1943 in ibid. See also von Papen-Bodek, "'Scholarly' Anti-Semitism," 170. See Asaf Atchildi, "Rescue of Jews of Bukharan, Iranian and Afghan Origin in Occupied France (1940–1944), *Yad Vashem Studies* 6 (Jerusalem, 1967): 257–81 as well as Levi Eligulashvili, "How the Jews of Gruzia in Occupied France Were Saved: Testimony of Levi Eligulashvili," *Yad Vashem Studies* 6 (Jerusalem, 1967): 251–5. See also Raul Hilberg, *Die Vernichtung der europäischen Juden* (Frankfurt: Fischer, 1989), 692; as well as von Papen-Bodek, "'Scholarly' Anti-Semitism," 169–70.

90. Grandinger an Legationsrat Dr. Rademacher am 16. Januar 1943 mit Anlage Abschrift von Euler's Denkschrift zur Frage der genealogischen Einordnung der sogenannten "portugisischen" Juden in den Niederlanden vom 12. Januar 1943 in NA Washington, 4666. Jacob Presser, who chronicled the persecution of Dutch Jewry, reports that by October 1941, census figures indicated 4,303 registered Portuguese Jews. See Jacob Presser, *Ashes in the Wind: The Destruction of Dutch Jewry* (Detroit: Wayne State University Press, 1988), 306. On February 1, 1944, Portuguese Jews were rounded up throughout Holland, and on February 25, 1944, 308 persons were deported to Auschwitz.

91. On Italian anti-Jewish research centers see Guiseppe Mayda, *Ebrei sotto Salò: La Persecuzione Antisemitica 1943–1945* (Milan: Feltrinelli Editore, 1978), especially the chapter "Pilato a Roma;" and Silva Gherardi Bon, *La Persecuzione Antiebraica A Trieste (1938–1945)* (Udine: Del Bianco,

1972), especially 167–74 and 230–8. On Preziosi see Guiseppe Chiusano, *Un Sacerdote altirpino Ministro di Stato: Giovanni Preziosi (1881–1941)* (Naples: Valsele Tipografica, 1987).

92. See Jahresbericht des Leiters der Außenstelle Frankfurt (Main) der Hohen Schule über das Jahr 1941 vom 10. Januar 1942 in CDJC, Paris CXLIII–293; and see Bericht für A. Rosenberg vom 2. September 1941 in BA Koblenz, NS 8/237.

93. See *Welt-Dienst,* No. 10/9 (May 1, 1943).

94. See Gerhard Volkmer, "Die deutsche Forschung zum osteuropäischen Judentum in den Jahren 1933–1945," in *Forschungen zur osteuropäischen Geschichte* vol. 42 Berlin 1989 (Wiesbaden: Otto Harrassowitz, 1989), 109–214.

95. See *Weltkampf,* Heft 3, October-December 1941, 182.

96. See his report on the Cracow opening, "Arbeitstagung des Instituts für deutsche Ostarbeit," *Weltkampf,* Heft 3, 1941, 177. See Steinweis, "Appropriation and Exploration."

97. See Claudia Steur, *Theodor Dannecker: Ein Funktionär der "Endlösung."* Schriften der Bibliothek für Zeitgeschichte N.F. Bd. 6 (Essen: Klartext Verlag, 1997), 199.

98. See Steur, *Theodor Dannecker,* 49.

99. See Exposé du 21 juin 1949 in CDJC Paris, LXXIV-14, p. 6.

100. On Klassen see Manfred Steinkühler, "'Antijüdische Auslandsaktion': Die Arbeitstagung der Judenreferenten der deutschen Missionen am 3. und 4. April 1944," in *Patient Geschichte,* hrsg. von Karsten Linne und Thomas Wohlleben (Frankfurt: Zweitausendeins, 1993), 256–79, here especially pp. 260–3 and 271.

101. See also John Fox, "German Bureaucrat or Nazified Ideologue? Ambassador Otto Abetz and Hitler's Anti-Jewish Policies 1940–1944," in *Power, Personalities and Policies: Essays in Honor of Donald Cameron Watt,* ed. Michael Graham Fry (London: Frank Cass, 1992), 175–232.

102. See the report by W. Becker of August 11, 1941, "Das Institut des Questions Juives," p. 1 in CDJC Paris, XIe-58. Becker indicated that Armenian Jews residing in Paris had Persian passports. So far we can only speculate whether the investigation about Iranian Jews in occupied France, which the German Foreign Office conducted in October 1942, was in any way related to Beckers report. Compare von Papen-Bodek, "'Scholarly' Anti-Semitism," 165.

103. See Steur, *Theodor Danneker,* 199.

104. See Josef Billig, *L'Institut d'Etude des Questions Juives,* officine francaise des autorités nazie en France. Inventaire commenté de la collection de documents provenant des archives de l'Institut conservés au CDJC

(Paris: CDJC, 1974), 155–8; as well as André Kaspi, "Le Juif et la France, une exposition à Paris en 1941," *Le Monde Juif*, Nr. 79, July-September 1975, 8–20.

105. See Abschrift Abetz am 5. September 1941 in CDJC, Paris, V-72; as well as W. Schwartz, "Zum Stand des Judenproblems in Frankreich," *Weltkampf*, Heft 2, April–June 1942, 161–2.

106. See André Kaspi, *Les Juifs pendant l'Occupation* (Paris: Editions du Seuil, 1997), 17.

107. In contrast to the number of visitors this refusal is corroborated by CDJC Paris, XXI-d-208a.

108. See *Weltkampf*, Heft 2, April-June 1942, 161–2.

109. See W. Schwartz, "Stand des Judenproblems in Frankreich," *Weltkampf*, Heft 2, April-June 1942, 161–2.

110. While Sézille assumed that 276,412 visitors had come to see the show, the embassy estimated 250,623 entrees. See Sézille to Dannecker on December 15, 1941, in CDJC Paris, XI-112, as well as Pierre André Taguieff, ed., *L'Antisémitisme de Plume 1940–1944: Etudes et Documents* (Paris: Berg International Editeurs, 1999), 444.

111. See Dr. Klassen am 18. März 1942 an Gesandten Schleier in NA Washington, 4742.

112. Lehmann had previously been published by the Parisian German Institute. See Eckhard Michels, *Das deutsche Institut in Paris 1940–1944: Ein Beitrag zu den deutsch-französischen Kulturbeziehungen und zur auswärtigen Kulturpolitik des Dritten Reiches* (Stuttgart: Franz Steiner Verlag, 1993), 41. See also Frank-Rutger Hausmann, *"Deutsche Geiteswissenschaft" im Zweiten Weltkrieg: Die "Aktion Ritterbusch" (1940–1945)* (Dresden: Dresden University Press, 1998), 285.

113. See Exposé du 21 Juin 1949 in CDJC Paris, LXXIV-14, pp. 17–18.

114. See Jean Laloum, *La France antisémite de Darquier de Pellepoix* (Paris: Editions Syros, 1979).

115. See his report of February 22, 1942, in CDJC, Paris XXVI-80, section e.

116. See Taguieff, *L'Antisémitisme de Plume*, 273.

117. See CDJC Paris, CXCV-205 examen ethnoracial du 21 aout 1943; CDJC Paris, CXCV-193 examen ethnoracial du 21 avril 1943; and CDJC Paris, XLII-59; and see the letter of one of his desperate clients of October 8, 1942, in CDJC Paris, CCXII-16. See also Marc Knobel, "L'éthnologie à la dérive: George Montandon et l'éthnoracisme," *Ethnologie française* 18 (1988): 107–13.

118. See La Séance Inaugurale de l'Institut d'Etudes des Questions Juives et Ethno-Raciales, 24. Mars 1943 in NA Washington, TM 120 4661. See also *L'Ethnie Française*, No. 8 (May 1943): 5–9; and Aufzeichnung für

Herrn Gesandten Rahn vom 25. September 1942 betr. Besetzung eines geplanten Lehrstuhls für die Geschichte des Judentums an der Sorbonne. See NA Washington, TM 120 4658, as well as "Ein Lehrstuhl für die Geschichte des Judentums an der Pariser Universität," *Welt-Dienst* 10/6 (March 15, 1943).

119. On Labroue see Claude Singer, "Henri Labroue, où l'apprentissage de l'Antisémitisme," in Taguieff, *L'Antisémitisme de Plume,* 233–46.

120. See CDJC Paris, XId-176.

121. See A. Linder, "Gespräch mit Henri Labroue. Juden und Judenforschung in Frankreich," *Pariser Zeitung,* December 22, 1942.

122. See Singer in Taguieff, *L'Antisémitisme de Plume,* 241. See also Hans Hagemeyer am 26. Mai 1944 in CDJC Paris, CXLIV-410.

123. See Frédérique Andreani, *La propagande antisémite dans la presse collaborationiste parisienne 1940–1944* (Métrise: Paris I, 1993).

124. See Prof. Dr. Henri Labroue, "Siebenmal wurden sie ausgewiesen: Die antisemitische Bewegung in Frankreich," *Deutsche Zeitung in den Niederlanden,* August 5, 1943, or "Kriegsschuld der Juden," *Deutsche Zeitung,* Budapest, March 24, 1944.

125. On Adolf Wendel see Peter von der Osten-Sacken, ed., *Das mißbrauchte Evangelium: Studien zu Theologie und Praxis der Thüringer Deutschen Christen* (Berlin: Institut Kirche und Judentum, 2002), 200–1.

126. See Abschrift Schwarz an den Sonderbeauftragten des Reichsschatzmeisters Herrn Reichsrevisor Franz Wick vom 18. Juli 1942 betr. Abteilung Ostjudentum in Litzmannstadt in IfZ, Munich, MA 251 Blätter 457–63.

127. See Kühn-Ludewig, *Johannes Pohl,* 68.

128. Patricia von Papen, "Antisemitic Research and its Political Applications: The Work of Klaus Schickert 1935–1945" (Paper given at the Association for Jewish Studies Conference, Chicago, 1999).

129. See Schickert's articles in the Hungarian Institute's organ: "Diskussion über die Judenfrage in Ungarn," *Mitteilungen über die Judenfrage,* April 23, 1937, Blatt 6; "Die Verjudung der ungarischen Presse," *Mitteilungen über die Judenfrage,* No. 12, August 5, 1937; "Jüdische Diktatur des Geldes in Ungarn," in *Mitteilungen über die Judenfrage,* Nr. 18 November 25, 1937, Blätter 3–4; "Umbruch in der Karpatho-Ukraine," in *Mitteilungen über die Judenfrage,* No. 442/44, December 22, 1938, Blätter 8–9.

130. See the review by Franz Ronneberger, Vienna, *Weltkampf,* Heft 1, 1944, 40–1. See also "Die Juden in Ungarn," *Welt-Dienst,* No. 11/9–10, May 1–2, 1944, front page and p. 2, which used Schickert's data.

131. See Dt. Gesandtschaft Pressburg an Auswärtiges Amt am 25. Februar 1944 in NA Washington, 4665.

132. See his introduction of December 1942 in *Die Judenfrage in Un-*

garn: Jüdische Assimilation und antisemitische Bewegung im 19. und 20. Jahrhundert (Essen: Essener Verlagsanstalt, 1943).

133. See Essener Verlagsanstalt to Schickert on May 24, 1944, in NA Washington, TM 120 4658. In his report to von Thadden of December 1943, Schickert had argued that one of the reasons for travelling to Hungary was the updating of his book for a third edition, then about to come out. See NA Washington, TM 120 4651.

134. See Patricia von Papen, "The Hungarian Institute for Research into the Jewish Question and its Participation in the Expropriation and Expulsion of Hungarian Jewry" (Paper given in honor of István Deák's Retirement Conference at Columbia University, 2000); the *Festschrift* is expected to appear in 2004. See also "Ungarisches Institut zur Erforschung der Judenfrage," *Welt-Dienst*, Nr. 10/7, April 1, 1943, 10, in which Bosnyák's brochures are listed.

135. On Seraphim see *Braune Universität: Deutsche Hochschullehrer gestern und heute*. Eine Dokumentation zusammengestellt und eingeleitet von Rolf Seeliger. Dokumentenreihe Heft 1, Selbstverlag, 1964, 66–8 and recently Hauke Janssen, *Nationalökonomie und Nationalsozialismus: Die deutsche Volkswirtschaftslehre in den dreißiger Jahren* (Marburg: Metropolis Verlag, 2000), 617.

136. "Ungarn's Judenfrage als wirtschaftliches und geistiges Problem," *Volk im Osten,* Hermannstadt, May-June 1943, 41–52.

137. Zoltán Bosnyák, "'Das Ungarische Institut zur Erforschung der Judenfrage' Wissenschaftliche Forschungsarbeit auf dem Gebiete der Judenfrage in Ungarn," *Europäischer Wissenschaftsdienst,* 3(1944): 10–14.

138. See Schickert's review of "Vitéz Kolosváry-Borcsa's A zsidókérdés Magyaroszági irodalma," *Weltkampf,* Heft 1, 1944, 41.

139. See Schickert über die in Vorbereitung befindlichen Schriften des Instituts am 23. Februar 1944 in BA Koblenz, NS8/266.

140. See Bericht über die Tätigkeit unseres Institutes zur Erforschung der Judenfrage am 8. März 1944 in CDJC, Paris, XXXIX-53.

141. "Gyilkold meg a keresztények legjobbját!" Pohl professzor, a világ legkiválóbb Talmud-tudósa beszél a "Függetlenségnek a világzsidóság háborús céljairól." In *Függetlenség,* July 2, 1944, 5.

142. See Kühn-Ludewig, *Johannes Pohl,* 261.

143. See *Welt-Dienst,* No. 11, 11–12, June 1 and 2, 1944.

144. See Von Thadden an Dt. Gesandtschaft Budapest am 28. April in NA Washington, 4665. Dt. Gesandtschaft Budapest an Auswärtiges Amt am 22. Mai 1944 in PA-AA Bonn, 5425 and Schleier an Büro Reichsaußenminister am 28. Juli 1944 in ibid.

145. See Schleier an die dt. Gesandtschaft Budapest z. Hd. des Juden-

referenten Herrn Konsul Dr. Grell/Budapest am 12. Juli 1944 in PA-AA, Bonn 5425.

146. See Protokoll über die Arbeitsbesprechung am 23. Juni 1944 im Gästehaus Eppenheim betr. Behandlung der Judenfrage in Ungarn, CDJC, Paris CXLIV-407, pp. 2, 5, 6, and especially 7a.

147. Schickert am 31. März 1944 betr. Quellen und Darstellungen zur Geschichte der antijüdischen Bewegung, in CDJC, Paris CXXXIX-52. It is noteworthy that SS-Untersturmführer Günther Franz, who since spring 1942 worked for the RSHA's Amt VII (Gegnerforschung), also commissioned Peter Aldag and Heinz Ballensiefen to write for the series *Quellen und Darstellungen zur Judenfrage*. See Wolfgang Behringer, "Bauern-Franz und Rassen-Günther: Die politische Geschichte des Agrarhistorikers Günther Franz (1902–1992)," in *Deutsche Historiker im Nationalsozialismus,* hrsg. von Winfried Schulze und Otto Gerhard Oexle (Frankfurt: Fischer, 1999), 124. See Fritz Zschaeck, "War Wilhelm Marr ein Jude?" in *Weltkampf,* Heft 2, May-August 1944, 94–8.

148. See Herwig Hartner-Hnizdo, *Das jüdische Gaunertum* (Munich: Hoheneichen Verlag, 1939).

149. See Theo Stengel and Herbert Gerigk, *Lexikon der Juden in der Musik* (Berlin: Bernhard Hahnefeld, 1940).

150. Volume 1 would have been Pohl's *Talmud Lexicon.*

151. See Willem de Vries, *Sonderstab Musik,* 64–70. It is noteworthy that Herbert Gerigk, one of the authors, who also led Rosenberg's *Kulturpolitisches Archiv,* also edited articles on music for *Meyers Konversationslexikon.* See Eva Weissweiler, *Ausgemerzt: Das Lexikon der Juden in der Musik und seine mörderischen Folgen* (Köln: Dietrich, 1999), 44.

152. It was out of print by April 1944.

153. Gerigk's ambitious goal was to list all of European Jewry, and thus to write the definite anti-Semitic music lexicon. See Weissweiler, *Ausgemerzt,* 93, 140.

154. Its preface stated unambiguously and clearly: "schließlich soll von unserer Seite ja nicht eine Verewigung der jüdischen Erzeugnisse geliefert werden, sondern eine Handhabe zur schnellsten Ausmerzung aller irrtümlich verbliebenen Reste aus unserer Kultur und unserem Geistesleben." See ibid., 8.

155. Ibid., 161–2. Gerigk received the *Kriegsverdienstkreuz erster Klasse ohne Schwerter* in May 1944.

156. See Elisabeth Frenzel, *Die Gestalt des Juden auf der neueren deutschen Bühne* (Bühl-Baden: Konkordia, 1940), idem, *Judengestalten auf der deutschen Bühne: Notwendiger Querschnitt durch 700 Jahre Rollengeschichte* (Munich: Deutscher Volksverlag, 1942); idem, *Der Jude im Theater: Schriften*

zur weltanschaulichen Schulungsarbeit der NSDAP, Heft 25 (Munich: Franz
Eher Nachfolge Verlag, 1943). After the war, Elisabeth Frenzel published
the best-selling standard work, with her husband, Herbert Frenzel, *Daten
deutscher Dichtung: Chronologischer Abriß der deutschen Literaturgeschichte*
(Köln: Kiepenheuer and Witsch, 1953); the second edition appeared in
1962, and the twentieth (paperback) edition (Munich: DTV, 1982).

157. As late as 1944 the Ministry of Education authorized the establishment of a chair for *Judenkunde* at Frankfurt University for the Tübingen extraordinarius Karl Georg Kuhn. Originally, Herr Reiffer of the *Welt-
Dienst* was interested in the job, but withdrew due to his lack of scholarly
credentials. (See Koeppen an Schickert am 31. Oktober 1944 in BA Koblenz,
NS 8/266). Schickert, however, maintained that anti-Jewish research remained an extra-universitary domain: "The research on the Jewish Question is thus organized in Germany such that individual teaching posts have
been assigned to the universities. But it would be erroneous to conclude, on
the basis of the small numbers of these teaching posts, a lack of vigor in our
work on the Jewish Question. The central location for the research on the
Jewish Question is outside the German university." (See Schickert, "Die Judenfrage in wissenschaftlicher Sicht," in CDJC Paris, CXXIX 57, p. 17)
The step had resulted from a local initiative. See Schickert am 25. Oktober
1944 Aktenvermerk betr. Errichtung eines Lehrstuhls für Judenkunde an
der Universität Frankfurt in CDJC Paris, CXXXIX-51.

158. Klaus Schickert, "Die Erforschung der Judenfrage im Südos-
traum," *Weltkampf: Die Judenfrage in Geschichte und Gegenwart,* Heft 1,
January-April 1944, 1–8.

159. See Lubomir Wladikin, "Die Judengesetzgebung in Bulgarien,"
Weltkampf, Heft 4, October-December 1942, 288–95. See also Schickert's
article "Josef Fadenhecht und der nationale Zusammenbruch Bulgariens,"
Weltkampf, Heft 3, September-December 1944, 169–75.

160. See Bericht über die Tätigkeit des Instituts vom 8. März 1944 in
CDJC, Paris, XXXIX-53.

161. See Dr. Koeppen Termin Hagemeyer beim Reichsleiter am
19.4.1944 in BA Koblenz NS 8/132 and Rosenberg an Bormann am
21.4.1944 in CDJC, Paris CXLIII.

162. See von Papen-Bodek, "'Scholarly' Anti-Semitism," 265–6. See
also the "Tentative List of Jewish Cultural Treasures in Axis-Occupied
Countries." By the Research Staff of the Commission on European Jewish
Cultural Reconstruction, *Jewish Social Studies* 8, No. 1, January Supplement, 1946. In addition, "Tentative List of Jewish Educational Institutions
in Axis-Occupied Countries," *Jewish Social Studies* 8, No. 3, July Supplement, 1946; as well as "Addenda and Corrigenda to Tentative List of Jew-

ish Cultural Treasures in Axis-Occupied Countries," *Jewish Social Studies,* Nr. 10, January Supplement, 1948.

163. See Jacqueline Borin, "Embers of the Soul: The Destruction of Jewish Books and Libraries in Poland during World War II," *Libraries and Culture* 28, No. 4 (fall 1993): 445–60, here p. 459.

164. See his fine abstract "Bestandsaufbau durch Plünderung Jüdischer Bibliotheken im RSHA 1936–1945" for the symposium "Raub und Restitution in Bibliotheken," held at Vienna's City Hall on April 23–24, 2003. See also Richard Hacken, "The Jewish Community Library in Vienna: From Dispersion and Destruction to Partial Restoration," *Leo Baeck Yearbook* (2002). I am indebted to Dr. Raphael Gross and Dr. Gabriele Rahaman for letting me read Professor Hacken's essay in advance. On the systematic confiscation of libraries and archives by the RSHA's Amt VII, see Jörg Rudolph, "Sämtliche Sendungen sind zu richten an: Das RSHA- Amt VII 'Weltanschauliche Forschung und Auswertung' als Sammelstelle erbeuteter Archive und Bibliotheken," in *Nachrichtendienst, politische Elite und Mordeinheit: Der Sicherheitsdienst des Reichsführers SS,* ed. Michael Wildt (Hamburg: Hamburger Edition, 2003), 204–40.

165. See Dov Schidorsky, "Confiscation of Libraries and Assignments to Forced Labor: Two Documents of the Holocaust," *Libraries and Culture* 33, no. 4 (Fall 1998): 347–88, here p. 354.

166. See *Handbuch der Romfrage,* Band A–K (Munich: Hoheneichen Verlag, 1940), for which Pohl wrote the article on the "Jewish Question," or the *Lexikon der Juden in der Musik.* See Weissweiler, *Ausgemerzt.*

167. See Protokoll über die Arbeitsbesprechung im Gästehaus Eppenheim am 23. Juni 1944 betreffs Behandlung der Judenfrage in Ungarn in CDJC, Paris CXLIV-407, p. 7a.

168. The immense rivalry between the Einsatzstab and the RSHA was evident as early as 1941 when an eyewitness, who had been forced to work for the RSHA's library, commented as follows: "There existed an incredible rivalry between the Office VII (the RSHA's library) and the Einsatzstab Reichsleiter Rosenberg. Each of them attempted to get hold of the best Judaica. I recall for example that one day an article appeared on the works of the Frankfurt Institute. The SS-leaders laughed immensely since they had captured all the precious publications and because the Einsatzstab in their opinion had only seized libraries of a lesser quality." See Kühn-Ludewig, *Johannes Pohl,* 146, but especially Gabriele Steinmacher, "Jüdische Bibliotheken," 9.

Konrad Jarausch

Unasked Questions: The Controversy about Nazi Collaboration among German Historians

DURING THE 1998 MEETING OF GERMAN HISTORIANS IN FRANKFURT, the public was surprised by charges of Nazi collaboration of leading West German historians of the postwar period. In a preliminary newspaper interview, the new president of the Deutsche Historikerverband, Johannes Fried, had felt forced to apologize for the complicity of his illustrious predecessors. Hundreds of scholars thronged into the lecture hall to find out more about this contentious issue, making it necessary to open a second auditorium to allow the overflow to follow the proceedings via closed-circuit TV. The tension in the room was palpable as younger scholars accused older colleagues of not asking tough enough questions about their mentors' contributions to war and genocide in the Third Reich. When some of the current leaders of the profession sought to explain that circumstances in the postwar years were not propitious for probing their teachers' Nazi backgrounds, the audience booed and hissed.[1] Delayed for too long, the self-cleansing of the historical profession erupted into a full-blown scandal.

The critics who were raising such uncomfortable moral questions were largely historians of the coming generation who had not yet obtained a secure academic position. Berlin historian-turned-journalist Götz Aly had for about a decade written about the role of academics as masterminds of National Socialist resettlement and genocide;[2] Basel geographer Michael Fahlbusch was finishing a massive study of the ethnic research organization that provided essential knowledge for the cleansing and remapping of occupied Europe;[3] Halle doctoral student Ingo Haar was preparing a monograph concerning the contribution of historians in the nationalities' struggles in the East;[4] and finally,

Parisian historian Peter Schöttler was working in the French Centre nationale de recherches scientifiques (CNRS) on the complicity of Western-area specialists in German expansionism.[5] Though somewhat differing in detail and intensity, their charges converged in the accusation that prominent historians had gone far beyond their patriotic duty in the Third Reich by actively helping to prepare genocide, serving not merely as accomplices but, in Aly's damning phrase, as *Vordenker der Vernichtung* (Pioneers of Destruction).

Rather ironically, the accused were the very left-liberal leaders of the German historical profession who in earlier years had, themselves, been outspoken critics of the establishment. For instance, the gifted polemicist Hans-Ulrich Wehler had been instrumental in establishing the new methodological paradigm of *Gesellschaftsgeschichte* in the 1970s and 1980s that sought to uncover the structural continuities of authoritarianism from the Second Empire on. Similarly, the accomplished comparativist Jürgen Kocka had helped promote the conception of a German *Sonderweg*, an exceptional line of development that deviated from the Western norm of democratic and capitalist modernization. And there were others, like the famous twins, Hans and Wolfgang Mommsen, who had time and again accused the German elites of nationalist complicity in the First World War and in the Nazi state.[6] In a curious reversal of fronts, these members of the so-called Bielefeld school were now caught in the unaccustomed role of having to defend themselves for not having been rigorous enough in their critiques, allowing personal respect to keep them from questioning their own teachers about their dubious roles in the Nazi regime.

Since the emotionalism of the public debate threatened to obscure the facts, the Berlin historian Rüdiger Hohls and I decided to launch an interview series in order to clarify the issues.[7] With the help of three masters students at the Berlin Humboldt-University, we interviewed seventeen prominent West German historians, two of them female, about the Nazi collaboration of their mentors. In order to get a handle on the tangled arguments, we differentiated three time horizons: (1) the actual behavior of scholars in the Third Reich, (2) their relationships to their students after the Second World War, and (3) the character of the current controversy about both. In selecting interview partners, we identified the power brokers through their institutional positions and aimed for some political diversity beyond the left-liberal spectrum. The interviews, divided into an unstructured autobiographical section and a standardized questionnaire on the present debate, were first put onto the electronic network H-soz-kult and then published as a book, called *Versäumte Fragen*.[8] The following remarks are based upon these texts as well as the numerous reviews, both printed and electronic, that have carried the debate further in the meantime.[9]

NAZI COLLABORATION

The public uproar was triggered by the discovery that Theodor Schieder, Werner Conze, and Karl-Dietrich Erdmann had collaborated with the National Socialists to a much greater extent than had previously been imagined. The three were not just ordinary scholars but had succeeded each other as presidents of the German Historical Association between 1962 and 1976, while Erdmann even chaired the international association of historians from 1975 to 1980. The evidence consisted of a chilling memorandum, compiled by Schieder in the autumn of 1939, which demonstrated that a group of historians in Eastern Germany was ready to help the Nazi project of ethnic cleansing by providing information on the nationalities-structure of the disputed Polish frontier regions.[10] Equally appalling was the racist language in Conze's dissertation on the German colony "Hirschenhof" in the Baltic and his *Habilitationsschrift* on agrarian structure and population in Lithuania and Belarus.[11] Even the cosmopolitan Erdmann had apparently penned a history textbook on the Third Reich that was further sharpened by the publisher; though never released, it contained more Nazi phraseology than seemed necessary.[12]

These incontrovertible materials made it impossible to uphold the fiction that only a small minority of historians had been involved in the National Socialist project. The traditional view, enunciated by Karl Ferdinand Werner in the mid-1960s, alleged that German historians had been so nationalist that they generally agreed with Hitler's revisionism and therefore did not need to be Nazified.[13] The few rabid Nazis who clustered around Walter Frank's Reichstinstitut für die Geschichte des neuen Deutschlands were not really respectable scholars and, at any rate, had been purged from the profession after 1945 through de-Nazification.[14] This reasoning also meant that core members of the discipline, represented by Gerhard Ritter or Friedrich Meinecke, had survived the Nazi regime unscathed and could therefore continue working in their previous positions with their time-honored methods.[15] The shocking proof that some of the brightest among the younger generation of historians who later assumed leading positions in the Federal Republic of Germany (FRG) had been much more deeply implicated in the Third Reich now threatened to destroy this apologetic consensus.

The controversy also drew attention to a pervasive trend toward an ethnic *Volksgeschichte* that had been largely ignored by earlier historiographical studies.[16] As a result of the disputed frontiers imposed by the Versailles treaty, many younger scholars in the 1920s turned away from grand politics but began to investigate nationalities issues, especially in Eastern Europe. Supported by geographers, ethnologists, or linguists, these historians sought to provide academic proof of the German-ness of disputed territories. Detailed demographic statistics could establish claims to a German *Volksboden*, areas where ethnic kin were dispersed beyond the borders of the Weimar Republic. Failing that, it might be possible to use the evidence of place names, building-styles of houses, or popular customs to show that certain regions were as least *Kulturboden* (i.e., influenced by German culture). The government therefore funded a dense network of interdisciplinary ethnic research organizations, both for the western and eastern regions. Inspired by their mentor, the half-Jewish German nationalist Hans Rothfels, in the late 1920s some of the most ambitious students, like Schieder, Conze, and Erdmann turned toward this innovative history.[17]

The key issue raised by the current critics is the extent and the character of the collaboration between various kinds of nationalist academics and the Nazis in their ethnic cleansing and genocide. Was the radical nationalism of many historians, as Hans Mommsen claims, really *identical* with National Socialism—or were both parallel projects that ultimately *diverged,* as his brother Wolfgang counters?[18] This is the point at which the debate tends to get muddled, because questions of evidence and morality become entangled with each other. Concerning the causal relationship, it is clear that the proponents of *Volksgeschichte* zealously contributed to a climate of opinion and a store of information that facilitated the racial projects of the SS. But it is less certain what impact the Schieder memorandum actually had on decision making, since it was quickly overtaken by events. The Conze studies could at best have had an indirect influence, while

Erdmann's textbook draft remained unpublished. Though any form of radical nationalism and of racial prejudice seems repugnant among academics, wedded to a rational ideal of research, do such sentiments already prove a complete identity with genocidal racism or are there gradations that careful scholarship ought to note?

The importance of making such interpretational distinctions can be illustrated by selected examples from my own family of Protestant academics. My aunt's brother, killed in April 1945, had received the golden Party emblem, and was clearly a rabid Nazi.[19] My uncle, the historian Franz Petri, was also a leading proponent of *Westforschung*, since his book on the Franco-German linguistic frontier attracted even Hitler's attention. Joining the party in 1937, he served as head of the university section in the Belgian occupation, but clashed repeatedly with the SS on whether to support radical Flemish autonomists.[20] In contrast, my father, a religious educator and journal editor, was not a Nazi and, according to recent testimony, actually protected some of his Jewish pupils. Though he enthusiastically supported Hitler's conquests, the systematic starvation of Russian POWs made him repudiate the war as inhuman a few weeks before his death in 1942.[21] My mother, a high school teacher of French and religion, was also a patriot, but she sympathized somewhat with opponents in the Confessing Church. While hindsight might condemn all these stances as nationalist involvement, the differences between them were so important to the contemporaries that they ought not simply be obliterated.

A final judgment on the degree to which historians were implicated in the Holocaust depends upon the analytical perspective that is used. If one restricts one's gaze to the leading professors of the older generation and the established journals or institutes, then the traditional perception that nationalist complicity was largely limited to expansionism is not completely inaccurate. But when one analyzes instead the interdisciplinary research networks outside academe or the new Reich universities that attracted ambitious members of the younger generation with their generous support, the contribution of historians to ethnic cleansing looms much larger. The conventional view that funding organizations like the Deutsche Forschungsgemeinschaft continued to carry on respectable research during the Third Reich has been conclusively refuted by the critics, who have pointed out the deep interest of scholars in many fields in pursuing in racist projects.[22] However, a look from the political expectations of the Nazi leadership toward the behavior of professional historians, offered by a critical Sicherheitsdienst memorandum of 1938, also reveals a considerable gap in style, rhetoric, and priority that seems to militate against their complete identity with the Party.[23]

POSTWAR SILENCE

One of the more irritating facets of the postwar period is the deafening silence with which most collaborators or perpetrators treated their own complicity with the Third Reich. Even regime opponents or struggling survivors were sometimes hushed, since the public did not want to be reminded of its own failings. Allied de-Nazification procedures and reeducation pressure made open admissions of individual guilt inopportune, as compromised individuals ran the risk of being dismissed on the basis of their own testimony. Within small circles of like-minded friends, veterans would freely talk about their war experiences, businessmen could brag about their not always legal "acquisitions," or administrators might reminisce about their policies in occupied lands. But among historians only a few exceptional individuals, like Reinhard Wittram or Hermann Heimpel, were courageous enough to confess publicly their personal culpability for serving war and repression.[24] This widespread reticence raises the question whether such silence was primarily a denial of responsibility or also a necessary cover for working through unresolved questions.

Part of the problem was the considerable continuity of personnel, since the FRG had to be constructed, so to speak, out of warped boards (i.e., with people who had been professionally active in the Third Reich).[25] In response to Soviet pressure, the East Germans cleansed house more radically, retaining only a few anti-Fascist bourgeois scholars and drafting Marxist intellectuals to create a new professoriate at the risk of losing much professional competence.[26] In the West, only pronounced Nazis like Ernst Anrich were permanently barred from teaching positions and forced to found para-academic institutions like the Ranke Society or Wissenschaftliche Buchgesellschaft. Other heavily involved historians, like Günther Franz, were dismissed, served time in internment camps, or struggled in odd jobs, but were allowed to resume academic positions after a decent interval on proof of change. Moderate nationalists continued to teach, and some historians in inner emigration (like the Catholic Franz Schnabel) were reinstated. But hardly any of the more than two dozen émigrés returned permanently, like Hans Rothfels, in order to help redirect historical scholarship.[27] In a university climate dominated by collaborators, open admissions of personal failings were not exactly welcome.

A halting learning process, nonetheless, seems to have taken place within the minds of most historians who were professionally concerned with the reasons for the German catastrophe. Especially those collaborators who were temporarily outside academe were compelled to repackage those nationalist ideas that had stalled their once promising careers. Unfortunately, this painful process of intellectual repositioning took place in private, leaving little written evidence of its struggles and stages. The published record makes clear that by the mid-1950s Theodor Schieder had turned toward historical theory, reexamining Marx and Weber to get his intellectual bearings. At the same time, Werner Conze had replaced the offensive word *Volk* with *Struktur,* amplifying his prior social interests into a new kind of structural history. Karl-Dietrich Erdmann had also expanded his horizon into Europe, putting the German past into a wider perspective. The negative example of the all-too-rapid metamorphosis of the literary scholar and SS-man Schneider into the postwar liberal stalwart Schwerte suggests that further research must therefore establish precisely how this reinvention proceeded in order to determine whether it was merely opportunist or actually genuine.[28]

Unfortunately, the transmission of the rethinking process to the students was largely blocked by the tradition of the *Ordinarienuniversität,* which privileged professorial authority. The interviews make it clear that in the 1950s full professors still thought of themselves as towering figures who were supposed to have all the answers and not betray any insecurity. Even those scholars who had established close working relationships with their pupils were therefore unwilling to bare their souls, lest they lose some of their nimbus. Moreover, doctoral students were caught in personal client relationships, since their future success depended upon the patronage of their masters in the form of financial support, access to publication, and job placement. Even favored students who had an inkling that something was amiss in the Nazi period were therefore unlikely to pose troubling questions to their mentors. Both sides, rather, concentrated on the results of the soul-searching, the new kinds of historical perspectives that professors could offer as explanation for the disastrous development of their nation. Instead of confronting their own complicity openly, historians dealt with it obliquely, preferring to do penance through changing their views of the past.[29] One of the scholars whose postwar work must be regarded as active contrition was, incidentally, Fritz Fischer.[30]

How is posterity to judge this frustrating unwillingness to speak up? To the young critics the silence of the Nazi generation smacks of a nationalist cover-up that sought to evade complicity in order to protect their position. The ample evidence that personal relationships, like the network of Rothfels students established at Königsberg in the 1930s, continued to function suggests not only a continuity of personnel, but also a continuation of Nazified thinking with barely altered vocabulary, thereby tainting the FRG.[31] To the defendants, embarrassed by their own sins of omission, the reticence is a product of those postwar compromises, necessary for drawing a skeptical war-chastened cohort into a democratic society, which a later moralizing time fails to comprehend. They emphasize instead the considerable body of printed work that changed historical methods, transformed interpretative perspectives, and embraced new, more humane values. At the same time, they imply that the liberality of their mentors in supporting new departures and their public engagement for Western-style democracy should compensate for their earlier missteps.[32] In effect, they suggest that this reticence had instead been an essential part of a process of "silent democratization."

The evaluation of the reorientation after World War II depends largely upon one's understanding of scholarly innovation processes in general. At first blush, the East German remaking of the historical discipline looks more rigorous, since the Socialist Unity Party ruthlessly purged personnel, constructed novel institutes, founded its own journals, and, in short, promoted a Marxist-Leninist conception that broke radically with the past. But the price of this thoroughness was a loss of standards, a rupture in memory culture, and a politicization that put historians at the service of a new dictatorship.[33] Ultimately the messier and incremental West German approach of a partial exclusion of Nazi historians, a gradual learning process of the remaining professoriate, and a competition between divergent conceptions that ranged from a chastened nationalism to a revived humanism, was more successful in redirecting historical thinking. Beyond some initial coercion, it banked on scholarly discussion to change interpretations, on generational succession to implant new perspectives, and on public debate to redirect memory culture. Ironically, in the long run such an indirect method produced more innovative scholarship, as well as democratic loyalty, than the direct imposition of a more thorough anti-Fascism from above.[34]

CURRENT CONTROVERSY

The present debate raises a number of further questions about the historical profession's belated acknowledgment of its Nazi complicity. To begin with, the timing is somewhat surprising, since other fields like medicine, theology, and anthropology had to confront these issues, with the help of critical historians, at an earlier time. In many ways the historical discipline is therefore only slowly catching up with a process of academic self-examination that was initiated through the generational rebellion of the late 1960s.[35] Begun by Michael Burleigh's path-breaking study of academic support for Eastern expansion in the Second World War, serious research on the National Socialist involvement of historians had already begun about a decade before the controversy erupted.[36] A number of interesting dissertations by Willi Oberkrome, Karin Schönwälder, and Ursula Wolf provided further evidence on the dimensions of political and scholarly collaboration of historians with National Socialism.[37] Why, then, did the long-overdue self-questioning erupt only in the late 1990s and a wider public suddenly pay attention to the failings of historians?

Part of the answer has to do with the conflict-ridden process of generational succession within the discipline that continued to change its priorities, values, and frames of reference. (1) The problematic great-grandfathers were the Weimar historians who, like Hans Rothfels, established the new paradigm of a nationalistic, interdisciplinary *Volksgeschichte*. (2) The implicated grandfathers were their favored students, like Theodor Schieder, Werner Conze, and Karl-Dietrich Erdmann, whose careers began in the Third Reich but who played a decisive role in modernizing historiography in the Federal Republic. (3) The embattled fathers are their star pupils, such as Hans-Ulrich Wehler, Jürgen Kocka, or the Mommsen brothers, who founded a new paradigm of historical social science that produced the critical conception of German exceptionalism, the *Sonderweg*. (4) The iconoclastic sons are their disillusioned students, such as Götz Aly, Michael Fahlbusch, or Peter Schöttler, who fault the left-liberals of the Bielefeld school for not having gone far enough in their critique of the tradition.[38] (5) And at present, yet another cohort of postunification students is coalescing, representing our interviewers, who are puzzled by the intensity of an uproar that they do not fully understand.

Some of the intensity of the controversy also derived from the institutional marginality of the critics who cast themselves as underdogs in fighting a professional establishment—an attractive pose for the media and the general public. The moral crusade of enlightening the discipline about its unsavory antecedents had a hidden agenda of displacing its current leaders so as to make room for the next academic cohort, still waiting at the gates. Since the left-liberals had gained influence by rejecting the national master narrative of their elders, there was an ironic logic in their own overachieving students' using the same strategy against them, accusing their mentors of not having lived up to their critical precepts.[39] This repetitive mechanism would also help to explain why the critics fastened upon the progressives as target rather than on powerful neotraditionalists like Lothar Gall or Klaus Hildebrand, let alone the more dangerous Right that sought to "renationalize" German outlooks after unification.[40] Not that the younger critics proceeded in bad faith, but their indignation also contained a touch of professional envy that seemed somewhat disingenuous.

The debate, moreover, gained some of its heat from the charge that the modernizing Bielefeld school had grown out of a set of unacknowledged "brown roots." Already Winfried Schulze had argued that the involvement of Schieder, Conze, and Erdmann in *Volksgeschichte* helped pave the way for their elaboration of a *Strukturgeschichte* during the 1950s that looked for social and political structures beyond individual persons and particular events.[41] Positing a direct transmission to the left-liberal societal historians, the critics therefore charged that their new approach of *Gesellschaftsgeschichte* contained an unrecognized Nazi legacy within itself and therefore ought to be rather suspect. From her British distance to the *querelles allemandes,* Mary Fulbrook has called the "implicit accusation of Nazi political associations . . . quite absurd," since it was precisely the project of the Bielefeld school to uncover the authoritarian continuities in German society in order to combat them. Moreover, the internal perspective also ignores the massive outside influence through the writings of Anglo-American scholars, student exchange experiences, and the teaching of returned émigrés like Hans Rosenberg and Dietrich Gerhard.[42] The

public's widespread credulity of the charges might finally be understood as a result of a laudable, but somewhat reflex-like, Holocaust
sensibility promoted by the media. Already the surprisingly positive
reception of Daniel Goldhagen's blanket indictment of complicity
in the face of scholarly caveats indicated that admissions of guilt had
become a touchstone that defined the identity of many German intellectuals.[43] The willingness to accept charges of responsibility without subjecting them to scrutiny is testimony to an extraordinary
transformation of public memory culture in the postwar period. By
unceasing efforts, a dedicated minority of anti-Fascist intellectuals
gradually succeeded in turning the recollections of regime opponents
and Nazi victims into the official public memory of the FRG. With
the help of the media and a revised school curriculum they superseded the personal memories of perpetrators, which were rarely expressed, and of collaborators, who claimed themselves to be victimized, and projected a critical set of recollections onto the whole.[44] As
a result, many young intellectuals have come to expect virtually all
Germans to be villains, since they lack the patience to untangle the
complicated pattern of complicity and reorientation of their own
personal forbears.

Hence the implications of the current controversy are productive
and troubling at the same time. On the one hand, the critics have broken through the structural generalizations of the Bielefeld school and
succeeded in raising the issue of personal responsibility for the crimes
of the Third Reich. Since the accused academics can no longer be interrogated directly, this shift calls for additional archival research on
the actions of individual historians under the Nazi regime and in the
postwar period in order to understand their ambiguous intentions
and motives. On the other hand, some of the accusations also contain an undercurrent of moralizing presentism that fails to appreciate
the complexity of earlier contexts, ranging from the chaotic Weimar
Republic to the disrupted postwar years. The historiographical challenge therefore consists of uncovering both the precise extent of
National Socialist complicity and of reconstructing the protracted
process of subsequent reorientation. Like the perplexing legacy of
the German Democratic Republic, the revolting record of the Nazi
period should not be confronted with self-righteous condemnation
but with a spirit of "critical historicization."[45]

ASSESSING COMPLICITY

The critics are undoubtedly to be applauded for raising the long-overdue question of the relationship between the historical profession and the Third Reich. Through their monographic work and the contribution of other scholars, like Matthias Beer, appalling findings have emerged that have shattered the retrospective complacency about the conduct of historians under the Nazi regime.[46] The rediscovery of the forgotten current of *Volksgeschichte* is an important addition to historiographical knowledge that raises the question of how to resolve the paradox of its methodological innovation and political servilitude. Moreover, the unearthing of the government-supported research networks of *Ost-* and *Westforschung*[47] has thrown shocking light on a whole institutionalized structure of radical nationalism outside the universities that was only too happy to serve German expansionism with scholarly information. Finally, the detection of an unsuspected degree of Nazi involvement among leading scholars of the FRG has brought the issue of continuities and new beginnings after 1945 into bolder relief. Hence, with their archival discoveries and interpretative arguments, Aly, Fahlbusch, Haar, and Schöttler have done German history a signal service.[48]

Yet differences of opinion persist in how to assess this new evidence of Nazi complicity among historians. There is little question that the professional establishment was only too glad to provide academic support for revisionism,[49] and offer historical arguments for territorial expansion and political hegemony over Europe.[50] Some of the brightest younger scholars also got so caught up in racism that they prepared materials for the Eastern-nationalities struggle that could be used for ethnic cleansing.[51] But does this large degree of support for Hitler's policies already constitute a direct involvement in genocide? The fresh evidence presented by Patricia von Papen-Bodek's essay in this volume and the forthcoming study of Alan Steinweis suggests that the Third Reich required a more specifically targeted *Judenforschung* largely outside academe in order to legitimize the Final Solution and to supply the instrumental information necessary for the Holocaust.[52] Hence it is not enough to posit a general agreement between radical nationalist aims and National Socialist policies; the precise linkage between professional historians and diverse National

Socialist policy makers must still be investigated in further detail so as to clarify who made what decisions on the basis of which knowledge.[53] It also does not suffice to point out the continuity of personnel and methods after 1945, if the changes in political uses are not pointed out as well.

Similarly, the problem of silence in the postwar period permits somewhat contradictory readings. Clearly, the unwillingness to admit complicity with the National Socialist regime does not speak well of the civic courage of the Schieders, Conzes, and Erdmanns, since their reticence made it more difficult to work through these issues. Also, the failure of the otherwise critical pupils to ask their powerful mentors embarrassing questions may have encouraged a structural approach to the Third Reich that tended to depersonalize guilt. The guildlike structure of the profession, with its long dependency on apprenticeship, its politicized appointment processes, and its corporate clubbishness, militated against a frank admission of mistakes and against a more insistent probing.[54] But it must not be forgotten that the West German historical discipline nonetheless opened more successfully than its Japanese counterpart to diverse viewpoints, modernized its methods, changed its topics, and produced a self-critical view of the German past. In spite of their faults, both cohorts played a crucial role in the messy effort of distancing from nationalism and conversion to democracy, since the National Socialist cohort initiated the self-questioning and the Hitler Youth generation completed the process.[55] Justified frustration with their pusillanimity ought not to overshadow an appreciation of this larger achievement.

The above controversy therefore suggests the need for greater self-reflexiveness among historians about the constraints of their own discipline. Moral rigorism is necessary and salutary, when it helps point to the many shortcomings of biased or opportunistic scholarship in the past. But it must also be complemented by a history-of-science perspective that views the discipline in a comparative light in order to establish some cognitive detachment. Put into broader terms, the problems of complicity and silence raise the question of the role of historians in political debate and policy advising. For instance, to prepare the peace talks after World War I, American scholars played a crucial role in formulating the proposals of the inquiry, which Woodrow Wilson sought to implement in the Versailles negotiations.[56] The temptation for historians to get involved in actively making history has therefore been considerable, and their judgments have not always been wise. The disastrous consequences of German scholarly support for Hitler's war also ought to caution against naïve calls for politicization in a reverse direction—however well intentioned they may be. The nationalist and racist self-delusion of professionals in the Third Reich ultimately reaffirms the importance of balancing an adherence to rational methods with a commitment to human rights as barriers against the perversion of scholarship.[57]

NOTES

1. The texts of this debate are reprinted with some additions in Otto Gerhard Oexle and Winfried Schulze, eds., *Deutsche Historiker im Nationalsozialismus* (Frankfurt, 1999). Cf. Johannes Fried, "Eröffnungsrede zum 42. Deutschen Historikertag," *Zeitschrift für Geschichtswissenschaft* 46 (1998): 869–74.

2. Götz Aly and Susanne Heim, *Vordenker der Vernichtung: Auschwitz und die deutschen Pläne für eine neue europäische Ordnung* (Hamburg, 1991). Cf. also Aly, *Macht—Geist—Wahn: Kontinuitäten Deutschen Denkens* (Frankfurt, 1997).

3. Michael Fahlbusch, *Wissenschaft im Dienst der nationalsozialistischen Politik? Die Volksdeutschen Forschungsgemeinschaften 1931 bis 1945* (Baden-Baden, 1999).

4. Ingo Haar, *Historiker im Nationalsozialismus: Die deutschen Geschichtswissenschaft und der "Volkstumskampf" im Osten* (Göttingen, 2000).

5. Peter Schöttler, ed., *Geschichtsschreibung als Legitimationswissenschaft 1918–1945* (Frankfurt, 1997), and "Deutsche Historiker im Nationalsozialismus—Zehn Thesen," *Werkstatt Geschichte* 17 (1997): 93–7.

6. Thomas Welskopp, "Die Sozialgeschichte der Väter: Grenzen und Perspektiven der Historischen Sozialwissenschaft," *Geschichte und Gesellschaft* 24 (1998): 173–98. Cf. also Georg G. Iggers, ed., *The Social History of Politics: Critical Perspectives in West German Historical Writing Since 1945* (Leamington Spa, 1985).

7. After the *Historikertag* the debate spilled over into other venues, such as additional newspaper interviews, local workshops, public lectures at the Wissenschaftskolleg in Berlin, and panel discussions such as the debate in Frankfurt/Oder in July 2000.

8. Rüdiger Hohls and Konrad H. Jarausch, *Versäumte Fragen: Deutsche Historiker im Schatten des Nationalsozialismus* (Stuttgart, 2000).

9. See the contributions of Mary Fulbrook, Robert Gellately, Wolfgang Jacobeit, Ralph Jessen, Ursula Meyerhofer, and Karen Schönwälder to

the review symposium on H-soz-kult (hsozkult.geschichte.hu-berlin.de) in the autumn of 2000. Cf. also the reviews by Manfred Hettling in *Die Zeit* (July 28, 2000), Christoph Jahr in *Neue Züricher Zeitung* (September 23, 2000), and Otto Köhler in *Konkret,* no. 9 (2000): 51–3.

10. Angelika Ebbinghaus and Karl-Heinz Roth, "Vorläufer des 'Generalplan Ost': Eine Dokumentation über Schieders Polendenkschrift vom 7. Oktober 1939," *1999: Zeitschrift für Sozialgeschichte des 20. und 21. Jahrhunderts* 7 (1992): 62–94. Cf. also his *Habilitationsschrift, Deutscher Geist und ständische Freiheit im Weichselland: Politische Idee und politisches Schrifttum von der Lubliner Union zu den polnischen Teilungen 1569 bis 1772/93* (Königsberg, 1940).

11. Werner Conze, *Hirschenhof—Die Geschichte einer deutschen Sprachinsel in Livland* (Berlin, 1934), his dissertation; and idem, *Agrarverfassung und Bevölkerung in Litauen und Weißrußland* (Leipzig, 1940), his *Habilitationsschrift.*

12. Martin Kröger and Roland Thimme, *Die Geschichtsbilder des Karl Dietrich Erdmann: Vom Dritten Reich zur Bundesrepublik* (Munich, 1996). The Third Reich textbook was never published due to reservations by some of the censors.

13. Karl Ferdinand Werner, *Das NS-Geschichtsbild und die deutsche Geschichtswissenschaft* (Stuttgart, 1967), was the first serious attempt to deal with the subject.

14. Helmut Heiber, *Walter Frank und sein Reichsinstitut für Geschichte des neuen Deutschland* (Stuttgart, 1966), concentrated on the outright Nazis in the profession.

15. Winfried Schulze, *Deutsche Geschichtswissenschaft nach 1945* (Munich, 1989). Cf. also Ernst Schulin, ed., *Deutsche Geschichtswissenschaft nach dem Zweiten Weltkrieg 1945–1965* (Munich, 1989).

16. Georg G. Iggers, *Deutsche Geschichtswissenschaft: Eine Kritik der traditionellen Geschichtsauffassung von Herder bis zur Gegenwart* (Munich, 1971), 318ff., does not mention *Volksgeschichte* at all, since it concentrates on the ideas of the mainstream of the profession.

17. Willi Oberkrome, *Volksgeschichte: Methodische Innovation und völkische Ideologisierung in der deutschen Geschichtswissenschaft 1918–1945* (Göttingen, 1993). For more evidence on Rothfels' prewar thinking, American transformation, and postwar influence, see the H-soz-kult symposium of February 14, 2003 and thereafter.

18. Hans and Wolfgang Mommsen interviews in Hohls and Jarausch, *Versäumte Fragen,* 163–217.

19. Bruno Jarausch, "Erinnerungen einer schlesisch-märkischen Familie" (Berlin, 1960), manuscript, in the author's possession.

20. Karl Ditt, "Die Kulturraumforschung zwischen Wissenschaft und Politik: Das Beispiel Franz Petri (1903–1993)," *Westfälische Forschungen* 46 (1996): 73–176. Cf. also the harsh indictment by the Dutch historian Hans Derks, *Deutsche Westforschung: Ideologie und Praxis im 20. Jahrhundert* (Leipzig, 2001).

21. War correspondence of Konrad Jarausch with his wife and brother, 1939–42, in author's possession.

22. See the discussion about Notker Hammerstein, *Die Deutsche Forschungsgemeinschaft in der Weimarer Republik und im Dritten Reich: Wissenschaftspolitik in Republik und Diktatur 1920–1945* (Munich, 1999).

23. Joachim Lerchenmueller, *Die Geschichtswissenschaft in den Planungen des Sicherheitsdienstes der SS: Der SD-Historiker Hermann Loeffler und seine Denkschrift "Entwicklung und Aufgaben der Geschichtswissenschaft in Deutschland"* (Bonn, 2001).

24. Some of the interviews in Hohls and Jarausch, *Versäumte Fragen,* mention such exceptions. Cf. also Ernst Schulin, *Hermann Heimpel und die deutsche Nationalgeschichtsschreibung* (Heidelberg, 1998).

25. This Kantian phrase was used by Gerhard A. Ritter in his interview in Hohls and Jarausch, *Versäumte Fragen,* 134.

26. Ralph Jessen, *Akademische Elite und kommunistische Diktatur: Die ostdeutsche Hochschullehrerschaft in der Ulbricht-Ära* (Göttingen, 1999); Mario Keßler, *Exilerfahrung in Wissenschaft und Politik: Remigrierte Historiker in der frühen DDR* (Cologne, 2001).

27. Winfried Schulze, "Der Neubeginn der deutschen Geschichtswissenschaft nach 1945: Einsichten und Absichtserklärungen der Historiker nach der Katastrophe," in Schulin, *Deutsche Geschichtswissenschaft nach dem Zweiten Weltkrieg,* 1–37. Cf. also Bernd Weisbrod, ed., *"Akademische Vergangenheitspolitik": Beiträge zur Wissenschaftskultur der Nachkriegszeit* (Göttingen, 2002).

28. Helmut König, Wolfgang Kuhlemann, and Klaus Schwabe, eds., *Vertuschte Vergangenheit: Der Fall Schwerte und die NS-Vergangenheit der deutschen Hochschulen* (Munich, 1997). Cf. Thomas Etzenmüller, *Sozialgeschichte als politische Geschichte: Werner Conze und die Erneuerung der westdeutschen Geschichtswissenschaft nach 1945* (Munich, 2001).

29. This is the consensus of the interviews in Hohls and Jarausch, *Versäumte Fragen.* See also Dirk Moses, "Grinding the Generational Axe," *H-soz-kult,* November 20, 2000.

30. Konrad H. Jarausch, "Der nationale Tabubruch: Wissenschaft, Öffentlichkeit und Politik in der Fischer-Kontroverse," in *Zeitgeschichte als Streitgeschichte,* ed. Martin Sabrow, Klaus Große Kracht, and Ralph Jessen (Munich, 2003), 20–36.

31. Michael Kater, *Doctors under Hitler* (Chapel Hill, N.C., 1989), 222ff., and idem, "Problems of Political Reeducation in West Germany, 1945–1960," *Simon Wiesenthal Center Annual* 4 (1987): 99–123.

32. The thesis that the democratic engagement of Schieder, Conze, and Erdmann after 1945 might atone for earlier sins was formulated by Hans-Ulrich Wehler in his interview in Hohls and Jarausch, *Versäumte Fragen*, 240ff., and his essay "Nationalsozialismus und Historiker," in Oexle and Schulze, *Deutsche Historiker im Nationalsozialismus*, 306ff.

33. Sascha-Ilko Kowalczuk, *Legitimation eines neuen Staates: Parteiarbeiter an der historischen Front. Geschichtswissenschaft in der SBZ/DDR 1945 bis 1961* (Berlin, 1997). For a more complex approach see Martin Sabrow, *Das Diktat des Konsens: Geschichtswissenschaft in der DDR, 1949–1969* (Munich, 2001).

34. Konrad H. Jarausch, "A Return to National History? The Master Narrative and Beyond?" in Konrad H. Jarausch and Michael Geyer, *Shattered Past: Reconstructing German Histories* (Princeton, N.J., 2003), 37ff. See also Konrad H. Jarausch, "The Failure of East German Anti-Fascism: Some Ironies of History as Politics," *German Studies Review* 14 (1991): 85–102.

35. Wolfgang Kraushaar, *1968: Das Jahr, das alles verändert hat* (Munich, 1968).

36. Michael Burleigh, *Germany Turns Eastward: A Study of Ostforschung in the Third Reich* (Cambridge, 1988), and Gabriele Camphausen, *Die wissenschaftliche Rußlandforschung in Dritten Reich 1933–1945* (Frankfurt, 1990).

37. Oberkrome, *Volksgeschichte*, passim; Karin Schönwälder, *Historiker und Politik: Geschichtswissenschaft im Nationalsozialismus* (Frankfurt, 1992); and Ursula Wolf, *Litteris et Patriae: Das Janusgesicht der Historie* (Stuttgart, 1996).

38. Konrad H. Jarausch and Rüdiger Hohls, "Brechungen von Biographie und Wissenschaft: Interview mit deutschen Historikern/Innen der Nachkriegsgeneration," in Hohls and Jarausch, *Versäumte Fragen*, 15–54. Cf. Dirk Moses, "The Forty-Fivers: A Generation between Fascism and Democracy," *German Politics and Society* 17 (1999): 94–126.

39. Konrad H. Jarausch, "Modernization, German Exceptionalism and Post-Modernity: Transcending the Critical History of Society," in Jarausch and Geyer, *Shattered Past*, 85ff.

40. For the power of centrist and conservative historians see Johannes Willms, "Das Treibhaus der Geschichte," *Süddeutsche Zeitung*, September 19, 2000. Cf. Konrad H. Jarausch, "Normalisierung oder Re-Nationalisierung? Zur Umdeutung der deutschen Vergangenheit," *Geschichte und Gesellschaft* 21 (1995): 571–84.

41. Winfried Schulze, "Der Wandel des Allgemeinen: Der Weg der

deutschen Historiker nach 1945 zur Kategorie des Sozialen," in *Teil und Ganzes: Zum Verhältnis von Einzel- und Gesamtanalyse in Geschichts- und Sozialwissenschaften,* ed. Winfried Schulze and Karl Acham (Munich, 1990), 193–216.

42. Mary Fulbrook, "Much Ado about Something Completely Different?" in *H-soz-kult,* November 2000. Cf. also Konrad H. Jarausch, "Die Provokation des Anderen: Amerikanische Perspektiven auf Deutsche Vergangenheitsbewältigung," in *Doppelte Zeitgeschichte: Deutsch-deutsche Beziehungen 1945–1990,* ed. Arndt Bauerkämper, Martin Sabrow, and Bernd Stöver (Bonn, 1998).

43. Bernd Giesen, *Intellectuals and the German Nation: Collective Identity in a German Axial Age* (Cambridge, 1998); and Hans-Julius Schoeps, ed., *Ein Volk von Mördern? Die Debatte zur Goldhagen-Kontroverse um die Rolle der Deutschen im Holocaust* (Hamburg, 1996).

44. Konrad H. Jarausch, "Survival in Catastrophe: Mending Broken Memories," in Jarausch and Geyer, *Shattered Past,* 317ff.

45. Hohls and Jarausch, "Brechungen von Biographie und Wissenschaft," 43f.

46. Matthias Beer, "Die Dokumentation der Vertreibung der Deutschen aus Ost-Mitteleuropa: Hintergründe, Entstehung, Ergebnis, Wirkung," *Geschichte in Wissenschaft und Unterricht* 50 (1999): 99–117. Cf. also Ursula Wiggershaus-Müller, *Nationalsozialismus und Geschichtswissenschaft: Die Geschichte der Historischen Zeitschrift und des Historischen Jahrbuchs 1933–1945* (Hamburg, 1998).

47. Compare Jan Pikorski, Jörg Hackmann, and Rudolf Jaworski, eds., *Deutsche Ostforschung und polnische Westforschung im Spannungsfeld von Wissenschaft und Politik* (Osnabrück, 2002), with Burkhard Dietz, Helmut Gabel, and Ulrich Tiedau, eds., *Griff nach dem Westen: Die "Westforschung" der völkisch-nationalen Wissenschaften zum nordwesteuropäischen Raum 1919–1960* (Münster, 2003). The latter triggered another heated symposium on *"Westforschung"* in HSK, beginning on May 13, 2003.

48. Robert Gellately, "Social Consensus and Germany's Educated Elite in the Shadow of Nazism," as well as the other reviews in *H-soz-kult,* September–October 2000.

49. Ulrich Heinemann, *Die verdrängte Niederlage: Politische Öffentlichkeit und Kriegsschuldfrage in der Weimarer Republik* (Göttingen, 1983); and Wolfgang Jäger, *Historische Forschung und politische Kultur in Deutschland: Die Debatte 1914–1980 über den Ausbruch des Ersten Weltkrieges* (Göttingen, 1984).

50. Heinrich-August Winkler, *Der lange Weg nach Westen: Deutsche Geschichte,* 2 vols. (Munich, 2000). The disastrous infatuation with Reich mythology was stronger for medievalists like Hermann Heimpel.

51. See texts by Schieder and Conze in nn. 10 and 11 and commentary in Oexle and Schulze, *Deutsche Historiker im Nationalsozialismus.*

52. Patricia von Papen, "Anti-Jewish Research of the Institut zur Erforschung der Judenfrage or Außenstelle of the High School of the NSDAP in Frankfurt am Main" (Frankfurt, 2000), manuscript. See also Alan E. Steinweis, "'Jewish Research' in Nazi Germany: Historiographical and Methodological Reflections" (Lincoln, Neb., 2000), manuscript.

53. The papers in the session on "Volksgeschichte und Kulturbodenforschung zwischen Versailles und Kaltem Krieg" at the Aachen Historikertag in September 2000 show that the initial emotionalism of the debate is subsiding, since the arguments are becoming more differentiated.

54. Wolfgang Weber, *Priester der Klio: Historisch-sozialwissenschaftliche Studien zur Herkunft und Karriere deutscher Historiker und zur Geschichte der Geschichtswissenschaft 1800–1970* (Frankfurt, 1984).

55. Georg G. Iggers, "Epilogue," in *The German Conception of History: The National Tradition of Historical Thought from Herder to the Present,* rev. ed. (Middletown, Conn., 1983), 269–93. See also Sebastian Conrad, *Auf der Suche nach der verlorenen Nation: Geschichtswissenschaft in Westdeutschland und Japan, 1945–1960* (Göttingen, 1999).

56. Larry E. Gelfand, *The Inquiry: American Preparations for Peace, 1917–1919* (New Haven, Conn., 1963).

57. Konrad H. Jarausch, *The Unfree Professions: German Lawyers, Teachers and Engineers, 1900–1950* (New York, 1990), 226ff.

Devin Pendas

The Historiography of Horror:
The Frankfurt Auschwitz Trial and the
German Historical Imagination

IN JULY 1962, THE ACADEMIC ADVISORY BOARD (*Wissenschaftliche Beirat*) of the Munich-based Institute for Contemporary History held its annual meeting. In keeping with the board's general supervisory role, it considered not only the institute's research activities but also its public, pedagogical endeavors as well. According to the board's report, "Individual members of the [academic] board and representatives of the foundation board (*Stiftungsrat*) raised the question as to what the institute could do to strive for greater public impact. In particular, people expected the institute to take a position on certain factual distortions of contemporary history (*Verzerrungen zeitgeschichtlicher Sachverhalte*). . . ."[1] However, professor Hans Rothfels, one of the editors of the institute's *Schriftenreihe,* protested that while public impact was one of the institute's goals, it ought not be the primary one, which should remain research. He argued that it was important that the members of the institute not disperse their efforts too greatly (*"sich verzetteln"*).[2] He worried that too much involvement in public controversies would merely distract the members of the institute from their scholarly work. Indeed, he wondered if "here and there, say in terms of public lectures, the problem is not that too much rather than too little has been undertaken."[3]

By the board's next meeting a year later, Rothfels had changed his mind. The institute's protocol summarized his new position as follows:

> As the result of a certain transformation in public opinion, the institute finds itself in a new situation. Publicity work, which he [Roth-

fels] had otherwise always sought to restrict, had become extremely urgent in the face of highly dubious apologetics, accompanied by defamatory attacks on the Institute and "all of us" by right-wing radicals. This constituted a change in mood that could not be taken seriously enough.[4]

Indeed, in reading the protocols of these meetings, one gets the impression that many of these historians studying the recent—that is, the Nazi—past in the 1960s felt that they were under siege. At the 1963 meeting of the foundation board, Rothfels had been even more specific as to the source of his growing concerns for public pedagogy, noting that the work of foreign historians, such as A. J. P. Taylor or the American revisionist David Hogan, was particularly disturbing.[5] But the historians of the institute were not simply concerned about erroneous or even malicious scholarship concerning Nazism; they were genuinely, though not hysterically, concerned about the apparent resurgence of the radical Right in Germany at the time.[6]

If there was an emerging consensus among the institute's board members that it had an obligation to counter historical distortions in the public sphere in the early 1960s, there was less agreement as to how best to achieve this goal. Indeed, there was a good deal of controversy over whether it was appropriate for the institute to provide *Gutachten* (expert advice or testimony) to private, nongovernmental parties. As a public (*öffentlich-rechtlich*) institution, the institute was required by law to provide such expert testimony to public agencies, including the judiciary. However, it was less clear whether it should—or even could, within the bounds of law—do the same for other parties. In particular, the governmental representatives on both the academic and foundation boards were concerned about the propriety of the institute's providing testimony to private parties, especially to some of the more frivolous popular publications. (The controversy was sparked when members of the institute authenticated some documents for the magazine *Stern*).[7] Such concerns on the part of at least some board members precluded anything like a major publicity campaign's being undertaken by the institute on its own initiative.

Therefore, if it wanted to reach out to the German public sphere to try to counteract what was perceived as a relatively systematic campaign of disinformation and distortion by the radical Right, the institute would have to find some other venue. The best-case scenario would be to find some highly public, officially sanctioned opportunity to set straight the record of the Third Reich once and for all. That opportunity came in early 1964, when historians from the institute gave expert testimony in the so-called Frankfurt Auschwitz Trial.[8]

A coincidence of interests emerged in the early 1960s between the Institute for Contemporary History and the Frankfurt prosecutor's office as it prepared for what was to be the largest and most comprehensive Nazi trial to date in West German courts. As early as May 1961, the prosecution team approached Hans Buchheim, then director of the institute, to discuss the possibility of obtaining historical *Gutachten* (opinions of experts) for use in the trial.[9] Buchheim agreed in principle and the details were left to be worked out in subsequent meetings. In October 1962 further general discussions took place and then, in early November, representatives from the federal state of Hesse, where the trial was being prepared, met with members of the institute to hammer out the details.[10]

The Hessian attorney general, Fritz Bauer, and the Frankfurt prosecutor's office had two reasons for seeking expert testimony from historians in Nazi cases. On the one hand, they were juridically concerned with mounting an effective prosecution. To do so, they felt it necessary to counter what they perceived to have been a potent defense strategy in earlier Nazi trials. Bauer noted that the defense had been able in these earlier trials to use procedural arguments to obscure the true meaning of such cases. "The defense brings to light the fact that things which, on the basis of recent history, actually ought to be able to be presumed as known to the court, cannot in fact be evaluated [by the court] without further ado if [these facts] are not actually introduced into evidence in a given trial."[11] In other words, unless historical facts were specifically entered into evidence, they could not be treated as legally proven, no matter how common the knowledge in question may in fact have been. To circumvent this difficulty, Bauer and the historians had already agreed in October that it made sense to have experts give background testimony covering the general political and historical events that formed the backdrop and indispensable context for these crimes.[12]

On the other hand, Bauer and his prosecutors were, like the historians from the Institute for Contemporary History, also deeply concerned about the general public understanding of the Nazi past. For Bauer, Nazi trials were clearly intended to be lessons in history and morality as well as judicial proceedings.[13] Therefore, the omission of history from prior Nazi trials was a problem not only for the successful prosecution of Nazi perpetrators but also for the public pedagogical value of such trials. At a high-level meeting of authorities involved in Nazi prosecutions the preceding October, Bauer had noted that "there is a further problem in that in previous trials, the defense has succeeded in dismembering the proceedings into small pieces, so that neither the jurors, trial observers nor the general public could get a general picture [of the events in question]."[14] Because they were not as strictly bound by the proceduralism of the legal process as prosecutors, in particular because they were not as constrained by the doctrine of legal relevance, expert witnesses could provide precisely the kind of general overview of Nazism and the Holocaust that had hitherto been impossible to present in Nazi trials. Such an overview was so valuable to the Hessian authorities that they were willing to risk being accused of orchestrating a show trial by deploying such evidence.[15]

A Nazi trial without an adequate historical dimension, Bauer implied, could succeed neither as a trial nor as a public event. "The meaning and purpose of the *Gutachten* should be to make the true intentions of the Nazi regime accessible to the court and the German public in the form of scholarly presentations."[16] These were to be academic rather than prosecutorial in character, pedagogical rather than evidentiary in the narrow sense. Above all, the *Gutachten* were seen by Bauer and the Frankfurt prosecutors as a way to compensate for what might be termed the "history deficit" in previous Nazi trials. They were to present the broad political, institutional, and historical context of the specific events on trial in a given case.

The institute was clearly delighted to have such a public forum in which to present the scholarly findings of its members. This is evinced by the following rather self-satisfied note in the institute's 1964 "activities report" describing the *Gutachten* in the Auschwitz Trial: "The expert testimony delivered by Dr. Broszat, Dr. Buchheim and Dr. Krausnick in the Auschwitz Trial met with an unusually high interest in the domestic and foreign press and in German radio, which was much to be desired in the best interests of the Institute."[17] While this assessment of the press coverage of the historical testimony in the trial is unfortunately overly optimistic, it clearly reflects what the institute hoped would be the result of its role in the trial.[18]

Altogether, five historians were asked to give testimony in the

Frankfurt Auschwitz Trial, three from the institute (Hans Buchheim, Martin Broszat, and Helmut Krausnick), one from Bonn University (Hans-Adolf Jacobsen, who was technically a political scientist), and one from the German Academy of Sciences in East Berlin (Jürgen Kuczynski). Broadly speaking, their testimony can be divided into two categories. The first and largest set of reports covered precisely the kind of general background information relevant to the trial. This group includes Buchheim's report on the history and structure of the SS; Broszat's two reports, one on the Nazi concentration camp system in general and one on Nazi policy in Poland; and finally, Krausnick's broad-ranging report on anti-Semitism and Jewish persecution both before and during the Third Reich. The second category of reports concerned more specific details of policy bearing either on the legal culpability of the defendants in the trial or on the structure of Auschwitz itself. This category includes Buchheim's analysis of authority and obedience in the SS (relevant to the defense by higher orders), Hans-Adolf Jacobsen's report on the so-called Commissar Order and the mass execution of Soviet POWs (relevant to the allegations against some of the individual defendants), and Kuczynski's account of the role of IG Farben at Auschwitz (relevant, or at least purportedly so, to the structure of the camp itself).[19] With the exception of Kuczynski's report, which was given at the request of the East German civil counsel, Friedrich Karl Kaul, and subsequently rejected by the court as biased, all six of these *Gutachten* had been explicitly requested in advance by the prosecution.[20]

The first point to note about the historical testimony in the Auschwitz Trial is that these historians presented well-constructed, cogent historical analyses based on extensive documentary evidence and representing the state of the historiographic field at that time. These reports were in the best philological tradition of German historiography, critically engaging with their sources in great detail. Each presented substantial, highly detailed, empirically grounded accounts of their specific topics.[21] Indeed, in the foreword to the published version of these reports, the authors asserted that this empirico-critical detail was in fact the defining scholarly *and* political facet of their work. They noted that a trial "demands a particularly high degree of rationality and sobriety," since these reports were not simply historical essays but also legal documents that would help determine the fate of the accused.[22] And it was precisely this extra degree of reason and sobriety that the authors hoped would render their reports especially "healthy" (*heilsam*) for a public sphere often too inclined to try to master the Nazi past in overly emotional terms. "'Rousing the conscience,' they call it. But a sleepy conscience is like a sleepy person: one can easily roust them from sleep with a good shake—but after a couple of half-awake moments, they go right back to sleep. By contrast, once human understanding (*Verstand*) has got a hold of something, it hangs on and will never lose it again."[23]

In testifying in the Auschwitz Trial, these historians thus pursued a dual goal: to assist the court in determining the legally relevant facts concerning criminal activity at Auschwitz, and to present the West German public with an irrefutable factual analysis of the Third Reich to stand as bulwark against a rising tide of right-wing revisionist apologias. Unfortunately, as it turned out, these goals were not always completely compatible.

From a legal standpoint, what was at stake in the trial was perforce the individual culpability of the defendants for specific, identifiable crimes committed at Auschwitz. The ultimate juridical value of the historians' testimony rested on their ability to situate that guilt—or a homologous innocence, as the case may be—in a specific historical context that illuminated the scope for individual agency, and hence responsibility, within that context.[24] To put it bluntly, from a legal perspective, what the historians had to say was of interest only to the extent that it bore, more or less directly, on the guilt of the twenty-two specific individuals on trial in Frankfurt. That the general historical context of Nazism was relevant to that guilt was agreed upon by all of the trial's participants, but only in the relatively restricted sense that that historical context established the playing field, so to speak, upon which the criminal drama of Auschwitz played out. As the presiding judge, Hans Hofmeyer, put it shortly after the conclusion of the trial, it was imperative to fit Nazi trials into the framework of [ordinary] criminal procedure—that is, so long as we do not view these trials as political trials but as murder trials in the sense of the criminal code, though admittedly ones in which the political situation which led the defendants to their actions cannot be lost from view but dare not become the centerpiece of the proceedings, either.[25] In this context, the task facing the historians testifying in the trial was to provide a summary of that important—but not overly important—political situation.

By contrast, from a historiographic, pedagogical perspective, what was at stake was to provide a systematic account of the interconnection between "the concentration camps and the mass murder of the Jews," on the one hand, and Nazism as a system of political domination, on the other.[26] Whether by reducing the issue to one of moral theology (Auschwitz as Hell) or criminal opportunism (Nazism as gangsterism), Germans had all too often lost sight of the essential connection between Nazism as a political form and the ideological mass crimes committed in the camps as the most horrifying content of that form. According to the historians, the great value of Nazi trials was that they placed the issue of this essential relationship between politics and criminality at center stage. "The actions of the individual defendant who participated in the crimes can only be properly understood and fairly judged if one understands the interconnection (*Geflecht*) between the spiritual, political and organizational preconditions that led to those actions."[27] Now, it is true that there is nothing inherently contradictory about this understanding of the role of the historian as expert witness and the legal understanding of that role. Indeed, the historians themselves asserted that their job was to portray the "historical and political landscape in which the individual events played out."[28] So there was a certain correspondence between the self-understanding of what the historians thought they were doing and what the court wanted them to do.[29]

The problem, at least in this case, sets in when one turns to the specific landscape being portrayed. Because Auschwitz was an SS institution par excellence, and because all save one of the defendants had been members of the SS (the remaining defendant having been an inmate *Kapo*), the political-landscape portrait necessarily concentrated on the SS. As the historians put it, the centerpiece of the testimony concerns an anatomy of the SS state. That means that it is less a question of what the SS *did* in detail but rather a matter of the origin and function of the power apparatus created by the unification of the SS and the police. In other words, how was totalitarian domination exercised in daily practice.[30] To describe these reports as an "anatomy," as their published version did, is supremely accurate because what they do, above all, is to dissect the structure and to describe the typology of the SS and its concentration camp system.

This is most obviously true of Buchheim's two reports on the SS proper and of Broszat's account of the concentration camp system.

Together these three reports form the core anatomical analysis of these reports. Thus, in describing what he termed the "revolutionizing innovation" of the Third Reich's constitutional structure, Buchheim, drawing on Ernst Fraenkel's earlier work, stressed the dual nature of Hitler's authority, that it was both *of* and *beyond* the state, as exemplified in his official title as Führer and Reich Chancellor.[31] Consequently, the Third Reich could not, on Buchheim's account, be understood as simply comprising a concentration and intensification of *state* power, nor even ultimately as a balancing act between competing forms of state power—say, between the legal and the party state. Rather, the history of the Third Reich was a process of *destatifying* public life (*"'Entstaatlichung' des öffentlichen Lebens"*).[32] Buchheim here makes an essentially classificatory argument: the Third Reich is not to be understood as a state at all, in the proper sense of that term (i.e., as a political entity bound by legal norms). Nor is it really to be understood as a political *party* masquerading as a state, because the Party itself represented at least a potential challenge to the supremacy of Hitler's own power and was incipiently "legalized"—that is, bound to positive norms, just like the state. This would have constrained Hitler's freedom to exercise power according to perceived laws of historical necessity, in his capacity as the embodiment of the *Volk*.[33] In the end, the Third Reich was, purely and simply, a manifestation of *Führergewalt*, of the leader's pure authority (with overtones of violence).

The role of the SS in this system was to operate as the Führer's executive, to implement, without reference to either positive law or state norms, whatever Hitler deemed to be historically necessary. "[I]n this way, the principle of *Führergewalt* was realized in its pure form over the years and the process of destatifying public life was driven forward. The historical meaning of the SS lay in having been the actual, adequate tool of *Führergewalt*, by virtue of being the Führer's executive."[34] The SS was an executive organ beyond normative regulation, which in practice tended to mean one that operated in overt opposition to all normative practice.[35] In this regard, to call the anatomy described by these historians an anatomy of the SS *state* might actually be a misnomer; it would perhaps have been more accurate to refer to them as an anatomy of the SS *anti-state*.

The remainder of these reports, with the significant exception of Krausnick's account of anti-Jewish policy, carry through this anatomy in great detail. Buchheim, for example, describes the intricacies of the bureaucratic hierarchy of the Nazi police apparatus, from Himmler through all of the many and varied subunits of the police and the SS. Broszat traces the trajectory of the concentration camp system from its initial function as a series of holding pens for political opponents to its apotheosis during the war as one of the central components of the economic organization of slave labor for the war effort, touching, though only briefly, on the role of the camps as sites of mass death. In both cases, the reports restricted themselves for obvious topical reasons to purely internal accounts of events and institutions between 1933 and 1945. Their character as an anatomy of the SS anti-state, the result of both the legal context and of the underlying interpretive schema, meant that the evolution of that anti-state was treated only immanently, on its own terms. It was never examined in relation to developments in German history prior to the Nazi seizure of power, nor comparatively, in relation to other aspects of German society during the period 1933–45 or to other forms of authoritarian governance. The result was a curious disassociation of the SS anti-state both from German history more generally and from German society as a whole. Indeed, the central thesis that the SS represented the negation of the state, its antithesis, means that, by implication, the state itself is exempted in some measure from the antinormative guilt accruing to the SS.

Historical developments are treated in very narrow, institutional forms. The following example can be taken as indicative. In describing the transition from the relatively chaotic early history of the concentration camps in the immediate aftermath of the Nazi seizure of power to the more closely regulated and regularized development of the camps in the years leading up to the pogrom of November 9, 1938, Broszat notes: "The protective custody decree of the Reich Ministry of the Interior [RMdI] of 12./26. April 1934 remained in effect as a guideline until January 1938. In the course of the further development of the concentration camps, however, it was not the tendency to terminate the state of emergency (*Ausnahmezustand*) but rather the contrary efforts to make it into a fixed and permanent arrangement that prevailed."[36] The failure of efforts to subordinate the camps to the regular judiciary is attributed primarily to personal opposition by Hitler.

In this brief account, we see the essential characteristics of this mode of historical argumentation. It focuses on the level of formal political action by government and/or party elites. Its subject matter is administrative regulations and institutional arrangements. To the extent that non-Nazi elements in German society (in this case, the judiciary and the civil service) are touched on at all, they are treated as at least limited opponents of the Nazis. The driving force of historical developments is the internal power struggles among German elites. (In this case, the civil administration loses to the Nazis and, among the Nazis, the Sturmabtejlung [SA] loses to the SS.) So to reiterate: To call this mode of argumentation an anatomy is perhaps more apt than its authors realized because its function is to trace a schema of typological connections internal to the "organism" in question, in this case, the SS and the concentration camps. To stretch the metaphor a bit: the evolutionary history of that organism per se is bracketed and left aside.

Among the historical reports presented in the Auschwitz Trial, there was one important exception to this purely internalist approach to the Third Reich. In his account of Nazi anti-Jewish policy, Helmut Krausnick ranged quite freely across European history, tracing the antecedents of Nazi anti-Jewish policy in the emergence of modern, nontheological anti-Semitism in the nineteenth century. In particular, Krausnick traced the origins of Nazi anti-Semitism to the doctrine of Social Darwinism as it emerged in the 1890s.[37] He also stressed the significant role played by Hitler's own pathological hatred of the Jews. Krausnick's report thus represented the sole effort to present a comprehensive history of at least one aspect of the Nazi regime and the Final Solution. But because it focused on only one aspect of Nazi Germany, albeit the one most directly pertinent in the given context, Krausnick's report, too, seemed somewhat detached from the broader history of Nazism and the Holocaust. There is a curious disconnect between Krausnick's report and the others. Anti-Semitism has a history that transcends not only Nazism but even—to an extent—Germany itself.[38] Otherwise, there is only the institutional history of the SS itself. In other words, anti-Semitism, as the ideological foundation of the Final Solution, is raised to the level of a transcendental, pan-European phenomenon while the Third Reich is reduced to the history of one of its constituent organizations. The only mediating link between the two is Adolf Hitler, who forms both the culmination of the cultural trajectory of anti-Semitism and the operative principle guiding the antinormative activity of the SS.

Much of this can obviously be attributed to the constraints of the juridical setting. For one thing, the range of topics addressed was considerably restricted by the demands of legal relevance. In addition to these initial background reports, two subsequent reports were accepted by the court concerning the problem of duress and higher orders and the so-called Kommissarbefehl ordering the execution of all Soviet commissars in the course of the campaign in Russia.[39] Taken together, then, these reports either addressed specific aspects of the Nazi regime deemed directly pertinent to the trial or evaluated technical legal considerations (duress, higher orders, and the specific order to kill Soviet commissars) from a historical perspective. In all cases, the reports' topics corresponded to the court's need for specific information deemed relevant to evaluating the individual guilt of the defendants. These topics, in turn, greatly restricted the scope of the historical analysis that could be undertaken. The historians were not free to evaluate the history of Nazism in general but rather *had* to evaluate, per their commission, only those aspects of it that might make a difference to the court's evaluation of the allegations against the individual defendants. The end result was not a history of Nazism, Nazi Germany, or even the Holocaust but only a structural anatomy of the institutional context of the individual guilt of the trial's defendants. It could not be otherwise.

That the SS state, or anti-state, was not necessarily coeval with or equivalent to the Nazi regime as such, much less with Nazi Germany as a whole, was to an extent indicated in these reports (e.g., in Broszat's interpretation of the concentration camps as the institutionalization of a "state of emergency"). But to the extent that the distinction between the SS and the remainder of German society emerges in these reports, it serves to highlight not their mutual entanglement but rather their mutual distinctiveness. Whatever one thinks of Buchheim's assertion that the SS, as the executive aspect of *Führergewalt,* became the indispensable instrument of Nazi domination, the fact remains that, at best, this interpretation leaves major dimensions of the Third Reich and the Holocaust unexplored. (At worst, it promotes a one-sided inflation of one aspect of the Nazi regime at the expense of other, equally important and, morally and historiographically more

disturbing, dimensions of German society in the years 1933–45).[40]
The historical portrait that emerged was narrowly focused and topi-
cally restricted, a contribution to, but not a substitute for, a more
comprehensive history of Nazism and the Holocaust.

This particular historical anatomy ultimately correlated strongly
with the "intentionalist," SS-oriented historical narrative presented by
the prosecution and the court in the Auschwitz Trial. These juridical
re-presentations of this historical narrative in turn gave an even more
reductionist, one-sided account of the Third Reich.[41] For obvious
reasons, the historical narratives presented in both the indictment
(*Anklageschrift*) and the judgment (*Urteil*) were considerably less
sophisticated and detailed than that presented by the historians.
Nonetheless, they likewise focused strongly on the internal history of
the SS and the concentration camps, especially Auschwitz itself. In
particular, these judicial histories stressed an intentionalist interpretation of the Holocaust that linked it directly to Hitler's own pathological hatred of the Jews.[42] This interpretation was already built into
the legal interpretation of the Holocaust as a crime committed at its
core by a handful of so-called "main perpetrators" (*Haupttäter*), primarily Hitler, Himmler, and Heydrich, aided and abetted by hundreds or thousands of co-perpetrators and accomplices.[43] According
to German legal interpretation, agency in the Holocaust remained
firmly in the hands of Adolf Hitler and those who actually carried out
the killing or who were instrumental in organizing it at a concrete
level could at most share some degree of that agency (and, in the process, make themselves culpable). To the extent that they internalized
Hitler's criminal motives, made his motives "their own," the actual
killers in the Final Solution could be considered co-perpetrators; but
if they simply acted out of obedience or convenience or moral lazi-
ness, they were, at worst, accomplices. Therefore, legally speaking,
the essential *historical fact* about the Holocaust and Auschwitz had to
be that it flowed directly from Hitler.

In this context, then, the argument that the essence of the SS lay
in its character as the executive branch of *Führergewalt* takes on new
meaning. Regardless of whether such historical arguments were deliberately constructed with legal categories in mind—and I tend to
doubt it, though the evidence gives no indication one way or the
other—there is a clear congruence. In this case, the historians and the
lawyers and judges constructed mutually reinforcing interpretations

of the Nazi past, one that depicted agency as flowing downward from Hitler to his minions but that also preserved a scope for autonomous, individual (indeed, monadic) evil within the SS as the agency of the Führer's will. However, if the model of the anti-state was already exculpatory in implication, the juridical model of the SS as an ersatz state directly operationalizing Hitler's personal will is even more so. On such an account, the SS becomes the primary institutional source of guilt for the defendants and, by extension, the primary—perhaps the sole—source of genuine (that is, criminal) guilt in Germany. Every other institutional locus of action becomes guilty of, at worst, poor judgment and bad luck. This means that the SS truly becomes an alibi for the remainder of the nation.

Such simplifications were picked up and amplified in the press, to the extent that they concerned themselves with the historical testimony in the trial at all, which was not very much. The following account of Krausnick's report from the *Frankfurter Allgemeine Zeitung* was perhaps the most extensive in the entire press. And, as one can see, it was not very extensive at all. From the expert testimony, one garners the following: serious consideration of interning the Jews even then; a "Germanic cult" was born, to which Richard Wagner contributed his bit; Houston Stewart Chamberlain pleaded for "maintaining the purity of the race"; and Social Darwinism outlined the principle of "natural selection and higher evolution through the continual struggle for survival." Humanity no longer counted in circles where the question was seriously discussed whether "elements not worthy of life" could be supported, where national utility took precedent over justice, where human beings were sterilized and "bred."[44] For the press, then, the lesson to be gleaned from the historical testimony in the Auschwitz Trial, contrary to Fritz Bauer's high hopes for the pedagogical value of such testimony, was little more than a series of buzzwords, ones that additionally served to ratify the growing impression in the press that defendants in the trial had been, by and large, sadistic monsters or devils.

In general, the strong focus on the SS in these *Gutachten* was a direct outcome of the trial's focus on Auschwitz. Auschwitz *was* an SS institution; indeed, it might be fair to say that it was *the* SS institution par excellence. However, as even the title of the published version of these reports indicates, this focus on the SS was quite expansive. This is not an anatomy of the SS within a Nazi or German state but an anatomy of the SS as a state or (as I have indicated), more precisely, an anti-state. This equation of the SS and the state or to a certain extent as its negation reflects the state of the discipline in the mid-1960s. (Broszat, for instance, notes that his is the first systematic account of the concentration camps since Eugen Kogon's very early history of the camps, called—appropriately enough— *The SS State*).[45] It is fully consonant with the totalitarian model prevalent throughout the 1950s, particularly in its stress on the opposition between Nazism as a "movement" and the ordinariness of the normative "state."[46] At the time, it presages the types of structural, polycratic analysis that were to emerge so forcefully at the end of the 1960s (e.g. Hans Mommsen's or Broszat's own later work).[47] At the same time, however, the interpretation presented in these reports also reflected a generalization of the mandatory legal focus on the specific site of the crime—Auschwitz—to a general historiographical principle.

As such, whether intentionally or not, this approach sustains an image of a non-Nazi domain outside the SS. There is a marked tendency to reduce German criminality to Nazi criminality and Nazi criminality to SS criminality. And this is as true of the historical testimony presented in the Auschwitz Trial as it is of the trial itself. To give but one particularly important example, this focus on anatomizing the SS, mandated by the specifics of the Auschwitz Trial but true of Nazi trials and their emergent historical narratives more generally as well, exempted from scrutiny the other great pillar of Nazi Germany: the Wehrmacht. This tendency to exempt the Wehrmacht from inclusion in the circle of mass criminality persisted with considerable vigor until quite recently. As late as 1989, Hans Mommsen could write:

> The mentality of the average *Landser* was characterized by soberness, rejection of the far-from-reality propaganda tirades, and by a firm will personally to survive. Certainly, under cover [*unter dem Vorzeichen*] of the commissar order there were grave encroachments by the army against the defenseless civilian population handed over to it and against prisoners of war; partisan war led to an unprecedented brutalization of the conduct of war by both sides. But the average soldier had little influence on this and could hardly find a way of avoiding the escalation of violence.[48]

It was only in the late 1970s, with the publication of the monumental quasi-official history of the war, that this view began to be fundamentally challenged.[49] And even then, it was not until the very late 1980s, if then, that this challenge can be considered a success, at least within the German academy.

It is an open question whether this challenge to the view of German criminality as residing exclusively with the SS has ever succeed more generally, as the controversy and public protests surrounding the so-called "Crimes of the Wehrmacht" exhibit demonstrate.[50] And while this myth of the "clean" Wehrmacht by no means originated with an academic orientation toward the study of the SS, such an orientation did much to sustain that myth (however unintentionally). The SS did become, in the words of one of its early historians, "the alibi of a nation."[51]

This is not to say that the SS was not a central power apparatus for Hitler's regime, nor that the SS did not expand parasitically to invade all arenas of public, and even private, life, especially in the regime's later years. Rather, as the polycratic model of Nazi power, which became dominant a few years after the publication of *Anatomy* indicates, the SS could be considered neither coterminous with a state that hardly existed in any unitary sense under the Nazis anyway, nor as the simple negation of a state that thereby remained innocent of all that was done in its name but behind its back. The SS was one power center among several, at times subordinate, at times dominant. And just as Nazi criminality cannot be reduced to Auschwitz, the perpetrators of the Holocaust cannot be reduced to the SS.

Above all, this focus on the SS, when coupled with the strong emphasis on atrocity that emerged in the trial, helped to sustain what might be termed a "minoritarian view" of Nazism. This view holds that the Third Reich was a criminal regime, imposed on the vast majority of indifferent or hostile Germans by a small minority of very brutal fanatics. A number of ordinary Germans may have been co-opted or reduced to providing support for the regime or to "implementing" its policies, but their heart was never in it. The bulk of Germans remained essentially apolitical, perhaps appreciative of the regime's material successes, while naïvely underestimating its brutality. And where this naïveté left off, the terror of the Gestapo began. At any event, the majority of Germans, in this view, were always far more committed to their own private interests and to *Germany* as such than to the Nazi regime itself.

In the end, the historical testimony in the Auschwitz Trial, for all its remarkable documentary insight, cannot help but point in the wrong direction. In and of itself, this is hardly fatal. Most histories, perforce, tell a partial story, focus on a specific issue or theme that does not and cannot encompass the whole. In the case of these reports, however, their connection with the Auschwitz Trial, which to a large extent grounds their restrictive focus, also gave them the status of an "official history." This was not just another history of the Nazi regime and its atrocities. This was a history produced by the IfZ, a governmentally sanctioned historical institute, and read into evidence at a state trial; this was as close as a democratic society ever comes to having a historiographical party line. And this party line pointed directly away from a view of the Holocaust as a total social act, one involving huge numbers of Germans in one way or another and, more significantly, the entirety of German society as an organized collectivity.

NOTES

1. Institut für Zeitgeschichte, Munich (hereafter IfZ), ED 105: Hausarchiv (30 July 1962), "Ergebnisprotokoll der konstituierenden Sitzung des Wissenschaftlichen Beirats des Instituts für Zeitgeschichte München," 7.

2. Ibid.

3. Ibid.

4. IfZ, ED 105: Hausarchiv (2 August 1963), "Ergebnisprotokoll der konstituierenden Sitzung des Wissenschaftlichen Beirats des Instituts für Zeitgeschichte München," 15.

5. IfZ, ED 105: Hausarchiv (1 August 1963), "Protokoll über die 4. Sitzung des Stiftungsrates," 9. See A. J. P. Taylor, *The Origins of the Second World War* (London: Hamilton, 1961); on Taylor's thesis more generally, see William R. Louis, ed., *The Origins of the Second World War: A. J. P. Taylor and His Critics* (New York: Wiley, 1972) and Gordon Martel, ed., *The Origins of the Second World War Reconsidered: The A. J. P. Taylor Debate after 25 Years* (Boston: Allen and Unwin, 1996). For Hogan, see David L. Hogan, *Der erzwungene Krieg: Die Ursachen und Urheber des 2. Weltkriegs* (Tübingen: Verlag der deutschen Hochschullehrer-Zeitung, 1961). This book was not published in English for nearly thirty years, and then by a notorious revisionist press, as David L. Hogan, *The Forced War: When Peaceful Revision Failed* (Cosa Mesa: Institute for Historical Review, 1989).

6. The following year (1964), the institute's director, Helmut Kraus-

nick, informed the board that he had had to obtain a temporary restraining order against the Deutsche National Zeitung for defaming him. And Rothfels, by now almost militant on these matters, noted that, "Insofar as there are [right-wing] blacklists, the Institute is on the blackest of them." IfZ, ED 105: (24 July 1964), "Ergebnisprotokoll der gemeinsamen Sitzung des Wissenschaftlichen Beirats und des Stiftungsrats des Instituts für Zeitgeschichte," 4, 17.

7. On the initial discussion of the *Stern* issue, see IfZ, ED 105: Hausarchiv (2 August 1963), "Ergebnisprotokoll der Sitzung des Wissenschaftliche Beirats des Instituts für Zeitgeschichte München," 16–17. The debate continued, however, in both the academic and foundation boards through at least 1965. See the relevant reports in IfZ, ED 105: Hausarchiv.

8. The Frankfurt Auschwitz Trial was, until the Majdanek Trial in the late 1970s, the largest and most comprehensive West German Nazi trial. It ran from December 1963 to August 1965. Twenty-two initial defendants (two were subsequently dropped for health reasons) were charged as either perpetrators of or accomplices to murder for crimes committed at Auschwitz. Seventeen were convicted and given sentences ranging from just over three years to life; three were acquitted. For a general overview, see Herman Langbein, *Der Auschwitz-Prozeß: Eine Dokumentation,* 2 vols. (1965; reprint, Frankfurt: Verlag Neue Kritik, 1995); and Bernd Naumann, *Auschwitz: A Report on the Proceedings against Robert Karl Ludwig Mulka and Others before the Court at Frankfurt* (New York: Frederick A. Praeger, 1966). For general overviews of the role of historians in the Auschwitz Trial, which depart in some respects from the interpretation presented here, see Norbert Frei, "Der Frankfurter Auschwitz-Prozeß und die deutsche Zeitgeschichtsforschung," in *Auschwitz: Geschichte, Rezeption und Wirkung,* ed. Fritz Bauer Institut (Frankfurt: Campus Verlag, 1996), 123–38; Irmtrud Wojak, "Herrschaft der Sachverständigen? Zum ersten Frankfurter Auschwitz-Prozeß," *Kritische Justiz* 32 (1999): 605–16; and Irmtrud Wojak, "Die Verschmelzung von Geschichte und Kriminologie: Historische Gutachten im ersten Frankfurter Auschwitz-Prozeß," in *Geschichte vor Gericht: Historiker, Richter und die Suche nach Gerechtigkeit,* ed. Norbert Frei, Dirk van Laak, and Michael Stolleis (Munich: C. H. Beck, 2000), 29–45.

9. Frankfurt Staatsanwaltschaft (hereafter FF StA), Handakten, Bd 5, "Vermerk, Hanns Großmann," 3 May 1961, B1. 865.

10. The representatives at the November meeting included: the Auschwitz Trial lead prosecutor Hanns Großmann; one of his associates, Joachim Kügler, who directly prepared the case; and the Hessian attorney general Fritz Bauer. Representing the IfZ were Helmut Krausnick, Hans Buchheim, and Martin Broszat. See Hessisches Hauptarchiv (hereafter

HHA), Abt. 631a, Nr. 1800, Bd. 84 (8 November 1962), "Vermerk über eine Besprechung der altpolitischen Dezernenten der Staatsanwaltschaft bei dem Oberlandesgericht und der Staatsanwaltschaften Frankfurt (M.) und Wiesbaden am 7. November 1962 bei Herrn Generalstaatsanwalt Dr. Bauer," B1. 85. The October discussion is referred to, though not described in detail, in the same document.

11. Ibid., B1. 86. The quote is a paraphrase of Bauer's comments entered into the protocol, not a verbatim transcript.

12. Ibid., B1. 87. Bauer also noted that such background testimony could also be very useful in clarifying the subjective dimension of Nazi crimes as well, in particular in demonstrating that the defendants were well aware of the criminal content of the orders they received and that they had not, in fact, thought that they were following ordinary, legally binding orders.

13. See, for instance, the comments by Bauer in a 1963 radio interview to the effect that such trials should serve to teach Germans once again that there is a law higher than human law, one that no power on earth can set in abeyance. Fritz Bauer, "Zu den Naziverbrecher-Prozessen: Gespräch im NDR," in *Die Humanität der Rechtsordnung: Ausgewählte Schriften,* ed. Joachim Perels and Irmtrud Wojak (Frankfurt: Campus Verlag, 1998), 113–7.

14. HHA, Abt. 503, Nr. 1161, "Protokoll der 4. Arbeitstagung der Leiter der Sonderkommissionen zur Bearbeitung von NS-Gewaltverbrechen in der Zeit vom 9. bis 10. Oktober 1963 in Wiesbaden," B1. 21. Again, the quote is a paraphrase rather than a verbatim transcription.

15. Ibid.

16. Ibid., B1. 21–2.

17. IfZ, ED 105: Hausarchiv, "Tätigkeitsbericht für die Zeit vom 1. Juli 1963 bis 30 Juni. 1964," 18.

18. On the press reaction to the Auschwitz Trial more generally, see Devin O. Pendas, "'I Didn't Know What Auschwitz Was': The Frankfurt Auschwitz Trial and the German Press, 1963–1965," *Yale Journal of Law and the Humanities* 12, no. 2 (2000): 397–446.

19. With the exception of Broszat's report on Nazi Polish policy, all of the reports by the West German historians were subsequently published in Hans Buchheim et al., *Anatomie des SS-Staates* (1967; reprint, Munich: DTV, 1994). For the English translation, see Hans Buchheim, Martin Broszat, Hans-Adolf Jacobsen, and Helmut Krausnick, *Anatomy of the SS-State,* trans. Richard Bary, Marian Jackson, and Dorothy Long (New York: Walker and Co., 1968). It is likely that Broszat's report was not included for publication because it is relatively similar to the book he had published a few years earlier under the auspices of the institute. See Martin Broszat, *Nationalsozialstische Polenpolitik, 1939–1945,* Schriftenreihe der Vierteljahrshefte

für Zeigeschichte no. 2 (Stuttgart: Deutsche Verlags-Anstalt, 1961). The original of Broszat's report is in the archives of the institute. See Martin Broszat, "Nationalsozialistische Polenpolitik," IfZ Archiv, MS244: 4851/72. Kuczynski's report was published in East Germany as Jürgen Kuczynski, "Die Verflechtung von sicherheitspolizeilichen und wirtschaftlichen Interessen bei der Einrichtung und im Betrieb des KZ Auschwitz und seiner Nebenlager," *Dokumentation der Zeit* 16, no. 308 (1964): 36–42.

20. This is made clear in a letter from prosecutor Vogel to civil counsel Henry Ormond, FF StA Handakten, Bd. 16, "Vogel to Ormond," 20 August 1963, Bl. 3429–30. Because the issues it raises are distinct, I will leave aside consideration of Kuczynski's testimony in this article. For a provocative, if ultimately unconvincing, attempt to rehabilitate Kuczynski's report as scholarship, see Florian Schmalz, "Das historische Gutachten Jürgen Kuczynskis zur Rolle der I. G. Farben und des KZ Monowitz in ersten Frankfurter Auschwitz-Prozess," in *"Gerichtstag halten über uns selbst . . .": Geschichte und Wirkung des ersten Frankfurter Auschwitz-Prozesses,* ed. Irmtrud Wojak (Frankfurt: Campus Verlag, 2001), 117–40.

21. Often enough, these reports represented not simply historiographic reviews summarizing the state of knowledge on a given topic but were themselves genuine scholarly achievements, presenting new and innovative accounts of their various themes. This is particularly true of Krausnick's report on anti-Jewish thought and activity, which was one of the first substantial treatments of the theme in Germany after the war. Buchheim's analysis of the SS and, depending on how one relates it to his later work, Broszat's account of the concentration camp system could also be considered path-breaking works.

22. Buchheim et al., *Anatomie,* 11. Unless otherwise noted, all citations are to the German edition and all translations are my own. While adequate for its purposes, the existing English translation seeks to present a fluid, readable text, sometimes at the cost of linguistic accuracy. I have therefore chosen to rely on the German text.

23. Ibid.

24. This tension between individual responsibility and historical context, between agency and structure, was one of the defining aspects of the Auschwitz Trial as a whole. See Devin Pendas, "Displaying Justice: Nazis on Trial in Postwar Germany" (doctoral diss., University of Chicago, 2000).

25. Hans Hofmeyer, "Prozessrechtliche Probleme und praktische Schwierigkeiten bei der Durchführung der Prozesse," in *Probleme der Vervolgung und Ahndung von Nationalsozialistischen Gewaltverbrechen: Sonderveranstaltung des 46, Deutschen Juristentages in Essen* ed. Ständigen Deputation des deutschen Juristentages (Munich: C. H. Beck'sche Verlagsbuchhandlung, 1967), 44.

26. "Vorwort," in Buchheim et al., *Anatomie*, 9.

27. Ibid.

28. Ibid., 10.

29. The use of historical experts in Nazi trials was by no means uncontroversial in the West German legal community in the 1960s. For example, at the Third Working Conference of Federal Prosecutors working on the Prosecution of Nazi Crimes of Violence in September 1966, Buchheim was forced to defend the role of historical experts in Nazi cases. In the discussion following a presentation by Hanns Großmann, a prosecutor from Berlin commented that he was of the opinion that courts should be cautious in their use of historical experts. According to the minutes, Buchheim replied that jurors, who, "in his opinion were often lacking in the most basic qualifications, had to be presented with an 'introductory course,' covering in the first instance questions of organization." See Zentrale Stelle der Landesjustizverwaltungen zur Aufklärung von nationalsozialistischen Gewaltverbrechen in Ludwigsburg, *Niederschrift über die Dritte Arbeitstagung der in der Bundesrepublik mit der Strafverfolgung von NS-Gewaltverbrechen befaßten Staatsanwälte in Konstanz,* 27–30 September 1966, 190.

30. "Vorwort," in Buchheim et al., *Anatomie*, p. 10.

31. Buchheim, "Die SS—das Herrschaftsinstrument," in *Anatomie*, 15. Cf. Ernst Fraenkel, *The Dual State: A Contribution to the Theory of Dictatorship* (London: Oxford University Press, 1941).

32. Buchheim, et al., *Anatomie*, 22.

33. Ibid., 26–7.

34. Ibid., 29.

35. "In practice, the anomically constituted authority of the leader (*Führergewalt*) had a norm dissolving impact and led to *anti-*normative action." Ibid., 19.

36. Martin Broszat, "Nationalsozialistische Konzentrationslager, 1933–1945," in Buchheim et al., *Anatomie*, 349.

37. Helmut Krausnick, "Judenverfolgung," in Buchheim et al., *Anatomie*, 555–64.

38. To be fair, Krausnick does stress the essential Germanness of the history of anti-Semitism that led up to the Nazi genocide of the Jews. Thus, with regard to Social Darwinism, he writes: "'Social Darwinism'—the application of Darwinian theories to social and political relations—was not, as is well known, a purely German phenomenon, indeed, not even primarily a German phenomenon. Nevertheless, if its foreign proponents remained essentially within the boundaries of practical social policy, its German interpreters . . . did not make Darwin's teachings simply into a foundation for political reform proposals but raised its theories increasingly to the level of a world view." "Judenverfolgung," 556.

39. Hans Buchheim, "Das Problem des Befehlsnotstandes bei den vom nationalsozialistischen Regime befohlenen Verbrechen in historischer Sicht" (2 July 1964) and Hans-Adolf Jacobsen, "Kommissarbefehl" (17 August 1964). Buchheim's essay is reprinted in Buchheim et al., *Anatomie,* 215–322.

40. To give but one example, recent work has demonstrated the extent to which the "terror" exercised by the SS was directed not against German society but against pariahs on the margins of that society, particularly Jews, on the basis of widespread popular support. In other words, the Gestapo was not an organ beyond or against German society but an expression of that society. See Eric A. Johnson, *Nazi Terror: The Gestapo, Jews, and Ordinary Germans* (New York: Basic Books, 1999); and Robert Gellately, *Backing Hitler: Consent and Coercion in Nazi Germany* (Oxford: Oxford University Press, 2001).

41. For my analysis of the historical accounts provided by the prosecution and the court, see Pendas, "Displaying Justice," 166–80, 324–34.

42. I am aware that to use the term "intentionalist" in this context is to risk anachronism, as that is a concept that only emerged somewhat later in the historiography of the Third Reich and the Holocaust, in the context of a debate with so-called "functionalists," of whom, ironically, Martin Broszat was one of the leading representatives. Nonetheless, because of the juridical imperative to focus on the specific motives of the accused in the context of Nazi trials, I would argue that intentionalism is, in fact, the proper term to describe this position. For a useful overview of these debates, see Ian Kershaw, *The Nazi Dictatorship: Problems and Perspectives of Interpretation,* 2nd ed. (London: Edward Arnold, 1985), 82–106.

43. On the legal doctrine of "main perpetrators" and its relationship to German Nazi trials, see Jörg Friedrich, *Die kalte Amnestie: NS-Täter in der Bundesrepublik* (Munich: R. Piper, 1994), 227–37.

44. Günther von Lojewski, "Der Weg bis zur biologischen Vernichtung," *Frankfurter Allgemeine Zeitung,* 18 February 1964.

45. Broszat, "Nationalsozialistische Konzentrationslager," in Buchheim et al., *Anatomie,* 323. Cf. Eugen Kogon, *Der SS Staat: Das System der deutschen Konzentrationslager* (Munich: Karl Alber Verlag, 1946), translated by Heinz Norden as *The Theory and Practice of Hell: The German Concentration Camps and the System Behind Them* (New York: Farrar, Straus and Co., 1950).

46. Cf., e.g., Arendt's analysis of this dynamic. Hannah Arendt, *The Origin of Totalitarianism,* new ed. (San Diego: Harcourt Brace Jovanovich, 1966), 389–92.

47. See Hans Mommsen, *From Weimar to Auschwitz,* trans. Philip O'Connor (Princeton, N.J.: Princeton University Press, 1991); or Martin

Broszat, *Der Staat Hitler: Grundlegung und Entwicklung seiner inneren Verfassung* (Munich: DTV, 1969).

48. Hans Mommsen, "Kriegserfahrungen," in *Über Leben im Krieg,* ed. Ulrich Borsdorf and M. Jamin (Reinbeck bei Hamburg: Rowohlt, 1989), 113. Cited in Omer Bartov, *Hitler's Army: Soldiers, Nazis, and War in the Third Reich* (New York: Oxford University Press, 1992).

49. See especially Horst Boog et al., eds., *Der Angriff auf die Sovjetunion, Deutsche Reich und der Zweite Weltkrieg,* vol. 4 (Stuttgart: Deutsche Verlags-Anstalt, 1983). Cf. also Christian Streit, *Keine Kameraden: Die Wehrmacht und die sowjetischen Kriegsgefangenen 1941–1945* (Stuttgart: Deutsche Verlags-Anstalt, 1978). For the most recent overview of this issue, see Wolfram Wette, *Die Wehrmacht: Feindbilder-Vernichtungskrieg-Legenden* (Frankfurt: S. Fischer Verlag, 2002).

50. Two moments in particular appear to have been decisive in bringing Wehrmacht participation in mass atrocity to the fore. The first is the publication of Omer Bartov's work. See Omer Bartov, *The Eastern Front, 1941–1945: German Troops and the Barbarisation of Warfare* (New York: St. Martin's Press, 1986) and idem, *Hitler's Army.* The second, and for Germans more important, was the traveling exhibit on Wehrmacht crimes organized in the late 1990s by the Hamburg Institut für Sozialforschung. See Hannes Heer and Klaus Naumann, eds., *War of Extermination: The German Military in World War II, 1941–1944* (New York: Berghahn Books, 2000). On the public reaction to the exhibit, see Theo Sommer, "Münchner Lektionenen: Die Rolle der Wehrmacht läßt sich nicht beschönigen," *Die Zeit,* 28 February 1997; Rudolf Augstein, "Anschlag auf die 'Ehre' des deutschen Soldaten?" *Der Spiegel* 53 (1997); and Johannes Klotz, "Die Ausstellung 'Vernichtungskrieg. Verbrechen der Wehrmacht 1941 bis 1944': Zwiscen Geschichtswissenschaft und Geschichtspolitik," in *Mythos Wehrmacht: Nachkriegsdebatten und Traditionspflege,* ed. Detlef Bald, Johannes Klotz and Wolfram Wette (Berlin: Aufbau Taschenbuch Verlag, 2001), 116–76.

51. Gerald Reitlinger, *The SS: Alibi of a Nation* (London: Heinemann, 1956).

IV. HISTORIOGRAPHY AND THE CHALLENGES TO HISTORIANS

Dan Michman

"Euphoria of Victory" as the Key: Situating Christopher Browning on the Map of Research on the "Final Solution of the Jewish Question"

CHRISTOPHER BROWNING CAN BE DEFINED AS THE LEADING EXPERT today on the issue of the decision-making process of the Final Solution of the Jewish Question. This definition stands, I believe, both for those who accept his theses on the issue entirely and for those who differ from him and argue with minor or major parts of them. That somebody can be defined as the "leading expert" on this issue is—from the point of view of the history of historiography of the Holocaust—somewhat surprising: in the beginning the facts seemed to be clear and did not raise any special problems.

ON THE HISTORY OF RESEARCH ON THE FINAL SOLUTION

During the first decade or so after 1945 it was quite clear to all that the physical eradication of the European Jews had been initiated by Adolf Hitler, that it had been thoughtfully carried out by his state machinery, and that anti-Semitism had played a major role in setting the process in motion. Two major causes led to the formation of this view.

1. The background of the trials of the major war criminals (the Nuremberg trials) supplied huge piles of documentation classified according to the aims of the trials to convict the accused. Because of judicial problems (deriving from international law and the local laws of the allied countries), not all crimes could be tried, unless planning—"conspiracy"—was proved. Conspiracy, at least for launching World War II, was also seen as tying the whole of the trials together.[1] Thus, the tactics of

"conspiracy and aggression" (as the series of volumes with documentation of the trials was titled later on) pursued by the prosecution in the Nuremberg trials shaped a first, historical overall view of Nazi politics.[2]

2. That first period—immediately after the downfall of National Socialism, but with Bolshevism still reigning in Eastern Europe—was the high tide of "totalitarian" explanatory theories.[3] Even though the concept "totalitarianism" was very much disputed,[4] totalitarian states were essentially viewed as being tightly organized; led by mighty, omnipotent leaders whose will is the law; and ruled by a frightening secret police using terror[5]— thus having firm control over developments and causing the state bureaucracy and the masses to act almost as marionettes.

To these two factors shaping the first conceptualization of the developments, one should add, perhaps, also a third, historiographical one: the quite common tendency to focus on the "grand personality," whether it is Jesus, Charlemagne, Napoleon, the Ba'al Shem Tov, Churchill, Stalin, or Hitler, and to view them as the forces driving history forth.

This context led to two paths of explanation for the Final Solution (which sometimes met): one, proclaimed by non-Jewish historians who dealt with Hitler and Nazism in general, portrayed Hitler as a traditional, ruthless tyrant seeking power for its own sake.[6] The other, consisting mainly of Jewish researchers who dealt with the fate of the Jews during the Nazi period, viewed Hitler as an ideological dictator obsessed with anti-Semitism. For the first, the Final Solution was not the central issue, but another manifestation of totalitarian brutality; for the last it was an essential, even though not main, issue of Hitler's *Weltanschauung*. Following an early typology of fascism,[7] this second approach of the first period can rightfully be called "proto-intentionalist."

Clear examples of the proto-intentionalist approach are *Harvest of Hate*, by Leon Poliakov, and *The Final Solution*, by Gerald Reitlinger. Even though their explanations of the motivation behind the murder of the Jews differed, both were sure that Hitler was the grand architect of the extermination project—a project that developed, they both agreed, in later stages of the Third Reich.[8] According to Poliakov, Hitler had used the Jews—the scapegoats in an age-old European Christian tradition—as "arch-enemy" (or *Gegenreich*) for the pseudo-religion he concocted, in order to manipulate the German masses: "the minds and souls of millions of Germans were more or less suffused with a sense of sacred horror," as he formulated it; this finally led to the decision to physically get rid of them.[9] According to Reitlinger, Hitler, being an obsessed anti-Semite—a "fact," (or better, an axiom) that did not need any further explanation in his eyes— "started the machine working."[10] It is true that Raul Hilberg, who wrote *The Destruction of the European Jews* shortly afterward, very much minimized the leading role of Hitler while explaining that the extermination of the Jews resulted from an escalating bureaucratic process. Hence he is often viewed as being a predecessor of what later came to be called "functionalism." Yet even Hilberg interpreted the event within the rigid parameters of a modern, organized totalitarian state, in which no political checks and balances exist. Says Hilberg:

> Hitler . . . did not have to originate any propaganda. He did not have to invent any laws. He did not have to create a machine. He *did* have to rise to power. A bureaucratic body, like an inanimate object, is subject to inertia. . . . It has to be started. . . . In 1933 the missing push [i.e. by Hitler] was applied, and the ball started to roll. The machinery of destruction was activated. The destruction process was set in motion. . . .[11] The destruction of the Jews did not proceed from a basic plan. . . . Yet the destruction process was a step-by-step operation . . . ([the steps being] definition, expropriation, and concentration). The path to annihilation leads directly through these age-old steps."[12]

As for the decision on the Final Solution, Hilberg claimed that, "basically, we are dealing with two of *Hitler's* decisions. One order was given in the spring of 1941, during the planning of the invasion of the USSR; . . . . Shortly after the mobile operations had begun . . . Hitler *handed down* his second order" (my emphases—D.M.).[13] And the reason for this whole development was, as Hilberg also ascertained, to scapegoat anti-Semitism: "the final product of an earlier age . . . For many centuries and in many countries, the Jews have been victims of destructive action."[14] Thus, Hilberg too thought the whole escalating process was basically linear; the decision—in two stages— to be given from above, by Hitler; and the reason to be age-old anti-Semitism. Consequently, Hilberg can also be seen as playing within the parameters of proto-intentionalism.

Therefore, contrary to what is commonly believed, the intention-alism as shaped in the first period of research after 1945 and common to such apparently differing approaches as Poliakov's, Reitlinger's, and Hilberg's did not claim that there was a clear, premeditated *planning* of the murder of the Jews. Rather, it agreed upon the view that there was a certain linear, logical development or escalation starting much earlier than the 1940s and culminating in a decision to murder all Jews, an act was taken by Hitler as a result of ideological, not cir-cumstantial, reasons—even though it was taken in certain circum-stances. To paraphrase the above-quoted description of Hilberg, there was a "direct path," followed "step-by-step."[15]

A second wave of intentionalism—what I would call "standard intentionalism"—promoted by German historians and stemming from research on National Socialism, not from Holocaust research, followed in the 1960s. Leading scholars in this wave were Helmut Krausnick and Eberhard Jäckel. The first defined the persecution of the Jews as "State-inspired. . . , planned with . . . diabolical consis-tency and carried through . . . cold-bloodedly and systematically."[16] Its origins were to be found in Hitler's anti-Semitism, already ex-pressed in his first political writing of September 16, 1919. But it had been developed in order "to build up and vindicate the totalitarian power structure of which he [Hitler] had dreamed. . . . There he was—the enemy: a concept which, evidently, no totalitarian system ever seems able to do without."[17] Hitler wanted to get rid of this en-emy. And thus, even though "the exact moment at which Hitler made up his mind that the Jews must be physically destroyed cannot be pre-cisely determined," it is certain that it *was* decided upon by Hitler and that it was linked to the preparation of the war against the Soviet Union—"the last possible enemy on the continent of Europe." At that historical moment the idea "with which he [Hitler] had been toy-ing . . . for a long period—of wiping out the Jews in the territories under his control"—matured.[18] Jäckel followed almost the same rea-soning, and was even more outspoken on the issue of intention—viewing *Mein Kampf* as the blueprint for all later developments.[19]

Later on an even more extreme brand of intentionalism, which might perhaps be called "radical intentionalism," developed; spokes-men for this approach were Lucy Dawidowicz in the 1970s and Daniel Jonah Goldhagen in the 1990s. Both spoke of an intention to solve the "Jewish Question" and to "get rid of the Jews" that had already emerged in European or German political culture early in the nineteenth century. Hitler, in their eyes, was the executor of this "grand," deeply ingrained, cultural and/or national "intention."[20]

But the intentionalist view gradually began to be attacked during the second half of the 1950s. The rise of social history and the extensive research carried out on aspects of the functioning of lower echelons of the bureaucracy of the Nazi state gave rise to the so-called functionalist—or structuralist—approach.[21] Emphasis was now put on the "struggle over competencies" (*Komptenzenstreit*) and the "mosaic of antagonizing interests and directions" ("ein widerspruchsvolles Mosaik antagonistischer Interessen und Richtungen")[22] among uncoordinated bureaucratic power centers in the Third Reich. Instead of a rigid, well-organized and -orchestrated totalitarian state, a picture of "organized chaos"[23] under a weak dictator (often led by radicals—as Hans Mommsen, for instance, claimed)[24] covered only by a (thin) layer of the "Hitler myth"[25] became dominant. Resulting from this view was the understanding that the Third Reich was characterized by "sudden and drastic decisions that had not been prepared in the governmental machine and thus both disrupted existing policies and practices and had quite unforeseen administrative and political results."[26] In this context, the former view of linear, consecutive, and logical developments leading toward the Final Solution had to be altered. Instead, the view of a "twisted road to Auschwitz" emerged.[27] This twisted-road approach pertained both to the development of anti-Jewish policies in general and to the very decision-making process on the mass murder of the Jews itself. Anti-Semitism as a central motive behind the escalating process became much less accentuated—in several cases, almost disappeared—and the decisive role attributed to Hitler faded. Instead, long-standing processes of modernization[28] including economic modernization within a nationalist-imperialist context,[29] on the one hand, or the barbarization of warfare, on the other,[30] were emphasized. Moreover, the embarking on the road to mass murder of all the Jews in Europe came to be viewed as an unforeseen, unplanned act, which "happened" in a situation of uncontrolled escalation. Broszat, who in the 1960s still had spoken about a "Befehl zur Endlösung der Judenfrage" (order for the Final Solution) as one of the examples of Hitler's way during the war years to act through a "verschleierte Führererlass" (veiled order of the Führer) on issues of major importance,[31] now pointed out that indeed "the first extensive liquidation act, the mass execution in the summer and fall of 1941, of hundreds of thousands of Jews in the occupied Soviet territories by the *Einsatzkommandos* . . . was no doubt carried out on the personal directive of Hitler."[32] Yet, after that first definite involvement of Hitler in a local act, "the physical liquidation of the Jews [throughout Europe] was set in motion not through a one-time decision but rather bit by bit."[33] Hitler was only partially involved in this process:

> It . . . seems that the liquidation of the Jews began not solely as the result of an ostensible will for extermination but also as a "way out" of a blind alley into which the Nazis had manoeuvred themselves. The practice of liquidation, once initiated and established, gained predominance and *evolved in the end* into a comprehensive "programme."[34] [my emphasis—D.M.].

Consequently—when not essentially linked to anti-Semitism and seen as having emerged accidentally, not as a consecutive stage of anti-Jewish policies of the 1930s—the murder campaign of the Jews was not perceived as exclusive any more. It was part either of the above-mentioned vague developments such as "modernity," or of much larger projects that included wholesale murder of a variety of populations. Moreover, the forces that propelled these processes were faceless: It was as if huge structures of concrete or stone had rolled downward in an oblique but wide and open field. In a conversation in Jerusalem several years ago, Peter Longerich claimed that while doing research for his latest book, he suddenly discovered that a linguistic habit of using passive modes—"actions were taken," "shootings occurred," and so on—had become dominant in German functionalist research literature dealing with the murder campaign of the Final Solution.[35]

Rivalry between functionalism and intentionalism peaked in the 1980s. In the 1990s, however, researchers of the younger generation as well as veterans have come closer, but differences can still be discerned. Outspoken intentionalists such as Jäckel have accepted many of the functionalist claims, as can be demonstrated in some of his recent studies.[36] On the other hand, functionalists such as Ian Kershaw, who decided to write a biography of Hitler,[37] and Peter Longerich, in his *Politik der Vernichtung*,[38] have accepted again the centrality of anti-Semitism and the major role played by Hitler. Moreover, a whole stream of research is now devoted to uncovering the entire biographies of many high- and low-ranking officials—including their lives and careers before the ascendance to power of Nazism in the Weimar and pre-Weimar periods, and after its downfall in postwar Germany.[39] Thus, the real actors with their human faces, the individuals, are re-installed in the picture.

Nevertheless, as said before, differences between the two basic approaches or schools still exist. These differences are, as I see it, due to the fact that both have precisely one trait in common: their search for an acceptable explanation for both the path to, and the decision-making process on, the Final Solution looks for a plausible *consistent* cause with inner logic. This logic might be long-standing intention or obsession; calculated acts deriving from a will for power; an escalating bureaucratic inertia; a more general leading thread—such as ideology or *Weltanschauung* (antisemitism, racism, fascism, or anti-Bolshevism); or even an abstract phenomenon such as economic modernization, the pathology of modernity itself, or the "spirit of science."[40] It might also be "rational" problems of the war situation, such as nutrition, a cause recently insisted upon by Christian Gerlach.[41]

CHRISTOPHER BROWNING'S EXPLANATION

It is in this respect that Christopher Browning has paved a special path. The issue that bothered Browning from the outset of his involvement during the 1970s in research on Nazi anti-Jewish policies is the feeling that neither of the two rivaling schools of research in their exclusivity provided a sufficient, convincing answer based on knowledge about *human* ways of acting, an answer that really explained the psychological transformation from the abstract idea to obviously organized and calculated mass murder ("the sheer magnitude and intended thoroughness of the Final Solution").[42] For Browning, intentionalists believe too much that vague or even clear ideas or ideologies can indeed motivate states and masses to carry out such extreme human acts as the Final Solution, while functionalists believe too much that things could have developed the way they did accidentally, without obvious steering, without some internal logic, or because of rational *ad hoc* needs (i.e., people—governments and thousands of executioners—do not "just" carry out large-scale criminal projects). In this context one should not forget that the annihilation of the Jews was total and comprehensive, including Jews all over Europe, and not only in Eastern Europe—the area on which almost all functionalists focus their research. Even if Browning did not mention Himmler's infamous speech in Posen (Poznan) on October 4, 1943, explicitly in his writings, its spirit must have been the trigger for Browning's long search for and research of "the missing link." On that occasion Himmler said the following:

> I am referring here to the evacuation of the Jews, the extermination of the Jewish people. This is one of the things that is easily said: "The Jewish people are going to be exterminated," that's what every Party member says, "sure, it's our program, elimination of the Jews, extermination—it'll be done." And then they all come along, the 80 million worthy Germans, and each one has his one decent Jew. Of course, the others are swine, but this one, he is a first-rate Jew. Of all those who talk like that, not one has seen it happen, not one has had to go through with it. Most of you men know what it is like to see 100 corpses side by side, or 500 or 1,000. To have stood fast through this and—except for cases of human weakness—to have stayed decent, that has made us hard. This is an unwritten and never-to-be written page of glory in our history. . . .
>
> We had the moral right, we had the duty towards our people, to destroy this people that wanted to destroy us. . . . We destroyed a bacillus. . . . We have carried out this most difficult of tasks in a spirit of love for our people.[43]

This speech reveals some essential ingredients of the Nazi "Final Solution" project: fanatic determination; the explicit declaration that the extermination of the Jews was a "task"; obvious links with former anti-Semitism; a biologistic mode of thought; and a radical shift regarding moral values.

Browning has spoken out loudly against the rivaling parties, claiming

> that neither an ultra-intentionalist interpretation reducing all but Hitler's plan to secondary status, nor an ultra-functionalist interpretation, excessively diminishing the role of Hitler, is satisfactory. The two ought not to be mutually exclusive; rather, the "final solution" was the result of a conjuncture of factors, which both the intentionalists and functionalists have helped illuminate.[44]

But if so, what was the glue that could make the factors stick together? Browning has defined himself a "moderate functionalist."[45] I think, however, that this self-definition is missing a central feature of the solution he has suggested to the historical problem as it has emerged from decades of intensive research by so many scholars. Browning joined the field of research on the Final Solution in his doctoral thesis on "The Final Solution and the German Foreign Office,"[46] written in the 1970s. Since then, two main issues in this field have bothered him: (1) how did the concept of and decision(s) on the murder campaign evolve, and (2) what was it that motivated such a broad variety of bureaucrats and others to willingly and efficiently participate in putting that campaign into practice? The two are, indeed, interrelated; Browning himself has explained that he attempted "to shed light on the emergence of the Final Solution by looking both from the top down and from the bottom up."[47]

As for the second issue, Browning indeed opted from the beginning for the functionalist approach. The conclusion of his book on Referat D III was that

> [t]he Foreign Office personnel involved in the Jewish question were a combination of opportunistic professional bureaucrats and an excessively ambitious and ruthless politician [Luther] who was Ribbentrop's number-one political infighter. They were primarily motivated by considerations of careerism, not racial ideology or fanatical and blind obedience to higher authority. The decisions which led to the original involvement of the Foreign Office in the Final Solution and later to pressing forward the Final Solution with increased urgency, resulted from the pressures exerted upon the Foreign Office by virtue of the intense internal political rivalry which was the essence of the Nazi system of government.[48]

But in his later studies on other groups of the lower echelons of Germans involved in the persecution of the Jews, such as the book *Ordinary Men,* Browning—while not abandoning functionalist insights— integrated many more intentional ingredients, such as anti-Semitism (in spite of Daniel Goldhagen's accusation that he did not pay enough attention to this aspect).[49]

Yet the key issue for Browning nevertheless remained the conceptual emergence of the Final Solution project and the decision-making process with which it was accomplished. A main trigger to focus so much on this issue was the invitation by Yad Vashem in 1980 to write the volume on the Final Solution in the comprehensive series on the history of the Holocaust it had then initiated. Browning carried out an impressive series of partial studies in order to explore the boundaries of the issue and the in-depth problems at stake. Two clusters of these studies have been published in *Fateful Months* and *The Path to Genocide*.[50] Recently, Browning published his overall study on the emergence of the Final Solution in the *Yad Vashem Comprehensive History of the Holocaust* series,[51] and another book—*Nazi Policy, Jewish Workers, German Killers*—consisting of a series of lectures held in the autumn of 1999 in Cambridge, England, and dealing with the same issues, has been published.[52] This body of publications allows us to analyze and understand the basics of his approach.

Except for painstaking research into detailed problems of the actual development—the sequence of events—which I will not survey here, the core of Browning's historical approach is that the hidden link holding the parts (ideology and action) and stages (the murder of the Soviet Jews and of the rest of Europe's Jews as well as the escalation of earlier stages of anti-Jewish policies) together is a mental state of "euphoria." As I will show, this concept combines—on the historiographical level—major segments of proto-intentionalism and functionalism.

When proposing his first overall view of the topic at the end of the 1980s, Browning stated that on the one hand,

> [t]here was no Hitler order from which the Final Solution sprang full grown like Athena from the head of Zeus. But sometime in the summer of 1941, probably before Goering's July 31 authorization, Hitler gave Himmler and Heydrich the signal to draw up a destruction plan, the completion of which inevitably involved the exploration of various alternatives, false starts, and much delay. Considerable "lead time" was needed, for the Nazis were venturing into uncharted territory and attempting the unprecedented.[53]

On the other hand, he fiercely attacked Arno Mayer for going "so wrong" as seeing the Holocaust as a by-product of the war against Bolshevism, for refusing "to understand the Final Solution for what it was—the Nazis' plan to kill every last Jew in Europe on whom they could lay their hands."[54] He has made clear that "the situation in early 1941" (i.e., before the invasion of the Soviet Union) had been entirely different: "The Nazi regime was committed to a solution to a self-imposed, European-wide 'Jewish problem.'" Former "solutions" had proved to be unrealizable, but with the war against the Soviet Union, the extended "Jewish problem" (now including Soviet Jews)

> was posed within the context of National-Socialism's confrontation with the ultimate ideological and racial enemy—"Jewish Bolshevism"—and the Nazis' bid to realize Germany's "manifest destiny" by waging a "war of destruction" to conquer the eastern *Lebensraum* necessary to underpin a one-thousand-year Reich.[55]

Thus, counter to most functionalists, he agreed that "the Jewish problem" was an issue apart, which occupied a special place in Nazi ideology already long before the invasion of Russia. Therefore, it was afterward "tenaciously and fanatically carried out [even] in the years of looming defeat."[56] He also insisted on Hitler's leading role in the decision-making process—that is, on Hitler's having set the process in motion. This was done, however, "as usual" by Hitler—"not [through] giving explicit orders," but through giving "a signal."[57] The war against the Soviet Union is, in Browning's eyes, not the *reason* for the Final Solution, but the *context enabling the transformation* from vague, utopian visions into concrete actions.

And what, then, was the trigger, the spark that set the fire? Counter to Arno Mayer and Philippe Burrin, who argued that the state of mind causing the transition to wholesale mass murder was depression resulting from the failure of the war against the Soviet Union in the late autumn or winter of 1941–42, Browning looked in the opposite direction: in his eyes it was "the intoxicating prospect" offered by "the fantastic victories over Russia" (as in *Fateful Months*).[58] In *The Path to Genocide* he clarified this point more extensively; there was, he maintained, "a rather consistent pattern between victory and radicalization, . . . dictating that the emergence of the Final Solution may have been induced as much by Hitler's fluctuating moods as by a fanatically consistent adherence to a fixed program."[59] Shortly afterward, in 1991, Browning decided that the best term for this jubilant mood pattern would be the "euphoria of victory";[60] this term consistently recurs in his further writings, up to today.[61]

The colligating concept of "euphoria" is indeed the key to comprehending the evolution of Browning's approach as well as to his entire view of the "event." If in the earlier stages of the crystallization of this understanding he pointed to only one occasion of "victory eu-

phoria," in midsummer 1941, he later modified this view slightly,
now writing of "an incremental, ongoing decision-making process
that stretched from the spring of 1941 to the summer of 1942, with
key turning points in the midsummer and early fall of 1941 that corresponded to the peaks of German victory euphoria and sealed the
fate of Soviet and European Jews, respectively."[62] Thus, the need to
modify his view of the actual developments due to new findings was
not blocked by a rigid understanding of the overall process; the
euphoria-of-victory concept was flexible enough to enable him rather
to include new details without being forced to change the general
contours and picture.

CONCLUSION AND EVALUATION

What, then, in my eyes, is Browning's major contribution to the field
of research on the Final Solution of the Jewish Question?

Browning has unearthed, of course, many unknown documents.
This, however, is not something unusual in historical research, even if
it is important. It is the "euphoria-of-victory" *concept* that should be
evaluated as *the* major insight he has contributed to our understanding. But it should be emphasized that this concept is not to be found
expressively in the documentation; it is something that Browning
sensed and that emerged in his mind after many years of research, years
of growing intimacy with the vast amount of Nazi documentation.

Even though Browning's almost entire *oeuvre* is focused on the
period 1939–42, the euphoria-of-victory concept links broader contours to the nucleus of the developments of 1941. Euphoria-of-victory
decision making was, according to Browning's analysis, the case on
not just one occasion, in 1941. It had been a consistent pattern apparent earlier, at the beginning of World War II, with the conquests
of Poland in the east (the Lublin reservation plan and the "ethnic
cleansing" in western Poland) and France in the west (the Madagas-
car Plan).[63] In all these cases anti-Jewish policies crystallized and escalated as a result of a state of mind created by political successes.
Consequently, a historically reasonable construction can be suggested
for the emergence of the Final Solution, binding together proto- and
moderate standard intentionalism as explaining the *essence,* with reasonable functionalism explaining the *climate,* in which it could ex-
plode. Hitler played a key role; the Jewish issue had a special place;

the murder of the Jews was not "merely" (if one can say so) ethnic cleansing or genocide but an unprecedented and unequaled project; the intention to get rid of the Jews had existed long before 1941—it was created by anti-Semitism and racism.[64] Yet "intention" is not what intentionalists as well as functionalists usually have in mind. There is no direct rational path from vague thoughts and expectations (intentions) to all-encompassing murderous projects (application). Hence, the decision-making process on this issue itself was "particular."[65] In order to make the leap(s) from intentions to application, a gluing link in the form of a certain state of the mind—a special mood—was needed. In Browning's approach, the euphoria of victory, like certain drugs, created such a state of the mind, in which there are grand visions on the one hand and a sense of no limits on the other. This state of mind is to be found in Hitler personally on the occasions mentioned above, but as policymaking in the Third Reich, it was shaped through "signaling" by Hitler on the one hand, and "working towards the Führer" on the other.[66] It beamed also to his entourage (as Göbbels' diary demonstrates in many instances) and penetrated probably also into the lower echelons operating in the field. Only such a behavioral pattern could translate vague, apocalyptic, murderous intentions into the readiness to really act.

I find this contribution of Browning's most interesting. It raises, however, additional questions. Did this pattern of functioning exist also before 1939? Can it, for instance, be applied to the process of seizing and consolidating power after 1933? If so, should the "emotional state" of Hitler and his regime be explored as a possible element colligating Nazi policies over the entire 1933–45 period? As said before, Browning's *oeuvre* has concentrated almost entirely on the years 1939 to 1942. Here his work has been very detailed. But he has neither extensively dealt with the prior years of the Third Reich nor with the larger issues of anti-Semitism, racism, modern bureaucracy, and so on. Therefore, his current achievements require a broader contextualization. Will Browning himself provide us with such a framework?[67]

NOTES

1. A. J. Kochavi, *Prelude to Nuremberg: Allied War Crimes Policy and the Question of Punishment* (Chapel Hill, N.C.: University of Chapel Hill Press, 1998), chap. 7, especially 225–6. See also C. R. Browning, *Nazi*

Policy, Jewish Workers, German Killers (Cambridge: Cambridge University Press, 2000), 116.

2. *Nazi Conspiracy and Aggression* (Washington: Office of the United States Chief of Counsel for the Prosecution of Axis Criminality, U.S. Government, 1946). I wish to thank Professor Shlomo Aronson for suggesting this insight in a discussion (about Kochavi's above-mentioned book), in which we both participated, at Bar-Ilan University in May 2000. See also his article "Yisrael Kasztner, OSS, ve-'te'oriyat rosh hahetz' be-nirenberg" [Israel Kasztner, OSS, and the 'Spearhead Theory' in Nuremberg], in *Mishpat ve-historiya* [Trial and History], ed. D. Gutwein and M. Mautner (Jerusalem: Zalman Shazar Center, 1999), 311. On the issue of the trials, see A. J. Kochavi, *Prelude to Nuremberg*.

3. In this respect, Hannah Arendt's 1966 "Preface to Part Three: Totalitarianism" of her republished *Origins of Totalitarianism* (New York: Harcourt, Brace, Jovanovitch, 1973), xxiii, is revealing. On the atmosphere in which she conceived and wrote her book she said: "The original manuscript of *The Origins of Totalitarianism* was finished in autumn 1949, more than four years after the defeat of Hitler Germany, less than four years before Stalin's death. The first edition of this book appeared in 1951. In retrospect, the years I spent writing it, from 1945 onwards, appear like the first period of relative calm after decades of turmoil, confusion, and plain horror—the revolutions after the First World War, the rise of totalitarian movements and the undermining of parliamentary government, followed by all sorts of new tyrannies, Fascist and semi-Fascist, one-party and military dictatorships, finally the seemingly firm establishment of totalitarian governments resting on mass support: in Russia in 1929, the year of what now is often called the 'second revolution,' and in Germany in 1933." For some background information, see also I. Kershaw, *The Nazi Dictatorship: Problems and Perspectives of Interpretation,* 2nd ed. (London: Edward Arnold, 1990), 12.

4. See D. Ohana, *Misdar hanihilistim* [The Order of the Nihilists] (Jerusalem: Magness Press, 1993), 18–22.

5. Arendt, Origins, part 3, especially chaps. 12 and 13; C. J. Friedrich, ed., *Totalitarianism* (Cambridge, Mass.: 1954).

6. See C. R. Browning, "Approaches to the 'Final Solution' in German Historiography of the Last Two Decades," in *The Historiography of the Holocaust Period,* ed. I. Gutman and G. Greif (Jerusalem: Yad Vashem, 1988), 59.

7. See E. Nolte, *Three Faces of Fascism* (New York: Holt, Rinehart and Winston, 1965); W. Wippermann, *Europäischer Faschismus im Vergleich 1922–1982* (Frankfurt am Main: Suhrkamp Verlag, 1983), especially 206.

8. L. Poliakov, *Harvest of Hate* (New York: Waldon Press, 1979), 284–

5; G. Reitlinger, *The Final Solution: The Attempt to Exterminate the Jews of Europe 1939–1945* (New York: A. S. Barnes, 1961), 3.

9. Poliakov, *Harvest,* 2, 8.

10. Reitlinger, *The Final Solution,* 4.

11. R. Hilberg, *The Destruction of the European Jews* (Chicago: Quadrangle Books, 1961), 18.

12. Ibid., 31–2.

13. Ibid., 177.

14. Ibid., 1.

15. My analysis of "intentionalism" is thus slightly different than the one presented by Browning in his "The Decision Concerning the Final Solution," in *Unanswered Questions: Nazi Germany and the Genocide of the Jews,* ed. F. Furet (New York: Schocken, 1989), 97. For approaches of leading historians of Jewish history in this period, see D. Michman, "Keitsad lemakem et hashoah bamirkam harahav shel toledot yisrael bazman hehadash? Nisyonot hitmoddedut shel historyonim movilim" [How to Situate the Holocaust in the Broader Context of Modern Jewish History? Approaches of Leading Historians], in *Hashoa bahistoriya hayehudit* [The Holocaust and Jewish History], ed. D. Michman (Jerusalem: Yad Vashem, 2004).

16. H. Krausnick, "The Persecution of the Jews," in *Anatomy of the SS State,* ed. H. Krausnick (New York: Walker and Company, 1968), 3.

17. Ibid., 22–3.

18. Ibid., 59–60.

19. E. Jäckel, *Hitlers Weltanschauung: Entwurf einer Herrschaft* (Stuttgart: Deutsche Verlags-Anstalt, 1981), chap. 3.

20. L. S. Dawidowicz, *The War Against the Jews, 1933–1945* (New York: Bantam Books, 1975); D. J. Goldhagen, *Hitler's Willing Executioners: Ordinary Germans and the Holocaust* (New York: A. Knopf, 1996). For an analysis of their view, see D. Michman, "'The Holocaust' in the Eyes of the Historians: The Problem of Conceptualization, Periodization, and Explanation," in *Holocaust Historiography: A Jewish Perspective. Conceptualizations, Terminology, Approaches and Fundamental Issues* (London: Vallentine Mitchell, 2003), 9–40.

21. See T. Mason, "Intention and Explanation: A Current Controversy about the Interpretation of National-Socialism," in *Der "Führerstaat": Mythos und Realität,* ed. G. Hirschfeld and L. Kettenacker (Stuttgart: Klett-Cotta, 1981), 23–42. For a recent, most interesting analysis of the background of the rise of functionalism, see N. Berg, *Der Holocaust und die westdeutschen Historiker: Erforschung und Erinnerung* (Göttingen: Wallstein, 2003); Idem, *The Invention of "Functionalism": Josef Wulf, Martin Broszat, and the Institute for Contemporary History (Munich) in the 1960s* (Jerusalem: Yad Vashem, 2003).

22. U. D. Adam, "Introduction," in *Judenpolitik im Dritten Reich* (Düsseldorf: Droste Verlag, 1972), 15–8, quotation from 17.

23. See G. Otto and J. Houwink ten Cate, eds., *Das organisierte Chaos* (Berlin: Metropol, 1998).

24. See H. Mommsen, "Hitlers Stellung im nationalsozialistischen Herrschaftssystem," in Hirschfeld and Kettenacker, *Der Führerstaat,* 43–69; H. Mommsen, "Die Realisierung des utopischen: Die 'Endlösung der Judenfrage' im 'Dritten Reich,'" *Geschichte und Gesellschaft 9,* no. 3 (Herbst 1983), 381–420. For an appalling recent example of his approach, see H. Mommsen, "Hitler's Reichstag Speech of 30 January 1939," in *Passing into History: Nazism and the Holocaust beyond Memory. In Honor of Saul Friedländer on His Sixty-Fifth Birthday,* ed. G. Ne'eman Arad *History and Memory* 9/1–2 (Special issue, Fall 1997): 147–61.

25. I. Kershaw, *The "Hitler Myth": Image and Reality in the Third Reich* (Oxford: Oxford University Press, 1990).

26. Mason, "Intention and Explanation," 25.

27. K. A. Schleunes, *The Twisted Road to Auschwitz: Nazi Policy toward German Jews, 1933–1939* (1970; reprint Urbana: University of Illinois Press, 1990).

28. Z. Bauman, *Modernity and the Holocaust,* paperback ed. (1989; 2nd printing) (Ithaca, NY: Cornell University Press, 1993).

29. G. Aly and S. Heim, *Vordenker der Vernichtung: Auschwitz und die deutschen Pläne für eine neue europäische Ordnung* (Hamburg: Hoffmann und Campe Verlag, 1991; paperback ed., Frankfurt am Main: S. Fischer Verlag, 1993).

30. J. Förster, "The German Army and the Ideological War against the Soviet Union," in *The Policies of Genocide: Jews and Soviet Prisoners of War in Nazi Germany,* ed. G. Hirschfeld (London: 1986), 15–29; O. Bartov, *The Eastern Front, 1941–45: German Troops and the Barbarization of Warfare* (New York: 1986); Idem, "Operation Barbarossa and the Origins of the Final Solution," in *The Final Solution: Origins and Implementation,* ed. D. Cesarani (London: Routledge, 1996), 119–36.

31. M. Broszat, *Der Staat Hitlers* (Munich: Deutsche Taschenbücher Verlag, 1969), 398–402.

32. M. Broszat, "Hitler and the Genesis of the 'Final Solution': An Assessment of David Irving's Theses," *Yad Vashem Studies* 13 (1979): 85 (the original, German version of this article was published in *Vierteljahrshefte für Zeitgeschichte* [Oktober 1977], nr. 4, 739–75.

33. Ibid., 84–5.

34. Ibid., 93.

35. On this tendency, see also Goldhagen, *Hitler's Willing Executioners,* 6, 475 n. 4. In my description and characterization of the functionalist

approach I differ from Browning's description as presented in his "Decision Concerning the Final Solution," 97. This relates especially to Broszat's view of Hitler's role, in which Browning depends on Broszat's earlier writings while neglecting the shift Broszat made in the 1970s. Longerich's remarks were made in a conversation with me at Yad Vashem in 1996.

36. E. Jäckel, "The Holocaust: Where We Are, Where We Need to Go," in *The Holocaust and History: The Known, the Unknown, the Disputed, and the Reexamined,* ed. M. Berenbaum and A. Peck (Bloomington: University of Indiana Press, 1998), 23–9.

37. I. Kershaw, *Hitler, 1889–1936: Hubris* (New York: Norton, 1998), xii: "My sympathies for the 'structuralist' [=functionalist] approaches to Nazi rule . . . were evident. There is no little irony, therefore, in my eventually arriving at the writing of a biography of Hitler in that I come to it, so to say, from the 'wrong' direction. [. . .] What follows is a work which reflects, through the medium of a biography of Hitler, . . . an attempt to bind together the personal with the impersonal elements."

38. P. Longerich, *Politik der Vernichtung: Eine Gesamtdarstellung der nationalsozialistischen Judenverfolgung* (Munich: Piper, 1998).

39. See U. Herbert, *Best: Biographische Studien über Radikalismus, Weltanschauung und Vernunft, 1903–1989* (Bonn: Dietz, 1996); H. Safrian, *Eichmann und seine Gehilfen* (Frankfurt am Main: A. Fischer Verlag, 1995); C. Steur, *Theodor Dannecker: Ein Funktionär der "Endlösung"* (Stuttgart: Klartext, 1997); M. Wildt, *Generation des Unbedingten: Das Führungskorps des Reichssicherheitshauptamtes* (Hamburg: Hamburger Edition, 2002); Idem, *Generation of the Unbound: The Leadership Corps of the Reich Security Main Office* (Jerusalem: Yad Vashem, 2002).

40. D. Peukert, "The Genesis of the 'Final Solution' from the Spirit of Science," in *Nazism and German Society 1933–1945,* ed. D. Crew (London: 1994), 274 ff.

41. "Die . . . Phase zwischen September und November 1941 bildete den Übergang von utopischen Völkermordplänen zu tatsächlich durchführbaren Massenmordprogrammen. [. . .] Ein wesentlicher Faktor für all diese Entwicklungen war die Kriegslage . . . um ganz materielle Dinge. [. . .] Eine besondere Rolle spielte die Ernährungslage" (C. Gerlach, *Kalkulierte Morde: Die deutsche Wirtschafts- und Vernichtungspolitik in Weissrussland 1941 bis 1944* [Hamburg: Hamburger Edition, 1998], 1132–3).

42. C. R. Browning, "Conclusion," in *Fateful Months: Essays on the Emergence of the Final Solution* rev. ed. (New York: Holmes & Meier, 1992), 86.

43. Nuremberg Documents, PS-1919; English translation in Y. Arad, Y. Gutman, and A. Margaliot, eds., *Documents on the Holocaust* (Jerusalem: Yad Vashem, 1981), 344.

44. Browning, "The Final Solution in German Historiography," *Fateful Months*, 72–3.

45. Browning, "The Decision," 99–100.

46. C. R. Browning, *The Final Solution and the German Foreign Office: A Study of Referat D III of Abteilung Deutschland 1940–43* (New York: Holmes & Meier, 1978). The first chapter of this book was already published in 1977: "Referat Deutschland, Jewish Policy and the German Foreign Office (1933–1940)," *Yad Vashem Studies* 12 (1977): 37–73.

47. Browning, *Fateful Months*, 7. See also Browning, *Nazi Policy*, 2: "Hitler was both the key ideological legitimizer and decision maker in this evolutionary process, which also depended crucially upon the initiatives and responses elicited from below."

48. Browning, *Foreign Office*, 185.

49. C. R. Browning, *Ordinary Men: Reserve Battalion 101 and the Final Solution in Poland* (New York: Harper Collins, 1992), 159–89.

50. Browning, *Fateful Months;* C. R. Browning, *The Path to Genocide: Essays on Launching the Final Solution* (Cambridge: Cambridge University Press, 1992).

51. C. R. Browning, *Die Entfesselung der Endlösung. Nationalsozialistische Judenpolitik, 1939–1942* (Propyläen Verlag: Munich, 2003); English version (University of Nebraska Press and Yad Vashem: Omaha, 2004); Hebrew version (Yad Vashem: Jersulem, 2004).

52. Ibid., n. 1.

53. Browning, "The Decision," 118; *Fateful Months*, 37.

54. C. R. Browning, "The Holocaust as By-Product? A Critique of Arno Mayer," in *The Path to Genocide*, 84.

55. C. R. Browning, "Prologue," in *Fateful Months*, xxi.

56. "The Euphoria of Victory and the Final Solution: Summer-Fall 1941," *German Studies Review* 17, no. 3 (1994): 478.

57. "The Euphoria of Victory," 474, 476.

58. C. R. Browning, "Conclusion," in *Fateful Months*, 86.

59. "Beyond 'Intentionalism' and 'Functionalism': The Decision for the Final Solution Reconsidered," in *The Path to Genocide*, 121; see also 113, twice.

60. See his review of P. Burrin's *Hitler et les juifs: genèse d'un génocide* (Paris: 1989), in *American Historical Review* 96 (1991): 1226: "Hitler played a key role in the decision-making process but not out of premeditation. Frustrated by the failure of previous solutions (emigration and expulsion), he opted for the Final Solution in the 'euphoria of victory' of midsummer 1941."

61. See "The Euphoria of Victory," 473–81; *Final Solution* ms., chap. 3 B 1; *Nazi Policy*, 2, 31, 38, 56.

62. *Nazi Policy,* 56; "The Euphoria of Victory," passim.

63. *Nazi Policy,* 2; "The Euphoria of Victory," 473.

64. This aspect should also be emphasized: Browning actually joins the camp of those who perceive the murder of the Jews as a singular enterprise even among the many other murderous activities of the regime, not as just one aspect of overall Nazi criminal behavior.

65. "The Euphoria of Victory," 480.

66. See I. Kershaw, *Hitler. [1] 1889–1936: Hubris* (New York: Norton, 1999), 527–91. Browning and Kershaw keep in close contact.

67. D. Michman, *Holocaust Historiography: A Jewish Perspective. Conceptualizations, Terminology, Approaches and Fundamental Issues* (Vallentine Mitchell: London, 2003), 91–126.

Gerhard Weinberg

Browning and the Big Picture

IT IS PROBABLY NOT VERY OFTEN THAT SOMEONE IS ASKED TO SPEAK AT a scholarly conference about the work of his own academic successor, but it only shows that the members of the History Department at the University of North Carolina at Chapel Hill are still as smart as they were when they invited me to join them twenty-seven years ago. When Paul Seabury published his path-breaking book on the German Foreign Ministry during the Nazi era in 1954,[1] he was able to include material on the Holocaust but only in an incidental way. His major concern was to illuminate the general contours of the internal development of the ministry and the German diplomatic service; in spite of its limitations, the book remains useful today. It was Christopher Browning who, in the revised version of his University of Wisconsin at Madison doctoral dissertation, published in 1978—please note: more than two decades later—delved into the way in which the German Foreign Ministry was deeply involved in the Holocaust and in a wide variety of other horrors of the regime.[2] The theme was taken up in an even more detailed way by German scholar Hans-Jürgen Döscher, who analyzed the relationship between the Foreign Ministry and the SS, having in the meantime located in the National Archives in Washington, D.C., microfilm of personnel records that were the equivalent of records that were at that time still illegally withheld by the Foreign Ministry of the Federal Republic in Bonn.[3]

There would be another example of a scholar in the German-speaking world (perhaps one should say *Landessprache*-speaking world, since he is an Austrian) taking up in detail a subject on which Browning did pioneering work. This is the role of the German armed forces in initiating on their own the mass killing of Jews in Serbia, already in 1941. Published in 1985 and again in 1991, his study of "Wehrmacht Reprisal Policy and the Murder of the Male Jews in Serbia" called attention to the extent to which the German army took the initiative within the general framework of Nazi policy to carry out the mass murder of people who had been selected as victims because they were Jews.[4] Documented in careful detail, this proved to be a stimulus, at least in part, to an ambitious and very important book by Walter Manoschek, *Serbien ist judenfrei: Militärische Besatzungspolitik und Judenvernichtung in Serbien 1941/42*.[5] Manfred Messerschmidt, then a key figure in the Military History Research Institute of the Federal Republic, which published Manoschek's book, noted in his "Foreword" that the findings of Browning, confirmed and elaborated by Manoschek, demonstrate that mass murder was initiated before, not after, the repulse of the German army on the Eastern Front in the winter of 1941, thus reinforcing the wide rejection of Arno Mayer's reversal of the chronology as nonsense.[6]

By a strange quirk of fate, there would be a sequel in which Browning's demolition appeared before rather than after the foolishness that needed correction. In 1992 there appeared a book that attracted worldwide attention, *Ordinary Men: Reserve Police Battalion 101 and the Final Solution in Poland*. I recall the attentive silence in the room when Browning at a meeting of the German Studies Association first read the paper, "One Day in Jozefow," subsequently published in the first of the *Lessons and Legacies* volumes.[7] In the book *Ordinary Men*, this event is placed in the context of the whole history of the unit's role in the Holocaust. There are aspects of *Ordinary Men* with which I do not agree, but the emphasis on the roles of conformity, peer pressure, and careerism is surely correct in Browning's analysis of those who became killers.

In this instance, the nonsense dealing in part with the same police unit appeared subsequently in the form of Daniel Goldhagen's *Hitler's Willing Executioners*, published in 1996.[8] The thesis propounded there required the author to convert Jewish judges in the Second Empire posthumously to Christianity, and Christians murdered in the death marches in the last part of World War II posthumously to Judaism, a procedure that ought in my opinion to have suggested that there might be something wrong with the thesis.[9]

But let me return to serious scholarship. Browning has published a large number of articles, many of them collected in two books, *Fateful Months: Essays on the Emergence of the Final Solution*,[10] and *The*

Path to Genocide: Essays on the Launching of the Final Solution.[11] They have been followed by the recent appearance of his Cambridge Trevelyan Lectures, *Nazi Policy, Jewish Workers, German Killers.*[12] What I would like to concentrate on are certain major aspects of Browning's work that underlie and inform all the pieces included in these books and that are likely to be of continuing significance for the future of Holocaust studies.

First, Browning has provided what I consider an especially important model for others in the field of Holocaust studies by seeking out and then carefully utilizing important groups of records that were previously either ignored or inaccessible. Let me illustrate this with a small number of examples. The account of Reserve Police Battalion 101 is based heavily on German judicial records not previously examined for their insight into the local realities of mass murder. It seems to me that more attention might have been given to the deliberate exclusion of references in the records to anti-Semitism because of the legal implications of such references in the context of German court proceedings, but no one reading *Ordinary Men* can fail to be impressed by what Browning has made of what might have looked to some as an unpromising batch of court records.

A second example is his utilization of materials, held at Yad Vashem, on the ghettos in Poland, in order to set up a differentiated analysis of the ghettos in the intermediate stage between ghettoization and killing, analyzing the moments where the Nazi leadership looked toward production and those where they anticipated murder.[13] A third example is the utilization of survivor testimony from the Starachowice Labor Camp in Poland to derive a clear and moving picture of what life and death were like in a labor camp that, but for its unusually high percentage of survivors, was probably typical of other such camps before all or almost all of their inmates had been killed.[14]

There are other instances of Browning's use of hitherto neglected or closed archives; the point that needs to be made is that in spite of the existence of a vast literature produced by scholars over the last quarter century, there are undoubtedly lots of other finds that remain to be made. Since the paper of the era involved is generally of very poor quality, the records must be examined very soon and/or microfilmed or they will be lost to scholarship forever by their sheer physical deterioration. This in turn raises another major issue to which the United States Holocaust Memorial Museum needs to pay close attention: microfilms without guides are close to useless. The vast quantities gathered by the museum need to be made accessible in practice as well as in theory by the preparation and publication of inventories.

Once again I want to return to Browning's work. In his scholarship, he has been careful to include two types of context for the new materials he has utilized. In the first place, there is a steady and thoughtful combination of existing published scholarship and related archival sources with the new. It is this feature of his work that will, in my judgment, give it a degree of permanent significance in the literature on the Holocaust. Second, he has tried to relate the specific questions, events, and problems he examines to the broader context of events in Germany and in World War II. Too much of the writing on the Holocaust has looked at those terrible events as through a pipe, disregarding the course of the war—a war that brought under German control well over 90 percent of those Jews killed while the fighting raged.[15] The confusions of such authors as Mayer, Sebastian Haffner, Christian Gerlach, and others are at least in part due to their failure to pay the close attention to the chronology of World War II that is needed. In a discussion some years ago I argued that Browning's explanation of the significance of specific events in the course of fighting on the Eastern Front for the evolution of decision making about the Holocaust was not the correct one;[16] what seems to me more important about his work in general is that he has consistently paid attention to the interrelation between the actual fighting at the front and stages and developments in the Holocaust.

There is, however, an aspect of the relationship between the war and the Holocaust that Browning does not engage sufficiently, and that is the broader nature and purpose of the conflict. The Germans did not go to war so that Hitler could visit the Eiffel Tower or so that the German Labor Front could launch a "Strength through Joy" cruise ship on the Caspian Sea. Hitler's pretense that the order for the so-called euthanasia program was signed by him on September 1, 1939, not weeks later, and his later claim that he had threatened that the Jews of Europe would be killed in a new war also on September 1, 1939, not on January 30 of that year, ought to be seen as a significant clue to his thinking. The demographic revolution on the globe was an integral part of the war; it was its principal purpose. No analysis of the Holocaust—as well as other facets of the great conflict—can really make sense unless this point is taken into consideration.

Both the initiation and the end of the Holocaust have to be seen within this framework. The genuinely held belief that Germany had lost World War I because of a "stab in the back" on the home front makes the effort to drive Germany's Jews out of the country in 1933–39 a portion of the general preparations of the country for war alongside the rearmament program. Military events that would bring masses of additional Jews under German control are central to the beginning of mass killing of the handicapped, the Jews, and the Sinti and Roma (Gypsies); the frantic desire of the Germans to complete as much of their main purpose as possible played a major role in its continuation into the last days of fighting.

The point that needs to be added to broaden the context that Browning does provide is the wider aim of the war from Germany's perspective. As Hitler himself explained in November 1941, Europe would be emptied of Jews country by country, and then would come the turn of the Jews in the rest of the world, what he described in the usual Eurocentric manner as Jews living among "*aussereuropäische Völker* [non-European peoples]." If the fate of the Jews of Palestine and other portions of the Middle East once the German army reached them was to be "*Vernichtung* [destruction]," to quote Hitler again, it should not be difficult to imagine the fate of those who had been removed from Europe.[17] We do not know precisely when Hitler began to think in these terms; one can find clues from prior statements going back to April 1920.[18] But concepts and implementation are certainly not the same thing, and Browning's very careful efforts to trace the precise stages in the decisions for the Holocaust are most helpful. It is, however, an inherent risk in any, even the best, study focused on a specific local situation, time frame, or segment of the killing apparatus that the wider context can be lost sight of all too easily—and with that loss comes a major reduction in the significance of what has been found. Browning is undoubtedly correct in rejecting the economic utilitarian explanation for the Holocaust offered by Götz Aly and Susanne Heim. Those scholars have indeed turned up some useful and important new materials, but their attempt to utilize German rationalizations for murder as a true indication of purpose, as opposed to the dominance of ideological presuppositions, cannot convince.[19]

Over the years, the influence of Browning's work on the historiography of the Holocaust has been threefold. In the first place, his presentations at professional meetings as well as to general public audiences have not only enlightened his listeners—they have certainly done so for me—but they have helped those in his audiences to understand matters that they had never seen as clearly before, because he has a gift for thoughtful, clear, and coherent exposition. Second, his publications, of which I have mentioned only some and of which there are some major ones yet to come, have enriched us all. Whatever the agreements or disagreements that others may have with Browning's work, they cannot help but be both impressed and assisted by what they read of it. Third, he has pointed the way to new directions in research, both by opening new questions and refining perspectives on old ones and also by calling attention to the availability and utility of materials that can offer additional insights.

There is a fourth dimension in which he can be expected to make a further contribution in the future. His prior academic appointment did not provide a substantial opportunity for him to direct graduate work and for those who want to pursue graduate work in the field of Holocaust studies to carry out their research under his guidance. May I conclude at the point at which I began: this has now been remedied, and we can hopefully look forward to a sequence of doctoral dissertations, subsequently turned into good books, by his future students at Chapel Hill.

NOTES

1. Paul Seabury, *The Wilhelmstrasse: A Study of German Diplomats under the Nazi Regime* (Berkeley: University of California Press, 1954). Seabury had earlier published some of his findings in "Ribbentrop and the German Foreign Office," *Political Science Quarterly* 64 (1951): 532–53.

2. Christopher R. Browning, *The Final Solution and the German Foreign Office: A Study of Referat D III of Abteilung Deutschland, 1940–43* (New York: Holmes & Meier, 1978).

3. Hans-Jürgen Döscher, *Das Auswärtige Amt im Dritten Reich: Diplomatie im Schatten der "Endlösung"* (Berlin: Siedler, 1987; Frankfurt am Main: Ullstein, 1991).

4. English text in *Fateful Months: Essays on the Emergence of the Final Solution* (1985; reprint, New York: Holmes & Meier, 1991), chap. 2.

5. Munich: Oldenbourg, 1993.

6. Arno J. Mayer, *Why Did the Heavens Not Darken? The "Final Solution" in History* (New York: Pantheon, 1988). This book has fortunately sunk into the obscurity it deserves.

7. Peter Hayes, ed., *Lessons and Legacies: The Meaning of the Holocaust in a Changing World* (Evanston: Northwestern University Press, 1991), 196–209, 365–6. In *Ordinary Men* (New York: Harper/Collins, 1992), the story is covered in chap. 7.

8. Daniel J. Goldhagen, *Hitler's Willing Executioners: Ordinary Germans and the Holocaust* (New York: Knopf, 1996).

9. A particularly dramatic example is the massacre at Gardelegen. The pictures of the burned victims reproduced by Goldhagen from the American army report naturally do not show that they did not wear the Yellow Star. See Joachim Neander, *Gardelegen 1945: Das Ende der Häftlingstransporte aus dem Konzentrationslager "Mittelbau"* (Magdeburg: Landeszentrale für politische Bildung Sachsen-Anhalt, 1998), especially 34–5. Among the Jewish judges in Imperial Germany who are posthumously converted by Goldhagen are at least three members of this author's family.

10. See n. 4 above.

11. New York: Cambridge University Press, 1992.

12. New York: Cambridge University Press, 1999.

13. *The Path to Genocide,* chap. 2.

14. *Nazi Policy,* chap. 4.

15. On this see Gerhard L. Weinberg, "The Holocaust and World War II: A Dilemma in Teaching," in Donald G. Schilling (ed.), *Lessons and Legacies,* vol. II. *Teaching the Holocaust in a Changing World* (Evanston: Northwestern University Press, 1998), 26–40, 197–8.

16. *German Studies Review* 17 (1994): 509–12.

17. *Akten zur deutschen auswärtigen Politik,* Serie D, XIII, 2. Nr. 515.

18. For the use of the term "Auszurotten" on April 6, 1920, see Eberhard Jäckel, ed., *Hitler: Sämtliche Aufzeichnungen 1905–1924* (Stuttgart: Deutsche Verlags-Anstalt, 1980), 120. Although there is now much additional information, Gerald Fleming's *Hitler and the Final Solution* (Berkeley: University of California Press, 1984) is still useful.

19. *The Path to Genocide,* chap. 3. See also Dan Diner, *Beyond the Conceivable: Studies on Germany, Nazism, and the Holocaust* (Berkeley: University of California Press, 2000), chap. 8, which engages the same issue.

Dariusz Stola

New Research on the Holocaust in Poland

POLAND WAS THE PRINCIPAL PLACE OF THE HOLOCAUST, POLISH JEWS were the first and largest group of its victims, and non-Jewish Poles were the largest group of the witnesses of the crime. Poland was also the country where the research on the Holocaust (*avant la lettre*) began, and recently the research has undergone an interesting evolution along a wider turn in attitudes toward the Jewish past of Poland. In recent years Polish historiography of the Holocaust and debates on Polish-Jewish relations during the Holocaust have themselves become a subject of interest and research. Several publications on this topic have appeared.[1] This article presents briefly the evolution of Polish historiography of the Holocaust and its conditions, and focuses on the "new" Holocaust studies in Poland—that is, those made public since the debate initiated by Jan Błoński in 1987.[2]

The choice of the Błoński debate is to some extent arbitrary and simplifying, since the turn in Polish approaches to the Polish-Jewish past, which the debate symbolizes, was in fact a longer process; it began several years earlier and probably would not have matured without the great changes of 1989. Yet the debate serves the purpose of periodization better than any other event and its choice emphasizes the role of the topic of Polish-Jewish relations in Polish studies and reflection on the Holocaust.

Polish and Jewish collective memories generated divergent and highly emotional images of the Second World War, which have played an essential role in shaping both groups' contemporary identity.[3] Confrontation of these "Jewish truths" and "Polish truths," as Krystyna Kersten termed them, caused especially high tensions in the sphere of the common theme of Polish-Jewish relations, primarily Polish attitudes toward the Jews during the Holocaust.[4] The controversy was more than a confrontation of different opinions. An unfortunate pattern of discussion, based on suspicion, mutual accusations, and apologetics, made it insoluble. "Jewish truth" was about pervasive Polish anti-Semitism resulting in indifference mixed with satisfaction with the solution of the Jewish problem by the Germans, the willing takeover of Jewish property, omnipresent Polish extortionists, numerous murders, and only sporadic instances of disinterested help. Poles positively rejected the charges as slanderous. They presented as typical the examples of heroic and selfless help to the Jews, and stressed that Poles were themselves victims of Nazis, and as such they did all, or almost all, they could to help. Often, they in turn accused Jews of treason and collaboration with the Soviets and persecution of non-communist Poles in 1939–41 and after the war. What such exchanges meant was expressed most clearly by Roman Zimand: "[E]ach side accused the other of collaboration—to the detriment of the other side—either with Nazism or with communism (in its Stalinist phase), that is, of collaboration with the most criminal regimes in the history of the world."[5]

Besides the complex legacies of the Polish-Jewish past (and of the past discussions of this past), a list of a few factors is in order here that had and have had an influence on Holocaust studies in Poland. First, World War II, including the Holocaust, is a major moment and among the most dramatic of Poland's history, its consequences difficult to overestimate and still visible. Second, because of the Holocaust and postwar emigration of most remaining Jews, Jewish culture in Poland almost discontinued and a Jewish presence has been marginal, which, among other things, contributed to the marginalization of historical narratives reflecting Jewish perspectives and experiences. Third, between the German occupation and 1989, Poland was under a communist regime, which meant the disappearance of freedom of speech and the emergence of large-scale efforts to manipulate the narratives and images of the past. As a consequence, some problems of the past could be discussed freely only relatively recently, in contrast to the long-standing discussions in the West.

Research on the destruction of Polish Jewry began in Nazi occupied Poland. The first studies and collections of documents came from the victims themselves, including Emmanuel Ringelblum and his colleagues in the Warsaw ghetto, who followed Simon Dubnov's call to "Write and document!" The first research by non-Jews was probably for the reports prepared by the Polish underground for the Polish government-in-exile in London. Immediately after the liberation from the Germans, survivors began large-scale documentary efforts. The Central Jewish Historical Commission, with its research institute and provincial branches, coordinated these efforts. The commission prepared research aids (guidelines and questionnaires) and in 1946 alone it conducted some 1,800 interviews.[6] Another institution, which soon began to collect important historical evidence, was the governmental Main Commission for Investigation of German Crimes. The first memoirs and studies of the Holocaust, in Polish and Yiddish, began to appear in print as early as 1945[7] and in the next two years they were already dozens. There also began a debate in the Polish press on Polish-Jewish relations during the occupation, mainly on their moral aspects.

Unfortunately, these trends were soon reversed. After the substantial emigration of Jews and along the accelerated Sovietization of Poland in 1948–50, the number of publications dramatically decreased, as well as the scope and intensity of research. Holocaust studies became themselves a kind of closed zone, cultivated almost exclusively in the Jewish Historical Institute. Heavy-handed censorship and propaganda influence gave the publications of the early 1950s a distinctive Stalinist flavor, noticeable even in the title of the most important one: *Hitlerite Policy of Extermination of Jews in 1939–1945 as a Manifestation of German Imperialism.*[8] Not just the interpretations but also the records of the past had to bow to the *Zeitgeist* of the period. For example, in 1952 editors "corrected" Ringelblum's chronicle of the Warsaw ghetto (later on, this distorted edition served as a basis for publications abroad).[9] The observation that, under the new regime, "the future is certain [because 'the laws of history' determine the victory of communism] but the past is not," applied also to the Holocaust.

The "thaw" of 1956 relaxed the Stalinist grip and brought a wave of war memoirs and other publications, including new editions of major earlier books. As in the 1940s, favorable conditions did not last long. Since the late 1950s the room for reliable research on recent history began to narrow again, although not to the extent that it did in the Stalin era. There was some room for less-ideological studies of German policies, the noncommunist underground, and Polish assistance to the Jews. This was true especially for the latter because the tendencies in propaganda and ideology in the 1960s drifted increasingly from a "revolutionary" to "nationalist-communist" bias. The nationalist tendency culminated in 1968 in the anti-Zionist campaign. The campaign meant openly anti-Semitic publications, a purge in the party and administration, serious blows to Jewish institutions (including the Jewish Historical Institute), an induced wave of emigration of Polish Jews (including historians, writers, and other bearers of memory), crude distortions in historiography, and censorship intervention, including the editing of Holocaust-related entries in encyclopedias.[10] As a consequence, the Jews were marginalized in public commemoration of the Nazi victims, in textbooks, and in research. Symbolic of this process was the de-Judaization of Jewish victims of Auschwitz, who were increasingly presented as "citizens of Poland and many other countries of Europe" or simply "human beings." This "universalistic" approach reflected a pattern developed in the Soviet Union and expressed in monuments of mass killing that did not mention the fact that their victims were Jewish, something that Shari Cohen called "state-organized forgetting."[11]

The authorities discontinued the campaign in a few months but its consequences weighed heavily on the next decade. It was only in the late 1970s that new winds were felt in discussions and publications on the Holocaust. The first signs of change could be found at the underground "flying university" and in early *samizdat* publications of dissident intellectuals.[12] But the period, which really changed Poles' way of thinking on many issues and greatly contributed to the turn in Polish approaches to the past, including the Holocaust, was the sixteen months of "Solidarity" in 1980–81. "Truth" was next to "Freedom" and "Justice" among the slogans of the movement. A dimension of its (meta)political struggle was "regaining the past," that is, building or restoring historical narratives different from the official narratives and "blank spots." This tendency was sometimes sentimentalist and had its own biases, but in any case it expanded the "free speech zone" and allowed for and demanded debate on history.[13] Besides, the glorious months of 1980–81 significantly strengthened the self-esteem of the Poles (and improved their image abroad), so they approached difficult moments in their past with less anxiety and a stronger sense of responsibility. This period weakened both censorship control and defensive attitudes within the Polish public, and it confirmed the saying that "only free people are open to the truth about themselves."

After the martial law of December 1981 the subject of the Holocaust reemerged in public discourse with the fortieth anniversary of the Warsaw ghetto uprising in 1983, when—in addition to official rituals—a number of articles appeared in the underground press and independent Catholic journals. The role of Catholic intellectuals and press is worth noting. The prior evolution of the Church's position toward the Jews, and the role played by Pope John Paul II, had a great impact on the Polish debates. Advocates of the revision of "Polish truths" on the Holocaust often referred to the example of the Church.

A parallel process, which embraced only a small group of people, was also of importance for our topic. This was a series of meetings of Polish and Jewish historians, of which the first took place in spring 1983 in New York, another in 1984 in Oxford, England, and the largest a conference in Jerusalem in 1988. The discussions were often difficult, indeed painful, but they broke the vicious circle of accusations and apologetics, self-protecting denials and counteraccusations. They also revealed that major points of debate were Polish-Polish, rather than Polish-Jewish, controversies. Besides, Polish scholars could watch the tide of interest in the Holocaust in the West and the impressive development of the field known as Holocaust studies. Domestically, Polish historiography benefited from the gradual softening of censorship in the late 1980s, which made possible the publication of a number of important sources. More important perhaps was the "moral emancipation" of historians, who became more willing to take on politically sensitive and controversial subjects.

One of the participants in the Polish-Jewish conferences was Professor Jan Błoński. With his article in the *Tygodnik Powszechny* in January 1987, he began a debate on Polish reactions to the Holocaust.[14] The debate has been invaluable both as an expression of opinions on the Polish-Jewish past and as a factor shaping them. Błoński began with a poet's reflection on the destruction of the Warsaw ghetto and ended with a call for symbolic compensation for Polish indifference. The ensuing debate focused primarily on moral questions; strictly historical investigation had only a minor, auxiliary role in the debate. The controversy was not about the facts: "It was clearly not a question of facts. There may have been differences over the facts, but this divergence [of opinions] was too great to be explained on this basis," noted Błoński. Yet, Antony Polonsky rightly stressed that the articulation of the moral problems at the center of the controversy made possible a much more effective analysis of the factual problems involved.[15] The study of Polish-Jewish relations and reactions to the Holocaust can thus become less of a field for emotional exchanges and can be advanced by the application of the traditional skills and techniques of the historian. Having begun with moral and philosophical considerations regarding the responsibility of the witnesses of radical evil, we can come back to the questions of facts and, through them, to the questions of methodology and professional ethics of the historian.

The Błoński debate reflected the progressive erosion of the Soviet-era regime and expansion of the "free speech zone" in the late 1980s. The great events of 1989, including the end of censorship, essentially changed conditions for public debate, historical research, and publishing. Freedom of speech matters, and this has been visible in Polish debates, research, and reflection on the Holocaust. Without going deeper into their content and meanings, the sheer frequency of the debates is telling. In the four decades between the late 1940s and the Błoński article, the topic of Polish-Jewish relations and the Holocaust was widely presented to the public only once, and that was as part of the infamous anti-Zionist campaign; in the last decade, there have been at least ten debates on the subject involving major national media.[16] In just a few years of the new Poland, probably more publications appeared on the subject than during the previous forty years.

The removal of political restrictions would not have been a sufficient factor for the development of research, publications, and reflection without substantial interest in the topic. Since the early 1990s many observers have noted in Poland a tide of interest in things Jewish. Major bookstores established and have maintained separate sections of Judaica, various Jewish topics appear frequently in journals and daily press, and cultural events such as the Jewish Culture Festival in Cracow or the exhibition of photographs of Polish Jews in Warsaw gather crowds. Even the interest in anti-Semitic publications may be, to some extent, a perverse aspect of this curiosity about the Jews. Those professionally involved in Polish-Jewish relations and their history were also surprised by the phenomenon, as were the jury members for a contest on Jewish history in 1993, who unexpectedly were flooded with essays and research reports from 4,000 students of secondary schools from all over Poland. Initially the interest was thought to be just a temporary fashion, yet ten years later it seems quite lasting. Also worth noting is that it coincided with the transformation of Poland into a market economy: the interest in things Jewish translated into demand. The publications and events turned out to be marketable and sold better than many other "cultural products," which in turn certainly contributed to their sustainability.

An important part of the interest in Jewish history is the Holocaust itself. Popular interest has probably resulted to large extent from the role the Holocaust has taken in contemporary Western culture (including Hollywood productions), which has massively poured into Poland since 1989. In the academy it has been influenced by and has benefited from the rise of Holocaust studies abroad. Indeed, the term "Holocaust" was imported as an English rather than a Greek word (as testified by its peculiar transliteration in Polish) and tends to replace the Polish term *Zagłada* (which is closer in meaning to *Shoah*).

Interest in the Holocaust seems also to have particular Polish roots. It is plausible that such events do not pass without a trace in the minds of their close witnesses, although what consequences exactly such witnessing brings is not clear (this is also a question for research).[17] An aspect of the new Polish approaches to the past, at least of many writers and historians in particular, has been the recognition of the Holocaust as a major fact of Poland's history and Polish history—of *our* history. This cross-fertilizes with the above observations of the Western recognition of the Holocaust, leading to the conviction that, in the Holocaust, our history is *the* History.

Moreover, the Holocaust is a disturbing part of Polish history. The frequency and intensity of Polish debates about Polish attitudes toward the Jews and the Holocaust leave no doubt that the Holocaust is a contemporary problem. The debates reveal three main elements of this problem. First is the burden of facing oneself: assessing how the "we" of the Polish imagined community responded to the tragedy of its Jewish neighbors. One ought to stress that for Polish history–rooted identity, solidarity with the past generations and especially with the generation of World War II seems particularly strong. Second is the problem at the center of controversies surrounding the presence of the Carmelites and crosses in Oświęcim (Auschwitz) expressed in the questions "Whose Auschwitz?" (which for most of the

Poles is the symbol of Polish martyrdom) and what is the appropriate way to commemorate its victims. Third is the problem caused by the sudden and dramatic disappearance of the Jews, who for centuries had been a part of Polish landscape and culture. "Post-Jewish emptiness" has both a symbolic aspect and a material aspect (i.e., the problem of Jewish property).

The progress in Jewish studies in the last decade would not have been possible without development of relevant institutions. The Jewish Historical Institute reversed the downward trend it had been in since 1968 and visibly strengthened. New centers for Jewish studies were established at the two most prominent Polish universities: Jagiellonian University in Cracow established the Center (now Department) of Jewish Studies headed by Professor Józef Gierowski; and Warsaw University the Mordechai Anielewicz Center headed by Professor Jerzy Tomaszewski. Jewish studies emerged also at other universities, in history or sociology departments. Significant institutions for education, publications, and research on the Holocaust have been the Auschwitz and Majdanek museums. Most recently, the Holocaust has been declared a priority for the newly established Institute of National Memory, which incorporates the former Main Commission for the Investigation of Nazi Crimes, an archival branch for the voluminous files of the communist period and a large research branch. The institutional buildup would not have been possible without foreign support. Thanks to grants and scholarships from foreign, institutional, and individual donors, Holocaust studies in Poland have been in a relatively fortunate situation compared to many other segments of underfinanced Polish research affected by the erosion of human capital and infrastructure.

The new academic centers do not face difficulties in attracting good students. The growth of interest in Polish-Jewish history, and the multi-ethnic past of Poland in general, was already visible among students in 1980s and proved not to be temporary. A survey of recent masters and doctoral theses in 1996 produced a list of 186 theses on Jewish topics.[18] As one member of the young cohort of Polish Holocaust scholars, who graduated in late 1980s, confessed to this author: "I chose the topic, but the topic chose me." Thus, a young generation has entered and keeps entering the field and has already left its mark on historiography. Generational change has also had an ethnic dimension: Holocaust studies are no longer an enclave of elderly Jewish scholars. In terms of its content or perspective, with new approaches to the Polish-Jewish past and generational changes, the traditional division of that past into Polish historiography and Jewish historiography in Poland no longer seems applicable. Fortunately, some of the new adepts of history learn Yiddish or Hebrew, which is a great novelty: probably for the first time even young Poles take classes in a Jewish language. This offers the prospect of overcoming the main linguistic barrier and basic weakness of the Polish Holocaust research today.

The new period in Polish studies on the Holocaust differs from the earlier ones in the greater availability of sources. Access to certain archival collections is no longer restricted for political reasons (as was the case, for instance, with the Polish underground documents that were kept closed in the Communist Party Central Committee archive) or is simply easier, thanks to improved archival infrastructure and the progressing efforts of archivists. Numerous documents have been recently found or revealed; a telling case is a collection of papers of the late Janusz Korczak.[19] Many primary sources have been published. Indeed, since the late 1980s Polish readers could have enjoyed a major wave of such publications; its intensity could be compared only to the one of the early postwar years. Indirectly, Polish scholars can benefit from a greater availability of sources from abroad, thanks to the declassification of documents in the former Soviet Union, the United States, and other countries, and the coincident progress in information technology. Also, secondary sources are much more accessible, thanks to translations and acquisition of foreign publications without political restriction; incomparably greater international scholarly contacts; and, again, information technology, which has greatly reduced the barrier of physical distance. In Poland, the growing number of new Holocaust-related studies itself creates research synergies.

The new wave of published primary sources consists of selected archival materials and various personal documents. Among the former, there is a number of most essential documents on the Holocaust from the Ringelblum Archive and the Auschwitz camp.[20] The published personal documents are much more numerous; in fact, a large part of the Ringelblum Archive also consists of such documents as diaries, memoirs, letters, and various accounts.[21] The timing and circumstances of their writing varied greatly. Some of these documents come from the war period, while their authors remained in the ghetto or in hiding on the "Aryan side." Such documents include accounts of well-known personalities, like Czerniakow's diary or Korczak's notes, as well as equally powerful memoirs of ghetto policeman Calel Perechodnik or of twelve-year-old David Rubinowicz. Other accounts were recorded in the early postwar period, several years ago, or just recently. Their authors had just left hiding, returned from the camps after the liberation, or were recalling the events from a perspective of decades; some of them only recently could overcome the barrier of past trauma. The list includes Józef Barski, Halina Birenbaum, Adina Blady-Szwajger, Michał Głowiński, Arnold Mostowicz, Helena Szereszewska, Noemi Szac-Wajnkranc, Stanisław Taubenszlag, M. M. Mariański, and many others.[22] There also appeared re-editions of memoirs that had first been published in the early postwar years, such as those of Marek Edelman and Władysław Szpilman.[23]

A separate group of this type of publications contains collections of testimonies and interviews: a selection of accounts from the Warsaw ghetto; two volumes of memoirs of the Children of the Holocaust Association; and interviews, of various types, by Anka Grupińska, Joanna Wiszniewicz, and Barbara Engelking-Boni.[24] Close to this group are Hanna Krall's "documentary tales" based on interviews with survivors and eyewitness.[25] There have been some overdue translations of memoirs from Yiddish or English, but most of the publications had been written originally in Polish. This feature of the recent wave of printed memoirs is worth noting. Publishing in Poland the personal documents of Polish-speaking Jews, while being simply easier and less expensive, also makes available and sometimes preserves the documents in their original language, without the translator's intervention that inevitably alters certain meanings and subtleties.

Also interesting, and not only for students of Polish-Jewish relations, are publications of Polish underground materials. The leading one is the volume containing 556 articles and notes from the Polish underground press on the Warsaw ghetto uprising, *Wojna niemiecko-żydowska* (German-Jewish War), edited by Paweł Szapiro.[26] Interesting individual documents can be found in the editions of the documents of the Home Army and the right-wing National Armed Forces.[27] There appeared also some relevant accounts of Polish witnesses, including the outstanding uncensored memoirs of Colonel Kazimierz Moczarski. After his distinguished wartime service in the Home

Army, Moczarski was imprisoned by the communists and could discuss the past with his cellmate—General Juergen Stroop, the man responsible for the final destruction of the Warsaw ghetto.[28]

Progress in Holocaust studies in Poland in the recent period has been impressive, especially for a medium-sized country with low spending on research and education; yet this cannot conceal the fact that the progress has been uneven and has not filled all the gaps it should. In spite of the publication of the valuable handbook *Najnowsze dzieje Żydów w Polsce* (Recent History of the Jews in Poland), with a chapter on World War II by Teresa Prekerowa, and recently a volume on the destruction of Polish Jewry by Marian Fuks, a comprehensive synthesis of the Holocaust in Poland is still missing.[29] It is a definite handicap for teaching and is an expression of the weakness of contemporary Polish historiography.

A number of studies on selected topics about the Holocaust have appeared, including works on the fate of various Jewish communities. Among them are monographs on German institutions and policies of terror, economic exploitation, and population engineering.[30] As a rule, they focus on what happened in occupied Poland, but there are a few studies that look outside the country, such as books by Karol Jońca (on Kristallnacht), Jerzy Tomaszewski (on the expulsion of Polish Jews from Germany in 1938), and Tomasz Szarota (on anti-Jewish riots in occupied Europe).[31] While some of the studies focus on specifically anti-Jewish policies or institutions (Jews in the Radom prison, camps for Jews in Lower Silesia), others are part of the general research on the history of Poland under German occupation while paying due (or at least greater) attention to its (anti-)Jewish aspects. A field of research that could develop in Poland only recently is studies on the Soviet occupation of eastern Poland in 1939–41.[32]

Thus, one can find information and analysis relevant for Holocaust research in studies on a variety of topics, from population displacement to Polish-Belorussian relations to operation of the Polish "blue" police. To stay with these examples, the latter book deals, although still in a defensive way, with the role of the police in implementing the *Endlösung*.[33] Detailed research on Polish-Belorussian relations under Soviet rule shows the complexity, dynamics, and powers of hate unleashed by the Soviet-imported revolution in a multiethnic environment, of which the Jews were part and were soon to become the most defenseless part.[34] The study of migrations in the

Lublin district makes clear that a major part of the displaced persons were Jews, and it shows how, because of their forced migrations and extermination, the district had a positive migration balance without population growth.[35] Such studies, although they do not focus on the Holocaust and their authors are often not familiar with Holocaust historiography, do provide useful information and contexts.

Such "territorialist" approaches, with a sensitivity for Jewish aspects of history, are well deserved and partially reactive against the ethnocentric tendency that marked many studies of Poland in the past. In the publications of the recent period (although unfortunately not all of them), one may note a greater sensitivity for other than Polish perspectives on the past. It seems that the repeated calls of historians such as Marcin Kula and Jerzy Tomaszewski to pay due attention to ethnic and religious minorities and to their role in and contribution to Poland's history eventually bore fruit. This is a fortunate turn from the ethnocentric Polish history that has dominated since the nineteenth century to a broader history of Poland. It means an effort to integrate the history of Polish Jews into Poland's history, including integration of the Holocaust—as the Jewish catastrophe—into the Polish narratives of Poland's past. Through examination of Polish reactions to the Holocaust and the consequences the Holocaust had, and has had, for the Poles comes the integration into the narratives of the Poles' past as well.

This integrative tendency influences not just interpretations but sometimes also new primary sources. In some Polish memoirs on World War II and the prewar period that have been published in the 1990s, one may notice a more frequent mention of Jews and their fate, a retrospective discovery of Jews in authors' pasts, and persons and events that the authors would probably not have mentioned (or even remembered) without a sensitivity that has emerged since the 1980s.

To make it more complex, this integrative tendency has had to coexist with difficult efforts to clarify and reemphasize the difference between the German policies toward Jews and Poles and the difference between the fates of Poles and Jews under the German occupation. Polish historiography had a tendency to blur these differences and the unique features of the Holocaust. This tendency was present already in the wartime reports and statements; it developed further under the communist-period distortions of a "universalistic" and "nationalist" variety; it was related to the peculiar Polish-Jewish "competition of victims" and the postwar symbolic appropriation of Auschwitz; it still marks popular images of the past.

While scholarly works have overcome this tendency, popular perceptions evolve more slowly. It will take time before more adequate images can be sufficiently absorbed by the wider public. The controversies about the Carmelites and crosses in Oświęcim in the 1990s *appear* to testify to the opposite (i.e., to a tendency for distortion of images and symbolic appropriation), but this is in fact not the case. More likely they are consequences of processes that took place much earlier but became manifest only later. The controversies followed the introduction of religious symbols, after the desecularization of Auschwitz, which the communists kept as a religious as possible through four decades. Religious signs (and the Carmelite nuns) were allowed in with the regime's erosion in the 1980s but the Polish perception of Auschwitz as the symbol of the martyrdom of Christian Poles had been well established long before that.

In the 1990s the messages of the Auschwitz monument and museum were changed. New approaches have replaced the earlier patterns of commemorating and presenting the past, including the "universalistic" distortions. The museum's publishing house provided a number of essential works on the camp, such as Danuta Czech's *Kalendarium wydarzeń w KL Auschwitz* (available also in German) and the five volumes of *Auschwitz 1940–1945,* edited by Wacław Długoborski and Franciszek Piper (available also in English and German).[36] The Museum has also devoted attention to the history of the genocide of Gypsies or Romany, the group of victims most marginalized so far.[37]

A highly welcome novelty in Polish research is the proliferation of studies on provincial Jewish communities. Their authors, often local historians, either attempt to write the missing Jewish part of a town history, including its last chapter, or focus on the Holocaust alone. The quality of such studies varies, yet jointly this grass-roots fact-finding effort generates a basis for comprehensive works of synthesis, including less fragmentary and more detailed knowledge of Jewish life and death in occupied Poland. The growing list of the publications includes books on Będzin, Białystok, Cracow, Dobrzyń, Gorlice, Kalisz, Kazimierz, Kielce, Krosno, Lublin, Łódź, Modrzejów, Ostrowiec, Pabianice, Płock, Poznań, Pułtusk and Maków Mazowiecki, Rymanów, Rzeszów, Skierniewice, Sochaczew, Tarnów, Tyśmienica,

Włoszczowa, Żywiec, the provinces of Ciechanów and Pomerania, and others.[38] The fate of the Jews of Warsaw has continued to attract the greatest attention. Studies on the Warsaw ghetto are the most advanced and to some extent derive from incomparably richer sources. Ruta Sakowska made valuable contributions to the general history of the people of the Closed Quarter (*Ludzie z dzielnicy zamkniętej*), while scholars of the younger generation have dealt with its specific aspects, such as the ghetto police or the "survival imperative."[39] A major work on the Warsaw ghetto, the voluminous *Getto warszawskie: Przewodnik po nieistniejącym mieście* (Warsaw Ghetto: A Guide to a Non-existing City), by Barbara Engelking-Boni and Jacek Leociak, with detailed maps, chronology, and descriptions of the ghetto institutions, has just appeared.[40]

A special group of Polish Holocaust studies consists of in-depth investigations of personal documents. In their careful examination of narratives, phrases, and words, as well as in their particular perspective on past events, these studies resemble archeology. Through such excavations in memoirs, diaries, letters, and interviews, Barbara Engelking-Boni, Jacek Leociak, Piotr Matywiecki, and (earlier) Ruta Sakowska have reached most interesting insights into the world of the ghetto, including better understanding of such essential notions as time, space, life and dying, and the character of literary representations of that world.[41] The authors take advantage of the relatively rich collection of personal documents in Polish, as well as of the rich methodological reflection of Polish humanistic sociology to develop an anthropology of the ghetto.

Polish-Jewish relations remain the leading theme of Holocaust studies in Poland. They continue to incite strong emotions, attract public (and international) attention, and pose extraordinary problems for research. This results from the complexity of the problem, its emotional, moral, and political burden. There have also been constraints on the research that could not be quickly removed by political revolution or soul-searching, such as the availability of sources and the consequences of the idle years with restrictions on research. Nazi-occupied Poland was a difficult and dangerous place to make independent records. For many aspects of life, especially for research that looks beyond the elite to larger social groups, the available evidence is scarce and fragmentary. The underground press, private diaries, and German reports often do not provide sufficient or reliable information for comprehensive historical presentation. This constraint can be only partially overcome with further, extensive queries and innovative research approaches. Such queries and analyses have begun only relatively recently, due to long-lasting political and psychological barriers.

The way the availability of sources affected research can be seen in a comparison of our knowledge of policies and attitudes of the two elements of the Polish wartime state: the government-in-exile and the "underground state" (i.e., the clandestine military and civilian organizations formally subordinate to the government-in-exile). The government-in-exile generated, as would any bureaucracy of this kind, relatively many sources. Its archives were preserved fragmentarily and dispersed, but they are incomparably richer than the documents generated by the underground leadership, which was extensively destroyed when Warsaw burned in 1944. After the war, the government-in-exile documents mostly remained abroad and as a rule were accessible, while the underground documents were kept closed in the archives of the Communist Party or the security forces. As a consequence, a number of studies of Polish-Jewish relations by Polish émigré or foreign scholars appeared abroad and used the government-in-exile files.[42] Scholarship on the topic "the government-in-exile and the Jews" was thus more comprehensive and detailed than those on "the underground and the Jews." New research in Poland on the former topic had a better starting point. There is a book on the Polish-Jewish political relations in exile, and books on the government devote separate chapters or sections to the topic.[43] At the same time, a book on the Polish underground and the Holocaust is still needed, although some new studies of the underground pay greater attention to Holocaust-related questions.[44] Paradoxically, the problem of attitudes toward the Jews is discussed in detail in new studies of the nationalist Right underground. They usually do not hide their apologetic character, but some of them try to keep to standards of academic publication and provide interesting evidence.[45]

Not surprisingly, the most often-presented pattern of Polish reactions to the Holocaust was assistance to the Jews. Research on this topic developed since the 1960s, with an inclination to inflate the scale of help. In the recent period a number of more balanced studies appeared, but a hagiographic tendency still pops up.[46] More significant has been the emergence of publications that discuss other-than-heroic Polish attitudes. Even highly sensitive topics are no longer avoided, and they attract public attention. Most recognized in this aspect have been Krystyna Kersten's *Polacy-Żydzi-komunizm* and Jan T. Gross' *Upiorna dekada*.[47] Recently, a new book by Gross, *Sąsiedzi*, opened another serious debate in the Polish media, and it may mark a new stage of research and reflection on Polish-Jewish relations and the Holocaust. The book goes far beyond the problem of Polish indifference, which has been discussed since the Błoński article. It focuses on direct participation in crime. Gross brought to the light the case of the mass murder of Jews in the town of Jedwabne in July 1941, committed, he claims, mainly by their Polish neighbors.[48]

Defensive attitudes and resistance to facing the most disturbing facts certainly remain; they probably contribute to the uneven development of research. Yet the parameters of these defensive attitudes are found elsewhere than they were at the time of the Błoński debate. Also, the instruments of the defense have changed, with arguments of historians—about factual findings, sources, and methodology—playing an increasing role.[49] This means a normalization of Holocaust studies in Poland. Constraints on the research remain, however, and new problems are likely to appear with the passing of the generation of witnesses. Their deaths will perpetuate the major research constraint: the barrier of silence that separates us from the majority of Poles who did not leave evidence to help us interpret their attitudes about the Holocaust. While the helpers and the wrongdoers expressed themselves in deeds or words, and records of some of these expressions are available for investigation, the motives of the passive and silent majority remain unclear. Speculation on their motives, on the cause of not acting, is largely *ex silentio*, with all its weaknesses.

The analysis of wartime Polish-Jewish relations has also benefited from new, substantial scholarship on Polish policies and attitudes toward the Jews before September 1939. These studies, mostly by historians of the younger generation, investigate solutions for the Jewish question proposed in the last years of independent Poland and the relevant positions of major political parties, the national Right in particular; they detail such topics as the anti-Jewish riots of the late 1930s and the "ghetto bench" at the universities.[50] Similarly, there are several studies on the early postwar years. The outbursts of anti-Jewish violence in that period have become no longer taboo, with books and articles published on pogroms in Kielce and Cracow, for example.[51]

In addition to book-size publications, there are periodicals that devote a substantial part of their space to the Holocaust. There is no specialized periodical for Holocaust studies in Poland, but there are journals or series that systematically publish relevant articles, approaching the Holocaust from various angles. The *Bulletin of the Jewish Historical Institute (Biuletyn Żydowskiego Instytutu Historycznego)* has been, since its establishment in 1940s, the main forum for presenting Holocaust-related articles. Many valuable papers have appeared in *Studia nad Faszyzmem i Zbrodniami Hitlerowskimi* (Studies in Fascism and Nazi Crimes), edited by Karol Jońca at the Wrocław University. Museums of the Auschwitz and Majdanek camps publish *Zeszyty Oświęcimskie* and *Zeszyty Majdanka*. The *Bulletin of the Main Commission for the Investigation of Crimes (Biuletyn Głównej Komisji Badania Zbrodni)* eventually left the shadow of its former "nationalist-communist" patrons.[52]

Finally, a survey of Polish scholarship cannot ignore the perverse side of the publications on the Holocaust—Holocaust denial. Among the variety of communist or nationalist distortions that have circulated in Poland in the past, there were attempts to blame the Jews for collaboration with the Nazis, or to justify anti-Jewish prejudice with their alleged collaboration with the Soviets, but this author knows of no cases prior to the collapse of the communist regime of complete denial of the fact of genocide. The scale of Jewish losses was underestimated in some of the underground reports during the war, but in the postwar period the numbers were rather inflated, as was the case with the alleged 4 million victims of Auschwitz. Denial of Nazi crimes was out of the question; it certainly could not pass the eyes of censors. To the contrary, the Nazis were held responsible for crimes they did not commit, such as the Katyń murders. It was also unthinkable to make such claims in a country where so many people had seen, heard, or smelled the "Final Solution," or had been witness to or victims of other mass crimes committed by the Germans.

Unfortunately, Holocaust denial in Poland only *seemed* unthinkable. The restoration of freedom of speech allowed for the eventual removal and correcting of communist distortions and "blank spots" and helped reduce defensive attitudes toward the controversial aspects of the past, but it equally opened the door for other distortions and lies, and eventually to a cacophony of opinions that flow from the media. A number of negationist articles, as a rule translations or adaptations from Western publications, appeared in the press of the extreme Right groups. These were low-circulation bulletins for highly particular audiences, and the wider public was not aware of them. Seventy percent of the respondents to a survey in 1995 had never heard negationist claims.[53] They became widely known thanks to Dariusz Ratajczak, Ph.D., who then taught history at the University of Opole. In 1999, his *Tematy niebezpieczne* (Dangerous Topics), presenting negationist claims (and a lot of anti-Jewish prejudice), attracted the attention of the national media (as well as the attention of a public prosecutor, because denying Nazi and communist crimes had been made punishable under a law of December 12, 1998). Ratajczak's line of defense was the freedom of academic research. He claimed he had merely presented various opinions in relevant literature, including those of such scholars as David Irving, a number of whose books had been translated and sold well in Poland.[54]

The debate around Ratajczak's case was about the limits of the freedom of expression and the rationale for the criminalizing of Holocaust denial. No one, to my knowledge, tried to question the fact of the genocide or the existence of gas chambers. Such claims seemed (still) just absurd to the participants. But the spread of the denial is increasingly possible due to some related processes. These are: generational change, as the witnesses pass away and ignorance about the war increases; relativism, encouraged by the recent wave of revisions of the "official truths" of the communist period ("If that was just a lie, other statements in textbooks may also be questionable," or simply, "Historians lie"); the rehabilitation of the anti-Semitic Polish Right as anti-Soviet and anti-German fighters (which they often were); and the decline of xenophobic attitudes toward the Germans, our new ally and friendly neighbor, which makes the horrors of the last war somehow less obvious.

NOTES

1. J. Tomaszewski, "Historiografia polska o Zagładzie," *Biuletyn ŻIH*, no. 2 (1999); and N. Aleksiun, "Polish Historiography of the Holocaust" (forthcoming in Gal-Ed) (these two provide annotated bibliographies of major publications). M. Steinlauf, *Bondage to the Dead: Poland and the Memory of the Holocaust* (Syracuse, N.Y., 1997); D. Blatman, "Polish Anti-

semitism and 'Judeo-Communism': Historiography and Memory," *East European Jewish Affairs*, no. 1 (1997), 23–43; A. Polonsky, ed., *"My Brother's Keeper?" Recent Polish Debates on the Holocaust* (London, 1990); S. Krakowski, "The Holocaust of Polish Jewry in Polish Historiography and Polish Emitter Circles," in *The Historiography of the Holocaust Period: Proceedings of the Fifth Yad Vashem International Conference, March 1983* (Jerusalem, 1988); idem, "Relations between Jews and Poles during the Holocaust: New and Old Approaches in Polish Historiography," *Yad Vashem Studies* 19 (1989), 317–40. See also M. Mazur, "Problemtyka żydowska na łamach Tygodnika Powszechnego i Więzi 1980–1989," *WSP Olsztyn* 1995; E. Koźmińska, "Polsko-żydowskie rozrachunki wojenne: Wyzwania Holokaustu. Analiza listów do redakcji 'Tygodnika Powszechnego' w odpowiedzi na dyskusję Błoński-Siła-Nowicki" (Warsaw University, Institute of Sociology, 1992); J. Żurek, "'Kwestia żydowska' w prasie polskiej w latach 1987–1989" (Silesian University, Institute of Political Science, 1991).

2. J. Błoński, *Biedni Polacy patrz¹ na getto* (1987; reprint, Cracow, 1994).

3. See, for example, *Pamięć żydowska, pamięć polska: Akta kolokwium, które odbyło sięw Krakowie 10–11 czerwca 1995* (Cracow, 1996).

4. K. Kersten, *Polacy-Żydzi-komunizm: Anatomia półprawd 1939–68* (Warsaw, 1992).

5. R. Zimand, "Wormwood and Ashes (Do Poles and Jews Hate Each Other?)" *Polin,* no. 4, (1989): 328.

6. Aleksiun, "Polish Historiography."

7. F. Friedman, *To jest Oświęcim!* (Warsaw, 1945); F. Friedman, *Zagłada Żydów lwowskich* (Lodz, 1945). The present article provides reference only to book-size publications (and does not exhaust their list); thus reference to articles, even important ones, may be missing.

8. A. Eisenbach, *Hitlerowska polityka eksterminacji Żydów w latach 1939–1945 jako jeden z przejawów imperializmu niemieckiego* (Warsaw, 1953).

9. Tomaszewski, "Historiografia polska o Zagładzie," 158.

10. D. Stola, *Kampania antysyjonistyczna 1967–1968* (Warsaw, 2000); P. Osęka, *Syjoniści, inspiratorzy, wichrzyciele: Obraz wroga w propagandzie Marca 1968* (Warsaw, 1999). Exemplary for 1968 writing are J. Kowalski, *Stosunki polsko-żydowskie wczoraj i dziś: Przyczynek do kampanii antypolskiej* (Warsaw, 1968); T. Walichnowski, *Izrael-NRF a Polska* (Warsaw, 1968). Relics of the 1968 style could still be found in publications as late as 1983; see J. Orlicki, *Szkice z dziejów stosunków polsko-żydowskich 1918–1949* (Szczecin, 1983).

11. S. J. Cohen, *Politics without a Past: The Absence of History in Postcommunist Nationalism* (Durham, N.C., 1999), 94–5.

12. T. Mazowiecki, J. Turowicz, and R. Zychiewicz, *Antysemityzm* (Warsaw, NOWA [Independent Publishing House], 1978[?]).

13. A key word of the revolutionary language of the period was *zakłamanie,* which means "entanglement in a web of lies," perceived as a major pillar of the regime. Its opposition was "to live in truth" (*żyć w prawdzie*).

14. The debate was made available to English readers by Polonsky, *"'My Brother's Keeper?'"*

15. Ibid., 22.

16. For such debates one may list the following: on the Carmelites in Oświęcim (which ended in 1993); on the rehabilitation of the extreme-Right National Armed Forces in 1992–93; the one in 1994 on the Michał Cichy article on the Warsaw uprising of 1944; on the commemoration of Auschwitz' liberation in 1945; in 1996, on the Kielce pogrom of 1946; on crosses in Birkenau in 1996–97; on Yaffa Eliach and Polonophobia in 1996; on crosses in the Auschwitz pit in 1998; on Jewish property claims in 1999; on Jan T. Gross's book on Jedwabne in 2000–01; and to some extent also the recurring debates on the location of a supermarket and a discotheque in Oświęcim.

17. See Steinlauf, *Bondage to the Dead.*

18. The list was far from complete; see J. Tomaszewski, ed., *Studia z dziejów Żydów w Polsce po 1945 roku* (Warsaw, 1997), 7.

19. A. Lewin, ed., *Janusz Korczak w getcie: nowe źródła* (Warsaw, 1992).

20. R. Sakowska, ed., *Archiwum Ringelbluma: Listy o Zagładzie* (Warsaw, 1997); idem, *Archiwum Ringelbluma: Getto warszawskie lipiec 1942–styczen 1943* (Warsaw, 1980); E. Ringelblum, *Stosunki polsko-żydowskie w czasie drugiej wojny światowej* (Warsaw, 1988); *Relacje z czasów Zagłady; Inwentarz archiwum ŻIH-INB, zespół 301,* vol. 1 (Warsaw, 1998); J. Dębski, ed., *Księgi zgonów z Auschwitz,* vols. 1–3 (Oświęcim, 1995; in English as *Death Books from Auschwitz,* vol. 7 [Munich, 1975], in German as *Sterbebücher von Auschwitz: Fragmente,* 3 vols. [Munich, 1995]); J. Pogonowski, *Listy z Auschwitz* (Oświęcim, 1998). See also *Raporty Ludwiga Fischera, gubernatora dystryktu warszawskiego 1939–1944* (Warsaw, 1987).

21. See M. Grynberg, ed., *Pamiętniki z getta warszawskiego: Fragmenty i regesty,* 2nd, expanded ed. (Warsaw, 1993).

22. Their incomplete list includes (in alphabetic order): J. Barski, *Przeżycia i wspomnienia z lat okupacji* (Wrocław, 1986); J. Bauman, *Nigdzie na ziemi* (forthcoming); J. Bauman, *Zima o poranku: Opowieść dziewczynki z Warszawskiego Getta* (Cracow, 1989); M. Berg, *Dziennik z getta warszawskiego* (Warsaw, 1983); H. Birenbaum, *Nadzieja umiera ostatnia* (Warsaw, 1988); A. Blady-Szwajger, *I więcej nic nie pamiętam* (1988; reprint, Warsaw,

1994); J. Brandwajn-Zieman, *Miłość w cieniu śmierci* (Lodz, 1995); I. Bronner, *Cykady nad Wisłą i Jordanem* (Cracow, 1991); S. Chaskielewicz, *Ukrywałem się w Warszawie* (Cracow, 1988); A. Czerniaków, *Dziennik getta warszawskiego 6 IX 1939–13 VII 1942* (Warsaw, 1983); J. Eisner, *Przeżyłam!* (Warsaw, 1988); Cz. Fater, *Aniołowie bez skrzydeł* (Warsaw, 1995); M. Głowiński, *Czarne sezony* (Warsaw, 1999); I. Birnbaum, *Non omnis moriar: Pamiętnik z getta warszawskiego* (Warsaw, 1982); M. Gray, *Wszystkim, których kochałem* (Warsaw, 1990); L. Guz, *Targowa 64: Dziennik 27 I 1943–11 IX 1944* (Warsaw, 1990); H. Hoffman, *Z Drohobycza do Ziemi Obiecanej* (Lublin, 1999); A. Janowska, *Krzyżówka* (Wrocław, 1996); S. R. Kałowska, *Uciekać, aby żyć* (Lublin, 2000); A. T. Kac, *Nowy Sącz: Miasto mojej młodości* (Cracow, 1997); S. Kraus-Kowalkowicz, *Dziewczynka z ulicy Miłej albo świadectwo czasu Holocaustu* (Lublin, 1995); N. Makower, *Miłość w cieniu śmierci: Wspomnienia z getta warszawskiego* (Wrocław, 1996); H. Makower, *Pamiętnik z getta warszawskiego, październik 1940–styczeń 1943* (Wrocław, 1987); M. & M. Mariańscy, *Wśród przyjaciół i wrogów: Poza gettem w okupowanym Krakowie* (Cracow, 1988); A. Meroz, *W murach i poza murami getta, Zapiski lekarki warszawskiej z lat 1939–1945* (Warsaw, 1988); B. Milch, *Testament* (Warsaw, 2001); A. Mostowicz, *Żółta gwiazda i czerwony krzyż* (Warsaw, 1988); L. Najberg, *Ostatni powstańcy getta* (Warsaw, 1993); C. Perechodnik, *Czy ja jestem mordercą?* ed. P. Szapiro (Warsaw, 1993); R. Reder, *Bełżec* (Oświęcim, 1999); E. Ringelblum, *Kronika getta warszawskiego* (Warsaw, 1983); D. Rubinowicz, *Pamiętnik* (Warsaw, 1987); K. Sakowicz, *Dziennik pisany w Ponarach od 11 lipca 1941 r. do 6 listopada 1943 r.,* ed. R. Margolis (Bydgoszcz, 1999); N. Szac-Wajnkranc, *Przeminęło z ogniem* (Warsaw, 1988); E. Szajn-Lewin, *W getcie warszawskim: Lipiec 1942–kwiecień 1943,* ed. M. Line and A. Grupińska (Poznań, 1989); H. Szereszewska, *Krzyż i mezuza* (Warsaw, 1993); L. Szmidt, *Cudem przeżylismy czas zagłady* (Cracow, 1983); B. Szatyn, *Na "aryjskich papierach"* (Cracow, 1993); S. Sznek-Bosak, *Wspomnienia z getta łódzkiego* (Lodz, 2000); S. Taubenschlag, *Być Żydem w okupowanej Polsce: Kraków-Auschwitz-Buchenwald* (Cracow, 1996); P. Wawer, *Poza gettem i obozem* (Warsaw, 1993); H. Z. Zimmermann, *Przeżyłem, pamiętam, świadczę* (Cracow, 1997).

23. M. Edelman, *Getto walczy* (1945; reprint, Lodz, 1991); W. Szpilman, *Pianista: Warszawskie wspomnienia 1939–1945* (1946; reprint, Cracow, 2000).

24. M. Grynberg, ed., *Pamiętniki z getta warszawskiego;* W. Śliwowska, ed., *Dzieci Holocaustu mówią . . .* (Warsaw, 1993); idem, *Czarny rok . . . , czarne lata . . .* (Warsaw, 1996); A. Grupińska, *Po kole: Rozmowy z żydowskimi żołnierzami* (Warsaw, 1991); idem, *Ciągle po kole: Rozmowy z żołnierzami getta warszawskiego* (Warsaw, 2000); [J. Wiszniewicz], *A jed-

nak czasem miewam sny: historia pewnej samotności Joannie Wiszniewicz opowiedziana (Warsaw, 1996); B. Engelking-Boni, *Na łące popiołów: Ocaleni z Holocaustu* (Warsaw, 1993); idem, *Czas przestał dla mnie istnieć. . . : analiza doświadczenia czasu w sytuacji ostatecznej* (Warsaw, 1996).

25. H. Krall, *Tam już nie ma żadnej rzeki* (Cracow, 1998); idem, *Dowody na istnienie* (Poznań, 1995); idem, *Taniec na cudzym weselu* (Cracow, 1994).

26. P. Szapiro, ed., *Wojna żydowsko-niemiecka: Polska prasa konspiracyjna 1943–1944 o powstaniu w getcie Warszawy* (London, 1992).

27. *Armia Krajowa w dokumentach,* vol. 6 (London, 1989); A. K. Kunert, ed., *Dokumenty i materiały Archiwum Polski Podziemnej 1939–1956* (Warsaw, 1993); M. Tyszkowa, ed., "Eksterminacja Żydów w latach 1941–1943: Dokumenty Biura Informacji i Propagandy KG AK w zbiorach Biblioteki Uniwersytetu Warszawskiego," *Biuletyn ŻIH,* no. 2–3 (1992); L. Żebrowski, ed., *Narodowe Siły Zbrojne: Dokumenty, struktury, personalia,* vols. 1–3 (Warsaw, 1994–96).

28. K. Moczarski, *Rozmowy z katem,* ed. A. K. Kunert (Warsaw, 1999). Also, the memoirs of Władysław Szpilman appeared re-edited; for example, in the first edition, the good German who had helped the author was made an Austrian. See also Z. Kossak, *Z otchłani* (1946; reprint, Oświęcim, 1998); W. Fejkiel, *Więźniarski szpital w KL Auschwitz* (Oświęcim, 1994); and others.

29. T. Prekerowa, "Wojna i okupacja," in *Najnowsze dzieje Żydów w Polsce,* ed. J. Tomaszewski (Warsaw, 1993), 213–386; M. Fuks, *Z dziejów wielkiej katastrofy narodu żydowskiego* (Poznań, 1999); see also D. Grinberg, ed., *Holocaust z perspektyw półwiecza: pięędziesiąta rocznica powstania w getcie warszawskim* (Warsaw, 1994).

30. *Żydzi i judaizm we współczesnych badaniach polskich,* vols. 1–2, ed. K. Pilarczyk (St. Gąsiorowski, 2000); L. Bończak-Bystrzycki, *Grabież mienia związków wyznaniowych na ziemiach polskich "wcielonych do Rzeszy" w okresie hitlerowskiej okupacji (1939–1945)* (Koszalin, 1999); J. Marszałek, *Obozy pracy w Generalnej Guberni w latach 1939–1945* (Lublin, 1998); J. Kazimierczak and S. Piątkowski, *Martyrologia Żydów w więzieniu radomskim 1939–1944* (Radom, 1997); A. Konieczny, *Tormsdorf, Grussau, Riebnig: Obozy przejściowe dla Żydów Dolnego Śląska z lat 1941–1943* (Wrocław, 1997); A. Grochowska, *Elementy prania mózgu w procesie zagłady Żydów* (Warsaw, 1996); GKBZ, *Rejestr miejsc i faktów zbrodni popełnionych przez okupanta hitlerowskiego na ziemiach polskich 1939–1945 (woj. zamojskie)* (Warsaw, 1994); J. Gulczyński, *Obóz śmierci w Chełmnie nad Nerem* (Konin, 1991); K. Dunin-Wąsowicz, *Warszawa w latach 1939–1945* (Warsaw, 1987).

31. K. Jońca, *"Noc kryształowa" i casus Herschela Grynszpana* (Wrocław,

1992); J. Tomaszewski, *Preludium Zagłady: Wygnanie Żydów polskich z Niemiec w 1938r.* (Warsaw, 1998); T. Szarota, *Zajścia antyżydowskie w okupowanej Europie* (Warsaw, 2000).

32. T. Strzembosz, ed., *Studia z dziejów okupacji sowieckiej: Obywatele polscy na kresach północno-wschodnich II Rzeczpospolitej pod okupacją sowiecką w latach 1939–1941* (Warsaw, 1997).

33. A. Hempel, *Pogrobowcy klęski: Rzecz o policji "granatowej" w Generalnej Guberni 1939–1945* (Warsaw, 1990).

34. M. Wierzbicki, *Polacy i Białorusini w zaborze sowieckim* (Warsaw, 2000).

35. J. Kiełboń, *Migracje ludności w dystrykcie lubelskim 1939–1944* (Lublin, 1995).

36. D. Czech, *Kalendarium wydarzeń w KL Auschwitz* (Oświęcim, 1992); W. Długoborski and F. Piper, eds., *Auschwitz 1940–1945: Węzłowe zagadnienia z dziejów obozu* (Oświęcim, 1999); F. Piper, *Ilu ludzi zginęło w KL Auschwitz* (Oświęcim, 1992); D. Wesołowska, *Słowa z piekła rodem: lagerspracha* (Oświęcim, 1996); A. Strzelecki, *Ostatnie dni obozu Auschwitz* (Oświęcim, 1995). A. Malcówna, *Bibliografia KL Auschwitz za lata 1942–1980* (Oświęcim, 1994), provides almost 2,000 bibliographical entries on relevant publications in Polish, English, French, and German.

37. W. Długoborski, ed., *50 lecie zagłady Romów w KL Auschwitz* (Oświęcim, 1994); idem, *Sinti und Roma in KL Auschwitz-Birkenau 1943–44* (Oświęcim, 1997); J. Parcer, ed., *Los Cyganów w KL Auschwitz-Birkenau* (Oświecim, 1994); State Museum of Auschwitz-Birkenau, ed., *Księga Pamięci: Cyganie w obozie koncentracyjnym Auschwitz-Birkenau* (Oświęcim, 1993).

38. W. Jaworski, *Żydzi będzińscy: dzieje i zagłada* (Będzin, 1993); A. Dobroński, *Białostoccy Żydzi* (Białystok, 1993); W. Boczoń, *Żydzi gorliccy* (Gorlice, 1998); A. Pakentreger, *Żydzi w Kaliszu 1918–1939* (Warsaw, 1988); A. Sas-Jaworski, *Dzieje Żydów kazimierskich* (Warsaw, 1997); K. Urbański, *Zagłada ludności żydowskiej Kielc 1939–1945* (Kielce, 1994); idem, *Leksykon dziejów ludności żydowskiej Kielc 1789–1999* (Cracow, 2000); A. Biberstein, *Zagłada Żydów Krakowa* (Cracow, 1985); E. Rączy, *Ludność żydowska w Krośnie 1939–1946* (Krosno, 1999); T. Radzik, *Lubelska dzielnica zamknięta* (Lublin, 1999); W. Puś and St. Liszewski, eds., *Dzieje Żydów w Łodzi, 1820–1944* (Lodz, 1991); P. Spodenkiewicz, *Zaginiona dzielnica: Łódź żydowska—ludzie i miejsca* (Lodz, 1998); J. Baranowski, *Łódzkie getto 1940–1944: Vademecum* (Lodz, 1999); M. Budziarek, ed., *Judaica łódzkie w zbiorach muzealnych* (Lodz, 1992); K. Urbański, *Powstanie, rozwój i zagłada gminy żydowskiej w Modrzejowie* (Kielce, 1998); W. R. Brociek, A. Penkalla, and R. Renz, *Żydzi ostrowieccy: Zarys dziejów* (Ostrowiec Świetokrzyski, 1996); R. Peska, *Skazani na zagładę: Żydzi w Pabi-*

anicach 1794–1998 (Pabianice, 1999); J. Przedpełski, *Żydzi płoccy: dzieje i martyrologia 1939–1945* (Płock, 1993); J. Sczepański, *Dzieje społeczności żydowskiej powiatów Pułtusk i Maków Mazowiecki* (Warsaw, 1993); A. Potocki, *Żydzi rymanowscy* (Krosno, 2000); S. Pelikan, *Żydzi miasta Tyśmienicy* (Lodz, 2000); F. Kotula, *Losy Żydów rzeszowskich 1939–1944: Kronika tamtych dni*, ed. Wanda Tarnowska (Rzeszów, 1999); E. Włodarczyk, *Z dziejów Żydów skierniewickich* (Skierniewice, 1993); P. Fijałkowski, *Żydzi sochaczewscy* (Sochaczew, 1998); A. Pietrzykowa and St. Potępa, eds., *Zagłada Żydów tarnowskich* (Tarnów, 1990); E. Gawron, *Vlotsheve: Żydzi we Włoszczowie w latach 1867–1942* (Włoszczowa, 2000); R. Caputa, *Okruchy pamięci: Z dziejów Żydów na Żywiecczyźnie* (Cracow, 2000); M. Grynberg, *Żydzi w rejencji ciechanowskiej 1939–1942* (Warsaw, 1984); M. Krajewski, *Byli z ziemi mojej: zagłada ludności żydowskiej Ziemi Dobrzyńskiej* (Bydgoszcz, 1990). Other known studies that provide information on Jewish communities and their destruction include those on Muszyna, Łowicz, Brańsk, Nowy Sącz, etc. A few studies reach outside prewar Poland, e.g., to the German town of Breslau, which became Polish Wrocław only after the war (L. Ziątkowski, *Dzieje Żydów we Wrocławiu* [Wrocław, 2000]).

39. R. Sakowska, *Ludzie z dzielnicy zamkniętej: Z dziejów Żydów w Warszawie w latach okupacji hitlerowskiej,* 2nd, enlarged ed. (Warsaw, 1993); A. Podolska, *Służba porządkowa w getcie warszawskim w latach 1940–1943* (Warsaw, 1996); T. Grosse, *Przeżyć! Obrona życia jako wartość podstawowa społeczności getta warszawskiego* (Warsaw, 1998); see also *Żydzi warszawscy 1939–1943* (Lublin, 1993) by two eminent witnesses, Władysław Bartoszewski and Marek Edelman.

40. B. Engelking-Boni and J. Leociak, *Getto warszawskie: Przewodnik po nieistniejącym mieście* (Warsaw, 2001).

41. B. Engelking-Boni, *Czas przestal dla mnie istnieć . . . : analiza doświadczenia czasu w sytuacji ostatecznej* (Warsaw, 1996), and her *Zagłada i pamięę: Doświadczenie Holocaustu i jego konsekwencje opisane na podstawie relacji autobiograficznych* (Warsaw, 1994); J. Leociak, *Tekst wobec Zagłady: O relacjach z getta warszawskiego* (Wrocław, 1997); P. Matywiecki, *Kamień graniczny* (Warsaw, 1994); R. Sakowska, *Dwa etapy: Hitlerowska polityka eksterminacji Żydów w oczach ofiar. Szkic historyczny i dokumenty* (Wrocław, 1986). See also T. Grosse, *Przeżyć! Obrona życia jako wartość podstawowa społeczności getta warszawskiego* (Warsaw, 1998). Joanna Wiszniewicz, using a similar approach, focuses mostly on postwar Jewish life in Poland, but the horrible past can be sensed behind the scenes.

42. The first book was K. Iranek-Osmecki, *Kto ratuje jedno życie . . . Polacy i Żydzi 1939–1945* (London, 1968). Others came in 1980s and early 1990s: Y. Gutman and S. Krakowski, *Unequal Victims: Poles and Jews during World War II* (New York, 1986); R. Lukas, *The Forgotten Holocaust: The Poles*

under German Occupation, 1939–1944, (Lexington, Ky., 1986; D. Engel, *In the Shadow of Auschwitz: The Polish Government-in-Exile and the Jews, 1939–1942* (Chapel Hill, N.C., 1987), idem, *Facing a Holocaust: The Polish Government-in-Exile and the Jews, 1943–1945* (Chapel Hill, N.C., 1993); and S. Korboński, *The Jews and the Poles in World War II* (New York, 1989).

43. D. Stola, *Nadzieja i Zagłada: Ignacy Schwarzbart—żydowski przedstawiciel w Radzie Narodowej RP, 1940–1945* (Warsaw, 1995); W. Michowicz, ed., *Historia dyplomacji polskiej,* vol. 5 (Warsaw, 1999); E. Duraczyński, *Rząd polski na uchodźstwie 1939–1945* (Warsaw, 1993); Z. Błażyński, ed., *Władze RP na obczyźnie podczas II wojny światowej* (London, 1994).

44. W. Borodziej *et al.,* eds., *Polska Podziemna 1939–1945* (Warsaw, 1991).

45. M. J. Chodakiewicz, *Narodowe Siły Zbrojne: "Ząb" przeciw dwu wrogom* (Warsaw, 1999); W. J. Muszyński, *W walce o Wielką Polskę: Propaganda zaplecza politycznego Narodowych Sił Zbrojnych (1939–1945)* (Warsaw, 2000).

46. E. Kurek-Lesik, *Gdy klasztor znaczył życie: Udział żeńskich zgromadzeń zakonnych w akcji ratowania dzieci żydowskich w Polsce w latach 1939–1945* (Cracow, 1992), and her *Żydzi, Polacy, czy po prostu ludzie* (Lublin, 1992); M. Grynberg, ed., *Księga sprawiedliwych* (Warsaw, 1993); K. Dunin-Wąsowicz, *Społeczeństwo polskie wobec martyrologii Żydów w latach II wojny światowej* (Warsaw, 1996); W. Bielawski, *Zbrodnie na Polakach dokonane przez hitlerowców za pomoc udzielaną Żydom* (Warsaw, 1987). Unfortunately, the late Teresa Prekerowa did not have time to publish a new version, expanded and free from censors' intervention, of her important study *Konspiracyjna Rada Pomocy Zydom w Warszawie* (Warsaw, 1982); the book, however, appeared in French as *Zegota: Commission d'aide aux Juifs* (Monaco, 1999).

47. K. Kersten, *Polacy-Żydzi-komunizm: Anatomia półprawd 1939–68* (Warsaw, 1992); J. T. Gross, *Upiorna dekada: Trzy eseje o stereotypach na temat Żydów, Polaków, Niemców i komunistów, 1939–1948* (Cracow, 1998).

48. *Sąsiedzi: Historia zagłady żydowskiego miasteczka* (Sejny, 2000; pub. forthcoming in English).

49. See, for example, M. J. Chodakiewicz, *Żydzi i Polacy 1918–1955: Współistnienie—Zagłada—komunizm* (Warsaw, 2000).

50. A. Landau-Czajka, *W jednym stali domu . . . Koncepcje rozwiązania kwestii żydowskiej w publicystyce polskiej lat 1933–1939* (Warsaw, 1998); J. Żyndul, *Zajścia antyżydowskie w Polsce w latach 1935–1937* (Warsaw, 1993); M. Sobczak, *Stosunek Narodowej Demokracji do kwestii żydowskiej w Polsce w latach 1918–1939* (Wrocław, 1998); O. Bergmann, *Narodowa Demokracja wobec problematyki żydowskiej w latach 1918–1929* (Poznań, 1998); M. Natkowska, *Numerus clausus, getto ławkowe, numerus nullus,*

"paragraf aryjski": *Antysemityzm na Uniwersytecie Warszawskim 1931–1939* (Warsaw, 1999); R. Michalski, *Obraz Żyda i narodu żydowskiego na łamach polskiej prasy pomorskiej w latach 1920–1939* (Toruń, 1997); W. Wrzesiński, ed., *Polska-Polacy-mniejszości narodowe* (Wrocław, 1992); W. Paruch, *Od konsolidacji państwowej do konsolidacji narodowej: Mniejszości narodowe w myśli politycznej obozu piłsudczykowskiego (1926–1939)* (Lublin, 1997); E. Koko, *W nadziei na zgodę: Polski ruch socjalistyczny wobec kwestii narodowościowej w Polsce (1918–1939)* (Gdańsk, 1995); W. Mich, *Obcy w polskim domu: Nacjonalistyczne koncepcje rozwiązania problemu mniejszości narodowych 1918–1939* (Lublin, 1994), and his *Problem mniejszości narodowych w myśli politycznej polskiego ruchu konserwatywnego (1918–1939)* (Lublin, 1992); B. Grott, *Nacjonalizm chrześcijański: Myśl społeczno-państwowa formacji narodowo-katolickiej w Drugiej Rzeczpospolitej* (Cracow, 1991); J. Majchrowski, *Silni-Zwarci-Gotowi: Myśl polityczna Obozu Zjednoczenia Narodowego* (Warsaw, 1985); M. Musielak, *Nazizm w interpretacjach polskiej myśli politycznej okresu międzywojennego* (Poznań, 1997); Sz. Rudnicki, *Obóz Narodowo-Radykalny: Geneza i działalność* (Warsaw, 1985).

51. B. Szaynok, *Ludność żydowska na Dolnym Śląsku 1945–1950* (Wrocław, 2000); G. Berendt, *Żydzi na gdańskim rozdrożu 1945–1950* (Gdańsk, 2000); A. Cichopek, *Pogrom Żydów w Krakowie 11 sierpnia 1945 r.* (Warsaw, 2000); E. Waszkiewicz, *Kongregacja Wyznania Mojzeszowego na Dolnym Śląsku na tle polityki wyznaniowej PRL, 1945–1968* (Wrocław, 1999); J. Śledzianowski, *Pytania nad pogromem kieleckim* (Kielce, 1998); J. Tomaszewski, ed., *Studia z dziejów Żydów w Polsce po 1945 roku* (Warsaw, 1997); A. Cała and H. Datner-Śpiewak, eds., *Dzieje Żydów w Polsce 1944–1968: Teksty źródłowe* (Warsaw, 1997); I. Hurwic-Nowakowska, *Żydzi polscy (1947–1950)* (Warsaw, 1996) (this is an old study that has remained on the shelf since the 1950s); S. Bronsztejn, *Z dziejów ludności żydowskiej na Dolnym Śląsku po II wojnie światowej* (Wrocław, 1993); *Antyżydowskie wydarzenia kieleckie 4 lipca* (Warsaw, 1992, 1994); B. Szaynok, *Pogrom Żydów w Kielcach 4 lipca 1946* (Warsaw, 1992).

52. The Main Commission for Investigation of Crimes has changed its name several times, to investigate first German crimes, then Nazi crimes, and, in the 1990s, "crimes against the Polish nation" (which include Nazi and communist crimes and crimes against humanity in Poland). It has also published documentary studies and inventories of German crimes. Currently the commission forms part of the Institute of National Memory.

53. J. Golub and R. Cohen, *Knowledge and Remembrance of the Holocaust in Poland* (New York, 1995). Poles (96 percent of respondents) were also the most certain that the Holocaust had actually happened.

54. A. Grabski, "Problemy z rewizjonizmem Holokaustu," *Biuletyn ŻIH*, no. 2. (2000), 33–47.

Christian Gerlach

Some Recent Trends in German
Holocaust Research

THE FOLLOWING STORY OF GENERAL EDUARD WAGNER MIGHT ILLUS-
trate why some of the shifts in German research about the Holocaust
in recent years took place. Born in 1894, Wagner joined the army in
1912 and became an artillery officer. In the 1930s Wagner reorganized
the supply services of the German army and became quartermaster
general of the ground forces. An unsuspicious position, as it seems.
In fact, Wagner belonged to the officers' opposition against Hitler
since 1939 and was especially active in that respect in the summer of
1944 because he was worried that the Red Army would occupy parts
of the German Reich. It was an airplane provided by Wagner that,
after his attempt on Hitler's life on July 20, 1944, Count Stauffenberg
used to fly from Hitler's headquarters to Berlin. Three days later Wagner killed himself because he had been involved in the coup.[1]

But his is not a hero's story. The importance of military supply
services had increased in the 1930s because of new concepts of a mobile war on the ground based primarily on tanks. Wagner and others
therefore linked the problems of supplies to the responsibility for occupied areas. As a consequence, the quartermaster general and his
subordinates enjoyed considerable power and had great responsibility in the German occupation policy. If one considers only the war
against the Soviet Union, the following points must be kept in mind.
Wagner and his men were in charge of the military administration
in all areas that were not under German civil rule (that was about
200,000 square miles, half of the occupied Soviet territories); they
were responsible for marking Jews with a yellow badge and creating
ghettos; and they were co-responsible for organizing forced labor, setting the minimal food rations of Jews and other inhabitants, and op-

pressing resistance. Wagner stood at the top of the occupation troops, many of whom killed hundreds or thousands of Jews (and other inhabitants). The Secret Military Police, which shot 33,000 people within fifteen months in the East, was under his control for some time, and Wagner was the officer principally responsible for antipartisan warfare until 1942 and still heavily involved in it afterward, more than once calling for or supporting the intensification of the use of violence that caused the death of hundreds of thousands of unarmed civilians.

Wagner knew before the German attack against the Soviet Union that there would not be enough troops to control his areas of occupation. So he asked for manpower support from the order police and accepted the fact that Himmler, who could not give him more police, sent instead his Waffen-SS Brigades. Moreover, Wagner integrated the Einsatzgruppen of Security Police and Security Service into his violent conception of occupation, negotiating with Heydrich about their deployment and tasks in March 1941. Months later, all these units murdered tens and hundreds of thousands of Jews. Further, Wagner personally advocated the killing of the mentally disabled to free up the hospitals for his troops.

Many of these activities were based on Wagner's conviction, long before the attack, that the campaign would produce massive, perhaps even decisive, supply problems for the Germans. The Soviet railway system was supposed to be too weak to carry enough German supplies in order to meet the requirements of 3 million troops on a giant theater of war. As a consequence, Wagner co-initiated the plan for a brutal occupation and exploitation policy that would starve to death 30 million people in the western Soviet Union. The victims were to be mainly the urban population, including virtually all Soviet Jews. The hope was that if the starvation scheme worked, the supply trains could be relieved from carrying food supplies and could carry more troops, ammunition, and fuel. Enforced imports from the Soviet territories would also solve the imminent general German food problem throughout the war. Although this plan fortunately failed, Wagner took active, deliberate measures to let 2 million Soviet POWs starve to death in autumn 1941. Wagner and his men were responsible for the POWs in their territories, too, and it was Wagner who lowered the food rations for nonworking prisoners immediately prior to the cold season. During a meeting of the chiefs of staff of all German army groups and armies at the Eastern Front on November 13, 1941, Wagner declared: "Non-working prisoners of war in the camps have to die of starvation" (*haben zu verhungern*). He was also a strong supporter of the siege of Leningrad, including the mass starvation of its population, where the victims eventually numbered 600,000. A low-ranking subordinate of Wagner, in charge of military supplies, even proposed to kill all 3 million civilians and troops in Leningrad by a bombardment with poison gas. His rationale was that this would be more efficient than starvation or a siege and that the German ammunition industry simply could not support a battle of attrition. Generally, the efforts to win—and later, at least not to lose—the war at any price created an atmosphere in which every measure seemed justified.

The case of Wagner suggests that different Nazi or German mass killings and policies of extermination were interconnected; that the actions taken by non-Nazis or even anti-Nazis were of disturbing importance for the destruction of humans, including the Holocaust; and that motives other than pure Nazi ideology—a questionable notion anyway—played a significant role in the politics and policies of mass violence. For Wagner, military, economic, or social policy considerations were of paramount importance. He was a key player as well in the efforts made during 1942–43 to introduce reforms in Nazi occupation policies in the Soviet Union in order to maintain control over these territories, but this did not mean a farewell to excessive violence. The aim that Wagner pursued above all was his notion of Germany's national interests: he did so as an opponent to Hitler, as a reformer of the occupation policy in the East, and as a co-initiator of mass killings on an unbelievable scale.

Within the last decade, extensive research about the Holocaust has been undertaken in Germany and elsewhere, and a strict geographical distinction no longer seems useful where international scholarly cooperation prevails. There were many different approaches that, however, were complementary rather than contradictory. Four elements were central to this research: (1) so-called "regional" studies about the events in several German-occupied regions of Europe; (2) the reconstruction of the political context of the Holocaust; (3) an investigation of the identities and motives of the perpetrators; and (4) in the 1990s, establishment of a new and broader empirical, documentary basis for research.

All these aspects—regional approach, contextualization, focus on the perpetrators, and empirical orientation—were obviously interrelated. They were nourished by the old questions: How could it happen? Who was responsible for the Holocaust? Which motives led to genocide? Many of the "regional studies" would better be labeled "country studies." Region is hardly the correct word for Serbia, Romania, Lithuania, or the General Government of Poland.[2] These country or regional studies proved to be a rewarding approach not only because they broadened our factual knowledge, of which we are still in dire need, but because of some general conclusions derived from them. One such result is that the murder of Jews was not simply the work of the SS and police units. The SS and police could not act independently with regard to extermination policies. Military and civil administrations in the occupied territories, where 95 percent of the victims lived, were "rediscovered" by scholars analyzing the context of the annihilation of the Jews, and it became evident that this crime could be seen as part of the larger policy of occupation. The basic lines of this policy were in fact less determined by the SS and police than by those administrations. The aims of occupation policy were closely linked to interests that can be briefly described as control and exploitation of a country or territory in the service of the war effort. Regional officials had some general instructions from central institutions but a great deal of autonomy in how to achieve these goals. Many of these interests had possibly nothing, or not much, to do with the persecution of the Jews and yet were connected to it. For the everyday professional service of these bureaucracies or military units, the general economy, public order, food, health, finance, or housing was often of greater significance and occupied more of their time than persecuting and killing Jews. Relatively few administrators were in charge of "Jewish affairs" only. The German term *Täter* is perhaps more comprehensive than the English "perpetrator"; beyond the actual killers in Einsatzgruppen or police battalions and guards of concentration camps, it includes the functionaries mentioned before. Many of them were not National Socialists (i.e., not members of the Nazi Party) but were nevertheless important initiators of destruction; this and the far-reaching acceptance of ideas to kill thousands of people were intimately connected with the interests of such functionaries as outlined above.

My following remarks do not attempt to provide a complete survey of the new developments of research in the field in Germany;[3]

rather, these are reflections on some general conclusions that can be drawn from recent studies and an attempt to identify some things that remain to be done and questions that have not been asked. My thoughts focus primarily on the historical contextualization of the Holocaust.

By the end of the 1980s, research about the Nazi period and the Holocaust still rested on four pillars of interpretation: (1) Nazi ideology; (2) the idea of "polyocracy"—namely, the radicalizing effects of overlapping competences, competition, and power struggles between different institutions and party agencies; (3) the way in which bureaucratic organizations worked and their efficacy; and (4) hierarchical structures, that is, orders and obedience. This framework of interpretation has recently been corrected, or supplemented, not only through an analysis of how the occupation worked in practice but also through investigations of important players other than those in the civil and military administrations.[4] Other actors include the scholarly intelligentsia;[5] the so-called SS intellectuals;[6] army officers and soldiers;[7] killers in police battalions and concentration camps; and reconsidered perpetrators in the Gestapo and Security Service.[8] The approaches used and results produced in these works varied widely. They demonstrated, though, that the middle level of functionaries—actually a wide range of positions, from, say, local commanders or civil district commissioners to state secretaries—was significant for the shaping of policy. The studies of Götz Aly and Susanne Heim, while still controversial, were pathbreaking in showing how influential scholarly advice was to the Nazi regime, although the ways of decision making were more twisted than Aly and Heim presumed. Most of all, Ulrich Herbert's exemplary biography of Werner Best proved that the contradictions between ideologues and pragmatists had been overrated by far—especially if both of these characteristics could be combined in the very same person.

All that paved the way for works that linked various political fields with the mass murder of Jews. The best-known study is probably Götz Aly's *Final Solution: Nazi Population Policy and the Murder of European Jews* (published in German in 1995),[9] which placed the Holocaust in the framework of monstrous resettlement plans in Eastern Europe and in the tradition of German and international attempts to overcome the order of the Paris treaties and to create ethnically homogenous states or territories. Aly attributed to the settlement of ethnic

Germans from Eastern Europe in the early years of the war a catalytic effect on the emergence of the Holocaust. Christopher Browning had pointed to such links a decade before.[10] It must be said, however, that the source material of both Aly and Browning referred chiefly to the Polish territories annexed by Germany (to a lesser degree to the General Government of Poland) and to the period through 1941. Such resettlement plans led to the Generalplan Ost, a scheme to resettle dozens of millions of eastern Europeans, of whom many were expected to die under extremely hostile living conditions. The complete versions of this plan came into being only in early and mid-1942; as research from the early 1990s shows, however, not much of it was really carried out except in western Poland and some isolated local areas, for example in Lithuania, Ukraine, and Lublin.[11]

Some authors have also pointed to the importance of food policy for the implementation of the Holocaust.[12] They argue that winning the war was the Nazis' (and the Germans') highest imperative if they were to realize any plans for the future, but that the war created a situation of increasing shortage and scarcity that resulted in extreme ruthlessness. The main points of reference for these scholars are the above-mentioned German intentions to let some 30 million people in the Soviet Union starve in 1941, including almost all Soviet Jews.[13] The aim of food deliveries for the German troops on the Eastern Front, considered a precondition for the smooth advance of a operationally risky military campaign, and the failure of the starvation scheme resulted in extended mass murders of Jews in decisive periods of accelerated destruction in 1941 and 1942, according to these scholars. There is at least no doubt about the importance of food policy for the deliberate destruction of 3 million Soviet POWs (2 million already in 1941), and even the big operations in the course of antipartisan warfare in Eastern Europe after 1942 have recently been seen as connected to the agricultural exploitation of certain territories. This implies that economic policy beyond the direct plunder of Jewish property must be taken into account in understanding the Holocaust, and it questions the older view that German economic interests with regard to the Jews were merely identical with the intention of gaining or preserving a workforce, especially during the most horrible periods of mass killings.

Historians like Sybille Steinbacher, Karin Orth, and Wolf Gruner,[14] who examined how Germans dealt with Jewish work and Jewish workers, demonstrated that precisely the introduction or expansion of forced labor was often a point of reference for (even more) mass murder because the principle of "selections" between the able-bodied and those considered unfit for work was often inherent in ideas about Jewish labor, at least after mid-1941. Jens Wagner has closed a part of the gap that existed in our knowledge about the forced labor of Jews and non-Jews in the final years of World War II (1943–45) in his work about the concentration camp Mittelbau-Dora.[15]

Further connections have been discussed or revealed. Susanne Willems dealt with the persecution of Jews, decisions on deportations, and housing policy in a case study about Berlin; Peter Longerich has argued that the anti-Jewish policy served to strengthen the cooperation of non-Germans in most of the sphere of influence. A wave of works about the plunder of Jewish assets suggests its significance at least in the early stages of persecution, if not for mass murder itself.[16] And the impoverishment of the Jews, which was an inevitable consequence, resulted in demands for "solutions" for eventual problems like deficiency diseases or black markets.

Where are the heated arguments that prevailed ten years ago between intentionalists and structuralists/functionalists and between supporters of economistic explanations of the Holocaust and those derived from the history of ideas? It seems that they have virtually vanished, and that the current absence of controversies between scholars with entirely different approaches to Holocaust research is based on the fact that many German (and of course not only German) historians no longer search for exclusive explanations—or the only true explanation—because the complexity of the roots of the Holocaust is more and more acknowledged. True, there are still different opinions, but present research is about *elements of explanation* and includes the attempt to actually understand the Holocaust as having had multiple causes.

This, however, is proving difficult. Resettlements, housing shortages, the danger of epidemics, German financial problems, suspected resistance, forced labor and selections, the attempt to fuel collaboration with Germany—these were the most widely divergent explanations, but in the end the result seems to have been always the same: the Jews were targeted.[17] This shows—it is often argued—that the initial, primary, real, or historically important reason for the Holocaust was in fact racial anti-Semitism. The other rationalizations—it is said—were made *post factum* to let the murders appear rational, and these rationalizations are considered at most second-rank or supportive factors or perhaps merely pretexts and not explanations at all. However, I would argue that what contradicts such a narrow focus on racial anti-Semitism is, first of all, the sequence of events in several German-occupied countries, the obviously horrendous influence of such "secondary" motives for the start or expansion of mass murder; and second, the structures, responsibilities, and practical distribution of power, represented by the political weight of the occupation administrations compared to the SS and the police. True, for the persecution of German or French Jews, food policy did not play a major role, nor were there resettlements in Greece or partisans in Denmark. But in most cases, issues existed that one would currently summarize under the term *Realpolitik,* which could let the mass murder of Jews appear not only desirable from the point of view of Nazis, but "necessary" from the point of view of many Germans engaged in trying to win a war. Nevertheless, the question as to whether ideology was the prime cause of the Holocaust remains a major line of distinction between different understandings in historiography. For this author, however, this question does not appear useful. My aim has not been to create a morally opaque mix of motives or to cause confusion in Holocaust research, but to think in terms of multicausality (as also suggested by the example of General Wagner at the beginning of this essay), which means that some necessary conditions had to be met. The processual combination and interplay of several motives, institutions, interests, and circumstances led from a long history of stigmatization and persecution of German and European Jewry to the Holocaust.

Anti-Semitic attitudes as driving forces for the policies of destruction seem so evident that they have not often been analyzed in a concrete sense. Yet leading experts like Christopher Browning and Karin Orth have run into trouble when trying to refine the actual motives of important groups of perpetrators.[18] How did anti-Semitism actually work? It seems to me that anti-Semitism has often been mistaken as an abstract dogma, which it was not, but instead should be understood as a *Weltanschauung,* or part of a *Weltanschauung,* world view, or perspective. This means that anti-Semites argued (and still argue) by appealing to segments of reality, which is precisely what makes anti-Semitism so dangerous and adaptable. It is therefore no wonder that anti-Semites in the Nazi era constantly related what they saw as the "Jewish Question" to political problems—problems that were real, or perceived as real, instead of being mere inventions or pretexts. As necessary as it is for historians to make a distinction for analytical purposes, to assess the weight of different factors—*weltan-schauliche* and pragmatic motives, ideology, and *Realpolitik*—were often not viewed by Germans at the time as opposites but as symbi-otic. Empirical studies about the concrete role of ideology for the policies of mass murder, like Isabel Heinemann's study on the Head Office for Race and Settlement of the SS, belong to a kind of work that will be necessary in the future.[19] It has reasonably been empha-sized by many scholars that ideology was a constant factor in annihi-lation policy. But it could also be argued that ideology underwent some gradual changes. German anti-Semitism of 1935 differed from the anti-Semitism of 1942.

The mass destruction of Soviet POWs was, though not com-pletely finished, considerably slowed down in the spring of 1942, whereas the later months of 1942 saw the peak of the Holocaust. The huge crematoria in Auschwitz-Birkenau were only commissioned in the summer of 1942, and construction was finished as late as spring 1943. Experts like Peter Longerich and Christopher Browning have recently emphasized that the mass murders of Jews were expanded in the spring and even summer of 1942, and I have offered food policy as one element of explanation.[20] Many of the discussions during the last two decades in Germany and elsewhere have concentrated on how the deliberate destruction of European Jewry started and how it was set into motion.[21] These debates were sometimes unbalanced, for they concentrated initially on the year 1941, but even when they were extended to the first half of 1942, they still did not answer such key questions as why annihilation went on and on, or why it was acceler-ated at certain periods and then stopped or slowed down. If mass murder and the policy of destruction against the Jews was less deter-mined by hierarchies, central orders, and plans, and if initiatives and interests from very different groups, institutions, and levels, as well as from different regions, played a major role, then the question why the mass murder—which was viewed as a uniform, homogenous pro-gram for a long time—was continued must be asked again.[22] A new way of answering this question would be that there were new inter-ests and initiatives that drove (or delayed) mass murder time and again, and that it was such initiatives that finally constituted the Holocaust as an overall program. One single order, or one decision, by Adolf Hitler and the help of his willing executioners were not enough to murder the Jews of Europe.

Some symptomatic open questions of Holocaust research—in Germany and elsewhere—should not be forgotten. We do not know much about the murder of about a million Jews in Ukraine (except eastern Galicia). An in-depth history of the death camps, especially in the General Government, remains to be written. There is no scholarly biography about Reinhard Heydrich, and none at all of Adolf Eichmann. Biographies of figures (Germans as well as non-Germans) such as the above-mentioned General Wagner could help us find out more about the connections between different mass killings, the often puzzling set or mixture of motives, and the way in which the distorted moral values of such persons worked when they were confronted with diverse political tasks. Yet perpetrator research (the question of the character and motives of the perpetrators) faces enormous methodological and source problems. And according to Yehuda Bauer, there is also a lack of empirical studies about the reaction of Jewish communities to persecution, threats, and mass murders.[23]

It is certain that German scholars must overcome their one-sided concentration on persecutors. The reason for this focus is evident: German researchers are committed to explaining the genesis of the society in which they are living and to trying to understand something about German identity. However, it should not be forgotten that there is another tradition in German historiography that deals with the victims, one rooted in oral history, local history, and the historiography of the German Democratic Republic. Beate Meyer's work about Jewish–non-Jewish couples and *Mischlinge* is an impressive example.[24] What is missing from research is what Meyer's book provides at least in part: the integration of the perspectives of victims and persecutors, as well as their interaction with those who are today, imprecisely, still called "bystanders" or "collaborators"—participants or witnesses from occupied countries like Poland, Ukraine, or the Netherlands. One way to do such research—not in order to pile up more details, but as one approach for in-depth studies—could be studies of the ghettos. Another would be the seemingly simpler, though in fact equally complex, task of writing biographies of Jews or describing the fates of Jewish families.[25] However, language barriers remain a serious obstacle to such integrative studies.

Assuming, however, that all these family stories will be written, what then of comprehensive interpretations? Outside Germany, there seems to be no lack of general interpretations of the Holocaust. For German historiography, it is remarkable that Peter Longerich, Wolfgang Benz, and Dieter Pohl have recently published the first general surveys about the Holocaust since Wolfgang Scheffler and Uwe Adam; and Peter Longerich wrote the first extensive and nearly comprehensive history of the entire course of the Holocaust by a German.[26] The broader empirical basis now available has provided the precondition for his work.

Even so, a serious explanatory weakness of the research about the Holocaust lies in the lack of *empirical* comparative works. To many scholars, such approaches still seem dangerous or inappropriate because of the fear that the Holocaust of European Jewry could thereby be diminished. I would argue that comparisons could be made between the Holocaust and other mass killings of civilians or noncombatants in history in general as well with other cases of Nazi violence (that does not mean to equate them). As for the latter, one reason for the lack of studies seems simple: the fate of murdered Soviet POWs or of Greek peasants does not really interest anybody in the "West."[27] In his masterly biography about Adolf Hitler, Ian Kershaw has included an excellent survey of the Holocaust, but to the destruction of 3 million Soviet POWs he dedicated one page; the siege of Leningrad (with its 600,000 victims) finds more or less mention in a footnote. Kershaw devotes a few brief remarks to antipartisan warfare and virtually no space at all to the deportation of 5 million civilian forced workers from all over Europe by the Germans.[28] The possible objection that the broad public could not be expected to have an interest in such matters does not make it better. Rather, it illustrates the problem. Only euthanasia, the mass murder of more than 200,000 disabled persons, mostly German, has attracted a scholarly interest similar to that in the annihilation of the Jews.[29] Comparisons about different policies of destruction could not only look at similarities or dissimilarities among killing methods or perpetrators, they could also search for common or different political or ideological roots, similar patterns, chronological parallels, links and mutual conditionalities, and the experience of victims, and could serve finally as a basis for the ongoing theoretical debates about the topic. Whatever one thinks about the thesis that the Holocaust was unique, the neglect of other German mass crimes can no longer be justified. The marginalization of other victim groups is an obstacle to a comprehensive understanding of the Holocaust, a goal historians are still struggling to reach today.

NOTES

1. For details about the case of Wagner, see Christian Gerlach, "'Militärische Versorgungszwänge,' Besatzungspolitik und Massenverbrechen: Die Rolle des Generalquartiermeisters des Heeres und seiner Dienststellen im Krieg gegen die Sowjetunion," in *Ausbeutung, Vernichtung, Öffentlichkeit: Neue Studien zur nationalsozialistischen Lagerpolitik,* ed. Norbert Frei, Sybille Steinbacher, and Bernd C. Wagner (Munich, 2000), 175–208.

2. Walter Manoschek, *"Serbien ist judenfrei": Militärische Besatzungspolitik und Judenvernichtung in Serbien 1941/42* (Munich, 1993); Radu Ioanid, *The Holocaust in Romania: the Destruction of Jews and Gypsies under the Antonescu Regime, 1940–1944* (Chicago, 2000); various works by Jean Ancel about the Holocaust in Romania; Christoph Dieckmann, *Deutsche Besatzungspolitik und Massenverrechen in Litauen 1941–1944: Täter, Zuschauer, Opfer* (Ph.D thesis, University of Freiburg, 2003). Classical "regional studies" are the parallel works of Dieter Pohl, *Nationalsozialistische Judenverfolgung in Ostgalizien 1941–1944: Organisation und Durchführung eines staatlichen Massenverbrechens* (Munich, 1996), and Thomas Sandkühler, *"Endlösung" in Galizien: Der Judenmord in Ostpolen und die Rettungsinitiativen des Berthold Beitz* (Bonn, 1996).

3. For a more comprehensive discussion, see Ulrich Herbert, "Extermination Policy: New Answers and Questions about the History of the 'Holocaust' in German Historiography," in *National-Socialist Extermination Policy: Contemporary German Perspectives and Controversies,* ed. Ulrich Herbert (New York, 2000), 1–52.

4. Dieter Pohl, *Von der Judenpolitik zum Judenmord: Der Distrikt Lublin des Generalgouvernements 1939–1944* (Frankfurt am Main, 1993); Bogdan Musial, *Deutsche Zivilverwaltung und Judenverfolgung im Generalgouvernement: Eine Fallstudie zum Distrikt Lublin* (Wiesbaden, 1999); Hannes Heer and Klaus Naumann, eds., *War of Extermination* (New York, 2000; German ed., 1995).

5. See Götz Aly and Susanne Heim, *Architects of Annihilation: Auschwitz and the Logic of Destruction* (Princeton, N.J., 2003; German version, 1991),

and many of their articles, mainly in the series *Beiträge zur nationalsozialistischen Gesundheits- und Sozialpolitik* (1985–1999).

6. Ulrich Herbert, *Best: Biographische Studien über Radikalismus, Weltanschauung und Vernunft 1903–1989* (Bonn, 1996); cf. also Jens Banach, *Heydrichs Elite: Das Führungskorps der Sicherheitspolizei und des SD 1936–1945* (Paderborn, 1998); Hans Safrian, *Eichmann und seine Gehilfen* (1993; reprint, Frankfurt am Main, 1995).

7. See Heer and Naumann, *War of Extermination.*

8. Christopher Browning, *Ordinary Men: Reserve Police Battalion 101 and the "Final Solution" in Poland* (New York, 1992); Michael Wildt, *Generation des Unbedingten: Das Führungskorps des Reichssicherheitshauptamts* (Hamburg, 2002); Karin Orth, *Die Konzentrationslager-SS: Sozialstrukturelle Analysen und biographische Studien* (Göttingen, 2000); the collection *Die nationalsozialistischen Konzentrationslager: Entwicklung und Struktur,* ed. Ulrich Herbert, Karin Orth, and Christoph Dieckmann (Göttingen, 1998), includes about fifty articles on 1,200 pages and gives an overview of present German and international research on concentration camps. For the genesis of the debate about perpetrators in Germany, Daniel Jonah Goldhagen's *Hitler's Willing Executioners: Ordinary Germans and the Holocaust* (New York, 1996) was also influential.

9. Götz Aly, *Final Solution: Nazi Population Policy and the Murder of European Jews* (London, 1999).

10. Christopher Browning, "Nazi Resettlement Policy and the Search for a Solution to the Jewish Question, 1939–1941," *German Studies Review* 9, no. 3 (1986): 497–519.

11. Mechtild Rössler and Sabine Schleiermacher, eds., *Der Generalplan Ost: Hauptlinien der nationalsozialistischen Planungs- und Vernichtungspolitik* (Berlin, 1993); Bruno Wasser, *Himmlers Raumplanung im Osten: Der Generalplan Ost in Polen* (Basel, 1993).

12. Christoph Dieckmann, "The War and the Killing of the Lithuanian Jews," in Herbert, *National Socialist Extermination Policies,* 240–75; Christian Gerlach, "German Economic Interests, Occupation Policy, and the Murder of the Jews in Byelorussia, 1941/43," in Herbert, *National Socialist Extermination Policies,* 210–39; Christoph Dieckmann, *Krieg, Ernährung, Völkermord: Forschungen zur deutschen Vernichtungspolitik im Zweiten Weltkrieg* (Hamburg, 1998).

13. Christian Gerlach, *Kalkulierte Morde: Die deutsche Wirtschafts- und Vernichtungspolitik in Weißrußland 1941–1944* (Hamburg, 1999).

14. Sybille Steinbacher, *"Musterstadt" Auschwitz: Germanisierungspolitik und Judenmord in Ostoberschlesien* (Munich, 2000); for a short version see her "In the Shadow of Auschwitz: The Murder of the Jews of East Upper

Silesia," in Herbert, *National Socialist Extermination Policies*, 276–305; Karin Orth, *Das System der nationalsozialistischen Konzentrationslager: Eine politische Organisationsgeschichte* (Hamburg, 1999); Wolf Gruner, *Der geschlossene Arbeitseinsatz deutscher Juden 1938–1943* (Berlin, 1997).

15. Jens-Christian Wagner, *Produktion des Todes: Das KZ Mittelbau-Dora* (Göttingen, 2001).

16. Susanne Willems, *"Der entsiedelte Jude": Albert Speers Wohnungs-marktpolitik für den Berliner Hauptstadtbau* (Berlin, 2002); Peter Lon-gerich, *Politik der Vernichtung: Eine Gesamtdarstellung der nationalsozialis-tischen Judenverfolgung* (Munich, 1998); Frank Bajohr, *"Arisierung" im Nationalsozialismus: Die Verdrängung der jüdischen Unternehmer 1933–1945* (Hamburg, 1997).

17. The notion that it was always the Jews who were targeted is in-complete but will prevail until other Nazi mass violence finally finds the at-tention that it deserves and is analyzed in depth.

18. Browning, *Ordinary Men;* Orth, *Die Konzentrationslager-SS*. The difficulties in finding conclusive interpretations without leaving solid em-pirical ground are mirrored by the articles in two recent collections: Chris-tian Gerlach and Ahlrich Meyer, eds., *Durchschnittstäter: Handeln und Mo-tivation,* vol. 16 in *Beiträge zur Geschichte des Nationalsozialismus* (Berlin, 2000); Gerhard Paul, ed., *Die Täter der Shoah: Fanatische Nationalsozialis-ten oder ganz normale Deutsche?* (Göttingen, 2002).

19. Isabel Heinemann, *Rasse, Siedlung, deutsches Blut: Das Rasse- und Siedlungshauptamt-SS und die nationalsozialistische Rassenpolitik im beset-zten Europa 1939–1945* (Göttingen, 2003); see also her "Another Type of Perpetrator: The SS Racial Experts and Forced Population Movements in the Occupied Territories," *Holocaust and Genocide Studies* 15, no. 3 (2001): 387–411.

20. Longerich, *Politik der Vernichtung,* 473–516; Christopher Brown-ing, A Final Decision for the 'Final Solution'? The Riegner Telegram Re-considered, *Holocaust and Genocide Studies* 10, no. 1 (1996): 3–10; Chris-tian Gerlach, *Krieg, Ernährung, Völkermord,* 167–257.

21. Longerich, *Politik der Vernichtung,* starts with the sentence: "The topic of this study is the decision-making process which led to the murder of the Jews of Europe" (p. 13). Another example is Ralf Ogorreck, *Die Ein-satzgruppen und die "Genesis der Endlösung"* (Berlin, 1996).

22. Cf. Christian Gerlach and Götz Aly, *Das letzte Kapitel: Realpolitik, Ideologie und der Mord an den ungarischen Juden 1944/45* (Stuttgart, 2002).

23. See Bauer's contribution in this volume.

24. Beate Meyer, *Jüdische "Mischlinge": Rassenpolitik und Verfolgung-serfahrung 1933–1945* (Hamburg, 1999).

25. An excellent recent example of this approach is Mark Roseman, *A Past in Hiding: Memory and Survival in Nazi Germany* (New York, 2001).

26. Longerich, *Politik der Vernichtung;* short surveys are Wolfgang Benz, *The Holocaust: A German Historian Examines the Genocide* (New York, 1999); Dieter Pohl, *Holocaust: Die Ursachen—das Geschehen—die Folgen* (Freiburg, 2000). See also Wolfgang Scheffler, *Judenverfolgung im Dritten Reich* (Berlin, 1964; the book was published in several editions, one considerably enlarged); Uwe Dietrich Adam, *Judenpolitik im Dritten Reich* (1972; reprint, Düsseldorf, 1979).

27. With regard to Soviet POWs, some new studies on camps were published during recent years. Newly discovered sources—particularly the registration files of those POWs who were held in the area of the German Reich found in Podolsk, Russia, and in Berlin—facilitate a much better analysis on a number of topics. Nonetheless, Christian Streit, *Keine Kameraden: Die Wehrmacht und die sowjetischen Kriegsgefangenen,* 4th ed. (Berlin, 1997; first published in 1978), remains the authoritative work in the field. For antipartisan warfare see Loukia Droulia and Hagen Fleischer, eds., *Von Lidice bis Kalvryta: Widerstand und Besatzungsterror: Studien zur Repressalienpraxis im Zweiten Weltkrieg* (Berlin, 1999).

28. Ian Kershaw, *Hitler 1936–1945* (Stuttgart, 2000). See, as a symptom, how rarely and in which way Fritz Sauckel, the chief organizer of the forced labor program, is mentioned (pp. 736, 740, 922, 1076). For Leningrad and the POWs, see p. 1197 n. 139, and p. 519.

29. Recently Heinz Faulstich's massive volume *Hungersterben in der Psychiatrie 1914–1949* (Freiburg, 1998) added a new accent on the debate, including the upward revision of the death figures.

Susannah Heschel

Does Atrocity Have a Gender? Feminist Interpretations of Women in the SS

CHRISTOPHER BROWNING'S STUDY OF A MOBILE KILLING UNIT COM-posed of civilian police officers who went from town to town mur-dering Jews in Poland, *Ordinary Men* (1992), aroused criticism among feminist historians for insufficient attention to the role of masculinity and male peer pressure in encouraging the men of the Einsatzgruppen to participate in acts of violence, even when offered the opportunity to return home. The cruelty displayed by these men, even when they themselves found their work repulsive, was attributed by Browning to group peer pressure, but feminists have viewed it as not untypical of male group behavior, which may foster displays of masculinity and group solidarity through expressions of physical violence.[1] The ques-tion that must also be raised, however, is how feminist scholars might subject atrocities committed by women to the same kind of gender analysis. Could acts of cruelty and physical violence committed by women guards at concentration camps be attributed to a comparable type of group pressure? Does female group behavior exhort displays of women's femininity and group solidarity through expressions of physical violence? Until now, feminist theory, when considering ques-tions of violence, has focused primarily on men as perpetrators and women as victims. The implied conclusion is that intensified expres-sions of masculinity elide into violence, while intensified expressions of femininity elide into nurturance and compassion.

Scholarship on Nazism and the Holocaust has paid almost no at-tention to female perpetrators. There is only one monograph on the (mostly female) nurses of the so-called euthanasia program, com-pared to numerous studies of the (mostly male) physicians; nothing on female-dominated professions, such as school teachers and social workers; almost nothing on the fate of German lesbians, compared to several studies of gay men. A recent anthology of scholarly articles on women and the Holocaust is typical in focusing entirely on the fate of Jewish women, and devoting only a few paragraphs to women perpetrators.[2] The focus of studies on women and the Holocaust is on female victims, with particular emphasis on how women's "feminine" emotional support and nurturance of one another in concentration camps enhanced their survival.[3] No comparable analysis has been made of the emotional support and other feminine conceits that might have encouraged groups of women perpetrators.

My question is how feminist theory can be used to analyze the role of perpetrators, both male *and* female, and how a study of Nazi perpetrators can illuminate deficiencies within feminist theory. Indeed, might a study of women guards at concentration camps be entitled "Ordinary Women"? As much as Browning's study, *Ordinary Men*, tends to normalize the killers, it is not my intention to demonize women, nor evoke patriarchal images of women as demonic. I should also note at the outset that all the women who served as SS guards were volunteers, like the male members of the mobile killing unit studied by Browning.

A study of women's involvement in Nazi atrocities begins with several unresolved historiographical problems. An ongoing debate, initiated primarily by work of Claudia Koonz and Gisela Bock, raises the broad question of National Socialism's attitude toward women: were they given new opportunities for political engagement, employment, and power in the Nazi party, in wartime Germany, and in the apparatus of racial policies (Koonz), or were they victims of a broad but often subtle anti-natalist and anti-woman policy, expressed through the sterilization program (Bock)?[4] The debate between Koonz and Bock led in Germany to a feminist Historikerstreit that began during the late 1980s over the question of women's participation in Nazism. Only in recent years have studies begun to be published delineating the actual role played by women at concentration camps, in Nazi political organizations, and as beneficiaries of Nazi racial policies. Today it is generally acknowledged, as Barbara Distel writes, that while women did not hold positions of power within the dictatorial hierarchy, they exerted great political influence as wives and *Handelnde* in the middle and lower levels of all institutions of the Nazi state, and that their indirect participation in genocide may not be undervalued.[5] A broadening of scholarly interest is called for in investigating the Jewish victims as well; a recent anthology on *Women in the Holocaust,* based on a conference, addresses Jewish women exclusively, with barely any attention to non-Jewish victims or perpetrators.[6] Examining the role played by women guards in the concentration camps leads to additional historiographical problems in interpreting the limited evidence available. Very few women were interrogated and tried after the war; the kind of evidence Browning gathered about men's backgrounds and their motivations is simply not available. Information gleaned from survivors' accounts is subject to cautious analysis, given the tendentious nature of postwar gender representations. Ultimately, however, what is troubling are the inadequacies of feminist theory that are brought to light by considering women as agents of atrocity.

Recent studies of female camp guards and wives of male camp guards provide a small amount of data. While it is clear that the decision-making process of sterilization, euthanasia, and the Final Solution, as well as the organization to carry out the murders, were in male hands, women also played key roles. In the sterilization and euthanasia programs, women most frequently carried out those orders, mostly as nurses, sometimes as doctors; 22 percent of the euthanasia program (T4) staff were female.[7] The precise number of women camp guards is not known, just as the precise number of camps is difficult to determine. There are records of 3,950 women guards in the Ravensbrück archives, but many more functioned as guards without having been trained there, suggesting that the number was much higher.

Although Ravensbrück served as the training center for many of the guards, it was not the exclusive training location. The training undergone by women was less systematic and did not last as long as the training of men, nor did women receive an apprenticeship in acts of violence. They were not SS members, but part of the SS staff (SS-Gefolge). Yet they were required, just as men, to take an oath of loyalty.[8] A census of January 1945 declares a total of 36,674 male guards and 3,517 female guards from the SS-Gefolge, indicating that approximately 10 percent of the guards were female.[9] At Auschwitz between 1940 and 1945 there were approximately 7,000 male guards and 200 female guards.[10] To date, no systematic survey of the Berlin Document Center collection of female SS cards has been undertaken to determine their demographic background. Irmtraud Heike argues that a surprisingly high percentage of women who volunteered for camp duty were professional social workers.[11]

Women served through the SS in a variety of capacities supervising female inmates. They worked as SS nurses, doctors, and office personnel, took charge of morning and evening roll call, handled the dogs, supervised the kitchen, and so forth.[12] While women guards were employed at camps with female prisoners, where they had direct supervision over women inmates, none were employed at the death camps Belzec, Chelmno, Sobibor, and Treblinka.[13] They were, however, at Auschwitz and Majdanek. The most important and best known concentration camps with women's divisions included Stutthof (opened in January 1941), Auschwitz (as of March 1942), Majdanek (August 1942), Mauthausen (October 1943), Dachau, Sachsenhausen, and Ravensbrück, which was a large women's camp north of Berlin with a gas chamber where approximately 350 women were deployed as guards.[14] Toward the end of the war, of the 1,202 satellite camps, 329 were women's camps.

Although there remains a tenacious belief to this day that women SS guards were not involved in murder, in fact they did participate in the selection of victims and in their murder, as well as in the accompanying torture and brutality.[15] Numerous memoirs attest to the brutality of women guards, including their arbitrary punishment and murder of inmates, and their selection of inmates for gassing.

From the beginning of 1940, women were issued a uniform: a gray outfit of jacket and pants, with the sign of the *Rechtsadler,* but not the *Totenkopf,* boots, and a cap. They were given a pistol, *Stöcken* (rod), and a whip, and often had dogs.[16] They lived in barracks outside the camps, or in a room on the camp premises. Married guards and mothers had the option, at least at Ravensbrück, of living outside the camp in private quarters.

There were, in addition, 240,000 women married to SS men, many of whom lived with their husbands at concentration camps, a group investigated in Gudrun Schwarz's recent book, *Eine Frau an Seiner Seite.* Many of those women used camp inmates as domestic servants, including for child care. In 1944 there were 794,941 men and 7,900 women working in the SS.[17] In addition, there were 10,000 women in the SS Helferinnenkorps, 15,000 women serving as *Polizeihelferinnen,* 500,000 women as *Wehrmachtsangehörige (ohne Sanitätspersonal),* and between 6 and 9 million women who were part of the Deutsche Frauenwerk, NS Frauenschaft, or NS Lehrerinnenverband.

There has been no systematic survey to date of the percentage of women guards, compared to men, who were investigated and put on trial after the war, and by whom. What is clear is that only a handful of women were tried. Five women guards from Auschwitz were tried and sentenced in Krakow, a few more at the trials of Bergen-Belsen and Ravensbrück. The largest number of women tried at one time occurred at the Belsen Trial, held at Lüneburg, at which twenty-seven men and twenty-one women were charged. Of the twenty-one women, sixteen were SS *Angehörige* and five were *Kapos.*

Several of the women tried became notorious figures in the press. Irma Grese, who had served as a guard at Ravensbrück, Auschwitz-Birkenau, and Bergen-Belsen, was tried at Lüneburg between September and November, 1945. She was convicted, sentenced to death by hanging, and executed in December 1945 along with two other guards, Dorothea Binz and Maria Mandel. Testimony at their trial from survivors detailed murders, tortures, cruelties, and sexual excesses. In addition to Grese's involvement in the selections for the gas chambers at Auschwitz, standing side by side with Mengele,[18] she was reputed to have been responsible for up to thirty murders a day, for continual beatings and whipping of concentration camp inmates, and for directing her dog to savage them.[19] Starting in the autumn of 1943, she served as *Oberaufseherin* (senior SS-supervisor) in Birkenau, the second-highest rank that an SS female could hold, supervising Polish Jewish women and later Hungarians. Her position allowed "virtual control of 30,000 women in Birkenau's C Lager, and . . . the power to exterminate literally thousands of human beings on a whim. According to a witness at her subsequent trial, she sent thousands and thousands of people, ill and in quite good health, to the gas chambers."[20] Born in 1923, she was only nineteen when she first arrived at Ravensbrück, twenty-two when executed.

The postwar popular press gave careful attention to the physical appearance of the few women guards put on trial, and also speculated about their sexuality. For example, *Newsweek,* in October 1945, described Irma Grese at the trial at Lüneburg: "In the prisoner's dock . . . Irma Grese bowed her pretty blond head and bit her lips." In 1948, *Time* magazine described Ilse Koch, wife of Karl Koch, commandant of Buchenwald, in an article entitled "The Bitch Again," as having "had men flogged for the pleasure it gave her."[21] Early articles described Koch's collection of tattooed skin, later articles emphasized her adulterous affairs and abuse of prisoners. A *Newsweek* article in 1967 about Koch's suicide in prison reported:

> At Buchenwald, Ilse bathed in Madeira wine and sported a large di- amond ring that Karl bought for her with some of his prison graft. And when "Karli," as she called him, was off on trips, which was frequent, Ilse indulged her insatiable sexual appetites with his young subordinates. She also liked to exhibit herself to the inmates in provocative clothes and then report for punishment those who dared to look. Men with tattoos particularly intrigued her, and in some cases—according to camp gossip—their skin ultimately turned up as lampshades in the Koch living room.

In the Soviet zone and the early German Democratic Republic (GDR), Ilse Koch was described similarly, as an "animal" or a "dehumanized creature" with unbridled sexuality.[22]

Both the memoir literature of survivors and the popular press present similar images of women guards, and both are subject to simi- lar methodological problems. As Karen Remmler has noted, there is a "dearth of critical writing on the significance of gender differences for both the remembrance and representation of the Holocaust."[23] Women guards are described almost uniformly as more cruel than men, not because of the nature of the atrocities they are said to have committed, but either because of the pleasure, usually erotic, they al- legedly enjoyed while tormenting women prisoners, or because the women's acts of cruelty either collide with their physical beauty or express their physical ugliness. Whatever the case, women's cruelty is presented with a sense of surprise, transgressing gender expectations, whereas men's cruelty is discussed without reference to their gender, as though the connection between atrocity and maleness is self-evident. The descriptions are written to satisfy our gender expectations: wom- en's cruelty is surprising, while men's is expected; women are basically innocent by nature, so an act of cruelty is viewed as abnormal.

The memoirs of Olga Lengyel and Gisella Perl employ similar language to describe Irma Grese; Perl wrote, "She was one of the most beautiful women I have ever seen. Her body was perfect in every line,

her face clear and angelic and her blue eyes the gayest, the most innocent eyes one can imagine. And yet, Irma Greze was the most depraved, cruel, imaginative sexual pervert I ever came across."[24]

Such imagery was maintained as recently as 1990, when this description of Grese appeared in Germany's *Evangelische Sonntagsblatt:*

> She shot women in cold blood, siced dogs on them, beat girls
> senseless. That's why she is standing in Lüneburg before a British
> military court. As a perpetrator, one of many? One of many, if she
> were not so lovely. The gruesomeness is not reflected in her face.
> She was a devil in disguise, a package of lies, a woman like a false
> promise. A charmer (bewitcher?) perhaps. Her photo, at any rate,
> hangs in the lockers of English soldiers, her name enlivens the
> headlines of the court reporter.

Susan Cernyak-Spatz wrote that "In my experience the matrons
were cruel, more vicious (sadistically vicious) than any SS man. These
women who, as I read later, ranged from baronnesses and countesses
to prostitutes, were the most vicious. You rarely found SS men who
played games with their dogs in which the point was for the dog to
get the prisoners' derrieres, but the matrons did."[25] Jolana Roth wrote
similarly of women guards at Auschwitz, "But the ones you did see—
they were worse than the men. I will never forget the one who would
stand at the peephole of the gas chamber just because she wanted to."[26]

Very few former SS women have written or spoken about their
experiences. One of the fifty women guards at a Buchenwald work
camp, who was trained at Ravensbrück, claimed, in an interview with
Alison Owings, that there was no violence against prisoners except an
occasional kick or punch, that the prisoners received adequate food
and medical care, and that the camp commander was "very humane."[27]
A more recent memoir, by Nanda Herbermann, a *Kapo* at Ravensbrück, is similarly circumspect about acts of violence she may have
committed, and tries to avoid any mention of her anti-Semitism, presenting her activities in the camp as a kind of social work for imprisoned prostitutes.[28]

Were women guards driven by the same motivations as men, and
can their behavior be explained by reference to the same factors invoked to explain male guards? Or, after considering the case of
women guards, do we have to reconsider the categories we use to interpret the motivations of men guards? Karin Orth, a historian who

has investigated the backgrounds of the male SS who served as camp guards, concludes that the overwhelming majority of male SS camp guards belonged to the "wartime generation" that grew up during the post–World War I era and were affected by the mythology regarding the war. Most had limited education, at best an apprenticeship, and achieved in the SS positions of prominence that would have been otherwise unattainable. "They belonged to the social strata most affected by the economic, political, and social crisis of the Weimar Republic, the ones that felt threatened by social decline." Most were early and young members of the Nazi Party, joining by September 1931. "Every second person was a member of both the Nazi Party and the SS by his mid-twenties."[29]

Orth argues that "compliance in deed formed the group and welded it together." Part of SS training for men involved witnessing and then carrying out public acts of brutality against inmates. Such acts of violence were undertaken primarily against Jewish prisoners, rather than political prisoners. Indeed, violence at the camps grew dramatically in the second half of 1938, as large numbers of Jews were arrested. Note, too, that camp commandants were described as "decent" in the memoirs of political prisoners, and it was political prisoners, rather than Jewish ones, who most often testified at postwar trials.[30]

Orth's observations about the educational and demographic backgrounds of male guards have not yet been systematically investigated in relation to women guards and SS wives, and their applicability to women remains a question. We might ask, for example, what impact the mythology of World War I had on women growing up in the postwar years, who bore the brunt of the catastrophic food shortage while maintaining their families on the home front. Obviously, the thrilling battle experience exalted by writers such as Ernst Jünger would not have the same meaning to young women. How did they react to returning soldiers, embittered and hostile toward the defeated civilian population?[31]

Virtually every historian assumes that the presence of other men in the SS unit was crucial for motivating acts of violence through a sense of peer pressure and display of machismo. This was matched, we are told, by the need the SS guards had to create a sense of their own decency. For that purpose, they employed inmates as household or personal servants to create a sense of normal life, its needs and satisfactions. Even more important in that respect would be the presence of their wives and families at the camp. Indeed, as Gudrun Schwarz has made clear, the SS was not simply a male organization, but a *Sippengemeinschaft* that investigated in detail the backgrounds of fiancées and wives, with the intention of creating a community of the Aryan elite.

Although we do not know what percentage of women guards were married or had children, nor anything about the backgrounds of their husbands, we might ask if any personal relationships or domestic arrangements provided the women guards with a comparable stability and moral reassurance enjoyed by SS men with their wives. Schwarz, in *Eine Frau an Seine Seite*, argues persuasively that the domestic normalcy SS wives provided gave stability and even moral sanction to SS guards, making the wives complicit in the deeds of their husbands. Yet we might ask similar questions about the consorts of women guards. Did the husbands of guards provide the same sort of reassurance that wives provided? In other words, are Schwarz's conclusions about moral sanction rooted in domesticity or in female gender?

Whatever their function, SS families constituted an on-site collection of public witnesses at the camps.[32] Eugen Kogon, a former Buchenwald inmate, testified in June 1949 that Ilse Koch and other SS wives watched the evening corporal punishment of inmates, and that their presence resulted in an intensification of the "wild excesses of the SS."[33] We have a few diaries, personal documents, and formal postwar interrogations of wives and husbands; the recently published excerpts from the diary of Himmler's wife find her repeating the phrase "Es war sehr nett." ("It was very nice").

In considering the moral and psychological reassurance offered by SS wives, we might also ask whether there are any links between the roles played by women guards and women prisoners, and women guards and SS wives, in relation to men. Sara Horowitz has suggested that acts of seduction among prisoners were also acts of restoration, restoring to men a sense of dignity and humanity, a claim similar to that made by Schwarz regarding SS wives. Is there a common thread of women's roles, a collaboration in the process of restoring maleness to the man? Does the brutal suffering of male victims have the same result of undermining "normal" male gender identity as the act of inflicting brutality? Does all femaleness restore maleness, or only a certain kind? In either case, what is women's political and moral responsibility? In this connection, it would be helpful to have a study of the

husbands of women guards, in order to learn how many lived with
their wives at the camps, whether they were also employed at a camp,
and how the relationship affected their wives. Again, is it domesticity
that provides the stability and moral sanction described by Schwarz,
or do they arise specifically from women?

Even historical and literary studies create gender narratives that
impose the political and social requirements of our era onto the period
we are studying. Postwar scholarship on women and the Holocaust
has had a fairly constant narrative since the 1983 Stern College conference, one that focuses primarily on women victims. This narrative
that avoids comparison between Jewish and non-Jewish women, avoids
studies of women perpetrators, glorifies women by comparison to men,
and tends to overgeneralize and to essentialize. The most important
dogma to emerge from the scholarship is the claim that women prisoners bonded and thereby provided one another with life-preserving
emotional nurturance. Failure to compare Jewish women prisoners
with non-Jews ignores contrary evidence, such as Rudolf Höss's observations that "women would let themselves go completely" and that
women who were criminal prisoners "surpassed their male equiva-
lents in toughness, squalor, vindictiveness and depravity."[34]

Much of our information about the behavior of camp guards depends upon testimony acquired in the immediate postwar years, in
preparation for trials. Since so few women guards were tried, very
little information about women SS was gathered. At the trials themselves, testimony was presented and evaluated in gendered and sexualized mythological language, and that language was repeated in postwar books about the women guards, making clarification of their
actual atrocities difficult.[35] Additional information comes in the memoirs written often decades after the war. In both cases, memories can
distort. For example, commenting on Eugen Kogon's testimony at
postwar interrogation that Ilse Koch's presence at the punishment of
prisoners resulted in the "wild excesses of the SS" becoming even
stronger, Alexandra Przyrembel wrote,

> Whether her presence spurred the SS on to further attacks or
> whether they were also recalled by inmates as key experiences be-
> cause her presence reminded them of a public outside Buchenwald
> cannot be determined on the basis of the available sources, any
> more than can the assumption that the presence of a woman at
> their public punishment might have represented a particular hu-

miliation for prisoners. . . . A "ritual" function, which condemned other prisoners to stand idly by.[36]

To what extent are the female guards constructed by a gendered cultural memory of inmates of their internments? For example, Catherine Bernard compares Livia Bitton Jackson's description of her hair being shaved at Auschwitz, which brought a loss of her identity, with Elie Wiesel's loss of God; for both, "it opens a gulf between them and any comprehensible order."[37] The differences in their descriptions may reflect their gendered identities, or their construction of an experience with an eye to the reader and the expectation that women will be more concerned about loss of hair, while men suffer the great theological crisis. In comparing the autobiographies of women and men, Bella Brodzki and Celeste Schenk argue that the former autobiography is the male universality, his representativeness of humanity, whereas women's style is self-effacing.[38] Perhaps women's memoirs are concerned with matters of the female domain to reassure readers that survivors of Auschwitz have not lost their gender identity. The reassurance of the survivor's intact femaleness is created, in part, by the monstrous image of the SS female.

The collaboration between historiography and memoir on this point is noteworthy; both have been written to meet contemporary social and cultural needs. In Holocaust memoir literature, women emphasize their bonding with other women. Scholars then conclude that women bonded more strongly than did men. Yet we can also argue that women have been socialized to value friendships, and therefore remember them in their memoirs as important, and perhaps also to reassure themselves and their readers that they remain "normal" females, despite their internment. Moreover, we as readers have our own desires about Holocaust literature, as well as our own desires for political confirmation, especially in our gender ideology. Most Holocaust memoirs were written during a period when women's roles experienced feminist questioning and change, especially within the Jewish community.

Within postwar Germany, for reasons related to the Cold War, as Elizabeth Heineman has argued, memories of the Nazi era were also gendered as female, in an effort to present Germany as a passive victim, and women were described as pure, untainted by atrocities. In a 1987 speech, West German President Richard von Weiszäcker declared: "World history forgets their [women's] suffering, their renunciation, and their quiet strength all too easily. . . . In the darkest years, they preserved the light of humanity from extinction. . . . But if the people did not crack inside under the destruction, the devastation, the horrors and the inhumanity, if they slowly came back to themselves after the war, then we owe it first of all to our women."[39] Many contemporary German feminists, until recently, have displayed a similar tendency, arguing that all German women were victims of Nazism, rather than complicit in it. As a result, women perpetrators have had to be described as deviant females, in order to preserve the innocence of German women—an effort, by the way, in which postwar Americans collaborated.

The desire to eroticize the guards, as well as the killing process overall, is a phenomenon that has been noted primarily in relation to men, although the eroticization of women guards and victims is a striking motif that links contemporary literature, film, the popular press, and serious works of historiography. Probably the best-known examples are the films: Lina Wertmüller's *Seven Beauties,* from 1976, and the 1974 porno film *Ilsa: She Wolf of the SS.* Less well known are the two Polish films: *The Passenger,* directed in the 1960s by Andrzej Munk, about a chance meeting on a cruise ship of a female guard at Auschwitz and one of her prisoners; and *The Last Stage,* filmed at Auschwitz in 1947 as an autobiographical account of the director, Wanda Jakubiowaska, a survivor. *Ilsa: She Wolf,* directed by an American, Dave Friedman, and showed in mainstream theaters in many countries, spawned a groundswell of porno films produced during the 1970s that used concentration camps as their setting, including *SS Extermination Camp* and *SS Hell Camp,* and the as-yet unfinished, *Schindler's Lust.*[40] Ilsa, who assumes the pose of Lola Lola, sexualizes Nazism and drains it of political content, as Andrea Slane has recently pointed out.[41] In the film, Ilsa as a commandant has sex with men and women, destroying both in the process, and thus becomes the demonic counterimage of the Virgin Mary, the icon of the woman who achieves immense power through her unleashed lust, or perhaps achieves destructive, uncontrolled lust as a result of her unbridled power. Her icon prepares for subsequent conservative American rhetoric that demonizes all but highly traditional sexual relations.[42] Thus, we have Rush Limbaugh's "Feminazi" appellation, and the 1990 made-for-television movie *Hitler's Daughter,* which suggests that ambitious career women may secretly be Nazis.[43]

Susan Sontag asked, "Why has Nazi Germany, which was a sexually repressive society, become erotic?" There are numerous illustrations of her point, one of the best-known being *The Night Porter* (1974), which also invokes the Lola Lola/Marlene Dietrich image in a postwar sadomasochistic relationship between a female survivor and a male guard. The androgyny and transvestism of Lola Lola are used to blur the boundaries not only of male and female, but of guard and prisoner. Who is carrying out the sadism of the camp, the male SS guard or the female former inmate? Are the atrocities inflicted or performed? In fact, *Night Porter* is less ambiguous than some argue; if there is hesitation or a limit to the violence, it comes from him, whereas she is the one who glories in it, seeking him out, egging him on, and fulfilling her wish by appropriating his role. The man may be ambivalent about being an SS officer, but she is enthusiastic about attaining the role for herself.

The eroticization of Nazism can occur even among those who protest most vehemently against it. Alvin Rosenfeld, in commenting on the final scene of D. M. Thomas's novel *The White Hotel*, in which a half-dead Jewish woman at Babi Yar is raped with a bayonet and killed, wrote:

> This . . . is a sickening but by no means singular instance of the literary imagination's perverse attraction to the Nazi atrocities, especially as these begin to take on a sexual character and feature the female victims of violent crime. . . . The sexual desirability of the mutilated woman is a recurring motif in fiction about the Jewish tragedy and is one of its most blatant exploitative strains.[44]

We might ask if rape-murder with a bayonet is, in fact, about sexual desirability, or about violence and hatred. Just as Thomas introduced a fictive sexual element into the Babi Yar account of Kuznetsov, has Rosenfeld introduced an erotic motivation? A strikingly similar eroticization comes from a very different kind of source, Daniel Goldhagen's book *Hitler's Willing Executioners*. Note here the emphasis on women guards:

> The Germans made love in barracks [in the camps] next to enormous privation and incessant cruelty. What did they talk about when their heads rested quietly on their pillows, when they were smoking their cigarettes in those relaxing moments after their physical needs had been met? Did one relate to another accounts of a

particularly amusing beating that *she* or he had administered or observed, of the rush of power that engulfed *her* when the righteous adrenalin of Jew-beating caused *her* body to pulsate with energy?[45]

In commenting on the photographs of David Levinthal, in which small, naked female figurines are shown about to be executed by Nazi guards,[46] Marianne Hirsch argues the contrary, that the victims were not eroticized by the Nazis, but desexualized. She wrote:

> In subjecting the scene of execution to a pornographic gaze, he moves it into a different register altogether. Levinthal says, and James Young agrees, that sexual humiliation in the victims' last moments was one of the tactics of the Nazi dehumanization of their victims. But wasn't it actually something altogether different— that the victims were *dehumanized* by being *desexualized,* robbed of any subjectivity and thus also robbed of their sexuality?[47]

If the gaze of the novelist, the literary critic, and the historian collaborate in creating an erotics of the Holocaust, is it an effort to rehumanize the victims or to shift the motives of the perpetrators to something more conventionally human and easier to understand, sexuality?

CONCLUSION

Finally, I want to turn to the question of feminist theory's adequacy in interpreting female violence. While much has been written by feminist theorists about violence done to women, almost nothing exists theorizing women's cruelty. Klaus Theweleit's classic study, *Male Fantasies,* suggests that fascism functions by way of abjection, and he reads the literature of Freikorps members expressing a rejection of sex and an embrace of purity and death. He has no counterpart regarding female fantasies and their political significance, but Theweleit does mention that "the beautiful young wife serves as a pretext for murder" and that "bodily love with a woman is associated with forgetting, and women are a means to that end," two motifs that certainly operate in the postwar reading of Nazi guards and executioners.[48] Still, the psychopolitical dynamics of Theweleit's work rest on male models and cannot simply be transferred to an explanation of women's attraction to Nazism.

Returning to the question asked of Browning's work, and whether male bonding serves as a stimulus to displays of masculine violence, we might ask whether, in the camp setting, bonding among female guards stimulated greater acts of violence, and if women guards were inspired to cruelty by the presence of male guards. In other words, there is a widely shared assumption that men's cruelty is, in part, an expression of masculinity, but no exploration into whether women's acts of cruelty are linked to expressions of their femininity, understanding both terms as social constructs. The realm of the camp belonged to the SS, a male organization. Did women guards join the realm of power reserved for the SS, or transgress it?

Gisela Bock argues that women guards attempted to enter a male arena, leaving behind the traditional domestic female sphere. Yet this presents the women guards as "male-imitative," as if evil resides exclusively or primarily in the domains controlled by men. Beatrice Hannsen's recent book, *Critique of Violence,* surveys major theories of violence formulated by twentieth-century male theorists, starting with Walter Benjamin, then turns in her last two chapters to feminist theory and focuses exclusively on violence done *to* women, not *by* women.[49] On the question of women's involvement in the Holocaust, Margarete Mitscherlich states while there were women working at concentration camps who committed horrible acts, violence and paranoia stem from male psychic structures, and women simply submit to them. Similarly, the German feminist theologian Christa Mulack has argued for twenty years that Nazi obedience to orders is analogous to Jewish obedience to divine commandments, a morality of obedience to authority that is typical for the male gender.[50] Likewise, the American feminist Robin Morgan, writing in *Ms.* magazine in 1991, claimed that women who participate in hate crimes are also victims of these crimes, since they must have been forced into them. In the 1979 feminist film by Helma Sanders-Brahms, *Deutschland: Bleiche Mutter* (Germany: Pale Mother), Nazism is not an anti-Semitic war against Jews, but a patriarchal war against women. In this film, which expresses views shared by many German feminists in the 1980s, the female victims manage to transform themselves into Germany's heroes. While the men march off to self-destruction in Nazi uniforms in a display of German nationalism, it is the women who embody and thereby preserve the meaning of being German. Seduced to enter the "house of murderers," German women are no more the perpetrators of Nazism than the innocent girls betrayed by evil men in the Grimm fairy tale of that title, narrated in the film by the mother to her daughter as an explanatory parable of Germany's fate.[51]

Such arguments suggest that women took on male roles when they became involved in the Nazi "functional elite," in Ulrich Herbert's term, directly participating in carrying out the Final Solution. Feminist theory has tended to portray women evil-doers as having entered a male realm. Indeed, that male realm is often portrayed as no longer human, but demonic. In some ways, feminist theory's suggestion that the women who committed crimes were asexual monsters rather than women is parallel to Christian theologians' arguments that the perpetrators were not Christians, but pagans. Feminist thought, when it begins to theorize the nexus between gender and women's violence, will also have to reconsider its conventional views of the male and masculine. Feminist consideration of women and atrocity also raises issues of women's roles in society, and ways in which femaleness shapes or is given expression through acts of atrocity. Ann Taylor Allen places the tension between the social realms assigned to women and men at the center of the relationship between the Holocaust and modernity put forward by, among others, Zygmunt Bauman. Allen notes that Bauman's historical precondition of the Holocaust, "the great divide . . . between reason and emotion," resulted from "the separation of spheres that identified the former with a masculine and public sphere, and the latter with a feminized and private sphere."[52] At the same time, the recent study by Isabel Hull, *Sexuality, State, and Civil Society in Germany, 1700–1815,* challenges our conventional dichotomy between the male/public and female/domestic spheres as fictions, viewing them as far more intertwined.[53] Hull argues that men's ability to take up a public role in society rests upon their status as rulers of their private, domestic families. She writes, "Men's autonomy (and therefore fitness for the new public of civil society) rested upon their presocial, private individuality, reckoned independently of society, whereas women's dependence derived precisely from the social, 'public' reckoning used to define their 'nature.' From the standpoint of determination, men were private, women, public."[54] Similarly, men's fitness to be part of the "functional elite" of Nazi society rested on qualifications based outside civil society—on their racial lineage, war experience, and so forth—whereas women's role within the Nazi state derived from the public, civic rhetoric defining their "nature."[55] In functioning as camp guards, then, women indeed expressed an aspect of their female identity, reconceived during the Nazi regime as having a public as well as private component.

Feminist theory of atrocity might include cross-cultural locations in women's lives in which cruelty is expressed, including competition among girls; the role of violence in motherhood; the societal demand that women conceal expressions of anger; the equation of femininity with docility that can create the so-called "apolitical female"; the wife as a person without an identity, as expressed, for example, in Chekhov's story "The Darling"; and more. Or perhaps a study of the women guards might take us in an altogether different direction. Elisabeth Beck-Gernsheim has described modern bourgeois women as gradually becoming freed from "existing for others" and "laying a claim to a life of one's own."[56] Within the League of German Girls (BDM) the goal was to produce a generation of hard-working, resilient, and unselfish women, independent of their families, who could assert themselves and "put their backs to the wheel without demur." "We stand alone" and "we have to make our way alone," they put it, and their presence on the Nazi stage was evidence of an emancipatory process unleashed by National Socialism.[57] At the same time, it is essential to recognize processes by which women received and internalized masculinist eroticized perspectives mediated by the brutalized discourse of the concentration camp universe. The language of the manuals used to train women guards at Ravensbrück was simple and avoided brutal images, but I would call attention to another level of discourse, that of the aural. While much has been theorized about the "gaze," and all guards were certainly witnesses to acts of brutality, suffering, and murder, little has been written about the role of the aural. What all those present at the camps experienced was a constant sound of human suffering. Does the sound of a man in pain have a different gender connotation than the sound of a woman in pain? How these differences would, in turn, be experienced by male and female guards is yet another question I would like to explore. The production of human sound—the voice—is intrinsically gendered. It is a cliché that men moaning or screaming in pain are expressing a violation of their masculinity. What would be comparable for women? The emphasis on cultivating women's voices to produce a sound that is strongly "feminine" might make the loud sound of women being tortured particularly jarring. Are women in pain perceived by listeners as all the more intensely enacting the feminine, as sufferers, or as transgressive of gender expectation, like men?

In addition, reinterpretations of social values and conscience in Nazi Germany indicate particular ways in which women could be encouraged to perform femininity in public, Nazified domains. For example, that women are traditionally expected to repress their opinions and follow those of the dominant male in their lives might make them more dutiful guards than men. Their displays of violence as guards might be seen as expressions of compliance, a traditional feminine attribute, one encouraged in particular by religious traditions. Women's ecstatic devotion to Hitler displayed at rallies might flag their feminine emotionality. Such expressions of female group behavior were performed with the awareness of the omnipresent male gaze. Indeed, in contrast to the all-male Einsatzgruppen or SA, all women's groups, whether the BDM or the women guards, were under male supervision and enacted their gender performances with that awareness. Whether SS women performed their gender differently when gathered in private in their barracks (which were quite spacious and comfortable at Ravensbrück) cannot be answered, though we might ask whether gender even exists in private. Historians since Koonz have recognized the double message at work in the Nazi propaganda concerning women: they belong in the kitchen, yet were given roles in the Nazi party, at the workplace, and in other public forums, such as the church. The Nazi encouragement of women's displays of physicality and strength as heroic, and the discouragement by the regime of fashion, cosmetics, gentleness, weakness, and other attributes promoted by the Wilhelmine bourgeoisie, clearly worked in creating a social atmosphere conducive to women's guard duty. Volunteering at a concentration camp, then, would not be an indication of women as "male imitators," but an expression of aspects of the peculiar femininity endorsed by the Nazi regime. Women's willingness to take part in atrocities, particularly against Jewish inmates, which was understood as a protection of Nazi Aryan society, might signify a maternal devotion to children, morally intensified by their violence.[58]

Within feminist theory, however, the complex dependence of the domestic on the public, and vice versa, is not always recognized. In the feminist Holocaust script, peer pressure among men elicits violence, while peer pressure among women elicits emotional nurturance. That almost no women guards were prosecuted after the war arose from a disbelief among the Allies that women could have committed atrocities, and from Germany's desire to rehabilitate its men by asserting the normalcy of its women. Ultimately, the story of the SS was gendered in relation to the narrative of Nazism and the Holocaust. In examining the role of women in the SS, the aim is to illuminate how the gender ideologies of bourgeois modernity, challenged and overthrown during the Nazi experience, intervened after the war to prevent adequate investigation and prosecution. The result was a sanctuary for SS women and a myth of women's neutrality or even victimhood that prevented our knowledge of what happened and distorted our understanding of the role of gender.

NOTES

My thanks to Marianne Hirsch and Doris Bergen, who have been extremely generous with their advice and criticisms. My deep gratitude as well to William Fontaine, Bibliographer for the Humanities at the Dartmouth College library, for finding much of the obscure material cited in this article. I would also like to extend appreciation to the Feminist Inquiry Seminar at Dartmouth College, for a thoughtful discussion of the paper.

1. Christopher Browning, *Ordinary Men: Reserve Police Battalion 101 and the Final Solution in Poland* (New York: HarperCollins, 1992).

2. Dalia Ofer and Lenore J. Weitzman, eds., *Women in the Holocaust* (New Haven, Conn.: Yale University Press, 1998).

3. A notable exception to this pattern is Ruth Klüger's memoir of Auschwitz, *Still Alive: A Holocaust Girlhood Remembered* (New York: Feminist Press at the City University of New York, 2001).

4. Claudia Koonz, *Mothers in the Fatherland: Women, the Family, and Nazi Politics* (New York: St. Martin's Press, 1987); Gisela Bock, *Zwangssterilisation im Nationalsozialismus: Studien zur Rassenpolitik und Frauenpolitik* (Opladen: Westdeutscher Verlag, 1986). On the feminist Historikerstreit, see Karin Windaus-Walser, "Gnade der weiblichen Geburt? Zum Umgang der Frauenforschung mit Nationalsozialismus und Antisemitismus," *Feministische Studien* 6 (November 1988): 102–15.

5. Barbara Distel, ed., *Frauen im Holocaust* (Gerlingen: Bleicher Verlag, 2001), 18.

6. Ofer and Weitzman, eds., *Women in the Holocaust*.

7. Michael Mann, "Were the Perpetrators of Genocide 'Ordinary Men' or 'real Nazis'? Results from Fifteen Hundred Biographies," *Holocaust and Genocide Studies* 14, no. 3 (Winter 2000): 331–66.

8. Gudrun Schwarz, "Wärterinnen in Konzentrationslagern," in Distel, *Frauen im Holocaust,* 333.

9. Irmtraud Heike, "Lagerverwaltung und Bewachungspersonal," *Frauen in Konzentrationslagern Bergen-Belsen, Ravensbrück,* ed. Claus Füllberg-Stolberg, Martina Jung, Renate Riebe, and Martina Scheitenberger (Bremen: Temmen, 1994), 221. Cited also by Schwarz, "Wärterinnen," 334.

10. Personal communication, Sybille Steinbacher.

11. Heike, "Lagerverwaltung und Bewachungspersonal," 223.

12. Schwarz, "Wärterinnen," 336.

13. Gudrun Schwarz, "SS-Aufseherinnen in nationalsozialistischen Konzentrationslagern Gross-Rosen" (1933–1945), *Dachauer Hefte* 10 (1994): 32–49, here p. 34.

14. Guste Zoener, ed., *Frauen-KZ Ravensbrück* (Berlin: VEB Deutscher Verlag der Wissenschaften, 1997); on male guards, see Helmut Krausnick, H. Buchheim, M. Broszat, and H.-A. Jacobsen, *Anatomy of the SS State* (New York: Walker, 1968), 600.

15. Schwarz, "SS-Aufseherinnen," 43–4.

16. Irmtraud Heike, "Lagerverwaltung und Bewachungspersonal," 222.

17. Article by David Marwell.

18. On the active participation of women guards, including Grese, in the selection of prisoners for death, see Schwarz, "SS-Aufseherinnen," 44–8.

19. R. Phillips, *The Trial of Josef Kramer and Forty-Four Others* (London: W. Hodge, 1949).

20. Daniel Patrick Brown, *The Beautiful Beast: The Life and Crimes of SS-Aufseherin Irma Grese* (Ventura, Calif.: Golden West Historical Publications, 1996); *Trial of Josef Kramer and Forty-four Others: The Belsen Trial,* ed. Raymond Phillips (London: W. Hodge, 1949), 105.

21. *Time,* October 4, 1948; cited by Alexandra Przyrembel, "Transfixed by an Image: Ilse Koch, the 'Kommandeuse of Buchenwald,'" *German History* 19, no. 3 (2001): 389.

22. Cited by Przyrembel, "Transfixed by an Image," 393.

23. Karen Remmler, "Gender Identities and the Remembrance of the Holocaust," *Women in German Yearbook* 10 (1994): 167.

24. Gisella Perl, *I Was a Doctor in Auschwitz* (New York: International Universities Press, 1948), 61.

25. Cited by Koonz, *Mothers,* 404.

26. Ibid., 405.

27. Alison Owings, *Frauen: German Women Recall the Third Reich* (New Brunswick, N.J.: Rutgers University Press, 1993), 323.

28. Nanda Herbermann, *The Blessed Abyss: Inmate #6582 in Ravensbrück Concentration Camp for Women,* ed. Hester Baer and Elizabeth R. Baer, trans. by Hester Baer (Detroit: Wayne State University Press, 2001).

29. Karin Orth, "Concentration Camp SS as Functional Elite," in *National Socialist Extermination Policies: Contemporary German Perspectives and Controversies,* ed. Ulrich Herbert (New York: Berghahn Books, 2000), 308.

30. Orth, "Concentration Camp SS," 320.

31. Richard Bessel, "The 'Front Generation' and Weimar," in *Generations in Conflict: Youth Revolt and Generation Formation in Germany 1770–1968,* ed. Mark Roseman (Cambridge: Cambridge University Press, 1995), 129–30.

32. Przyrembel, "Transfixed by an Image," 373.

33. Ibid., 385.

34. *KL Auschwitz Seen by the SS: Höss, Broad, Kremer,* ed. Jadwiga Bezwinska and Danuta Czech (Oświęciem: Auschwitz Museum, 1972), 76.

35. For examples, see Przyrembel, "Transfixed by an Image," 371 nn. 11–13.

36. Ibid., 385–6.

37. Catherine A. Bernard, "Tell Him That I: Women Writing the Holocaust," *Other Voices* 2, no. 1 (February 2000). The quotation is from the online version at http://www.othervoices.org/2.1/bernard/womanwriting.html.

38. Bella Brodzki and Celeste Schenck, eds., *Life Lines: Theorizing Women's Autobiography* (Ithaca, N.Y.: Cornell University Press, 1988).

39. Cited and analyzed by Elizabeth Heinemann, "The Hour of the Woman: Memories of Germany's 'Crisis Years' and West German National Identity," *American Historical Review* 101 (1996): 354–95.

40. See, for example, *Last Orgy of the Third Reich* (1976); *Love Camp 7* (1967): *Madam Kitty* (1973); *Nazi Love Camp #27* (1975); *Red Nights of the Gestapo* (1977); *She Devils of the SS* (1973, a.k.a. *Cutthroat Commandos*); *SS Extermination Camp* (1976); *SS Girls* (1975); *SS Hell Camp* (1977); *SS Hell Camp #5: Woman's Hell* (1976); *SS Special Section Women* (1977).

41. Andrea Slane, *A Not So Foreign Affair: Fascism, Sexuality, and the Cultural Rhetoric of American Democracy* (Durham, N.C.: Duke University Press, 2001).

42. Ibid., 250.

43. Ibid., 279–80.

44. Alvin H. Rosenfeld, *Imagining Hitler* (Bloomington: Indiana University Press, 1985), 58; D. M. Thomas, *The White Hotel* (New York: Viking Press, 1981).

45. Daniel Goldhagen, *Hitler's Willing Executioners: Ordinary Germans and the Holocaust* (New York: Knopf, 1996), 339.

46. David Levinthal and Garry Trudeau, *Hitler Moves East: A Graphic Chronicle, 1941–43* (New York: Laurence Miller Gallery, 1989).

47. Marianne Hirsch, "Nazi Photographs in Post-Holocaust Art: Gender as an Idiom of Memorialization," in *Phototextualities*, ed. Andrea Noble and Alex Hughes (Albuquerque: University of New Mexico Press, 2002) reprinted in *Crimes of War: Guilt and Denial*, ed. Omer Bartov, Atina Grossman, and Molly Noble (New York: New Press, 2002).

48. Klaus Theweleit, *Male Fantasies*, trans. Stephen Conway. Vol 1, *Women, Floods, Bodies, History* (Minneapolis: University of Minnesota Press, 1987), 34, 41.

49. Beatrice Hanssen, *Critique of Violence: Between Poststructuralism and Critical Theory* (London: Routledge, 2000).

50. Margarete Mitscherlich, *Die friedfertige Frau* (Frankfurt: Fischer Verlag, 1985); Christa Mulack, *Jesus: der Gesalbte der Frauen* (Stuttgart: Kreuz Verlag, 1987), 155–6.

51. I would like to thank Professor Doris Bergen for bringing this film to my attention and for pointing out its proto-nationalist elements.

52. Ann Taylor Allen, "The Holocaust and the Modernization of Gender: A Historiographical Essay," *Central European History* 30, no. 3 (1997): 361.

53. Isabel Hull, *Sexuality, State, and Civil Society in Germany, 1700–1815* (Ithaca, N.Y.: Cornell University Press, 1996); see my application of Hull's work to the study of modern Jewish women: Susannah Heschel, "Nicht nur Opfer und Heldinner," in *Jüdische Geschichtsschreibung Heute*, ed. Michael Brenner (Munich: Beck Verlag, 2002), pp. 139–62.

54. Hull, *Sexuality*, 411.

55. "Nazi elite," as defined by Ulrich Herbert, determines membership by proximity to and responsibility for the terror and extermination policies of the Nazi regime. See Ulrich Herbert, "Rückkehr in die Bürgerlichkeit? NS-Eliten in der Bundesrepublik," in *Rechstradikalismus in der politischen Kultur der Nachkriegszeit. Die verzögerte Normalisierung in Niedersachsen*, ed. Bernd Weisbrod (Hanover: Hahn, 1995), 159, 157–73.

56. Elisabeth Beck-Gernsheim, "Vom 'Dasein für andere' zum Anspruch auf ein Stück 'eigenes Leben,' Individualisierungsprozesse im weiblichen Lebenszusammenhang," *Soziale Welt* 34 (1983): 307–40; cited by Dagmar Reese, "The BDM Generation: A Female Generation in Transition from Dictatorship to Democracy," in *Generations in Conflict: Youth Revolt and Generation Formation in Germany 1770–1968*, ed. Mark Roseman (Cambridge: Cambridge University Press, 1995), 231 n. 11.

57. Reese, "The BDM Generation," 240.

58. Irmtraud Heike notes that Lagerfeld raised strenuous objections to the maltreatment of German prisoners, while engaging in brutal violence against Jewish prisoners.

V. T·R·I·A·L·S C·O·M·P·E·N·S·A·T·I·O·N AND J·E·W·I·S·H A·S·S·E·T·S

Hilary Earl

Scales of Justice: History, Testimony, and the Einsatzgruppen Trial at Nuremberg

INTRODUCTION

MOST HISTORIANS AGREE THAT THE MASS MURDER OF SOVIET JEWRY BY units of the SS-Einsatzgruppen in the summer of 1941 marks a watershed in Nazi racial policy toward Europe's Jews. Some even view their activities as the beginning of Hitler's plan for the "Final Solution." But when exactly did the leaders of the Einsatzgruppen receive the order to murder all Soviet Jews—men, women, and children— an order the defendants, the prosecution, and the judges in the Einsatzgruppen trial in 1947 all referred to as the *Führerbefehl?*[1] Was the order given before the units were deployed in the Soviet Union on June 22, 1941, as Otto Ohlendorf, the principal defendant in the trial, testified? Or was it given later, in the late summer or early fall of 1941, some weeks or months after units of the Einsatzgruppen departed from their assembly point in the border town of Pretzsch on the Elbe river, in Saxony? The question of the timing of the murderous order is at the heart of a fierce debate amongst scholars of the Final Solution, in which the men of the Einsatzgruppen unquestionably played a vital role. In fact, the issue of timing is part of the larger intentionalist-functionalist debate that arose mainly because documentary evidence of an order by Hitler to murder Europe's Jews has not been uncovered.[2]

The intentionalist-functionalist debate centers on the question of whether Hitler had a plan, a blueprint, to murder Europe's Jews. The question arose largely because of a lack of clear documentary evidence to support when and by whom the decision for the Final Solution was taken. In the absence of a clear record of the decision-making process, not only have interpretations of the origins of the Final Solution varied considerably, but the documentary void has also led many postwar historians to search for alternate evidence that might help them pinpoint the timing of Hitler's decision to murder eastern Jewry. Some historians found that evidence in the postwar testimony of Otto Ohlendorf, leader of Einsatzgruppe D, who, when tried for his crimes at Nuremberg in 1947, testified that the order to murder Soviet Jewry was given to the leaders of the Einsatzgruppen by Bruno Streckenbach, head of Office I (Personnel) of the Reichssicherheitshauptamt (RSHA), before the invasion of the Soviet Union in the summer of 1941. Ohlendorf's testimony about the nature and timing of the *Führerbefehl* suggested to historians that the order was more than Hitler's "wish" or "desire," and was part of a well thought-out and concrete plan to murder Europe's Jews.

The historical controversy about the timing and nature of the order to murder Soviet Jewry developed when, in the 1980s, Alfred Streim, former chief prosecutor at the Central Office for the Investigation of National Socialist Crimes in Ludwigsburg, Germany, detected discrepancies in Ohlendorf's testimony. After reviewing a number of affidavits given by former members of the Einsatzgruppen, Streim concluded that the Hitler-order to murder all Jews had not been issued prior to the invasion of the Soviet Union in June 1941. Rather, it most probably had been given some weeks later, between early August and September 1941, the precise date of which cannot be determined without further documentary evidence. What is certain, according to Streim, is that the Einsatzgruppen's murderous behavior escalated from partial to complete genocide sometime between June and September 1941, but that the genocidal murder of Soviet Jews had not been planned at the outset of Operation Barbarossa, as Ohlendorf had testified in 1947. From the evidence available, Streim concluded that Ohlendorf's testimony had been perjured; Ohlendorf had lied as a defense strategy to escape a death sentence. Since Streim highlighted the issue of timing in the 1980s, it has become a point of contention in the historiography on the origins of the Final Solution, and while further research has helped clarify the issue of timing, no definitive date for the order to murder all Soviet Jews has been established.[3]

Central to this issue is why historians accepted Ohlendorf's testimony at face value. This paper will show that his testimony on the issue of the timing and nature of the *Führerbefehl* was believed because it was from a major, self-proclaimed participant of the Final Solution who seemed to be more honest and straightforward than most of the other accused. Even though he was a self-confessed mass murderer, his personality was such that perjury appeared to be beneath him. In short, he seemed credible as a witness and thus a good source of historical evidence. Significantly, historians were not the only ones guilty of accepting Ohlendorf's testimony as fact. Indeed, even the prosecutors and presiding judge of the trial at Nuremberg failed to challenge the veracity or consistency of Ohlendorf's testimony on the issue of the *Führerbefehl*.[4] Why? Partly for the same reasons that historians accepted it: In Anglo-American jurisprudence, when documentary evidence is lacking, facts are established through the direct testimony of witnesses.[5] In other words, judicial procedure places a great amount of "faith in the veracity of the spoken word," and in 1947 Ohlendorf seemed a more credible witness than most others.[6] But this was not the only reason Ohlendorf's testimony went unchallenged. The timing of the order—whether it was promulgated in June, July, or August 1941—was not germane to the case the prosecution was preparing.[7] Mass murders had been committed and the Einsatzgruppen leaders had been indicted. The task of the prosecution was to prove that the accused had committed these crimes and of the court to determine whether they had understood the illegal nature of the order. In other words, the timing of the order had no significant legal relevance for the prosecution's case. The prosecutors would be satisfied if they proved to the court that the men on trial had committed the crimes with which they were charged. Hence, a vigorous cross-examination, the one method the court has to test witness testimony, was not employed.[8] That Ohlendorf's testimony was not subjected to scrutiny directly contributed to the ambiguity of the historical record, especially to our current understanding of the events that led to the murder of Soviet Jewry in the summer of 1941.

It is ironic that the planners of the Einsatzgruppen trial identified historical truth as one of the explicit goals of the trial. Not only did they want to punish the perpetrators, but as important was their wish to expose the criminal history of Nazism and the Third Reich for all to see.[9] In the early postwar years it was believed that the trial of Nazi war criminals would clarify what these men did, how they did it, and why. As Telford Taylor, the American chief of counsel for war crimes and the individual responsible for prosecuting Nazi war criminals, expressed it, "many of these [trial] documents, now have a gloss on them in the form of supplementary testimony by the men . . . who were mentioned in them, thus creating an immense overlay of additional information and comment that in many settings is of great historical importance."[10] But, for the historian, this "overlay of additional information" (as Taylor called it) can be extremely disconcerting, especially when it is found that the additional information is uncorroborated or even untrue. Taylor and the other planners probably did not realize it at the time, but in the context of a legal proceeding, the dual goals of punishment and education are frequently incompatible.[11] After all, criminal trials are adversarial, and testimony is most frequently given in an attempt to establish legal exculpation, and not to document historical truth. By their very nature criminal trials can act as strong impediments to historical truth when, by excluding or altering historical facts, a defendant can demonstrate innocence, or a prosecutor, guilt. This is exactly what happened in the Einsatzgruppen trial in 1947 and 1948, and it is this distortion of fact that is at the heart of the current historical controversy. For this reason it is important to return to the context in which these factual errors were made and to determine, if possible, why the accused distorted the truth.[12]

The issue of the so-called Hitler-order is of extreme importance historically. However, it is beyond the scope of the present chapter to investigate when or even if an actual order was given to the leaders of the Einsatzgruppen; this must be left to those who study the origins of the Final Solution.[13] Rather, the aim of this chapter is to show how and why the prosecutors of the Einsatzgruppen leaders failed to accurately assess the importance of when the order to murder Soviet Jews was given, and how and why the distortion of this fact occurred in the context of a legal proceeding. This is a complex and at times complicated issue involving more than just perjured testimony and historical misrepresentation.[14] Not all of the pertinent factors can be addressed here. Rather, the goal of this chapter is two-fold: first, to trace the development of Otto Ohlendorf's testimony on the issue of the *Führerbefehl* and to determine how and why American authorities never challenged its authenticity; and second, to examine the issue of the *Führerbefehl* in the context of the Einsatzgruppen trial and to relate how the order was used as a defense strategy and how this strategy backfired. The material presented here leads to the conclusion that the so-called *Führerbefehl* was an important, even critical, factor in determining the outcome of the trial. Whereas the defense intended to use the existence of the *Führerbefehl* to demonstrate a lack of criminal intent on the part of the defendants, to the prosecution the existence of the order was proof that the accused had carried out genocide and that the impetus for this act came from Hitler. That the court came to view the existence of the order as fact, despite evidence to the contrary, can be directly attributed to the credibility and assertiveness of Ohlendorf as a witness.

OTTO OHLENDORF, EARLY INTERROGATIONS, THE IMT AND THE QUESTION OF ORDERS

The matter of the *Führerbefehl* was first articulated, albeit vaguely, by Otto Ohlendorf in his first interrogation by Allied authorities in October 1945 in preparation for his testimony at the first Nuremberg trial before the International Military Tribunal (IMT).[15] During this day-long interrogation Ohlendorf described in detail the organizational structure of the Einsatzgruppen, including the composition of the groups and their relationship to the army, and twice briefly referred to their orders. The first order, he informed his interrogator, Lieutenant Colonel Smith Brookhart, was given verbally to the four leaders of the killing units in early May 1941, just days before the Einsatzgruppen units crossed into Soviet territory at the beginning of Operation Barbarossa.[16] At this time Ohlendorf did not say who gave the order to murder Soviet Jews, nor did Brookhart ask.[17] The second order he said, was delivered by Himmler personally during the Reichsführer's visit to the eastern front in September 1941. It is important to bear in mind that during this early interrogation, Ohlendorf never explicitly revealed the contents of the first order, whereas he did tell Brookhart that the second order from Himmler called for the "extermination" of *all* Jews, without exception, in the Russian theater of war.[18]

The following day, Ohlendorf was interrogated a second time. Before Brookhart could begin questioning him, however, Ohlendorf spent some time correcting "facts" he had given the previous day. He had, he told Brookhart, mistakenly believed that Operation Barbarossa began in May, but now realized he had been wrong.[19] He also explained that the directive to "liquidate" Soviet Jews had been given by

Hitler, but that Himmler only informed him of the Führer's decision approximately four weeks before the units were deployed.[20] Presumably, here he was referring to the general assignment of the Einsatzgruppen in the east and not specifically to the *Führerbefehl*.[21] In any case, he did not elaborate or reveal any further details of this matter during this second interview, nor did his interrogator ask.

During these early interrogations, Brookhart mainly was interested in obtaining specific details about the activities of the Einsatzgruppen, such as how victims were lured to their deaths, and the precise manner in which they were killed and the bodies disposed of. Ohlendorf's claim that Hitler had given the order to murder did not seem out of the ordinary to Brookhart, which is hardly surprising considering Allied presumptions about the hierarchical structure of the totalitarian Reich and the power Hitler wielded within it. That Brookhart missed an opportunity to question Ohlendorf about such an historically important issue is also not remarkable given that at this early date the Allies had few details of what had transpired on the eastern front, and thus were not aware of how important the issue would later become.[22] Moreover, the case the Americans were preparing at Nuremberg was based on the assumption that criminal decisions were conceived at the highest levels of the party, and thus Ohlendorf's claims merely confirmed their preconceived view that Hitler was at the center of the decision-making process with respect to mass murder.[23] In this context it makes sense that Brookhart would not have questioned him on the issue of timing. Instead, he listened intently while Ohlendorf willingly and dispassionately offered information about atrocities, always making certain that the interrogator was aware of how "humane" his method of execution was compared to the practices of his colleagues who commanded the other three units.[24] In a subsequent interview Ohlendorf seemed "particularly anxious," Brookhart later noted, to distinguish between those SS officers who acted under superior orders and those who did not. Ohlendorf believed he was one of the former and had therefore acted "legally." But again, Brookhart did not question how or even if it was possible for the SS units to take independent action; he merely accepted Ohlendorf's assertions at face value.[25]

In criminal proceedings, generally speaking, the more time that elapses between a criminal act and witness testimony about it, the less clear and reliable that testimony is judged to be by the court.[26] Ironically, this was not the case with Ohlendorf. In fact, the opposite is true. The more he spoke on the issue of the *Führerbefehl* and its contents, and the more assertive he became about it, the more the Americans accepted his testimony as "truthful." After dozens of interrogations by American authorities, Ohlendorf's recollection of events became more specific. Forgotten details were remembered, names recalled, and new facts added until his "story" became "the truth" not only to himself, but most significantly to American authorities as well. Yet it was not until he was called as a prosecution witness at the first Nuremberg trial in January 1946 that he articulated the full contents of the groups' initial orders, and even then his statement, while legally compelling, was ambiguous as historical fact.

On January 3, 1946, Ohlendorf appeared at the Palace of Justice in Nuremberg as a witness for the prosecution in their cases against the German High Command and the only representative of the SS on trial, Ernst Kaltenbrunner. The interrogations of the previous year formed the basis of his testimony. Colonel John Harlan Amen, who had personally conducted several interviews with Ohlendorf, also acted as the examiner when Ohlendorf took the stand. He had Ohlendorf explain to the tribunal how the negotiations with the German Army and the Reich Security Main Office (RSHA) resulted in the formation of the Einsatzgruppen. Ohlendorf was next asked to explain how the Einsatzgruppen were expected to deal with Soviet Jews and communist functionaries. He explained that Einsatz and Kommandoführer were "orally instructed [by Bruno Streckenbach, Head of Personnel in Office I of the RSHA, to murder Jews and Soviet political commissars] before their mission."[27] It is important to note here that Ohlendorf did not explicitly state that the *Kommandos'* instructions were to kill *all* Jews, although this could certainly be inferred from his testimony; rather, he simply stated that the leaders of the *Kommandos* were told, before their mission, that Jews were to be "liquidated."[28] Amen did not question Ohlendorf further on this matter, accepting as reasonable the idea that the men who led these groups would be informed of their task before they were deployed[29]— not too outrageous a legal assumption, especially considering that a major, self-proclaimed participant of the mass murder stated it as fact, but certainly a proposition extremely important to our historical understanding of the events of June 1941. Besides, Ohlendorf was a witness for the prosecution, not the defense. His testimony was meant to corroborate prosecution claims that the German Army co-operated with the Einsatzgruppen in their murderous activities in So-viet Russia and that Kaltenbrunner personally knew of the criminal actions of the Einsatzgruppen in Soviet territory.

The prosecution could not have asked for a more credible witness than Ohlendorf, who not only was able and willing to divulge much information about the criminal workings of the regime, but did so in a convincing manner.[30] Undoubtedly Ohlendorf's confidence during the trial influenced the court's perception of the veracity of his testi-mony. As one judicial figure remarked, "Whatever offenses Ohlen-dorf may have to answer for, he will never need to plead guilty to eva-siveness on the witness stand. With a forth-rightness which one could well wish were in another field of activity, Otto Ohlendorf related how he received the Fuehrer-Order and how he executed it."[31] From an "evidentiary standpoint," as Taylor later recalled in his memoir of the trial, Ohlendorf's testimony was "a real blockbuster."[32] From the perspective of defendants such as Göring, Ohlendorf was seen as a traitor, "selling his soul to the enemy," but to Hans Frank and Walther Funk he was admired for his honesty.[33] Whether he was seen as a trai-tor or star-witness, in 1946 there was no doubt in anyone's mind that Ohlendorf was speaking the truth.

Ohlendorf's testimony about the existence and timing of the *Führerbefehl* at the IMT became his mantra and would be repeated in substance one year later in affidavits entered into evidence at his own trial and during direct testimony.[34] This evidence was so compelling and his testimony so assertive that those directly involved in his pros-ecution a year later accepted his statements at face value, even though the assertiveness of a witness is not always the best gauge of truth.[35] Yet, from this point onward, the existence of the *Führerbefehl* became a given and no further efforts were made to determine whether it really existed—again leaving this important historical question unanswered.

DEFENSE ARGUMENTS, THE *FÜHRERBEFEHL*, AND TESTIMONY AT THE EINSATZGRUPPEN TRIAL

The trial of the Einsatzgruppen leaders began with their arraignment in September 1947, to which each entered a plea of "not guilty, in the sense of the indictment."[36] What the accused meant by this was to be-come clear two weeks later when the trial began in earnest. The prosecution's case took only two days to present since their evidentiary basis was entirely documentary.[37] Given the incriminating nature of the evidence, mainly the Einsatzgruppen's own reports, coupled with Ohlendorf's earlier confession to the crime, the defense attorneys were forced to use very imaginative arguments to prove their clients' innocence.[38] This strategy proved highly problematic for the defense in general, and their difficulty was compounded by the fact that there were twenty-two defendants on trial, not just one. As a result, the defense had to come up with a common line or, as the prosecution called it, "organized hypocrisy," that was applicable to all accused regardless of their position in the Einsatzgruppen.[39] Thus, the attorneys for the defendants employed a variety of strategies, and while this "shotgun" approach was probably necessary under the circumstances, rather than helping their clients, it created a sense of incredibility and desperation and ultimately weakened the basis and presentation of their case.

Dr. Rudolf Aschenauer, the attorney for Ohlendorf, made the opening statement for the defense on October 6. To everyone's surprise, Aschenauer acknowledged that "executions" had occurred in the Soviet Union and that most of the accused would not deny they had committed the acts with which they were charged; but these executions were legally justified, he argued, because they were carried out in *presumed* self-defense on behalf of a third party—the German Reich—during a *presumed* state of emergency.[40] In American law this argument is referred to as putative justification or self-defense, which suggests that an individual's criminal action was predicated on "the reasonable belief that a feared aggressor is about to attack."[41] More importantly, justification assumes that the crime committed "outweighs the harm of the offense—either because a greater harm is avoided or because a greater social interest is furthered."[42] As Aschenauer interpreted it, a defendant's actions were justified if he could prove that he had acted in self-defense to protect Germany, even if his presumption of a threat was mistaken.[43] The accused had killed innocent civilians, but they did so believing their actions were for the greater good of the German Reich, not only to save Germany from Bolshevism, but also to ensure the continued existence of Germany, which was threatened by the war with the Soviet Union.[44]

As a second line of defense, Ashenauer and the other attorneys intended to prove that the leaders of the Einsatzgruppen took their

orders from the military commanders to which their units were attached, and that the so-called *Führerbefehl* demanded obedience. In
law, this argument is exculpatory when it can be confirmed that an
"excusing condition" existed in connection with the criminal act. In
this case, it would have to be shown that either the accused did not
know their conduct was wrong at the time of the crime or that their
criminal actions were the result of coercion.[45] Under Control Council Law No. 10, the law under which the defendants were tried, neither putative justification nor superior orders were applicable, but Aschenauer hoped the tribunal would consider them since both had
long pedigrees in German legal theory and law.[46] With the putative
self-defense argument Aschenauer aimed to show that while the defendants' acts were criminal they were nonetheless legally justified. If
the court did not find this defense reasonable, he hoped they would
legally excuse the defendants on the grounds that they were acting
under duress on the orders of their superiors.[47] But by making these
arguments he implicitly acknowledged the criminal acts of those accused, and thus the burden of proof was now placed squarely on the
shoulders of the defense.

To this end, the defense had to demonstrate that the defendants
were soldiers, carrying out the most difficult of soldierly tasks—protecting their state—in a military but humane fashion during the
war.[48] To prove the validity of putative justification, Aschenauer introduced expert testimony as well as entered into evidence a radio
broadcast by Stalin of July 3, 1941, in which the Soviet leader called
for the most extreme measures against the German Reich, including
partisan warfare and the total destruction of the German fascist state.[49]
In Aschenauer's words, "[the] solution of the problem 'Bolshevism
versus Europe' could only be brought about by a 'solution' of the Jewish problem and in . . . [the Einsatzgruppen's] particular sphere, [*sic*]
only by unreserved execution of the Fuehrer-Order," that is, the murder of Soviet Jewry.[50] But Aschenauer's argument was misleading as
well as inherently flawed. While these men undoubtedly took their
orders from their superiors, could they really be considered soldiers,
given their lack of military training and the political and ideological
nature of their task?[51] Moreover, the defense claim that the Einsatzgruppen murdered Russian Jews to protect Germany from Soviet
aggression (as articulated in Stalin's July 1941 radio speech) was implausible, since it was Germany who was the aggressor and not the

other way around. Thus, if any nation could argue putative self-defense, it was the Soviet Union and not the Third Reich.

On the witness stand most of the men assisted in their defense by claiming they believed that Bolshevism and Jews were synonymous. For instance, Ohlendorf stated that he believed the Jews "played a disproportionately important role" in the Soviet state. And, in what can only be called a pathetic attempt to prove the link between the two, he made the ridiculous claim that "Jews who were executed went to their death singing *The International* [sic] and hailing Stalin." Singing, he dubiously argued, was confirmation that the Jews posed an imminent and grave threat to the Reich.[52] The putative self-defense argument proved unconvincing to the tribunal, particularly after Ohlendorf admitted he was morally opposed to the order to murder Russian Jews.[53] As the presiding judge, Michael Musmanno, pointed out, either Aschenauer defended Hitler's order as justifiable under the circumstance of total war, or he defended his client Ohlendorf, who testified that he carried out the order under duress because he objected to it on moral grounds. But he should not argue both positions.[54] At the same time, while Musmanno did not limit the scope of defense counsels' representation (in fact, he acknowledged their right to put forth mutually exclusive defenses especially given the gravity of the charges), he did emphasize that in doing so both defenses were "inevitably weaken[ed]."[55]

Werner Braune, head of Einsatzkommando 11b, also could not deny murdering Jews, especially given Ohlendorf's earlier testimony. Thus he, too, attempted to argue putative self-defense by making the link between Bolshevism and the Jews, but his testimony was even more ineffective than Ohlendorf's. He told the tribunal that as far as he understood it, "the vast majority of Jews supported Bolshevism," but Musmanno was not convinced. Logically, the chief judge replied, if the majority supported Bolshevism, that meant that a minority of Jews did not. Braune had to agree, but this number was small, he said, perhaps as low as 10, 20, or 30 percent. Musmanno demanded to know why, then, if this were the case, all Jews were killed, even the minority who did not support Bolshevism. Musmanno's logic silenced Braune, whose only explanation was that "the possibility [to save them] did not exist."[56] For Musmanno this was demonstrable proof that the putative self-defense claim was fraudulent, as he concluded in his judgment, "[t]he record shows . . . that when it came to a Jew, it did not matter whether he was a member of the Communist Party or not," and even if all the Jews in the Soviet Union were shown to be Bolsheviks, murder for holding differing political opinions is still murder.[57]

Given the utter failure to prove putative justification, the defense was compelled to argue their back-up case: superior orders. Legally, if the defendants did not know that carrying out the *Führerbefehl* (i.e., the murder of innocent civilians) was illegal or if they had been coerced, they could not be convicted of a crime. Ohlendorf, as the lead defendant in the case, took the stand first. Under direct examination he reiterated his earlier testimony about the nature and delivery of Hitler's order and emphatically stated that anyone who disobeyed the Führer "would have met immediate death."[58] Hitler's orders were so compelling, he claimed without hesitation, that had he been ordered to do so, he would have murdered his own sister.[59] Ohlendorf was consistent and insistent, and as hard as the prosecution tried they could not crack his resolve. He appeared confident about his testimony. On the witness stand he presented himself as assured, credible, and, above all, right. The fact is that Ohlendorf's audaciousness, coupled with a weak cross-examination, did little to discredit the defense of obedience to orders. But there was more than one man on trial, and as far as the tribunal was concerned it took but one accused to demonstrate the weakness of the defense. On the issue of "superior orders" this happened when Willy Seibert, Ohlendorf's deputy chief in Einsatzgruppe D, testified.

Under direct examination by his attorney Dr. Hans Gawlik, Seibert explained that he was not responsible for what took place in Soviet Russia because he merely followed orders; after all, he said, he was a soldier and a soldier's first duty is obedience.[60] Under further questioning by the presiding judge, he was asked if he understood that killing unarmed civilians in occupied areas, without trial, is murder under the recognized laws of war (not to mention the laws of humanity). Seibert responded that he "simply didn't know [anymore] where murder start[ed] and murder end[ed]." Killing when one was ordered to do so, Seibert concluded, was not the same as murder.[61]

Unsatisfied, Musmanno probed further into the issue. He asked the defendant a hypothetical question, which, in a criminal trial in the United States, would have been disallowed, but given the unusual combination of American and Continental law employed at Nuremberg he was well within his rights to do.[62] He asked Seibert whether, if he were ordered to, he would shoot his own parents.[63] Seibert stumbled. He could not or would not respond to the question. As Musmanno recalled later, "[T]he faces of the other defendants in the dock dropped. 'Why, you idiot,' they seemed to say, '*that* is our whole case.'"[64] Since Seibert refused to answer the question and Musmanno refused to continue the trial until he did, the court was held in recess until the following day, at which time Seibert was instructed that he must answer the question.[65] The next day Seibert, looking exhausted from a night of no sleep, took the stand.[66] Musmanno repeated the question: "[I]f . . . the military situation made it necessary for you, after receiving an order . . . from a superior officer, to shoot your own parents, would you do so?" Averting his eyes from the other defendants, and in what can only be described as an agonizing moment, Seibert responded, "Mr. President, I would not do so . . . it is inhuman to ask a son to shoot his parents."[67] In one sentence Seibert, for whatever reason unwilling to lie, had destroyed the defense's case. A German soldier is not, as Musmanno phrased it in the judgment, "a fettered slave"; rather, he is a "reasoning agent," and as such he does have some latitude in his actions. Some orders, particularly inhuman ones, he keenly noted, may be disobeyed, and because they could be disobeyed, the only reasonable conclusion he could draw was that the defendants had freely engaged in mass murder.[68]

Willy Seibert's was not the only testimony to contradict Ohlendorf's on the issue of superior orders. In fact, most historians of the Final Solution who deal with the issue of timing point to the testimony of Erwin Schulz, head of Einsatzkommando 5, as proof that Ohlendorf lied about the nature and timing of the order.[69] Of all the defendants to take the stand, only Schulz refused to acknowledge the existence and timing of the *Führerbefehl.* In doing so, he provided the prosecution with an unexpected opportunity to probe into an obvious factual inconsistency, something they did not do, despite their stated aim to provide an accurate account of what happened. Why they did not is another matter. The simple fact is that by the time Schulz took the stand the prosecution was already convinced that Hitler had issued an order to murder all Soviet Jews, and besides, legally the issue was irrelevant to their case. Since Schulz was the only accused to make such a contradictory claim, the preponderance of evidence was clearly on the side of Ohlendorf, who to begin with appeared a far more credible witness than Schultz.

On the stand, Schulz not only refused to acknowledge that he'd carried out any illegal murders (all murders were legal, he argued, because they were preceded by thorough investigations and trials), but more importantly, he disputed the timing, delivery, and nature of the Führer's order. When asked by his attorney about the so-called Hitler-order, Schulz explained that the first time he had heard of it was during his interrogation on Good Friday in 1947, and it was Ralph Wartenberg, the prosecution's chief interrogator, who told him about it.[70] It was not until August 1941, he stated, that he was given the order to murder *all* Jews, including women and children, and then the order was given to him by Otto Rasch, commander of Einsatzgruppe C, not Bruno Streckenbach as Ohlendorf had maintained.[71] Everything Schulz said on this issue of orders was at odds with Ohlendorf's testimony, which should have raised a red flag for the prosecutors. But the truth was, as Arnost Horlik Hochwald's cross-examination of Schulz demonstrated, that the prosecution was reticent to accept Schulz's version of events, preferring instead Ohlendorf's testimony on the existence and timing of the Hitler-order.

> Horlik Hochwald: You made here a differentiation between the Hitler order as testified to by the defendants Ohlendorf and Naumann and the order of Jeckeln which was handed down to you by Rasch?
> Schulz: That is right.
> Horlik Hochwald: . . . will you tell the Tribunal where you see this *colossal* difference between these two orders?[72]

Schulz's inability to respond with any authority undoubtedly suggested to the prosecution that he was lying. Clearly, the prosecutors had made up their minds: the Einsatz- and Kommandoführer knew about their tasks before they were deployed in the summer of 1941 and, in any event, it made no legal difference, as Horlik Hochwald pointed out, whether the order was given in Pretzsch by Streckenbach or a month later by Rasch in the Soviet Union; in either case, it was still Hitler's order and innocent people still lost their lives.[73] In short, even had the prosecution been willing to entertain Schulz's assertions it is unlikely it would have had an impact on their case, the point of which was to prove the defendants had committed murder, and not when they had been ordered to do so. Thus, while historians might lament this lost opportunity to explore a matter crucial to historical understanding, the court found Schulz's testimony less than convincing, which ultimately helped the judges decide his and the other defendants' fate.

Following Ohlendorf's lead, one by one, the defendants took the stand and testified that they were not legally responsible for the mass murder of Soviet Jewry, because they were soldiers, following orders, and as such had no choice but to obey. Thus, it seems that Ohlendorf's detractors are correct in one sense after all.[74] Obedience to orders was a defense strategy, used in a desperate attempt to save the lives of mass murderers who otherwise had not a legal "leg to stand on."

But of course, putative self-defense and superior orders were not the only arguments put forward by a defense team desperate to prove that their clients were not responsible. In fact, scores of different arguments were advanced during the trial, many of which contradicted the two principal defenses. For instance, Franz Six maintained that while he was only a professor and knew nothing of the murder of the Jews, he still tried his best to be released from his duty as head of a *Kommando*.[75] Moreover, he stated that his group, Vorkommando Moscow, was not a killing unit, but an "archival-Kommando," and thus under his command documents were collected, but no "people" were killed.[76] When asked why he did not ask to be released from his duties, Waldemar Klingelhöfer, Six's replacement as head of Vorkommando Moscow, claimed that it was a useless endeavor and therefore he had never even tried.[77] Werner Braune, head of Einsatzkommando 11b, agreed with Klingelhöfer, that it was pointless to evade one's duty, but he also claimed that his actions were no worse than those of the Allies, who had indiscriminately killed thousands of German civilians during the war.[78] Therefore, he reasoned, the Americans were just as guilty of murder as the Germans.[79] Then there were those defendants who claimed they had not killed innocent persons, but only partisans, and then only after thorough investigations. Adolf Ott went so far as to claim that he had not killed any Jews because there were none left by the time he arrived in Russia in January 1942.[80] The most outrageous argument, however, came from those who claimed that had they not done the killing someone else surely would have. But as Musmanno aptly rebutted, "The defendants are accused here for their own individual guilt. No defendant knows what his successor would have done."[81] While unconvincing individually, the combination of all these varying arguments constituted what can only be con-

sidered a "shotgun" defense, which added to the appearance of desperation on the part of the accused and ultimately led the tribunal to
conclude that the defendants were guilty. As a line of defense it was
an utter failure. In fact, defense efforts to coordinate their strategy not
only failed to benefit their clients, but actually helped the prosecution, as did the weak testimony of defendants such as Seibert and
Braune.[82] In the end, the irony is that this defense strategy, which was
intended to save the lives of the accused, did little if anything to help
them win their case. Indeed, it did the opposite. Testimony on the existence of the *Führerbefehl* confirmed in the minds of the prosecution
and the tribunal that these men had committed genocide as ordered
by the most powerful man in Germany. As Musmanno stated emphatically, "there is no doubt . . . the order [to murder the Jews] was
issued by the Head of the State,"[83] and thus it proved to him that Jews
were not killed because they were communists or even because they
were a threat to the Reich; they "were killed simply because [they
were] Jews."[84] As such, the defendants were guilty of Crimes against
Humanity; that is, genocide.

CONCLUSION

What can be concluded both historically and legally about Ohlendorf, the *Führerbefehl,* and Nuremberg? From this example we can see
that war-crimes trials, while interesting history themselves, do not
always provide accurate or complete accounts of the past, nor do they
always enhance the historians' understanding of the events they purport to recount. In this case, the trial actually complicated historical understanding. One reason for this, of course, is that judicial proceedings are adversarial, designed to establish guilt or innocence for a
particular crime, and only incidentally to promote historical truth,
despite the prosecution's contentions to the contrary.[85] By their very
nature criminal trials can act as strong impediments to historical
truth when, by excluding or altering historical facts, a defendant can
demonstrate innocence. Clearly this is what the defense attempted to
do by claiming superior orders at Nuremberg. While due process and
historical accuracy are not necessarily mutually exclusive, the fact is
that prosecutors and historians seldom ask the same questions. For
instance, Ohlendorf and several of his codefendants were ready to admit at trial that they had played a key role in mass murder, because

their defense hinged on the argument that they had acted legally, as soldiers, under direct orders from their superiors. Under Article II of Control Council Law No. 10 (the law under which the defendants were indicted and tried), the Allies precluded "superior orders" as a defense, although it could be "considered in mitigation" when sentencing.[86] Thus, the order to murder Soviet Jewry was legally important for the defense, since it could be ruled exculpatory. But in 1947 the prosecution was never seriously interested in addressing the issue of motivation, and therefore whether the defendants had followed orders or acted on individual initiative was never considered, despite the legal framework for such a defense. On the other hand, the issue of timing is important historically; knowing when and by whom the order was given could help us better understand the overall way in which the Holocaust developed. In the end, however, the court never considered the historical relevance of the matter one way or the other despite the (persistent and futile) hopes of defense counsel and, one might add, historians. This should also remind us that questions and issues that we privilege today in our historical analyses of the Third Reich are not always the same as the ones that the court or prosecution emphasized at the time. Of course, all of this is not to suggest that all trial testimony is untrue and therefore unworthy of historical consideration; but it is certainly a warning that testimony should be evaluated carefully, in the context of the trial it comes from, and that we as historians should make clear distinctions among the legal process, legal fact, and historical accuracy, especially when it comes to the use of trial testimony as historical evidence.[87]

Ultimately, for historians the issue of the timing of the Hitler-order is significant. A decisive date would settle an extremely contentious issue; more importantly, it would better explain the origins of the Holocaust and Hitler's role in it—but legally, judges can consider only the facts as they appear in court and not what actually happened. Given the paucity of facts available to the prosecution and the tribunal, when Ohlendorf told about the existence of the *Führerbefehl*, the tribunal was unable to gauge his level of truthfulness, and, in any case, it really did not matter to them. They knew from other evidence (mainly the reports of the Einsatzgruppen) that these men had ordered, witnessed, and participated in the mass slaughter of about three-quarters of a million innocent people. When it came right down to it, because Ohlendorf's testimony appeared credible, no one ever questioned him about its veracity. Given this situation, the only reasonable legal conclusion for the tribunal was that his testimony corroborated the evidence and the evidence corroborated his testimony: the murder of the Jews was, in the court's judgment, the result of an order by Hitler given prior to the deployment of the mobile killing units, in the spring or early summer of 1941. Thus, while it is tempting to accept Ohlendorf's testimony as accurate, to do so is historically dangerous without considering the context in which that testimony was given.

NOTES

1. At the trial of the Einsatzgruppen leaders, the order to murder Soviet Jewry was at various times referred to as the "Hitler-order," the "Hitler-befehl," the "Führerbefehl," and the "Führer-order." In this paper, all of these various forms are used.

2. Initially there were two schools of thought concerning the origins of the Final Solution. Intentionalists such as Lucy Dawidowcz, *The War against the Jews* (New York, 1975), and Gerald Fleming, *Hitler und die Endlösung: "Es ist des Führers Wunsch . . ."* (Wiesbaden, 1982), strongly believe that there is a clear link between Hitler's early anti-Semitic ideology and his later anti-Semitic practice; in other words, they see a straight path from Hitler's hatred of the Jews to his policy of "extermination." Proponents of this view support their argument with Hitler's writings and speeches that highlight his early commitment to "annihilate" the Jews. Hitler hated the Jews, he repeatedly stated in his speeches and writings, and the Jews were eventually murdered; therefore, they argue, his intention had always been murder. This view highlights the important role of Hitler in initiating the murder of European Jewry. More moderate intentionalists such as Karl Dietrich Bracher, *The German Dictatorship* (New York, 1966), and Eberhard Jäckel, *Hitlers Weltanschauung: Entwurf einer Herrschaft* (Stuttgart, 1971), however, do not focus so much on the idea of a "blueprint" for murder as they do on the centrality of anti-Semitism in Hitler's world view. They see the murder of the Jews as part of Hitler's long-range goals; each policy he implemented, from the 1933 boycott to the invasion of the Soviet Union in 1941, was part of his overall aim to achieve a Europe free of Jews. Functionalists, on the other hand, ascribe a lesser role to Hitler while emphasizing the function of the SS and other organizations in the decision to murder European Jewry. Adherents to this view argue the policy of "extermination" was developed piecemeal and in stages. Gradually, as the Nazis consolidated their power, Jewish policy became increasingly radicalized,

until 1941 and the invasion of the Soviet Union, when it was decided the best way to solve the "Jewish problem" was through mass murder. For classic statements on the functionalist position see Karl Schleunes, *The Twisted Road to Auschwitz: Nazi Policy toward German Jews 1933–1939* (Urbana, Ill., 1990), and Uwe Dietrich Adam, *Judenpolitik im Dritten Reich* (Düsseldorf, 1972). In recent years the issue has become less polarized, tempered by such nuanced interpretations as those by Christopher Browning, who classifies himself as a "moderate functionalist," and Phillip Burrin, who calls his approach "conditional intentionalism." For elaboration and explanation of the terms initially coined by Tim Mason, see his "Intention and Explanation: A Current Controversy about the Interpretation of National Socialism," in *Der Führerstaat: Mythos und Realität. Studien zur Struktur und Politik des Dritten Reiches,* ed. Gerhard Hirschfeld and Lothar Kettenacker (Stuttgart, 1981), 23–40. See also Ian Kershaw, *The Nazi Dictatorship: Problems and Perspectives of Interpretation,* 3rd ed. (New York, 1993), 80–107; Christopher Browning, "Beyond 'Intentionalism' and 'Functionalism': The Decision for the Final Solution Reconsidered," in *The Path to Genocide: Essays on Launching the Final Solution* (New York, 1992), 86–121, idem, "The Decision Concerning the Final Solution," in *Fateful Months: Essays on the Emergence of the Final Solution,* rev. ed. (New York, 1991), 8–38; and Michael R. Marrus, *The Holocaust in History* (Toronto, 1987), 31–54.

3. For a full accounting of the debate about timing, see especially Alfred Streim, "The Tasks of the SS Einsatzgruppen," in *Simon Wiesenthal Center Annual* 4 (1987): 309–28; and Helmut Krausnick and Alfred Streim, "Correspondence," in *Simon Wiesenthal Center Annual* 6 (1989): 311–46. See also Helmut Krausnick et al., *Anatomy of the SS State* (Frogmore, England, 1965, 1973), 59–75; Alfred Streim, *Die Behandlung sowjetischer Kriegsgefangener im "Fall Barbarossa": Eine Dokumentation* (Heidelberg, 1981), 74–93; and idem, "Zur Eröffnung des allgemeinen Judenvernichtungsbefehl gegenüber den Einsatzgruppen," in *Der Mord an den Juden im Zweiten Weltkrieg: Entschlußbildung und Verwirklichung,* ed. Eberhard Jäckel and Jürgen Rohwer (Stuttgart, 1985), 107–19. For various positions on the issue of timing and the role of the Einsatzgruppen in the Final Solution, see Browning, *Fateful Months,* 8–38; Helmut Krausnick and Hans-Heinrich Wilhelm, *Die Truppe des Weltanschaunngskrieges: Die Einsatzgruppen der Sicherheitspolizei und des SD, 1938–1942* (Stuttgart, 1981), 150–72, 622–37; Peter Longerich, "Vom Massenmord zur 'Endlösung': Die Erschießungen von jüdischen Zivilisten in den ersten Monaten des Ostfeldzuges im Kontext des nationalsozialistischen Judenmords," in *Zwei Wege nach Moskau: Vom Hitler-Stalin-Pakt zum "Unternehmen Barbarossa,"* ed. Bernd Wegner (Munich, 1991), 251–4; Philippe Burrin, *Hitler and the Jews: The Genesis of the Holocaust* (London, 1989), 93–113; Ronald Head-

land, "The Einsatzgruppen: The Question of Their Initial Operations," *Holocaust and Genocide Studies* 4, no. 4 (1989): 401–12; Yaacov Lozowick, "Rollbahn Mord: The Early Activities of Einsatzgruppe C," *Holocaust and Genocide Studies* 2, no. 2 (1987): 221–41; and most recently Ralf Ogorreck, *Die Einsatzgruppen und die "Genesis der Endlösung"* (Berlin, 1996), whose entire book addresses this issue.

4. For example, both Ohlendorf's attorney and the presiding judge in the trial referred to the order as fact. See Eidesstattlich Versicherung des Rudolf Aschenauer, 11.11.1949, N642 (Aschenauer), box 62, Bundesarchiv-Militärarchiv (BA/MA from here forward), Freiburg. See also conversation between Michael Musmanno and James Heath, 14 October 1947, in *The United States of America v. Otto Ohlendorf et al.*, National Archives Microfilm Publication M895, roll 2, 636–7 (from here forward simply *Trial*, roll, page).

5. On this issue see Lawrence Douglas, "Wartime Lies: Securing the Holocaust in Law and Literature," in *The Holocaust's Ghost: Writings on Art, Politics, Law and Education*, ed. F. C. Decoste and Bernard Schwartz (Edmonton, Alberta, 2000), 17–18.

6. Ibid.

7. This short, six-week time frame is at the heart of the issue of timing.

8. Douglas, "Wartime Lies," 17–18.

9. For example, Telford Taylor, chief of council for war crimes, wrote that one of the purposes for publishing the records of the twelve subsequent Nuremberg trials was "[t]o promote the interest of historical truth. . . ." See Taylor, *Final Report to the Secretary of the Army on the Nuernberg War Crimes Trials under Control Council Law No. 10* (Washington, D.C., 1949), 101.

10. Telford Taylor, quoted in Headland, *Messages of Murder*, 177. For a discussion of the historical significance of the Einsatzgruppen reports, see Ronald Headland, *Messages of Murder: A Study of the Reports of the Einsatzgruppen of the Security Police and the Security Service, 1941–1943* (Rutherford, N.J., 1992), pp. 177–204.

11. Lawrence Douglas disagrees. He argues that war-crimes trials can serve a didactic end. See Lawrence Douglas, *The Memory of Judgment: Making Law and History in the Trials of the Holocaust* (New Haven, Conn., 2001), 1–7.

12. Helge Grabitz long ago called for the continuation of National Socialist trials in order to punish those who were responsible, as well as to better understand the historical facts brought out in the trials. See Helge Grabitz, "Problems of Nazi Trials in the Federal Republic of Germany," *Holocaust and Genocide Studies* 2, no. 3 (1988): 209.

13. As Saul Friedländer has observed, not until all of the evidence has been considered (including German, Jewish, and Soviet sources) "will it be

possible for a more or less complete picture . . . to appear." Friedländer, "Introduction," in Burrin, *Hitler and the Jews,* 5–6.

14. For example, Streim writes that "Ohlendorf lied when deception was useful, and he spoke the truth when honesty was profitable." See Streim, "Reply to Helmut Krausnick," 338–9.

15. Letter from Lieutenant Colonel Smith Brookhart Jr. to Colonel Amen, 24 October 1945. National Archives Microfilm Publication M1270 (Interrogation Records Prepared for War Crimes Proceedings at Nuremberg, 1945–1947, OCCPAC Interrogations), roll 13, 1–2 (from here forward simply M1270, roll, page).

16. Ohlendorf's recollection regarding the leaders of the four groups was incorrect. He mistakenly identified Max Thomas as the leader of Group C when the units were first formed in Pretzsch, but it was Otto Rasch who led Einsatzgruppe C in June 1941. Ohlendorf later corrected this error in an affidavit. See affidavit of Otto Ohlendorf, 5 November 1945 (PS 2620), in *Trial,* Prosecution Documents, roll 11, frames 0044–5.

17. Vernehmung des Otto Ohlendorf by Lieutenant Colonel Smith W. Brookhart Jr. and Colonel John H. Amen, 26 November 1945, in M1270, roll 13, 13.

18. Interrogation Summary, 24 October 1945, in M1270, roll 13, 3.

19. Vernehmung des Otto Ohlendorf by Lieutenant Colonel Smith W. Brookhart Jr., October 25, 1945, in M1270, roll 13, 1–2.

20. M1270, roll 13, 8; and affidavit of Otto Ohlendorf (PS 2620), 5 November 1945, in *Trial,* roll 8, frame 0054, in which Ohlendorf stated: "Im Juni 1941 wurde ich von Himmler bestimmt, eine der Einsatzgruppen zu fuehren, die demals gebildet wurden, um den deutschen Armeen in russischen Feld zug zu folgen. Ich war der Chef der Einsatzgruppe D . . . Himmler erklaerte, dass ein wichtiger teil unserer Aufgabe in der Beseitigung von Juden, Frauen, Maennern und Kindern, und Kommunistischen Funktionaeren bestuende. Ich wurde etwa vier wochen vorher ueber den Angriff auf Russland benachrichtigt."

21. Richard Breitman argues that information concerning the murder of the Jews in the Soviet Union was shared on a "need-to-know basis" only, and then only orally. Given Ohlendorf's high position it is possible that he met with Himmler some weeks prior to the invasion. See Richard Breitman, "Himmler and the 'Terrible Secret' among the Executioners," in *The Impact of Western Nationalisms,* ed. Jehuda Reinharz and George L. Mosse (London, 1991), 77–97.

22. The Soviets did not participate in the planning or preparation of this trial, despite having been asked by the Americans.

23. This idea was confirmed by Michael Marrus, who wrote, "'Intentionalism,' it may be supposed, was born in Nuremberg in 1945 when

American prosecutors first presented Nazi war crimes as a carefully orchestrated conspiracy, launched together with the war itself. American legal experts hoped to prove that there had been a deliberate *plan* to commit horrendous atrocities as well as other breaches of international law. . . ." in
Michael Marrus, "The History of the Holocaust: A Survey of Recent Literature," *Journal of Modern History* 59 (1987): 120.

24. For example, see interrogation of Otto Ohlendorf by Lieutenant
Colonel Smith W. Brookhart Jr., 24 October 1945, in M1270, roll 13, 14–
16. See also Interrogation Summary of Otto Ohlendorf, 24 October 1945,
in M1270, roll 13, 3, in which Ohlendorf claims his job was to "prevent
cruelties," one example of which was safeguarding the possessions of the victims until after they were executed; another was ensuring that the victims did
not have to wait an excessive amount of time before they were shot. This, he
assured Brookhart, was done to prevent them from dwelling on their fate.

25. Vernehmung des Otto Ohlendorf by Lieutenant Colonel Smith
W. Brookhart Jr., 27 October 1945, and Brief of Interrogation of Otto
Ohlendorf by Lieutenant Colonel S. W. Brookhart, 29 October 1945, in
M1270, roll 13.

26. Brian A. Grossman, "Testing Witness Reliability," *Criminal Law
Quarterly* 5 (1962–63): 321.

27. Ibid., 316–7.

28. Ibid., 316. Compare with Ralf Ogorreck's assessment of Ohlendorf's testimony in *Die Einsatzgruppen und die "Genesis der Endlösung,"* 48.

29. On this issue see Headland, "The *Einsatzgruppen:* The Question
of Their Initial Operations," 401–12, who argues that even if the so-called
Führerbefehl was not given before Operation Barbarossa, at the very least
the leaders of the Einsatzgruppen generally knew in June 1941 that their
task in the Soviet Union was to murder Jews. Breitman's interpretation
agrees with this conclusion; Breitman, "Himmler and the 'Terrible Secret'
among the Executioners," 80–1.

30. Taylor, *Final Report,* 60.

31. Opinion and Judgement of the Tribunal, 8 April 1948, in *Trial,* 132.

32. Telford Taylor, *The Anatomy of the Nuremberg Trials: A Personal
Memoir* (Toronto, 1992), 246.

33. G. M. Gilbert, "The Anglo-American Prosecution Concludes, 3
January 1946," in *Nuremberg Diary* (reprint: New York, 1995), 101; and
Taylor, *Anatomy,* 248.

34. For example, see his interrogation of November 15, 1946.
Vernehmung von Otto Ohlendorf durch Mr. Wartenberg, 15 November
1946, in NARA Microfilm Publication M1019 (Records of the United
States Nuernberg War Crimes Trials Interrogations, 1946–1949), roll 50,
20–1, and his affidavit of April 1947, in which he asserted, "On the basis of

orders which were given by former Brigadefuehrer Streckenbach, Chief of Amt I of the RSHA, by order of the head of the RSHA, to the Chiefs of the Einsatzgruppen and the Kommandofuehrers at the time of the formation of the Einsatzgruppen in Pretzsch [sic] (in Saxony) and which were given by the Reichsfuehrer SS to the leaders and men of the Einsatzgruppen and Einsatzkommandos who were assembled in Nikolajew in September 1941 a number of undesirable elements composed of Russians, Gypsies, and Jews and others, were executed in the area detailed to me." See Affidavit of Otto Ohlendorf, 2 April 1947 (NO 2856), in *Trial,* Prosecution Documents, roll 11, frames 0797–8. See also Testimony of Otto Ohlendorf, 14 October 1947, in *Trial,* Prosecution Documents, roll 2, 631–7.

35. Grosman, "Testing Witness Reliability," 324–5.

36. See Arraignment, 15 and 22 September 1947, in *Trials of War Criminals before the Nuernberg Military Tribunals under Control Council Law No. 10,* vol. 4 (Washington, D.C., 1951), 23–9. This became the standard response of war criminals to charges of mass murder. As Hannah Arendt aptly observed at the trial of Adolf Eichmann in Israel when he pled the same, "In what sense then did he [Eichmann] think he was guilty? In the long cross-examination of the accused . . . neither the defense nor the prosecution nor, finally, any of the three judges ever bothered to ask him this obvious question." The same can be said of the Einsatzgruppen trial. See Hannah Arendt, *Eichmann in Jerusalem: A Report on the Banality of Evil.* (New York, 1965) p. 21.

37. The decision to call no witnesses was Ferencz's. He reasoned that because very few individuals survived the murderous actions of the Einsatzgruppen it might be difficult to locate those who did. Moreover, he felt witnesses were "unreliable . . . those who would testify against any Nazi defendant would be blinded by rage and pain. Besides," he emphasized, "I didn't need them. I was going to hang the murderous gang by their own documents." Letter from Benjamin Ferencz to Hilary Earl, 27 February 1997. On the issue of the use of the Einsatzgruppen reports as legal evidence at the trial see Headland, *Messages of Murder,* 159–76.

38. Headland, *Messages of Murder,* 165.

39. Brief for the Prosecution, Analysis of the Defense Presented on Behalf of the Accused, February 1948, in *Trial,* roll 29, frame 0014. On the issue of a common defense, see Ogorreck, Die Einsatzgruppen und die "Genesis der Endlösung," 53–5, who points to evidence that strongly suggests Ohlendorf did pressure the other defendants to plead a common defense of "superior orders" and "putative necessity." See also Klaus-Michael Mallmann, "Die Türöffner der 'Enlösung,'" in *Die Gestapo im Zweiten Weltkrieg,* ed. Gerhard Paul and Klaus-Michael Mallmann (Darmstadt, 2000), 437–44.

40. It was impossible for Aschenauer to argue otherwise, given the existence of the reports and the tribunal's ruling that they were authentic.

41. George P. Fletcher, *Basic Concepts of Criminal Law* (New York, 1998), 88. Legally, justification pertains to the permissibility of an act that violates the law. If the act is illegal, but was carried out for self-defense, the act is justifiable and must prevail legally. On the other hand, the legal concept of "excuse" speaks to the culpability of the perpetrator of the criminal act. For example, if the perpetrator acted under duress in carrying out a criminal act, he cannot be considered personally responsible for his act. On this issue of justification versus excuse see also George P. Fletcher, "The Right and the Reasonable," in *Justification and Excuse: Comparative Perspectives I,* ed. Albin Eser et al. (Freiburg, 1987), 76–81. For German perspectives, see Winfried Hassemer, "Rechtfertigung und Entschuldigung im Strafrecht: Thesen und Kommentare," in Eser et al., *Justification and Excuse,* 175–227; and Claus Roxin, "Rechtfertigungs- und Entschuldigungs- gründe in Abgrenzung von sonstigen Strafausschließungsgründen," also in *Justification and Excuse,* 230–62.

42. Paul H. Robinson, "Causing the Conditions of One's Own Defense: A Study in the Limits of Theory in Criminal Law Doctrine," in Eser et al., *Justification and Excuse,* 660 n. 3.

43. Rudolf Aschenauer, Opening Statement for the Defendant Ohlendorf, 6 October 1947, in *Trials of War Criminals,* 60. German law has long recognized that a perpetrator may not be punished if his actions were committed because of "confusion, fear or fright." This does not alter the wrongfulness of the act, but legally it does erase personal blame. On this issue see Albin Eser, "Justification and Excuse: A Key Issue in the Concept of Crime," in *Justification and Excuse,* 31 n. 19, 51–6.

44. The legal basis for "necessity" comes from the notion that in doing so the action benefits society as a whole. For an explanation of the history of "legal necessity" see Fletcher, *Basic Concepts of Criminal Law,* 138–42.

45. Robinson, "Causing the Conditions of One's Own Defense," 661 n. 5.

46. Rudolf Aschenauer, Opening Statement for the Defendant Ohlendorf, 6 October 1947, *Trials of War Criminals,* 54–5. On the issue of putative self-defense in law see Fletcher, *Basic Concepts of Criminal Law,* 88–91.

47. As Dr. Willi Heim, attorney for Paul Blobel, contended in his opening statement, had these men disobeyed their orders, they would have been subjected to military court martial and in all likelihood lost their own lives; thus they had no choice but to follow orders. See Willi Heim, Opening Statement for the Defendant Blobel, 6 October 1947, in *Trials of War Criminals,* 85.

48. On the issue of the legal defense of superior orders see Aubrey M.

Daniel, "The Defense of Superior Orders," *University of Richmond Law Review* 7, no. 3 (spring 1973): 477–509, who examines the case of American Lieutenant William L. Calley Jr. for his role in the My Lai Massacre in 1968.

49. Ohlendorf Document 39, Transcription of Radio Broadcast of Joseph Stalin, 3 July 1941, in *Trial*, roll 26, 567.

50. Rudolf Aschenauer, quoted in Opinion and Judgement of the Tribunal, 8 April 1948, in *Trial*, 69.

51. Opinion and Judgement of the Tribunal, 10 April 1948, in *Trial*, 102.

52. Testimony of Otto Ohlendorf, 8 October 1947, in *Trial*, roll 2, 522.

53. Discussion between Michael Musmanno and Rudolf Aschenauer, 15 October 1947, in *Trial*, roll 2, 759–65.

54. Ibid., 760.

55. Ibid., Opinion and Judgement of the Tribunal, 10 April 1948, in *Trial*, 60, 75.

56. Testimony of Werner Braune, 26 November 1947, in *Trial*, roll 4, 3069–72.

57. *Trial*, 765; Opinion and Judgement of the Tribunal, 8 April 1948, in *Trial*, 70, 75.

58. Later he contradicted himself on this issue, testifying that he forbade men who were emotionally unable to cope with the task of murder from carrying out executions. Some were so traumatized by their job, he said, he sent them back to Berlin for reassignment. Importantly, no one questioned Ohlendorf on this issue. Testimony of Otto Ohlendorf, 8 October 1947, in *Trial*, roll 2, 523, and 14 October 1947, in *Trial*, 592. Since there is neither documentary evidence nor cross-examination of this issue, it is impossible to know for certain whether the men of the Einsatzgruppen found themselves in the same or similar position as Police Battalion 101. On this subject see Christopher R. Browning, *Ordinary Men: Reserve Battalion 101 and the Final Solution in Poland* (New York, 1992).

59. Testimony of Otto Ohlendorf, 15 October 1947, in *Trial*, roll 2, 740–52.

60. Gawlik was to become the head of the Koordinierungsstelle zur Förderung des Rechtsschutzstelle für die deutschen Gefangenen im Ausland, an organization that was founded in 1949 with the establishment of the German Basic Law to help so-called "prisoners" convicted by foreign governments.

61. Michael Musmanno, *The Eichmann Kommandos* (London, 1961), 128.

62. Musmanno took every available opportunity to directly question witnesses during the trial. In his memoirs he noted that his role was as both judge and jury. See ibid., 128.

63. Questioning of defendant Willy Seibert by Michael Musmanno, 19 November 1947, in *Trial*, roll 4, 2671–3.

64. Musmanno, *Eichmann Kommandos,* 129.

65. Questioning of defendant Willy Seibert by Michael Musmanno, 19 November 1947, in *Trial,* roll 4, 2674.

66. Musmanno, *Eichmann Kommandos,* 132.

67. Testimony of Willy Seibert, 20 November 1947, in *Trial,* roll 4, 2676. See also Opinion and Judgement of the Tribunal, 8 April 1948, in *Trial,* 79–81.

68. Opinion and Judgement of the Tribunal, 8 April 1948, in *Trial,* 77; Musmanno to defendant Seibert, 20 November 1947, in *Trial,* roll 4, 2676.

69. For example, see Ogorreck, *Die Einsatzgruppen und die Genesis die Endlösung,* 52; Streim, "Tasks of the SS Einsatzgruppen," 214; Browning, *Fateful Months,* 17, 19; and Burrin, *Hitler and the Jews,* 101–4. Interestingly, historians have overlooked the testimony of Adolf Ott, who tried in vain to make the distinction between the Hitler-order to murder Soviet Jews and the Hitler-order to murder all European Jews. See Testimony of Adolf Ott, 10 December 1947, in *Trial,* roll 5, 3716–62. Even Telford Taylor, the chief of counsel for war crimes, did not understand the difference between partial and total genocide, reporting that, "The notorious 'final solution of the Jewish question,' the objective of which was nothing less than extermination of European Jewry, was the basis of the 'Einsatz case.'" See Taylor, *Final Report,* 69.

70. Testimony of Erwin Schulz, 17 October 1947, in *Trial,* roll 2, 933.

71. Testimony of Erwin Schulz, 21 October 1947, in *Trial,* 1073.

72. Ibid., 1077.

73. In response to Schulz's claim the prosecutors wrote, "The evidence shows that the *Einsatzkommando* 5, under the command of the defendant Schulz, participated in the program of genocide, as set forth in the Fuehrer-order." Furthermore, "not only the evidence in the Record, but also Schulz's own statements on the witness stand prove that this defense of his is entirely untrue and cannot be believed." "Trial Brief for the United States of America against Erwin Schulz, January 1948," in John Mendelsohn, ed., *The Holocaust 17: Punishing the Perpetrators of the Holocaust. The Brandt, Pohl and Ohlendorf Cases* (New York, 1982), 8–9, 17.

74. Streim, "Tasks of the SS Einsatzgruppen," 313.

75. Testimony of Franz Six, 24 October 1947, in *Trial,* roll 3, 1325–35.

76. Ibid., 1345–52.

77. Testimony of Waldemar Klingelhöfer, 11 December 1947, in *Trial,* roll 5, 3811–2.

78. Testimony of Werner Braune, 25 November 1947, in *Trial,* roll 4, 3053.

79. Ibid., 3042–4.

80. Testimony of Adolf Ott, 11 December 1947, in *Trial,* roll 5, 3782.

81. Opinion and Judgement of the Tribunal, 10 April 1948, in *Trial,* roll 96.

82. On the issue of defense strategies and coordination, see, for example, Ogorreck, *Die Einsatzgruppen und die "Genesis der Endlösung,"* 54–5; and Streim, "Tasks of the SS-Einsatzgruppen," 313. Both argue that Ohlendorf tried to persuade his codefendants to testify as he did.

83. Discussion between Musmanno and Heath, 14 October 1947, in *Trial,* roll 2, 636–7.

84. Opinion and Judgement of the Tribunal, 8 April 1948, in *Trial,* 70.

85. For example, Telford Taylor, chief of council for the prosecution of war criminals, wrote that one of the purposes of publishing the records of the twelve subsequent Nuremberg trials was "[t]o promote the interest of historical truth. . . ." See Taylor, *Final Report,* 101.

86. In fact the tribunal did consider the issue of superior orders in its judgment, but it found that the defendants were not compelled to act and therefore had a measure of independence in their actions. Control Council Law No. 10, 20 December 1945, quoted in *Trials of War Criminals,* xvi–xix. To a degree, Control Council Law No. 10 was based on established principles of international law that held that individuals, and not abstract states, were responsible for criminal acts, especially murder. In this sense the defense of following superior orders was ruled inadmissable by the judges of the IMT and subsequently by Tribunal IIa (later renamed Tribunal II) in the Einsatzgruppen case.

87. Goldhagen writes, "[I]t is easy to demonstrate that [the perpetrators] do lie rampantly, by word and by omission, in order to minimize their physical and cognitive involvement in the mass slaughters. Because of this, the only methodological position that makes sense is to discount *all* self-exculpating testimony that finds no corroboration from other sources." For elaboration on this issue see, Daniel Jonah Goldhagen, *Hitler's Willing Executioners: Ordinary Germans and the Holocaust* (New York, 1996), 467.

Rebecca Wittmann

Legitimating the Criminal State: Former Nazi Judges and the Distortion of Justice at the Frankfurt Auschwitz Trial, 1963–65

BETWEEN 1945 AND 1992, WEST GERMAN JUDICIAL AUTHORITIES INVES-
tigated over 100,000 suspects allegedly involved in Nazi crimes. Of
these, only 6,487 were tried and convicted.[1] Of all 6,487 defendants,
13 were sentenced to death, 163 to life imprisonment (a murder conviction), 6,197 to temporary prison terms, and 114 to fines.[2] These
sentences handed down in postwar West German Nazi trials were extremely lenient, and generally did not reflect the massive crime of the
systematic mass murder of the Holocaust. Some argue that judges in
postwar West Germany found ways to reduce convictions and sentences out of fear that they would be investigated as former members
of the Nazi party, or worse, because of persistent and lingering Nazi
beliefs.[3] Others contend that it was the result of an extreme reluctance on the parts of the government, the Ministry of Justice, local
courts, and the German public to try the "murderers in their midst."[4]
These arguments may hold true for certain district courts and states
where ex-Nazis held positions of authority and influence. However,
they are generalizations that do not present a complete picture of the
complexities of trying Nazi criminals in postwar Germany using the
West German criminal justice system.

I would argue that the stipulations of the West German penal
code and the pretrial and trial testimony of the former judges whom
the SS sent to Auschwitz in 1943 in the form of a special investigative
commission (*Sonderkommission*) to investigate corruption among
the guards, demonstrate that the limitations of the law tied the hands
of the prosecution and the judges at the Auschwitz Trial, making

them dependent on the same standards of illegality used by the Nazis themselves when investigating criminal activity in the camps. This legitimated the criminal Nazi state and set a standard for illegal behavior in the 1960s Frankfurt courtroom that eerily echoed the laws of the Third Reich. The statements of these judges about the brutality of such defendants as Wilhelm Boger, known as the "Devil of Birkenau" and accused of torturing thousands of people, shifted the focus in the courtroom away from Nazi genocide to individual acts of cruelty, suggesting that Nazi orders were more acceptable and "legal," and therefore that those who herded thousands into the gas chambers were not as guilty as those who shot prisoners without a legal death sentence handed down by Nazi desk officials in Berlin. Some defendants benefited from such a distortion of justice, as they were convicted only of aiding and abetting murder for standing on the selection ramp. This was the result for Robert Mulka and Karl Höcker, the defendants who had occupied the most senior positions of anyone on trial as adjutants to commanders Höss and Baer, respectively. These SS witnesses signified a turning point of sorts in the trial, for only the most grotesque and shocking of crimes were heavily punished, while mass murder conducted through the machinery of genocide, the gas chambers, and the crematoria was pushed into the background.

The transcripts, audio tapes and most especially the extensive pretrial files of postwar West German Nazi trials paint a vivid picture of Germany's judicial attempt at *Vergangenheitsbewältigung* (coming to terms with the past), and exhibit the deficiencies of the law in rendering a fair judgment for the crimes of the Holocaust. The Auschwitz Trial took place in Frankfurt am Main, West Germany, between December 1963 and August 1965. The trial of twenty Auschwitz perpetrators by the public prosecutor's office of the state of Hesse represented a cross-section of criminals who participated in the atrocities at the camp between 1940 and 1945, and lasted more than 180 days. It involved approximately 400 witnesses and produced 30,000 pages of files, not including the trial record itself, which is now being transcribed from audiotape. The trial was not the first criminal proceeding against Nazi perpetrators (and one prisoner *Kapo*) in Germany. After the Nuremberg trials of the 1940s, West German state prosecution offices began taking up cases in the early 1950s. Only in the late 1950s, though, did these trials really address the "Final Solution" and receive widespread public attention.[5] They were not conducted according to the international criminal laws established at Nuremberg, but according to the West German criminal justice system. The Germans decided to use their own penal code (StGB—*Strafgesetzbuch*) for numerous reasons. Specifically, the German penal code had existed since 1871 (the year of German unification) and was in place throughout the Nazi period. The existence of these laws made murder illegal throughout the Third Reich and circumvented the harshly criticized use of retroactive or ex post facto laws. In addition, it allowed the new democratic West German state to demonstrate its ability to deal with its own past through its own laws. And finally, it removed the politics present at Nuremberg and made the activities of former Nazis a purely criminal matter.[6]

The West German criminal code was subject to many restrictions that hindered the state in its attempt to render justice for crimes of such magnitude. Briefly, there were three basic problems with the use of this penal code. First, the murder charge stipulated that the prosecution prove the subjective inner motivation of the defendant. Elements of intent in paragraph 211 included sadism, lust for murder, sexual drive for killing, treachery, malicious intent, cruelty, and finally, base motives (which the postwar German courts defined for the Nazi trials as "race hatred"). Second, the distinction between perpetrator and accomplice in the penal code (paragraphs 47–9) specified that the primary perpetrator must show individual initiative and knowledge of the illegality of the act. This meant that the state had to prove beyond doubt that each defendant had acted individually and with personal initiative in order to be convicted of murder. Otherwise, he or she could be convicted only of aiding and abetting murder, which generally received a much lighter sentence. So, despite the illegality of the orders to kill at Auschwitz (as was determined by expert testimony at Nuremberg), the lack of personal initiative led to a lesser charge.[7]

Third, and finally, the statute of limitations prevented the courts from using the manslaughter charge. Beginning in the late 1950s, the *Verjährungsdebatte,* or "debate on the statute of limitations," in the federal parliament dominated political discussion of Nazi trials in West Germany. This complex controversy dealt with the limitations on murder (twenty years), manslaughter (fifteen years), and aiding and abetting charges, and was at the heart of the early years of West German attempts to deal with the Nazi past. The courts were very much at the mercy of the decisions made in parliament, and they could

charge the defendants only according to the decisions brought down
in the *Verjährungsdebatte*. This meant that in 1963, for example,
manslaughter was no longer an option as a charge, which made the
state's task much more difficult because it was limited to proving
murder or the far lesser charge of aiding and abetting. The debate had
an enormous effect on the proceeding of the trial, and the decision to
disallow the manslaughter charge represented a huge disadvantage to
the prosecution, which, headed by Attorney General Fritz Bauer, had
the unique goal of putting the entire "Auschwitz complex" on trial.

The former SS judges who testified at the Auschwitz Trial—Konrad Morgen (head of the special commission), Gerhard Wiebeck, and
Wilhelm Reimers—were part of a "Special Commission and Police
Court" in Krakow. Reichsführer SS Himmler sent them to Auschwitz
at the end of 1943 to investigate alleged corrupt practices by SS guards.
This included the theft of valuables from new transports (stored in
the "Canada bunker" of the camp) and excessive cruelty and murder
not ordered by the officials of the RSHA (Reichssicherheitshauptamt, the Central Security Department of the Reich) or the WVHA
(Wirtschafts und Verwaltungshauptamt, the SS Economic and Administrative Office) in Berlin.[8]

The accepted norms of prisoner treatment at Auschwitz were preserved in document form and used in the Nuremberg trials. The
prosecutors in Frankfurt obtained these documents and included
them in the indictment of the trial. The official laws of the concentration camps showed which of the defendants' actions were allow-
able and which would be investigated by someone like Morgen, who
was concerned with guards who went above and beyond orders in
their actions. For example, the indictment included a statement from
October 10, 1933, by Theodore Eicke, at that time the commander
of the Dachau concentration camp. In 1934 he was promoted to Inspector of Concentration Camps. The excerpt not only listed various
laws regarding the crimes that would lengthen or intensify the imprisonment terms in Dachau, but also stipulated the punishment
that would be inflicted. For example, paragraph 6 stated:

[w]ith eight days strict arrest and with twenty-five cane lashes at the
beginning and the end of punishment, the following crimes are to
be punished:
1. whoever makes critical or mocking remarks to an SS officer,
or purposely fails to salute, or through any kind of behavior makes

it known that he won't submit to the force of discipline and order. . . .[9]

The list of paragraphs also included more serious crimes, such as instigation of political insurrection and mutiny or sabotage, which were to be punished by hanging or shooting (or both!).

A memo sent out to the political departments of the camps (where prisoners suspected of communist activity or sabotage were interrogated) listed the types of punishments that were enforceable in the case of "criminal" behavior within the camp. These regulations directly affected defendants from the political department, particularly Boger, Pery Broad, Klaus Dylewski, Johann Schobert, and Hans Stark. The presence of these regulations in the indictment set a standard for determining what constituted individual initiative. They applied to prisoners who were sentenced to death or to solitary confinement, and they clearly fell within acceptable Nazi practices of "intensified interrogations" (*verschärfte Vernehmungen*). The court would therefore presumably not have considered these actions by a defendant to qualify as sadistic, excessive behavior. The relevant paragraph states:

> Arrest will be carried out in a cell, with harsh conditions, and water and bread. Every four days the prisoner will get warm food. Work detail includes hard physical labor or especially dirty work under special supervision.
>
> As extra punishment the following come into consideration:
>
> Exercise drills, corporal punishment (beatings), withholding of mail, deprivation of food, hard quarters, tying to a post, reprimands and warnings. All punishments will be recorded.
>
> Arrest and hard labor will prolong protective custody by not less than eight weeks; secondary punishment will prolong protective custody by not less than four weeks.
>
> Prisoners in solitary confinement will not be released within a foreseeable period.[10]

These special regulations became standard for all of the camps. The inclusion of these laws in the indictment gave the courts a model of what was considered acceptable in the camps; according to historian Martin Broszat,

> the object of [these] regulations was to lay down in writing and to stress that caning could not be carried out arbitrarily by individual guards and that it was a regular form of punishment. Because the

caning was carried out by several SS men the ill-treatment became impersonal and anonymous and every member of the guard formations was accustomed from the beginning to this act which he might at any time be ordered to perform.[11]

Breaking the chain of command was not tolerated. In fact, as we will see from the SS investigation into illegal acts, breaking the rules in favor of more violent behavior was punished more harshly than refusing to carry out a task at all. Guards were not supposed to sink to the level of depraved sadists. In order to prevent this, the regulations included details of permissible torture in "intensified interrogations." For example, "hits with a leather whip in quick succession, in which the hits are counted, is allowed; de-clothing of prisoner or certain body parts is strictly prohibited. The prisoner may not be tied down, but is to lie on the bench voluntarily. He can only be hit on the behind or the upper thigh."[12]

The defendants and their attorneys could not use these documents to demonstrate the "superior orders" (or *Befehlsnotstand*) defense used by many guards who insisted that they were only following orders. This defense had been ruled invalid at Nuremberg through documentation that proved that no SS officers had ever been investigated or punished for refusing their orders. The prosecution used the camp laws to show that the actions of the defendants on the stand were undertaken with individual initiative and with knowledge of the illegality of the act, and could therefore be tried and punished as perpetration of murder. Thus the ironic situation arose in which the standard of the Nazi state was adopted in the courtroom in Frankfurt in order to try the very crimes committed under that state. The judge, Hans Hofmeyer, had to refer to Nazi documents and Nazi laws about what was acceptable at Auschwitz in order to convict the defendants on the stand in Frankfurt. The absurdity of this situation was not lost on Hofmeyer, who repeatedly had to ask witnesses which actions had been ordered by Berlin or the camp commanders, knowing full well that this lent an air of legality to the command to murder millions in Auschwitz. This line of questioning was at its most extreme during the testimony of Dr. Morgen.

Georg Konrad Morgen was already familiar with war crimes proceedings. He was a witness at the Nuremberg trial in August 1946, where he testified for the defense on the question of the criminality

of the SS as an organization.[13] Morgen was first interviewed for the
Auschwitz investigation on March 8, 1962. He was interrogated by
the court's investigative judge, Dr. Heinz Düx, in the "interim trial
phase," after the prosecution had submitted its case to the district
court of Frankfurt and the court took over the investigation and proceeded with its own inquiry to determine the validity of the prosecution's case. This was not the first time Morgen appeared in the files.
His testimony from another case—against two guards at the district
court in Cologne in January 1961—appeared in the pretrial files of
the Auschwitz Trial at the same time. In that interrogation, Morgen
described his educational history and his entrance into the Nazi Party
and then the SS. According to Morgen, he became a member of the
judicial office in June 1943, where he was an official in the Reich's
Criminal Police Department (Reichskriminalpolizeiamt), which was
part of Office 5 of the RSHA. He worked on cases of capital crime and
his first job was as part of an investigation of corruption at Buchenwald.[14] Morgen's testimony on his duties at Buchenwald set the parameters for what was to be considered questionable guard behavior,
both for the Nazis and for the court at Frankfurt. He reported:

> During my investigations at individual camps, I pursued numerous
> criminal offences which were made known to me and which were,
> in my opinion, pursuable. It was not possible for me to press charges
> against people who had carried out the orders of my own court su-
> periors (Gerichtsherren), for example the executions that had been
> ordered by Reichsführer Himmler, or the carrying out of euthana-
> sia, which after all went back to an order by Hitler. "Gerichtsherr"
> is an institution of the war crimes investigation law, which gave the
> military commanders [i.e., Hitler and Himmler] jurisdiction in
> the widest sense, including the opening of investigations, the is-
> suing of arrest warrants, indictment, appeals, confirmation or dis-
> missal of a sentence, its execution, and the power to pardon. How-
> ever, insofar as I was informed of crimes against life or limb that
> occurred on the private initiative of an SS member, I began inves-
> tigations against them.[15]

In his interrogation for the Auschwitz Trial, Morgen was more
specific about the circumstances of the camp. He stated that he went
to Auschwitz on his own accord after his investigations at Buchenwald led him to suspect that similar corrupt activities must have also

been going on at the much larger camp. After seeing that the SS in the Canada bunker at Auschwitz were a "bunch of demoralized and brutalized parasites," and finding heaps of stolen gold and jewelry in their coats, he requested that a *Sonderkommission* be created to investigate corruption. He immediately arrested the guards who had been stealing, and Boger was among them. His supposed heroic activities continued when he decided to widen the investigation to offences of excessive brutality after discovering that Commander Höss had had an affair with a female prisoner named Hodys. When he found out that she was pregnant, Höss had her put into a standing cell where she was left to die of starvation. Luckily, Morgen "came just in time to save this woman and had her transferred to a clinic in Munich."[16] Höss was then transferred away from Auschwitz. Still, Morgen defended Höss: "I don't mean to imply that Höss was in principle a bad person. . . . The entire circumstances in Auschwitz . . . at that time demoralized him as well. No person can bear to rule boundlessly over life and death, to turn a person into ashes from one minute to the next."[17]

Morgen's pretrial testimony was a carefully crafted response in which he did not give away many specific details about the defendants, while attempting to present himself as a tireless and courageous pursuer of justice. He did not remember Franz Hofmann, although the latter had guided Morgen through the camp, and he remembered only the possibility of having investigated Boger for corruption and murder offences. He could no longer remember the trial in Weimar in 1944 of Maximillian Grabner, the head of the Political Department at Auschwitz, who was notorious for excessive cruelty. This was implausible, as Grabner's arrest was a central part of the SS investigative commission's activities, and at one point Morgen insisted that he had arrested Grabner himself. Yet, he presented himself as the instigator of reform. He saw the gassings, and while he could not say for sure, he thought it possible that "because of my report in 1944, the gassings were discontinued."[18] At the very least, he imagined that he was responsible for ending the secrecy surrounding the gassings and making them public knowledge. He could not do more than this, however, because in the end, the final authority was Hitler's.

Morgen referred to the overriding authority of Hitler and Himmler once again in the trial. He did so with such eloquence and certainty that his testimony commanded authority. When asked by Judge Hofmeyer about the atrocities that took place in the camp, and why he did not take everyone with any power and responsibility and arrest them, he insisted that he did not have the power to arrest. In normal law, he would have sent a proposal to the public prosecutors of a district, and it would have gone through all of the channels of justice as part of a bureaucratic chain. However, during the SS era, according to military jurisdiction (*Kriegsgerichtbarkeit*), all judges were responsible to Hitler and Himmler. Therefore, he would have had to ask Hitler and Himmler to open an investigation against themselves; Hitler would be the judge, the prosecutor, and the law enforcer. According to Morgen, Hitler was the "chancellor of the Reich, the president, the chief commanding officer of the Wehrmacht, the lawmaker, and the highest officer of the law (*Oberstgerichtgeber*)."[19]

Morgen insisted both in the pretrial interrogations and in the trial that he had absolutely no power beyond his duty to investigate acts of private initiative, including theft, brutality, and unordered murder. The blame for everything else lay squarely on the shoulders of Hitler and was determined by the complex laws of military jurisdiction. In a remarkable performance, Morgen expressed with remorse his disgust at the slaughter going on at Auschwitz and his regret that it was impossible for him to do anything to stop it. Instead, he claimed that he had used his small role to investigate and prosecute the "unordered crimes," hoping that he would at least take some of the killers out of the system.[20] In this way, according to Morgen's noble version, he began investigating corruption at Auschwitz.

Morgen testified that to his surprise (because, he maintained, he had no prior knowledge of what Auschwitz was and how many millions of people were being murdered), his office intercepted a box filled with three pieces of gold that had been sent by a medical orderly at Auschwitz to his wife. Morgen discovered that this was high-carat tooth gold, melted together into fist-sized clumps. Morgen realized that "twenty, fifty, one hundred thousand corpses must have made up this one package." This was a chilling thought; but for Morgen's purposes, "what was even more unbelievable was that the perpetrator managed to keep a quantity without being noticed."[21] Morgen managed to convert his appearance on the stand into the story of his ignorance about this camp called Auschwitz. He said, "From this viewpoint

I comprehended for the first time, that the at-that-time unknown Auschwitz . . . must have been one of the largest places of human destruction that the world had ever seen."[22]

Morgen insisted that he would have liked to investigate and try everyone involved in the killing at Auschwitz. But because it had been ordered by his superiors, he could investigate only the corruption of those orders.[23] He claimed to know, for example, that Oswald Pohl, head of the WVHA, stole the gold as well, as Pohl and his closest workers set up a system whereby some of the gold that was sent to Degussa—a gold and silver melting company in Frankfurt—was redirected into an account there from which Pohl could siphon hundreds of thousands of marks. Obviously Pohl was above Morgen and therefore above investigation, so Morgen started with the smaller men.

During his time at Auschwitz Morgen became aware of the horrifying activities in the Political Department, especially the "Stalin-swing" (presumably his mistaken name for the "Boger-swing," a torture device created by defendant Wilhelm Boger). According to Morgen, defendant Boger and Maximilian Grabner were among the most brutal guards and took part in executions "on their own accord; they were not ordered to do so and they didn't give any notices of death to their bosses."[24] Morgen testified that he decided to try these "intensified interrogations" as murder, and he had Grabner arrested. He was then ordered to see Lieutenant General Heinrich Müller, chief of police at the RSHA in Berlin. In his portrayal of events, Müller severely reprimanded Morgen for his activities at Auschwitz, particularly the arrest of the head of the Political Department.[25] Müller told him that he "had no understanding of his duties as part of the State Police." Morgen, in what he presented as a moment of immense moral courage, pleaded with Müller: "After all, we still live in a constitutional state, and there are limits that even the Gestapo has to hold themselves to." Müller turned "as white as calcium" and threw Morgen out of his office. In yet another courageous act, Morgen went back "into the lion's den" and tried a new approach with Müller. Asking for advice, in a deferent tone, the conversation according to Morgen was as follows:

Morgen: Herr Müller, isn't it the Führer, and you, the chief of the Gestapo, who has the ultimate decision on every sentence?

Müller: Yes.

Morgen: Well, how would you judge it, if someone went far beyond your orders, and without informing you, through his own decision, killed a hard working prisoner?

Müller: That's impossible, that just doesn't happen!

Morgen: You see, Lieutenant General, sir, that is how people are ignoring your authority in the camps, that is what Grabner did, and that is why I arrested him.

Müller: Well, this is very different, this I understand. (Müller then recalled some of Grabner's disobedience himself.)[26]

Grabner was indicted for murder in at least two thousand cases. Morgen was able to open investigations against Rudolf Höss, camp commander; Hans Aumeier, camp leader; and others, including Boger. The trial against Grabner, however, was dismissed midway through the proceedings and Grabner was transferred to Berlin.[27]

Morgen's impassioned performance and informed description of what was one of the only channels for punishing the crimes of the Holocaust were so convincing that he helped to reinforce and legitimate the Nazi rules of behavior at Auschwitz. He argued that the Nazi laws of procedure were so ruthlessly enforced that it was impossible for him to investigate anyone but the guards who took the law into their own hands and undermined the authority of people like Müller. Regardless of whether the SS command actually punished guards for sadistic behavior, Morgen's testimony lent credibility to Nazi regulations and diminished the legal responsibility (according to the West German law) of those who carried out the orders of their superiors, focusing the attention on those who went above and beyond those orders.

The question-and-answer exchange between Judge Hofmeyer and Dr. Morgen brought the limitations of the West German penal code glaringly to the fore. During his appearance on the stand, Morgen suddenly found himself unable to remember any specific details about any of the defendants. For example, he knew only vaguely about the "Boger-swing," and the fact that it was illegal because not one protocol was taken during any of the interrogations. When the judge addressed the subject of the injection of prisoners with phenol (euphemistically termed *abspritzen,* which meant "injecting to death"), Morgen was also reticent. When reminded that defendant Josef Klehr was a medical orderly involved with the injections, Morgen remembered that Klehr had taken part in secret injections with fake death certificates. He knew that Klehr was doing something illegal. Morgen said that those who had orders "did not have to fear the light of day"; but that people like Klehr, who "tried to throw sand in the eyes" of the commanders and conducted the injections with such secrecy, knew that it was forbidden. The interrogation continued:

Hofmeyer: Were all of the injections unlawful?
Morgen: In some of the euthanasia cases, they were done legally,
          if they were incurably ill. "14F13"—the heading for
          death cases—was also a euphemism for the euthana-
          sia program.
Hofmeyer: Was it ordered?
Morgen: Yes, it went out from the Reich head doctor, von
          Grabitz.[28]

Hofmeyer moved to the subject of "intensified interrogations." To the noticeable irritation of the audience in the courtroom, he asked Morgen "what was allowed, when was it allowed, and who allowed it?" Morgen answered by reciting almost verbatim the camp regulations for interrogation that appear earlier in this chapter. The prosecution's greatest stride forward with Morgen came in the form of an answer to Hofmeyer's question about the "Boger-swing":

Hofmeyer: Was the swing officially or unofficially allowed in the
          framework of the intensified interrogations?
Morgen: As far as I know, it was not allowed. After Grabner's ar-
          rest, Müller did not say it was allowed.
Hofmeyer: So you arrested Grabner for murder, but also for using
          the swing?
Morgen: Yes.
Hofmeyer: So what about Boger. . . ?
Morgen: I can't remember any details.[29]

Hofmeyer's voice registered annoyance that Morgen could not give any specific details about Boger. Morgen appealed to Hofmeyer as a colleague, saying that after twenty years it was difficult to remember and "you, as fellow judges, would understand this."[30] Still, Hofmeyer was relentless. On the subject of the "Black Wall," an execution site at Auschwitz between blocks 10 and 11, Hofmeyer pressed Morgen on his pretrial testimony about Boger's participation in executions there along with another guard. Morgen insisted on the stand that his memory "[was not] reliable anymore."

In retrospect, Hofmeyer's questioning seems preposterous. His queries about what was allowed and when it was allowed deflected the blame and shifted the focus to the crimes *not* allowed by the Nazis. This occurred once again in Hofmeyer's questions about the Political Department. According to Morgen, every member of the Political Department had a piece of paper in his pocket that said "only the *Führer* decides the fate of enemies of the state." Hofmeyer then asked him: "Let's say, if here in this trial, we had to establish that this or that defendant killed prisoners without this specific order from Lieutenant General Müller, would it be allowed or not?" Morgen insisted that what Müller did not allow was considered illegal.[31]

Hofmeyer was clearly exasperated with these distinctions. He began to talk freely to Morgen, complaining about the unbelievable contradictions in Auschwitz: the difference between official and unofficial activity, and the desire for healthy people who could work, and at the same time the experiments in which people were injected with measles, brought to the point of death, and then brought back to life, only to be shot at the Black Wall. Morgen acknowledged that Auschwitz was a place of "grotesque contradiction" where there was "backwards rule" and "everything was possible." This was a result of the huge changes in prisoner numbers that occurred monthly—first they needed people to work very badly, then they suddenly had thousands too many. Morgen seemed genuinely disgusted with the hypocrisy of the laws at Auschwitz, as did Judge Hofmeyer and the prosecution. However, those laws were constantly reiterated and legitimated in the Frankfurt courtroom. Public prosecutor Kügler asked about the suspension of the case against Grabner, and wanted to know if it was dismissed because either the defendants or the witnesses had said "what do you want, anyway? Why would you go after us for a few shootings when thousands are killed every day in Auschwitz? Wouldn't that mean we didn't do anything wrong?" Morgen responded: "But no—the subtle but essential distinction is this: with the ordered executions or gassing, any initiative disappears, it was simply the carrying out of orders. But for the other shootings, the defendants couldn't use an order as their defense and they . . . they did it out of personal motive."[32] This legal distinction for SS investigators was the exact distinction between perpetrator and accomplice to murder in the West German penal code.

The defense and the prosecution battled over these differences. Defense lawyers tried to argue that the rules for "intensified interrogations" changed in 1943, when a relaxing of procedure made more torture permissible. Morgen conceded to this possibility. The defense also tried to establish that there may have been special regulations for each camp, in which special situations meant that the commanders could order executions themselves. Morgen said this was possible only in the case of open resistance or the attack of an SS man. He insisted that it was always clear to him which guards acted on their own initiative, as they created a whole "theatre" around their actions— they destroyed proof, they behaved secretly, and most especially, they falsified death certificates.

The question of falsified death certificates brought the courtroom to a new level of absurdity. The defense and prosecution not only tried to determine which deaths had been ordered, but which false explanations of these deaths had been ordered. Defense attorney Naumann asked Morgen to clarify what these death certificates were: some concealed ordered murder (injections), some concealed illegal murder (the "swing"); if Morgen admittedly knew that these death certificates were mendacious, how could he use them for his investigations? And was it not possible that if the orders to create false death sentences came from above, then the orders to kill did, as well? Morgen insisted that some falsifications were indeed ordered, but for Grabner's activities, for example, neither the mode of killing nor the false cause of death were ordered.

Finally, Hofmeyer questioned Morgen on SS duties in general, hoping to bring to the fore the relationship between morality and murder. He asked Morgen about the military penal code (*Militär Strafgesetzbuch*) and particularly paragraph 47, which stated that an order that constituted a crime should not be followed. Morgen confirmed that this law was in place throughout the Nazi period (despite Himmler's infamous 1943 Posener Rede, which could be interpreted as issuing a formal exemption from this law), but it was very difficult to determine what a crime meant in this "situation," particularly in war. A soldier could not criticize a political decision, as this would mean that everyone who murdered on the Russian front, if this was defined as a crime, was guilty of murder. Hofmeyer was outraged at the comparison. In reference to earlier testimony about an SS guard who killed children without an order, he told Morgen:

> There can be discussion about that; but there can be no
> discussion about whether or not a soldier should follow
> an order to throw innocent little children into burning
> fires. It must be clear to a soldier that this is a crime.

Morgen: You are absolutely right about that, Director Hofmeyer. . . . But I cannot imagine, and I hope I'm right,
that that kind of thing happened, because it contradicts
the entire direction [of the Nazi regime].[33]

We know now, from witness testimony at the trial and from countless
survivor accounts, that such things happened all the time. Morgen
steadfastly defended the laws of the SS, arguing that individual and
sadistic murder "was beneath a true German; and despite everything
that everyone says about them, despite everything that happened,
the SS never ordered or demanded such cruelties. On the contrary."[34]
This supposed principle of the SS was reinforced as a truth—despite
the existence of evidence of incredibly cruel treatment—by the limitations of the law in Frankfurt.

The pretrial testimonies of Gerhard Wiebeck and Wilhelm Reimers,
also judges on the SS commission, echoed much of what Morgen reported. Wiebeck went to work for Morgen in February of 1944, after
the Auschwitz investigation was already underway. He interrogated
Boger for the Grabner investigation and could remember Boger's
proclamation: "we killed far too few. Everything should be done for
the *Führer* and the Reich."[35] Reimers also worked on the investigation of the "illegal killing of prisoners" in the Political Department,
but he insisted that this had nothing to do with the *Judenaktionen*
(mass murder of the Jews). His role was simply to look into the "illegal theft" of Jewish belongings. He claimed that he constantly attempted to maintain secrecy about his role there so that he would not
arouse suspicion. However, the SS guards soon came to know what
he was doing, and they hated him. They attempted to bribe him into
dismissing certain investigations, but he stoically refused. In this capacity he witnessed executions of men, women, and children (by
shooting) in a large room attached to the small crematorium. However, he insisted that he "couldn't clamp down on these shootings—
i.e. prevent these actions, because my power of authority did not go
that far. My job was only to establish what was going on at Auschwitz
and then to report it."[36] Reimers testified more readily about the ar-

rival and subsequent gassings of transports at Auschwitz and gave relatively specific details about such actions that he witnessed. He reported them matter-of-factly, his interrogation betraying no hint of remorse or disgust with what he saw. In fact, the way he saw it, prisoners who had been gassed looked very peaceful and had normal expressions on their faces, "as though they had died a natural death."[37] At the end of his interrogation Reimers discussed the "spiritual burden" of being at Auschwitz, where people had lost all regard for human life. However, his tone was one of a server of the state doing his duty and asking no questions beyond this. After all, precisely that kind of behavior (taking the law into his own hands) was what he was investigating.

Reimers did not appear on the stand at Auschwitz, but Gerhard Wiebeck did. Judge Hofmeyer asked him what constituted an action worth investigating, whether "the 'general line' (*Generallinie*) ended at unauthorized killing." Wiebeck responded: "You could say that. The investigation of general killing was not authorized. I heard that the extermination of the Jews had been verbally ordered by Hitler." The commission, then, did not investigate such activities as gassings. When asked why by prosecutor Kügler, Wiebeck replied, "That didn't interest us at that time. Those were 'supreme acts beyond justice' (*justizfreie Hoheitsakte*)."[38] Ironically, gassings became "supreme acts beyond justice" at the Auschwitz Trial as well.

The claims of all of the SS judges to have done their very best to bring about some form of justice were reiterated on the stand by Dr. Werner Hansen, the former SS judge who had presided over the trial against Grabner in Weimar. Hansen reported that Morgen told him about the mass murder at Auschwitz and assumed that "obviously orders from the highest levels of rule were involved." He continued, contending that "these actions lay outside of the realm of power of justice. An investigation proceeding of this mass murder was therefore absolutely out of the question. . . . The best that could be done was to indict Grabner."[39] Grabner therefore stood trial for 2,000 unordered murders and 2,000 falsified causes of death.

There was, therefore, heavy emphasis in the courtroom on a handful of SS judges who investigated and proceeded against a handful of SS guards accused of theft or murder at Auschwitz. Morgen had, of course, worked on a commission that investigated and punished people who stole goods that had already been stolen from millions of Jews, who tortured and killed people who had already been selected for torture and death. The purpose of the *Sonderkommission* seemed ridiculous at the trial. However, Morgen served a very important role for the prosecution and judges in Frankfurt: As a member of the court (he was at the time a lawyer in Frankfurt) he gave specific details about the activities that showed individual initiative and murderous intention, and his authority made the cases against Boger, Klehr, and the other unrepentant sadists stronger. These judges appeared on the stand with some measure of dignity and authority, as they had retained legal positions after the war. Their testimonies carried immeasurable weight and significance and they legitimated the Nazi laws and Nazi justice on the one hand and exonerated themselves on the other. There was irony in the fact that such detail about an "unordered" shooting had to be pursued so vigorously and meticulously despite its seeming irrelevance. How could it be that only those murders undertaken without an official order were emphasized in the Auschwitz Trial? Was not the entire camp a place of murder? Were these defendants on the stand for murdering millions of innocent men, women, and children, or for disobeying the command of the Nazi rulers? Increasingly, the latter outshone the former as the central focal point of the trial. The sadists became the main targets of scrutiny, just as they had been in 1943 in Auschwitz itself. This was not, however, the result of reluctance on the part of the judge or the public prosecutor's office. Both were equally determined to find the truth about the defendants' activities. The prosecution, a team of young lawyers headed by Attorney General Fritz Bauer, had high hopes that all of the defendants would be convicted of murder. But they were bound by the very restrictive West German penal code, which itself was considerably limited by the loss of the manslaughter paragraph and by the narrow definitions of murder and participation in murder. For these reasons, the courtroom used standards that resembled those of the Nazi state. This is most evident in the fact that only those who had disobeyed Nazi orders were convicted of murder at the Frankfurt Auschwitz Trial. According to these standards, none of the major war criminals at the Nuremberg trial would have been convicted of murder. The West German criminal justice system was woefully insufficient and inefficient for crimes of such magnitude.

NOTES

1. Official statistics of the Zentrale Stelle der Landesjustizverwaltung zur Verfolgung nationalsozialistischer Verbrechen in Dick de Mildt, *In the Name of the People: Perpetrators of Genocide in the Reflection of Their Postwar Prosecution in Germany, The "Euthanasia" and "Aktion Reinhard" Trial Cases* (The Hague: Kluwer Law International, 1996), 20–1.

2. De Mildt, *In the Name of the People,* appendix A.1, 403.

3. Ingo Müller, *Hitler's Justice: The Courts of the Third Reich,* trans. Deborah Lucas Schneider (Cambridge: Harvard University Press, 1991), 255.

4. Hannah Arendt, *Eichmann in Jerusalem: A Report on the Banality of Evil* (New York: Viking Press, 1964). Historian Dick de Mildt voices similar sentiments, pointing to a 1952 survey by the U.S. High Commission for Germany that showed that only one in ten Germans wanted further Nazi war crimes trials, stating that "the main reason for this much debated popular aversion was undoubtedly formed by the deeply rooted unwillingness among the German population at large to face up to the vilest aspects of a political system they had so enthusiastically supported. . . ." De Mildt, *In the Name of the People,* 23.

5. A complete list of trials and judgments can be found in Adelheid L. Rüter-Ehlermann and C. F. Rüter, eds., *Justiz und NS-Verbrechen: Sammlung deutscher Strafurteile wegen nationalsozialistischer Totungsverbrechen,* 22 vols. (Amsterdam: University Press Amsterdam, 1945–1999). These volumes show very clearly that West German trials did not consistently deal with crimes against the Jews until 1958.

6. According to legal historian Adalbert Rückerl, Germans were tired of Allied interference in German affairs. He states that "the reason why they regarded the murder of millions of Jews, political opponents and insane persons as a political act rather than a primarily criminal one may be found in the reporting of the trials mounted by the IMT [International Military Tribunal] in Nuremberg and its enormous impact on public opinion. The trials were characterized by an intermingling of military, political and purely criminal events in a manner which rendered it virtually impossible for an unprejudiced observer to obtain the facts they needed to unravel the tangle of evidence." Adalbert Rückerl, *The Investigation of Nazi Crimes 1945–1978: A Documentation,* trans. Derek Rütter (Hamden, Conn.: Archon Books, 1980), 35–6.

7. For a more in-depth discussion of the German penal code, see Rückerl, *Investigation of Nazi Crimes,* and Nigel G. Foster, *German Law and Legal System* (London: Blackstone Press, 1993).

8. The confiscation of Jews' belongings and the relationship of this practice at Auschwitz to "Aktion Reinhard" is dealt with in Bertrand Perz

and Thomas Sandkühler, "Auschwitz und die 'Aktion Reinhard' 1942–45: Judenmord und Raubpraxis in neuer Sicht," *Zeitgeschichte* 5 (September-October 1999): 283–316. The authors briefly discuss the appearance of Dr. Morgen to investigate individual guards suspected of stealing goods.

9. Nuremberg Document 778-PS, in *Anklageschrift* (Indictment), the Public Prosecutor's Office at the District Court of Frankfurt am Main, 4Js 444/59 (hereafter StAFfM), 78:14741.

10. Ibid., 78:14744. This passage appears verbatim and with new accompanying explanations in Helmut Krausnick, Hans Buchheim, Martin Broszat, and Hans-Adolf Jacobsen, *The Anatomy of the SS State,* trans. Richard Barry, Marian Jackson, and Dorothy Long (New York: Walker and Company, 1968).

11. Broszat, *Anatomy of the SS State,* 432.

12. StAFfM, 78:14801. A memo of April 4, 1942, from the WVHA, Administrative Section D, signed by SS Lieutenant Colonel Liebehenschel, at the time head of the Central Office and later commander of Auschwitz, ordered that a new policy on corporal punishments would go into effect: "The *Reichsführer* SS and the chief of German Police has ordered that during the execution of corporal punishment (for both male or female protective custody prisoners), when the word 'intensified' (*verschärft*) is added, the punishment should be carried out on an unclothed behind. In all other cases, proceed as already ordered." Nuremberg Document 2199-PS in StAFfM, 78:14802.

13. At Nuremberg, Morgen told a bizarre version of events in which the extermination camps were not run by the SS but by an officer of the Hitler Chancellory (Christian Wirth). He was not taken seriously and not cross-examined by the prosecution. Gerhard Reitlinger, *The Final Solution: The Attempt to Exterminate the Jews of Europe 1939–1945* (Northvale, N.J.: Jason Aronson, 1987), 123–4.

14. Konrad Morgen, January 26, 1961, 30 UR 9/58 LG Köln in StAFfM, 48:8515–6.

15. Ibid., 48:8517–8.

16. Konrad Morgen, March 8, 1962, in 4 Js 444/59, StAFfM, 63:11716.

17. Ibid.

18. Ibid., 63:11718.

19. Konrad Morgen, *Strafsache gegen Mulka und andere,* 4Ks 2/63. First Frankfurt Auschwitz Trial, December 20, 1963–August 8, 1965, jury trial at the District Court, Frankfurt am Main (hereafter APO), March 9, 1964, Tape # 4A. The trial itself was taped rather than transcribed; the transcription that appears in this paper (in translation) is my own. Listening to

the tapes enhanced my understanding of the atmosphere in the courtroom and provided invaluable insight into the changing tone of the proceedings.

20. Ibid.

21. Ibid.

22. Ibid.

23. Gerhard Reitlinger corroborates this representation of Morgen in his book on the Final Solution. Reitlinger recalls Morgen's appearance at the Nuremberg trial and says that "he seems to have been a boastful man of some integrity, though not enough. Although he knew how to keep his mouth shut when the clues became dangerous, he got the reputation of a Nosey Parker in SS circles. . . . In the end Morgen's fellow-captives overcame their repugnance, recognizing in him a man whom the Allies might consider respectable." Reitlinger, *Final Solution,* 123–4.

24. Morgen, APO.

25. According to Gerhard Reitlinger, Himmler's decision to send Morgen to Auschwitz was a strange one, for "he must have known that he would come up against Kaltenbrunner, Nebe and Müller." In fact, in his pretrial interrogation in March 1962, Morgen addressed the question of opposition to his work there: "[A]s far as I know, the sharpest resistance came from General Pohl, the chief of the Gestapo, Lieutenant General Müller, and the head of the RSHA, General Dr. Kaltenbrunner. They tried every conceivable way to stop me, first gently and then with offers of a fabulous career in another section of the SS, then through typical military measures, through complaints to the *Reichsführer SS* and the Reich criminal police, through massive threats and finally through an attack on my investigative commission, in which our entire office barracks and files were destroyed through arson." Morgen, StAFfM, 63:11721. Reitlinger seems to believe Morgen's contention that he genuinely wanted to punish the atrocities of Auschwitz, stating that "he believed that if he brought a charge against some of the individual murderers in the camp, the official system of mass murder at the crematoria would have to come to light, too." Reitlinger, *Final Solution,* 453. This characterization contradicts his earlier comments about Morgen's mendacity.

26. Morgen, APO. It is quite telling that Morgen was not punished for his disobedience directly in the face of one of the highest officials of the SS. We already know that no one was ever punished for refusing to follow his or her orders; presumably, Morgen was reprimanded for doing his duty with too much zeal and without proper ordinance from Berlin. This was also the standard by which Morgen himself investigated the guards at Auschwitz.

27. After the war, Grabner was tried by a Polish tribunal in 1947, where he was sentenced to death and executed.

28. Morgen, APO.

29. Ibid.

30. Ibid.

31. Ibid.

32. Ibid.

33. Ibid.

34. Ibid.

35. Gerhard Wiebeck, March 23, 1960, in StAFfM, 28:4752. He repeated this statement on the stand in his trial testimony.

36. Wilhelm Reimers, June 6, 1961, in STAFfM, 51:9132.

37. Ibid., 51:9133.

38. Gerhard Wiebeck in Hermann Langbein, *Der Auschwitz-Prozess, Eine Dokumentation,* 2 vols. (Frankfurt am Main: Verlag Neue Kritik, 1995), 336.

39. Dr. Werner Hansen in Langbein, *Der Auschwitz-Prozess,* 338.

Constantin Goschler

German Compensation to Jewish Nazi Victims

WHILE THE ISSUE OF GERMAN COMPENSATION FOR NAZI VICTIMS HAS been a topic of minor public interest for most of the time since the end of the Second World War, it has featured more prominently over the last few years, especially in the United States. Several aspects are combined in the debate: While some ask to what extent Germany has sufficiently fulfilled its historical obligations toward the Nazi victims, others focus on the connection between German compensation and questions of Jewish identity. This debate takes place at a time when most of the individually concerned survivors of the Holocaust and other Nazi crimes are either already dead or very aged. Therefore the current debate seems to be a symptom of a change from material to symbolic claims, especially with respect to the suffering of Jewish Nazi victims.

In contrast to the present situation, at the end of the Second World War and for a long time thereafter the racial persecution of Jews, which culminated in the Holocaust, was considered only one aspect of the vast array of human and material destruction caused by Nazi Germany. At the same time a basic assumption prevailed that it would be impossible for the Germans to pay for every crime they had committed. Thus Jewish claims referring to Nazi persecution competed with many other demands from inside and outside Germany: claims of German refugees from the East, war veterans, and the like on the one hand; and claims for war reparations and such on the other hand—hence the historical process that led to compensation for Jewish Nazi victims was marked by its improbability, especially since it had been without historical precedence. The attempts to deal with the claims of Holocaust victims after 1945 may not be considered as the result of a superhistorical sense of justice that reacted to a new quantity and quality of crimes against humanity. Rather, they might be explained as the result of a combination of specific political circumstances and gradually evolving perceptions, which will be explained in this chapter.

In the following sections I want to deliver both a short survey and an analysis of the German attempts to settle compensation claims of Jewish Nazi victims. The latter notion has to be handled with care, at least with respect to the German Reich, insofar as it also refers to gentiles who had been considered as Jews by the Nazis on racial grounds even though they did not identify themselves as Jews.[1] My first guiding question aims at the motives behind the attempts to compensate Jewish Nazi victims, which are far less than obvious. Thus we will ask to what extent competing perceptions existed regarding Nazi persecution and its victims. Second, I will inquire into the role of changing political frames and patterns of political and legal actions with regard to the compensation of Jewish Nazi victims. Third, what were both the material and symbolic results and effects of compensation for Jewish Nazi victims (which includes the question of the shortcomings)? What is the meaning of restitution for German society, on the one hand, and for Jewish individuals and communities, on the other? And what were the consequences of the process of compensation for the relationship between German society and Jews in Germany and abroad?

The chapter is arranged in seven parts: The first part deals with discussions on compensation for Jewish Nazi victims before the end of Nazi rule, the second with the attempts at restitution of Jewish property, the third with the settlement of Jewish collective claims, the fourth with compensation for personal damage for Jewish individuals, the fifth with settlements of German companies for Jewish forced labor, and the sixth with additional settlements after the German reunification. Finally, there are some concluding remarks.

DISCUSSIONS ON COMPENSATION FOR JEWISH NAZI VICTIMS BEFORE THE END OF NAZI RULE

Plans for the compensation of Jewish Nazi victims had evolved already before the end of Nazi rule. Even inside Germany such ideas can be found, though they were very limited in scope and focus first on stopping the persecution. The group of conservative German officers who failed to kill Hitler on July 20, 1944, had planned to abolish the anti-Jewish measures enacted since the beginning of the war. This also indicates both the scope and the limits of consensus in the non–National Socialist part of German society with Nazi anti-Jewish politics. In case of a successful revolt, Carl Goerdeler, the designated head of a new German government, had intended not only to announce to the German people the immediate halt of the persecution of Jews, but also to condemn the enrichment with Jewish property.[2] Yet the revolt failed and Goerdeler and many of his companions were killed in an orgy of revenge.

In the same year, Nehemiah Robinson, a Jewish expert in this field, published a book in the United States on *Indemnifications and Reparations*, wherein he analyzed the then known ideas of the German resistance's referring to a future compensation of persecuted Jews. In his book he was acutely aware of a dilemma within the German resistance: Robinson stated these plans primarily aimed at keeping the German overall burden as low as possible. This resulted from the German resistance's belief that the construction of a new democratic society should not be hampered by excessive reparations, as had been the case at the time of the Weimar Republic.[3] Thus the German resistance strictly rejected being considered a proponent of a new Versailles treaty that would promote their political isolation within German society. This attitude naturally strictly limited the scope of any claims for compensation for Nazi victims.

Jewish reflections on possible ways of compensation after the war naturally were less hampered by such considerations of the capacity of the Germans to accept financial burdens. Plans that aimed at restitution and indemnification for Jewish Nazi victims emerged especially in the environment of Jewish organizations in Palestine, the United States, and Great Britain.[4] A decisive step was made by Nahum Goldmann, who represented both the World Jewish Congress (WJC) and the Jewish Agency for Palestine, at the Pan-American Conference of the WJC in Baltimore in November 1941. On that occasion he declared the Nazi persecution of German Jews to be part of a war against the Jewish people, thus justifying a claim for collective reparations.[5] Already before the end of the war a strong tendency had emerged in American Jewish organizations and the Jewish Agency, which thought that future compensation claims should primarily be devoted to the purpose of Jewish settlement in Palestine. Hence from the beginning there existed a strong link between Jewish compensation claims and Zionism.

However, other organizations in the United States, like the Axis Victims League or the American Association of Former European Jurists, propagated a strictly non-Zionistic and universalistic approach: Even though they mainly consisted of persecuted Jewish emigrants from Germany or Europe, they placed the plight of Jews and of other groups under Nazi rule into a common framework. These organizations, which were dominated by former German lawyers like Hugo Marx and Bruno Weil, took a decidedly alternative stance against American and other international Jewish organizations: They focused mainly on individual claims for former German Jewish nationals.[6] This foreshadowed conflicts among different Jewish groups, which became even more important after the end of the war.

In his aforementioned 1944 book Nehemiah Robinson pinpointed the different approaches to the question of Jewish restitution claims. He differentiated between "restorative" and "constructive" measures. The former aimed at individual compensation and restitution, whereas the latter were directed at collective claims: They were based on the assumption that the Jewish people as a whole was a victim of Nazi persecution and therefore wanted to use the received compensation for its reconstruction.[7] All together, while the aforementioned universalistic (and also individualistic and German-centric) approach of groups like the Axis Victims League was politically marginalized at the end of the war, the international Jewish organizations had agreed upon the idea of a separate and collective compensation claim that focused on the Jewish people.[8]

The Allies' plans for compensation of Jewish Nazi victims were mainly fueled by the refugee problem, which was considered an undesired export of social problems from Germany and thus regarded as an attack on the stability of the international order.[9] These plans were championed by the United States. Since 1943 the U.S. administration had considered how Germany might be made responsible for the refugee problem it had caused after the war. However, plans to solve the question of compensation for Jewish and other Nazi victims as part of the reparation problem faltered in the course of internal discussions. There was one important exception: Already before the end of the war, the American Military Government for Germany was instructed to take care of the future restitution of Jewish property that was forcefully withdrawn during the Nazi era. The first step should be to put all former Jewish assets under property control.[10] This was partly motivated by Minister of Finance Henry Morgenthau, who was afraid of a recurrence of the situation in Northern Africa, where the French were only reluctantly proceeding with the restitution of stolen Jewish assets.[11] Even before the end of the war, the thousands of requests to the U.S. administration from former German Jews who had become naturalized U.S. citizens had engendered a certain sensibility toward that issue. So far, there is no evidence that the other Allies considered similar steps in their occupation zones in Germany.

THE RESTITUTION OF LOOTED JEWISH PROPERTY

On May 8, 1945, the Allied powers assumed total control in occupied Germany, which subsequently was divided into four zones of occupation. At first, German governments and administrations worked under the severe auspices of their respective military governments. Then in 1949 two German governments were established that, for the next forty-one years, coexisted in a state of unfriendly kinship. It was not until the mid-fifties that they assumed sovereignty, which in some respects still was not complete until German reunification in 1990. Under these circumstances compensation for Jewish Nazi victims could not be settled in a bilateral manner between Jews and Germans, as the influence of the Allied powers was always at hand, though it gradually became less so after the fifties. However, Allied interests were far from identical (for which the Cold War gave clear evidence). While immediately after their defeat Germans enjoyed only a minimal scope of independent action, the growing tensions between East and West contributed significantly to increase their political mobility.

The restitution of Jewish property that was seized under duress between 1933 and 1945 was the first step in dealing with the consequences of Nazi persecution of Jews. A decisive momentum for that was the desire to settle unrest in the realm of property circumstances, which was considered a precondition for a stable economic development. This affected not only Jewish assets, but also the property of trade unions, political parties, and social and charitable organizations that had been confiscated soon after 1933. From the German perspective the latter categories very often figured as preeminent, and in a way they worked as a motor for considerations about restitution of property taken away during the Nazi era.

Several German state administrations made plans for restitution laws, and in one case even a state law was passed for that purpose. As early as September 14, 1945, the Soviet military government in Thuringia enacted a restitution law that had been written by the German administration.[12] (The law originated at the time when this state still belonged to the American zone of occupation.) According to this law, identifiable properties that had previously belonged to Jews, or had been the property of former parties, trade unions, or political, religious, or other organizations, were liable to restitution. Such properties included estates, houses, business companies, and so forth. Until 1948 this restitution law was effective, yet it increasingly collided with the political changes in the Soviet zone of occupation, which led in direction to socialization of private property.

While the enforcement of the Thuringian restitution law highlights the changes in the political and economic system in East Germany, at the same time the spirit of this law reveals much about the German rationale and the envisioned scope of restitution. It also indicates interpretations of the nature of Nazi persecution of the Jews. A common feature of this law and similar drafts originating in German state administrations at that time was that they intended to make only such identifiable property liable to restitution that had been taken away by measures of the German state, the Nazi party, or affiliated organizations. Thus the broad scope of cases, where Jewish property went into non-Jewish hands due to the general atmosphere of persecution, remained excluded. This implied an image of anti-Jewish Nazi politics that focused on state terrorism while the role of German society was not taken into account.

Presumably there might have been some restitution of Jewish property in Germany after 1945, even without Allied influence. (However, such a counterfactual argument has to struggle with the problem that in such a scenario the Germans would have been able to get rid of Nazi rule without the Allies.) In any case the scope of such purely "homemade" restitution would have been much narrower than that which finally resulted from Allied pressure. This argument is supported by the fact that since Germany was able to articulate itself again politically (i.e., since the foundation of the Federal Republic), voices against the restitution of Jewish property out of private hands dominated at first. They were silenced only after the restitution of identifiable property had been widely accomplished in the mid-fifties.[13]

The Allies, primarily the United States, were the decisive agent for the enactment of restitution laws dealing with Jewish property in postwar Germany. However, the aims of the four Allied powers were quite divergent with respect to restitution: The French government was not very concerned about restitution of Jewish property. The model for restitution in the French zone of occupation was the respective measures in Northern Africa and in liberated France, which served to redress the measures against Jewish property during the war (and which were considered highly unsatisfying by Jewish observers, as mentioned before). The British stance on this question was also marked by domestic problems. On the one hand they were deeply concerned about possible burdens for the British taxpayer; on the other hand, they were also worried about the impact of any transfer of Jewish assets abroad to the conflict in Palestine, where the British mandatory power was challenged by the Jewish underground army.

What is more, both France and Britain considered the possible restitution of Jewish property in close relation to their own claims for war reparations. They shared this view with the Soviet Union, which became apparent during the Allied Control Council's deliberations on the issue of a common restitution law, which ended without success in 1947. During these talks the United States delegation found itself repeatedly isolated.[14] The United States was the only participant of the Second World War not to have been economically weakened; neither had they suffered destruction on their own territory as had all European countries. Thus it could afford a less rigorous stance on the reparations issue than could their former wartime partners. What is more, they championed the return to a liberal, free-market society, which was closely linked with a strong belief in the sanctity of private property—which also clearly was not the case for the Soviet Union.

It has already been mentioned that the U.S. administration had already been concerned about the restitution of Jewish property before the end of the war. Consequently in 1946 it instructed the state administrations in the American zone of occupation to draft a restitution law for identifiable Jewish property (i.e., estates, houses, companies, etc.). During these negotiations American Jewish organizations managed to attain a decisive influence. The turning point came in the form of talks among American Military Governor Lucius D.

Clay and five American and Palestine Jewish organizations (the nucleus of the later Jewish Conference on Material Claims against Germany, or in short, the Claims Conference), which took place in Washington, D.C., in autumn 1946. On that occasion Clay granted far-reaching guarantees referring to the scope and enactment of the restitution of identifiable Jewish property.[15] Yet, when he tried to press for accomplishment of this maximum program, his administration was not able to receive the consent of either the German state governments or the other Allied powers. There were three major points of dispute: First, which losses of Jewish property should be considered as consequence of improper actions and thus be liable to restitution? Should it be considered possible that in Nazi Germany at least in some cases, Jewish property had been sold without discrimination on the part of the vendor? After fierce controversies it was decided that every transaction of Jewish property after September 15, 1935 (the day the Nuremberg racial laws were enacted), should be automatically disputable. Furthermore, the last owner of the property in dispute was made liable, even if he had not been directly involved in the transaction.

Second, there was a great deal of argument about the Jewish demand for a strong Allied element in the restitution courts, which finally also were established in American Military Law No. 59. A third major point of dispute arose from the question of how to proceed with heirless Jewish property resulting from the murder of whole families. Agreement existed that the German treasury should not profit from this situation. However, the desire of the aforementioned committee of Jewish organizations to put Jewish successor organizations in charge of these assets met with fierce resistance from many sides. The Germans—and also some of the Allied powers—were opposed to the idea of transferring these assets abroad for the purpose of the reconstruction of Jewish life around the world (and especially in Palestine), implying an unbearable financial drain from Germany. Yet there were other opponents to this idea, including the newly established Jewish communities in Germany, who competed with the international Jewish organizations for the property of former Jewish communities that had been eliminated by the Nazis. The struggle that emerged from this conflict was marked at times by the desire of international Jewish organizations to dispute any legitimacy of Jewish communities on German soil at all. Then there were the members of the former German Jewish communities living abroad. They either disputed the right of the newly established Jewish communities to be the legitimate heirs to their tradition and property (especially as they consisted mainly of Jews who had immigrated only after 1945 from Eastern Europe to Germany), as well as the right of foreign Jewish organizations to claim these assets.

Basically the committee of Jewish organizations achieved what they had been promised earlier by Clay. As they were not ready to compromise with the other Allied powers (which the U.S. military governor clearly would have preferred), Clay enacted the draft of the restitution law that he had agreed upon with the American Jewish organizations in November 1947 as a unilateral military government law. Earlier, the German state governments had refused to enact this law because they were not ready to provide democratic legitimacy to what they considered to be an American *octroi*. The French Military Government followed the next day with its own law for their occupation zone which was inspired by domestic restitution legislation, while the British Military Government enacted a modified version of the American law two years later. While in West Berlin in 1949 the Western Allies agreed on a common restitution law based on the American-British law, in the Soviet zone nothing of this sort happened.

The Allied High Commission, namely the United States, urged the newly established Federal Republic on to a speedy and fair enforcement of the Allied restitution laws.[16] They were in a strong position insofar as the highest restitution court of appeal was dominated by Allied judges. By far the greatest part of the restitution of identifiable property affected former Jewish assets; however, there were other categories, like the property of political parties, trade unions, churches, and charitable organizations. The bulk of claims was settled during the fifties. The total amount of restored assets in the Federal Republic, including West Berlin, was estimated at DM 3.5 billion. However, a considerable number of unregistered out-of-court settlements also existed, which mostly affected the restitution of huge enterprises.[17]

The enactment of the restitution of identifiable property met with fierce resistance within German society. By publishing astronomical sums that allegedly were transferred to Jewish successor organizations outside Germany, the enemies of restitution fueled fears of the ruin of the German currency and economy among the German people.[18] An estimated number of 100,000 German individuals were liable to return Jewish assets[19] and received in return the money they had formerly paid—yet due to the effects of the currency reform, they got a bad deal. In the early fifties, organizations of those under obligation for restitution lobbied intensively in German political parties and parliaments, particularly blaming American Military Government Law No. 59 as draconian. Their major criticism was that this law was not concerned with the role of "goodwill," which a considerable number of the purchasers of Jewish property in the Nazi era claimed to have exercised.[20] These groups enjoyed considerable sympathy not only from a broad spectrum of political parties, but also from the general public. A poll in West Germany from August 1949 recorded that 54 percent of those questioned were in favor of compensation for German Jews. But when asked for their opinion on restitution of Jewish property (i.e., where it really did hurt) the number significantly declined: Only 39 percent opined claims were justified in such cases where a non-Jew had bought a Jewish shop after 1933 and where the former owner demanded restitution on equal terms.[21]

Yet the Western Allied restitution laws covered only a part of the problem of Jewish property that had been taken away between 1933 and 1945, as they referred only to identifiable assets within West Germany and West Berlin. An unresolved problem of highest priority was the assessment of damage for nonidentifiable Jewish assets taken away by the German Reich, its authorities, the Nazi Party, and similar institutions. Such claims referred especially to the series of robberies committed by the German treasury, whose booty consisted of huge amounts of Jewish stocks and shares, gold, silver, jewels and jewelry, pieces of art, and household goods.[22]

The talks on revision of the West German occupation statute that took place in the early fifties provided an opportunity to find a solution to this problem. In short, these negotiations were a "self-obligation versus sovereignty" deal. The negotiations on the relinquishment of Allied reserved powers resulted in the "Contractual Agreements" of 1952. It constituted an important part of the "Treaty on Germany" of 1955, which granted the Federal Republic far-reaching sovereignty. There were several important provisions. Among others, the Federal Republic committed itself to handle the existing Allied restitution legislation in a fair and speedy manner and furthermore to creating new laws in favor of former Nazi victims. First, West Germany was required to improve legislation concerning indemnification for

Nazi victims (to which we will come back later). Second, the Federal Republic agreed to enact a solution for the question of assessment of claims for nonidentifiable Jewish assets taken away under the responsibility of the German Reich.

For the accomplishment of the latter obligation, in 1957 the Federal Republic enacted the Federal Restitution Law.[23] With respect to other financial burdens that Western Germany was expected to assume (namely, the expenses for its military contribution to the North Atlantic Treaty Organization [NATO]) the Western Allies initially had agreed to limit the total amount to be paid under this law to DM 1.5 billion. However, this restriction was later dropped, and finally a total amount of circa DM 4 billion was remunerated.[24] Yet this was still far away from the actual losses of Jewish property during the Nazi era, since there were other severe limitations. First, the law provisioned an upper limit for each claimant. Second, the claimants were to provide evidence that the assets in question had reached the territory of the Federal Republic or Berlin. While there was a good chance of such proof in the case of looted assets from France, the Netherlands, or Belgium, in the case of Eastern European countries claimants struggled with a massive lack of evidence.[25]

In East Germany there was almost no restitution of Jewish property. After the establishment of the German Democratic Republic (GDR) in 1949, restitution of private property was considered a relic of a bourgeois conception of legality. Restitution of Jewish property conflicted with both the aim of socialization of private property and the priority of reparations for the Soviet Union. Furthermore, there were also the aftereffects of the stereotype of a close connection between Jews and capitalism. When in 1952 Paul Merker, who had struggled for a kind of reconciliation between restitution of Jewish property and a socialist transformation of society, was indicted as an agent of a capitalist-Jewish world conspiracy,[26] restitution of Jewish assets definitely became a taboo.

Jews from abroad striving for restitution of their property in East Germany were provided with no assistance, and in 1954 the Foreign Office of the GDR formally decided not to answer any such requests.[27] Restitution claims also produced counterproductive effects. Insofar as these assets were still in private hands, such efforts tended to effect state confiscation instead of restitution to former Jewish owners. The Jewish communities in the GDR also fought with minor success only for the restitution of Jewish property.[28] As compensation for the re-linquishment of restitution claims to the property of Jewish communities taken away during the Nazi era, the state provided them with maintenance and also cared for synagogues, Jewish cemeteries, old people's homes, and so on.

The 1970s and 1980s saw some further attempts to settle the restitution of former Jewish property in the GDR.[29] After its admission to the United Nations in 1973, the GDR also endeavored to establish diplomatic relations with the United States. However, the U.S. State Department adopted the request of the Claims Conference that any diplomatic relations were dependant on a previous settlement of Jewish restitution claims. This referred especially to the considerable property both of Jewish communities and Jewish individuals in East Berlin. As a result the GDR entered into talks with representatives of the Claims Conference. The outcome was far from satisfying for the Jewish side: In 1976 the GDR tried to close the case by sending U.S.$1 million to the Claims Conference as a single contribution in favor of needy Nazi victims living in the United States. This offer was considered totally inadequate, and the money was instantly sent back. Yet as the GDR kept on trying to improve its trade relations with the United States and especially sought admittance to the most-favored nation clause, there were ongoing efforts by the Claims Conference and the World Jewish Congress for a settlement of the restitution issue. But again, all endeavors seemed fruitless, until in the wake of the GDR's agony there were signs of a new readiness to deal with Jewish claims. In the end, this obvious attempt to win the highly overestimated Jewish influence in the world in order to rescue the GDR proved to be futile. It was up to the Federal Republic to handle the unresolved questions referring to Jewish compensation claims, which included matters not only of restitution but also of a Jewish collective claim that had been established in the early postwar era.

REPARATIONS FOR THE JEWISH PEOPLE? THE
SETTLEMENT OF JEWISH COLLECTIVE CLAIMS

Immediately after the end of the war the World Jewish Congress, the Jewish Agency, and the American Jewish Conference set up a joint committee for the purpose of promoting a Jewish reparation claim.[30] Similar propositions were forwarded by the American Jewish Committee to the State Department, which also aimed at a share of the German reparations for stateless European Jews. The U.S. administration was interested in allocating independent, non-American funds to finance international aid for stateless German and Austrian Nazi victims. Hence, when eighteen nations debated on the allotment of reparations from the Western zones of occupation in Germany at the Paris conference on reparations in November 1945, the U.S. delegation struggled to get a share for stateless, nonrepatriable Nazi victims. As a result of their efforts, article 8 of the Paris Agreement on Reparation stipulated that all nonmonetary gold (i.e., valuables such as jewels and jewelry, dental gold, etc., taken away from murdered Nazi victims) which had been recovered by the Allied armies in Germany should be devoted to the rehabilitation and resettlement of nonrepatriable Nazi victims. German assets in Sweden, Switzerland, and Portugal, and the heirless property of deceased Nazi victims in neutral countries were also intended as an additional source of income for that purpose.[31] Another conference in Paris in June 1946 decided that the bulk of this reparation share should be devoted to Jewish refugees. The American Joint Distribution Committee (JDC) and the Jewish Agency received 90 percent of the total amount of circa U.S.$30 million that was finally collected for nonrepatriable Nazi victims under this regulation. Given the modesty of this sum, it was rather a symbolic success for the Jewish organizations that had fought for a Jewish reparation share.

The issue was put back on the political agenda only after the establishment of two German states in 1949.[32] After that there were a number of clandestine approaches to German officials, in both the West and the East, by Jewish representatives to investigate possibilities of a settlement of a collective Jewish claim. The main driving force behind these contacts was the economic crisis of the State of Israel, which had been established in 1948. However, these were extremely sensitive issues, if only because of the psychological problems that affected any contacts between Germans and Jews at that time. Therefore the Jewish side would have preferred the Allies fetch the chestnuts out of the fire for them. Yet as the Allies strictly refused to do so, there was no alternative to approaching the Germans directly. While the Federal Republic agreed to such talks on a Jewish collective claim, the GDR refused to enter into negotiations on that issue, pointing to the fact, among others, that they had carried their burden and paid significant reparations to the Soviet Union and Poland. Another excuse was the alleged eradication of fascism and anti-Semitism in their territory and also the care they provided to Jewish communities in their territory.[33] (The latter two arguments were not particularly convincing at that time, when great numbers of Jews were fleeing from the GDR due to the fear of a new rise of anti-Semitism.)

After a series of clandestine contacts between representatives of the State of Israel and the Federal Republic, the German Chancellor Konrad Adenauer finally paved the way for official talks with the State of Israel and the Claims Conference, which rallied twenty-three Jewish organizations from around the world. The latter had been established in the immediate aftermath of an official declaration made by Adenauer before the West German Parliament on September 27, 1951. Previously he had refused to publicly express German collective guilt as the Jewish side wished.[34] Yet on the occasion of his speech he asserted the readiness of the Federal Government "to strive for a solution to the material compensation problem [. . .] together with representatives of Jewry and the State of Israel." At the same time he highlighted the "limitations of the German financial capacity due to the bitter necessity to provide for the countless war victims and to care for refugees and exiles" from the East.[35] On the occasion of a secret meeting in London in December 1951 with Nahurm Goldman, the president of the Claims Conference, Adenauer made the far-reaching decision to accept the Israeli claim to U.S.$1 billion as a basis for negotiations.[36] This happened to be two-thirds of the total amount that had been claimed from Germany, while the remaining third had been unsuccessfully demanded from the GDR.

The negotiations between the delegations of the State of Israel, the Claims Conference, and the Federal Republic, which began in March 1952 in Wassenaar, the Netherlands, were extremely complicated. They were overshadowed by fierce demonstrations and street battles in Israel, where a widespread sentiment against any such talks with Germany existed. This was overruled only by the even more urgent need for money to save the beleaguered existence of the State of Israel. While the Israeli claim for U.S.$1 billion was based on the expenses spent on 500,000 Jewish Nazi victims in Israel, the Claims Conference justified an additional demand of U.S.$500 million for claims for heirless Jewish property. Another demand was for the improvement of the German compensation legislation.

The German delegation's insistence on a link with another conference that took place at the same time in London turned out to be a major problem during negotiations: The issue at stake in these parallel talks was German prewar and postwar commercial foreign debt. Yet the Jewish side dwelled on their own claims' priority, which they considered to be at a moral nature, while in London only commercial claims were discussed. After a deep crisis in the Wassenaar deliberations, the Germans finally went ahead. It has been said that they reacted only to American pressure. However, in the first instance it was Chancellor Adenauer himself, who had a vital interest in a settlement, even if not at any price. But when he met strong resistance within his own government both during and after the negotiations, the United States assisted him several times by putting the German adversaries of an agreement under political pressure. At the same time, the U.S. administration was anxious not to assume political and financial responsibility for the outcome and therefore carefully limited their degree of political engagement.

On September 10, 1952, Adenauer, Israeli Foreign Minister Sharett, and Goldmann finally signed the achieved agreements in Luxembourg. In addition to a treaty between the Federal Republic and the State of Israel on a lump-sum payment of DM 3 billion (at that time, the USD-to-DM ratio was 4.2 to 1), two protocols with the Claims Conference were also approved. Protocol No. 1 comprehended the agreed principles for improvements in the existing German compensation legislation for Nazi victims. Protocol No. 2 settled a lump-sum payment for the Claims Conference of DM 450 million. Of the total amount of DM 3.45 billion, which was to be conferred over a time span of fourteen years, one-third had to be provided by the delivery of German goods, and a further third was devoted to the payment of crude oil.[37]

Fierce Arab protests, fearing a bolstering of the Israeli position with the help of German supplies, which continued until ratification of the treaties, again fueled the German adversaries of such a settlement. To win the decisive ballot of the Federal German Parliament on March 18, 1953, Chancellor Adenauer, the head of the Christian-Democratic Party, needed the help of the opposing Social Democratic Party, which was the only party to vote unanimously for the agreement. On the other hand, there was a considerable number of abstentions from the rows of the governing conservative coalition.[38] The German discussion was divided by financial and foreign policy considerations. The Luxembourg agreements were not a ticket for the political integration of the Federal Republic into the West. Yet after Adenauer had raised hopes for an agreement with Israel and the Claims Conference both publicly and in secret talks, a failure of the negotiations would have been regarded as the breaking of a promise. Thus, doubts about the credibility of the Federal Republic might have arisen that would not have been helpful for its claim to being a new and democratic Germany. In the end, the symbolic and material results were equally important for both sides. On the one hand, they were considered an expression of the Federal Republic's will to provide compensation to Jewish Nazi victims. On the other hand, German deliveries to Israel not only bolstered the German export industry but also accelerated Israeli economic development. Several hundred thousand former Jewish Nazi victims received individual indemnification payments, among them circa 250,000 in Israel. There were several further agreements between the Federal Republic and Israel that might also be regarded as elements of an individual and collective compensation. However, in most cases they were not made publicly known, partly because of their effect on the strategic situation in the Near East.[39]

COMPENSATION FOR PERSONAL DAMAGE

Immediately after the surrender of the German Reich there had been an urgent need for care of Nazi victims who had been liberated from concentration camps, prisons, and so on. As said before, steps toward the restitution of Jewish property were speedily established by the Allied authorities, at least in the Western occupation zones. But it took until the late 1940s for further steps to be taken toward settling the compensation of personal losses of Nazi victims. Due to the lack of a central authority, these regulations normally were established on a state level, which led to a multitude of highly diverse regulations.

From the beginning there had been a widespread consensus on who was a Nazi victim: those who had suffered from racial, political, or religious persecution. Yet increasingly in East and West Germany divergent interpretations of the Nazi past emerged. In the East, a two-class system was established whereby communist "fighters" were considered more honorable than Jewish "victims." Conversely, in the West Jews were considered to have been the main target of the Nazi attack, while communists increasingly faced problems receiving compensation for their suffering during the Nazi era. The diversity of social principles also marked the compensation issue. While in East Germany Nazi victims, including Jews, received preferential supplementary benefits—provided they lived in the territory of the GDR—West Germany took another path: "compensation west" was characterized by an attempt to provide indemnification in relation both to the damages resulting from persecution and to the former social position of the claimant. Furthermore, it was not restricted to Nazi victims living in the territory of the Federal Republic but—at least in principle—to those who at the time of their persecution had been Germans, and who were not unfortunate enough to live on the "wrong" side of the Iron Curtain. In short, while the effects of compensation for Nazi victims in West Germany were socially differentiated and politically leveling, in East Germany supplementary benefits dominated that were politically differentiated and socially leveling. Thus there were two contrasting principles of social relations: social security in the East, and restoration of damaged rights in the West.[40]

Benefits for Jewish Nazi victims in East Germany since October 1949 after based on the "Order for the Safeguarding of the Legal Position of Approved Persecutees of the Nazi Regime."[41] As indicated earlier, it affected only those Nazi victims who lived in East German territory, and few Jews did so. This order provided preferential supplementary benefits within the framework of social insurance. It granted benefits referring to pensions, housing and household goods, medical treatment, and so on. Taken together, this happened to be a system of paternalistic care and distribution of privileges, which was typical for the social system of the GDR.[42] While communist resistance fighters stood at the top of the list, Jewish Nazi victims were by no means excluded and—at least from a strictly material aspect—suffered no discrimination.[43] However, the number of Jews who could benefit from these regulations steadily diminished. In 1957 there was a total number of 28,730 approved Nazi victims in the GDR. Among them were only 2,555 (i.e., 9 percent) who had been racially persecuted as Jews.[44] This reflected the Jewish exodus from East to West Germany that had been a consequence of the anti-Semitic wave in the early fifties in the Eastern bloc, and which deeply affected the GDR.[45]

In the 1950s and early 1960s the communist Nazi victims frequently complained about what they considered the privileged situation of the Jewish Nazi victims in the GDR. The main reason for their complaints was that the amount of benefits was dependent on the claimant's former income, which on average had been higher among mainly middle-class Jewish Nazi victims than among political fighters with a commonly working-class background. These grievances finally resulted in a change of the respective legislation. In 1965 a new law was passed in the GDR that paid tribute to the communist Nazi victims, insofar as it established a two-class system: The so-called Honorarium Order no longer granted benefits within the frame of the social security system, but as a pension from the state. Thus the benefits no longer were dependent on former income, but on the claimant's status as a "fighter" or a "victim." Having arrived at retirement age, which was five years lower for both these groups, "fighters" initially received 800 Mark, and "victims" 600 Marks. In comparison to GDR standards of income, those who could benefit from these honorariums were wealthy.[46] However, in 1966 this group encompassed only approximately 35,000, and by 1988 this number had diminished to approximately 10,000. Among them were only about 11 percent who had been persecuted for racial reasons—that is, because they had been considered Jews by the Nazis.[47] (The proportion of them who regarded themselves as Jewish was much lower, both because the GDR had initially attracted mostly communist believers and because, in general, the GDR did not encourage the display of religious identity.) All in all, only a marginal group of Jewish Nazi victims existed that could benefit from some sort of compensation by the GDR, yet this group was, at least with respect to GDR standards, extremely privileged.

These developments sharply contrasted with those in West Germany. Until the establishment of the Federal Republic, only state laws existed that settled the compensation for Nazi victims on a very different level. Therefore, both national and international organizations representing the interests of former Nazi victims and the Allied High Commission urged the Federal Republic to come up with a federal law to provide substantial improvements. This was also part of the regulations of the Contractual Agreements and Protocol No. 1 signed in Luxembourg. To fulfill these obligations, in 1953 the federal Parliament passed the Supplementary Federal Compensation Law.[48] From the beginning this law was considered liable for revision, but it nevertheless established some basic principles that deeply affected the compensation of Nazi victims by the Federal Republic: it was especially important that the federal indemnification legislation did not aim at full compensation for the damages that were inflicted upon Nazi victims between 1933 and 1945. Hence it did not provide compensation according to the principles of the civil law, but aimed at limiting compensation payments.[49] The attempts by the Federal Government to settle claims of Nazi victims were considered to be a compromise between an unavoidable moral obligation and the limited financial and economic abilities of the Federal Republic.

As early as 1956 the revised Federal Compensation Law[50] was passed. This law may be regarded as the pivotal effort of the Federal Republic to settle compensation claims from Jewish and other Nazi victims. As a result of the Federal Compensation Law almost 80 percent of the total money spent for that purpose was yielded.[51] This law, which until 1965 was repeatedly going to be revised, is exhaustive and extremely complicated. Yet sometimes even tiny variations in the wording of the law made a decisive difference for hundreds of thousands of former Nazi victims. The Federal Compensation Law included only some of those people who had suffered persecution by the Nazi regime in the widest sense. A first restriction was imposed by the fact that only those who were considered victims of racial, political, or religious persecution between 1933 and 1945 could apply—which was clearly the case for Jews. An even more important restriction was that only those who had lived in the area of Germany (within the borders of December 1, 1937) or those who later moved to the Federal Republic within certain deadlines were entitled to apply. In short, the Federal Compensation Law primarily focused on those who currently were German nationals or who had been German nationals at the time of their persecution by the Nazis. A third important restriction was provided by the fact that only those who currently were living in states that entertained diplomatic relations with the Federal Republic were entitled to a claim. This restriction excluded mostly claimants from Eastern Europe and the GDR. There were only a few exceptions to the last rule, including primarily the displaced persons and the so-called "special groups" of persecutees, among them especially refugees and stateless Nazi victims who enjoyed restricted claims.[52]

The Federal Compensation Law established a number of categories of damages, and claimants could apply separately for each of them. These categories were damage to life, to body and health, to freedom, to property (especially as a consequence of the payment of special taxes and duties for Jews), and also damage to professional and economic advancement. With respect to damage to property there was sometimes competition with the Federal Restitution Law. This affected especially the recently much-debated question of unpaid life insurance claims resulting from Nazi persecution. Even if there was still a lot of criticism of this law, twenty years after the end of the Nazi regime hundreds of thousands of Jewish and other Nazi victims finally were eligible to file claims.

However, while the enforcement of the Federal Compensation Law finally gained momentum, there were again political struggles on the issue of compensation. On the one hand, representatives of the Nazi victims demanded further improvements of the existing legislation. The Claims Conference, which played a pivotal role within this process, urged for access to the law for further groups of Nazi victims that so far had been excluded.[53] They also put pressure on the German government by organizing public protest rallies in the United States, a weapon to which Bonn was particularly sensitive. On the other hand, there were attempts to foster a negative mood among the German population against compensation payments for Nazi victims: Among others, several German federal ministers of finance were eager to point out the possible negative effects on German economic stability that compensation payments going abroad would have, thus making use of the deep-rooted German inflation trauma. One of the most problematic consequences of such campaigns was the encouragement of a negative attitude toward compensation claims and a tendency toward more restrictive decisions among the German compensation bureaucracy.[54]

In 1965 the federal Parliament finally passed a revision of the Federal Compensation Law that got the demonstrative suffix "final law,"[55] thus expressing the firm will that this law should never again be liable to any changes. This was related to a broad consensus in the Federal Republic that it was time to look forward and to draw the final line under the Nazi past. For the next two decades the climate was unreceptive to calls for further improvements of the existing compensation legislation. Even Nahum Goldmann declared that with the enactment of the Federal Compensation Final Law, all future demands of the Claims Conference were obsolete, for which he was highly criticized by other organizations representing the interests of former Nazi victims.[56]

As a result of intense negotiations, mainly with the Claims Conference, the Federal Compensation Final Law comprised more than 100 amendments. Part of this was a compromise on the question of those Jews who had not emigrated from Eastern European countries until the respective deadline of the Federal Indemnification Law. For this group a special fund with DM 1.2 billion was created, after Goldmann threatened to launch international protests.[57] By creating this kind of special fund the German government had avoided opening the Federal Compensation Law to this group—this strategy also became a model for settling future demands for an increase in compensation.

The Claims Conference also succeeded in a number of other cases: There were important improvements for the widows of Nazi victims, for those who had suffered damage to their health or to their professional advancement, and so on. For the filing of claims a final deadline at the end of 1969 was established.[58] Any future attempts at improvements in the law or at achieving access for groups of Nazi victims who so far had been excluded were fruitless. As already mentioned, whenever the German government saw the necessity to react to demands for further improvements in the compensation of Nazi victims, they decided to set up a special fund or to settle these questions in related laws. Yet the Federal Compensation Final Law was no longer liable to any changes, which sharply contrasted with several laws dealing with other financial aspects of the Nazi past.

The available statistical information on the assessment of the Federal Indemnification Law is very sketchy. This is partly the effect of deliberate decisions by the German authorities. While they are anxious to provide impressive figures to demonstrate the German efforts toward compensation of Nazi victims, they are also afraid of a public discussion on the scale of these payments. The individual payments varied—depending on the categories of claims—from extremely modest to extremely generous. This may be illustrated by two extremes: For one month spent in a concentration camp, only DM 150 for damage to freedom could be claimed. A prospective engineer who was prevented by the Nazis from finishing his exams could claim DM 10,000 for damage to education, while any lawyer in the same situation received a lifelong judge's pension, provided he declared that it had been his will to enter into that career (this could total hundreds of thousands of deutsche Marks).[59] These disparities also hint at the varying capacity of different groups to establish their particular interests within the law.

Included in the little information provided by the official statistics is the total amount of expenses paid according to the Federal Compensation Law until today. Even though no more claims could be filed since the end of 1969, there are still ongoing payments for about 100,000 Nazi victims receiving pensions. Thus, until today about DM 80 billion have been paid in the execution of this law.[60] According to estimates, about one million Nazi victims benefited from the Federal Compensation Law. Due to the nature of existing statistics, it is not possible to indicate the exact share of Jewish claimants. However, it may be assumed that it is a mirror image of the situation in the GDR, where in later years only about 10 percent of the approved Nazi victims had suffered racial persecution.[61] A strong indicator for the overwhelming share of Jewish claimants is that about 80 percent of the approved payments went abroad, mostly to the United States or Israel.

The Federal Indemnification Law has in many ways been important for the overall impression of German efforts to compensate Jewish Nazi victims. Besides the financial aspects, another aspect was of greatest importance for this: as in the case of the Federal Restitution Law, the claims assessment procedure generated encounters between the former victims and the German bureaucracy. Especially during the first decades these encounters produced much frustration and hardship. This even led to the accusation that the compensation procedure turned out to be a "second persecution."[62] Even if this may be considered to be an exaggeration, there can be no doubt that considerable problems overshadowed the meetings. For example, in the 1960s the number of rejected claims for damage to health, which of course is extremely sensitive to the way medical expertise is used, differed in several states—from 15 percent in Berlin to 66 percent in Baden-Wurttemberg.[63] (The German states were in charge of the enactment of this law as there was no federal compensation administration.) However, in later years a more positive attitude seems to have prevailed among the compensation authorities.

Of course, it is extremely difficult to provide a fair assessment of this situation in only a few words. Yet it may be helpful to hint at a structural problem that affected this critical encounter between Nazi victims and the compensation bureaucracy: Beyond all individual injustices that certainly can be discovered by close scrutiny of the enactment of the German compensation legislation, a deeper conflict exists between the holistic approach to the issue by individual Nazi victims and the structure of the German compensation administration, which, by its very nature, could proceed only within the limits of a bureaucratic rationality. This quite naturally produced conflicts on a communicative level. However, as the example of the regional variety of rejected claims for damage to health clearly reveals, the German indemnification administration was also influenced by a mixture of prejudices and financial considerations.

SETTLEMENTS OF GERMAN COMPANIES
FOR JEWISH SLAVE LABOR

At the heart of German compensation legislation, as it evolved during the postwar years, lay the distinction between compensation for German nationals and reparations for foreign nationals. In a way, the path to compensation for Nazi victims had been entered into for the reason that German nationals who had suffered Nazi persecution were not entitled to reparation claims. As a consequence, however, many Nazi victims had no chance to claim compensation, simply because they were not German nationals. There were several attempts to shatter this legal wall. However, on this issue the German government could for many years rely on the aid of the United States: Washington repeatedly frustrated attempts from Paris and London to include foreign nationals in the German compensation legislation.[64] For the sake of German financial capacity during the first postwar decade, the U.S. administration insisted on a strict separation between internal compensation and external reparations. They were concerned not only about a German military contribution to NATO, but also about their own financial interests.

Hence at the London conference on German foreign debts in 1952, where Germany's pre- and postwar commercial debts were debated, an open conflict emerged between the delegations of the United States and the Netherlands. The latter urged the inclusion of individual compensation claims of their nationals who had suffered Nazi persecution. This referred especially to claims for unpaid wages of forced laborers from the Netherlands who had been employed, for example, by the IG Farben company. Yet the U.S. delegation thwarted this attempt, since it was not ready to accept any reduction in its own demands. As the United States had been a major creditor, they had an overwhelming interest in the repayment of credits they previously had provided to Germany.[65] As a result, any claims resulting from the Second World War from states who had been at war with or occupied by Germany, as well as any such claims from nationals of these states, against the German Reich or institutions or persons acting on behalf of it were delayed until a final settlement of the reparation issue.[66] In short: any compensation claims from foreign Nazi victims were prevented until the enactment of a peace treaty with Germany. This meant a postponement *ad calendas graecas.* Article 5 (2) of the London Agreement on Foreign Debts from 1953 proved to be a rock-solid legal bulwark against all future foreign individual compensation claims— at least until German reunification radically altered the scene. This affected especially the compensation claims of foreign former concentration camp inmates or the claims for unpaid wages of foreign forced laborers.[67]

Among the forced laborers who had been "employed" during the Second World War predominantly by German industry and agriculture, there were three major groups. The first group embraced about 9.5 to 10 million foreigners, who were forced to work in Germany during the years between 1939 and 1945. A second group of forced laborers consisted of concentration camp inmates (among them a considerable number of Jews), and a third group of European Jews who were forced to work for the Germans in the occupied countries. So far, any numbers on the size of the latter groups are highly speculative, but certainly they comprised hundred of thousands.[68] In numbers, Jews constituted only a minor proportion of the whole number of forced workers. But their fate was the worst, since for them work was intended to be a means of murder, which was not the case for forced workers as a whole.

However, all groups of forced laborers until recently had in common that they were not entitled to claim compensation. The Federal Compensation Law did not consider forced labor to be a specific Nazi persecution but rather persecution for reasons of nationality. Only a minor share of forced laborers could claim compensation for damage to freedom, provided they belonged to the above-mentioned groups that had access to this law.[69] The German government considered claims of foreign forced laborers as part of the international claims of their respective states against the German Reich. Therefore, until recently, the London Agreement on Foreign Debts effectively blocked any such claims. For several decades the German companies concerned also made use of this situation. They unanimously argued that they had been forced by the German Reich to employ forced laborers or that they had simply acted on orders from the Reich.[70]

In the 1950s and 1960s several former forced laborers filed lawsuits in Germany against their former employers to receive compensation for wages and damage to health. German courts admitted that these claims were justified, yet they decided that they came either too early or too late. The first case affected the bulk of slave laborers, who were nationals of a foreign state that formerly had been at war with Germany or occupied by the Reich during the war. In this case their claims were postponed by the London Agreement on Foreign Debts until a German peace treaty. German claimants seemed to be in a better position, yet in their case the courts went the other way around: they regularly argued that these claims were lapsed. There was one single exception, when a German court in 1965 conceded a Jewish prisoner a compensation of DM 178.80 for unpaid wages for six months of forced labor.[71]

Since civil law actions of individual forced laborers against German companies were more or less futile, the Claims Conference chose another approach that was successful in a number of cases. Using a blend of diplomatic persuasion and economic pressure, between 1957 and 1962 it prevailed upon several German companies (I. G. Farben in Liquidation, Krupp, A.E.G., Siemens, and Rheinmetall) to settle claims of Jewish forced laborers from concentration camps employed by these companies during the war. After difficult negotiations they agreed to pay amounts between DM 2.5 million (Siemens) and DM 52 million (I. G. Farben in Liquidation), which came to a total amount of circa DM 51.5 million that was to be distributed by the Claims Conference.[72] Yet the respective companies explicitly rejected any legal or moral obligation in connection with these agreements, and the Claims Conference had to relinquish any future claims against them. Thus any prejudgment against other German companies was to be avoided. Three other companies followed in the 1980s and the early 1990s: The Deutsche Bank paid DM 5 million in favor of former Jewish forced laborers of the newly acquired Feldmühle Nobel AG to the Claims Conference. The Daimler-Benz AG paid DM 20 million, of which the Claims Conference received DM 10 million. Thus they settled a claim that Flick had reneged on about twenty years earlier. Finally, the Volkswagen AG paid DM 12 million in favor of their formerly employed forced workers to organizations in their respective home countries. What German companies so far had agreed to was primarily the result of anxieties about public opinion in the United States, which was highly relevant for their business interests. This was the main reason other organizations of forced laborers from the former Eastern bloc could not compete with the success of the Claims Conference.[73]

In the 1980s, a growing interest in the issue of forced laborers and other so called "forgotten victims"—Gypsies, homosexuals, deserters from the Wehrmacht, people who were forcefully sterilized, and so on emerged in West Germany. Jews were not a particularly important group within this public discourse: The general impression was that Jewish claims had been resolved relatively fairly within the existing compensation laws, while some other groups had been less effective in settling their claims. At that time there was also a remarkable difference in styles of political action: The Claims Conference kept to its traditional model (i.e., confidential talks with the German administration that were closed to the public, combined with hints at the potential mobilization of the American public). On the other hand, advocates of the so-called forgotten victims aggressively tried to mobilize the German public against the German administration. However, substantial changes were not produced by German society but by major events in the realm of international politics.

ADDITIONAL SETTLEMENTS AFTER GERMAN REUNIFICATION

As a consequence of the end of the Cold War, the compensation issue reappeared on the agenda.[74] There were several reasons for this: First, the claims of former Nazi victims from countries behind the Iron Curtain could no longer simply be ignored by the Federal Republic. Second, a number of questions that hitherto had not been settled by the GDR now fell under the jurisdiction of the Federal Republic when, as one of the major results of the end of the Cold War, German reunification became possible. In the years before, the political elites of the Federal Republic paid lip service to this political aim but in general had not really anticipated that reunification would become reality. Once it took place it stirred up not only joy, but also a nightmare: What would happen to the postponement of reparation requests that had been established by the 1953 London Agreement on Foreign Debts? As said before, this question also affected many aspects of the compensation issue, especially claims from Nazi victims from Eastern Europe.

There are still several aspects of the diplomatic process of German reunification that are not well researched by historians, including the question of how the Federal Republic managed to get rid of its sword of Damocles—that is, the peace-treaty clause of the London Agreement on Foreign Debts, during the so-called "Four-Plus-Two-Talks" among delegations of the United States, the Soviet Union, Great Britain, France, and Germany. Yet the Federal Republic managed to establish an agreement that the existing rights and obligations of the four victorious powers with respect to the international status of Germany were to be superseded by a final agreement according to international law. This document was signed in Moscow on September 12, 1990.[75]

Several traditional aspects of peace treaties remained excluded from this agreement, including the settlement of border, property, reparation, and compensation issues. To the detriment of claims from former Nazi victims, the Federal Republic obtained security against the necessity to settle a number of "open questions" that had been postponed for decades. However, the Federal Republic did not receive this concession free of charge: While a number of considerable obligations toward the former victorious powers are known that the Federal Republic had to assume (and many more are rumored), at least some settlements in favor of Nazi victims after 1990 may be considered to belong to this context.

In the course of this process, the Federal Republic started negotiations with the Soviet Union and Poland to settle claims of Nazi victims from these countries. In the early 1990s the Federal Republic agreed to pay approximately DM 1.5 billion for this purpose; however, the dissolution of the Soviet Union complicated the assessment since many more countries reemerged on the European landscape.[76] The Claims Conference also entered into a new series of negotiations during the unification process. Yet the talks on the hitherto unresolved question of looted Jewish property in the GDR were complicated by the fact that initially two German governments with divergent interests participated. The West German government considered the question of restitution of looted Jewish property in the broader framework of the restitution of property of East Germans who pre-

viously had gone to West Germany, and therefore it preferred restitution *in natura*. On the other hand, the East German government
was interested in providing then–East Germans security after reunification and therefore preferred indemnification to restitution. The
final outcome was the Law for the Settlement of Open Property
Questions, which was passed by the last Parliament of the GDR. This
law, which was primarily devoted to property questions related to the
history of the GDR, also decided the settlement of Jewish restitution
claims referring to the Nazi era.[77] With respect to the latter, the federal government revised this law in 1992 to adapt it to the standards
of the Allied restitution laws, which meant giving priority to restitution over indemnification. Since then, restitution of Jewish property
in the territory of the former GDR has been effectively enforced and
has led to generally satisfying results. In general, it affects either the
heirs of Jewish Nazi victims or—in cases where there are no more
heirs—the Claims Conference. Therefore, the restitution of Jewish
property today is carried out in a much more regular "business style"
than in the 1940s or 1950s, when a much higher degree of personal
affection was involved in these cases.[78]

Another important point on the agenda of the Claims Conference was unresolved compensation issues. Among others, this referred primarily to the claims of Jewish Nazi victims who so far had
not yet received compensation because they had lived behind the
Iron Curtain. A first step was an agreement in October 1992, based
on article 2 of the Agreement of September 18, 1990, of the Unification Treaty between the Federal Republic of Germany and the GDR.[79]
This agreement affected Jewish Nazi victims from Central and Eastern Europe who were then living in Germany, the United States, Australia, or Western Europe and who had not yet received any compensation and were living in a state of economic emergency. Yet the
Claims Conference requested that survivors who were still living in
Central and Eastern Europe should also get German pensions. The
Federal Republic agreed to a settlement only after a public campaign
in the United States: The American Jewish Committee confronted
the public with pictures of a Baltic SS soldier and a Baltic Jewish Nazi
victim, rhetorically asking which one of them received a German
pension. Again, public opinion in the United States proved to be the
strongest weapon in the struggle for compensation. In early 1998 the
Federal Republic agreed to pay DM 500 million to survivors of the

Holocaust in Central and Eastern Europe (starting in 1999) and for the first time accepted monthly payments.[80]

An additional weapon strengthened the arsenal of those who struggled for German compensation payments in the 1990s. The filing of the first class-action lawsuit in the U.S. federal court against Swiss commercial banks in October 1996 initiated the use of litigation as a tool in the United States for Nazi-era claims. Since this was taken seriously both by the courts and by the defendant banks, the same lawyers also filed lawsuits against German and other European enterprises. While this pressured these companies to move toward a greater readiness to compensation, this legal instrument can also be regarded as a double-edged sword, as it provoked discomfort that compensation politics were increasingly characterized by a kind of blackmail.[81] The recent aggressive campaigns may be justified by their success at overcoming the stubborn attitude of German companies or the German government in the compensation question. In the end, it was the German attitude considering compensation claims from Nazi victims as a kind of debt to be collected from the debtor at his residence that was responsible for the requirement of such methods. However, they also provoke questions as to how far the results reflect a tendency that those who are able to use the instruments of U.S. public opinion and courtrooms most effectively will receive the most favorable compensation.

These effects can also be seen in the case of the recent struggle over the foundation "Remembrance, Responsibility and Future." This foundation, which is to serve the main purpose of compensating former Nazi forced laborers and other Nazi victims, was established in summer 2000 by the enactment of a German federal law. It received a donation of DM 10 billion, provided by the German government and German industry. The Claims Conference will receive approximately DM 2 billion to settle the claims of former Jewish forced laborers and also DM 274 million for social purposes to benefit Holocaust survivors. The International Commission on Holocaust-Era Insurance Claims will receive DM 150 million to settle unpaid life insurance claims resulting from Nazi persecution, plus DM 350 million for its humanitarian fund.[82] The bulk of the money will thus go to partner organizations in Central and Eastern Europe to settle claims of former (non-Jewish) forced laborers.

In the preamble of this law, the German Federal Parliament clearly expressed the expectation that German companies will no longer suffer the threat of being sued before American courts for their improper actions during the Nazi era. However, at the present time the German side does not yet consider the guarantees provided by the American side to be sufficient and therefore is reluctant to start paying off. The rationale behind this is that both the German government and German business regard this law as drawing the line under the long story of dealing with the liabilities resulting from Nazi crimes.

However, one might ask whether this foundation really will put an end to the story of German compensation for Nazi victims, or whether it will just be another part of a serialized novel. As we have seen, as early as 1965 the West German Parliament passed a revision of the Federal Compensation Law that was explicitly labeled "final law." Given the fact that it is simply impossible to compensate Nazi crimes in an encompassing sense, the answer to the question of when compensation to the victims will be adequately settled will always be of a political nature. At least with respect to Jewish Nazi victims, one might say that over time the question of compensation has shifted more and more from individuals who had personally suffered from Nazi persecution to their individual and collective heirs. With this, the shift from restoration of individual biographies of Jewish Nazi victims to the establishment of Jewish identity becomes more and more dominant. However, as we have seen with the discussion of the earliest Jewish plans to settle compensation claims, the aspect of a collective claim aiming at the future of the Jewish people played an important role from the beginning, while alternative, universalistic concepts finally did not prevail.

CONCLUDING REMARKS

The issue of German compensation for Jewish Nazi victims after 1945 refers to the historic circumstances defining actual models of "justice": As I have tried to show, there was more than one possible solution given the fact that in an absolute sense it was impossible to make good what had happened. Compensation had also been a highly disputed issue within different Jewish groups, representing different approaches to "justice," which also reflected different attitudes to Jewish identity. At the same time, these groups managed to show unity against the Germans, thus both using and reinforcing Germans' traditional fear of a mighty "world Jewry." Therefore, at least as far as international Jewish organizations were concerned, compensation and restitution basically were not considered a means of reeducation of the German people, but a means of restoring the lives of Jewish individuals and the Jewish people outside Germany.

Furthermore, the issue of compensation for Jewish Nazi victims points to the question under which the very conditions that moral claims for justice can prevail. As we have seen, the United States played a decisive role in the political process leading to German compensation from the beginning until today. It repeatedly pressed Germany to compensate, especially Jewish Nazi victims, displaying and wielding a range of instruments of power, from direct control in the immediate postwar era to economic pressure in the following decades. At times, however, it also protected Germany from foreign pressure to assume further financial burdens by improving existing compensation for Nazi victims, for which the London Agreement on Foreign Debts gives an example. Yet the United States always considered claims from Jewish Nazi victims against Germany in the broader framework of its own overall national interest, which sometimes meant that it had other priorities.

The ultimate reason, however, that the United States and some major Jewish organizations came to play the roles they did was that, all in all, Germany did not regard the compensation of Nazi victims—Jewish as well as others—as a debt for which they should actively seek a solution. Instead they showed a strong tendency to wait for claims first and then to try to beat down the price. Thus, while in the end the Federal Republic has spent enormous amounts for compensation, especially of Jewish Nazi victims, there remains an impression of an oddly assorted set of settlements that seem to reflect the bargaining power of individual groups rather than mirror the historical structure of Nazi crimes and related questions of justice.

This is not a consequence only of German political pragmatism, but also of a substantial difference in the meaning of compensation for Nazi victims. On the German side, compensation efforts have always been considered a process that one day or another should terminate. In other words, from a German perspective, paying compensation has always implied the desire to settle the case, at least in a material sense. On the Jewish side, however, things are put differently. Due to the very nature of the Holocaust, indemnification has always been considered an open-ended process that can never come to a close. With respect to this controversy, one might argue that as long as there are still individual survivors of Nazi persecution who have not been adequately compensated, there is no question that these are legitimate claims. But what will happen in a not-too-distant future, when the last survivors will have died? To put the question in the words of Henry Rousso:

> What shall we do after reparations? How to deal with a collective suffering which will be handed on from generation to generation? How is a guilt to be paid off which can neither be eradicated by collective consciousness . . . nor by the after all considerable progress of historical knowledge nor by the symbolic, juridical and financial acknowledgement of these crimes? Maybe the only acceptable answer will be to keep the question itself alive without trying to answer it.[83]

NOTES

I am very indebted to Marilyn Henry who provided me with valuable comments on this article.

1. This distinction became relevant when the Jewish Claims Conference refused to assume responsibility for those former forced workers of the German war industry who had been persecuted because of their Jewish descent, but had no Jewish denomination.

2. "Regierungserklärung: Anlage zu Bericht Ernst Kaltenbrunners an Martin Bormann, 5.8.1944." Printed in *Spiegelbild einer Verschwörung: Die Kaltenbrunner-Berichte an Bormann und Hitler über das Attentat vom 20. Juli 1944. Geheime Dokumente aus dem ehemaligen Reichssicherheitshauptamt,* ed. Archiv Peter (Stuttgart: Seewald, 1961), 149.

3. Nehemiah Robinson, *Indemnification and Reparations: Jewish Aspects* (New York: Institute of Jewish Affairs of the American Jewish Congress and World Jewish Congress, 1944), 224.

4. For the following see Nana Sagi, *German Reparations: A History of the Negotiations* (Jerusalem: Magnes Press, 1980), 14–27; and Constantin Goschler, *Wiedergutmachung: Westdeutschland und die Verfolgten des Nationalsozialismus, 1945–1954* (Munich: Oldenbourg, 1992), 38–48.

5. Nahum Goldmann, *Mein Leben als deutscher Jude* (Munich: Langen-Müller, 1980), 372.

6. See, for example, Hugo Marx, *The Case of the German Jews vs. Germany: A Legal Basis for the Claims of German Jews against Germany*

(New York: Egmont Press, 1944); and Fritz Moses, *Aus der Geschichte der Wiedergutmachung: Zu Bruno Weils siebzigstem Geburtstag. Bruno Weil, ihrem Gründer und Präsidenten überreicht im April 1953 von der Axis Victims League* (New York: Axis Victims League, 1953). See also Goschler, *Wiedergutmachung*, 4ff.

7. Robinson, *Indemnifications and Reparations*, 244ff.

8. Goschler, *Wiedergutmachung*, 41–4.

9. Ibid., 49–52.

10. Ibid., 60ff.

11. See *Morgenthau Diary (Germany)*, vol. 2. prepared by the Subcommittee to Investigate the Administration of the Internal Security Act and Other Internal Security Laws of the Committee on the Judiciary United States Senate (Washington, D.C.: USGPO, 1967), 1243ff.

12. See Thomas Schüler, "Das Wiedergutmachungsgesetz vom 14. September 1945 in Thüringen," *Jahrbuch für Antisemitismusforschung* 2 (1993): 118–38; for the results of the enforcement of the law, see Lothar Mertens, *Davidstern unter Hammer und Zirkel, Die jüdischen Gemeinden in der SBZ/DDR und ihre Behandlung durch Partei und Staat 1945–1990* (Hildesheim: Olms, 1997), 229–37; Angelika Timm, *Hammer, Zirkel, Davidstern: Das gestörte Verhältnis der DDR zu Zionismus und Staat Israel* (Bonn: Bouvier, 1997), 68–80; and the articles by Ralf Kessler, Philipp Spannuth, Angelika Timm, and Christian Meyer-Seitz, in *"Arisierung" und Restitution: Die Rückerstattung jüdischen Eigentums in Deutschland und Österreich nach 1945 und 1990*, ed. Constantin Goschler and Jürgen Lillteicher (Göttingen: Wallstein, 2002).

13. See Walter Schwarz, *Rückerstattung nach den Gesetzen der Alliierten Mächte*, vol. 1 in *Die Wiedergutmachung nationalsozialistischen Unrechts durch die Bundesrepublik Deutschland* (Munich: Beck, 1974), 69–95. This book belongs to a semi-official series of six volumes published under the auspices of the Federal Ministry of Finance; see also Constantin Goschler, "Die Auseinandersetzung um die Rückerstattung 'arisierten' jüdischen Eigentums nach 1945," in *Die deutsche Bevölkerung und die Judenverfolgung im Dritten Reich*, ed. Ursula Büttner (Hamburg: Christians, 1992), 339–56. For the history of restitution of Jewish property in West Germany see also Constantin Goschler, "Die Politik der Rückerstattung," in Goschler and Lillteicher, *"Arisierung" und Restitution*, 99–125; Jürgen Lillteicher, "Rechtsstaatlichkeit und Verfolgungserfahrung: 'Arisierung' und fiskalische Ausplünderung vor Gericht," in Goschler and Lillteicher, *"Arisierung" und Restitution*, 127–59; Jürgen Lillteicher, "West Germany and Compensation for National Socialist Expropriations: The Restitution of Jewish Property by the Treasury, 1947–1964," in *Coming to Terms with the Past in West-Germany: The 1960s*, ed. Philipp Gassert and Alan Steinweis (forthcoming).

14. Goschler, *Wiedergutmachung,* 114–22.

15. Ibid., 111 ff. These organizations were the World Jewish Congress, the American Joint Distribution Committee (JDC) the Jewish Agency for Palestine, the American Jewish Committee, and the American Jewish Conference.

16. Ibid., 172. See also Jürgen Lillteicher, "Die Rückerstattung jüdischen Eigentums in Westdeutschland: Eine Studie über Rechsstaatlichkeit, Vergangenheitsbewältigung und Verfolgungserfahrung" (diss., University of Freiburg, 2002).

17. Schwarz, *Rückerstattung,* 360, 364f. In 1957 in the former U.S. zone of occupation, 44 percent of the claimants came from the United States, 18 percent from Germany, 9 percent from Great Britain, 5 percent from Switzerland, 5 percent from Israel, and 8 percent from Central and South America. See Schwarz, *Rückerstattung,* 366. The non-Jewish claims presumably are included in the number of claims from Germany. See ibid., 366.

18. See, as an example, Helmut Köhrer, *Entziehung, Beraubung, Restitution: Vom Wandel der Beziehungen zwischen Juden und Nichtjuden durch Verfolgung und Restitution* (Baden-Baden: JUS-Verlagsgesellschaft, 1951), S. 170.

19. Schwarz, *Rückerstattung,* 368.

20. Ibid., 71 ff., 275f.; Goschler, "Auseinandersetzung um die Rückerstattung."

21. Elisabeth Noelle and Erich Peter Neumann, *Jahrbuch der öffentlichen Meinung: 1947–1955* (Allensbach: Verlag für Demoskopie, 1956), 130; see also the results in Report No. 113 (5 Dec. 1951), "German Opinions on Jewish Restitution and some Associated Issues," in *Public Opinion in Semisovereign Germany: The HICOG Surveys, 1949–1955,* ed. Anna Merritt and Richard L. Merritt (Urbana: University of Illinois Press, 1980), 146.

22. Walter Schwarz, "Die Wiedergutmachung nationalsozialistischen Unrechts durch die Bundesrepublik Deutschland: Ein Überblick," in *Wiedergutmachung in der Bundesrepublik Deutschland,* ed. Ludolf Herbst and Constantin Goschler (Munich: Oldenbourg, 1989), 33–54, here 34, 39f.; Otto Küster, *Erfahrungen in der deutschen Wiedergutmachung* (Tübingen: Mohr, 1967), 9f.

23. "Bundesgesetz zur Regelung der rückerstattungsrechtlichen Geldverbindlichkeiten des Deutschen Reichs und gleichgestellter Rechtsträger," in *Bundesgesetzblatt* 1 (1957): 734ff.

24. Hermann-Josef Brodesser et al., *Wiedergutmachung und Kriegsfolgenliquidation: Geschichte—Regelungen—Zahlungen* (Munich: Beck, 2000), 249. This volume provides a semiofficial account of the compensation issue and also the official statistical survey.

25. See Schwarz, "Überblick," 39ff.; Friedrich Biella et al., *Das Bundesrückerstattungsgesetz,* vol. 2 in *Die Wiedergutmachung nationalsozialistischen Unrechts durch die Bundesrepublik Deutschland* (Munich: Beck, 1981).

26. See Jeffrey Herf, *Divided Memory: The Nazi Past in the Two Germanys* (Cambridge: Harvard University Press, 1997), 106–61.

27. Angelika Timm, *Jewish Claims against East Germany: Moral Obligations and Pragmatic Policy* (Budapest: Central European University Press, 1997), 89–91.

28. See Mertens, *Davidstern unter Hammer und Zirkel,* 245f.; Timm, *Jewish Claims against East Germany,* especially pp. 17ff., 64ff.

29. For the following paragraph see the detailed account by Timm, *Jewish Claims against East Germany,* 94–180.

30. For the following see Goschler, *Wiedergutmachung,* 64ff.

31. Final Act and Annex of the Paris Conference on Reparation, part I, art. 8: "Allocation of a Reparation Share to Non-Repatriable Victims of German Action," in *Department of State Bulletin* 14, no. 343 (27 January 1946): 118f.

32. For the following see Sagi, *German Reparations to Israel;* Lily Gardner Feldman, *The Special Relationship between West Germany and Israel* (Boston: Allen and Unwin, 1984); Ronald Zweig, *German Reparations and the Jewish World: A History of the Jewish Claims Conference,* 2nd ed. (London: Frank Cass, 2001), 50–68; Goschler, *Wiedergutmachung,* 257–85; and Yeshayahu A. Jelinek, ed., *Zwischen Moral und Realpolitik: Deutsch-israelische Beziehungen 1945–1965. Eine Dokumentensammlung* (Gerlingen: Bleicher, 1997).

33. See Timm, *Jewish Claims against Israel,* 85ff.

34. Kai von Jena, "Versöhnung mit Israel? Die deutsch-israelischen Verhandlungen bis zum Wiedergutmachungsabkommen von 1952," in *Vierteljahrshefte für Zeitgeschichte* 34 (1986): 457–80, here pp. 463f.; Yeshayahu A. Jelinek, "Political Acumen, Altruism, Foreign Pressure or Moral Debt: Konrad Adenauer and the 'Shilumim,'" in *Tel Aviver Jahrbuch für deutsche Geschichte* 19 (1990): 77–102, here pp. 87f.; and Tom Segev, *The Seventh Million: The Israelis and the Holocaust* (New York: Hill and Wang, 1993).

35. Verhandlungen des Deutschen Bundestags, 165. Sitzung, 27 September 1951, in *Stenographische Berichte* (Bonn: Bonner Universitäts-Buchdruckerei), vol. 9, 6697f.

36. Konrad Adenauer to Nahum Goldmann, 6 December 1951, printed in Jelinek, *Zwischen Moral und Realpolitik,* 177.

37. Documents Relating to the Agreement between the Government of Israel and the Government of the Federal Republic of Germany (signed on 10 September 1952 at Luxembourg), ed. by the State of Israel, Ministry of Foreign Affairs, 1953, 125–68.

38. Verhandlungen des Deutschen Bundestags, 255. Sitzung, 18 March 1953, in *Stenographische Berichte,* vol. 15, 12362–6.

39. For the enactment and the effects of the agreement see Sagi, *German Reparations,* 194–201; Zweig, *German Reparations,* 67–185; Segev, *Seventh Million,* 189–210; Jelinek, *Moral und Realpolitik.* The Federal Republic not only provided considerable military assistance to Israel but, for example, established extremely advantageous possibilities for certain Israeli nationals to enter the German social security system and thus acquire the right to German pensions. The latter arrangement later became a matter of public interest because it produced a considerable number of frauds.

40. See Ralf Kessler and Hartmut Rüdiger Peter, *Wiedergutmachung im Osten Deutschlands: Grundsätzliche Diskussionen und die Praxis in Sachsen-Anhalt* (Frankfurt am Main: Peter Lang, 1996), 228.

41. "Verordnung zur Sicherung der rechtlichen Stellung der anerkannten Verfolgten des Naziregimes," in *Zentralverordnungsblatt: Amtliches Organ der Deutschen Wirtschaftskommission und ihrer Hauptverwaltungen sowie der Deutschen Verwaltungen für Inneres, Justiz und Volksbildung* 14, no. 89 (October 1949), 765f. See also Kessler and Peter, *Wiedergutmachung im Osten Deutschlands,* 191f.

42. Compare with Sigrid Meuschel, "Überlegungen zu einer Herrschafts- und Gesellschaftsgeschichte der DDR," in *Geschichte und Gesellschaft* 19 (1993): 5–14, here pp. 12f.; Hans Günter Hockerts, "Grundlinien und soziale Folgen der Sozialpolitik in der DDR," in *Sozialgeschichte der DDR,* ed. Hartmut Kaelble, Jürgen Kocka, and Hartmut Zwahr (Stuttgart: Klett-Cotta, 1994), 519–44, here p. 529ff.

43. "Durchführungsbestimmungen zu der Anordnung zur Sicherung der rechtlichen Stellung der anerkannten Verfolgten des Naziregimes vom 10. February 1950," in *Gesetzblatt der DDR,* no. 14, 87–92; "Richtlinien für die Anerkennung als Verfolgte des Naziregimes," in *Gesetzblatt der DDR,* no. 14, 92–4.

44. Constantin Goschler, "Nicht bezahlt? Die Wiedergutmachung für Opfer der nationalsozialistischen Verfolgung in der SBZ/DDR," in *Wirtschaftliche Folgelasten des Krieges in der SBZ/DDR,* ed. Christoph Buchheim (Baden-Baden: Nomos, 1995), 169–91, here p. 183; Olaf Groehler, "Integration und Ausgrenzung von NS-Opfern: Zur Anerkennungs- und Entschädigungsdebatte in der Sowjetischen Besatzungszone Deutschlands 1945 bis 1949," in *Historische DDR-Forschung: Aufsätze und Studien,* ed. Jürgen Kocka (Berlin: Akademie Verlag, 1993), 105–27, here p. 127.

45. For the following cf. Constantin Goschler, "Paternalismus und Verweigerung: Die DDR und die Wiedergutmachung für jüdische Verfolgte des Nationalsozialismus," in *Jahrbuch für Antisemitismusforschung* 2 (1993): 93–117, here pp. 103f.; Mario Keßler, *Die SED und die Juden:*

zwischen Repression und Toleranz. Politische Entwicklungen bis 1967 (Berlin: Akademie-Verlag, 1995), 85–105; Mertens, *Davidstern unter Hammer und Zirkel,* 54–61; and Timm, *Hammer, Zirkel, Davidstern,* 111–26.

46. "Verordnung über Ehrenpensionen für Kämpfer gegen den Faschismus und für Verfolgte des Faschismus sowie deren Hinterbliebene vom 8. April 1965," in *Gesetzblatt der DDR,* 2 (1965): 295; "Erste Durchführungsbestimmung vom 8. April 1965," in *Gesetzblatt der DDR* 2 (1965): 295.

47. Goschler, "Allein bezahlt," 188.

48. "Bundesergänzungsgesetz zur Entschädigung für Opfer der nationalsozialistischen Verfolgung (BergG)," *Bundesgesetzblatt* 1 (1953): 1387ff. Already in 1951 the Federal Parliament had passed a special Federal Compensation Law for Public Servants (Gesetz zur Regelung der Wiedergutmachung nationalsozialistischen Unrechts für Angehörige des öffentlichen Dienstes, or BWGöD). This law served for the settlement of the claims of those civil servants who were forced by the Nazi government out of their jobs after 1933, among them many Jews.

49. See Ernst Féaux de la Croix, "Vom Unrecht zur Entschädigung: Der Werdegang des Entschädigungsrechts," in *Der Werdegang des Entschädigungsrechts unter national- und völkerrechtlichem und politologischem Aspekt,* Ernst Féaux de la Croix and Helmut Rumpf, vol. 3 in *Die Wiedergutmachung nationalsozialistischen Unrechts durch die Bundesrepublik Deutschland* (Munich: Beck, 1985), 1–118; Christian Pross, *Wiedergutmachung: Der Kleinkrieg gegen die Opfer* (Hamburg: Athenäum, 1988); and Goschler, *Wiedergutmachung.*

50. "Bundesgesetz zur Entschädigung der Opfer der nationalsozialistischen Verfolgung (Bundesentschädigungsgesetz)," *Bundesgesetzblatt* 1 (1956): 559ff.

51. By the end of 1998 DM 78.4 billion had been paid according to the Federal Compensation Law. The total amount spent for compensation of Nazi victims by the Federal Republic and the German states was at that time DM 105.9 billion. See Brodesser et al., *Wiedergutmachung und Kriegsfolgenliquidation,* 249.

52. Compare with Hans Giessler, "Die Grundsatzbestimmungen des Entschädigungsrechts," in *Das Bundesentschädigungsgesetz: Erster Teil (§ 1 bis 50 BEG),* ed. Walter Brunn et al., vol. 4 in *Die Wiedergutmachung nationalsozialistischen Unrechts durch die Bundesrepublik Deutschland* (Munich: Beck, 1981), 1–116, here pp. 50–74; Gerhard Kraus, "Entschädigung für Nationalverfolgte," in *Entschädigungsverfahren und sondergesetzliche Entschädigungsregelungen,* ed. Hugo Fink et al., vol. 5 in *Die Wiedergutmachung nationalsozialistischen Unrechts durch die Bundesrepublik Deutschland* (Munich: Beck, 1987), 171–264, here p. 71; and Ulrich Herbert, "Nicht entschädigungsfähig? Die Wiedergutmachungsansprüche der Aus-

länder," in Herbst and Goschler, *Wiedergutmachung in der Bundesrepublik,* 273–302.

53. Féaux de la Croix, "Vom Unrecht zur Entschädigung," 99, 102.

54. Pross, *Wiedergutmachung,* 111f.; Kurt R. Grossmann, *Die Ehrenschuld: Kurzgeschichte der Wiedergutmachung* (Frankfurt am Main: Ullstein, 1967), 149f.

55. "Zweites Gesetz zur Änderung des Bundesentschädigungsgesetzes: BEG-Schlußgesetz," *Bundesgesetzblatt* 1 (1965): 1315ff.

56. Grossmann, *Ehrenschuld,* 144.

57. Ibid.; Féaux de la Croix, "Vom Unrecht zur Entschädigung," 108f.; Pross, *Wiedergutmachung,* 121f.; Cornelius Pawlita, *"Wiedergutmachung" als Rechtsfrage? Die politische und juristische Auseinandersetzung um Entschädigung für die Opfer nationalsozialistischer Verfolgung (1945 bis 1990)* (Frankfurt am Main: Lang, 1993), 312–7.

58. Féaux de la Croix, "Vom Unrecht zur Entschädigung," 109f.; Laszlo Schirilla, *Wiedergutmachung für Nationalgeschädigte: Ein Bericht über die Benachteiligung von Opfern der nationalsozialistischen Gewaltherrschaft* (Munich: Kaiser, 1982), 67–89; Pross, *Wiedergutmachung,* 122; Pawlita, *"Wiedergutmachung" als Rechtsfrage?* 311.

59. Karl Heßdörfer, "Die Entschädigungspraxis im Spannungsfeld von Gesetz, Justiz und NS-Opfern," in Herbst and Goschler, *Wiedergutmachung in der Bundesrepublik,* 231–48, here pp. 239f; Walter Schwarz, "Die Wiedergutmachung nationalsozialistischen Unrechts durch die Bundesrepublik Deutschland: Ein Überblick," in Herbst and Goschler, *Wiedergutmachung in der Bundesrepublik,* 33–54, here p. 48.

60. See Brodesser et al., *Wiedergutmachung und Kriegsfolgenliquidation,* 249.

61. Karl Hessdörfer, "Die finanzielle Dimension," in Herbst and Goschler, *Wiedergutmachung in der Bundesrepublik,* 55–9.

62. See Pross, *Wiedergutmachung.* This study is highly critical of German compensation and was directly opposed to the self-congratulatory six-volume account sponsored by the Federal Ministry of Finance.

63. H. J. Herberg, *Die Beurteilung von Gesundheitsschäden nach Gefangenschaft und Verfolgung* (Herford: Nicolaische Verlagsbuchhandlung, 1967), 7f. Other categories of damages (especially loss of life) showed a similar regional pattern of rejection. See Grossmann, *Ehrenschuld,* 81.

64. Goschler, *Wiedergutmachung,* 241–7.

65. See "Informelle Besprechungen über die Regierungsanfragen zu dem Entwurf des Abkommens über die Deutsche Auslandsschulden," print: Bundestags-Drucksache 1/4478 (1953), Anlage 3, especially pp. 7f., 10f., 42, 53–6, 71. See also Herbert, "Nicht entschädigungsfähig," 280; Christoph Buchheim, "Das Londoner Schuldenabkommen," in *West-*

deutschland 1945–1955, ed. Ludolf Herbst (Munich: Oldenbourg, 1986), 219–29, here p. 223. See also Hans-Peter Schwarz, ed., *Die Wiederherstellung des deutschen Kredits: Das Londoner Schuldenabkommen* (Stuttgart: Belser, 1982).

66. "Art. 5 Abs. 2, Londoner Schuldenabkommen," in *Bundesgesetzblatt* 2 (1953): 331ff.

67. Herbert, "Nicht entschädigungsfähig," 278ff.

68. Ulrich Herbert, "Zwangsarbeiter im 'Dritten Reich': ein Überblick," in *Entschädigung für NS-Zwangsarbeit: Rechtliche, historische und politische Aspekte,* ed. Klaus Barwig, Günter Saathoff, and Nicole Weyde (Baden-Baden: Nomos, 1998), 17–32, here pp. 17f., 31f.

69. See the following: Benjamin B. Ferencz, *Less Than Slaves: Jewish Forced Labor and the Quest for Compensation* (Cambridge: Harvard University Press, 1979); Constantin Goschler, "Controversy about a Pittance: The Compensation of Forced Laborers from Concentration Camps by Germany's Post-War Industry," in *Dachau Review* 1 (1988): 157–76; Barwig, Saathoff, and Weyde, *Entschädigung für Zwangsarbeit;* Diemut Majer, "Die Frage der Entschädigung für ehemalige NS-Zwangsarbeiter in völkerrechtlicher Sicht," in *Archiv des Völkerrechts* 29 (1991): 1–26.

70. Ferencz, *Less Than Slaves.*

71. Ibid., 172ff.

72. See the statistical survey in Ferencz, *Less Than Slaves,* 210ff. Until 1973, approximately 15,000 former, mostly Jewish, forced laborers received a compensation (Ibid.). See also Hermann-Josef Brodesser et al., *Wiedergutmachung und Kriegsfolgenliquidation: Geschichte—Regelungen— Zahlungen* (Munich: Beck, 2000), 250.

73. See Goschler, "Controversy about a Pittance."

74. See also Hans Günter Hockerts, "Wiedergutmachung in Deutschland: Eine historische Bilanz 1945–2000," *Vierteljahrshefte für Zeitgeschichte* 49 (2001): 167–214, here pp. 209ff. This article provides an excellent survey on the history of reparations of Nazi victims from 1945 to 2000.

75. "Vertrag über die abschließende Regelung in Bezug auf Deutschland," in *Bundesgesetzblatt* 2 (1990): 1318ff.

76. For example, the Federal Republic initially overlooked the fact that there were three Baltic states which finally resulted in new negotiations. These states finally got lump-sum payments of DM 2 million each.

77. See especially section 1, article 6, "Gesetz zur Regelung offener Vermögensfragen," in *Bundesgesetzblatt* 2 (1990): 1159ff.

78. See Philipp Spannuth, "Rückerstattung Ost: Der Umgang der DDR mit dem 'arisierten' Vermögen der Juden und die Gestaltung der Rückerstattung im wiedervereinigten Deutschland," in Goschler and Lillteicher, *"Arisierung" und Restitution,* 241–63; and Christian Meyer-Seitz,

"Die Entwicklung der Rückerstattung in den neuen Bundesländern seit 1989: Eine juristische Perspektive," in Goschler and Lillteicher, *"Arisierung" und Restitution,* 265–79.

79. Constantin Goschler, "Paternalismus und Verweigerung: Die DDR und die Wiedergutmachung für jüdische Verfolgte des National-sozialismus," in *Jahrbuch für Antisemitismusforschung* 2 (1993): 93–117, here p. 112.

80. Jewish Nazi victims living in Central and Eastern Europe benefiting from these agreements receive DM 250 monthly, while those living in Western countries receive DM 500 monthly.

81. See the discussion of this issue by Gabriel Schoenfeld, "Holocaust Reparations: A Growing Scandal," in *Commentary Magazine* September 2000, 25–34; and also "Holocaust Reparations: Gabriel Schoenfeld and Critics," *Commentary Magazine* January 2001, 10–21. Schoenfeld's article was an answer to Norman Finkelstein's book, *The Holocaust Industry: Reflections on the Exploitation of Jewish Suffering* (London: Verso, 2000).

82. "Gesetz zur Errichtung einer Stiftung 'Erinnerung, Verantwortung und Zukunft,'" in *Bundesgesetzblatt* 1 (2000): 1263ff.

83. Henry Rousso, "Frankreich," in *Verbrechen erinnern: Die Auseinandersetzung mit Holocaust und Völkermord,* ed. Volkhard Knigge and Norbert Frei (Munich: Beck, 2002), 253–61, here p. 261.

Jonathan Steinberg

Compensation Cases and the Nazi Past:
Deutsche Bank and Its Historical Legacy

IN DECEMBER 1997, THE DEUTSCHE BANK AG, FRANKFURT AM MAIN, AP-
proached me to ask if I would serve on a Historical Commission to look
into the bank's activities during the Nazi regime and the Second World
War. The other members of the commission were Dr. Avraham Barkai (Jerusalem), Professor Gerald D. Feldman (California/Berkeley),
Professor Dr. Lothar Gall (Frankfurt), and Professor Harold James
(Princeton). At the first meeting of the commission on January 31,
1998, in the Historical Institute of Deutsche Bank AG, it was agreed
that the most immediate question was the significance of the gold purchased from the Reichsbank by the Deutsche Bank during the Second World War, and I was asked to prepare a report on the question.

I had trained in banking at M. M. Warburg & Co. (then Brick-
mann, Wirtz & Co.) in Hamburg in 1957 and 1958 and then worked
for E. M. Warburg & Co., Inc., in New York. I knew German banking practices and felt comfortable, even nostalgic, as I looked at the
musty folders and yellowed correspondence that emerged from the
Deutsche Bank archives. I had a "feel" for that particular past. What
I had no feel for was the tormented present and the ambiguities into
which I had walked as if half-asleep. After thirty-five years as a professional historian I thought I understood my trade, its obligations
and ethical issues. Nothing had prepared me for the difficulties, pressures, and anxieties of historical research carried out in the pay of a
giant German multinational banking group under the scrutiny of the
world's press.

But first, a preliminary word: In 1995, Deutsche Bank had published an official history to mark the 125th anniversary of its establishment in 1870. Unlike most anniversary publications, this was not

a glossy volume with pictures of the founders in high collars and bowler hats standing outside the first bank building; it was a thoroughly researched piece of scholarship by five internationally recognized authors.[1] Three of its authors, who had written chapters in the official history, now returned to join the new Historical Commission. At first glance it might seem odd—and to those of a suspicious disposition it did seem odd—that the bank needed to form yet another committee to look into many of the same issues that one of our number had covered in his chapter in that volume. In order to explain that, the reader needs to know the curious story of Nazi gold and its appearance as an international issue of high, if temporary, urgency. The events tell us a great deal about historical research, its use and misuse in the public arena, and quite a lot about the difficulty of trying to study the Holocaust with the tools of conventional business history.

On December 13, 1996, an independent commission of experts (the Bergier Commission) was set up in Switzerland to look into the "general problem of unclaimed assets deposited by the Nazi regime and its intermediaries in Switzerland."[2] This was the result of increasingly strident criticism of the Swiss government and the Swiss National Bank (SNB) for collaborating with the Nazis during the war. The most flagrant form of that cooperation was the purchase of huge quantities of gold, presumably looted, from the Reichsbank. In 1995–96, how much gold and where it came from were not yet known. An American interagency task force under Stuart E. Eizenstat, under secretary of state for economic, business, and agricultural affairs, was set up to look at existing American records on the same issue. William Slany, the historian of the State Department, took charge of a team of experts. Under his direction, all known records bearing on the subject, some 15 million pages of documentation, were lodged in the National Archives. As he reported to the London Conference on Nazi Gold in December 1997, "Nearly a million pages of very important records from several agencies were declassified during the last month of 1996, one of the largest single declassification actions ever accomplished."[3]

The American government published the two Eizenstat reports, the first, "U.S. and Allied Efforts to Recover and Restore Gold and Other Assets Stolen or Hidden by Germany during World War II," in May 1997, and the second, "U.S. and Allied Wartime and Postwar

Relations and Negotiations with Argentina, Portugal, Spain, Sweden and Turkey on Looted Gold and German External Assets and U.S. Concerns about the Fate of the Wartime Ustasha Treasury," in June 1998. Clearly the U.S. government does not favor eye-catching titles. The British government published the proceedings of the December 1997 London Conference on Nazi Gold, which ran to 833 pages. The Bergier Commission published its interim report, "Switzerland and Gold Transactions in the Second World War," in May 1998, 191 pages long with four appendices. Both Deutsche Bank and Dresdner Bank published histories of their own wartime gold transactions in 1999.[4] The former, of which I was principal author, ran to 176 pages, and the latter to 232. Peter Hayes's book on Degussa, the company that melted and refined the looted gold on orders from the Reichsbank, will be published in English and German in the near future.[5] The American, Swiss, and German publications amount to well over 2,000 pages of highly intensive research on only one form of asset looted by the Nazis. If one considers the systematic theft of Jewish securities, art collections, jewels, coins, rare books, and libraries, and the forced sale of Jewish businesses to "Aryan" competitors,[6] the sums involved and the sheer number of articles stolen make Nazism the greatest act of larceny in human history—and also make it virtually impossible to imagine that the normal activities of professional historians based in universities and research institutes will ever remotely approach an adequate account of the scale of the theft. A crime so vast becomes, by its very enormity, in effect, unknowable.

Gold was the first of the stolen assets to cause a big international fuss, and its story is instructive for my purposes. The historical studies commissioned by governments and private firms showed that gold was an essential element in the Nazi war economy. It allowed the Nazi regime, which teetered on the edge of international insolvency for its entire history, to gain access to a vital source of convertible and internationally acceptable currency, the Swiss franc. Switzerland acted as the Nazi's international banker. According to the Bergier Commission, during World War II, Switzerland was the most important conduit for gold originating from countries occupied or controlled by the Third Reich. Roughly 79 percent of all gold shipments from the Reichsbank to other countries was routed through Switzerland. In terms of volume, the SNB accounted for 87 percent of this bar, with

Swiss commercial banks handling the remaining 13 percent. Although there are differences in the figures, the value of the gold delivered by the Reichsbank to the SNB was between SFr 1.6 and 1.7 billion. The SNB, which took over the gold transactions from the private banks in 1941, carried out 92 percent of the purchases. Private clients were not directly involved in such transactions, so individual asset claims did not arise.[7]

The same could not be said of private banks. Gold has an undeniable glamour that unclaimed bank accounts cannot match, and the idea of looted billions in gold held in vaults in Switzerland caught the public's imagination. In the midst of my work on the Deutsche Bank's report, in June 1998, Edward Fagan, an American lawyer who has made Holocaust asset claims into an industry, lodged a suit against the Deutsche and Dresdner banks for $18 billion in damages (18 is a symbolic number; the Hebrew letter equivalents spell the word "life.") The suit claimed that dealings by Deutsche Bank had been in gold taken from concentration camp victims.[8] It was my first experience of this overheated world and, as the historian responsible for the bank's gold report, I found myself facing journalists. On June 4, 1998, I stated categorically at a press conference in the name of our Historical Commission: "The point is that the Deutsche Bank and, in fact, none of the commercial banks could have known the origin of the gold. There is no proof and I expect to find none that Deutsche Bank knew anything."[9]

The statement turned out to be both right and wrong. In the strict sense, the bank knew nothing. By June 1998 our research had reached its first, preliminary stage. The records of gold transactions by the Reichsbank had turned up in the archives of the U.S. Treasury and had been declassified. The Reichsbank ledgers, which had mysteriously disappeared in 1957 from the Bundesbank archive in Frankfurt, had luckily survived on not-very-legible U.S. microfilm copies. These ledgers recorded every purchase and sale of gold. Gold bars can be identified by their precise weights (measured to four decimal points) and various internal numbering systems. Two things became clear in the painstaking process of reconstructing the transactions: first, that the internal lists derived from Deutsche Bank files tallied so closely with the Reichsbank ledgers that we could safely assume that the gold transactions of the Deutsche Bank had been more or less accurately located. Second, it became clear that at least 744 kilograms of fine gold (kgf in what follows) in gold bars sold to Deutsche Bank were taken originally from victims of concentration camps. This gold has become known as "Melmer-Gold," after SS Hauptsturmführer Bruno Melmer, who delivered the consignments to the Reichsbank. Regular deliveries began in late summer 1942 and were extremely carefully concealed. Melmer wore civilian clothes and carried the boxes and crates personally. The Reichsbank then had the task of processing the foreign currency, gold coins, silver of various sorts, teeth fillings, eye-glass frames, fountain pens, securities, stamp collections, and other valuables collected from the victims of the gas chambers. These items had to be sorted and turned into transferable assets while the gold had to be made negotiable by converting the lumps and pieces into standard-sized gold bars of internationally recognized fine quality. Degussa carried out that refining. Some 744 kgf, which is about 16 percent of the gold consigned to Deutsche Bank by the Reichsbank,[10] represented gold from concentration camp victims—that is, "victim gold" (*Opfergold*). The remainder of the 4,446 kgf delivered to Deutsche Bank from the Reichsbank cannot be definitely identified. There are indications that some further deliveries may have been victim gold, but we cannot be certain.

Since the gold came directly from the Reichsbank and in standardized bars, no private clients were involved and in the strict sense the bank could not have known where the gold came from. What the directors of Deutsche and Dresdner banks knew about "concentration camp gold" or did not know has not been established. There is no evidence to implicate them directly, but it seems hard to believe that top insiders like Hermann Josef Abs did not "know" in some general sense that they were trafficking in blood-stained commodities. Much of the gold had in any case been robbed from the central and private banks in the occupied countries, so even gold not from concentration camps had been tainted. There was a curious footnote to the story: 323 kgf remained in a Swiss safe after the war. On every occasion when directors of the new, postwar Deutsche Bank tried to get Hermann J. Abs to sell the gold, Abs replied that "wir die Depots ruhig liegen lassen sollen" (we should let the depots lie quietly).[11] Abs died in 1993. Four years later, before I or my team got involved in the research, Deutsche Bank decided that the very existence of what might have been tainted gold required an act of gratuitous restitution. The bank sold the gold for DM 5.6 million and gave the proceeds in equal parts to the World Jewish Restitution Organization and the March of the Living Foundation.[12]

The research on both Deutsche and Dresdner banks showed that the gold went into commercial sale on the Turkish free market—Turkey was neutral until late 1944—and served to supply the German government or private clients in Istanbul or Ankara, who could not exchange Reichsmarks in ordinary foreign-exchange transactions. Rather to my surprise, very little gold was used to finance the activities of German firms. The Deutsche and Dresdner studies taken together filled the archival gaps. The conclusion is clear: gold sales in Turkey were a "normal" banking activity known as "arbitrage." Deutsche and Dresdner bought gold at official fixed rates from the Reichsbank and paid for it with Reichsmarks accumulated from their customers. A quirk of the Turkish foreign exchange regulations made this a risk-free transaction. Foreign currency could not be imported to Turkey, but gold could. Hence the two German banks could charge whatever they liked because desperate holders of increasingly devalued Nazi currency and assets could not afford to haggle. The Reichsmarks then went back to Berlin to be exchanged at the artificially maintained price and the gold bars shipped via the Credit-Anstalt in Vienna to the Deutsche and Dresdner affiliates in Turkey. True to the best traditions of postwar Austria, the Credit-Anstalt denied in a letter to Deutsche Bank that it had an archive. Today a team of historians is studying this "nonexistent" historical source.

Deutsche Bank certainly made a neat profit—about 18 percent on sales—from the gold arbitrage. In the years between 1941 and 1943, for which records survive, the Deutsche Bank's Istanbul branch earned RM 938,156.16 from gold transactions. In the same years the Deutsche Bank as a whole earned RM 629 million,[13] so the gold trade, though lucrative, was a tiny part of the bank's activities.

Gold has now ceased to be a central topic in asset or restitution claims. Nevertheless the story of gold, the Holocaust, and world public opinion tells us some important things about Holocaust assets and the struggles for restitution, and to these more general issues I would now like to turn.

First, there is the role of the lawyers. The final plenary session of the international committee, which established the German foundation to deal with Holocaust asset claimants, took place on July 17, 2000. Stuart Eizenstat, speaking for the American government, declared:

> We must be frank. It was the American lawyers, through the lawsuits they brought in U.S. courts, who placed the long-forgotten wrongs by German companies during the Nazi era on the international agenda. It was their research and their work which highlighted these old injustices and forced us to confront them. Without question, we would not be here without them. The settlement we reached of 10 billion DM will help hundreds of thousands of victims, beyond those whom the lawyers represent, live out their declining years in more comfort. For this dedication and commitment to the victims we should always be grateful to these lawyers. But they have also worked diligently to find solutions to seemingly intractable problems and to cooperate in finding ways to achieve legal peace for German companies. The legal fees they will receive are far less than would normally be received for such a large settlement and represent only about 1 percent of the total Foundation sum. This is eminently reasonable given their contribution.[14]

There is a sense in which that statement is right. The huge suits that lawyers like Edward Fagan brought against German, Austrian, and Swiss firms were not legal cases in the usual sense. They were quite literally publicity stunts, intended to get headlines. Mr. Fagan, who claims to represent 82,000 victims, liked to bring frail, elderly survivors with him as he stood outside the gleaming glass tower of some powerful German company and demanded some unthinkable sum in restitution. The strategy worked and continues to work. On April 17, 2000, ABC News reported:

> Austria is reeling from an $18 billion claim for compensation launched in the U.S. courts by Jewish Holocaust victims. The sum would "bankrupt the Austrian state," said Maria Schaumayer, the Austrian government's recently appointed special envoy for World War II compensation claims. Austria's Chancellor Wolfgang Schüessel calls the claim "ridiculous." The lawsuit alleges the companies conspired with the Nazis in the theft of property from Holocaust victims and in the exploitation of wartime slave labor. It was filed in New York Thursday by attorney Edward Fagan, who specializes in Holocaust suits. Court documents allege that the Austrian companies continue to conceal their wrongdoing while

failing to account for assets that once belonged to Holocaust victims, whom the lawsuit seeks to certify as a class.[15]

Now, as it happens, Austrian companies actually behaved as Mr. Fagan said they did and would undoubtedly have continued to do so, had not Jörg Haider gained such international notoriety. The formation of the Black-Blue Coalition between the conservative Austrian People's Party and Haider's neo-fascist Freedom Party took place on February 4, 2000. As Austria suddenly found itself a European pariah, it rediscovered its past. Less than three weeks after the neo-fascists joined the coalition, on February 22, 2000, Dr. Maria Schaumayer, former president of the Austrian National Bank and now special representative for restitution and slave labor issues, received Mr. Fagan in Vienna. With astonishing speed archives appeared, commissions were set up, government statements of public regret were made. The official press release of January 17, 2001, which marked the signing in Washington, D.C., of the Austrian Restitution Agreement, noted:

> Recalling the statement by Federal Chancellor Wolfgang Schüssel, on the occasion of the 55th anniversary of the re-establishment of the Republic of Austria, at the meeting of the Council of Ministers on April 28, 2000, affirming that Austrians stand by the onerous heritage of their country and acknowledging that, when it comes to questions of restitution, compensation, and material reparation, the Second Republic was often too hesitant.[16]

"Lying" would have been a more accurate description than "too hesitant," but at least the government had changed its stance. Mr. Fagan's activities had, it seemed, been successful, but he himself emerged with less credit than he might have wished. As the *New York Times* reported on September 8, 2000:

> The final outrage from Fagan came this summer, in Berlin, when he held up the final formal signing of the German slave labor settlement, in part because of a dispute over how many millions would be given to the lawyers. With several hundred people and top German and American officials waiting in the next room, Fagan, still wearing a 20/20 microphone, could be heard haggling over the fees, and then boasting of his success to first one lawyer. "I got the legal fees up," he said. And then to another lawyer, he said, "We did great, we did great, we just got another, we just got some more money."[17]

The real key to the success of Mr. Fagan and others rested less on his talent for publicity than on other, less dramatic factors: the first of these is the class action suit in America. There is a Web site that tracks actions against firms on securities matters called the Securities Class Action Clearing House. It provided a useful table of this one thicket in the wood of American litigation. It shows that between December 22, 1995, and the middle of 2003, 1,761 federal securities-fraud class actions had been brought in federal courts, 489 in the year 2001 alone.[18] If one adds product liability, professional negligence, and medical or hospital malpractice cases, and also adds the cases in state rather than federal jurisdiction, there must be many thousands of cases tracked on other Web sites that engage battalions of lawyers. (There is a special site for class actions against Microsoft alone.)

The class action would be an American foible, were it not for the second vital factor: globalization. Of course, I knew that Deutsche Bank was only partially interested in the pure search for truth when forming the historical commission on which I served. By December 1997, Nazi gold was a "hot issue" on the front pages of the world's press. Deutsche Bank's Vorstand (its executive board) were certain that, when the media, lawyers, and Jewish organizations finished pounding the Swiss, the Germans would be next. In addition, though none of us knew it in January 1998, when our commission met for the first time, Deutsche Bank intended to take over Bankers Trust, Inc., of New York for the tidy sum of $9.5 billion. The fusion needed permission from the Federal Reserve Bank and approval from New York state and city banking authorities. A nasty story about its Nazi past was not ideal public relations for the takeover.

The bank needed a historical commission as prominently staffed and lavishly supported as possible. A handful of historians, staying at the Frankfurter Hof and getting retainers that were high by their standards (but not the bank's), was a form of accident insurance and cheap at the price. On May 20, 1999, the bank collected its payment. The Federal Reserve System issued an order "approving an application [by Deutsche Bank] to become a bank holding company." The Fed took account of the objections made to the fusion by "individuals and organizations that expressed concern about certain activities of Deutsche Bank during World War II." The Fed noted, however, that "Deutsche Bank has provided substantial information about the steps that the bank has taken and is taking to address its activity during World War II." A footnote followed that refers to the Historical Commission and our "Gold Report." They got what they paid for.[19]

Deutsche Bank is not unique. Daimler-Benz, BMW, the big Swiss banks, Nestlé, Hoffmann-Laroche, Novartis, the German insurance and chemical companies, and Austrian banks and machine tool companies all need to operate in the greatest market in the world: the United States. They simply cannot afford to have their licenses revoked or their mergers blocked by regulatory authorities at the state or federal level, nor their legal departments tied up for years in messy class action litigation.

The world has changed for companies and their governments, and not just because of terrorism. Globalization has many complex and contradictory facets. In the "good old days," European companies and states could simply lie low or ignore claims for asset restitution. In the period after 1945, the Swiss government could afford to drag its feet and haggle about how much gold it would or not return to the victims of Nazi atrocities or even to central banks like the Dutch or Belgian banks that the Nazis had looted. On June 25, 1949, as Peter Hug describes it,

> the Federal Council [the Swiss executive—JS] exchanged confidential letters with the Polish government in which it agreed that "heirless" assets held in Switzerland belonging to missing Polish nationals would be transferred to the Polish central bank's "nationalization compensation account" at the Swiss National Bank for the benefit of Swiss citizens whose property had been nationalized by Poland.[20]

The Swiss government, in effect, agreed to barter the unclaimed assets of what were almost certainly victims of the Holocaust to pay off its own citizens, who had lost assets as a result of actions by the new communist regime in Poland. On December 7, 1949, the *New York Times* reported the story, as did the Toronto *Globe and Mail*. International protests from governments and nongovernmental agencies arrived at Swiss embassies and directly at the Federal Political Department in Bern, but nothing actually happened. The 1950s passed and the Swiss did nothing. Questions were asked in the Swiss parliament but the international and domestic outcry had no effect. The "immoral" agreement, which even the Swiss Neue Zürcher Zeitung called "a complete violation of the depositors' property rights or the rights of their private heirs and . . . [a] blatant contradiction of our private law,"[21] continued to operate. No such outcome would be conceivable today. Mr. Fagan would ensure that the fuss would not die down, and the vulnerability to American pressure on the governments and companies involved would ensure that his cries were heard.

The collapse of the Soviet Union made the emergence of the Holocaust asset industry possible. The publication of new documentary sources and the opening of archives transformed the evidential bases of claims against companies. The files of several of the Nazi economic ministries had landed in Russian hands in 1945 and had been transferred to secret archives in Moscow. These were now open to public inspection, but high copying charges and low incomes of archivists created an ideal situation for the big consumer of new material. Companies could afford the dollar-a-page copying fees; the private researcher could not. In addition, the emergence of successor states played a part. In the years 1989 to 1992 the governments of Ukraine, Belarus, and the Baltic Republics attempted to gain international respectability by offering their archives and procurators as aids in the war crimes trials that began in 1991 and 1992 in Australia, England, and Canada. In his concluding remarks in July this year, Under Secretary Eizenstat paid tribute to "the five central and eastern European governments—Belarus, the Czech Republic, Poland, Russia, and Ukraine"—that had played an important part in bringing the slave labor compensation negotiations to a conclusion. Belarus and Ukraine, in particular, bankrupt and threatened as they are, need the support for their citizens who suffered as slave laborers and the funds that they hope will flow from the German Foundation eastward to Minsk and Kiev.

The collapse of the Soviet Union changed the climate in which Holocaust matters were treated. The official doctrine had always been that the crimes of Nazism had to do with the existence of fascism, an extreme form of capitalism. Since capitalism had been abolished in the socialist states, they had no cause to look to their own pasts. Many really important contributions were made by historians working in Eastern Europe, but they tended to be ignored by Western historians for equal, if opposite, reasons. Work published in Eastern Europe, Westerners believed, must be distorted by ideology (of which, of course, Western historians were free) and therefore could not be used.[22]

Other, less tangible changes have made it possible to pursue the issue of asset restitution. The first is simply the passage of time. If elderly criminals are to be brought to justice or equally elderly victims to be compensated, there is no time to lose. Time has been instrumentalized by the exploitation of anniversaries: the fiftieth anniversary of the outbreak of the Second World War in 1989 or of its end in 1995. The books, films, documentaries, and shows that accompanied these events flowed into the general turbulence of the media in the 1990s and may have produced the extraordinary reception that Daniel Goldhagen's book *Hitler's Willing Executioners: Ordinary Germans and the Holocaust* enjoyed. The book appeared in hardcover in March 1996. By the beginning of April 1996 Goldhagen was a national celebrity. By the end of April he undertook promotional tours in Britain and Germany and became within two months an international celebrity. Whatever merits or demerits academic historians may see in the work, nobody has put the issue of collaboration by the great mass of the German people in Nazi crime as vividly as Daniel Jonah Goldhagen. One of my German graduate students told me that she had seen people reading the book on the streetcars in Hannover, her hometown. If in these media-saturated days attention has become a rare commodity, Goldhagen grabbed a lot of it.

Genocide in neighboring Yugoslavia during the 1990s has kept the genocide in World War II alive. Croatian massacres of Serbs during the period 1941 to 1944 have left an indelible stain on Serbian self-definition and prompted what Serbs saw as justifiable reprisals in return. Terms like "ethnic cleansing," a contemporary version of Nazi euphemisms for murder, hold up the greater Holocaust as the measure of lesser ones. Indeed, the term "Holocaust" itself has become part of the speech of many victims and groups who wrap their claims in the shrouds left outside Auschwitz and Sobibor. Many of the investigators and prosecutors who learned their trade in the war crimes trials in Australia or Canada in the early 1990s, where the defendants had killed Jews, now investigate or prosecute Serbs, Croats, or Bosnians in The Hague tribunal.

Yet more general and even harder to define has been the emergence of groups determined to gain control of their own pasts. In a book published in 2000 called *The Guilt of Nations,* Elazar Barkan suggests that the world is watching "the attempts of groups . . . to redress the past," and he continues: "the novelty in the discourse of restitution is that it is a discussion between perpetrators and their victims . . . a new form of political negotiation that enables the rewriting of memory and historical identity in ways that both can share."[23]

My instincts tell me that Barkan is right. Every victim group now finds its voice in the struggle in Barkan's phrase "to redress the past." The struggle to establish the provenance and amounts of assets stolen and looted between 1939 and 1945 certainly has a real, material foundation, but by now, when so many have died uncompensated, it has merged into a wider process of redressing the past that we see all around us but cannot yet quite define or explain.

Finally, there is the impact of the Holocaust industry on the historians who work in it and the discipline they represent. Very unpleasant accusations have been hurled at those of us who work on these issues and are paid by the German, Swiss, or Austrian governments or companies for doing so. My own experience has been that such charges, even when not malicious, are certainly groundless. No sooner had our Gold Report been completed than the lawyers for the Holocaust survivors were using it—a better proof of its "objectivity" than any claim I could make. The charge that the bank had concealed evidence of gold transactions about which it knew is false. The 1995 official history of the Deutsche Bank did not discuss the gold deliveries, because the evidence only became available in 1997.

That curious truth, in turn, arises from the very nature of modern historical research—the sheer size of the enterprises being studied. A good example was the discovery by Deutsche Bank itself—not by us on the Historical Commission—in February 1999, just before our Gold Report appeared, of the accounts of commercial finance provided by four Deutsche Bank branches to firms and suppliers involved in building Auschwitz. These files from the Kattowitz branch in what was then German Silesia and is now Poland turned up in the basement of Deutsche Bank's Hannover affiliate. How they got there and why is not absolutely clear. In September 2000, Professor Manfred Pohl, director of the Historical Institute of Deutsche Bank AG in Frankfurt, gave an interview to the *Frankfurter Rundschau* in which he revealed that Deutsche Bank's Leipzig branch had employed slave labor to clear up bomb damage. The Gestapo charged the bank RM 3,989.70 for the workers, who were supplied at an hourly wage of RM 0.60.[24] Did we on the Historical Commission manage to "miss" these spectacular discoveries? The answer is yes, but the omission was honest. The main reason is the sheer scale of the archives of the Altbank (as the Deutsche Bank which ceased trading in 1945 is called), which run to more than nine kilometers. The other is that historical research resembles a huge jigsaw puzzle. Those who work on it have no picture on the box nor any idea how many pieces are missing. In the case of Auschwitz financing, we did think about it but assumed that it would not have happened under the direct aegis of Deutsche Bank. We knew that the wartime Deutsche Bank had no branches in areas where the death camps were located and we interpreted the bank's policy to mean that it wanted its foreign subsidiaries to deal with dirty business from the concentration camps. In October 1998, Betrand Perz had revealed in Austria that the Creditanstalt/Bankverein of Vienna, a partly owned subsidiary of Deutsche Bank during the war, had engaged in "Holocaust business" through its Cracow branch. We failed to note that those parts of Poland that had been annexed to Hitler's Greater German Reich, such as Upper Silesia, would have had Deutsche Bank branches as part of the domestic network. Hence branches of the Deutsche Bank, although technically not in Poland, could be and (we now know) were busy financing the death camp nearest to them: Auschwitz. The slave labor in Leipzig was overlooked because we did not know that the files existed, and neither—until September 2000—did the Deutsche Bank itself. Finally, suspicious critics should notice that Professor Pohl and Deutsche Bank, in my experience, always publish such discoveries, no matter how damning.

The simple charges against us have no foundation, but other moral and historiographical problems remain. The critics have been too crude, too fond of conspiracy theories, to see the real issues. What are they? First, the Holocaust in its pedantic thoroughness created a unique legacy, combined with terrifying atrocities and accurate record keeping, of gold wrenched from victims' teeth and balance sheets recording the collecting and valuation of the resulting lumps. What we were doing was counting and weighing those lumps, tracing their conversion into fine gold bars, and following their progress. To the impatient critic, we seem to lack the requisite moral outrage. These crimes ask, in Arno Mayer's memorable phrase, why the heavens did not darken. We were instead calculating evidence to the fourth decimal point.

Yet there is a morality in this precision, which is no less real for being undramatic. Those who work on these matters employ a kind of "forensic positivism." Trials and lawsuits are never far from our work. The need to get things precisely right exerts its influence. The Deutsche Bank's board, shrewder than our critics, bought my professionalism. If the report was damning but professionally presented, the Federal Reserve was more likely to accept the bank's commitment to face its past. I am proud of my handiwork. I am also certain that my main critics have not bothered to read the actual report, because that would force them to acknowledge a more complicated reality than they choose to see.

But what about us? Have we, in a subtler sense, been bought? Here the answer is less clear cut. First, I have not done all the research myself. Documents have been found for me and often summarized. I trust Jutta Heibel and Martin Mueller, my coworkers in the gold research; but can they replicate my thirty-five years of experience? Did they see what I might have noticed? I cannot answer that. We got our report out in just over a year, and I am proud of that, too—but also uneasy. The tight deadlines were set by the needs of Deutsche Bank, not of historical scholarship. I was shown cards from the files of the controversial director, Hermann Josef Abs, the official responsible for foreign business of Deutsche Bank from 1938 on and undoubtedly the most influential German banker of his generation, but I did not rummage in the Abs papers. Had I insisted on having access, what would have happened? Professor Pohl, the director of the Historical Institute, assures me that the archive is "open" to members of the commission but not yet to outsiders. I accept that but feel uneasy about that, too. An archive should be open to all, not just to a select few.

The critics wag their fingers and complain that we were well paid for our work, as if the lawyers, bankers, and insurance agents who worked on these matters were not. The money was good and the travel agreeable. I have nothing against four-star hotels. I hope that if I felt compromised, I would have resigned on the spot, but, as the late Fats Waller observed, "one never knows, do one?" It is hard to assess how corruptible one is. As I examine my behavior, I cannot see signs that the work has changed anything except my relationship to the tax collector. I did work for a fee that I would have done for nothing. I studied an aspect of the Holocaust, the central problem of our century and of my life.

Feeling "important" can be a form of corruption to which academics are peculiarly subject. Most historians share, but few confess, doubts about the value of their research or even the practice of history as such. I have been hired as a historical consultant at a good fee by a big company on an important matter, so my work *must* be important. It is not every day that I get a footnote in the protocols of the Federal Reserve System. I am certainly not immune to the charms of the view from the top floor of the Deutsche Bank tower in Frankfurt. Yet, ultimately, had I wanted to run a bank, to be rich and powerful, I would have stayed with the Warburg bank. What I really wanted to do was to try to understand how the Holocaust could have happened and I have spent most of my professional and a part of my personal life in that quest.

The grief, the pain, and the horror of the Holocaust will not be lessened by publication of a small report on a minute part of the "Final Solution of the Jewish Question," but it seems to me that by doing as honest a job as I can and by trying to tell unpleasant truths in their full complexity, I assert the value of human thought against those who would suppress it. Our report with its footnotes and tables says that human affairs are complicated and that simple explanations conceal what they pretend to reveal. Precise and balanced historical analysis, however small its contribution, affirms our humanity, our right to question and to judge.

Six years have passed since I received the call from Frankfurt to ask if I would serve on the commission looking into Deutsche Bank's gold transactions during the Second World War. The English version of the Gold Report has been duly remaindered and the Historische Kommission, which produced it, was dissolved early in 2003. The world in which the events described in this essay took place has changed radically. The attack on the World Trade Center certainly altered the international agenda but, and much more important, the same globalization that made the Holocaust investigations possible and desirable has now made them an unnecessary expense. The great boom of the 1990s has given way to the stagnation of the first years of the new millennium. Deutsche Bank has a new head of its executive committee, who has to save money, not spend it. Large, dramatic fusions of great financial, media, or high-tech conglomerates have turned sour and the stench of corporate corruption rises from the daily newspaper. History has returned to the obscurity of the lecture hall. The story of Deutsche Bank, its gold transactions, and its instrumentalization of historical scholarship is over. Justice for the victims of Nazi genocide turns out be dependent on the economic climate. This is another lesson and legacy of the story of Nazi gold and a great German bank.

NOTES

1. Lothar Gall, Gerald D. Feldman, Harold James, Carl-Ludwig Holtfrerich, and Hans E. Büschgen, *Die Deutsche Bank 1870–1995* (Munich: C. H. Beck Verlag, 1995), English ed. *The Deutsche Bank, 1870–1995* (London: Weidenfeld and Nicolson, 1995).

2. "Switzerland," in *Nazi Gold: The London Conference* (London: HM Stationery Office, 1998), 494.

3. William Slany, "Research into U.S. and Allied Efforts to Recover and Restore Gold and Other Assets Stolen or Hidden by Germany during World War II," in *London Conference,* 710.

4. Jonathan Steinberg, "Verbindung mit den Mitgliedern der Historikerkommission zur Erforschung der Geschichte der Deutschen Bank in der N S-Zeit Avraham Barkai," in *Die Deutsche Bank und ihre Goldtranskationen während des Zweiten Weltkrieges,* ed. Gerald D. Feldman, Lothar Gall, and Harold James, aus dem Englischen übersetzt von Karl Heinz Siber (Munich: C. H. Beck Verlag, 1999); Johannes Bähr, *Der Goldhandel der Dresdner Bank im Zweiten Weltkrieg,* unter Mitarbeit von Michael C. Schneider. Ein Bericht des Hannah-Arendt-Instituts. Gustav Kiepenheuer Verlag GmbH. (Leipzig, 1999).

5. Peter Hayes, *From Cooperation to Complicity: Degussa in the Third Reich* (Cambridge: Cambridge University Press, forthcoming).

6. Harold James, *Hitler's Willing Investment Bankers* (Cambridge, 2001), provides information on Deutsche Bank's role in those forced transfers of Jewish businesses assess to Aryan owners.

7. Unabhängige Expertenkommission Schweiz-Zweiter Weltkrieg (Bergier Commission), *Die Schweiz und die Goldtransakationen im Zweiten Weltkrieg* (Bern, 1998), 80.

8. "Milliardenklage irritiert Banken," *Die Welt,* June 5, 1998.

9. Press release, Deutsche Bank, Frankfurt am Main, June 4, 1998.

10. Bergier Commission, Table 2, p. 128 in English ed., and Tabelle 2. S. 143 in German ed.

11. Jonathan Steinberg, *The Deutsche Bank,* 66.

12. Ibid.

13. Ibid., 13–14.

14. "Holocaust Issues," available online at http://www.state.gov/www /regions/eur/holocausthp.html.

15. "abcNEWS.com, April 18, 2000," available online at http://www .abcnews.go.com/sections/world/DailyNews/austria000417_holocaust.html.

16. "Joint Settlement Statement on Holocaust Restitution, January 17, 2001," available online at http://www.usembassy-vienna.at/final.html.

17. "Prominent Holocaust Claims Lawyer Accused of Neglecting Clients," *New York Times,* September 8, 2000.

18. Securities Class Action Clearinghouse, Stanford University School of Law, available online at http://securities.stanford.edu/.

19. Federal Reserve System, Deutsche Bank AG Frankfurt am Main, "Order Approving an Application to Become a Bank Holding Company and Notice to Acquire Nonbanking Companies," Federal Reserve Release, May 20, 1999, 16–17 and n. 27.

20. Peter Hug, "Unclaimed Assets of Nazi Victims in Switzerland: What People Knew and What Else They Ought to Know," in *Switzerland and the Second World War,* ed. Georg Kreis (London and Portland, OR: Frank Cass, 2000), 82.

21. Neue Zürcher Zeitung, March 7, 1950, in Kreis, *Switzerland,* 85.

22. That such attitudes are not dead can be seen in the attacks made on Thomas Kuczynski, a leading economic historian in the former German Democratic Republic. Kuczynski published a study of the compensation that German firms owed to slave laborers under the Nazis, which came to the sum of DM 180 billion. As he pointed out in his reply to his critics, nobody had seriously criticized the underlying calculations or even objected to the possible bases by which the value added by slave laborers could be converted to contemporary values. If there were 14 to 15 million slave workers at various stages, then the amount of compensation per head amounts to roughly DM 12,000, hardly a princely compensation for the horrors of slave work in the Third Reich. See Thomas Kuczynski, "Entschädigungsansprüche für Zwangsarbeit im Dritten Reich auf der Basis der damals erzielten zusätzlichen Einnahmen und Gewinne," *1999 Zeitschrift für Sozialgeschichte des 20. und 21. Jahrhunderts,* Heft 1, 2000, 15–64, and his "Zwischen den Muhlsteinen: zu eigigen Hintergründen der Verhandlungen über Entschädigungen für Zwangsarbeit," *Junge Welt,* June 3–4, 2000, 10–11.

23. Elazar Barkan, *The Guilt of Nations: Exploring the Global Politics of Restitution from 1945 Germany to Present-Day Bosnia* (New York: Norton, 2000), x, xviii.

24. E-mail to Mitglieder der Historikerkommission, from Manfred Pohl, Tuesday, September 26, 2000, re: "Beschäftigung von Zwangsarbeiter und Kriegsgefangenen."

Helen Junz

Holocaust-Era Assets: Globalization of the Issue

ON JANUARY 3, 1996, THE U.S. CONGRESS UNANIMOUSLY PASSED A RESO-
lution demanding that the government declassify all information
concerning persons suspected of war crimes. In doing so they recalled
that "during the 104th Congress America had celebrated the 50th anniversary of the end of Word War II and the end of the Holocaust,
one of the worst tragedies in human history."[1] This resolution resulted in the War Crimes Disclosure Act, which not only opened archives but also provided the wherewithal for their analysis. Peter Bich-
sel, commenting on President Bill Clinton's signing of the act in the
German paper *Die Zeit,* noted that "President Clinton may well be
the first U.S. President without a Zurich bank account."[2] This remark
illustrates the extent to which questions regarding the treatment of
Holocaust assets had become a public issue, perhaps for the first time
in two generations.

Five months earlier, on May 2, 1996, the Jewish community had
reached agreement with the Swiss banks to look into the question of
assets that had lain dormant in Swiss banks since the Holocaust. On
that date the Swiss Bankers Association, the World Jewish Restitution
Organization, and the World Jewish Congress, on behalf of allied
Jewish organizations, established a committee that was mandated to
ascertain the fate of the dormant accounts of Nazi victims in Swiss
banks and to assess their treatment, to the extent that this was feasible
given the passage of time. It was the first time since 1945 that the resolution of the dormant-account question had been placed into the
hands of an internationally recognized group. Obviously, the committee—the Independent Committee of Eminent Persons (ICEP),
under chairmanship of Paul A. Volcker—came into being only after
lengthy negotiations. Its gestation period reached back into 1995.

What happened between then and August 12, 1998, when class action lawsuits against Swiss banks that ran into billions of U.S. dollars were settled, is a matter of history. Part of this history is how the establishment of the Volcker Committee triggered what would become a virtually worldwide search for the facts of the treatment of Holocaust-era assets—assets that, unlike their owners, needed neither visa nor faced "Eintritt für Juden und Hunde verboten" signs.

DORMANT ACCOUNTS, DORMANT ISSUES

While the amount of U.S.$18 billion, an oft-repeated number, was understood to be symbolic—the number "18" in Hebrew stands for the letters that make up the word "life" (*chai*)—the ICEP still was faced with widely divergent claims and counterclaims regarding the total amount of assets that might actually be involved. This led Paul Volcker to look for a benchmark against which the plausibility of the wide range of numbers that were being bandied about could be tested. He therefore asked what the total amount of assets at the disposal of the Jewish populations in Nazi-dominated Europe might have been at the eve of the war and, more specifically, how much of these assets could have been movable.

Clearly, one could have expected that a few weeks of research would provide a reasonably well-founded answer. After all, the questions of the extent of Nazi looting, of what was recovered and what had been lost, had been with us for more than fifty years. And almost a quarter of a century had passed since a number of countries, including Germany and the United States, had basically closed their official books on the issue. Yet, there were no readily available answers and, in the end, a considerable amount of green field research, reaching into archival and economic records on three continents, was required.

The underlying question thus concerned not only the issue of what accounts of Nazi victims were still lying dormant in Swiss banks, but a much broader one: namely, why had the issue of the incomplete accounting for the spoliation of Nazi victims itself been allowed to lie dormant for more than two generations? It is not that these questions suddenly sprang, like Athena from Zeus's head, fully blown onto the scene. Many of the facts that eventually led to the setting up of the Volcker Committee had been well known and well researched much before 1995.

The story of the Swiss accounts—the flow of Nazi-looted gold through the neutral countries and the litany of abortive efforts to obtain an accounting of the amounts involved—had been the subject of a considerable body of scholarly and investigative work. Aside from contemporary analyses of the Swiss-American Accords, which dealt with the treatment of German and victims' assets in Switzerland, much of what is known about the Reichsbank's gold today was already set out by Stanley Moss in 1956.[3] In the 1980s there was a mini-explosion of research on the subject: among the historians, notably by Werner Rings and Arthur L. Smith Jr.; among the investigative reporters, by Ian Sayer, Douglas Botting, and Nicholas Faith; and a little later in fiction, by Paul Erdman in *The Swiss Account,* possibly the only novel of its kind to be festooned with scholarly footnotes.[4] The latter is perhaps less surprising given the fact that Erdman received his doctorate from the University of Basel in 1956 with a dissertation that delved, in part, into the Swiss-American Accords.[5] In March 1985, the Swiss National Bank itself published an account of its gold transactions with the Reichsbank.[6] While the author was able to draw on documents that, under the Swiss thirty-five-year rule, had not been accessible before the 1980s, the article did not add to the basic facts already set out by other authors. Much, in fact, dated back to testimonies taken from Reichsbank officials immediately after the war and public since the Nuremberg trials. What was new was that this material was now cited in a Swiss National Bank publication and that the author could depict the bank as having put a "naive trust in the good faith of the Reichsbank."[7] But none of this knowledge and none of this research led to remedial action until the mid-1990s.

This inaction was not for a lack of attention-focusing opportunities in the intervening years. Indeed, there were several milestones that could have served to trigger action. Foremost was the capture of Adolf Eichmann in 1960 and his subsequent trial by the Israelis in 1961–62. This ignited a virtually worldwide debate around the issues of the treatment of persecutees, of acquiescence and collaboration by victims themselves and by their fellow countrymen at large, and of historic fact and the truth of personal recollections. While the trial succeeded in its aim of heightening the awareness of the facts of the Holocaust, especially among the younger generation in Israel, it may also have been the opening move for a number of countries in the process of confronting their own histories. In Germany, where this process had already been in train for some time, it added impetus. But clearly, the time was not ripe for anything approaching the concerted search for objective facts such as was initiated in the 1990s.

Second, in 1967 the Six-Day War, more than anything else, established Israel as the focus of Jewish awareness, especially in the United States. And this greater awareness, in turn, also sharpened that with respect to the Holocaust. Still, it took until 1993 with the opening of the Holocaust Memorial Museum in Washington for broader interest to be both recognized and generated.[8]

While the arts produced a spate of Holocaust-related works, from the *Diary of Anne Frank* to the *Shoah* television series, these were largely personal history based and tended to treat the subject more from an ethnic/cultural angle rather than as part of recent national history.[9]

SEARCH FOR HOLOCAUST-ERA ASSETS: WHY THE MID-1990S BOOM?

What, then, was so special in 1995 that it could break this inertia and set in motion a wholesale questioning of the economic facts of the Holocaust—a questioning that, in the end, would spark virtually worldwide efforts to trace what had happened to the assets of victims of the Nazi regime both during its reign and after its defeat?

Obviously, there is no one factor that can explain why over the past six years dozens of entities, including twenty-four national commissions,[10] have engaged in documenting their part of this history. Rather, a confluence of circumstances prepared the ground. A core set of explanatory factors, though different observers will assign different weights to individual components, figures in all accounts.

First, everybody's list includes the fall of the Berlin Wall and the disappearance of the East-West divide, which helped open archives hitherto inaccessible to Western researchers. Suddenly masses of valuable material on the Nazi period, especially that held in the archives of the former German Democratic Republic (GDR) and in some Eastern European countries, became available. Although access to important files of the financial/economic institutions of the Nazi regime, which the Soviets had removed from Berlin to Moscow, remained difficult, it no longer was foreclosed. And in this instance supply created its own demand.

More directly, the collapse of communism removed the political barriers that had prevented the flow of restitution from West to East. Together with the restoration of private property rights in the former communist countries, this meant that those Nazi victims, or their heirs, who had lived behind the Iron Curtain finally could lodge claims for restitution and compensation. And those who lived in the West could, together with everyone else, pursue efforts to reclaim property in the East. Still, it took until 1995 for the United States to consider these developments sufficiently important to name Stuart E. Eizenstat, then ambassador to the European Union in Brussels, as the government's special envoy for property claims in Central and Eastern Europe—a portfolio that he took with him when he returned to Washington to hold executive posts in the Department of Commerce, the State Department, and the Treasury and that made him the government's lead in the expanding area of restitution claims activity.

Second, the fiftieth anniversary of the end of World War II triggered both reminiscences and a new flow of information. The release of official documents, sealed for half a century, added further to the stock of newly available archival information.

Third, and crucially important, the passage of half a century had sharpened the awareness that no time was to be lost if living memory was to be passed on, if forgotten or buried truths were to be brought to the surface, and if justice was to be done. Among nations, it renewed the hunt for, and prosecution of, war criminals; among survivors it brought home the realization that the next generations were owed a share in the memory and helped break the barrier of silence that had divided many from their children and grandchildren. Psychologists have attempted to explain why that silence, kept until recently by so many Nazi victims or their heirs, also extended to the recovery of their material possessions. Prominent among the reasons given was the desire to seal off a past too difficult to be dealt with and the need to rebuild their own existence and, indeed, to rebuild their devastated families. Survivor guilt alone explained much of the reluctance to pursue, or even raise, matters of property with any vigour. Moreover, the less-than-hospitable environment may have caused survivors to seek to put a distance between themselves and the Nazi caricature of the Jew as a shylock, bent upon coining money.

Fourth, over the past generation there has been broad acceptance of general precepts regarding civil and human rights that made pursuit of individual rights a matter of course. Historians recently have augmented the psychological explanations for the reluctance on the part of many Nazi victims to engage in an active fight for their property rights by pointing out that the postwar environment in which victims, or their heirs, had to pursue their claims was inauspicious, to say the least.[11]

Obviously, when in 1947 the U.S. Military Government in Germany imposed a restitution law in the U.S. zone of occupation,[12] claimants could not expect to be welcomed. It is not surprising, then, that at the outset many either eschewed engagement with a rigid, and not always fully de-Nazified, German bureaucracy altogether or were discouraged by the cumbersome machinery. Nevertheless, eventually restitution efforts of the Federal Republic of Germany (which, until reunification in 1990, covered claims against West Germany only) reached thousands of victims, and by January 1997 payments amounted to just over DM 100 billion.[13]

However, it is noteworthy that the overwhelming share—more than 90 percent—of these expenditures was for compensation claims, that is, for loss of health, pensions, professional pursuit, schooling, and so on, while just under 4 percent, DM 3.94 billion, covered restitution claims proper, that is, claims for loss of property.[14] Professor Walter Schwarz, in his contribution to the monumental analytical documentation of the restitution process in West Germany published by the Federal Ministry of Finance, concludes that "[I]t follows that the value of restituted property, even if confined to West Germany only, represented but *part* of the assets lost as a consequence of persecution."[15] Although the amounts quoted for restitution payments can only be approximations because of valuation problems and because some restitution was in kind and some bypassed the restitution machinery altogether, there can be little doubt about either the relative shares or the validity of Professor Schwarz' assessment.

Perhaps most surprising, and therefore more daunting, was the unfriendly environment in which restitution claims had to be pursued in countries where victims could have expected an amicable reception. This was especially so with respect to the United States. After all, the United States was a driving force behind, if not the initiator of, the provisions of the London Declaration of January 1943, which warned that transfer of property rights under direct or indirect duress might be reversed; of those in the Final Act of the Paris Conference on Reparation in 1945, which began to recognize, at least with respect to the neutral countries, that heirless assets of victims of Nazi policy should not escheat to the state in which they were held; of the peace treaties with Hungary and Romania, which explicitly required that property looted from persecutees be restituted to the original owners or their heirs or, in the absence of any heirs, to representatives of the surviving members of the victimized group in question.[16] As noted above, it single-handedly laid the basis for the German Restitution Law when in 1947 it ensured the adoption of such a law in the U.S. zone of occupied Germany (Military Government Law No. 59). This law put the reversal of the transfer of property under duress on a legal basis; recognized that property left by victims without heirs should not, as normal, escheat to the state, but be assigned to a successor organization that represented the group of persecutees of the victim in question and that would use the assets for the benefit of the survivors of that group; and, finally, emphasized the need for speedy restitution.[17]

Thus, the intent of U.S. policy with respect to property looted from, or abandoned under duress by, victims of Nazi persecution was clear from the end of hostilities onward: a full and speedy return to the original owners or their heirs or, in the absence of designated heirs, to an officially designated successor organization, which was mandated to utilize these assets for the benefit of the population group to which the original owners had belonged.

However, neither of these principles appeared to govern the treatment of those victims' assets that had come under the control of the U.S. authorities within their own territory. The United States, early in the war, had moved under its Trading with the Enemy Act (TEA) to

1. prevent the Axis from fueling its war effort with the external assets of its own nationals, or of those held by the populations in the countries and territories they came to control, and

2. divert the use of such assets to the United States' own war purposes, including the eventual provision of funding to satisfy war claims.

Inevitably, victims' assets were caught in this program. Indeed, the sequestering of victims' assets was seen as a way of "protecting and preserving the property of our allies and friends, the victims of our enemies. . . ."[18] But, when it came to relinquishing control, many survivors or their heirs may have wondered about the effects of this act of friendship.

Abraham S. Hyman, a former acting adviser on Jewish affairs to General Lucius D. Clay,[19] wrote in a draft article in 1953: "As a general rule people are more circumspect about their behaviour at home than about their conduct abroad. However, in dealing with the heirless property of victims of persecution, the Congress of the United States has made it appear that the reverse of this rule appeals to the United States."[20] He might have broadened his dictum to include the U.S. executive branch with the U.S. Congress, and to cover survivors and their heirs as well.

It seemed ironic to him that the U.S. government, which had been the driving force in wresting recognition of both the rights and the plight of the victims of Nazism from its sometimes unwilling allies and from a generally unwilling Germany, should turn out to be lagging in acting on their behalf at home. The slowness with which victims' assets were released after the war clearly was at extreme odds with the precepts the U.S. authorities had pushed in international fora. Thus, it took victims on average 3.5 years to get the Office of Alien Property to return title to their assets. And it took many attempts stretching over the number of years for a postwar child to reach its majority—eighteen—for Congress to pass legislation that released heirless assets to the designated successor organization. At the same time, the amounts involved had been whittled down from U.S.$3 million in the early legislative proposals to the paltry U.S.$500,000 that was finally paid out in 1963.

In contrast, in 1954 Congress passed a law, introduced by senators Dirksen of Illinois and Langer of North Dakota and supported by Secretary of State John Foster Dulles, that aimed to return all German private property taken under the TEA to the Federal Republic of Germany, as if, in the confiscation of these assets, no distinction had been drawn between friend or foe. This action—but for President Eisenhower's veto of the bill—would have allowed the German state to fall heir to the assets of Nazi victims!

At the state level, several attempts were made, notably in New York State, to pass legislation to assign unclaimed property of Nazi victims that had, under law escheated to the state, to designated successor organizations. However, all these attempts died in the legislature. And even when victims' or successor organizations' quest for restoration of property rights met with a sympathetic response, these concerns figured low on the agenda of a world focused on Cold War and economic reconstruction issues. The scope for victims, their heirs, and their successor organizations to pursue material property claims forcefully and successfully was clearly limited within the United States as well as abroad.

The elements that flowed from the four factors enumerated above, to wit,

> 1. the revival of the issue of property claims as the implosion of the communist regimes enabled Nazi victims, or their heirs, who had lived behind the Iron Curtain to lodge such claims;
>
> 2. the release of information and documentation following the fall of the Berlin Wall and the fiftieth anniversary of the end of World War II;
>
> 3. the sense of urgency to deal with the unfinished business of the war two-score and ten years after its end, and the realization that this was the last call to transmit living memory and right individual wrongs; and
>
> 4. the greater predisposition toward activism that came with the passage of generations and the change in the general climate toward support of individual rights

all helped prepare the ground for the snowballing demands for the facts regarding the treatment of Holocaust-era assets worldwide.

But was this enough to explain the precipitate ending of the Swiss banks' fifty-year record of successfully fending off private and official pressures for the release of more than a token amount of information on the dormant accounts still on their books, let alone the unclaimed funds themselves? This record of noncompliance, obfuscation, and *de minimis* action throughout the period is well documented. So it was not surprising that the banks believed that another token effort to ascertain the volume of dormant accounts, which in the spring of 1995 produced 775 accounts with a value of SFr 38.7 million (roughly $32 million at the then-prevailing exchange rate), would put the matter to rest, as two earlier searches had done in the past.[21] However, 1995 turned out not to be business as usual. For one, the business situation had shifted dramatically since 1962, when the last such search of the banks' accounts took place. With globalization, any would-be player on the international scene had to become global. Growth-oriented financial institutions could no longer be satisfied with a branch or agency in the United States. Network building and mergers and acquisitions were *de rigueur,* in all of which the large Swiss banks were set to participate and all of which required the fiat of the U.S. federal and state regulators. This meant that for the first time in the postwar period, the weight of leverage lay with those outside Switzerland.

Second, the growing acceptance that it was more than proper that individual rights should be asserted and defended, together with the litigiousness of American society, had made the class action suit a typical and favored avenue for seeking remedies in that respect.

Last, but not least, at the same time that all these factors combined to create a propitious environment for victims and their spokespersons to be heard, a formidable combination of personalities was in place to make it happen. The World Jewish Congress, under Edgar Bronfman Sr. with Israel Singer and Elan Steinberg, set off the avalanche. They looked to congressional support from the senator from New York and chairman of the Senate Banking Committee, Alfonse M. D'Amato. And from there on matters took a dramatically different turn as compared with a quarter of a century earlier. Then, in December 1969, Liba Weingarten, vice president of the Jewish Nazi Victims Congregation of New York, raised the question of the dormant bank accounts in Switzerland with Senator Jacob Javits of New York. She wrote: "You must be aware of the fact that Switzerland is still holding on to all the property [incl.] money in banks—left by Jews, who perished during World War Two [thru] the Nazis and their helpers . . . and this heirless property has not been released yet by Switzerland almost 25 years after the end of the terrible war. Does the American Government also intend to do something about it?" Senator Javits' office passed the letter routinely to the State Department.[22] Clearly, the short answer to her question was "no."

On December 7, 1995, faced with essentially the same question, Senator D'Amato, who coincidentally had succeeded Javits in his Senate seat, replied, "We'll hold hearings. We'll research it and we'll look into the problem."[23] And this time the executive branch was poised to act as well, with then–Under Secretary of Commerce Stuart E. Eizenstat, already appointed special envoy for property claims in Central and Eastern Europe. Finally, state banking regulators, to name but one, Alan Hevesi in New York, the state most important for the Swiss banks, were fully engaged.

From this point the avalanche of research that focused on the treatment of Holocaust-era assets gathered breadth and speed: It spread to Britain, where Greville Janner, a Member of Parliament and vice president of the World Jewish Congress in Britain, asked Foreign Secretary Malcolm Rifkind for a review of intelligence material on Word War II–related Swiss financial activities. This request led to the publication, in September 1996, of the Foreign and Commonwealth Office's (FCO's) history note entitled "Nazi Gold: Information from the British Archives."[24] This report proved crucial in three respects:

 1. It drew attention to the fact that the Reichsbank's monetary gold, much of which was sold to and through Switzerland, contained not only resmelted gold looted from the central banks of occupied countries, but also "tainted" gold—that is, gold taken from Nazi victims;[25]

 2. it helped set off a massive research effort with "the British, U.S. and Swiss governments . . . all engaged in further activity to investigate the question of Nazi gold";[26] and

 3. it led the Jewish organizations to request that the residual gold still on the books of the Tripartite Gold Commission (TGC), in the words of the FCO, "be used to compensate individual victims of Nazism."[27] The FCO went on to say: "We are concerned to ensure that the outcome of these discussions should fulfil not only our legal obligations in connection with the Commission gold, but also our moral obligations: the question of compensation for survivors of the Holocaust is an important one, which it is right for us to review regularly."[28]

All this constituted a sea change from the earlier period of, at best, "benign neglect"—a period summed up bluntly in 1998 by the French commission la Mission d'Étude sur la Spoliation des Juifs de France (the Matteoli Commission). In describing their task, they wrote:

> The field of enquiry was vast and largely unexplored. This was so because during the Occupation, the entire category of individuals defined as Jewish by the German occupation authorities and by the French state fell victim to looting and pillage of their property, which took many forms. After the Liberation, the French Republic . . . arranged for the restitution of the stolen assets. However, the genuine endeavours made to return to the rightful owners what could be returned . . . *peter out at the beginning of the 1950s in a climate of general indifference.* [emphasis provided by author][29]

But perhaps it was most striking that, finally, after two and a half generations of pragmatism, the question of justice—and justice to the

individual—moved center stage. Robin Cook, Britain's foreign secretary, in opening the London Conference on Nazi Gold in December
1997 and speaking of "the distribution of gold immediately following
the Allied victory," said, "The records tell a story of genuine efforts by
the Allies to do the right thing in the midst of post-war chaos. The needs
of the survivors were urgent, and decisions were taken that allowed those
needs to be met. Those decisions were not perfect, or exact. With the
20/20 vision of hindsight we might have done things differently."[30]

Indeed, not only were the needs desperate, but they competed
with many other concerns, which were accorded at least an equal and
often a higher priority. Both the wholesale plunder of the occupied
countries and the breadth of the war the Nazis waged against European Jewry and others they considered undesirable were well known
before the war ended. The figure of 10 million people in concentration camps and of 21 million displaced persons (i.e., those in the
camps plus those conscripted into supporting Germany's war work)
had been variously cited,[31] as had the systematic spoliation of victims'
assets. However, no planning could fathom the full extent of the consequences: theoretical knowledge was one thing, grasping the enormity
of the practical implications quite another. Not surprisingly, the result was a pragmatic approach that subordinated, for very good practical reasons, making good to individuals—who throughout the
Hitler years had been stripped not only of their assets, and too often
their lives, but also of their individuality—to making good to the
community of victims. The choice of what was practical in favor of
what were the rights of individuals is the thread that runs through the
formulation and implementation of postwar restitution policy during the entire twenty-year period from its inception through the sixties, when it was thought the chapter could be closed, at least as far as
the official community was concerned.

How different, then, in 1997, to hear Robin Cook continuing his
opening remarks: "[T]he real victims of the Nazis were not the Central Banks. They were individuals. Countless individuals, who died
because of their religion, their race, their beliefs. And we must always
remember that they were individuals, because the Nazis tried so hard
to reduce them to numbers, to remove their humanity."[32] At the same
time that Robin Cook stressed the individuality of victims, Stuart
Eizenstat, then under secretary of state, speaking for the United States,
rang the parallel theme of justice.[33]

It was the questions raised by the issue of Swiss dormant bank accounts that gave the immediate impetus to a focused search for what had remained unknown about the treatment of Hitler's victims and their possessions. The Volcker Committee's work itself, in attempting to fill in the gaps in knowledge about these accounts, centered on the two core points reiterated at the London conference: justice and recognition of individual rights. The committee thus saw its work, though "focused on a specific banking issue: the fate of funds entrusted to Swiss banks by victims of Nazi persecution," as having "[m]ost directly, the objective to provide for simple justice for those victims (and their heirs) with unsatisfied claims on accounts in Swiss banks. It is also a matter of great importance for those banks themselves and their reputation. But it has significance beyond the people and the institutions directly involved."[34]

And, indeed, it did. It spawned a huge, globe-spanning effort in historical research and moral self-assessment. Twenty-four national commissions, from Argentina to Latvia to the United States, have since sought—or are still seeking—to document and assess their handling of Holocaust-era assets and issues. In almost every case it has not proven possible, after the passage of now more than two and a half generations, to put definitive numbers on the quantity of assets concerned. But the widespread acceptance of the need for an accounting of how governments, businesses, and individuals were involved in or dealt with the persecution, dispossession, and destruction of whole peoples in itself helps provide a certain measure of justice. The need to know, indeed, is paramount. Thus, the fact that we are here today to discuss (what seems to many "yet again") the discovery of the facts of Nazi spoliation of European Jewry is not only part of a belated righting of wrongs; it is part of our need to know "why," if "never again" is to have any meaning. I, therefore, am not bothered by the fact that this issue has attracted a number of actors who are playing out their own agendas: Where money and politics are involved that is hardly surprising. It does not bother me because—and that is the answer to those who write pejoratively about a "Holocaust industry" and who indignantly argue that all this is "just about money"—in the last analysis it is about the restoration of property rights and the recognition of individual rights: in short, about some return of the individuality that was one of the most precious assets stolen from the victims of Nazism.

NOTES

Much of this presentation also appears in Helen B. Junz, *Where Did All the Money Go? Pre-Nazi Era Wealth of European Jewry* (Berne: Staempfli Publishers Ltd., 2002).

1. Jean Ziegler, *Die Schweiz, das Gold und die Toten* (Munich: C. Bertelsmann Verlag, 1997), 15.

2. Ibid., 16.

3. Stanley Moss, *Gold Is Where You Hide It: What Happened to the Reichsbank Treasure?* (London: Andre Deutsch Ltd., 1956).

4. Werner Rings, *Raubgold aus Deutschland: Die "Golddrehscheibe" Schweiz im Zweiten Weltkrieg* (Zurich: Artemis Verlag, 1985); Arthur L. Smith Jr., *Hitler's Gold: The Story of the Nazi War Loot* (Oxford: Berg, 1989); Ian Sayer and Douglas Botting, *Nazi Gold* (New York: Congdon and Weed, 1984); Nicholas Faith, *Safety in Numbers: The Mysterious World of Swiss Banking* (London: Hamish Hamilton, 1982); Paul Erdman, *The Swiss Account* (London: Andre Deutsch Ltd., 1991).

5. Paul Erdman, *Swiss-American Economic Relations, Their Evolution in an Era of Crises* (Basel: Kyklos-Verlag, 1959).

6. Robert Vogler, "Der Goldverkehr der Schweizerischen Nationalbank mit der Deutschen Reichsbank 1939–45," Schweizerische Nationalbank, *Geld, Währung und Konjunktur,* Quartalsheft No. 1, March 1985.

7. In fact, Reichsbank Vice President Emil Puhl, the key contact in the Swiss National Bank's gold dealings with Germany, was sentenced mainly because of his involvement in the Reichsbank's handling of gold looted by the SS, including concentration camp gold (the Melmer deliveries). See also Arthur L. Smith Jr., *Hitler's Gold,* 42–7.

8. Although planning for the museum was initiated in 1979.

9. For this and the foregoing see, for example, Ido de Haan, *Na de ondergang* (The Hague: Sdu Uitgevers, 1997).

10. Argentina, Austria, Belgium, Brazil, Croatia, Czech Republic, Estonia, France, Germany, Greece, Israel, Italy, Latvia, Liechtenstein, Lithuania, the Netherlands, Norway, Portugal, Slovakia, Spain, Sweden, Switzerland, Turkey, United States.

11. Through the 1970s, the issue of the restitution of property to victims of the Nazi regime hardly figured on the horizon of historians tracing the period of the U.S. occupation of Germany. A perusal of the indexes to a number of studies that have achieved core status in the literature shows that, when restitution is mentioned at all, it generally refers to the return to relevant governments of property the Nazis looted from countries or territories outside Germany (generally known as "external restitution"), and the topic as such receives a couple of mentions at best. See, for example, John

Gimbel, *The American Occupation of Germany: Politics and the Military,*
1945–1949 (Stanford, Calif.: Stanford University Press, 1968); Earl F.
Ziemke, *The U.S. Army in the Occupation of Germany, 1944–1946* (Washington, D.C.: Center of Military History, U.S. Army, 1975); Harold Zink,
American Military Government in Germany (New York: MacMillan, 1947).

12. Military Government Law No. 59, which eventually was also
adopted in the British and French zones and thereby became the basis of the
German Restitution Law.

13. Statement of German Delegation, "German Restitution for National Socialist Crimes," in Foreign and Commonwealth Office, *Nazi Gold:*
The London Conference (London: HM Stationery Office, 1998), 286–92.

14. The remainder, about 6 percent, reflects a mixture of compensation and restitution payments under governmental agreements: DM 3.45
billion under the Israel Agreement and DM 2.5 billion under global agreements with sixteen nations. Statement of German Delegation, "German
Restitution for National Socialist Crimes," 291.

15. Walter Schwarz, *Rückerstattung nach den Gesetzen der Alliierten*
Mächte: Die Wiedergutmachung nationalsozialistischen Unrechts durch die
Bundesrepublik Deutschland, Band I, published by the Federal Ministry of
Finance in cooperation with Walter Schwarz (Munich: Verlag C. H. Beck,
1974). Author's translation.

16. See U.S. State Department, *Bulletin* 14 (January 27, 1946), Paris
Conference on Reparation, Final Act, article 8, subsection C. The actual
wording was "governments in neutral countries shall be requested to make
available for this purpose (in addition to the sum of 25 million dollars)
assets in such countries of victims of Nazi action, who have since died and
left no heirs"; and Treaty of Peace with Hungary, article 27; Treaty of Peace
with Rumania, article 25 (and article 24.3, for an example of "duress"
clause), in Charles Bevans, compiler, *Treaties and Other International Agree-*
ments of the United States of America, 1776–1949, vol. 4, *Multilateral,*
1946–1949, 411, 413, 465.

17. Military Government Law No. 59, *Military Government Gazette,*
Germany, United States Army Area of Control, Issue G, 10 November
1947, established as one of the basic principles "the speedy restitution of
identifiable property . . . to persons who were wrongfully deprived of such
property within the period from 30 January 1933 to 8 May 1945 for reasons of race, religion, nationality, ideology or political opposition to national Socialism. . . ."

18. Paul V. Myron, "The Work of the Alien Property Custodian," *En-*
emy Property, Law and Contemporary Problems (School of Law, Duke University) 11 (winter-spring, 1945), 91.

19. General Clay served from the end of March 1945 to May 16, 1949,

first as deputy and later as military governor of the U.S. Zone of Occupation of Germany.

20. Abraham S. Hyman, "The Heirless Paradox," draft article, 5/25/53, Central Archives for the History of the Jewish People, Jerusalem, JRSO, NY, 916B.

21. These surveys, conducted by the banks themselves, sought to identify possible victims' accounts. The one conducted shortly after the war yielded a total value of less than SFr 1 million; the 1962 search, ordered by the Swiss government, came up with 739 accounts valued at SFr 6.2 million. Source: Independent Committee of Eminent Persons, *Report on Dormant Accounts of Victims of Nazi persecution in Swiss Banks,* December 1999.

22. Gregg J. Rickman, *Swiss Banks and Jewish Souls* (Brunswick: Transaction Publishers, New Brunswick, N.J., 1999), 39.

23. Ibid., 41.

24. Foreign and Commonwealth Office, *Nazi Gold: Information from the British Archives,* Historians, Library, and Research Department, History Notes No. 11, September 9, 1996.

25. It also, through an error (reading $ for SF), magnified the issue by indicating that in negotiations with the Allies in March 1946 an official of the Swiss National Bank had let slip that the Swiss banks still held $500 million equivalent in German gold, an amount more than twice the $200 million estimated by the Americans. The correct figure should have been SFr 500 million, which, in fact, at the exchange rate of the day, at $118 million would have been below the U.S. estimate. This error was corrected in the second edition of the report.

26. Foreign and Commonwealth Office, *Nazi Gold: Information from the British Archives,* Historians, Library, and Research Department, History Notes No. 11, 2nd ed., January 1997, Foreword.

27. Ibid.

28. Ibid.

29. Mission d'Étude sur la Spoliation des Juifs de France, "Introduction," *Extracts from the Second Progress Report of the Study Mission into the Looting of Jewish Assets in France.*

30. Foreign and Commonwealth Office, *Nazi Gold: The London Conference* (London: HM Stationery Office, 1998), 6.

31. See, for example, Ziemke, *The U.S. Army in the Occupation of Germany, 1944–1946.*

32. Foreign and Commonwealth Office, *Nazi Gold: The London Conference,* 7.

33. Ibid., 10.

34. Independent Committee of Eminent Persons, *Report on Dormant Accounts,* 2.

VI. C·O·N·F·R·O·N·T·I·N·G
T·H·E P·A·S·T

Ian Buruma

The Innocent Eye: Childlike, Childish, and Children's Perspectives on the Holocaust

A WITNESS ACCOUNT, FROM POLISH ARCHIVES:

> They deported us to Russia on February 10, 1940. It was very cold. In our transport at the station there were one hundred freight cars; 3 locomotives pulled the train. They didn't give us water on the way. Lice bit us. I chopped wood in the settlement but often I was hungry. I never got meat at all. At school they said there was no Lord God and to throw religious medaillions in the stove. I didn't. The clothes we had from Poland we traded for flour. One whole family of 9 people died of hunger. I got typhus and my father died of hunger. It was good in the Polish army. Many Polish children died in the settlement, about forty.
> Grade 2 B.
> I am 12[1]

Compare this to another childhood memory in a highly successful recent movie, which begins with the words: "This is a simple story. But it is not easy to tell. Like a fable, there is sorrow, there is wonder and happiness."[2] What follows is not *like* a fable, it *is* a fable, about an Italian Jew being sent to a Nazi death camp with his small son and Christian wife. It is in fact a comedy, with no pretension of realism about being sent to a Nazi death camp. The comedy in Roberto Benigni's *Life Is Beautiful* consists of an elaborate ruse by the father, a Chaplin-esque figure, to shield his son from terrible reality. They are in a death camp. But the father pretends their experience is all part of an extraordinary game: nothing is real; the bad Nazis are only playing roles. If the little boy does his best, and makes the right moves, he will outwit the others and win the game—that, is, he will survive. By the time the movie is over, the father is dead, but the boy survives. He has won the game. Riding on top of a tank, waving his arms in triumph, he still has no idea that his survival was more than a game.

It is, of course, a sentimental conceit. Children who actually survived such horrors knew perfectly well they were not part of some game. And there was little room for wonder or happiness in their experiences, either. What strikes one about the children's accounts of terror in Poland, or anywhere else, is an emotional numbness, which Bruno Bettelheim explained as follows: "[E]motions require a great deal of energy; the greater the demands made on one's resources for sheer survival, the less energy one has available to experience feelings."[3]

What Benigni does in his movie is childish rather than childlike. He prolongs the state of innocence. He pretends that if we can maintain our innocence, and act as if life is a game, we will be better equipped to survive the bitterness of the adult world. This is part of his comic performance; even off-screen Benigni likes to behave like a child, an innocent, suffused with feelings of wonder and happiness.

Another movie director with a childish (and childlike) view is Stephen Spielberg. It may be no coincidence that he has become the most famous Hollywood fabulist of the Holocaust. The quickest, most effective way to our hearts (and our tear ducts) is to appeal to our nostalgia for lost innocence, for the child in us. And since the terrors of childhood are as vivid as the wonders and joys, it is perhaps not by chance either that the childlike view of horror should speak to us so readily.

Spielberg's *Schindler's List* is not told from the point of view of a child. And unlike Benigni's film, it aims to be realistic. But it is sentimental and childish nonetheless. The very idea that one can make a film about the Holocaust and make people feel good when they leave the cinema, because of the redemptive heroism of the main character, is childish. Not just that, but the hero, Oskar Schindler, a shady opportunist in real life, is presented as a kind of Father Christmas to "his Jews," who behave like a bunch of grateful children. We cry at the end of the picture, partly because in some deep place we still like to believe in Father Christmas. No matter how bad things get, the man with the white beard will come to our rescue. To get the full flavor of this, the terrors that come before the release must look real, and Spielberg's skill at providing shock effects is part of his essentially childlike vision.

There is a world of difference between real, numbing shock, as experienced in real life, and a shock effect, as experienced in the cinema. The latter always ends in a release. Real life is almost never so obliging. Take the famous scene in the showers of Auschwitz. In reality, the fake bathroom that promised the bliss of warm water delivered nothing but murderous gas. There is no gas in Spielberg's film. By some miracle, the menacing faucets just gush warm water. That is the difference between death and a shock effect.

Spielberg's other film about World War II, more interesting, in my opinion, than *Schindler's List,* is told from the point of view of a child, an English boy whose comfortable colonial life in Shanghai is suddenly turned upside down when he is put in a Japanese concentration camp. *Empire of the Sun,* based on the novel by J. G. Ballard, is also about innocence and wonder. In fact, the boy, Jim, lives in a world of fantasy, of brave Japanese fighter pilots who soar in the skies, high above the real world. Jim observes the violence and chaos of Chinese life through the windows of his father's chauffeur-driven limousine, as though the Chinese were exotic figures in a fabulous stage show. His fantasies of war and fighter planes are actually more real to him than the real thing. When he finally gets to see an actual Japanese fighter on the ground, he strokes it, as though it were a pet, or some magic toy. This is what makes the story so perfect for the Spielberg treatment: everything is seen through a gauze of childlike wonder.

Life in the camp, as the helper of an English doctor and a gang of American low-lifes, is brutal enough to divest any child of innocence. Yet Jim still dodges in and out of his fantasy world, and sometimes seems surprised when fighter aircraft or guns shoot with real bullets. Still, by the end of the war, he has become a hardened survivor: an adult in the body of a child. Ballard's novel, much less sentimental than Spielberg's film, ends with Jim feeling like a stranger to his parents after they are reunited. He "had wanted to explain . . . everything that he and the doctor had done together, but his mother and father had been through their own war. For all their affection for him, they seemed older and far away."

In the movie, however, Jim's smartly dressed parents do not look a minute older than they did in the beginning. Jim touches his mother's hair with the same wonder he displayed when he stroked the Zero fighter, and melts into her arms, as though the comforts of childhood can be magically restored in one maternal embrace.

In fact, of course, childhood can never be restored, not by all the tricks in Spielberg's magic box. That is precisely the point of the ending of Imre Kertesz's extraordinary novel, *Fateless*. Kertesz is a Hungarian Jew who survived Auschwitz and Buchenwald as a boy. His novel is really a memoir presented in a novelistic form. The horror of Kertesz's experience, of coming of age in Nazi camps, is that the camp regime becomes the norm. He, too, is emotionally numb, like the Polish children. It is the world outside the camps, to which he returns after liberation, that seems out of kilter. He quickly realizes that his experiences can never be fully understood by those who did not share them. He learns another thing, too: that life is more than fate, that each human being, in order to be fully human, has to feel responsible for his own life. When he is told, back in Budapest, to "forget" about "the terrors," he wonders how a person can ever "forget" such experiences, not only because they were terrible, but because they were a part of one's life. To forget about one's life is like the wave of a fairy's wand, comforting perhaps, but unreal.

The loss of innocence, or growing up, is one of the basic human stories, beginning with the expulsion of Adam and Eve from the Garden of Eden, which was perhaps the first *Bildungsroman*. The list of novels and films that repeat this story in one way or another is almost endless. Whether you believe that man is born a sinner depends on your religion. Confucian Chinese believe that man is born good, and society corrupts. But whatever the faith or culture, the corrupt nature of adult life is manifest. When the American gangsters in Spielberg's film ask Jim what he has learned from them, Jim answers that he now knows that "people will do anything for a potato."

The child's view of real or imagined atrocities, then, appeals to our nostalgia as well as our desire for a higher morality, for some way to transcend or purify the corruption of adult society. Many—perhaps most—stories about loss of innocence are rooted in the same source as religious beliefs. The actual historical context is often lost. These stories become pure parables of good and evil. The religious element can shine through even the most secular narratives.

Consider a Spanish movie released in the United States in 2000 entitled *Butterfly*, directed by José Luis Cuerda. The setting is rural Galicia in the years leading up to the Spanish Civil War. The politics are secular, socialist, republican. The hero is a middle-aged schoolteacher who tries to transfer his faith in science, literature, and liberty to the children in his charge. If just one generation of Spaniards, he exclaims, can be educated in freedom, then things will turn out all right. The local priest accuses him of corrupting young minds with knowledge and luring his pupils away from the Church. The local landowner suspects him of encouraging rebellious thoughts and anarchist schemes. But one intelligent little boy, nicknamed "Sparrow," soaks up his teacher's lessons with a naïve and loving passion; Sparrow's father, a tailor with socialist sympathies, gives the teacher a new suit as a token of his gratitude.

The scenes of Sparrow's childhood are deliberately shown as a kind of bucolic paradise, with village orchestras, festivals, and picnics in glorious, undisturbed nature. There are only hints of menace—the bullying landowner, the oily priest, the Guardia Civil lurking in the woods. But the menace suddenly explodes into violence when the war begins. Republicans, like Sparrow's father, hastily burn their socialist papers. People disappear in the night. The teacher is arrested. Sparrow's mother tells her boy that his father never made a suit for the teacher. But he did, says the boy. No he did not, says the mother. And at that moment, the son loses his innocence, not because of his teacher's secular learning, but because he has become aware of the price of survival. The boy is told to denounce his teacher, lest his own family get into trouble. The teacher, from being a model of goodness and enlightenment, becomes a fearful figure to be exorcised. In the last, harrowing shot of the movie, we see the teacher, standing on a truck, his hands bound, on his way to execution; and he sees, with tears in his eyes, how his favorite pupil picks up a stone to throw at him, while shouting "Atheist! Traitor! Red scum!" just as his mother had told him to do. And in that unforgettable image, the teacher, the paragon of secularism, is suddenly transformed into Jesus Christ, betrayed by his disciples.

There is much scope for sentimentality in this film, but the saccharine potential is undermined by our identification, not with the teacher, but with those who betray him: the mother, who wishes to save her family; the father, who cries "Traitor!" with tears in his eyes; and even with the boy, who learns his bitter lessons. In these circumstances there can be no extension of our stay in the Garden of Eden. This is much closer to reality than a manipulated identification with innocence.

What of Anne Frank's *Diary?* Does it belong to the literature of lost innocence, too? I believe it does. But not in the same way as a Spielberg movie.

Anne Frank's diary contains humour, malice, anger, confusion, and a depth of reflection well beyond her years (confined in an attic, her life under threat, she too grew up fast), but they are never sentimental. And yet the cult that has grown around Anne Frank is not only quasi-religious but highly sentimental. Her death transformed her from a sharp-eyed teenager into a martyr, an innocent cut down by cruel men—in a word, a saint. Saints are figures who retain their innocence in adult life—that is why female saints are almost always untainted by carnal knowledge; the fateful snake passed them by. Anne Frank died before she could become corrupted by adult life.

The fact than young girls from Amsterdam to Tokyo identify with Anne Frank is not surprising. It is actually a tribute to her literary talent. Under extraordinary circumstances, she managed to express such universal feelings as budding sexual desire, rebelliousness, and so on. In Japan the teenage identification with Anne Frank went so far that a clever manufacturer coined the word "Annes" for sanitary napkins. It is to be expected, then, that many of the pilgrims who make their different ways to the Anne Frank House in Amsterdam should be young and female.

More disturbing is the wider identification with Anne Frank's fate. Her story has become such a prominent part of Dutch school education that by now she has become a kind of Dutch Joan of Arc. Her innocence is Dutch innocence. Just as she was a victim of Nazi Germany, so was her adopted country. And this despite the fact that only Poland lost a higher percentage of Jews than Holland; despite the fact that the Dutch bureaucracy did much to help the Germans bring this about (mostly out of stupidity and cowardice, rather than ideological malice); and despite the fact that Anne Frank's family was betrayed by a Dutch person (and hidden by an Austrian).

There are various reasons that the Anne Frank story should have become a centerpiece of contemporary education, not only in Holland. One of them has to do with the tendency to move away from narrative national history, which begins with the first inhabitants to crawl out of their caves, and to move toward social studies with no historical education. And social studies tend towards morality tales—about racism, for example. Anne Frank has become a morality tale, a kind of modern Bible story. The result is unhistorical, frequently sentimental, and to the extent that Dutch people are encouraged to identify with her innocence, childish.

Holland is not the only country to cloak itself in holy innocence. The loss of national innocence, as though nations grow up, like humans, is a constant theme even in the United States. No one is quite sure when exactly Uncle Sam lost his innocence—the U.S. Civil War, Hiroshima, the Vietnam War, the Kennedy assassinations, Watergate; but whenever it was, the idea is there, mulled over, debated, or lamented in TV shows, history books, and Hollywood movies.

A more dramatic example, however, is Japan. A nationalist historian once expressed the opinion that Japan's twentieth-century wars were all the consequence of being dragged into the corrupt world of Western powers, as though Japan in the mid–nineteenth century was still a child among adults. Bliss it was to be in the gilded isolation of the Tokugawa Period. But after the country of Kabuki actors, rice farmers, woodblock artists, and samurai became a modern nation-state, with armies dressed in Western-style uniforms and imperialist ambitions to match, the Japanese became corrupted by politics and the Darwinist struggle for survival. It is complete nonsense, of course, but I have heard this view in different variations from a good number of Japanese.

The modern—that is, post-Meiji—system of Japanese emperor worship, with the emperor playing the twin roles of divine patriarch and Prussian-style monarch, turned out to be a lethal form of childishness. The late emperor Hirohito called his subjects "his children." He did not believe in popular sovereignty. His children owed him absolute obedience, and thus were not responsible citizens. No wonder, then, that when the war was over, and the terrible damage done to millions of Asians, including the Japanese, few people felt responsible. And when public opinion was manipulated—with the active participation of the U.S. occupation staff under General MacArthur—to believe that the emperor himself had been an innocent child, deceived by cruel militarist cliques, the childishness became institutionalized once more. Japanese were encouraged to identify themselves with the emperor; if he was innocent, so were they.

Japan since the late 1940s was no longer seen by many Japanese as a nation that was guilty of unleashing a terrible war in Asia, but as a nation of victims—victims of Western power politics, victims of Japanese military cliques, and finally, victims of the two atom bombs. There are more novels and films in Japan about Hiroshima and Nagasaki than about any other events in the war. Many are sentimental.

And one of the most famous, a novel entitled *Black Rain,* by Ibuse Masaji, is about an innocent girl of about Anne Frank's age who dies of radiation before she can fully become a woman.

And this brings me back to the film I spoke of in the beginning: Roberto Benigni's *Life is Beautiful.* Benigni has often spoken about his own father, who had been a prisoner in a German camp. His father was an innocent too, whose torment was made even more maddening, because he did not know what he had done wrong. And, like the character in the movie, Benigni's father shielded his family from hearing about the terrible truth by coating his experiences with a sugary gloss. Instead of the truth, he told funny stories. A touching inspiration, then, for a touching film.

But the American scholar of Italian culture, Ruth Ben-Ghiat, dug up the real story behind Benigni's inspiration, which complicates matters somewhat. Luigi Benigni, Roberto's father, was neither innocent nor Jewish, but a soldier in the Italian fascist army who had been taken prisoner with other Italians, after Italy surrendered to the allies. This is not to suggest that Luigi was a war criminal. But to retell his story as a fable about Jewish suffering is like the Dutch identification with Anne Frank: there is an element of bad faith; it is as though all Italians were Jews, or at least shared their fate. The fact that the movie character's wife is a Christian who willingly accompanies her husband to the death camp can only strengthen that impression.

The problem about representing the Holocaust, or any other horrific historical experience, is not a problem of realism or fable. The problem is one of false identification, of the refusal to look truth in the face. And the truth is that to glorify innocence is often a way of ducking responsibility, or, like Peter Pan, of refusing to grow up.

NOTES

1. Irena Grudzinska-Gross and Jan Tomasz Gross, *War Through Children's Eyes.* Stanford, CA: Hoover Institution Press, 1981.

2. See the superb article by Ruth Ben-Ghiat, "The Secret Histories of Roberto Benigni's *Life is Beautiful,*" *Yale Journal of Criticism* 14 (Spring 2001): 253–266.

3. Grudzinka and Gross, *War Through Children's Eyes,* Foreword.

Jeffrey Herf

How and Why Did Holocaust
Memory Come to the United States?
A Response to Peter Novick's Challenge

FOR MOST OF THE PERIOD SINCE THE HOLOCAUST, A CLEAR AND UNAM-
biguous dichotomy stood at the center of all discussion of its memory. On the one side were those who stood in favor of memory, which
was synonymous with searching for truth about what happened,
bringing criminals to justice, and recognizing the suffering of victims.
On the other side stood those who benefited from and advocated
silence, avoidance, repression, and denial if not outright lying. The
task of historians was straightforward and clear: to place the discipline of history in the service of memory of that which a complacent
present would prefer to forget, and, as the title of this series states,
to learn lessons and pass on legacies so that these or similar horrors
will not be repeated. In recent years historians of memory, even when
taking the side of the victims and seeking to recall truths about past
crimes, have drawn our attention to some ambiguous features of
memory. In casting a sardonic gaze on the presence of Holocaust
memory in American society in recent years, Peter Novick in *The
Holocaust in American Life* in part reflects this broader reconsideration of memory among his fellow historians, yet pushes this reconsideration beyond what even his own evidence will bear.

Historians who have worked on the memory of the Holocaust in
the two postwar Germanys, of World War II in the Soviet Union, of
the Nazi occupation of France and Western Europe and the resistance
or the paucity thereof against it, and of the American Civil War in
those postwar decades have drawn our attention to elements of memory of a more mundane nature.[1] Memory may be the victim's truth-

ful recollection of past crimes, but even in that case memory is, after all, by definition, a recollection of what has happened to an individual or a group. It is inherently narcissistic or, in less pejorative terms, it is about what we know from our own experience. It is not about others. Hence, a focus on memory may set off Hobbesian struggles for recognition in which various memories compete rather than complement one another. Memory may serve the interests of justice and decency, but it may also be the plaything of manipulators who stoke the flames of resentment and hatred by pointing to past, and largely imagined, wrongs in order to launch new cycles of violence and aggression or to justify new examples of dictatorial rule. Indeed, historians of Nazism itself point to the importance Hitler attributed to the "memory" of a "stab-in-the-back" by "the November criminals" during World War I as a prime example of the misuse of memory in precisely this manner. Finally, historians of memory have pointed out that in any society there will be a variety of memories, and that, as a result, the alternative facing a society at any given point is generally not that of remembering or forgetting, speech or silence, recovery or repression. Rather, at every point there are different stories and public memories to tell about the past. The issue of which ones receive or fail to receive a public hearing is always a matter both of intrinsic interest and truth content as well as political power and influence.

Which of the many memories present come to the fore in a broad public at a particular time is a result both of what actually happened in the past and of politics in the present that influence what aspects of the past a society chooses to publicly remember. Memory does not just "come." Its advocates must make great efforts, inside and outside the political arena, to see that the memory of their particular experience finds a hearing in the larger public. This is a part of what politics in a democracy, especially a multi-ethnic democracy, is about. In short, to the extent to which the memory of the Holocaust has become more prominent in American society since the 1960s, it is a result of efforts of American Jews to bring this about. The result is not one of which Novick approves. Just as the prominence of the Holocaust is something he finds regrettable, so too are what he sees as its causes. Why, he asks, did the Holocaust attain greater public presence in American society from the 1960s to the 1990s?[2] Why has an event that was a part of European, more than American, history become so prominent in American society? Why, in a country whose defining national disgrace has been slavery, segregation, and racism against African-Americans, did the Holocaust Memorial Museum in Washington, D.C., precede construction of a memorial museum devoted to the history of black enslavement? What does the prominence of this memory say about the political and moral outlook of American Jewry and its national organizations?

Novick's core argument is the following. The greater presence of the Holocaust is one consequence of a regrettable transformation of the values and identity of American Jews away from the universalist, left-liberalism, and leftism of the early postwar decades to more conservative politics resting on narrower ethnic identity and stories of past victimization. This shift in identity and toward identity-based politics has gone hand in hand with a conscious political strategy pursued by national Jewish organizations to use the memory of the Holocaust to deflect criticism of Israel following the Six-Day War of 1967 and the Yom Kippur War of 1973. "Turning the Holocaust into the emblematic Jewish experience" has been "closely connected to the inward and rightward turn of American Jewry in recent decades."[3] American Jewish organizations gave enhanced and unprecedented attention to the Holocaust because its memory was effective in deflecting "any legitimate grounds for criticizing Israel, to avoid even considering the possibility that the rights and wrongs were complex."[4] Citing literature produced by the American Israel Public Affairs Committee and other Jewish lobbying organizations, Novick argues that this strategy of political instrumentalization was decisive in bringing the Holocaust to greater prominence in American society. In addition to the shift to the right and the deflection of criticism of Israel, Novick argues that the Holocaust's prominence was a response to a decline in Jewish religious belief to the point at which the Holocaust became "virtually the only common denominator of American Jewish identity in the late twentieth century."[5] Jewish identity focused on the Holocaust became "dominant, because it was, after all, virtually the only one that could encompass those Jews whose faltering Jewish identity produced so much anxiety about Jewish survival."[6]

Before proceeding to discuss Novick's argument in more detail, it is clear that each of these key causal factors has a strikingly pejorative nature. Reading the work, one is struck that Novick gives very short or no weight to possible alternative, non-pejorative (from even his perspective) causal factors. For example, he does not consider the possibility that some of those who gave weight to the memory of the Holocaust may have done so because of involvement in the civil rights and anti-war protests of the 1960s, just as the willingness of non-Jewish Americans to pay attention to this memory may have been due to a decline in racism and anti-Semitism in American society. That is, he does not examine whether the emergence of the Holocaust is due to the persistence of Jewish liberalism and the expansion of tolerance in American society generally. He also does not address a seemingly obvious point, namely, that the generation of survivors of the Holocaust, having established families and careers, turned to this issue in their mature years in the determination that memory of these events would persist after this generation had died. Moreover, and quite surprisingly given his previous work on the American historical profession, he also neglects to consider the equally obvious hypothesis that as Jewish scholars, intellectuals, and artists made advances in the universities, the media, and film, they would devote their talents to bringing this history and its narratives into historical scholarship, print and electronic media, and Hollywood films.

Yet even those who will take strong issue with Novick's explanation for the emergence of the Holocaust since the 1960s will benefit from his pointed insights into the wartime and immediate postwar years. He takes issue with the view that the United States "abandoned" the Jews. Instead, he cites officials in the Roosevelt administration's Office of War Information who sought to convince the American public that Nazi Germany was "everyone's enemy." In so doing they sought to "to broaden rather than narrow the range of Nazi victims" because they believed that if American intervention were justified as a war to save the Jews it would have narrowed support for the anti-Nazi struggle, played into the hands of isolationists, and appeared to confirm Nazi propaganda about Jewish influence on Roosevelt.[7] He recalls the anti-Semitism of some Republican Party campaign slogans of 1940, such as "It's Your Country—Why Let Sidney Hillman Run it?" along with attacks on the "Jew Deal" and "President Rosenfeld." As other historians of World War II have pointed out, in light of the German control of the continent from 1940–41 to 1944, practical prospects for rescue were "dim." Yet the issue of what the Allies, the Soviet Union, no less than the United States and Great Britain, could have done to save the Jews remaining alive in Europe in spring 1944 remain important ones and cannot be dismissed as easily.

Novick's discussion of the tension between the memory of the Holocaust and political culture of Cold War anti-communism is generally very good but will not come as news to historians of postwar Europe and West Germany. As the United States mobilized to contain the Soviet Union, its former ally in the war against Nazism, and to reintegrate its former enemies now in West Germany into the Western alliance "talk of the Holocaust was not just unhelpful but actively obstructive;" indeed, it was the "wrong atrocity" with which to mobilize anti-Soviet sentiment. In other words, the memory of the Holocaust was an uncomfortable and politically inconvenient memory in the conservative climate of the 1950s. Moreover, he points out, as others have previously, that the theory of totalitarianism, at least some forms of it, focused attention on the the political rather than ethnic, racial, or religious identity of Nazism's victims, thus contributing to marginalization of the Holocaust. It also stressed the commonalities between Nazism and communism. "Conversely, any suggestion that the Nazi murder of European Jewry was a central, let alone defining, feature of that regime would undermine the argument for the essential identity of the two systems [Nazism and communism—JH]. As a result, one will search in vain through the vast literature on totalitarianism for any but the most glancing and casual mention of the Holocaust."[8] Novick has in mind the interpretation of totalitarianism voiced by Carl Friedrich and his students, such as Zbigniev Brezinski. In this form of the literature on totalitarianism, he correctly notes, one indeed could "search in vain" for mention of the Holocaust. It is peculiar, however, that Novick does not mention the single most important contribution to "the vast literature" on totalitarianism, one which came from the pen of a former member of his own University of Chicago's Committee on Social Thought. That was, of course, Hannah Arendt's 1950 *The Origins of Totalitarianism*. In this classic, anti-Semitism, the death camps, and the genocide of European Jewry stood in the center of analysis and did so at a time when both Marxist and conventional political science analysts of totalitarianism were unable or unwilling to understand and explain the impact of Nazi ideological fanaticism.

While Novick is correct that in general the Holocaust did not fit well into the mentality of Cold War anti-communism, he is less convincing when he writes that for American Jewish organizations seeking to dissociate themselves from communism, "in matters having to

do with Germany there was a virtual taboo on mention of the Holocaust." Instead, discussion of the Holocaust remained largely a "private, albeit widely shared, Jewish sorrow" that did not become "a
public communal emblem. . . ."[9] He pushes this point too far. As I
have written and as the Israeli historian Shlomo Shafir has pointed
out in greater detail, such staunch Cold War anti-communist organizations as the American Federation of Labor argued vehemently during the 1950s in favor of restitution for Jewish survivors.[10] The restitution disputes entailed considerable discussion of Nazi persecution.

The postwar American "forgetting" of the Holocaust and the
German war on the Eastern Front in World War II, the premature
reintegration and amnesty of accused or convicted Nazi war criminals
in West Germany, and the cold-hearted approach of many West German government officials and leaders of industry toward restitutions
claims are familiar and well-documented themes.[11] The acquiescence
of the American government in the climate of premature amnesty in
West Germany in the 1950s has been well described by historians.
Among other things, this policy reflected the lack of political clout of
both the state of Israel and American, not to mention European, Jews.
Nevertheless, the Western governments did not pursue policies that
were actively anti-Jewish or anti-Semitic. It was the anti-communist
West Germans, not the "anti-fascist" communist regimes in East Germany, that offered financial restitution and financial support for Israel in the 1950s. Novick's only comment about the attacks on Jews
in the "anti-cosmopolitan" purges in Eastern and Central Europe of
this period is to criticize a press release from the American Jewish
Committee for presenting what he calls the "grotesque fabrication"
that the East German government was rounding up non-Aryans
based on principles of selection resting on Nazi racial legislation.[12] In
fact, in the winter of 1952–53, the East German government did
purge many Jewish members of the party and government and did
frighten Jewish community leaders enough so that most fled to the
West. Though the winter purge did not rest on Nazi racial legislation
and was not directed at "non-Aryans" or all Jews, the anti-Semitic aspects of the purge were clear to anyone reading the attacks in East
Germany's government-controlled press on an alleged international
conspiracy of Zionists, capitalists, and imperialists. Novick focuses
his indignation on the American Jewish Committee for getting some
facts wrong about the purge—facts that were hard to come by, given

the East German dictatorship's ability to close off access to accurate information—rather than on this burst of anti-Semitic politics in Europe less than a decade after the Holocaust. In West Germany, and in the United States, it was the liberal press, especially the left-of-center *Frankfurter Rundschau* in the Federal Republic and the *New York Times,* respectively, not the conservative papers, that reported on the "anti-cosmopolitan purge" in most detail.[13] In the early 1960s, the flagship of American conservatism, the *Wall Street Journal,* editorialized that the Eichmann trial in Jerusalem risked reviving anti-German sentiment, would benefit the communists, and was pervaded by "an atmosphere of Old Testament retribution."[14] William F. Buckley's *National Review* argued that communists would benefit from the "Hate Germany movement" being furthered by the Eichmann trial.[15] The Holocaust was, as Novick aptly put it, "the wrong atrocity" for conservative anti-communists who did not want to dwell on Germany's dark past. Novick finds that fear about this conservative backlash during and after the McCarthy period made leaders of Jewish organizations wary of emphasizing the Holocaust.

Many readers will agree with Novick that the Arab-Israeli wars of 1967 and 1973 were important for the emergence of the Holocaust in American public consciousness. While the Six-Day War of 1967 fostered a renewed Jewish consciousness and pride internationally, the Yom Kippur War, though it culminated in Israeli victory, underscored Israel's vulnerability. Followed as it was by the Arab oil boycott and the United Nations' 1974 resolution equating Zionism with racism, it also underscored Israel's international political isolation and the key role of the United States as its defender. It was at this moment of Israel's political vulnerability that American Jewish organizations gave unprecedented attention to the Holocaust because they saw doing so as an effective means to build political support for Israel and to immunize it against criticism. Novick views this as a misuse of the past but does not interrogate his own assumption. Why, after all, in the face of armed hostility of the Arab world and the infamous United Nations resolution, was it unreasonable for Jews and non-Jews to recall that, in fact, the Holocaust happened not so long ago and that anti-Semitic prejudices were a component of international hostility to the Jewish state? Novick sees this effort as an indicator of a move to the right, and, to be sure, it was very much at odds with the anti-imperialist and anti-Zionist mood of the American and international left. Yet between left and right lies liberalism, and one could easily and plausibly see American support for Israel as a continuation of the liberal tradition of such support beginning in the 1940s under FDR and continuing with President Harry Truman.[16]

Of course, for a variety of reasons, including the anti-Israeli hostility of the Soviet Union and parts of the Western new Left, some American Jewish intellectuals and organizational leaders did indeed contribute to American neo-conservatism. It is also the case that some of the scholars who wrote widely noted books about the Holocaust, such as Lucy Dawidowicz, published essays and reviews in the neo-conservative flagship journal *Commentary*.[17] Certainly she and like-minded colleagues deserve a great deal of credit for bringing the Holocaust to the fore in American society and intellectual life. Yet, to take Dawidowicz as one example, both of her two most well-known works on the Holocaust, *The War against the Jews* (1975) and *Historians and the Holocaust* (1981), are firmly within a liberal historiography in which the role of ideas and ideology is given prominence as a causal factor in opposition both to the social and economic determinism that shaped so much of Marxist and functionalist analyses of Nazism and to the conservative neglect of the Holocaust that Novick also criticized.

Though in the 1970s, social historians paid too little attention to the causal significance of ideological and cultural factors, there was nothing inherently conservative or "right wing" about Dawidowicz's work. On the contrary, in the discipline of history, a methodologically conservative if politically liberal standpoint of conventional political historians had dominated much scholarly and almost all popular accounts of World War II. These narratives focused on the political and military dimensions of struggles between states fought in major battles—Battle of Britain, Pearl Harbor, Stalingrad, Iwo Jima, Midway, D Day, Hiroshima, and so on—and addressed the Holocaust, if at all, only briefly.[18] From the perspective of historians of Europe—and Novick began his career as a historian of twentieth-century France—bringing the history of the Holocaust from the margins to the center of a narrative of the war did not represent a move to the Right. In the face of opposition from conservatives, sometimes Marxists, often nationalist apologists, this shift represented one of many efforts in the historical profession of recent decades to bring the stories of subordinate groups of all kinds out of the shadows cast by past historical convention, focused as it was on the stories of nations and their national leaders.

Perhaps the most surprising aspect of *The Holocaust in American Life* is that its author is the preeminent historian of the fragmentation of the conventional political narrative of American history. In his much-discussed 1988 work, *That Noble Dream: The "Objectivity Question" and the American Historical Profession,* Novick argued that the entry of Jews, blacks, and women had been a driving force in bringing about a more complex and inclusive narrative of American history.[19] Yet only a decade later, Novick regrets rather than celebrates the inclusion of the Jewish catastrophe into the main narratives of German and European history even though this achievement was due, in part, to the labors of the very same American Jewish historians whose entry into the discipline he had welcomed in *That Noble Dream.* One wishes that he had mentioned, as part of his history of the emergence of the Holocaust in American life, the contributions of major liberal German-Jewish refugee historians such as Raul Hilberg, George Mosse, and Fritz Stern. They wrote classic works about the implementation of the Holocaust, and about anti-Semitism and the background to Nazism and the Holocaust, at a time in the early 1960s when German historians in Germany and non-Jewish historians of Germany in the American historical profession, with a few exceptions, avoided the topic. These works were published before arguments about Israel became publicly prominent in the wake of the 1967 and 1973 wars.[20]

In *That Noble Dream,* Novick demonstrated that a more accurate picture of American history was due, in part, to the growing ethnic and gender diversity of the American historical profession. One wishes he had applied his own argument to the role of American and American-Jewish historians in bringing the Holocaust from the periphery to the center of German and European history. Had he done so, he would have had to qualify his assertions concerning the ethnic provincialism attached to Holocaust memory. To be sure, one can point to examples of the memory and history of the Holocaust that fit the pattern of narrow identity politics. Yet a balanced account would also point to the work of histories in which the emergence of the Holocaust is part of an increasingly cosmopolitan and less provincial America-centric history of the Second World War. Despite their differences about dates, the arguments of Christopher Browning and Richard Breitman as well as that of Phillip Burrin regarding the timing of the decision to launch the Holocaust have deepened the links between the history of World War II and that of the Holocaust.[21] Gerhard Weinberg and Omer Bartov have advanced this integration among military and diplomatic historians of the war.[22] The incorporation of the Holocaust along with the Eastern Front and the war on the Asian mainland has been one of the significant developments in the American historical profession's history of World War II. For these historians, the emergence of the Holocaust has been associated with the very universalism and cosmopolitanism whose weakness Novick regrets. One wishes Novick had explored this aspect of the Holocaust in American life but also that he had asked whether similar motivations might be at work in its emergence in popular consciousness beyond the confines of the historical profession. It is a plausible, though yet-unproven, hypothesis that the more Americans learn about the Holocaust, the more aware they might become of those aspects of the Second World War in Eastern Europe and the Soviet Union and Asia that did not directly affect American soldiers and the majority of non-Jewish Americans.

It is a commonplace that the emergence of race as a focus of interest among American historians is inseparable from the changes that have taken place in American society since the 1960s. No one to my knowledge has suggested that this emergence is due to the increasing conservatism or primarily to narrow forms of identity politics. Yet historians who brought the Holocaust into the main narratives of German and European history had to fight some battles that were in principle similar to those that led to the prominence of race as a category of American historiography. In the post-1960s political climate, the Holocaust did not fit well into the leftist intellectual life on either side of the Atlantic. To be sure, there were traditionalists, such as Dawidowicz or the younger Andreas Hillgrüber, who grasped the ideological dimension when social historians refused to admit its importance, just as there was a Marxist or two (notably Timothy Mason, who sought to understand the primacy of politics in Nazi Germany as an exception that proved the rule of Marxist theories of the state).[23] Among West German historians, two liberals, Karl Bracher and Eberhard Jäckel, in the late 1960s and into the 1970s published the key texts that first brought anti-Semitism and the Holocaust into the central political narratives of twentieth-century German history.[24] In the New Left generation in West Germany, historian Dan Diner and sociologist Detlev Claussen argued to emancipate the history of the Holocaust and European and German anti-Semitism from dismissal in the era of a revived Marxism.[25] Conversely, in antifascist East Germany, early efforts by dissident communists to raise the issue of the Holocaust were crushed in the anti-cosmopolitan purges, after which the official Marxist-Leninist ideology left little if any room for a full-fledged historical analysis of anti-Semitism and the Holocaust.[26] One central conclusion of my history of public discussion of the Holocaust in both Germanys after 1945 is that a focus on the Holocaust, be it in historical scholarship, political public memory, or judicial investigation, has consistently found the most support from left-liberals and Social Democrats (with some exceptions in the Left and moderate Right). They, too, in public life, fought a battle against a forgetful, hard-hearted, and more recently nationalistic Right, and at times against first the communist and then the neo-Marxist New Left. There is considerable evidence that a similar argument applies to the emergence of the Holocaust in American life and again, one wishes Novick had explored that hypothesis.

The alternative hypothesis, which Novick did not examine and which remains to be examined, is the following: The Holocaust emerged in American life because the United States became a less anti-Semitic and less racist society. Declining anti-Semitism meant that non-Jewish Americans were more willing to look at the facts of the Holocaust while Jewish leaders were less fearful of the conservative backlashes they sought to avoid in the 1950s. Memory of past persecution, including the Holocaust, played a major role in nourishing the liberalism of American Jews, including their disproportionate support for the Civil Rights movement. The Jewish focus on the Holocaust since the 1960s drew on similar sentiments and was a complement to, not a diversion from, a continuing liberal concern over racial and religious hatred and the forgetfulness of the political culture of the 1950s. The protest movements of the sixties and their aftermath expanded American interest in and willingness to acknowledge all manner of past injustices. In such a climate, it would have been odd if the Holocaust had not found greater presence in American life. Opponents of the war in Vietnam and its conduct evoked the memory of the Nuremberg war crimes trials and those reflections in turn influenced some of the current generation of American historians of the Holocaust.[27] As Novick's interesting discussion of the American response to the Eichmann trial in Jerusalem in 1961 illustrates, the same conservative voices opposed the Civil Rights movement criticized the Eichmann trial and its focus on the genocide of European Jewry. One wishes Novick had drawn out the corollary of his evidence regarding conservative hostility to discussion of the Holocaust and acknowledged liberal sources of the Holocaust's subsequent greater American presence.

Another important and plausible hypothesis to account for the presence of the Holocaust in American life that Novick does not explore concerns the most obvious motivations and initiatives of American Jews. It is that, as the generation of survivors aged and were able to establish careers and families, they and their children were able to turn their energies to see that the memory of the Holocaust did become a part of the public life of the world's most important multiethnic democracy. In so doing, they behaved as all other ethnic groups have in American life. It is a plausible hypothesis worth exploring that Jews, inside and outside their religious and secular institutions, did so because they felt morally compelled to do so and were, for the first time in the postwar era, in a social, political, and financial position to bring their hopes to fruition. It is equally plausible that many, if not most, of those involved in making films, writing novels, organizing school curricula, and founding the Holocaust Memorial Museum, did so because they thought it was intrinsically right and necessary to do so and not primarily because they calculated that it would also immunize Israel from criticism or would bring young people into or back into the Jewish community. Certainly the Holocaust would not have assumed more presence in American life without the initiatives of the Jewish community and its leadership. The archives of these organizations await a historian willing to entertain the possibility that Jewish focus on Holocaust memory rested on such intrinsic motivations rather than primarily on the hypothesis of the cynical "uses" of the Holocaust that Novick presents.

Novick's analysis of the self-regarding nature of Holocaust memory in contrast to a presumed previous universalism is evident in his discussion of Elie Wiesel, recognized as the most prominent public face of Holocaust survivors. He draws on a multitude of criticisms from Wiesel's Jewish critics who are unhappy with the way he has linked suffering and redemption in ways that resonate with his Christian admirers and for surrounding the Holocaust with an aura of sacred mystery, outside the mundane causal influences of history and politics. He takes Wiesel to task for insisting that the Holocaust Museum in Washington focus on the six million Jews rather than on "eleven million" noncombatants said by some to have been killed by the Nazis, and takes Wiesel and others to task for seeming selfishness in refusing to share the stage with others.[28] One could dismiss Novick's concerns here, as he treats the serious historical arguments about the uniqueness of the Holocaust far too cavalierly. Here, fairness to Elie Wiesel requires recalling that at the opening ceremonies of the Holocaust Memorial Museum, he urged then-reluctant President Clinton to use American military force to stop the ongoing Serbian program of ethnic cleansing directed against Bosnian Muslims. Wiesel, like the editors and writers of the pro-interventionist *New Republic,* made the case for American military intervention with explicit reference to the consequences of appeasement of Nazism in the 1930s and lack of effort to stop the Holocaust in the 1940s.[29] Novick does not mention this expansive, universalist "use" of the memory of the Holocaust. It is a stiking omission, given his view that Holocaust memory makes us less concerned about subsequent horrors that do not match its extremity, or leads us to avoid painful memories of racial persecution of African-Americans that are, in contrast to the Holocaust, part of American history.[30] Eli Wiesel's impassioned plea for American intervention in the Balkans, articulated at the opening ceremonies of the United States Holocaust Memorial Museum, would seem to suggest that among those most active in fostering memory of the Holocaust there were prominent advocates of the universalist and expansive implications of its memory.

In Israel, where the memory of the Holocaust has indeed played a major role in political debate, criticism of the political Right for its instrumentalization has been a long-standing theme. As Israeli historian of Germany Moshe Zuckermann has recently argued, in making common cause with his fellow historian, Yehuda Elkana, the memory of the Holocaust does not justify policies in the present that neglect or even cause the suffering of the Palestinians. In a much discussed "Plea for Forgetting" published in the flagship of Israeli liberalism, *Haaretz,* Elkana criticized the use made of the memory of the Holocaust by conservative politicians in Israel.[31] Zuckermann, however, while critical of the use made of the Holocaust by those who failed to grasp its key implications, recalled Theodor Adorno's recasting of Kant's categorical imperative: Act in such a manner so that neither Auschwitz nor anything like Auschwitz can ever be repeated. Rather than appeal for a forgetting of Auschwitz, he argued that true and full recollection of the Holocaust was part of a liberal program and was incompatible with an intransigent Israeli nationalism. Zuckermann's intervention recalls a point relevant for the emergence of the Holocaust in American life, namely that (as Novick argues) it can be used to serve mundane political purposes but also that (as Novick is reluctant to acknowledge) its memory contains lessons that really are not compatible with the narrow-minded identity politics to which Novick objects.

In the past decade, historians of memory in Israel, Europe, and the United States have arrived at a disillusioned, sober conclusion: memory of past horror and injustice, though it is a fundamental moral obligation, does not insure a humane future. It may be the handmaiden of a renewed ethnocentrism and nationalism. Indeed, cultivation of past suffering, real and imagined, has been a key feature of some of this century's most evil regimes. Yet if Holocaust memory does not guarantee a humane future, its absence would be a terrible loss, an offense against those who died and a blow to the hopes of preventing a future repetition. Its emergence in American public life represents one of the most surprising and welcome pieces of evidence of seriousness in a society well known for its sunny, shallow optimism and of growing religious and ethnic tolerance in an overwhelmingly Christian population that especially before World War II and the Holocaust, accepted anti-Semitic sentiment as a norm.[32] Peter Novick chose not to pursue a range of plausible alternative hypotheses to account for the presence of the Holocaust in American life. These unexamined hypotheses leave a substantial body of work for another historian or historians to do. In the wake of the terrorist attacks of September 11, 2001, the extent to which the memory of the Holocaust transcends the categories of Left and Right, in which so much debate has taken place, also again comes into view. The memory of the Holocaust, whatever short-term political benefits it may or may not have given some of its advocates, has been and will remain the memory of radical evil in the modern world. Now that Americans have experienced at home what radical evil means, albeit on a scale far smaller than that of the Holocaust, its continuing place in an America more serious and more burdened with tragedy seems assured. Perhaps a future historian will find that the American memory of the Holocaust since the 1960s grew in part because it resonated with those undercurrents in American culture that, beneath the famous facile optimism, had an unexpected appreciation for the presence of radical evil in the world.

NOTES

1. See David Blight, *Race and Reunion: The Civil War in American Memory* (Cambridge: Harvard University Press, 2001); Jeffrey Herf, *Divided Memory: The Nazi Past in the Two Germanys* (Cambridge: Harvard University Press, 1997); Charles Maier, *The Unmasterable Past: History, Holocaust and German National Identity* (Cambridge: Harvard University Press, 1988); Harold Marcuse, *Legacies of Dachau: The Uses and Abuses of a Concentration Camp, 1933–2001* (Berkeley: University of California Press, 2001); Henry Russo, *The Vichy Syndrome* (Cambridge: Harvard University Press, 1991); and Moshe Zuckermann, *Zweierlei Holocaust: Der Holocaust in den politischen Kulturen Israels und Deutschlands* (Göttingen: Wallstein Verlag, 1998).

2. Peter Novick, *The Holocaust in American Life* (Boston: Houghton-Mifflin, 1999).

3. Ibid., 10.

4. Ibid., 155.

5. Ibid., 7.

6. Ibid., 187.

7. Ibid., 27.

8. Ibid., 87.

9. Ibid., 96.

10. On this see Shlomo Shafir, *Ambiguous Relations: The American Jewish Community and Germany since 1945* (Detroit: Wayne State University Press, 1999); and Jeffrey Herf, *Divided Memory.*

11. The literature is considerable. See Ulrich Brochhagen, *Nach Nürnberg: Vergangenheitsbewältigung und Westintegration in der Ära Adenauer* (Hamburg: Junius Verlag, 1994); Norbert Frei, *Vergangenheitspolitik: Die Anfänge der Bundesrepublik und die NS-Vergangenheit* (Munich: C. H. Beck Verlag, 1996); Ulrich Herbert, *Best: Biographische Studien uber Radikalismus, Weltanschauung und Vernunft* (Bonn: J. H. W. Dietz Verlag, 1996);

Jeffrey Herf, *Divided Memory;* Thomas Schwartz, *America's Germany: John J. McCloy and the Federal Republic of Germany* (Cambridge: Harvard University Press, 1991).

12. Novick, *The Holocaust in American Life,* 99.

13. On the anti-cosmopolitan purges in East Germany and its West German and American reportage, see Herf, *Divided Memory.*

14. Novick, *The Holocaust in American Life,* 129.

15. Ibid., 130.

16. On Truman and American support for the new state of Israel, see Alonzo Hamby, *Man of the People: A Life of Harry S. Truman* (New York: Oxford University Press, 1995).

17. See Lucy Dawidowicz, *The War against the Jews* (New York: Holt, Rinehart and Winston, 1975); *The Holocaust and the Historians* (Cambridge: Harvard University Press, 1981).

18. An excellent account that displays this conventional structuring of the narrative is Peter Calvocoressi, Guy Wint, and John Pritchard, *Total War: The Causes and Consequences of the Second World War,* 2nd rev. ed. (Hammondsworth, Middlesex, England: Viking, 1989). On this, see the excellent "Bibliographical Essay" in Gerhard Weinberg, *A World at Arms: A Global History of World War II* (New York: Cambridge University Press, 1994), 921–44.

19. Peter Novick, *That Noble Dream: The Objectivity Question and the American Historical Profession* (New York: Cambridge University Press, 1988).

20. See George Mosse, *The Crisis of German Ideology: The Intellectual Origins of the Third Reich* (New York: Grosset and Dunlap, 1964); Fritz Stern, *The Politics of Cultural Despair: A Study in the Rise of Germanic Ideology* (New York: Doubleday Anchor, 1965).

21. See, for example, Christopher Browning, *Paths to Genocide: Essays on the Launching of the Final Solution* (New York: Cambridge University Press, 1992); and Richard Breitman, *The Architect of Genocide: Himmler and the Final Solution* (Hanover, N.H.: University of New England Press, 1992); Phillip Burrin, *Hitler and the Jews: The Genesis of the Holocaust* (London: Edward Arnold, 1994). On the integration of intellectual, cultural, international, and social history with political history, see Jeffrey Herf, "Not So Boring After All: Recent Trends in Political History of Twentieth Century Germany," *Tel Aviver Jahrbuch für deutsche Geschichte* 28 (1999): 13–31.

22. See Gerhard Weinberg, *A World at Arms;* Omer Bartov, *Hitler's Army: Soldiers, Nazis and War in the Third Reich* (New York: Oxford University Press, 1992).

23. See Lucy Dawidowicz, *The Holocaust and the Historians.* Before his

regrettable contributions that became part of the *Historikerstreit*, Hillgruber had recognized the role of racial anti-Semitism in the 1960s when young West German leftist historians did not want to focus on such cultural and intellectual factors. See Andreas Hillgrüber, *Hitler Strategie: Politik und Kriegführung, 1940–1941*, 2nd ed. (Munich: Bernard and Graefe, 1982); Timothy Mason, *Nazism, Fascism and the Working Class*, ed. Jane Caplan (New York: Cambridge University Press, 1995).

24. In West Germany, the key figures who brought these issues into the mainstream of German historiography were Karl Dietrich Bracher and Eberhard Jäckel. See Karl Bracher, *The German Dictatorship*, trans. Jean Steinberg (New York: Praeger, 1970); and Eberhard Jäckel, *Hitler's World View: A Blueprint for Power*, trans. Herbert Arnold (Cambridge: Harvard University Press, 1981).

25. See Dan Diner, *Beyond the Conceivable: Studies on Germany, Nazis and the Holocaust* (Berkeley: University of California Press, 2001). On debates about the Holocaust within the new Left in West Germany, see Dan Diner, ed., *Zivilisationsbruch: Denken nach Auschwitz* (Frankfurt am Main: Fischer Verlag, 1988); and Anson Rabinbach and Jack Zipes, eds., *Germans and Jews since the Holocaust* (New York: Holmes and Meier, 1986).

26. See Jeffrey Herf, *Divided Memory;* Helmut Eschwege, *Fremd unter Meinesgleichen: Erinnerungen eines Dresdner Juden* (Berlin: Ch. Links Verlag, 1991); and Olaf Groehler and Ulrich Herbert, *Zweierlei Bewältigung: Vier Beiträge über den Umgang mit der NS-Vergangenheit in den beiden deutschen Staaten* (Berlin: Ergebnisse, 1992).

27. Telford Taylor, *Nuremberg and Vietnam: An American Tragedy* (Chicago: Quadrangle Books, 1970).

28. The self-regarding, narcissistic tendency of group and national memories is a topic that has received increasing attention among historians. See Henry Russo, *The Vichy Syndrome* (Cambridge: Harvard University Press, 1991); Jeffrey Herf, *Divided Memory;* Sarah Farmer, *Martyred Village: Commemorating the 1994 Massacre at Oradour-sur-Glane* (Berkeley: University of California Press, 1999); Pierre Nora, *Realms of Memory: Constructions of the French Past* (New York: Columbia University Press, 1997); and David W. Blight, *Race and Reunion*. I have examined the interaction of narcissism, zero-sum games, and universalism as they emerged in the debates over the Holocaust Memorial in Berlin in Jeffrey Herf, "Abstraction, Specificity and the Holocaust: Recent Disputes over Memory in Germany," *German Historical Institute Bulletin*, 22, no. 2 (November 2000): 20–35.

29. Another, very prominent, and very public example of how the memory of the Holocaust served to energize political arguments in favor of American military intervention to stop ethnic cleansing in Bosnia is offered

by the articles and editorials in *The New Republic*. They are collected in Leon Wieseltier, "Afterward," *The Black Book of Bosnia: The Consequences of Appeasement*, ed. Nader Mousavizadeh (New York: Basic Books, 1996).

30. Peter Novick, *The Holocaust in American Life*, 240.

31. Moshe Zuckermann, *Zweierlei Holocaust.*

32. On the difficulty in American culture of acknowledging the unredeemed and tragic nature of the Holocaust, see Lawrence Langer, *Admitting the Holocaust: Collected Essays* (New York: Oxford University Press, 1995).

Pieter Lagrou

Facing the Holocaust in France, Belgium, and the Netherlands

THE HOLOCAUST TOOK PLACE IN EUROPE: IT WAS PERPETRATED ON EUropean soil and it is part of European history. Compared to the question of the presence of the Holocaust in North America, the question for its presence in Europe is obvious and seems to call for straightforward answers. European countries have to account for events that took place at least partially within their own borders. They have to integrate these events into their national histories; and they cannot escape the question of national responsibility. Since 1945, the question of their responsibility has been both a question of historical understanding and a question of social justice. Geography is central to both, yet at the same time the Holocaust defies geographical location. It is not merely part of German history exported to other regions by the accident of war and occupation, nor is it, as has insistently been repeated in many European countries during the first postwar years, a proof of how un-European German history really is. This convenient interpretation has been entirely abandoned by historians, politicians, and the wider public in most Western European countries.

Yet, however welcome national amendments to this interpretation have been, it remains a central truth that without a German occupation, the massacre of local Jewish communities in Western Europe would have been unthinkable. Moreover, the geographical dislocation of mass murder to distant centers of mass death is central to the understanding of how the Holocaust took place and how it was perceived, both by contemporaries and in the aftermath of war. The "territoriality" of the Holocaust, or rather, its extraterritoriality, is at the heart of the complex nature of its posterity in Europe, too. Poles are justifiably outraged at the expression "Polish death camps." This observation is even more central for the occupied countries of Western Europe, where the distance between the killing and the persecution was the greatest. These countries are part of a "European periphery" of the Holocaust. They are not the heartland where most of the killing took place (Poland, Belarus, Ukraine), not the homeland of the perpetrators (mainly Germany and Austria), and not the place where most survivors ended up (Israel and the United States). Still, the fact that these countries were somehow peripheral to the Holocaust does not imply that the Holocaust was peripheral to their national histories.

About 200,000 Jews were deported from occupied Western Europe and murdered in German-occupied Poland.[1] Two-thirds of the victims were massacred in Auschwitz during the second half of 1942. Deportation had been preceded by anti-Semitic measures imposed by the German occupier, or in the French case, taken by the national authorities before German requests to do so. Part of the deportations took the form of brutal manhunts, but the actual killing took place in the East. Beyond this basic similarity, national differences were fundamental. Half of all victims from the occupied countries of Western Europe were deported from the Netherlands. They represented 73 percent of the Jewish community in the Netherlands. Of the remaining 100,000 victims, three-quarters were deported from France and one-quarter from Belgium. They represented 25 and 40 percent of their national Jewish communities, respectively. Victims of the genocide in Denmark and Norway number 116 and 750, respectively, due to the privileged status of the former, to proximity of neutral Sweden (facilitating escape), and to the very small size of their prewar Jewish communities. In Italy, with about 5,600 victims, four-fifths of the Jewish community of the first fascist nation survived.

Differences of scale between the former three countries and the latter three are huge. As far as the Netherlands, France, and Belgium are concerned, deportation rates contradict expectations based on the social composition of local Jewish communities or on the strength of anti-Semitism as a theme in domestic politics. Only 17 percent of the Dutch Jewish community were recent immigrants of foreign nationality, compared to 93 percent of first-generation immigrants in Belgium and 75 percent in France.[2] Xenophobia and anti-Semitism were virtually absent from Dutch prewar politics; they were certainly stronger in Belgium, and they were a cornerstone of the ideology of the Vichy regime. Deportation rates, demography, and political climate are three different realities, and establishing a causal relationship among them is problematic and moreover not the object of this chapter. It still remains an important observation that recent immigrants living under an officially anti-Semitic regime in France had three times more chances of survival than citizens of a country without any tradition of political anti-Semitism and whose ancestors had lived in the same country for many generations in the Netherlands. Recent research in Belgium, revealing important differences between Antwerp and Brussels, suggests that national borders are not necessarily the appropriate framework for understanding local realities.[3] Even in Western Europe, the legacy of the genocide in terms of assessing national responsibilities in a continental massacre is by no means a straightforward issue and it never has been. The official recognition in 1995 by Queen Beatrix of the Netherlands and president Jacques Chirac of France of national responsibilities in the persecution, deportation, and subsequent killing of Jewish citizens have not put this matter to rest, as if a simple historical truth had finally been admitted after half a century of stubborn refusal.[4]

Yet, crucially, the presence of the Holocaust in Western Europe since 1945 has never been merely a matter of historical understanding. The historical understanding that what had happened to its Jewish population was different from the afflictions of war that hit other groups, of what only decades later came to be known in wider circles as the Holocaust, was only very partial and where it existed, it was formulated very hesitantly. Yet, in the immediate wake of the event, forms of remembrance of the genocide were not limited to historiography, to commemorations or monuments. What was at stake in the Western European societies that had been home to 200,000 of the victims of the continental tragedy, in all its immediacy, was social justice, much more than historical truth. Before they recognized the event, the central challenge for liberated countries in Western Europe was to recognize the victims and to enunciate the modalities of the reintegration of the survivors in postwar society. To what kind of society did the survivors return—the few thousands who survived deportation and the tens of thousands who had survived in hiding?

A first obvious issue is the disappearance or continued existence of Jewish life in different European countries after 1945. The Netherlands and France, who, taken together, account for almost 90 percent of all western victims, offer in this regard two very different tales. In the Netherlands, the remembrance of the Jewish tragedy eventually emerged in the virtual absence of a Jewish community.[5] The country had been home to one of the oldest and, relative to the total population, largest Jewish communities in Western Europe. The German occupier killed 100,000 of the 140,000 individuals it considered as *Volljüden*. Postwar emigration to Israel and the United States was particularly strong among this decimated community, pushing one out of every five survivors to leave the country after 1945. Jewish cultural organizations estimated that the postwar Jewish community in the Netherlands consisted of approximately 25,000 individuals, about half of them affiliated with religious organizations. France, on the contrary, was home to the largest Jewish community in Europe after 1945.[6] Some 230,000 Jews had survived the persecutions and by the late 1950s, demographic growth and immigration from Eastern Europe brought this number close to 300,000 (which was the estimated number of Jews living in France in 1939). The exodus, between 1956 and 1962, of North African Jews to France almost doubled the postwar community. Even if the colonial wars were much more central to the personal experience of the French than the Holocaust that took place in Europe, it was the legacy of the Nazi genocide and the French participation in it that conditioned the terms of cohabitation of their identities as both Jews and French citizens, a situation not wholly different from that in Israel.

Secondly, differences were not merely of a quantitative nature. Jewish citizens had always occupied a peculiar and segregated position in Dutch society, because of the predominant role of confessional affiliation in all spheres of public life. Catholics and the different Protestant churches had separate political parties and trade unions and, moreover, a separate cultural life, separate sports manifestations, and separate sociabilities, a segregation that had contributed to the difficulty of survival in the face of persecution because of the limited exchanges and solidarities between different communities. The secular French Republic relegated confessional affiliation to the private sphere and sought to reduce the role of religious organizations in public life. Assimilation into French society was perceived as a danger by traditional Jews and anti-Semites—for very different reasons—but it was also positively an opportunity seized by many Jews. This difference contributed to the different definition in both societies of "national" experiences of war.

In the Netherlands, the genocide accounted for 55 percent of all war-related deaths, including the war against Japan (compared to one out of every six war dead in France).[7] This brutal fact was absolutely incompatible with the representations put into place during and immediately after the war of a country united in its collective suffering and stubborn resistance.[8] In these representations, the last winter of war, when only the southern part of the country was liberated while the rest suffered cold, flooding, and hunger, occupied an inordinate place. The Dutch remembrance of the occupation is a stark example of a centralized policy of memory, pursued by a broad national coalition in power all through the first postwar decade. The construction of public monuments was subjected to approval by a central commission, which vetoed the inscription of names on monuments and recommended abstract forms as a means of enhancing national cohesion. The organization of public commemorations was the exclusive competence of local and national authorities, who consulted the official representatives of all major social, political, and religious authorities. The war historiography was entrusted to a State Institute for War Documentation, which eventually produced an officially endorsed series of TV documentaries broadcast in the early 1960s, and one single, authoritative multivolume history, published in the 1970s and 1980s. On the political level, only the Communist Party and the conservative Calvinists of the Anti-Revolutionary Party did not partake of this national consensus.

More importantly, all other agents of remembrance emerging outside the tightly controlled networks of Dutch civil society were excluded. Organizations of former resistance fighters were boycotted as a divisive form of activism, prejudicial to the national unity and to the urgent task of reconstruction. Despite unrelenting militancy, resistance fighters were not awarded with official decorations (until 1980) and they did not benefit from any special social legislation to compensate for their wartime service nor were they awarded priority recruitment in civil service, as happened in most formerly occupied countries of Europe. A similar fate awaited the different groups of repatriates, a great majority of them conscript workers sent to the German industrial centers for labor service.

The postwar governments rejected, per principle, special measures for special categories of war victims. In a situation of generalized scarcity, the available goods and funds were distributed on an egalitarian basis, regardless of the wartime trajectories of individuals and groups. The only exception to this rule was reserved for the victims of the resistance, executed or deported for their heroic action on Dutch soil.[9] They were taken in charge by a special charitable foundation, endowed with government funding, whose explicit aim was the reparation of wartime suffering. At no point in the discussions on the law for victims of the resistance was the fate of the victims of genocide even mentioned. They faced long procedural battles facing hostile administrations to recover their stolen property. The fact that only communist organizations took their defense, both on the material and the symbolical level, only increased their isolation. Commemorations by the Auschwitz Committee were boycotted by the cabinet, and during the 1960s the Dutch government was the only European government, except that of Greece, to refuse any financial contribution to the Auschwitz monument. The first national legislation recognizing a right to reparation and social assistance was voted into effect in 1972. By that time, Dutch involvement in the genocide had become a national historical obsession. After almost three decades of official silence and neglect, state-funded group therapy (increasingly for second-generation survivors as well) was offered as a belated form of national recognition for Jewish suffering in the Netherlands.

Remembrance of the occupation in France was much more fragmented than traditional interpretations of French memories of the war suggest. On the political level, Gaullist and communist discourses were more peripheral to the national narrative than usually portrayed, partly because both political forces were absent from central power in the crucial years between 1947 and 1958, and partly because of the genuine appeal of other, dissonant memories. Most noticeably, though, because of the fragmented political economy of the Fourth Republic and a less docile civil society, public memories of the war escaped governmental control. Social organizations of former POWs and repatriates, resistance veterans, and victims of persecution proliferated and competed for public recognition. In order to do so they conformed to the model of the veterans of the Great War, who had obtained social legitimacy, political leverage, and a substantial level of entitlements to reparations and public assistance in the course of the interwar years. The generation of 1940–45 emulated their mass organizations, rituals, and symbols and aspired to obtain similar legal recognition.

The contest for national recognition for veterans and war victims after 1945 became a debate on the nature and symbols of French patriotism. The inclusion or the exclusion from organizations, public assistance, legislation, or official tributes of Vichy's enemies was at the heart of this debate: what Vichy defined as *"l'anti-France"*—Bolsheviks, foreigners, masons, Jews.[10] Official recognition of victims of the genocide was a central object of litigation between Gaullist forces, defending an exclusive tribute to a fighting elite, and a self-proclaimed anti-fascist coalition in which the Communist Party played a central role, defending an inclusive tribute to all enemies of fascism, be it of their own choice or not. Unlike in the Dutch debate, references to Jewish victims were most explicit in the discussions in Parliament and in the various organisations of Nazi victims. The xenophobic patriots who opposed any form of entitlement for victims of the genocide stood accused of anti-Semitism. In the course of 1948, both parties to the conflict obtained their own pieces of legislation: a law for the deported resistance fighters and a law for all other victims of deportation and internment, including foreign nationals living in France since 1939, with only slightly inferior entitlements. Until the return to power of de Gaulle in 1958, the suffering of deportation was more central as a symbol of the French war experience than the heroical resistance.

In Belgium, memories of the occupation years were even more polarized and politicized. In 1940, the king had decided to stay in the country while his government continued the war from exile, at the side of the British. His choice was not unrelated to his political sympathies at the time, but his ambitions for the creation of an authoritarian regime with German support never materialized, for lack of interest from the German side. After the war, a broad left wing considered him an unacceptable head of state, at the very least for his guilty silence while his country was occupied and his population oppressed, deported, and murdered. The Catholic party defended the king, idealizing his attitude as both a personal sacrifice and an attempt to protect the Belgian population through neutrality. The conflict would paralyze Belgian politics until 1950, when the king was finally forced to abdicate in favor of his son. The two sides harbored different memories of the war and different concepts of the Belgian nation: on the one hand, a coalition of secularized, democratic, and anti-fascist forces; on the other hand, royalist, Catholic, and traditionalist forces. In this conflict, a militant commemoration of resistance and Nazi persecution was a political strategy against the king and his Catholic defenders. An anti-royalist coalition governed the country with a narrow minority from 1945 to 1947, and it enacted a broad legislation recognizing different groups of Nazi victims, most often against the Catholic opposition. Jewish victims obtained entitlement to reparation benefits as war victims, but the opposition maneuvered to exclude them from the symbolic tribute in the law, reserved for "national martyrs." More importantly, reparation benefits were limited to Belgian nationals, who constituted a mere 5 percent of Jews deported from Belgium during the occupation.

The polarization of war memories also became entangled in the regional and linguistic conflicts that divided Belgian society. The Flemish part of the country was the stronghold of Catholic and royalist opinion. Alienated by the identification of the anti-fascist legacy with the secularized left wing, gradually Flemish opinion increasingly identified with the radical fringe of Flemish nationalism that had sided with the Nazi occupier and that was portrayed, in the years 1950–90, as a victim of a vengeful Belgian state, suppressing Flemish aspirations. The threatening electoral success of the xenophobic Flemish extreme Right in the course of the 1990s showed the dangers of this political strategy to mainstream Flemish parties. Through successive waves of constitutional reform, the Belgian state has transferred most of its competencies to the regions. Regional polarization of the memories of the war have thereby lost their *raison d'être,* thus creating a new framework for a belated debate on national, regional, and local responsibilities in the Holocaust.

The modalities and the discourse by which victims of the Holocaust were recognized as national victims in France and Belgium did not carry any recognition of the specific nature of their experience. On the contrary, even their persecution was assimilated a service to the nation—in the terms of the law, they had "contributed to the salvation of the Nation." As victims of the national enemy they had become honorary citizens and as victims of fascism part of the anti-fascist struggle. The national remembrance honored the dead and provided aid for the survivors as victims of deportation—as French nationals and anti-fascists, not because of their extermination as Jews. That being said, no other forms of social recognition were available at the time, as the Dutch example eloquently illustrates. The anti-fascist discourse offered a formal legal recognition to survivors of the Holocaust, with both symbolic and material benefits; it offered social support and sociability through organizations capable of delivering a powerful sense of mission. Specific recognition of Jewishness, even through the recognition of a tragically distinctive persecution, was not what many survivors, whose survival had depended on the opposite, asked for at the time. Anti-fascism was also a powerful narrative, a heroic and dynamic posture, a means of overcoming the appallingly arbitrary affliction that had hit them and thus because a way to take possession of their own destiny. Forced assimilationism and ideological hegemony were not incompatible with receptivity among Jewish survivors for this discourse. The alternatives to anti-fascist assimilation were exclusion from any form of recognition and patriotic contempt as practiced by nationalist, anti-communist, and pro-colonial milieus in most Western European countries. Until the late 1960s, moreover, there was no incompatibility between a pro-communist and a Jewish allegiance. The Six-Day War in 1967 and the anti-Semitic purges in Poland one year later would create an irrevocable rupture.

Accordingly, during the first quarter-century after 1945, a measure of social justice for victims of the Holocaust in postwar Western Europe did not depend on the establishment of the historical truth about the distinct experience of their persecution. On the contrary, only insofar as they presented themselves as anti-fascists and patriots could they legitimately claim public attention and official recognition. The anti-fascist amalgamation has been denounced as an intended and forced de-Judaization. In the terms of the immediate postwar period and from the perspective of the survivors, the conflict between an identification as Jew or anti-fascist was also a conflict between a categorization by the persecutor and a free-floating categorization whereby the victim could choose her or his identification. To the extent that anti-Semitic hyperpatriots pleaded for the exclusion of Jewish victims from postwar legal recognition on precisely this basis, historical untruth collided with social injustice. Western European Holocaust survivors who had internalized a militant anti-fascist identity spoke a language that was understood by their contemporaries, that provided social legitimacy, self-esteem, and a sense of purpose. In their aspiration for justice, they inscribed their personal experience in collective narratives and escaped moral solitude. This implied con-

forming to the codes and paradigms capable of providing social legitimacy, first of all that of the fighter and the militant, of the hero.
Recognition for their historically specific suffering was dependent on
their identification with universal values of patriotism, anti-fascism,
and humanism.

History did not end in the late 1960s. On the contrary, from the
perspective of today, it seems that it accelerated. Heroes are decidedly
out of fashion and the status of victim of the Holocaust, which failed
to provide a narrative and a meaning, a legitimacy, and an interpretation to Jewish survivors in Western Europe prior to the late 1960s, has
now become a universal source of narratives, of legitimacy, of identity. Whatever this reveals about contemporary Western societies, what
is so striking about Western Europe is not the fact that the Holocaust
has become the yardstick of evil and injustice, the ultimate frame of
reference by which crime or lesser forms of discrimination are judged.
It is instead the obsessive character of many attempts not just to compare current or past events to the Holocaust, but to inscribe them historically into the event. Binjamin Wilkomirski's and Bruno Dössekker's
trajectory is only the most recent example of this.[11] No other event
could have provided a middle-aged Swiss man in quest for an identity with a more powerful myth of origin, with a wider and more respectful audience, with a more indisputable legitimacy than that of a
child survivor of Auschwitz. Dutch gay activists or French associations of Gypsies have tried insistently, not just to claim that all forms
of intolerance and discrimination are evil and therefore have somehow something in common with the Holocaust, but to identify historically certified examples of victims of Nazi persecution from their
own communities, however counterproductive their efforts have generally been. (Persecution of homosexuals as existed in the Reich was
not extended to the occupied regions of Western Europe, in spite of
a limited decree to that extent in the Netherlands of July 31, 1940.[12]
Persecution of Gypsies in the same region did not witness a systematic exterminatory plan, in spite of the murderous Z Convoy from
Mechelen to Auschwitz of January 15, 1944).[13] This time, recognition of the universal values they proclaim seems to be made dependent on their identification with a historically specific suffering. The
concreteness of historical and geographical location is not an antidote
against a generalized recourse to Auschwitz as the Saint Anthony of
modern humanitarianism: it might even act as a perverse attraction.

In Western Europe, too, the Holocaust is often used as a bad argument for a good cause.

Historians cherish the ideal that by trying to establish the historical truth, they contribute to establishing social justice. Yet the contradiction between the singularity of a historical event, in its chronological, geographical, and social situation, and the universal meaning it might hold are such that truth and justice are bound to collide. Examples call for emulation, for the better and for the worse. However much individuals and groups aspire to become retroactively part of a historical event, the past is irrevocably past and belongs, increasingly, to the dead only. With the settlements of the last claims of spoiled assets, the remaining issues of social justice relating to the Holocaust reach a final stage. The Holocaust as a master narrative of the twentieth century, however, will continue to be appropriated and expropriated by claimants of various causes. In this, what Charles Maier called in a recent conference in Buchenwald the "unmooring" of the Holocaust, geography is bound to lose much of its relevance and Western Europe some of its singularity.[14]

NOTES

1. Among an abundant literature, see Wolfgang Benz, ed., *Dimension des Völkermords: Die Zahl der jüdischen Opfer des Nationalsozialismus* (Munich, 1996); Bob Moore, *Victims and Survivors: The Nazi Persecution of the Jews in the Netherlands, 1940–1945* (London, 1997); Maxime Steinberg, "Le paradoxe français dans la solution finale à l'Ouest," *Annales* 3 (1993): 583–94; Hans Blom, "The Persecution of the Jews in the Netherlands: A Comparative Western Perspective," *European History Quarterly* 19 (1989): 333–51; Pim Griffioen and Ron Zeller, "La persécution des Juifs en Belgique et aux Pays Bas pendant la seconde Guerre Mondiale," *Cahiers d'Histoire du Temps Présent* 5 (1999): 73–132.

2. Moore, *Victims and Survivors,* 37.

3. Lieven Saerens, *Vreemdelingen in een wereldstad: Een geschiedenis van Antwerpen en zijn joodse bevolking (1880–1944)* (Tielt, 2000).

4. See *Discours et messages de Jacques Chirac, maire de Paris, premier ministre, président de la République en hommage aux Juifs de France victimes de la collaboration de l'État francais de Vichy avec l'occupant allemand* (Paris, 1998). Belgian Prime Minister Guy Verhofstadt stopped short of such an apology in his speech at the Dossin Barracks in Mechelen on September 24, 2000. See http://premier.fgov.be/topics/speeches/n_speech39.html.

5. See the excellent study of Ido de Haan, *Na de Ondergang: De herinnering aan de Jodenvervolging in Nederland, 1945–1995* (The Hague, 1997), 61–77.

6. See Anne Grynberg, "Après la tourmente," in *Les Juifs de France de la Révolution française à nos jours,* ed. Jean-Jacques Becker and Annette Wieviorka (Paris, 1998), 267–76; and Michel Abitol, "La cinquième République et l'accueil des Juifs d'Afrique du Nord" in Becker and Wieviorka, *Les Juifs de France,* 287–327.

7. See Pieter Lagrou, "The Nationalisation of Victimhood: Selective Violence and National Grief in Western Europe, 1940–1960," in *Life after Death: Approaches to a Cultural and Social History of Europe during the 1940s and 1950s,* ed. Richard Bessel and Dirk Schumann (New York: Cambridge University Press, 2003), 243–58.

8. The following paragraphs synthesize the argument developed in Pieter Lagrou, *The Legacy of Nazi Occupation: Patriotic Memory and National Recovery in Western Europe, 1945–1965* (New York: Cambridge University Press, 2000).

9. See also Pieter Lagrou, "Victims of Genocide and National Memory: Belgium, France and the Netherlands, 1945–1965," *Past & Present* 154 (1997): 181–222.

10. See also Pieter Lagrou, "Die Wiedererfindung der Nation im befreiten Westeuropa: Erinnerungspolitik in Frankreich, Belgien und den Niederlanden," *Transit* 15 (1998): 12–28.

11. See Elena Lappin's article in *Granta* 66 (summer 1999) (trans. into German as *Der Mann mit zwei Köpfen* [Zurich, 2000]); and Binjamin Wilkomirski, *Bruchstücke: aus einer Kindheit 1939–1948* (Frankfurt, 1995).

12. See Louis de Jong, *Het Koninkrijk der Nederlanden in de tweede Wereldoorlog,* vol. 14, *Reacties* (The Hague, 1991), 556–60.

13. See José Gotovitch, "Quelques données relatives à l'extermination des Tsiganes de Belgique," *Cahiers d'Histoire de la deuxième Guerre Mondiale* 4 (1976): 161–80; and Denis Peschanski, *Les Tsiganes en France, 1939–1946* (Paris, 1994).

14. Charles S. Maier, "Die 'Aura' von Buchenwald," in *Verbrechen Erinnern: Die Auseinandersetzung mit Holocaust und Völkermord,* ed. Volkhard Knigge and Norbert Frei (Munich, 2002), 327–41.

Suzanne Brown-Fleming

Excusing the Holocaust: German Catholics and the Sensation of Cardinal Aloisius Muench's "One World in Charity," 1946–59

ON JUNE 2, 1945, BARELY ONE MONTH AFTER THE END OF WORLD WAR II in Europe, Pope Pius XII made a statement regarding the relationship between the German people and Nazi atrocities. He declared that most Germans, and especially Catholics, were not responsible for the atrocities of the recently ended war.[1] Similarly, in August of 1945, at their annual gathering in Fulda, Germany's Catholic bishops collectively drafted a pastoral letter addressing the issues of guilt and responsibility for Nazi crimes. The Fulda pastoral acknowledged that some individual Germans, including Catholics, cooperated with the regime and therefore deserved condemnation. But, argued the Fulda pastoral, most did not.[2] In January 1946, the first installment of another pastoral letter entitled *One World in Charity* appeared in the United States. It surfaced in occupied Germany one year later. *One World* referred to Allied authorities as "hate mongers . . . other Hitlers in disguise who would make of a whole nation a crawling [Bergen-] Belsen." Only a few criminals perpetrated the heinous crimes carried out under the Nazi regime, argued *One World*. Why, then, asked its author, should women and children suffer, because "some [Allied] policy makers in top levels revived the Mosaic idea of an eye for an eye?"[3] The author of *One World* was German-American Aloisius Muench,[4] then bishop of Fargo, North Dakota. Pope Pius XII's Rome address, the German bishops' Fulda pastoral, and Cardinal Aloisius Muench's *One World in Charity* represent concrete statements by the highest Catholic offices in Rome, Germany, and the United States. All three statements, made within a year of one another, rejected the idea of "collective guilt."[5] The statements also put to words a popular myth that would linger until Pius XII's death in 1958: that most German Catholics were victimized by Nazism, or, alternatively, resisted it.[6]

This essay examines the role of Cardinal Aloisius Muench in the articulation and propagation of the postwar myth that German Catholics stood apart from Nazism and the Holocaust. Aloisius Muench of Fargo, N.D., was Pope Pius XII's apostolic visitor (1946),[7] head of the Vatican[8] relief mission (1947–49),[9] apostolic regent (1949–51),[10] and, finally, apostolic nuncio to Germany (1951–59).[11] Put simply, he was the pope's personal diplomat to the German Catholic Church for thirteen years. Cardinal Muench was the most powerful American Catholic figure in Germany during the late 1940s and throughout the 1950s, with access to German politicians and religious hierarchy, Allied occupation personnel, the Vatican's innermost sanctum, German war criminals, and war victims.[12]

The circumstances by which Cardinal Muench left the diocese of Fargo for occupied Germany were rooted in the recently ended war. During Nazi rule, the Holy See's nunciature to Germany was located in Berlin and headed by Archbishop Cesare Orsenigo (1873–1946).[13] Pope Pius XII (Eugenio Pacelli) was former papal nuncio to Bavaria (1917–25) and the Weimar Republic (1920–29) and, thereafter, Vatican secretary of state (1930–39). During his papacy (1939–58), Pope Pius XII was known in Vatican circles as *il papa tedesco,* "the German Pope," due to his love for the Germans. He remained a stout Germanophile before, during, and after the Third Reich.[14] After his contact with the German bishops was interrupted by the Allied capture of Rome in March 1944, Pope Pius XII sought ways to keep up with the situation of the Catholic Church in increasingly devastated Germany. To this end, he dispatched what is dubbed the "first Vatican mission" to Germany in early June 1945, with American Monsignor Walter Carroll at its helm. In September 1945, the pope ordered the "second Vatican mission" to Germany, and in October 1945, the "third Vatican mission." The end result of the third Vatican mission was its establishment as a permanent fixture in occupied Germany. It was to set up household in Kronberg, on the outskirts of Frankfurt am Main. The aim of the Kronberg mission, officially established at the Villa Grosch, was to alleviate the suffering of displaced persons and prisoners of war. The Kronberg Vatican mission had no diplomatic recognition. The Allied powers authorized its existence strictly for relief purposes.[15]

Prior to the end of the war, on February 8, 1945, Nuncio Cesare Orsenigo had moved what remained of his household to Eichstätt, a town located in the middle-Franconian region of central Bavaria.[16] German defeat in May 1945 meant that the nunciature lost its official status. What had once been Germany was now an occupied, nonsovereign territory. The Allied Control Council in Berlin, consisting of American, British, French, and Russian deputies, determined that Archbishop Orsenigo could remain in Eichstätt. The French deputy quipped that the archbishop, no longer recognized as a diplomat by the Allies, would be accredited only to "Her Majesty, Human Misery." Nonetheless, the Allied Control Council's decision pleased Pius XII, who desired the continuity of the Eichstätt nunciature in Germany, even if unofficially. But Archbishop Orsenigo died on April 1, 1946, leaving only Monsignor Carlo Colli, the archbishop's aide de camp, to maintain the link between Pius XII and German Catholicism. In January 1947, Monsignor Colli, too, died, leaving only the nunciature's secretary, Monsignor Bernard Hack of Berlin, in Eichstätt.[17]

In the meanwhile, then-Bishop Aloisius Muench of Fargo, N.D., arrived in Germany in late July 1946. He was Pope Pius XII's hand-picked choice to go to Germany in the capacity of apostolic visitor. Cardinal Muench toured the French, British, and American zones of Germany from September to December 1946 in order to converse with German bishops about the state of the Catholic Church in battered Germany. Cardinal Muench's stint as apostolic visitor neared its end in January 1947 and thus coincided with Monsignor Colli's death and the collapse of the Eichstätt nunciature. Pope Pius XII could appoint no new nuncio until Germany's political status changed.[18] He solved this dilemma by keeping Cardinal Muench in Germany. Apostolic visitor Muench submitted his findings to the Holy Father in February 1947 expecting to return home to Fargo. But by the end of their audience, Cardinal Muench sensed the pope's desire that he remain in Germany "for an indefinite period."[19] In order to keep him in Germany, Pope Pius XII named Cardinal Muench head of the Vatican's mission for refugees, expellees, and displaced persons in Kronberg. From Kronberg, Cardinal Muench was to fill the gap left in the Eichstätt nunciature by Archbishop Orsenigo's and Monsignor Colli's deaths. Pope Pius XII used the Villa Grosch in Kronberg as an unofficial and makeshift nunciature until a permanent one could be reestablished.[20] The secretary of the Eichstätt nunciature, Monsignor Hack, traveled weekly from Eichstätt to Kronberg with documents and correspondence to be signed and approved by Cardinal Muench.[21]

In May 1949, the Basic Law formed a constitutional basis for the new Federal Republic of Germany, which convened its first operating parliament in September 1949. In accordance with the Federal Republic's new status, Pope Pius XII designated Cardinal Muench apostolic regent to Germany in October 1949. Cardinal Muench told good friend Martin Salm that his appointment as regent "did not involve any change of title or address," because the "nunciature" had always continued to function. Cardinal Muench noted: "We [in Kronberg] took over the work."[22] One and a half years later, in March 1951, the Allied High Commission permitted the Federal Republic to form an independently operating foreign affairs ministry. Now Pope Pius XII could officially name a nuncio to Germany again. On March 12, 1951, the nunciature was officially reestablished in Bad Godesberg, a suburb of Bonn. On April 4, 1951, Aloisius Muench became the first diplomat to be accredited to the Federal Republic.[23]

Whatever his changing title, from the summer of 1946 until the pope's death in 1958, Cardinal Muench was Pius XII's eyes and ears in Germany. Further, he was in the unique position of serving both the Holy Father in Rome *and* the American military government, for Cardinal Muench was also the U.S. National Catholic Welfare Conference's (N.C.W.C.'s) liaison representative to the U.S. Army in occupied Germany from the summer of 1946 until the end of occupation in 1949. Occupation statutes made clear that he was not to "assume responsibilities in the functional fields of operation directed and supervised by religious affairs officers of military government." He was "not attached to the office of military government" in the sense that he was a "representative of [his] respective faith in the United States and functionally responsible to the United States agenc[y] that paid [his] salar[y]." He was not to "operate within the framework of nor under the functional direction of Military Government."[24]

His position meant that Cardinal Muench had plentiful and regular access to the Religious Affairs Branch (a branch of the Education and Religious Affairs Division of the Office of Military Government–United States [OMGUS]) and other branch and division officers, and to General Lucius Clay and his political advisor, Robert Murphy, in particular.[25] Ambassador Murphy had studied German in the past and at one point served as the American consul in Munich.[26] Cardinal Muench forged a good relationship with Ambassador Murphy, telling Bishop Vincent Ryan of Bismarck, North Dakota as early as November 1946, "planners were making a fiasco over here [in Germany]," that "the bureaucracy was terrible," but "fortunately, [the cardinal] got good help from Ambassador Murphy."[27]

When appointed bishop of the diocese of Fargo in 1935, Cardinal Muench had begun the practice of preparing an annual pastoral letter to be read from pulpits across the diocese in five installments, beginning on the Sunday following Shrove Tuesday and ending on Passion (Palm) Sunday.[28] He kept up this practice, even through his tenure in Germany. In December 1945, in preparation for the Lent season of 1946, and prior to any knowledge of his impending appointment as papal emissary and military government liaison in Germany, Cardinal Muench drafted a pastoral letter entitled *One World in Charity*.[29] As *One World* became a sensation in Germany by 1947, it bears close scrutiny and analysis. Cardinal Muench entitled the first section of *One World* "An Eye for an Eye." He commented on the "barbaric cruelties" conducted during World War II, and deemed the atrocities carried out during the war unique—"no age record[ed] similar brutalities." He condemned a variety of disparate actions and events, so that German crimes appeared heinous, but no more so than acts committed by the Allies or even by the Catholic Church. "Let no one venture even as much as to mention again the Inquisition or Bartholomew's Night,"[30] wrote Muench. "Maidanek, Belsen[,] Buchenwald,[31] Lidice,[32] Hiroshima, and Nagasaki[33] will cry out to their victims to arise and tell their story of horrible bestialities," Muench claimed, thus equating the U.S. atomic attacks on Japan in the last month of the war with the Nazi concentration and death camp systems.[34]

Cardinal Muench proceeded to describe "the bombing of civilians in unfortified cities, the holocausts[35] in [cities] of defenseless men, women, and children [and] the forced migration of millions from their homes and lands," a reference to ethnic Germans (and others) affected by the Potsdam Agreement (August 1945).[36] Citing the case of Soviet-occupied Lithuania (June 1940 to June 1941),[37] Muench detailed the deportation of 40,000 Lithuanians under Soviet occupation on June 14–17, 1941. "Children and old people, women and men, were crammed into cattle cars without food or water. Large numbers died in the railroad stations before the trains even moved. Nothing more was ever heard of those who were deported."[38]

"Hundreds of thousands of Poles" suffered a fate "just as tragic" as that of Lithuanians under Soviet occupation,[39] wrote Muench. "Wives were separated from their husbands, and children from their parents . . . the dispersal of Polish refugees is one of the most horrifying episodes in the historical annals of nations," he claimed. "What terrible things befell civilian populations through bombing from Warsaw[40] to Rotterdam,[41] from Coventry,[42] London,[43] Cologne, Berlin and Dresden[44] to Hiroshima and Nagasaki, need not be told," declared the bishop. "Hundreds of thousands" are "forced to work in [Soviet] mines and factories under conditions of slavery not much different from that practiced [under the] Roman [Empire]," he continued. Worse off, argued Muench, were the "approximately 20,000" Poles, Hungarians, Baltic nationals, and ethnic Germans expelled westward under the Potsdam Agreement.[45] Jews were absent in Muench's litany of victims. The "chaotic conditions" of war were partially to blame for such unprecedented suffering, said Cardinal Muench. But also to blame was what he called "a cold, calculated policy of revenge, brought against millions of people, for the most part persons not responsible either for the outbreak of the war or its horrors."[46] Muench's imagined "one world" would "never be built by those who hate, and hating take their inspiration from the hard teaching of an eye for an eye and a tooth for a tooth. It will have to be built by those who believe in Christ's law of love."[47]

The second section of Muench's pastoral letter dealt with the topic of mercy.[48] "In some quarters it is not popular to make a plea for mercy," wrote Muench. "It may be difficult to put aside the pagan within us with his hard and cruel law of an eye for an eye and a tooth for a tooth, and put on Christ with His law of mercy, kindness, and love, but we have no option. We have to be either for or against Christ," he told his diocese. "As Christians and as Americans we raise our voice in indignation against an official inhumanity which does not permit the United Nations Relief and Rehabilitation Administration (UNRRA) to ship relief supplies either to Germany or to Japan," wrote Muench. "Having condemned the atrocities of the Nazis we can not now make ourselves guilty of similar atrocities."[49] "Shall we not sit in judgment now of the atrocities that are being committed in the name of retributive justice, which in actual fact, however, is not justice but plain revenge. We condemn, too, a conspiracy of silence on the part of a large influential segment of our press for not making known to the American people the real plight of the European peoples. Our people are generous: they would respond with full hands," Muench declared.[50] Again, he did not name the imagined enemy with undue influence in the American press. He left this to the imagination of his listeners.

In the third section of *One World,* "Bread on the Waters," Muench pursued the theme of guilt, focusing on Germans specifically. Muench denied the validity of "collective" guilt, stating that "the indictment of an entire nation can not be justified in the light of principles of democracy."[51] Not stopping at the rejection of "collective" guilt, he went further and claimed that "countless" anti-Nazis, many more than "the American people generally knew," including representatives of the Catholic Church, suffered under the regime. Here, he took the tact already being perpetuated in German Catholic circles and by the pope himself in his June radio address.[52] Cardinal Muench finished the third section of *One World* with barely veiled references to the Morgenthau school of postwar planning, which called for territorial losses, harsh reparations policy, de-industrialization, and "pastoralization" of Germany. "To strip a people, not only of its household goods, but also of its tools and machinery of production impoverishes them," admonished Muench.[53] "Mr. [Bernard] Baruch's plan to make Germany a nation of goat-herders and foresters" is "immoral, uneconomic, and unworkable," Muench said, quoting from the *London Economist.*[54] Treasury Secretary Henry Morgenthau Jr. and Bernard Baruch were Jewish Americans who initially advocated a harsh peace for Germany.

In the fourth section of *One World,* Cardinal Muench again juxtaposed ideas of revenge against love and mercy, but portrayed mercy as a Judeo-Christian tradition by the tenth century: "To the Jews of old the Lord said: If thy enemy be hungry, give him to eat; if he thirsts; give him water to drink, for thou shalt heap hot coals upon his head, and the Lord will reward thee."[55] Victor nations, wrote Muench, needed to heed the words of the Old Testament (Jewish) Psalmists. Muench still clearly differentiated between Old Testament (Jewish) and New Testament (Christian) traditions, however. "To Christians, too, come commands of mercy and love to a fallen foe," Muench wrote several paragraphs later. He cited Christ in the New Testament to bolster his point: "But I say to you who are listening," cried out Christ in his Sermon on the Mount, "love your enemies, do good to those who hate you."[56] Muench concluded, "happily few in numbers [were] those who reject this teaching of the God of Israel and of His Christ."[57] Those in the United States "advocating the decimation of the German population" by means of starvation and pastoralization "could certainly not be called Christians, nor even Americans," argued Muench, likely referring again to Morgenthau and Baruch.

In the fifth and final section of *One World,* called "The New Order in Christ," Muench returned to his pre–December 1941 pacifist sentiments. He criticized the current American administration for "putting to work a powerful machine of propaganda urging the maintenance of armies and navies on a scale larger than ever before." The alternative, he argued, was "taking the leadership among nations to bring about progressive disarmament and abolition of peacetime military training."[58] "Balance of power" arrangements such as those now being made by the Truman administration sacrificed small nations "such as Finland, Lithuania, Estonia, Latvia, or the Balkan states" on what Muench called "the alter of expediency."[59] Poland, "partitioned by her own Allies,"[60] could not call her soul "her own."[61] Financial resources should go to churches, schools, justice, and charity, not toward developing atomic weapons, he wrote. The small minorities of Catholics in Russia, Lithuania, Latvia, and Estonia, and the Catholic Church in Poland, were given no consideration in "Big Power" conferences, and suffered under totalitarianism. Cardinal Muench finished this section in characteristic language, with a final plea that all men "submit themselves to the law of love of God and of neighbor."[62]

To conclude this analysis of *One World,* two points bear mentioning. First, Cardinal Muench only acknowledged the mass murder of European Jewry twice in the entire twenty-five–page text, and never directly. In one of two examples, Muench wrote,

[I]n Europe and Asia gangsters of a new type, pitiless and savage, rose to positions of power. They boasted of their totalitarian power with reason, for they controlled not only a strong secret police but also military might of unheard of proportions. These overlords set up concentration camps, the real horrors of which came to light only after the war, exterminated millions of persons because of theories of race inferiority and dragged into slave labor men whose countries they overran with lightning invasion.[63]

Cardinal Muench claimed that Hitler found criminal Germans to carry out the Final Solution based on planning *no different in its nature* from those postwar occupation policies that allowed for starvation or communist infiltration in Europe. He did not differentiate between ghettoization, mass shooting, gassing, and cremation, major Nazi tactics used to murder at least six million European Jews, and food rationing by the Allies in postwar Germany. In a second example, and the only time Cardinal Muench referred to Jews by name in the context of victimization, he argued for mercy toward *Germans*. "We expressed our horror when the Nazis proclaimed the doctrine of racial guilt against all the Jews. Rightly we condemned such a doctrine. Shall we now profess it in the kind of peace we are making?" asked Muench.[64]

The most popular passage extracted from *One World* by Germans and repeated time and again between the appearance of *One World* in Germany in 1947 and Cardinal Muench's retirement in 1959 was this:

> Are we not making ourselves partners in the crimes of Hitler by now doing the very thing we once condemned and fought against? The hypocrisy is colossal. The fact that this forced labor goes now under the name of human reparations does not alter the fact that it is nothing less than labor slavery. We are wretched hypocrites if we do not denounce as a crime what we were quick to denounce when done by the enemy. The law of justice has no double yardstick for measuring misdeeds of friend and foe.[65]

Germans cited this passage to remember the Nazi past in a particular way: as *regrettable but fully comparable* to acts committed by the Allies, especially the expulsion of ethnic Germans from eastern territories and de-Nazification and war crimes procedures. And, inevitably, German accountability tended to become lost in these comparisons to Allied acts.

Cardinal Muench's pastoral letter, originally twenty-five typeset and single-spaced pages (approximately 10,200 words), was translated into German and printed in its entirety in at least two, and probably three, German-language newspapers in the United States. The first reprint appeared in the monthly Techny, Illinois periodical *Familienblatt* in 1946.[66] At least two other translations also appeared in U.S. publications. The first of the five installments of *One World* appeared in the German-language *Nord-Dakota Herold* on March 8,

1946. The version appearing in the *Herold* was an exact replica of Cardinal Muench's original text written for Fargo Catholics and was not modified in any way.[67] *Herold* editor Cornelius Sittard translated the English text of *One World* into German for *Herold* readers, and considered this task "an honor and a privilege." A German-American with sisters and brothers in Aachen, he was convinced that "a willful order" was behind delays in the care packages he sent to Aachen. It was Sittard's opinion that "a mentality just as despicable as the motives and actions of the former enemy [Axis] leaders" existed now in the United States. He agreed with *One World*'s argument that Germans should not be burdened with guilt, telling Cardinal Muench that "a burden of hate" still "rest[ed] heavily on millions of innocent people [meaning Germans] under the pretext that [Nazism must be] eradicat[ed]."[68] One year later, German-language newspapers in the United States remained interested in *One World*. The periodical *Der Wanderer* in Saint Paul, Minnesota expressed interest in publishing the letter in April 1947.[69] Sudeten German priest Emmanuel J. Reichenberger approached *Wanderer* editor Alphonse J. Matt to suggest "hundreds of thousands of copies [of *One World*] be translated and distributed in Germany." Father Reichenberger wished to give "moral and spiritual comfort to a people driven to . . . despair . . . by physical suffering but even more by the feeling of being abandoned . . . by their fellow Christians around the world."[70] *Saint Josefsblatt* in Mount Angel, Oregon also reprinted it in five installments that replicated exactly the version distributed in Fargo parishes.[71]

Some time between its appearance in the *Familienblatt, Nord-Dakota Herold,* and *Saint Josefsblatt* and the first months of 1947, *One World* migrated across the Atlantic Ocean to Germany. What circulated in Germany was *not* a reprint of *One World* as distributed in Fargo or U.S. German-language newspapers, but multiple truncated versions of it. While the multiple circulating versions differed in length, all had three features in common. The first was retention of Cardinal Muench's comments exonerating the majority of Germans of guilt or responsibility. The second common feature was the retention of the lengthy passages on the suffering of ethnic Germans and the German civilian population; and, third, the equation of Allied nations and Nazi "crimes."

Archbishop of Cologne Joseph Cardinal Frings[72] mentioned one version of the circulating pastoral letter in January 1947, noting that it "wandered through Germany like a ghost."[73] Other sources also trace its distribution back to the city of Cologne. *One World* was available in Cologne as early as January 2, 1947. Old friend to Cardinal Muench and economist Franz Lauter wrote him that "a pastoral letter is circulating here, titled *Die Einwelt in der Liebe,* and you are showed to be its author. I too have a copy of it, sixteen single-spaced pages."[74] Lauter traced its dissemination in Germany to Clemens August Graf Cardinal von Galen,[75] the so-called Lion of Münster. Lauter wrote that "talk went around last year [in 1946], that [Cardinal] von Galen got hold of [*One World*] in Rome, though later this [rumor] proved to be false."[76] Another old friend of Cardinal Muench's hinted as to how it might have appeared in Cologne. In a letter to Muench, Father Gabriel Vollmar relayed an exchange between himself and the director of the Borromäus Verein in Bonn.[77] The director asked Vollmar whether Cardinal Muench had granted permission to publish *One World.* Vollmar replied that as of January 1947, Cardinal Muench had not, but conjectured that perhaps Cardinal Muench granted his permission after January, due to the growing problem of hunger in the Rhineland.[78] The Verein director then relayed a bit of hearsay; rumor had it that a priest "with a Polish-sounding name" had approached the archiepiscopal vicar general's office in Cologne, asking that *One World* be granted imprimatur.[79] At first the Cologne office expressed reservations. The "Polish-sounding" priest then presented a letter, supposedly signed by Cardinal Muench, granting authorization. Upon seeing this alleged letter of permission, the Cologne office granted imprimatur.[80]

Cardinal Muench wrote back to Vollmar, denying the story related by the Borromäus Verein director. "I have never granted permission for the publication of this pastoral letter, and I ask that you tell this to the director of the *Borromäus Verein,*" said Cardinal Muench. "Nor will I grant it in the future," he continued. "I discussed this matter with you once earlier. With best wishes," he finished.[81] As Cardinal Muench did indeed grant permission to the *Familienblatt* in the spring of 1946, we can assume that he meant the "sixteen single-spaced" version Lauter saw in Cologne and supposedly distributed by the archiepiscopal vicar general's office.

Cardinal Muench openly alluded to the fact that "newspapers report[ed] on a pastoral by him discussing conditions in Germany" in a February 1947 interview with N.C.W.C. correspondent Max Jordan. Cardinal Muench acknowledged it to be his pastoral *One World in Charity,* and accounted for the mistaken impression that it was a new publication due to the fact that Vatican radio had referred to it recently. Military government officials were already aware of its existence and illegal distribution by February 1947, for a version of it was already in circulation in the states of Wuerttemburg-Baden and Hesse. Official Karl Arndt became concerned enough to contact John O. Riedl, acting head of the office of Religious Affairs. Upon investigation, Riedl could discern only that the *Familienblatt* in Techny, Illinois reprinted it in 1946, and that this version "somehow" reached Germany.[82]

Evidence shows that the dissemination of *One World* in Germany was a grass-roots movement among German Catholic clergy and laity, a fact of great importance to the question of how German Catholics understood their own culpability for the Holocaust. According to *One World,* they had no culpability. In 1952, Father Gabriel Vollmar wrote to Cardinal Muench, "[H]ow happy I am today to have distributed your wonderful pastoral letter of February 1946."[83] Monsignor Joseph Kamps kept a borrowed copy obtained from a priest of the Gesellschaft Jesu in Beuren, Westphalia.[84] In April 1947, Sister Maura of the Mission for the Poor and Sick (Missionare der Armen und Kranken) in Dortmund read *One World* while hospitalized in St. Joseph's hospital, Dortmund-Hörde. Struck by it, she asked her fellow nuns "to pray for [Cardinal] Muench every day, so that his great work on behalf of Germans would be supported." After showing it to her doctor, she ordered it to be copied and distributed in "academic circles."[85] Sister Alodia of the Missionare told Cardinal Muench that "her friends and acquaintances read his pastoral with great interest and wonderment." The Missionare "had the pastoral copied again, for the poor German people were no longer used to such understanding and deeply shared sympathy."[86] A Munich schoolteacher claimed she got the pastoral "from friends who themselves received it from an employee of the military government."[87] Such examples illustrate that various translations of *One World* acquired a life of their own and became something of an underground sensation.

That April 1947, a rash of excerpts from *One World* appeared in secular newspapers across Germany. Extensive passages appeared in the April 4 edition of the *Aachener Nachrichten.* On April 24, a brief excerpt appeared on the front page of the *Berliner Tagesspiegel.* On

April 25, the *Rhein-Ruhr Zeitung* and the *Kölnische Rundschau* did the same.[88] Cardinal Muench, quite concerned about U.S. reaction to his comments on the Allies, dispatched Father Stanley Bertke to Political Advisor Robert Murphy's office in Berlin "in order to explain to him under what circumstances the pastoral letter had been written." Father Bertke was to tell Murphy that Cardinal Muench authored the pastoral letter in December 1945, *before* learning of his position as liaison representative. Further, added Cardinal Muench, Allied policy toward Germany had improved a great deal since 1945, so much so that he believed his complaints in *One World* to now be outdated.[89]

Two months later, on June 13, a "Father John LaFarge of New York" paid a visit to Kronberg, noted Muench.[90] Father LaFarge carried a copy of *One World,* translated into the French language, and asked Cardinal Muench's permission to circulate it. Cardinal Muench claimed to have denied Father LaFarge permission.[91] He was referring to American Jesuit John LaFarge, who was an important figure among American Catholic leaders for several reasons. First, he was one of two authors of the famous encyclical *Humani Generis Unitas,* commissioned by Pope Pius XI in August 1938. The encyclical condemned racism and racial anti-Semitism specifically, but was never published.[92] Father LaFarge was also the most influential Catholic spokesman on black-white relations in the United States. He was on the editorial staff of the weekly Catholic journal *America* from 1926 until his death in 1963, and from 1944 to 1948 he was its editor in chief.[93] From 1933 onward, *America* was one of the few American Catholic journals to provide continuous coverage of Nazi anti-Semitism and the Holocaust, publishing fifty-six articles and forty editorials on the subject.[94]

Cardinal Muench's diary dated Father LaFarge's visit to June 13 but included no details about the visit. In a letter to German priest Georg Meixner a week later, Cardinal Muench acknowledged that the two discussed not *One World,* but an article entitled "Bayern und die Hitlerbewegung," concerning the National Socialist movement in Bavaria.[95] Father LaFarge would later write Cardinal Muench and, similarly, recall that the two discussed the topic of Catholic Bavaria and Nazism.[96] Frustratingly, neither Father LaFarge nor Cardinal Muench specifically mentioned *One World* in their letters to each other after the visit. But Father LaFarge's autobiography offers potential insight. On June 12, one day before traveling to Frankfurt, Father LaFarge visited French priest (Father) Du Rivau in Offenburg. Du Rivau ran a German-French cultural center and its monthly magazine, *Dokumente,* consisting of German articles translated into French.[97] It is possible that on June 12 Father Du Rivau gave Father LaFarge a copy of *One World* translated into French. Father LaFarge probably brought this copy to Cardinal Muench the next day.

Whether it was the particular French translation of *One World* presented to Cardinal Muench by Father LaFarge in June is unclear, but a French translation did eventually circulate in the French zone that summer. It was so widely disseminated that Military Ordinary to French Chaplains in Germany (Bishop) Picard de la Vacquerie sent Cardinal Muench a letter on the subject in early September.[98] Cardinal Muench replied that he had composed the letter in December 1945, and gave it to the printer "toward the end of January 1946." He released it to Fargo pastors "about the middle of February," while still in Rome with Cardinal Stritch. Upon his return to the United States on March 4, he "found" that his pastoral letter "had not only been circulated in [his] diocese but had also gone through the Catholic press of the United States."[99] In the case of its release to the *Familienblatt,* these statements were false, in that Cardinal Muench gave Father Markert specific permission to translate and print it. One wonders then about the veracity of Cardinal Muench's claim that he rejected Father LeFarge's suggestion to circulate a French translation.[100] He lied to Sister Maura of the Missionare when telling her in June 1948 that he himself had "no" copies of illegally circulating translations, and that he "never received one, even though," he acknowledged, "the pastoral was distributed all across Germany."[101] Though Lauter did not appear to enclose a copy of the sixteen-page translation circulating in Cologne in January, Bishop de la Vacquerie and others sent Cardinal Muench a copy of the five-page French translation in the summer and fall of 1947.

In mid-September 1947, U.S. intelligence officials again reported that "a pastoral letter allegedly written by Bishop Aloisius Muench of Fargo, U.S.A." was being circulated, this time in Schwabach, Bavaria. It was not the "sixteen-page" version that Lauter claimed circulated in Cologne. It was, rather, a six-page German translation. United States intelligence officials "doubted its authenticity," as it was "too well adapted to German psychology." (!) The letter, the report stated, "severely criticize[ed] U.S. occupation policies in Germany[,] comparing [them] with brutalities committed by the Hitler organizations." Because the letter was not dated and contained press commentary from December 1945, intelligence officials correctly surmised that it was not of recent issue.[102]

By the end of August 1947, a Dutch translation of *One World* existed in Holland.[103] In Landkries Offenburg (French zone), the Stadtpfarrer of St. Cyriakus church in Oberkirch mimeographed 500 copies of *One World*, or, to be more exact, of a twelve-page extraction from it. He distributed it not only to his parish members but also to "the most prominent personalities and families . . . in the Baden *Landtag* and *Gemeinde*."[104] But Muench's biggest troubles began when the five-page French translation referenced by Bishop de la Vacquerie reached the French military governor in Germany, (General) Pierre Joseph Koenig. On September 23, 1947, Koenig wrote to his counterpart in the American zone, Lucius Clay, including a reproduction of the five-page French version of *One World*. Koenig described it as signed by "Monsignor," versus the higher and correct rank of "Bishop," "addressed [with the date of] April 1946, to the Catholics of the diocese of Fargo at the time when he was quitting it." Koenig reported that it enjoyed wide circulation in the French zone, especially in Baden-Baden. Like OMGUS officer Riedl, Koenig traced the translation back to the *Familienblatt*, and also to "the English journal *Universe* of 17 January 1947."[105]

Nearly two weeks after Koenig sent his missive to Clay, Riedl contacted Muench to ask for clarification on *One World*. "We are frequently asked for an opinion in regard to it and to other emendations of it, and do not have the information necessary to give a factual answer," noted Riedl.[106] But Riedl's concerns were eclipsed by anxiety on much higher levels. On October 6, Muench flew to the United States with Clay in his private plane, none the wiser about the French military governor General Koenig's complaint to Clay.[107] Unbeknownst to Muench, Clay carried the inflammatory letter from Koenig in his personal pouch,[108] but had decided not to discuss Koenig's letter with Muench at this time.[109] Instead, he asked his political advisor, Robert Murphy, to conduct a quiet investigation of the affair in order to "get the facts."[110] In the first few days of October, Murphy contacted Francis Cardinal Spellman of New York to ask for an invitation to the upcoming Alfred E. Smith Memorial Foundation dinner in New York

City. Among other things, he hoped to discuss the Muench pastoral letter with Spellman.[111]

Spellman was one of five American archbishops who were elevated to the coveted rank of cardinal together with Stritch in February 1946. Cardinal Spellman's fame was such that he was dubbed "the American pope" after Vatican Secretary of State Eugenio Pacelli's visit to Washington in 1936. Spellman accompanied Pacelli everywhere, including Pacelli's audiences with President Franklin D. Roosevelt. Spellman and Roosevelt developed a close relationship, and Spellman came to be regarded as "the" intermediary between Rome and Washington.[112] This explained Murphy's decision to contact Spellman about the *One World* matter. On November 12, with Muench still in the United States, Spellman "had a short visit with [then-]Bishop Muench and showed him an information note" sent by Murphy.[113] Spellman appeared to Muench "overworked and quite nervous."[114] Spellman disclosed to Muench that "the French accused [Muench] of having written a letter to the German bishops in the French zone," but Spellman did not yet know more details.[115] Muench, apparently not yet wise to the Koenig-Clay exchange, immediately suspected that Spellman referred to the distribution of *One World* in the French zone. Muench, already alerted to its distribution by Bishop Picard de la Vacquerie in letters dated September 5 and October 24, was not taken by surprise.[116]

Clay spoke to Cardinal Spellman about Muench and *One World* around mid-October, 1947.[117] Clay warned Spellman that he "would ask for [Muench's] recall." Spellman discouraged Clay from dismissing Muench, conjecturing that "maybe the letter [was] not authentic." To verify its authenticity, Spellman asked Clay to send him a copy of the translation included in Koenig's September 23 letter. Because Spellman had heard nothing further by November 12, he assumed the matter was "settled." Murphy apparently relayed to Spellman that "Clay [was] a hot-head [and went] off half-cocked," and therefore Spellman should not be too worried.[118] But Spellman's assumption that the matter was settled was false. In a letter dated October 24, Murphy again prompted a discussion of the matter with Spellman and enclosed the five-page French translation of *One World*.[119] Murphy's letter reached Spellman on November 17.[120] Hoping to ease Murphy and Clay, Spellman asked Muench to write a formal explanation of *One World*, which Muench did, on that very day.

In his explanation, Muench emphasized first and foremost that he wrote the letter in December 1945 and gave it to the printer in January 1946, prior to his leaving for the Stritch ceremony in February and therefore several months before he heard of his assignment in Germany.[121] As to the anti-Allied excerpts, Muench claimed they were torn from their context, and they were therefore "unfair." In his November 17 letter to Spellman, Muench shed no light on how *One World* might have appeared in Germany. He said only that "extensive excerpts . . . appeared in German translation without [his] authorization," though he acknowledged that "a request came to [him] from an (unnamed) publication in Bonn" to print it, which he claimed to have rejected.[122]

On November 25, Spellman formally replied to Murphy's October 24 query, and included a copy of the two-page explanation by Muench.[123] Murphy "showed the enclosure [by Muench] to Clay" and thereafter assumed the matter to be "satisfactorily closed."[124] Though no documentation of this conversation between Clay and Murphy is available, it appears that Murphy intervened on behalf of Muench. One possible explanation for such an intervention might be their shared views on ethnic German expellees. As for Muench, he never showed remorse for his authorship of *One World*. "I regret only that merely excerpts [of *One World*] have appeared," Muench told Bishop de la Vacquerie.[125] He told Central Catholic Verein of America (CCVA) member Mary Filser Lohr that he felt glad of the fact that his pastoral "brought much comfort to the German people," and had "gone through all Germany," mimeographed again and again by "people who wished to get it circulated." He was "naturally happy" that "so much good [was] done by means of it."[126] It gave him "great joy" that the letter provided consolation and encouragement to Germans.[127] In his diary, he privately mused that he "would fight [his own] recall based on calumny" concerning his pastoral.[128]

American military government intelligence analysts in Kreis Schwabach believed that "[*One World*'s] attacks on American policies in Germany provid[ed] welcome reading material for certain dissatisfied elements of the people." According to Schwabach military government officials, "quite a number of the [German] population" believed that the U.S. withheld material aid from Germany out of spite; that "German reconstruction and rehabilitation [were] being obstructed by dilatory policies on the part of the Allies," resulting in "many ready customers" for such a letter.[129] But citing American interpretations of *One World*'s popularity is hardly necessary, as Germans spoke for themselves clearly enough. Cardinal Frings of Cologne summarized *One World*'s effects on German Catholics most succinctly in a conversation with Muench: "[N]o bishop in the world is so welcome [here] as you."[130] A number of other German bishops wrote letters of praise about Muench to the pope.[131] The Stadtpfarrer of St. Cyriakus in Oberkirch called the pastoral letter "courageous," showing "how justifiable it was, that His Holiness Pope Pius XII named [His] Excellency Muench apostolic visitor to Germany." The parish of St. Cyriakus sent deepest thanks, but did not stop there, mimeographing and circulating 500 copies of the pastoral letter.[132] Scores of letters to Muench from German Catholics indicate widespread knowledge of and support for *One World*, indicating also the rejection of notions of German guilt or responsibility for Nazi crimes. "Daily I express my deepest respect for Your Excellency's valiant and resolute pastoral letter, a copy of which came into my hands. It is an apostolic speech which cannot be ignored," Auxiliary Bishop Höcht of Regensburg wrote to Muench in 1946.[133] Many German Catholics interpreted *One World* as proof that they had done nothing wrong, even if they had an undeniable level of involvement with the Nazi party.

More than anything else, *One World* was the document that established Muench's reputation among German Catholics early on. "I always had a wish to meet and get to know a foreigner (*Ausländer*) of good will [toward Germans] who has a position of weight and influence," Elisabeth Baumgart of Selingen told Muench after reading his pastoral.[134] At a time when only "cries of hate" could be heard toward Germans, argued Theodor Lebeda of Limburg, Muench's pastoral calling for charity and mercy toward Germans was a welcome change.[135] Further examples elucidate similar sentiments. Franz Lauter of Munich, mentioned previously with regard to the distribution of *One World* in Cologne, urged Muench excitedly, "[I]f this letter is authentic, [I] recommend it be spread further, for today it is important and cheering for us German Catholics to know [the message of] the pope and his representative."[136] Lauter's comment demonstrated his awareness of Muench's position as Pius XII's papal visitor (July 1946–January 1947). Lauter may also have been alluding to the pope's June 1945 radio address rejecting German "collective" guilt and praising

Catholic anti-Nazi efforts. "Just an hour ago I read your pastoral in the *Tagesspiegel*," wrote Sudeten expellee Franz Münnich, now of Ostlutter. "No one feels its truth like we *Flüchtlinge* (refugees) and *Ausgewiesenen* (ethnic German expellees)," he insisted.[137] Master builder Franz Grübert, an ethnic German expellee from Silesia residing in Furth im Wald, elaborated more on what made it so cheering: It validated his belief that the majority of Germans now paid for the crimes of the few. "Again, the great masses, who had no influence on [Germany's] fate and yet were exposed to its promises and led astray by it, now suffer for it," objected Grübert, "and I am one of these," he added.[138] Elisabeth Baumgart of Selingen, after thanking Muench for his *One World,* wrote indignantly, "admittedly, the Nazis plunged the world into this chaos. But, does that give others the right to use the same means employed by the Nazis? The Nazis were not the German people."[139] H. Mertens, an ethnic German Sudeten expellee now living in Kreis Hersfeld, claimed to have read an excerpt of *One World* in *Der Ruf* in September 1947. He, too, soundly rejected the idea of "collective" guilt. A convert to Catholicism in 1936, Mertens wrote, "We did not contribute to the many things for which Germans are today reproached. We refused to contribute, held high our faith and therefore are not guilty for the many things that have so besmirched the German name in the world today."[140]

A strong sense of victimization was certainly not limited to ethnic German expellees. It also extended to so-called Reich Germans. Barbara Vincenz, teacher in a Koblenz *Volksschule,* obtained a copy of Muench's pastoral in February 1947. "Why is one German treated like the next? There are so many, who wanted nothing to do with Hitler. I was not in the party, but I am punished. Why don't people like myself get more to eat," asked Vincenz.[141] Therese Wagner, a teacher in Munich, read an excerpt from *One World* in the *Isar Post* in March 1947. "On your extended trip through Germany [in winter 1946], you saw our distress and you know . . . that the majority of the German people were not susceptible to National Socialism, were against National Socialism," she told Muench.[142]

A deeply distressing response to *One World* came from Hedwig Rohmer of Munich, a teacher in a Munich public school. "We understand that other peoples shrink from our deeds, thinking we [are] all of bad character," acknowledged Rohmer. "It is deeply humiliating and depressing, though we did not know anything, most of us, of those cruel acts and places [revealed after the war's end]," she continued. Her sense of victimization bordered on paranoia. "There are real plans to kill millions and millions of Germans," she insisted. "We all wish to give satisfaction to those countries suffering from us and to help those victims of the past time. But we presume that the idea is of killing us in a slow way instead of doing it with gas. Sometimes we think it more merciful to die like them in the KZ [*Konzentrationslager*]," she wrote.[143]

In the eyes of some of its German Catholic readers, *One World* put Muench on par with the likes of the famous anti-Nazi Cardinal von Galen and even with the Holy Father himself. Master builder Franz Grübert of Furth im Wald linked *One World* to speeches by von Galen. "Reading your words, my thoughts quickly go back to the now-famous preaching of Cardinal Count (*Graf*) Galen. He, too, was a brave confessor in a godless state," noted Grübert.[144] Priest Franz Weimar drew a similar connection. "Yours were the most powerful lines written since the most holy bishop of Münster against the Nazis some years ago," insisted Weimar.[145] Priest Franz Schmal of Todtnauberg told Muench that *One World* embodied "the spirit of Pope Pius XII." He insisted, "I cannot remember an Episcopal manifesting in such a high degree the very mentality of our Holy Father."[146]

Even after making a splash in 1947, the fame of *One World* and the reputation it imparted to its author continued to spread. In telling his friend Muench about a new booklet published by the Neuberg Abbey in September 1951, Vollmar noted that the last page referred to a word (*Liebe,* translated as "charity") from the Holy Scripture, a noble tradition that Muench, too, stressed in his 1946 *One World.*[147] Vollmar called Muench's *One World* "a heroic act and a document of historical importance [written] in a time of hate" against Germans.[148] In December 1952, Dr. H. Hassenbach wrote Muench to request additional copies of *One World,* noting, "among the colleagues in his circles, there was a great interest for it."[149] Hassenbach did not specify which of the many circulated versions he wanted.[150] In response, Father Howard Smith, Muench's secretary at the nunciature, wrote to the home diocese in Fargo requesting more copies of *One World* (also not specifying which version). "The archbishop occasionally receives requests for a copy of his 1946 pastoral *One World in Charity,* [and] we have only one copy here," wrote Smith. Smith went on to request that a dozen copies be sent to the nunciature in Germany, for distribution when the request arose. (!)[151] Allied censorship ceased with the end of military occupation in 1949, so Muench's willingness to distribute *One World,* while now legal, showed lack of change in his openly pro-German position.

In 1957, *ten years* after the initial appearance of *One World* in Germany, German Catholics remembered Muench for it. Josef Hering, a Nazi Party member (*Parteigenosse*) and prison guard in Amberg from 1936 to 1945, wrote to complain about his treatment under American internment. He cited a passage from *One World* to repudiate the behavior of the Americans: "Let us not become party to the crimes of Hitler, in that we now do what we so harshly judged and fought the Nazis for doing . . . no double-standard should be applied to the law of justice!" Not surprisingly, Hering vehemently rejected any notion of guilt or responsibility. "I once saved the life of an American flier," claimed Hering. "[Mine] was the face of the so-called criminal . . . who had to suffer through the most difficult of circumstances with his family for crimes committed by others."[152]

When Muench retired from the nunciature in Bad Godesberg in December 1959 to join the College of Cardinals in Rome, he still remained famous for *One World.* In an article entitled "Friend and Champion of the Germans," the *Kirchliche Nachrichten Agentur* quoted the very same passage Hering had chosen two years earlier to capture the spirit of Muench.[153] *One World* was viewed by a great many German Catholics as "bread for the hungry soul," as one Nuremberg Catholic, Barbara Muschweck, described it.[154] It greatly helped spread Muench's fame as a pro-German figure of German parentage, sympathetic to German Catholics, who held a great deal of power as the Vatican emissary to German Catholics. *One World* made him accessible in the eyes of German Catholics, to whom he even became a sort of "confessor." One ironic illustration of Muench's powerful reputation as a friend to all Germans was the myth of his association with Adolf Eichmann. In 1961, the *Chicago Daily Tribune* and the New York *Daily News* reported that the defense lawyer to Adolf Eichmann, Dr. Robert Servatius, planned to approach Muench on behalf of his client. Servatius held the erroneous belief that Muench was the Vatican's nuncio to Germany during World War II, and that "Muench visited Eichmann several times during the war to help Jews escape

Nazi persecution."[155] Servatius reportedly said that he hoped Muench "would testify, and [Muench's] evidence will show Eichmann is not the monster he is made out to be."[156]

The New York *Daily News* printed a correction several weeks later, acknowledging that Monsignor Cesare Orsenigo was papal nuncio from 1930 until his death in March 1946. A recheck by *Daily News* correspondent for Jerusalem Joseph Fried revealed that Servatius had based his false statement on Eichmann's police interrogation. Purportedly asked about his church contacts, Eichmann said, "I can remember that the then permanent—what was the man who was executive of the Fulda Bishops Conference[157]—the then Bishop Muench. I believe that later he was dean of the diplomatic corps in Bonn and I believe he is the same who a short time ago was appointed cardinal by the Pope." Eichmann claimed to have met Muench "twice a month in 1943."[158] Perhaps Eichmann met with pro-Nazi Nuncio Cesare Orsenigo? In any case, Eichmann mistook Muench for Orsenigo, a strangely illustrative misunderstanding. It demonstrated the degree to which Muench enjoyed broad acceptance across Germany, and was viewed as having positive ties with Germans, and especially with Catholics.

NOTES

1. Ludwig Volk, "Der Heilige Stuhl und Deutschland 1945–1949," *Stimmen der Zeit* 194 (1976): 802.

2. "Die deutschen Bischöfe: Erster gemeinsamer Hirtenbrief nach dem Krieg, Fulda, 23 August 1945," in *Dokumente deutschen Bischöfe: Hirtenbriefe und Ansprachen zu Gesellschaft und Politik 1945–1949*, vol. 1, ed. Wolfgang Löhr (Würzburg: Echter Verlag, 1985), 40–5.

3. Aloisius Muench, *One World in Charity: A Pastoral*, 7. I thank the librarians of the Aloisius Cardinal Muench Seminary in Fargo, N.D., for sending me a copy of the pastoral letter's original edition. A second edition version of *One World* is available in Aloisius Muench Collection (hereafter cited as HM 37), Box 93, Folder 4 (hereafter, HM 37/93/4), Archives, John K. Mullen Memorial Library, The Catholic University of America (hereafter ACUA), Washington, D.C. In this passage, Muench quoted the second and third books of the Old Testament, Exodus 21:24 ("eye for eye, tooth for tooth, hand for hand, foot for foot") and Leviticus 24:20 ("fracture for fracture, eye for eye, tooth for tooth"). Exodus and Leviticus contain laws recorded during the year that Israelites, having fled Egypt, camped

at Mount Sinai, when God directed the prophet Moses to organize Israel's worship, government, and military forces.

4. Aloisius Muench was ordained to the Roman Catholic priesthood in 1913. Father Muench reached the rank of monsignor in September 1934. On August 10, 1935, Pope Pius XI named Monsignor Muench bishop of the diocese of Fargo, N.D. Given the title of archbishop by Pope Pius XII in 1950, he remained the diocesan bishop of the diocese of Fargo until 1959, while also fulfilling his duties in Germany (1946–59). In 1959, Pope Pius XII gave him the title of cardinal, which bestows upon its bearer extreme significance and power in the universal Roman Catholic Church (he was one of roughly seventy cardinals in the Catholic Church worldwide). I will use the title of cardinal when referring to Aloisius Muench throughout this article, but it should be noted that he held the rank of bishop and (after 1950) archbishop during nearly all of his tenure in Germany.

5. "Collective" guilt means that "all" Germans bore culpability or guilt. The notion of German "responsibility" does not imply wrongdoing, but does imply moral *accountability*. Individual Germans who may not have supported the Nazi regime (and hence did not bear "guilt") still had the obligation to help Nazism's victims. The concept of German "collective" responsibility, then, means that Germany as a nation bore the obligation to help Nazi victims after the war, regardless of variations in degree of "guilt" within the German population itself. Hannah Arendt describes collective responsibility as follows: "[E]very government assumes political responsibility for the deeds and misdeeds of its predecessors and every nation for the deeds and misdeeds of the past." See Hannah Arendt, *Eichmann in Jerusalem: A Report on the Banality of Evil* (New York: Penguin Books, 1964), 298. See also Friedrich Meinecke, *Die deutsche Katastrophe: betrachtungen und erinnerungen* (Zürich: Aeo-Verlag e.g., 1946).

6. While this model of resistance and victimization applied to anti-Catholic measures, on the whole, it did *not* apply to measures against Jews. One illustrative example is Michael Mann's recent study of 1,581 German war criminals, which demonstrates that Catholic Holocaust perpetrators outnumbered their Protestant counterparts. See Michael Mann, "Were the Perpetrators of Genocide Ordinary Men or Real Nazis? Records from Fifteen Hundred Biographies," *Holocaust and Genocide Studies* 14, no. 3 (winter 2000): 331–66. For Mann's religious data, see pp. 347–50 and 356–7.

7. An apostolic visitor, also referred to as a "papal visitor," is a papal representative to a particular church, government, or internationally accredited council. Apostolic visitors differ from other papal legates in that the pope summons them for special emergencies only, and their missions are generally of short duration.

8. The Vatican is the independent city-state in Italy where the Bishop

of Rome (the pope) resides, but I use the term here as a shorthand expression for the central authority of the Roman Catholic Church: the pope, the Roman Curia (bureaucracy), and the Vatican city-state together (as is now common). Technically, the pope and persons and departments of the Roman Curia, which assist in governance and administration of the universal Roman Catholic Church, are the "Holy See," also called "Apostolic See." Throughout this article I will use the terms "Holy See" and "Vatican" interchangeably to signify the authority of the Catholic Church in Rome.

9. For a discussion of the postwar Vatican relief office in Kronberg, Germany, see Ludwig Volk, "Der Heilige Stuhl und Deutschland 1945–1949," *Stimmen der Zeit* 194 (1976): 795–823.

10. The role of the Vatican regent was in practice that of a nuncio, but due to the Federal Republic of Germany's lack of full autonomy in 1949, no diplomats (and hence no papal nuncio) could, in principle, operate there. This changed in 1951, when the Federal Republic established an independently operating Foreign Ministry and received foreign diplomats for the first time.

11. The Holy See employs its own ambassadors, called "nuncios," to represent the pope to hundreds of civil governments. Nuncios hold the rank of ambassador and also hold the honorary title "dean of diplomatic corps" in nation-states adhering to the Congress of Vienna (1815). In each nation-state, nuncios operate from their nunciature, or diplomatic headquarters.

12. Spanning his stay in Germany between 1946 and 1959, Vatican liaison to Germany Aloisius Cardinal Muench received tens of thousands of letters from German and American Catholics. Of these, approximately 100 letters written by U.S. Catholics and army, military government, or embassy officials commented directly and unambiguously on the Holocaust, its survivors, and Jewish refugees in Germany or already in the United States. In addition, Cardinal Muench kept a diary throughout his stay in Germany. In it, he recorded several dozen private conversations with military and ecclesiastical officials regarding Jews specifically. Select U.S. Army officials and American Catholic hierarchy, clergy, and laity in contact with Cardinal Muench viewed Jewish immigrants who entered the United States after 1933 as "alien" or "recent" Americans, unfamiliar with "American" standards of fairness, incapable of true "loyalty" to the United States, and "in control" of American policymaking vis-à-vis Germany. Cardinal Muench and many in his intimate circles believed those Jews who emigrated to the United States during or after the war, Holocaust survivors, and Jewish refugees in displaced persons camps in Europe to be "avengers" who wished to harm Germans and who were careless with property, immoral, and excessively involved in leftist and black-market activities.

13. Born in Olginate, Italy, Cesare Orsenigo was appointed Apostolic Nuncio to the Netherlands on June 23, 1922, and subsequently Apostolic Nuncio to Hungary in 1925. On April 25, 1930, he succeeded Eugenio Pacelli as Apostolic Nuncio to Germany. He died on April 1, 1946.

14. Frederic Spotts, *The Churches and Politics in Germany* (Middletown, Conn.: Wesleyan University Press, 1973), 29. The debate on the nature of Pius XII's relationship to Germans and to the Holocaust began in 1963 with the premier of Rolf Hochhuth's play, *Der Stellvertreter* (The Deputy), which criticized Pius XII's inaction with regard to the Holocaust. Books discussing relations between the Vatican and Judaism in general or Pope Pius XII and the Holocaust specifically are numbered in the hundreds. Recent important publications are: James Carroll, *Constantine's Sword: The Church and the Jews* (Boston: Houghton Mifflin, 2000); John Cornwell, *Hitler's Pope: The Secret History of Pius XII* (New York: Penguin Books, 2000); David Kertzer, *The Popes against The Jews: The Vatican's Role in the Rise of Modern Anti-Semitism* (New York: Knopf, 2001); Ernst Klee, *Persilscheine und falsche Paesse: Wie die Kirchen den Nazis halfen* (Frankfurt am Main: Fischer Verlag, 1991); Michael Phayer, *The Catholic Church and the Holocaust, 1930–1965* (Bloomington: Indiana University Press, 2000); Ronald Rychlak, *Hitler, the War, and the Pope* (Huntington, Ind.: Our Sunday Visitor, 2000); and Susan Zuccotti, *Under His Very Windows: The Vatican and the Holocaust in Italy* (New Haven, Conn.: Yale University Press, 2000).

15. Volk, "Der Heilige Stuhl und Deutschland," 795–6; (Father) Colman S. Barry, O.S.B., *American Nuncio: Cardinal Aloisius Muench* (Collegeville, Minn.: Saint John's University Press, 1969), 53–6. Barry cites the date of the first Vatican mission as late May 1945 and the second as August 1945.

16. Volk, "Der Heilige Stuhl und Deutschland," 795.

17. Barry, *American Nuncio*, 67.

18. Volk, "Der Heilige Stuhl in Deutschland," 795.

19. Letter from Aloisius Muench, Rome, to Terry Muench, Milwaukee, 18 February 1947. HM 37/32/2, ACUA.

20. "Der Visitator konnte seine Werk nich auf offizielle Weise angehen." See Ludwig Volk, "Bilanz einer Nuntiatur 1946–1959: Schlussbericht des ersten Nuntius in der Nachkriegszeit," *Stimmen Der Zeit* 195 (1977): 149.

21. Barry, *American Nuncio*, 67.

22. Letter from Muench, Kronberg, to Martin Salm, Chilton (Wisc.), 17 November 1949. HM 37/15/1, ACUA.

23. Volk, "Bilanz einer Nuntiatur," 152.

24. Report entitled "Religious Affairs," 24–5, dated August 1946; Basic Documents, Box 158, Religious Affairs Branch (hereafter RA), Education

and Religious Affairs Division (hereafter ECR), Record Group 260: Office of Military Government–United States (hereafter RG 260-OMGUS), National Archives II, College Park, Maryland (hereafter, NARA).

25. Joseph Bendersky cites evidence showing that both Military Governor Lucius Clay (March 1946–May 1949) and his political advisor in the State Department, Robert Murphy, viewed Jewish colleagues as untrustworthy. See Joseph W. Bendersky, *The "Jewish Threat": Anti-Semitic Politics of the U.S. Army,* (New York: Basic Books, 2000), 364–71. Bendersky persuasively shows that many high-ranking officers and officials in postwar Germany and back in the United States believed that "Jewish refugees in American uniforms unduly affected American policy toward Germany in a variety of detrimental ways," 364.

26. Ibid., 370. Some suspected him of anti-democratic and even "fascist" sympathies. Other studies describe him as "an outspoken Catholic suspected of exhibiting favoritism toward Catholics" and as being "greatly mistrusted" by Treasury Secretary Morgenthau. See Rebecca Boehling, *A Question of Priorities: Democratic Reform and Economic Recovery in Postwar Germany* (Providence, R.I.: Berghahn Books, 1996), 44.

27. Letter from Muench, Kronberg, to Bishop Vincent J. Ryan, Bismarck, 15 November 1946. HM 37/8/4, ACUA.

28. Shrove Tuesday is the day before Ash Wednesday, the beginning of the Lenten fast. Lent, derived from the Anglo-Saxon word *lencten,* meaning spring, refers to the time of forty days of fasting before Easter. During the period between Shrove Tuesday and Easter, Catholics prepare for the Feast of the Resurrection, or Easter, Jesus Christ's return from the dead. Passion Sunday is celebrated on the second Sunday before Easter.

29. The term "charity" has a long history in Catholic theology. In essence, charity means love directed toward God *and neighbor* as the highest purpose of any Catholic. The Latin root of "charity," *caritas,* means "love." Charity is the third and most important of the three theological virtues (faith, hope, and charity). Theologians define it as the highest form of Christian love. For a discussion of how Berlin seminarians trained during the Weimar period understood the concept "who is neighbor," that is to say, who was included in the category "neighbor" and who was excluded, see (Father) Kevin Spicer, C.S.C., "Choosing between God and Satan: The German Catholic Clergy of Berlin and the Third Reich" (doctoral diss., Boston College, 2000), 86–114. Cardinal Muench's focus on the term "charity," meaning (Christian) love, raises the issue of its opposite: hate or contempt toward God and neighbor. Alleged Jewish contempt for and rejection of the Son of God manifested in his human form, Jesus Christ, has been the basis of Christian anti-Judaism, as Christians believed that Jesus was the Messiah sent by God and rejected by the Jewish people.

30. The Inquisition was an institution in Catholicism for the eradication and punishment of heresy. The Fourth Lateran Council (1215) called for secular authorities to help with the eradication of heresy. In 1231 Pope Gregory IX issued a papal bull, *Excommunicamus,* establishing procedures for identifying heretics in various parts of Europe. Traveling tribunals went to Germany, France, and Italy and examined those suspected of formal heresy. By the fourteenth century, the tribunals lost their vigor. But, in 1479, Catholic monarchs of Spain Ferdinand and Isabella created the Spanish Inquisition. The aim of this centralized office was to seek out heretics and ferret out converted Jews and Muslims who still covertly practiced their own religion. Though it was most vigorous in the late sixteenth century, this institution lasted in Spain until 1834. Pope Paul III established the Roman Inquisition in 1542 as part of the church's response to the Protestant Reformation. It was the final tribunal of the church dealing with matters of heresy. In 1965, as part of the Second Vatican Council, the Roman Congregation of the Inquisition was renamed the Congregation for the Doctrine of the Faith. Bartholomew's Night is a reference to the murder of thousands of Huguenots in Paris and of Protestant men, women, and children all over France beginning on August 24, 1572 (Saint Bartholomew's Day). The Catholic king of France, Charles IX, ordered these murders, urged to do so by his mother Catherine de Medici and the Catholic Guises.

31. Majdanek was a POW and extermination camp located on the outskirts of Lublin in southern Poland. Majdanek began operation in October 1941 as one of the largest camps in Eastern Europe, with seven gas chambers. Inmates included Soviet POWs, imprisoned and deported Belorussians and Poles, and Jews. Approximately 360,000 inmates perished there, roughly 215,000 from starvation, abuse, exhaustion, and disease; and roughly 145,000 from gassing or shooting. Majdanek ceased operation in July 1944 upon the arrival of the Red Army. Bergen-Belsen was a concentration camp near Celle in northwest Germany. Originally designed as a POW and transit camp with capacity for 10,000 prisoners, by the last weeks of the war, it held 41,000. Some 35,000 inmates died of starvation, overcrowding, and disease, or were murdered. Bergen-Belsen was the first camp to be liberated by the Western Allied forces (April 15, 1945). The best recent study on Bergen-Belsen, including its role as a camp for so-called exchange Jews, is Eileen-Alexandra Wenck, *Zwischen Menschenhandel und "Endlösung": das Konzentrationslager Bergen-Belsen* (Paderborn: F. Schöningh, 2000). Buchenwald was a concentration camp near Weimar, Germany, established in 1937. About 239,000 Germans and foreign nationals, mostly political prisoners, were interned there. No gassing facilities existed at Buchenwald, but disease, malnutrition, exhaustion, ill-treatment, and physical abuse killed approximately 43,000 inmates. Most SS personnel

fled on April 11, 1945, after which the prisoners seized control of the camp from the remaining guards.

32. Lidice (Liditz) was a Czech miners' settlement near Kladno, west of Prague. After the assassination attempt against Reinhard Heydrich (May 27, 1942), Adolf Hitler ordered German police and SD men to surround Lidice on the evening of June 9, 1942. Though no link between the assassination and Lidice could be proved, 198 adult males were shot execution style, 184 women were transported to Ravensbrück concentration camp in Germany, and 90 children were taken to the Reich *Gau* Wartheland (Warthegau), a region of German-occupied Poland to the south of the Vistula and Netze rivers.

33. In the final month of the Second World War, the United States dropped the first atomic bomb on Hiroshima, Japan, on August 6, 1945, and three days later a second on Nagasaki, Japan.

34. *One World,* 2. Muench made no reference to the fact that Nazis targeted Jews for gassing in the POW and extermination camp Majdanek, nor did he cite the especially low value placed on the lives of Jewish prisoners in the concentration camps Buchenwald and Bergen-Belsen. In fact, Muench described Buchenwald as a place where "Germans tortured Germans," making no mention of any other national group incarcerated there.

35. Usage of the term "holocaust" in 1946 referred to large-scale destruction, especially by fire.

36. *One World,* 3.

37. The Republic of Lithuania was founded on December 11, 1917. The German-Soviet Non-aggression Pact of August 23, 1939, ceded Lithuania to the Soviet sphere of influence, and on June 15, 1940, the Soviets annexed Lithuania. Occupied by the Germans at the onset of the Russian campaign beginning June 22, 1941, Lithuania was incorporated into the Reich Commissariat Ostland (Eastern Land). In July 1944, the Red Army once again annexed Lithuania.

38. *One World,* 4. Though Lithuanian Jews also endured deportation by rail (often cattle) car under the German occupation of Lithuania (late June 1941 to July 1944), and in greater numbers, Muench never mentioned Jews by name. Jews, approximately one-third of the Lithuanian population in 1939, were especially concentrated in Vilna (Vilnius) and Kovno (Kaunus). A world center of *halakha* (rabbinic law), Vilna's Jewish community was second in importance in Europe only to the Warsaw community. In Vilna alone, Jews numbered about 57,000. The Lithuanian Jewish community was the first target of the Final Solution, and it fared the worst. As early as the end of 1941, 80 percent of Lithuanian Jews had been killed, and the death toll reached 96 percent by the end of the war. Yet Muench ignored the fate of Jews in wartime Lithuania. See Leni Yahil, *The Holocaust:*

The Fate of European Jewry, trans. from the Hebrew by Ina Friedman and Haya Galai (New York: Oxford University Press, 1990), 274–5.

39. Adolf Hitler unleashed his war on Poland on September 1, 1939, marking the beginning of World War II. Germany and the Soviets divided up Poland between them, and the territories occupied by the Germans were incorporated into the Greater German Reich (Danzig–West Prussia and the Wartheland). The remainder was organized as the General Government (October 10, 1939). The Soviets occupied the remaining portions of eastern Poland.

40. On September 1, the main body of the activated German army (fifty-seven divisions) attacked in two assault columns with about 2,500 tanks concentrated in the direction of Warsaw. They were supported by Air Fleets One and Four, with a total of 1,017 aircraft.

41. Rotterdam, the largest port city in the Netherlands, was the target of a May 14, 1940, German air attack that killed over 900 civilians and destroyed the historic Old City.

42. German bombers (449 in total) attacked Coventry, a British industrial city in the Midlands southeast of Birmingham, on the night of November 14–15, 1940. German pilots dropped 500 tons of explosive bombs and 30 tons of firebombs, killing 554 civilians, wounding 865, and destroying the Old City's gothic cathedral.

43. The first bombs fell on London on August 24, 1940, as part of the 1940–41 Air Battle for England between the German Luftwaffe and the British Royal Air Force (RAF). By August 31, 1940, the Luftwaffe had flown, 4,779 missions and dropped 4,638 tons of bombs. On September 7, 1940, the Luftwaffe launched a massive attack on London that continued by evening over the next sixty-five nights. Intermittent nighttime attacks continued until May 29, 1944 (this excluding V1 "flying buzz bombs," which continued through March 1945).

44. Cologne, Berlin, and Dresden, Germany, were all targets of severe British and American bombing attacks. On February 13–14, 1945, British and American air forces attacked Dresden in three waves. An estimated 35,000 civilians lost their lives, and Dresden became a symbol for atrocities against civilians from the sky, criticized harshly even from the Allied side.

45. *One World,* 5.

46. Ibid., 6.

47. Ibid., 7. Muench juxtaposed the Old Testament laws of Moses and Israel (the laws of Jews) to those of Christ, of love, of the New Testament, of Christians. Not only did Muench exclude Jews from his litany of victims, he indicted them as the harbingers of revenge.

48. It was titled "Intervention of Mercy." Though he did not specify which "quarters" decried "mercy," his listeners could easily infer that Jews

were among them. By constructing sharp opposites that wove through centuries of familiar anti-Jewish teaching (love vs. hate, mercy vs. vengeance, kindness vs. cold-heartedness), Muench did not have to speak the word "Jew" for his listeners to hear it.

49. *One World,* 9.

50. Ibid., 10–11.

51. Ibid., 13.

52. Ibid., 14. Muench cited a 1945 edition of *Petrusblatt,* a Berlin Catholic newspaper, claiming that prior to its abolition by the Nazi regime in 1938, it "did not bow before the spiritual terror of National Socialism. For five long years, from 1933 to 1938, [*Petrusblatt*] waged a journalistic battle against race-hatred, lies, and injustice. Persecutions of Christians, oral and written warnings, interrogations, threats—nothing deflected us from the course charted for us by our bishops," the editorial claimed. If applied to Catholic resistance efforts based on Nazi *anti-Catholic* policy, the *Petrusblatt* editorial rang true, though its focus on resistance to Nazis' anti-Catholic measures was and is highly misleading. Catholic resistance to Nazi measures curtailing Catholic schools, newspapers, associations, politics, and institutions is a historical fact, as is the Catholic outcry against Nazi slander of Catholic clerics, and, perhaps best known, resistance to euthanasia policy in the sermons of Clemens August von Galen, the so-called Lion of Muenster. Aware of this record, Muench wrote in *One World* that "an amazing story" of Catholic resistance to Nazism would be told in years to come. The historical record on German Catholic resistance to Nazism between 1933 and 1945 has been told. See, among others, Helmreich, *The German Churches under Hitler,* 237–96 and 347–68; Heinz Boberbach, ed., *Berichte des SD und der Gestapo über Kirchen und Kirchenvolk in Deutschland, 1934–1944* (Mainz: Grünewald Verlag, 1971); Conway, *The Nazi Persecution of the Churches 1933–1945;* Kurt Nowak, *Geschichte des Christentums in Deutschland* (Munich: Beck Verlag, 1995), 243–90. Muench did not separate those Catholic anti-Nazis who were also rabid anti-Semites from the (few) Catholic anti-Nazis motivated in part by opposition to Nazi crimes against Jews. This problem appears not only in *One World,* but in much of the literature exonerating Catholics on the premise of their "resistance" record. The crucial question is not *whether* some Catholics resisted (they did), but *why* they resisted. The major issues that motivated most Catholics determined to take risks in a potentially life-threatening regime did not include a high-priority concern for the fate of Jewish Germans.

53. *One World,* 15.

54. Muench does not specify his source further.

55. Here, Muench quotes from the Old Testament book of Proverbs

25:21–2. These words are accredited to David's son and successor Solomon (ca. 961–922 B.C.). Quoted in *One World*, 17.

56. From the New Testament Gospel of Luke 6:27–34. Quoted in *One World*, 18.

57. This is consistent with Muench's outlook on religious and practicing Jews, which was often favorable, especially when compared to his views of Jews he considered "materialistic," "communistic and socialistic," "vengeful," or "greedy." See *One World*, chaps. 4 and 5.

58. Ibid., 21.

59. Muench referred here to the 1945 Potsdam Accords, which can be interpreted as having ceded all territory east of the Oder-Niesse line to Soviet influence.

60. Again, a reference to the specifics of the Potsdam Accords as affecting Poland.

61. *One World*, 22.

62. Ibid., 23–5.

63. Ibid., 4.

64. Ibid., 13–14.

65. Ibid., 5.

66. Despite numerous attempts, I have been unable to obtain the *Familienblatt* in order to compare its translation of *One World* to the original distributed in Fargo.

67. "Eine Welt in der Liebe," *Nord-Dakota Herold* (Dickinson, N.D.), March 8, 1946. I thank the State Historical Society of North Dakota for making the *Herold* available to me.

68. Letter from Cornelius Sittard, Dickinson, to Muench, Kronberg, 18 November 1946. HM 37/14/5, ACUA.

69. Founded in Saint Paul, Minn., in 1867, *The Wanderer* had been in the editorial hands of the Matt family since 1899. Joseph Matt, who took it over at that time, was one of the principal leaders of the Central Catholic Verein of America (CCVA) and remained greatly interested in its social reform projects. Despite this, *The Wanderer* was highly conservative on political and religious issues. Gleason, *The Conservative Reformers*, 4.

70. Letter from Alphonse J. Matt, Saint Paul, to Muench, Kronberg, 16 April 1947. HM 37/25/1, ACUA. Muench replied that the idea of mass distribution was acceptable, the only question being that he "would not know who would foot the bill . . . [would] the CCVA? Or would the [American] bishops? Or, maybe a group of donors—friends of the Church in Germany?" See letter from Muench to Matt, 24 April 1947. HM 37/25/1, ACUA.

71. The first installment of *One World* appeared in German on July 15,

1946; the second on July 22; the third on July 29; the fourth on August 5; and the fifth and final installment on August 12, 1946. My thanks to the University of Oregon for making microfilm copies of the *Saint Josefsblatt* available to the University of Maryland.

72. Born February 6, 1887, Joseph Cardinal Frings was ordained to the priesthood on August 10, 1910. On May 1, 1942, he was appointed archbishop of Cologne, but did not actually receive the title of bishop until June 21, 1942. On February 18, 1946, he was elevated to cardinal. He was retired from his position as archbishop of Cologne on February 10, 1969 and died on December 17, 1978.

73. Muench diary entry dated 21 January 1947, vol. 5, p. 50, in HM 37/1/1.

74. Lauter did not include a copy of this particular "sixteen single-spaced" version, and no copy of this version exists in the National Archives.

75. Born on March 16, 1878, Clemens August von Galen was ordained to the priesthood on May 28, 1904. He was appointed bishop of Münster on September 5, 1933, and ordained bishop on October 28, 1933. On February 18, 1946, he was elevated to cardinal. He died on March 22, 1946.

76. My translation: letter from Franz Lauter, Cologne, to Muench, Kronberg, 2 January 1947. HM 37/23/4, ACUA.

77. Founded in 1845 as a society to promote good reading, the Borromäus Verein was the leading Catholic library organization in Germany. See Margaret S. Dalton, "The Borromäus Verein: Catholic Public Librarianship in Germany, 1845–1933," *Libraries and Culture* 31, no. 2 (spring 1996), 409–421.

78. We know that Muench granted permission to the German-language newspaper *Familienblatt* some time prior to June 7, 1946.

79. The Catholic imprimatur (literally, a word placed at the beginning or end of a published document), grants "permission to print." It is the license required of all writings that treat doctrine, morality, canon law, or scripture. Imprimatur, are issued by a diocese and require approval of the diocesan bishop. See *The Concise Catholic Dictionary,* s.v. "imprimatur."

80. My translation: letter from Gabriel Vollmar, Bonn, to Muench, Kronberg, 17 March 1947. HM 37/96/7, ACUA.

81. My translation: letter from Muench to Vollmar, 15 April 1947. HM 37/96/7, ACUA.

82. Letter from John O. Riedl to Karl Arndt, April 24, 1947, in John O. Riedl Collection, Series 1, Box 3, Marquette University. No copy of the version referenced by Riedl is available, hence it is not clear whether Riedl refers to the sixteen-page version circulated in Cologne or to another version.

83. My translation: letter from Vollmar, Bonn, to Muench, Bad Godesberg, 23 April 1952. HM 37/90/3, ACUA.

84. My translation: letter from Monsignor Joseph Kamps, Beuren, to Muench, Kronberg, 25 January 1948. HM 37/92/5, ACUA.

85. My translation: letter from Sister Maura, Dortmund, to Muench, Kronberg, 3 April 1947. HM 37/37/6, ACUA.

86. My translation: Sister Alodia, Dortmund, to Muench, Kronberg, 18 April 1947. HM 37/37/1, ACUA.

87. Letter from Hedwig Rohmer, Munich, to Muench, Kronberg, 14 January 1947. HM 37/9/2, ACUA.

88. News clipping saved by Muench. HM 37/162/7, ACUA.

89. Letter from Muench, Chicago, to Cardinal Francis Spellman, New York, 17 November 1947. HM 37/69/13, ACUA.

90. Muench diary entry dated 13 June 1947, vol. 6, p. 19.

91. Letter from Muench to Spellman, 17 November 1947.

92. Phayer, *The Catholic Church and the Holocaust*, 2–4, 13.

93. David W. Southern, *John LaFarge and the Limits of Catholic Interracialism 1911–1963* (Baton Rouge: Louisiana State University Press, 1996), xiii–xiv.

94. Phayer, *The Catholic Church and the Holocaust*, 12–13.

95. My translation: letter from Muench, Kronberg, to Georg Meixner, Bamberg, 21 June 1947. HM 37/139/4, ACUA.

96. Letter from Father John LaFarge, New York, to Muench, Kronberg, 11 July 1947. HM 37/9/3, ACUA.

97. John LaFarge, *The Manner Is Ordinary* (Garden City, N.Y.: Image Books, 1957), 278–9.

98. Letter from Picard de la Vacquerie, French zone, to Muench, Kronberg, 5 September 1947. HM 37/69/13, ACUA. De la Vacquerie attached a copy in French, which came to five single-spaced pages.

99. Letter from Muench to de la Vacquerie, 30 September 1947. HM 37/69/13, ACUA.

100. Muench made this claim in his explanatory letter to Spellman dated November 17, 1947.

101. My translation: letter from Muench, Kronberg, to Sister Maura, Dortmund, 19 July 1948. HM 37/37/6, ACUA.

102. "Weekly Intelligence Report for Schwabach," 12 September 1947. Folder "Intelligence Reports," Box 1479, Correspondence of Schwabach Resident Liaison and Security Office, 1945–49, Records of the Field Operations Division, RG-260-OMGUS, NA.

103. Muench diary entry dated 30 August 1947, vol. 6, p. 46.

104. Letter from Stadtpfarrer Ruh, Oberkirch, to Muench, Kronberg, 6 September 1947. HM 37/92/4, ACUA. This particular twelve-page version is not available in the Muench collection or in the National Archives.

105. Letter from General Pierre J. Koenig, French zone headquarters,

to General Lucius Clay, Berlin, 23 September 1947. In folder entitled "December 1947" (#9), Box 37 (October-December 1947), CGCPA, OPAG-B, RG 84-State Department, NARA. See appendices for full text.

106. Letter from John Riedl, Religious Affairs, to Muench, Kronberg, 8 October 1947. In folder entitled "Religious Affairs Miscellaneous part II," Box 164, RA, ECR, RG 260-OMGUS, NARA.

107. Muench diary entry dated 6 October 1947, vol. 6, p. 79. See also Phayer, *The Catholic Church and the Holocaust,* 155.

108. Muench diary entry dated 21 December 1947, vol. 7, pp. 30–1.

109. Muench heard of this later, both from Spellman and from Murphy. In a private conversation dated January 29, Murphy told Muench of Clay's ultimate decision to remain silent about the complaint on the October 6 plane ride. When Muench inquired as to why Clay did not simply approach him then, directly, Murphy replied that Clay had a "complex mind," and, further, it was inappropriate in that Muench was Clay's guest on the trip. See Muench diary entry dated January 29, 1948, vol. 8, pp. 66–7.

110. Muench diary entry dated 21 December 1947.

111. Telegram, Spellman to Murphy, 9 October 1947. In folder 7 entitled "October 1947," Box 7 (October-December 1947), CGCPA, OPAG-B, RG 84-State Department, NARA.

112. Zoeller, *Washington and Rome,* 171; Hennesey, *American Catholics,* 276.

113. Letter from Spellman to Murphy, 25 November 1947. In folder 9 entitled "December 1947," Box 37 (October-December 1947), CGCPA, OPAG-B, RG 84-State Department, NARA.

114. Letter from Muench to Stanley Bertke, 13 October 1947. HM 37/55/6, ACUA.

115. Muench diary entry dated 12 November 1947, vol. 6, pp. 97–9.

116. Letter from De la Vacquerie to Muench, 24 October 1947. HM 37/69/13, ACUA.

117. Muench diary entry dated 17 November 1947, vol. 7, p. 4.

118. Muench diary entry dated 12 November 1947.

119. Letter from Murphy to Spellman, 24 October 1947. In folder 9 entitled "December 1947," Box 7 (October-December 1947), CGCPA, OPAG-B, RG 84-State Department, NARA.

120. Muench diary entry dated 17 November 1947.

121. Letter from Muench to Spellman, 17 November 1947, appendixes to letter from Spellman to Murphy, 25 November 1947, in folder 9 entitled "December 1947," Box 37 (October-December 1947), CGCPA, OPAG-B, RG 84-State Department, NARA.

122. No other documents mention a request from a "publication in Bonn."

123. Spellman asked Muench's permission to do so. See letter from Spellman to Muench, 25 November 1947. HM 37/69/13, ACUA.

124. Murphy wrote to Spellman, "I have taken the liberty of showing the enclosure to General Clay. I believe this satisfactorily closes the matter. This is an interesting example of what may happen when words are taken out of their context and detached from the date on which they were used. . . . I shall look forward to Bishop Muench's return [to Germany] and will acknowledge his memorandum when I see him." Letter from Murphy to Spellman, 16 December 1947, in folder 9 entitled "December 1947," Box 7 (October-December 1947), CGCPA, OPAG-B, RG 84-State Department, NARA. This letter is also available in the private papers of Francis J. Cardinal Spellman, Archives, Archdiocese of New York (AANY), Saint Joseph's Seminary, Yonkers, N.Y. See Robert Murphy, London, to Francis Spellman, New York, 16 December 1947; in AANY, S/D-12, Folder 21, Fargo. I thank Archivist Sister Marguerita Smith for making a photocopy of this letter available to me. The Spellman papers are closed, though the archive will allow individual requests.

125. Letter from Muench to De la Vacquerie, 30 September 1947.

126. Letter from Muench, Kronberg, to Mary Filser Lohr, New York, 10 May 1947. HM 37/26/10, ACUA.

127. Letter from Muench to "Stadtpfarrer Ruh," 13 September 1947. HM 37/92/4, ACUA.

128. Muench diary entry dated 12 November 1947.

129. "Weekly Intelligence Report for Schwabach," 12 September 1947. In folder entitled "Intelligence Reports," Box 1479, Correspondence of Schwabach Resident Liaison and Security Office, 1945–49; Records of the Field Operations Division, RG 260-OMGUS, NARA.

130. Muench diary entry dated 21 January 1947.

131. Letter from Muench, Kronberg, to his sister Terry Muench, Milwaukee, 18 February 1947. HM 37/32/2, ACUA.

132. Letter from Stadtpfarrer Ruh to Muench, 6 September 1947.

133. Letter from Weihbischof (Auxiliary Bishop) Höcht, Regensburg, to Muench, Kronberg, 1946. HM 37/142/6, ACUA.

134. Letter from Elisabeth Baumgart, Selingen, to Muench, Kronberg, 24 July 1947. HM 37/20/10, ACUA.

135. Letter from Theodor Lebeda, Limburg, to Muench, Kronberg, 7 October 1947. HM 37/116/15, ACUA.

136. Letter from Franz Lauter to Muench, 2 January 1947.

137. Letter from Franz Münnich, Ostlutter, to Muench, Kronberg, 26 April 1947. HM 37/20/9, ACUA.

138. Letter from Franz Grübert, Furth, to Muench, Kronberg, 2 January 1947. HM 37/83/1, ACUA.

139. Letter from Elisabeth Baumgart to Muench, 24 July 1947.

140. Letter from H. Mertens, Hersfeld, to Muench, Kronberg, 26 September 1947. HM 37/128/3, ACUA.

141. Letter from Barbara Vincenz, Koblenz, to Muench, Kronberg, 5 February 1947. HM 37/20/9, ACUA.

142. Letter from Therese Wagner, Munich, to Muench, Kronberg, 5 March 1947. HM 37/20/9, ACUA.

143. Letter from Hedwig Rohmer, Munich, to Muench, Kronberg, 14 January 1947. Two copies, one in German and one translated copy, exist in the collection. See HM 37/9/2 and 55/3, ACUA.

144. Letter from Gruebert to Muench, 2 January 1947.

145. Letter from Father Franz Weimar to Muench, Kronberg, 11 October 1947. HM 37/53/7, ACUA.

146. Letter from Father Franz Schmal, Todtnauberg, to Muench, Kronberg, 18 April 1947. HM 37/92/3, ACUA.

147. Letter from Vollmar to Muench, 3 December 1951. HM 37/96/8, ACUA.

148. Letter from Vollmar to Muench, 23 April 1952. HM 37/90/3, ACUA.

149. Letter from H. Hassenbach, Frankfurt am Main, to Muench, Kronberg, 22 December 1952. HM 37/21/8, ACUA.

150. Many versions of *One World* existed. They included the original twenty-five page (typed) English version for Fargo Catholics released during Lent 1946 and the translations appearing in the German-American periodical *Familienblatt* and other U.S. German-American newspapers in 1946 and 1947. The versions circulating in Germany included the "sixteen-page" (single-spaced, typed) German translation in Cologne in January 1947, the "six-page" (typed) version seized by American officers in Schwabach, and the "twelve-page" version distributed by Stadtpfarrer Ruh in the French zone. Finally, there was the five-page French translation obtained by De la Vacquerie and Koenig, subsequently translated into English by General Clay's office. Many more may have existed.

151. Letter from Father Howard Smith, Bad Godesberg, to a "Dave," Fargo, 29 December 1952. HM 37/63/6, ACUA.

152. Letter from Joseph Hering, Amberg, to Muench, Bad Godesberg, 1 August 1957. HM 37/131/4, ACUA.

153. "Freund und Anwalt der Deutschen," *Kirchliche Nachrichten Agentur (KNA) Beilage.* HM 37/45/2, ACUA.

154. Letter from Barbara Muschweck, Nuremberg, to Muench, Kronberg, 7 July 1947. HM 37/20/10, ACUA.

155. "Cardinal Muench Asked to Testify for Eichmann," *Chicago Daily Tribune,* 22 April 1961. HM 37/30/5, ACUA.

156. When Muench heard of the clipping, he was indignant. "If this Wechtenbruch, assistant of the lawyer Servatius, comes here [to Villa Salvator Mundi, Vatican City] to see me, I would refuse to see him because no matter what I say it will be twisted," Muench wrote to his sister Terry. See letter from Muench, Rome, to his sister Terry, Milwaukee, 29 April 1961. HM 37/30/5, ACUA.

157. Fulda, a city in central Germany (now Hesse) on the Fulda River, was the site of a German (Benedictine) monastery founded in 744 by Saint Wynfrith Boniface (ca. 675–754) and his pupil Sturmius. Its importance to German Catholicism deemed Fulda the location of the annual conference of the Catholic bishops and archbishops of Germany (Fulda Bishops Conference). Adolf Cardinal Bertram (1859–1945), archbishop of Breslau, was chair (*Vorsitzender*) of the Fulda Bishops Conference from 1920 to 1945. See Werner Marschall, *Adolf Cardinal Bertram: Hirtenbriefe und Hirtenworte* (Cologne: Böhlau Verlag, 2000), vii.

158. "Cardinal Never Met Eichmann," *Daily News,* 5 May 1961. HM 37/60/10, ACUA.

James E. Young

Germany's Holocaust Memorial
Problem—and Mine

ONCE, NOT SO LONG AGO, GERMANY HAD WHAT IT CALLED A "JEWISH
problem." Then it had a paralyzing Holocaust memorial problem, a
double-edged conundrum: how would a nation of former perpetrators mourn its victims? How would a divided nation reunite itself
on the bedrock memory of its crimes? In June 1999, after ten years
of tortured debate, the German Bundestag voted to build a national
"Memorial for the Murdered Jews of Europe" on a prime, five-acre
piece of real estate between the Brandenburger Tor and Potsdamer
Platz, a stone's throw from Hitler's bunker. In their vote, the Bundestag also accepted the design—a waving field of pillars—by American architect Peter Eisenman that had been recommended by a five-
member *Findungskommission,* for which I served as spokesman.

Proposed originally by a citizens' group headed by television talk-
show personality and journalist Lea Rosh and World War II historian
Eberhard Jäckel, the memorial soon took on a fraught and highly
politicized life of its own. Although I had initially opposed a single,
central Holocaust memorial for the ways it might be used to compensate such irredeemable loss, or even put the past behind a newly
reunified Germany, over time I began to grow skeptical of my own
skepticism. Eventually, I was invited to join the five-member *Findungskommission* charged with choosing an appropriate design for Germany's national memorial to Europe's murdered Jews, the only foreigner and Jew on the panel. Here I would like to tell the story of
Germany's national Holocaust memorial and my own role in it, my
evolution from a highly skeptical critic on the outside of the process
to one of the arbiters on the inside. I find that as the line between my
roles as critic and arbiter began to collapse, the issues at the heart of

Germany's memorial conundrum came into ever sharper, more painful relief.

Along with a private citizens' initiative they had organized, Lea Rosh and Eberhard Jäckel at first hoped to place their memorial on the *Gestapo-Gelande,* a scarred wasteland and former site of the Gestapo headquarters in a no-man's land near the wall in the center of Berlin. But the "Gestapo-terrain" had long been enmeshed in a complicated debate over its own future and how to commemorate all the victims of the Gestapo in a single place.[1] With the fall of the wall in 1989, however, the project gained the backing of both the federal government and the Berlin Senate, who recognized that such a memorial might serve as a strategic counterweight to the *Neue Wache.* Shortly afterward, the government designated an alternative site for the memorial, also at the heart of the Nazi regime's former seat of power. Bordered on one side by the *Todesstreifen,* or "death-strip," at the foot of the Berlin wall, and on the other by the Tiergarten, the former site of the "Ministerial Gardens" was still a no-man's land in its own right, slightly profaned by its proximity to Hitler's bunker and the Reichs Chancellory. But in its 20,000 square meters (almost five acres) at the heart of a reunified capital, it would also become one of Berlin's most sought-after pieces of real estate—and was thus regarded as a magnanimous, if monumental, gesture to the memory of Europe's murdered Jews.

In 1994, about a year after the dedication of the *Neue Wache,* a prestigious international competition called for designs for Germany's national "Memorial to the Murdered Jews of Europe," and some 528 designs were submitted from around the world. Submissions ran the gamut of taste and aesthetic sensibilities, from the beautiful to the grotesque, from high modern to low kitsch, from the architectural to the conceptual. There was, for example, Horst Hoheisel's proposal to blow up the Brandenburger Tor, as well as Dani Caravan's proposed field of yellow flowers in the shape of a Jewish star. Berlin artists Stih and Schnock proposed a series of bus stops whence coaches would take visitors to the sites of actual destruction throughout Berlin, Germany, and Europe. Other designs included numerous variations on gardens of stone, broken hearts, and rent Stars of David. Round, square, and triangular obelisks were proposed, as well as a gigantic empty vat (130 feet tall), an empty vessel for the blood of the murdered. One artist proposed a Ferris wheel composed of cattle-cars instead of carriages, rotating between "the carnivalesque and the genocidal."[2]

The jury was composed of some fifteen members, both experts and laypeople, appointed by the three sponsoring agencies now involved—the Bundestag, the Berlin Senate, and the original citizens' group. Though the deliberations had been shielded from public view, many of the jurors subsequently told of rancorous, biting debate, with little meeting of the minds. The citizens' group resented the intellectuals and experts on the jury, with what they regarded as their elitist taste for conceptual and minimalist design. "This is not a playground for artists and their self-absorbed fantasies," Lea Rosh is reported to have reminded her colleagues on the jury. Meanwhile, the intellectuals sniffed at the lay-jurors' middlebrow eye for kitsch and monumental figuration, their philistine emotionalism; and the Bundestag's appointees glanced anxiously at their watches as the right political moment seemed to be ticking away.

In March 1995, organizers announced the jury's decision: first prize would be shared by two teams who had submitted similarly inspired designs—one led by Berlin artist Christine Jacob-Marks and the other by a New York artist living in Cologne, Simon Ungers. Of these two, only that proposed by Jacob-Marks would be built, however, possibly with elements incorporated from the other, and an additional eight projects would be recognized as finalists in the competition. Jacob-Marks's winning design consisted of a gargantuan, twenty-three-foot-thick concrete gravestone, in the shape of a 300-foot-square, tilted at an angle running from six feet high at one end to twenty-five feet high at the other. It was to be engraved with the recoverable names of 4.5 million murdered Jews, and in the Jewish tradition of leaving small stones at a gravesite to mark the mourner's visit, it was to have some eighteen boulders from Masada in Israel scattered over its surface.

Its literal-minded and misguided symbolism seemed to have paralyzed a jury as unable to resist it as to love it. Since eighteen is the Hebrew number representing *chai*, or life, the number of stones seemed right. But according to Josephus, Masada was the last stronghold against the Romans at the end of the Jewish revolt of 66–73 C.E. and also the site of a collective suicide of Jews that prevented the Romans from taking them as slaves. A German national Holocaust memorial with Jewish self-sacrifice as part of its theme? Within hours of the winner's announcement, the monument's mixed memorial message of Jewish naming tradition and self-sacrifice generated an avalanche of artistic, intellectual, and editorial criticism decrying this "tilted gravestone" as too big, too heavy-handed, too divisive, and finally just too German. Even the leader of Germany's Jewish community, Ignatz Bubis, hated it and told Chancellor Kohl that the winning design was simply unacceptable. Kohl threw up his hands in exasperation, pronounced the design as "too big and undignified," and obligingly rescinded the government's support for the winner of the Holocaust memorial competition. Germany's "Memorial for the Murdered Jews of Europe" seemed to have been sunk by its own monumental weight—and once again, Germany was left pondering its memorial options.

Between the announcement of the winner and its subsequent rejection, the organizers showed all 528 designs in a grand memorial exhibition at Berlin's Stadtratshaus. Good, I wrote at the time. Better a thousand years of Holocaust memorial competitions and exhibitions in Germany than any single "final solution" to Germany's memorial problem. This way, I reasoned, instead of a fixed icon for Holocaust memory in Germany, the debate itself—perpetually unresolved amid ever-changing conditions—might now be enshrined. Of course, this was also a position that only an academic bystander could afford to take, someone whose primary interest lay in perpetuating the process itself.

MY HOLOCAUST MEMORIAL PROBLEM

After yet another year of stormy debate over whether a new competition should be called, whether a new site should be found, or whether the winners should be invited to refine their proposals further still, the memorial's organizers once again took the high road. They called for a series of public colloquia on the memorial to be held in January, March, and April 1997, which they hoped would break the memorial deadlock and ensure that the memorial could be built before the Holocaust receded further into the history of a former century. Toward this end, they invited a number of distinguished artists, historians, critics, and curators to address the most difficult issues and to suggest how the present designs might best be modified. Among those invited to speak at the last colloquium in April 1997, I was asked to explore the memorial iconography of other nations' Holocaust memorials in order to put the Germans' own process into international perspective.

The first two colloquia, in January and March 1997, roused considerable public interest on the one hand, but as the exchanges between organizers of the memorial and invited speakers grew more acrimonious, a gloomy sense of despair gradually settled over the proceedings. The organizers, led by Lea Rosh, insisted that the "five aims" of the project remain inviolable: (1) this would be a memorial only to Europe's murdered Jews; (2) ground would be broken for it on January 27, 1999, Germany's newly designated "Holocaust Remembrance Day," marked to coincide with the 1945 liberation of Auschwitz; (3) its location would be the 20,000-square-meter site of the Ministerial Gardens, between the Brandenburg Gate and Potsdamer Platz; (4) the nine finalists' teams from the 1995 competition would be invited to revise their designs and concepts after incorporating suggestions and criticism from the present colloquia; and (5) the winning design would be chosen from the revised designs of the original nine finalists.[3]

Not only did the designs continue to come under withering attack by the invited experts, but the aims of the project itself were now called strongly into question. Among other speakers at the first colloquium, historian Jürgen Kocka suggested that while there was an obvious need for a memorial to Europe's murdered Jews, the need for a memorial to encompass the memory of the Nazis' other victims was just as clear. Other speakers, such as Michael Stürmer, then questioned the site itself, whether its gargantuan dimensions somehow invited precisely the kind of monumentality that had already been rejected. Other critics focused more narrowly on the first colloquium's theme: "Why There Should Be a Holocaust Memorial in Berlin," concluding that with the authentic sites of destruction and memory scattered throughout Berlin, there should not be a central memorial at all.

These vociferous challenges to the memorial were met by a seemingly stony indifference from the speaker of the Berlin Senate, Peter Radunski, who had been appointed to convene the proceedings. Since these criticisms had no place on the agenda, he said, they did not need to be addressed there. Lea Rosh's response was less measured. She opened the third colloquium with a bitter attack on what she called the "leftist intellectual establishment" responsible for undermining both the process and, by extension, memory of Europe's murdered Jews. The aim here was how to go forward, she said, not to debate the memorial's very *raison d'être*, which was already established. Her angry words, in turn, merely served to antagonize the critics and harden the positions of the memorial's opponents, who included many of Germany's elite historians, writers, and cultural critics, among them

Reinhart Koselleck, Julius Schoeps, Salomon Korn, Stefanie Endlich, Christian Meier, and eventually Günter Grass and Peter Schneider.

By the time I spoke at the third colloquium in mid-April, both the organizers and a large public audience at the Stadtratshaus in Berlin had grown visibly and audibly agitated by the spectacle of their tortured memorial deliberations. Over and over again, the other speakers—senators, art historians, and artists—bemoaned the abject failure of their competition. All of which was compounded by their acute embarrassment over the incivility of it all, the petty bickering, the name-calling, the quagmire of politics into which the whole process seemed to be sinking. Bad enough we murdered the Jews of Europe, one senator whispered to me, worse that we cannot agree on how to commemorate them.

When my turn to speak came, I began by trying to reassure the audience: decorum is never a part of the memorial-building process, not even for a Holocaust memorial. "You may have failed to produce a monument," I said, "but if you count the sheer number of design-hours that five hundred twenty-eight teams of artists and architects have already devoted to the memorial, it's clear that your process has already generated more individual memory-work than a finished monument will inspire in its first ten years." I then proceeded to tell the stories of other, equally fraught memorial processes in Israel and the United States: the furious debate in Israel's Knesset surrounding the day of remembrance there; the memorial paralysis in New York, Los Angeles, and Washington that had eventually resulted in several competing memorials, all of them contested. I could almost hear the collective sigh of relief.

In fact, here I admitted that until that moment I had been one of the skeptics. Rather than looking for a centralized monument, I was perfectly satisfied with the national memorial debate itself. Better, I had thought, to take all these millions of deutsche Marks and use them to preserve the great variety of Holocaust memorials already dotting the German landscape. Because no single site can speak for all the victims, much less for both victims and perpetrators, the state should be reminding its citizens to visit the many and diverse memorial and pedagogical sites that already exist: from the excellent learning center at the Wannsee Conference House to the enlightened exhibitions at the Topography of Terror at the former Gestapo headquarters, both in Berlin; from the brooding and ever-evolving memorial landscape at Buchenwald to the meticulously groomed grounds and fine museum at Dachau; from the hundreds of memorial tablets throughout Germany marking the sites of deportation to the dozens of now-empty sites of former synagogues—and all the spaces for contemplation in between.

Here I also admitted that with this position, I had made many friends in Germany and was making a fine career out of skepticism. Most colleagues shared my fear that Chancellor Kohl's government wanted a "memorial to Europe's murdered Jews" as a great burial slab for the twentieth century, a hermetically sealed vault for the ghosts of Germany's past. Instead of inciting memory of murdered Jews, we suspected, it would be a place where Germans would come dutifully to *unshoulder* their memorial burden, so that they could move freely and unencumbered into the twenty-first century. A finished monument would, in effect, finish memory itself.

On the one hand, I said, we must acknowledge the public need and political necessity for a German national Holocaust memorial; at the same time, we must also recognize the difficulty of answering this need in a single space. If the aim of a national Holocaust memorial in Berlin is to draw a bottom line under this era so that a reunified Germany can move unencumbered into the future, then let us make this clear. But if the aim is to remember for perpetuity that this great nation once murdered nearly 6 million human beings solely for their having been Jews, then this monument must also embody the intractable questions at the heart of German Holocaust memory rather than claiming to answer them. Otherwise, I feared that whatever form the monument near the Potsdamer Platz took would not mark the memory of Europe's murdered Jews so much as bury it altogether.[4]

These were persuasive arguments against the monument, and I am still ambivalent about the role a central Holocaust monument will play in Berlin. But at the same time, I said, I have also had to recognize that this was a position of luxury that perhaps only an academic bystander could afford, someone whose primary interest was in perpetuating the process itself. As instructive as the memorial debate had been, however, it had neither warned nor chastened a new generation of xenophobic neo-Nazis—part of whose identity depends on forgetting the crimes of their forebears. And while the memorial debate has generated plenty of shame in Germans, it is largely the shame they feel for an unseemly argument—not for the mass murder once committed in their name. In good academic fashion, we had become preoccupied with the fascinating issues at the heart of the memorial process and increasingly indifferent to what was supposed to be remembered: the mass murder of Jews and the resulting void it left behind.

The self-righteous and self-congratulatory tenor of our position had also begun to make me uneasy. Our unimpeachably skeptical approach to the certainty of monuments was now beginning to sound just a little too certain of itself. My German comrades in skepticism called themselves "the secessionists," a slightly self-flattering gesture to the turn-of-the-century movement of artists, many of whom would be Jewish victims of the Nazis. What had begun as an intellectually rigorous and ethically pure interrogation of the Berlin memorial was taking on the shape of a circular, centripedally driven, self-enclosed argument. It began to look like so much hand-wringing and fence-sitting, even an entertaining kind of spectator sport. "But can such an imperfect process possibly result in a good memorial?" parliamentarian Peter Conradi asked me at one point. I replied with an American aphorism that was altogether unfamiliar to his German ears: "Yes," I said, "for perfect is always the enemy of good." To this day, I am not sure he understood my point.

And here, I realized, my own personal stake in the memorial had begun to change. The day after I returned from that third colloquium in April, Berlin's minister of culture, Senator Peter Radunski, called to ask if I would join a *Findungskommission* of five members appointed to find a suitable memorial design. Who were the other four? I asked. He replied with the names of the directors of the German Historical Museum in Berlin (Christoph Stoelzl) and the Museum of Contemporary Art in Bonn (Dieter Ronte), as well as one of Germany's preeminent twentieth-century art historians (Werner Hoffmann) and one of Berlin's most widely respected and experienced arbiters of postwar architecture (Josef Paul Kleihues)—all authorities he believed to be above reproach. We would be given free rein to extend the process as we saw fit, to invite further artists, and to make an authoritative recommendation to the chancellor and the memorial's organizers. I was to be the only true expert on Holocaust memorials, he said. And, as I then realized, I would be the only foreigner and Jew.

Before answering, I had to ask myself a series of simple, but cutting, questions: Did I want Germany to return its capital to Berlin *without* publicly and visibly acknowledging what had happened the last time Germany was governed from Berlin? With its gargantuan, even megalomaniacal restoration plans and the flood of big-industry money pouring into the new capital in quantities beyond Albert Speer's wildest dreams, could there really be no space left for public memory of the victims of Berlin's last regime? How, indeed, could I set foot in a new German capital built on the presumption of inadvertent historical amnesia that new buildings always breed? As Adorno had corrected his well-intentioned but facile (and hackneyed) "Nach Auschwitz . . ." dictum, maybe it was also time for me to come down from my perch of holy dialectics and take a position.

But as one of the newly appointed arbiters of German Holocaust memory, I would also find myself in a strange and uncomfortable predicament. The skeptics' whispered asides echoed my own apprehensions: a mere decoration, this American Jew, a sop to authority and so-called expertise. I asked myself: was I invited as an academic authority on memorials, or as a token American and foreigner? Is it my expertise they want, or are they looking for a Jewish blessing on whatever design is finally chosen? If I can be credited for helping arbitrate official German memory, can I also be held liable for another bad design? In fact, just where is the line between my role as arbiter of German memory and my part in a fraught political process far beyond my own grasp?

So when asked to serve on this *Findungskommission* for Berlin's "memorial to the murdered Jews of Europe," I agreed but only on the condition that we write a precise conceptual plan for the memorial. Perhaps the greatest weakness in the first competition had been its hopelessly vague conceptual description of the memorial itself, leaving artists to founder in an impossible sea of formal, conceptual, and political ambiguities. In contrast, we would be clear, for example, that this memorial would not displace the nation's other memorial sites, and that a memorial to Europe's murdered Jews would not speak for the Nazis' other victims, but might, in fact, necessitate further memorials to them. Nor should this memorial hide the impossible questions driving Germany's memorial debate. It should instead reflect the terms of the debate itself, the insufficiency of memorials, the contemporary generation's skeptical view of official memory and its self-aggrandizing ways. After all, I had been arguing for years that a new generation of artists and architects in Germany—including Christian Boltanski, Norbert Radermacher, Horst Hoheisel, Micha Ulmann, Stih and Schnock, Jochen Gerz, and Daniel Libeskind—had turned their skepticism of the monumental into a radical countermonu-mentality. In challenging and flouting every one of the monument's conventions, their memorials have reflected an essentially German ambivalence toward self-indictment, where the void was made palpable yet remained unredeemed. If the government insisted on a memorial in Berlin to "Europe's murdered Jews," then could not it too embody this same countermonumental critique?

Rather than prescribing a form, therefore, we described a concept of memorialization that took into account a clear definition of the Holocaust and its significance; Nazi Germany's role as perpetrator; current reunified Germany's role as rememberer; the contemporary generation's relationship to Holocaust memory; the aesthetic debate swirling around the memorial itself. Instead of providing answers, we asked questions: What are the national reasons for remembrance? Are they redemptory, part of a mourning process, pedagogical, self-aggrandizing, or inspirational against contemporary xenophobia? What national and social ends will this memorial serve? Just how compensatory a gesture will it be? How anti-redemptory can it be? Will it be a place for Jews to mourn lost Jews, a place for Germans to mourn lost Jews, or a place for Jews to remember what Germans once did to them? These questions must be made part of the memorial process, I suggested, so let them be asked by the artists *in* their designs, even if they cannot finally be answered.

Here I also reminded organizers that this would not be an aesthetic debate over how to depict horror. The Holocaust, after all, was not merely the annihilation of nearly 6 million Jews, among them 1.5 million children, but also the extirpation of a thousand-year old civilization from the heart of Europe. Any conception of the Holocaust that reduces it to the horror of destruction alone ignores the stupendous loss and void left behind. The tragedy of the Holocaust is not merely that people died so terribly but that so much was irreplaceably lost. An appropriate memorial design would acknowledge the void left behind and not concentrate on the memory of terror and destruction alone. What needs to be remembered here is what was lost as much as how it was lost.

In addition, I suggested that organizers must be prepared to accept the fact that this memorial was being designed in 1997, more than fifty years after the end of World War II. It would necessarily reflect the contemporary sensibility of artists, which includes much skepticism over the very appropriateness of memorials, their traditional function as redemptory sites of mourning, national instruction, and self-aggrandizement. To this end, I also asked organizers to encourage a certain humility among designers, a respect for the difficulty of such a memorial. It is not surprising that a memorial such as Jacob-Marks's was initially chosen: it represented very well a generation that felt oppressed by Holocaust memory, which would in turn oppress succeeding generations with such memory. But something subtler, more modest and succinct might suggest a balance between being oppressed by memory and inspired by it, a tension between being permanently marked by memory and disabled by it. As other nations have remembered the Holocaust according to their founding myths and ideals, their experiences as liberators, victims, or fighters, Germany will also remember according to its own complex and self-abnegating motives, whether we like them or not. Let Germany's official memorial reflect its suitably tortured relationship to the genocide of Europe's Jews, I said.

Before proceeding, we also had to address two further concerns shared both by us, as members of the *Findungskommission,* and the memorial's opponents: should it be a contemplative site only, or pedagogically inclined, as well? By extension, would this memorial serve as a center of gravity for the dozens of memorials and pedagogical centers already located at the actual sites of destruction, or would it somehow displace them and even usurp their memorial authority? Because we did not see Holocaust memory in Germany as a zero-sum project, we concluded that there was indeed room in Berlin's new landscape for *both* commemorative spaces and pedagogically oriented memorial institutions. In fact, Berlin and its environs were already rich with excellent museums and permanent exhibitions on the Holocaust and other, more contemporary genocides—from the Wannsee Conference House to the Topography of Terror, from the new Jewish Museum on Lindenstrasse and the proposed Institute for the Study of Anti-Semitism, to the critical and insightful exhibitions at Buchenwald and Sachsenhausen.

The question was never whether there would be only a memorial or a museum. But rather: in addition to these already existing pedagogical houses of memory, was there room as well for a commemorative space meant for memorial contemplation and national ceremonies? Again, we concluded that in Berlin's constellation of memorial sites, there was indeed room for a central memorial node in this landscape, one that would inspire public contemplation of the past, even as it encouraged the public to visit and learn the specifics of this past in the many other museums nearby and throughout the country.

In fact, though still suspicious of the monument as a form, I also began to see how important it would be to add a space to Germany's restored capital deliberately designed to remember the mass murder of Europe's Jews. This would not be a space for memory designed by the killers themselves, as the concentration camp sites inevitably are, but one designed specifically as a memorial site, one denoting the current generation's deliberate attempt to remember. Of course, the government must continue to support the dozens of other memorial and pedagogical sites around the country. But these are, after all, already there. To build a memorial apart from these sites of destruction, however, is not merely the passive recognition and preservation of the past. It is a deliberate act of remembrance, a strong statement that *memory must be created* for the next generation, not only preserved.

Finally, I would have to reserve the right to dissent publicly over any final design which I could not stand by. I would agree to serve on such a *Findungskommission* even as I still held strong doubts that a resolution was even possible. I would suspend judgment on whether such a resolution was desirable until the end. If, in the end, we arrived at nothing we could justify to the organizers, then my early skepticism would have been justified. But if we did find something in a collaborative effort with artists and architects, it would be our responsibility to explain our choice to the public. For if we could not justify it formally, conceptually, and ethically, then how could we expect the public to accept it?[5]

THE DESIGNS

In weighing the power of concept against formal execution in a final group of designs, the members of the *Findungskommission* unanimously agreed that two proposals, one by Gesine Weinmiller and the other by Peter Eisenman and Richard Serra, far transcended the others in their balance of brilliant concept and powerful execution. Though equally works of terrible beauty, complexity, and deep intelligence, the proposals by Weinmiller and Eisenman/Serra derived their power from very different sources. The choice here was not between measures of brilliance in these two works but between two very different orders of memorial sensibilities: Weinmiller's was the genius of quietude, understatement, and almost magical allusiveness; the collaboration of Eisenman and Serra resulted in an audacious, surprising, and dangerously imagined form. One was by a young German woman of the generation now obligated to shoulder the memory and shame of events for which she was not to blame; the other was by two well-known Americans, architect and artist, one of whose Jewish family left Germany two generations ago. Together, we felt, these two designs would offer the public, government, and organizers of the memorial an actual and stark choice. Their cases were equally strong, but in the end one would have to gather the force of consensus over the other.

In Gesine Weinmiller's three-sided plaza, visitors would descend into memory and wend their way through eighteen wall-segments composed of giant sandstone blocks scattered in a seemingly random pattern in the square. The walls surrounding the area on three sides created a rising horizon as one came further into their compass, slowly blocking out the surrounding buildings and traffic noise. This space would be both part of the city and removed from it. And only gradually would the significance of these forms and spaces begin to dawn on visitors: the eighteen sections of stone wall recall *life* in Hebrew gematria (*chai*); the descent into memory space countered the possible exaltation of such memory and suggested a void carved out of the earth, a wound; the stacking of large stone blocks recalled the first monument in Genesis, a *Sa'adutha* or witness-pile of stones, a memorial cairn; the rough texture and cut of the stones visually echoed the stones of the Western Wall in Jerusalem, the ruin of the temple's destruction; their rough fit would show the seams of their construction; the pebbles on which visitors tread would slow their pace and mark their visit in sound, as well as in the visible traces their steps would leave behind.

Then there was a striking, yet altogether subtle perspectival illusion created from the vantage point in one corner above the plaza: the seemingly random arrangement of scattered wall segments would suddenly compose themselves into a Star of David, and then fall apart as one moved beyond this point. The memory of Jews murdered would be constituted momentarily in the mind's eye before decomposing again, the lost Jews of Europe reconstituted only in the memorial activity of visitors here. Built into this design was also space for historical text on the great wall at the bottom of the decline into memory. Such a text would not presume to name all the victims of the crime but would name the crime itself. Built into this space was the capacity for a record of Holocaust history and for the changing face of its memory.

In its original conception, the proposal by Peter Eisenman and Richard Serra also suggested a startling alternative to the very idea of the Holocaust memorial. Like Weinmiller's, theirs was a pointedly antiredemptory design: it found no compensation for the Holocaust in art or architecture. In its waving field of 4,000 pillars, it at once echoed a cemetery, even as it implied that such emblems of individual mourning were inadequate to the task of remembering mass murder. Toward this end, it took the vertical forms of its pillars—sized from ground level to five meters high, spaced ninety-two centimeters apart—and turned their collected mass into a horizontal plane. Rather than pretending to answer Germany's memorial problem in a single, reassuring form, this design proposed multiple, collected forms arranged so that visitors have to find their own path to the memory of Europe's murdered Jews. As such, this memorial provided not an answer to memory but an ongoing process, a continuing question without a certain solution.

Part of what Eisenman called its *Unheimlichkeit,* or uncanniness, derived precisely from the sense of danger generated in such a field, the demand that we now find our own way into and out of such memory. And because the scale of this installation would be almost irreproducible on film shot from the ground, it demanded that visitors enter the memorial space and not try to know it vicariously through their snapshots. What would be remembered here are not photographic images but the visitors' actual experiences and what they remembered in situ. As might have been expected in a piece partly designed by Richard Serra, this design also implied a certain physical danger in such memory, a danger meant to remain implicit but so close to being actualized in its scale and forms as to suggest something more than a mere figure of threatening memory.

Before long, public consensus (though far from unanimous) gathered around the design by Peter Eisenman and Richard Serra. It was reported that Chancellor Kohl also strongly favored the design by Eisenman and Serra and even invited the team to Bonn to hear them personally explain their proposal. During their January 1998 visit with the chancellor, Eisenman and Serra were asked to consider a handful of design changes that would make the memorial acceptable to organizers. As an architect who saw accomodation to his clients' wishes as part of his job, Eisenman agreed to adapt the design to the needs of the project. As an artist, however, Richard Serra steadfastly refused to contemplate any changes in the design whatsoever. As a result, he withdrew from the project, suggesting that once changed, the project would in effect no longer be his.

While we were sorry to see Richard Serra withdraw from the project, we could also fully understand the artist's prerogative to resist recommended changes in what he regarded as a finished work. Here, in fact, the artist's and the architect's modes of operation may always diverge: where the architect generally sees an accomodation to the clients' requests as part of his job, the artist is more apt to see suggested changes, however slight, as a threat to his work's internal logic and integrity. This conflict, too, is normal in the course of collaborations between artists and architects.

Despite our enthusiastic recommendation of Eisenman and Serra's design, in the sheer number of its pillars and its overall scale in proportion to the allotted space, the original design left less room for visitors and commemorative activities than we had wanted. Some of us also found a potential for more than figurative danger in the memorial site: at five meters high, the tallest pillars might have hidden some visitors from view, thereby creating the sense of a labyrinthine maze, an effect desired neither by designers nor commissioners. The potential for a purely visceral experience that might occlude a more contemplative memorial visit was greater than some of us would have preferred.

Therefore, among the modifications we requested of Peter Eisenman, now acting on his own, we asked for a slight downscaling of both the size of individual pillars and their number. In June 1998, I spent a day in Peter Eisenman's New York City studio to hear his rationale and to see the changes he had made, a day before he sent his newly designed model off to Berlin for safekeeping. Shortly after, I could report to the other commissioners that our suggestions had not only been expertly incorporated into the design by Peter Eisenman, but that they worked, in unexpected ways, to strengthen the entire formalization of the concept itself. Here I also found that I had, in effect, collapsed my roles as arbiter, critic, and advocate—all toward finding the language that the chancellor himself might use in justifying his decision to a still-skeptical public.

In Eisenman's revised design, I found that he had reduced both the number of pillars (from 4,200 to about 3,000) and their height, so that they would now range from half a meter tall to about three meters or so in one section of the field. Where the "monumental" has traditionally used its size to humiliate or cow viewers into submission, this memorial in its humanly proportioned forms would put people on an even footing with memory. Visitors and the role they play as they wade knee-, or chest-, or shoulder-deep into this waving field of stones will not be diminished by the monumental but will be made integral parts of the memorial itself, now invited into a memorial dialogue of equals. Visitors would not be defeated by their memorial obligation here, nor dwarfed by the memory-forms themselves, but rather enjoined by them to come face to face with memory.

Able to see over and around these pillars, visitors will have to find their way through this field of stones, on the one hand, even as they are never actually lost in or overcome by the memorial act. In effect, they will make and choose their own individual spaces for memory, even as they do so collectively. The implied sense of motion in the gently undulating field also formalizes a kind of memory that is neither frozen in time, nor static in space. The sense of such instability will help visitors resist an impulse toward closure in the memorial act and heighten one's own role in anchoring memory in oneself.

In their multiple and variegated sizes, the pillars are both individuated and collected: the very idea of "collective memory" is broken down here and replaced with the collected memories of individuals murdered, the terrible meanings of their deaths now multiplied and not merely unified. The land sways and moves beneath these pillars so that each one is some three degrees off vertical: we are not reassured by such memory, not reconciled to the mass murder of millions but now disoriented by it.

In practical terms, the removal of some 1,200 pillars from an originally proposed 4,200 or so has dramatically opened up the plaza for public commemorative activities. It has also made room for tourist buses to discharge visitors without threatening the sanctity of the pillars on the outer edges of the field. By raising the height of the lowest pillar-tops from nearly flush with the ground to approximately a half-meter tall, the new design also ensures that visitors will not step on the pillars or walk out over the tops of pillars. Since the pillars will tilt at the same degree and angle as the roll of the ground-level topography into which the pillars are set, this too will discourage visitors from climbing or clambering over them. In fact, since these pillars are neither intended nor consecrated as tombstones, there would be no actual desecration of them were someone to step or sit on one of these pillars. But in Jewish tradition, it is also important to avoid the appearance of a desecration, so the minor change in the smallest pillars was still welcome.

In their warm, sandy tone, the concrete-form pillars will reflect the colors of the sun and sky on the one hand and remain suggestive of stone, even sandstone, on the other. The concrete will not have the rough lines of their pour forms but will be smooth, close to the texture of a sidewalk. They can also be impregnated with an anti-graffiti solution to make them easy to clean. Over time, it will be important to remove graffiti as it appears, in order not to allow it to accumulate. The crushed-stone ground surface is also an excellent idea, in that it inhibits running, frolicking, or lying on the ground, even as it marks the visitors' own footsteps in both sound and space.

The architect prefers that the pillars, though stonelike, remain underdetermined and open to many readings: they are alternately stones, pillars, blank tablets, walls, and segments. This said, in their abstract forms, they will nevertheless accomodate the references projected onto them by visitors, the most likely being the tombstone. This is not a bad thing and suggests the need to keep these pillars blank-faced. With written text, they might begin to look very much like tombstones, in fact, and so might generate a dynamic demanding some sort of formal treatment as tombstones, even symbolic ones.

For this reason, I suggested that a permanent, written historical text be inscribed on a large tablet or tablets set either into the ground or onto the ground, tilted at a readable angle, separate from the field of waving pillars. Their angled position will bring visitors into respectful, even prayerful repose as they read the text, with heads slightly bowed in memory. These could be placed at the entrance or on the sides, under the trees lining the perimeter of the field, leaving the integrity of the field itself formally intact, while still denoting exactly what is to be remembered here. Thus placed, the memorial texts will not create a sense of beginning or end of the memorial field, leaving the site open to the multiple paths visitors take in their memorial quest. This, too, will respect the architect's attempt to foster a sense of incompleteness; it will not be a memorial with a narrative beginning, middle, and end built into it.

On June 25, 1999, the German Bundestag took a series of votes on the matter of the memorial. It finally passed three principal motions: (1) The Federal Republic of Germany will erect in Berlin a "memorial for the murdered Jews of Europe"; (2) The design for this memorial will be the field of pillars proposed by Peter Eisenman, to which an information center will be added; and (3) A public foundation made up of the directors of other memorial institutions, as well as representatives from the organization of Jews in Germany, will be established by the Bundestag to oversee both the building of the memorial and its information center in the year 2000.

Now that Germany's "Memorial for the Murdered Jews of Europe" has been dedicated, is this the end of Germany's Holocaust memory-work, as I had initially feared? Obviously not. Debate and controversy continue unabated. Moreover, now that Parliament has decided to give Holocaust memory a central place in Berlin, an even more difficult job awaits the organizers: defining exactly what it is to be remembered here in Peter Eisenman's waving field of pillars. What will Germany's national Holocaust narrative be? Who will write it and to whom will it be written? The question of historical content begins at precisely the moment the question of memorial design ends. Memory, which has followed history, will now be followed by still further historical debate.

On the dedication of the memorial in January 2000, fittingly fraught as always, the debate continued. Some, like Mayor Eberhard Diepken, stayed home like a petulant child who did not get his way; others stayed home out of the deeply felt conviction that no memorial will ever be adequate to the task. Of those who came to the dedication, most came to remember, some to mourn, and some to share in the memorial's unflattering political limelight. Had I been able, I surely would have come—both to mourn and to watch with some satisfaction as Berlin continued to wrestle with its memorial demons.

From this American Jew's perspective, this last year has been a watershed for German memory and identity. No longer paralyzed by the memory of crimes perpetrated in its name, Germany is now acting on the basis of such memory: it participated boldly in the North Atlantic Treaty Organization's (NATO's) 1999 intervention against a new genocide perpetrated by Milosevic's Serbia; it has begun to change citizenship laws from blood- to residency-based; and it has dedicated a permanent place in Berlin's cityscape to commemorate what happened the last time Germany was governed from Berlin. Endless debate and memorialization are no longer mere substitutes for actions against contemporary genocide but reasons for action. This is something new, not just for Germany but for the rest of us, as well.

For whether Germans like it or not, in addition to their nation's great accomplishments over the last several centuries, they will also always be identified as that nation that launched the deadliest genocide in human history, which started a world war that eventually killed some 50 million human beings, and which used this war to screen its deliberate mass murder of some 6 million European Jews. It is not a proud memory. But neither has any other nation attempted to make such a crime perpetrated in its name part of its national identity. For this space will always remind Germany and the world at large of the self-inflicted void at the heart of German culture and consciousness—a void that at once defines national identity, even as it threatens such identity with its own implosion.

NOTES

This is adapted from James E. Young, *At Memory's Edge: After-Images of the Holocaust in Contemporary Art and Architecture* (New Haven, Conn.: Yale University Press, 2000).

1. For more on the debate surrounding the discovery of ruins on the *Gestapo-Gelande* and subsequent architectural competitions to memorialize this site, see James E. Young, *The Texture of Memory* (New Haven, Conn.: Yale University Press, 1993), 81–90.

2. See *Denkmal fur die ermordeten Juden Europas: Kunstlierischer Wettbewerb: Kurzdokumentation* (Berlin: Senatsverwaltung fur Bau und Wohnungswesen, 1995).

3. From Peter Radunski's "Opening Remarks" to the First Colloquium on Berlin's Memorial to the Murdered Jews of Europe, January 11, 1997.

4. For articulate arguments against the memorial, see Reinhard Kosellek, "Wer das vergessen werden? Das Holocaust-Mahnmal hierarchisiert die Opfer," *Die Zeit,* no. 13 (19 March 1998); Gyorgy Konrad, "Abschied von der Chimare: Zum Streit um das Holocaust-Denkmal," *Frankfurter Allgemeine Zeitung* (26 November 1997): 41.

5. I raised many of these same issues, in slightly different form, in James E. Young, "Gegen Sprachlosigkeit hilft kein Kreischen und Lachen: Berlins Problem mit dem Holocaust-Denkmal-und meines," *Frankfurter Allgemeine Zeitung* (2 January 1998): 28.

Notes on Contributors

Yehuda Bauer is professor (emeritus) at Hebrew University and the author of many studies of the Holocaust, including *Rethinking the Holocaust,* published in 2001. He is an academic advisor to Yad Vashem and a member of the Israeli Academy of Science.

Richard Breitman is professor of history at American University and editor in chief of *Holocaust and Genocide Studies.* He is the author of several books on the Holocaust, including *Architect of Genocide: Himmler and the Final Solution* and *Official Secret: What the Nazis Planned, What the British and Americans Knew,* and he is the coauthor of a forthcoming book-length report by independent historians for the Nazi War Criminal and Imperial Japanese Records Interagency Working Group.

Suzanne Brown-Fleming is program officer for the University Programs Division, Center for Advanced Holocaust Studies, United States Holocaust Memorial Museum. Her work has appeared in *Die USA und Deutschland im Zeitalter des Kalten Krieges, 1945–1968* and *The Society for Historians of American Foreign Relations Newsletter.*

Ian Buruma is a writer based in London and is also Luce Professor of Democracy at Bard College. He has written about both Asian and European affairs for *The New York Review of Books, The New Yorker,* and other publications. He is the author of several books, including *The Wages of Guilt* and, most recently, *Bad Elements: Chinese Rebels from L.A. to Beijing.*

Jeffry M. Diefendorf is professor of history at the University of New Hampshire, and he has published extensively on German urban history, including *In the Wake of War: The Reconstruction of German Cities after World War II* and, most recently, *Rebuilding Urban Japan after 1945*.

Hilary Earl teaches at Wilfrid Laurier University in Waterloo, Ontario. She is a former fellow at the Center for Advanced Holocaust Studies at the United States Holocaust Memorial Museum.

Christian Gerlach is assistant professor of history at the National University of Singapore, having been a visiting assistant professor at the University of Freiburg and a postdoctoral research fellow in the Department of History of the University of Maryland. He has authored major studies of the relationship between German military, food, and demographic policies and the Holocaust, including *Kalkulierte Morde: Die deutsche Wirtschafts- und Vernichtungspolitik in Weißrußland 1941–1944,* and, with Götz Aly, *Das letzte Kapitel: Realpolitik, Ideologie und der Mord an den ungarischen Juden 1944/45*.

Jonathan Goldstein is professor of history at the State University of West Georgia and research associate of Harvard University's John K. Fairbank Center for East Asian Research. His books include *The Jews of China* and *China and Israel, 1949–1998: A Fifty Year Retrospective*.

Constantin Goschler teaches at the Humboldt University in Berlin. He is the author and editor of several books about indemnification and restitution for Nazi victims and also works on cultural history and the history of science in the nineteenth century.

Jeffrey Herf is professor of history at the University of Maryland at College Park. His publications include *Reactionary Modernism: Technology, Culture and Politics in Weimar and the Third Reich* and the prize-winning *Divided Memory: The Nazi Past in the Two Germanys*.

Susannah Heschel is Eli Black Associate Professor of Jewish Studies at Dartmouth College and serves as chair of the Jewish Studies Program. She is the author of numerous studies of modern Jewish thought, including *Abraham Geiger and the Jewish Jesus*.

Konrad Jarausch is professor of history at the University of North Carolina, Chapel Hill, and the author of numerous books on modern German history.

Paul B. Jaskot is associate professor of Art History at DePaul University and the author of *The Architecture of Oppression: The SS, Forced Labor and the Nazi Monumental Building Economy*. He is currently working on a study of the political reception of the Nazi past and postwar German art and architecture.

Helen Junz served as an economist with the U.S. government and the International Monetary Fund. Her work on Holocaust assets research started in 1997 with a project for the Independent Committee of Eminent Persons (Volcker Committee). She also was a member of the Independent Commission of Experts, Switzerland (Bergier Commission), director of research on non-gold financial and economic assets for the Presidential Advisory Commission on Holocaust Era Assets in the United States, and an advisor to the International Commission on Holocaust Era Insurance Claims.

Pieter Lagrou is a historian at the Institut d'Histoire du Temps Présent, Centre National de la Recherche Scientifique in Paris. He is the author of *The Legacy of Nazi Occupation: Patriotic Memory and National Recovery in Western Europe, 1945–1965*.

Yehudi Lindeman, the founder and past director of Living Testimonies, the Holocaust Video Archive at McGill University in Montreal, has recently retired from the McGill Department of English. He has published widely on Renaissance poetry and translation. He is also a child survivor who spent three of the war years in various places in hiding in rural Holland.

Dan Michman is professor of modern Jewish history and chairman of the Arnold and Leona Finkler Institute of Holocaust Research, Bar-Ilan University, and Chief Historian at Yad Vashem. He is the author of many books and articles on Holocaust history, most recently *Holocaust Historiography from a Jewish Perspective.*

Patricia von Papen-Bodek is an independent scholar who received her doctorate from Columbia University. She is a board member of the Swiss Johanna Heumann Foundation, where she is responsible for beneficiaries' relations with North American universities, and she has published several articles on Nazi-era research on the so-called Jewish Question.

Devin Pendas is assistant professor of history at Boston College. He is completing a book on the Frankfurt Auschwitz Trial and its role in the politics of memory in postwar West Germany.

Sybille Steinbacher is assistant professor at the Ruhr University in Bochum. She has published studies on the relationships between concentration camps of Dachau and Auschwitz and their neighboring towns, including *Dachau—Die Stadt und das Konzentrationslager in der NS-Zeit. Die Untersuchung einer Nachbarschaft* and *"Musterstadt Auschwitz" Germanisierungspolitik und Judenmord in Ostoberschlesien.*

Jonathan Steinberg is Walter H. Annenberg Professor of Modern European History at the University of Pennsylvania. He was the principal author of the 1999 report on gold, *The Deutsche Bank and its Gold Transactions during the Second World War* and author of *All or Nothing: The Axis and the Holocaust, 1941 to 1943.*

Dariusz Stola is a fellow at the Institute for Political Studies, Polish Academy of Sciences, a professor and vice rector at the Collegium Civitas in Warsaw, and a fellow at the Center for Migration Research, Warsaw University. Having published widely on contemporary Polish history, he was recognized by the Minister of Culture for distinguished service to Polish culture.

Gerhard Weinberg is professor (emeritus) of history at the University of North Carolina, Chapel Hill. He is the author of numerous works on German history and, in 1994, of *A World at Arms: A Global History of World War II.*

Lenore Weitzman is Robinson Professor of Sociology and Law at George Mason University. In Spring 2002 she was a Miles Forman Fellow for the study of Jewish resistance at the United States Holocaust Memorial Museum.

Rebecca Wittmann is assistant professor of history at the University of Toronto at Mississauga. Her book *Beyond Justice: The Auschwitz Trial, the Law, and the Holocaust* is forthcoming from Harvard University Press.

James E. Young teaches in the Department of Judaic and Near Eastern Studies at the University of Massachusetts, Amherst. He is the author of *At Memory's Edge, The Texture of Memory,* and *Writing and Rewriting the Holocaust.* An expert on memorials, he was appointed by the Berlin Senate to the five-member commission that selected the design for Germany's national "Memorial to the Murdered Jews of Europe."